2003

CHRONOLOGICAL HISTORY OF U.S. FOREIGN RELATIONS

CHRONOLOGICAL HISTORY OF U.S. FOREIGN RELATIONS

Volume III
1989–2000

by Lester H. Brune

Richard Dean Burns, Consulting Editor

Routledge
Taylor & Francis Group
NEW YORK AND LONDON

Editorial Staff:
Laura Kathleen Smid, *Project Editor*
Jeanne Shu, *Senior Production Editor*
Edward Cone, *Copyeditor*
Cynthia Crippen and Melanie Belkin, *Indexers*
Dennis Teston, *Production Director*
Jennifer Crisp, *Cover Designer*
Indiana University Graphic Services, *Cartographer*
Kate Aker, *Director of Development*
Sylvia K. Miller, *Publishing Director, Reference*

Published in 2003 by
Routledge
29 West 35th Street
New York, NY 10001
www.routledge-ny.com

Published in Great Britain by
Routledge
11 New Fetter Lane
London EC4P 4EE
www.routledge.co.uk

10   9   8   7   6   5   4   3   2   1

Library of Congress Cataloging-in-Publication Data

Brune, Lester H.
　　[Chronological history of United States foreign relations]
　　Chronological history of U.S. foreign relations / by Lester H. Brune ; Richard
Dean Burns, consulting editor.
　　　　p. cm.
　　Rev. ed. of: Chronological history of United States foreign relations. New York :
Garland, 1985–1991.
　　Includes bibliographical references and index.
　　Contents: v. 1. 1607–1932 – v. 2. 1933–1988 – v. 3. 1989–2000.
　　ISBN 0-415-93914-3 (set : alk. paper) – ISBN 0-415-93915-1 (vol. 1 : alk. paper) –
ISBN 0-415-93916-X (vol. 2 : alk. paper) – ISBN 0-415-93917-8 (vol. 3 : alk. paper)
　　1. United States—Foreign relations—Chronology. I. Burns, Richard Dean. II. Title.

E183.7 .B745 2002
327.73′002′02—dc21
　　　　　　　　　　　　　　　　　　　　　　　　　　　　　　　　　　2002023693

Printed on acid-free, 250-year-life paper
Manufactured in the United States of America

Contents

XVII.   CONTINUING U.S. FOREIGN INTERVENTIONS

1 9 8 9

January 4, 1989

U.S. fighter planes shoot down two Libyan aircraft.

The United States and Libya had been involved in an ongoing dispute regarding the Gulf of Sidra's international status (see August 19, 1981). Libya claimed all of the Gulf of Sidra was part of its territory, while the United States argued that only the southern part of the gulf was within Libyan borders. On January 4, two U.S. F-14 combat aircraft were patrolling the northern part of the Gulf of Sidra, which the United States considered part of the Mediterranean Sea, when two Libyan fighter MiG-23s appeared, "armed and hostile," and were shot down by the American pilots. Although Libya claimed its aircraft were unarmed, the U.S. Defense Department released some film on January 5 that showed that the Libyan MiGs had, in fact, been armed.

See August 19, 1981.

January 6, 1989

Cambodia's president indicates that Vietnamese forces will leave by September if a peace agreement is reached.

Vietnam had begun its troop withdrawal in 1988, but Hanoi awaited plans for a new Cambodian government to end the civil war. Cambodian President Heng Samrin wanted to encourage truce discussions by making his January 6 announcement. On July 6, 1989, an important step was made when U.S. Secretary of State James Baker supported talks between Heng's government and Prince Norodom Sihanouk, who represented the opposition. Washington had previously refused to recognize the Cambodian regime backed by Vietnam.

See July 25, 1988.

January 7, 1989

Delegates from 149 nations reaffirm the Geneva protocol against chemical weapons.

French President François Mitterrand called this meeting to revive a 10-year U.N. effort to gain agreement on curbing or abolishing all chemical weapons. The Geneva Protocol of 1925 was an agreement not to use these weapons, but it did not ban their production or stockpiling.

At this Paris meeting all nations present agreed not to use chemical weapons, but some raised qualifications. U.S. Secretary of State George Shultz failed in an attempt to stop the export of chemical technology, such as that which Libya had recently obtained from West Germany. In addition, an attempt by Arab delegates to ban nuclear as well as chemical weapons was not accepted. Many Third World nations argued that poison gas was the "poor man's atomic bomb," but the superpowers rejected this comparison.

During the meeting, Soviet Foreign Minister Eduard Shevardnadze announced that the USSR would unilaterally destroy its chemical stockpile of 50,000 tons and urged others to do so as well. Although the United States claimed that the Soviets had 200,000 tons, a revised 1990 CIA study showed that the Soviet total was indeed 50,000. Under President George Bush, the United States continued to produce binary nerve gas weapons until June 1, 1990, when Bush and Soviet leader Gorbachev signed an agreement to stop production of chemical weapons, and its ratification was awaited. Thus, the January 1989 Paris meeting did not end the production of chemical weapons.

January 12, 1989

Congress begins to dispute the deal with Japan on the FSX fighter plane.

Although the U.S.-Japanese fighter aircraft venture had been discussed for more than a year, Congress paid little attention until the *Wall Street Journal* on January 12 gave details of recent decisions by Mitsubishi Industries, the prime contractor, and General Dynamics, whose F-16 would be the prototype plane used in the $1.2 billion program. Claiming that General Dynamics's share of the work was indefinite and that advanced U.S. technology needed protection, Congress proposed to restrict the deal.

Rather than pass a resolution against the deal that could have ended it, congressional opponents passed a law with restrictions to guarantee 40% of the work for Americans. President Bush vetoed the bill, and a Senate vote upheld the veto on September 13, 1989. Plans for the FSX went ahead.

See October 2, 1987.

January 15, 1989

The Soviet Union reports that its last troops have left Afghanistan.

While the United States gave military assistance to the Afghan rebels, Soviet aid continued to the Afghan government. When President George Bush took office in 1989, he insisted that Afghanistani President Najibullah and his aides go into exile before supervised elections chose a new government. The Soviet Union rejected this position, and the fighting in Afghanistan continued between the rebels and government forces.

Since agreeing to withdraw its forces, the Soviet Union kept the fixed timetable. Attempts by the Kabul government to negotiate with the rebels had not been successful, however, and the United States continued to supply the rebels even though they failed to unite. During a meeting in Islamabad, Pakistan, on January 10, the negotiations were suspended because of disputes between Pakistan-based and Iranian-based rebels.

See April 14, 1988.

January 15, 1989

Demonstrations in Czechoslovakia led by Václav Hável are dispersed by police using water cannons.

The demonstrations in Prague celebrated the twentieth anniversary of a student's suicide to protest the August 1968 Soviet-led Warsaw Pact invasion of the city (see August 20, 1968). Led by Hável, a dissident playwright, protests continued for six days with over

400 protesters being arrested including Hával himself. The Czech protests heralded 1989 as the year during which other Soviet satellite nations moved to end their communist regimes.

On later Czechoslovakian developments, see November 28, 1989.

January 15, 1989

Thirty-five nations approve a comprehensive agreement on human rights in Europe and North America.

The third follow-up meeting to the Helsinki Accords of 1975 began on November 4, 1986, in Vienna and concluded on January 15. The first Helsinki sessions and the second in Madrid prepared the way for more specific agreements on all forms of human rights and government performance to respect them. In the 79-page agreement, provisions were made to continue meetings on confidence and security-building measures among all European states as well as negotiations on the reduction of conventional armed forces in Europe between the NATO and Warsaw Pact alliances.

See April 28, 1992.

January 19, 1989

President Reagan permits U.S. oil companies to resume business in Libya but still blames Libya for supporting terrorism.

In January 1986, Reagan imposed economic sanctions against Libya for allegedly plotting the Rome and Vienna airport terrorist attacks of December 1987. He permitted five U.S. oil companies to resume business to prevent Libya from nationalizing them and to stop Libyan leader Mu'ammar al-Gadhafi from receiving the oil profits. Reagan's orders permitted the U.S. managers to operate, sell, or transfer ownership of the companies.

On January 18, the State Department reported that Libya continued to assist terrorists. According to the report, since the U.S. air raid of April 15, 1986, Libya had supported an average of one terrorist attack each month and was linked to attacks on U.S. information libraries in Colombia, Peru, and Costa Rica, using Panama as a base.

January 20, 1989

George Bush is inaugurated as the 41st president of the United States.

Unlike President Reagan, whose first inaugural of 1981 shared headlines with Iran's release of American hostages, Bush faced national economic problems, the waning of the Cold War, and decisions about Soviet leader Mikhail Gorbachev's policies of glasnost and perestroika, which sought, among other things, cooperation between East and West.

January 27–29, 1989

Delegates at a Moscow conference reveal that U.S. President Kennedy made concessions to the Soviets during the Cuban missile crisis of 1962.

The Moscow conference was one in a series of meetings featuring the 1962 crisis participants and scholars to record and analyze their statements at the time. American officials participating in the crisis initially met at Hawks Cay, Florida, in January 1987. They also joined three Soviet participants at a Cambridge,

President George H. W. Bush. National Archives

Massachusetts, session in October 1987. Because the Cold War was winding down, the January 1989 conference in Moscow included Americans, Russians, and a Cuban delegation.

The meeting was especially revealing by disclosing that President John F. Kennedy did not take a firm stance against Soviet Premier Nikita Khrushchev, as traditional accounts had claimed. Rather, on October 27, 1962, Kennedy offered concessions to Krushchev with a definite pledge to withdraw U.S. nuclear missiles from Turkey in exchange for the withdrawal of Soviet missiles from Cuba. Although scholars previously hinted at Kennedy's willingness to compromise, Theodore Sorensen told the Moscow delegates that he deleted Kennedy's promise to remove the Turkish missiles when he edited Robert Kennedy's memoir of October's *Thirteen Days*, published in 1969. Robert promised that his brother the president would withdraw the Turkish missiles during an October 27 meeting with Soviet Ambassador Anatoly Dobrynin. The Soviet ambassador agreed to keep the promise secret for fear of the reaction of the NATO allies of the United States.

In addition to the sessions at Hawk's Cay, Cambridge, and Moscow, there was a conference in Havana, Cuba, in January 1992.

At Havana, the Soviets revealed that contrary to CIA estimates in October 1962, they had 35 nuclear warheads in Cuba between October 16 and 28, 1962, which could be used if the United States tried to invade Cuba. These sessions were supplemented with declassified documents by the United States, the Soviets, and Cuba that provided other important details about the 1962 Cuban missile crisis.

February 3, 1989

Paraguayan General Andrea Rodríguez ousts President Stroessner.

After ruling Paraguay since 1954, President Alfredo Stroessner was overthrown and sent into exile by his former aide, General Andrea Rodríguez, whose army troops fought and defeated Stroessner's Presidential Escort Battalion. After gaining control of Paraguay, Rodríguez called for elections in May 1989. In these elections, Rodríguez's Colorado Party gained control of Congress, although the elections were marked by extensive fraud. Nevertheless, the May elections became a first step in liberalizing the Colorado

Party's control over Paraguay as well as reforming the election process, freedom of the press, and freedom of association in Paraguay.

See April 22, 1996.

February 6, 1989

The Polish government agrees to hold talks with opposition leaders.

The Polish government inaugurated talks with opposition groups to negotiate political and economic reforms. An agreement was reached during a January 27 meeting among government representatives, leaders of the Roman Catholic Church, and Solidarity trade union leader Lech Wałęsa.

See August 31, 1988.

February 10, 1989

President Bush and Canadian Prime Minister Mulroney discuss air pollution.

Because Mulroney feared acid rain drifting into Canada caused by U.S. industrial pollution, President Bush agreed to push for laws to reduce such pollution. The president asked Congress to amend the 1970 Clear Air Act, but the process was complex. Congress needed data on the level of pollutants to reduce the effect of regulation on the health

and safety of the coal miners whose output was the primary cause of acid rain.

See November 15, 1990.

February 14, 1989

Lebanese Christian forces led by General Anoun fight rival Christians led by General Geagea.

Although Muslim factions of Syrian-backed Amal and Iranian-backed Shiites accepted a cease-fire among themselves, the Christian forces of General Michel Anoun began fighting rival Christians led by Samir Geagea. On February 17, the United States evacuated 12 of its embassy workers from Beirut to Cyprus after Christian army shellfire struck the embassy.

See November 24, 1989.

February 14, 1989

Iran issues a fatwa to kill Indian author Salman Rushdie.

Iranian religious leader Ayatollah Ruholla Khomeini's *fatwa* (religious finding) urged Muslims to "execute" Indian-born novelist Rushdie. Khomeini called Rushdie's novel, *The Satanic Verses* "blasphemous." As a result, Britain broke diplomatic relations with Iran and the European Community recalled its

Prime Minister Brian Mulroney and President Bush meet at Walker's Point to discuss acid rain problems. George Bush Presidential Library

ambassadors from Teheran. The United States had already terminated relations with Iran on April 7, 1980. Rushdie, who was living in England, went into hiding after the *fatwa* was issued.

February 23, 1989

The United States approves formation of a rebel government in Afghanistan.

The Afghan exile government in Pakistan was made up of seven rebel leaders who elected moderate Sibghatullah Mojaddidi president and radical Muslim leader Abdul Rasul Sayaf premier. In February, President Bush rejected Soviet leader Mikhail Gorbachev's offer to embargo arms shipments to Afghanistan because the United States claimed the Soviets left stockpiles of arms for Afghanistan's pro-Soviet government when they withdrew on January 15, 1989.

See June 5, 1989.

February 25, 1989

Soviet troops disperse demonstrators in the Soviet republic of Georgia.

In Tbilisi, Georgia, 15,000 people led by the National Democratic Party staged a protest against the Soviet Union on the anniversary of Georgia's annexation by the Soviets in 1921. To quell the protests, Soviet police arrested over 500 dissidents. Later, from April 9 to 14, 1989, Soviet soldiers killed 20 demonstrators and arrested many others before forcing Georgia's Communist Party leader to resign. He was replaced on April 14 with Georgia's KGB chief, Givi Gumbaridzhe.

February 27, 1989

President Bush attends burial services for Japanese Emperor Hirohito.

Bush began a week's visit to East Asia by joining 700 foreign dignitaries for burial ceremonies for Emperor Hirohito, who died on January 7. Hirohito's position was taken by Crown Prince Akihito. Following the ceremonies, Bush visited China and South Korea. In China, Bush received assurances that Soviet leader Mikhail Gorbachev's forthcoming visit to Beijing would not result in a new Soviet-Chinese alliance. Bush's visit was marred by China's refusal to allow the dissident Fang Lizhi to attend a banquet Bush

hosted. In Seoul, Bush urged South Korea's National Assembly to promote a free-market economy by ending protectionist trade policies.

February 27, 1989

Protests in Venezuela oppose austerity measures adopted for the IMF.

After being inaugurated on February 1, President Carlos Andrés Pérez sought to resolve the nation's debt problem—a difficulty faced by other Latin American countries as well. On February 17, he adopted the austerity program proposed by the International Monetary Fund by increasing transportation fare by 50 percent and gasoline prices by 90 percent. Riots broke out in Caracas by opponents of the IMF measures, which called for cutting social programs and reducing wages. In response to the protests, Pérez renounced the IMF's austerity program by again levying price controls and providing wage increases to restore order in Venezuela.

March 2, 1989

The European Community agrees to ban by 2000 chlorofluorocarbons that deplete the ozone layer.

The EC decision to ban these gases anticipated a March 7, 1990, conference of 123 nations meeting in London to approve this ban. The decision also complemented a May 2 meeting of 80 nations in Helsinki that supported the 1987 Montreal Protocol to end the production of chlorofluorocarbons no later than 2000.

March 11, 1989

The United States and Israel announce a peace plan to moderate the *Intifada* uprising.

Hoping to bring some sort of peace to its occupied territories on the West Bank and in Gaza, Israel agreed to stop the detention and deportation of Palestinians in the territories and reduce its troops in Palestinian areas. At the same time, the United States would urge Yasser Arafat's Palestine Liberation Organization (PLO) to moderate the *intifada*'s uprising and stop PLO raids from south Lebanon into Israel.

Israel also encouraged peace on March 15 by returning Taba beach to Egypt, a part of the Sinai retained by Israel under the 1979 agreement.

See May 5, 1979; December 9, 1987; July 28, 1989.

March 10, 1989

The United States seeks to reduce debts of developing countries and nations adopting free-market reforms.

U.S. Treasury Secretary Nicholas F. Brady suggested a plan under which international financiers would reduce debts of developing countries and the IMF/World Bank would aid debt reductions in countries adopting free-market reforms and austerity policies comparable to the Reagan program introduced in the 1980s.

March 17, 1989

The Senate approves Richard Cheney as defense secretary.

President Bush's national security team was completed when the Senate approved Cheney as secretary of defense. James A. Baker and Brent Scrowcroft were already approved by the Senate as secretary of state and national security adviser, respectively, but Bush's nomination of John G. Tower as defense secretary had been rejected by the Senate on February 23 following an FBI investigation of his alcohol problems and charges of sexual misconduct.

March 20, 1989

The State Department says U.S. relations with El Salvador require its new government to respect human rights and democracy.

Because El Salvador's March 19 elections had problems with dissidents protesting El Salvador's human rights violations, the United States said future diplomatic relations depended on the newly elected President Alfredo Cristiani's policy on human rights. Rebels in the Farabundo Marti National Liberation Front (FMLN) boycotted El Salvador's March elections because they wanted to delay elections for six months. Cristiani won the election with 54 percent of the vote against the Christian Democratic Party's Fidel Chivez Mena, who gained 36 percent; the remaining votes were won by three small parties.

On February 3, 1989, U.S. Vice President J. Danforth ("Dan") Quayle visited Salvador to emphasize U.S. concerns for human rights and to urge the FMLN and other parties to participate in the elections. After the FMLN refused, the civil war continued between the rebels and the government despite additional cease-fire negotiations in Mexico City on September 7 and in Costa Rica beginning on October 16.

See November 20, 1989.

March 23, 1989

Serbia adopts illegal terms by claiming Kosovo's assembly approved amendments to Serbia's constitution.

Kosovo and Vojvodina were two autonomous provinces within the Serb Republic as established by the Federated Republic of Yugoslavia's 1974 constitution. Under the 1974 constitution, six of the eight seats on the Yugoslav Presidency's were occupied by one delegate from each of the six Yugoslav Republics: Serbia, Slovenia, Croatia, Bosnia-Herzegovina, Montenegro, and Macedonia. The Presidency's other two seats were for one representative from Kosovo Province and one from Vojvodina Province. In addition, the 1974 constitution provided that the provincial assemblies of Vojvodina and Kosovo must vote by a two-thirds majority whenever the Republic of Serbia proposed amendments to the Serb Republic's constitution. Thus, when the Republic of Serbia's National Assembly approved amendments to its constitution in 1988, Serbian President Slobodan Milošević had to persuade assemblies of Vojvodina and Kosovo to approve those amendments by a two-thirds vote (see November 8, 1988).

In early 1989, when Warren Zimmermann became U.S. Ambassador to Yugoslavia, he quickly realized the unity of Yugoslavia was threatened owing to economic disputes among the three most prosperous republics: Slovenia, Serbia, and Croatia. Although the Bush administration decided Yugoslavia was no longer of strategic importance to the United States, Ambassador Zimmermann warned Washington that Serb President Milošević endangered Yugoslav unity. Zimmermann informed the State Department that the threat to Yugoslav unity came from Milošević's call for a Greater Serbia that would include Serbian minorities living in Croatia, Bosnia-Herzegovina, Montenegro, and Macedonia as well as Serbia's autonomous province of Kosovo, where nearly 90% of the population were ethnic Albanian (Kosovars). Both Milošević and Kosovo's 10% Serbian population believed a Greater Serbia was destined to be established by Serb control over Kosovo as a sacred homeland where Serbian armies fought Ottoman Turks during a historic battle in 1389. Furthermore, the Patriarch of the Serbian Orthodox Church resided in Pec, a city in Kosovo.

As for Vojvodina, ethnic Serbs were nearly 50% of the population, with the other 50% being ethnic Hungarians. Thus, Milošević easily persuaded Vojvodina's provincial assembly to approve the Serb Republic's amendments to the constitution, but Kosovar demonstrations and strikes opposed to the amendments broke out in Kosovo during November 1988. The protest movements escalated in 1989 as the date approached for Kosovo's assembly to vote on the amendments.

In response to the protests, Milošević declared martial law in Kosovo on February 20, 1989. Despite strong objections to martial law from the governments of Slovenia and Croatia, Milošević sent two battalions of soldiers from the Serb-dominated Yugoslav National Army (YNA) to enforce martial law and end Kosovo's "disorders." Thus on March 23, while Kosovo's provincial assembly met to vote on the amendments that would end Kosovo's autonomy, YNA tanks, artillery, and armored personnel carriers surrounded the assembly building. Inside, officials from Belgrade mingled with the assembly delegates to check on how each person voted and, allegedly, cast illegal ballots.

Under these circumstances, a majority of assembly votes approved the amendments but failed to get the two-thirds required by the Yugoslav constitution of 1974. When Milošević received news about Kosovo's vote, he took another illegal step by declaring a simple majority, not the required two-thirds, was sufficient to approve the amendments. He also ordered the YNA and the Serb Republic's Minister of the Interior to replace all Kosovar officials with Serbian officials, including the police, judges, and all criminal justice officers. The March 1989 events enabled Milošević to gain control of four seats on Yugoslavia's eight-member presidency. By April 1989, Milošević appeared to be on the way toward completing his dream of a Greater Serbia, but leaders of Croatia, Slovenia, and Bosnia-Herzegovina blocked the way toward Milošević's Greater Serbia.

See November 8, 1988; January 23, 1990.

March 26, 1989

Multi-candidate elections in the Soviet Union result in mixed results for Communist Party candidates.

First Secretary of the Communist Party of the Soviet Union Mikhail Gorbachev decided to call for multi-party election in March 1989 as another step toward his program to democratize the Soviet Union's shift to a civil society. As defined by the Communist Party's Central Committee, the March elections would choose members for a new Soviet Congress of People's Deputies as a parliament to meet twice a year. Of the 2,250 members being elected for the Congress of People's Deputies, 1,500 would represent people from all of the Soviet republics. The Communist Party's Central Committee selected the other 750 members during its January 10, 1989 meeting in Moscow.

In the March 26 elections, Communist Party members won 1,200 of the 1,500 at large seats in the Congress of People's Deputies. Of the remaining seats in Congress, 300 represented various parties scattered throughout the Soviet Union and, of course, the Central Committee's candidates made up the remaining 750 members, giving a total of 2,250 delegates to the Congress of People's Deputies. Notably, Leningrad's Communist Party chief, Yury F. Solovyev, lost in the election because 130,000 voters used their right to cross out Solovyev's name on the ballot while only 110,000 people voted for Solovyev. Boris Yeltsin chose to run for one of Moscow's seats, correctly believing he could win because of his popularity among Muscovities.

See May 29, 1989.

March 28, 1989

Iraq compensates families of Americans killed in the 1987 Exocet missile attack.

The U.S. State Department announced it would accept Iraq's offer to pay $27.3 million in compensation to families of 37 Americans killed when an Iraqi Exocet missile hit the USS *Stark* during the Iran-Iraq war.

See May 17, 1987.

April 9, 1989

A military coup in Haiti fails to oust President Avril.

An army coup failed in Haiti because loyal palace guards rescued President Prosper Avril. The elite battalion of officers attempting the coup opposed Avril's dismissal of four army officers accused of drug trafficking. The elite battalion began the coup on April 2 and continued fighting against Avril's loyal troops until April 9.

See December 16, 1990.

April 25, 1989

The Soviet Union begins pulling its troops out of Eastern Europe.

The Kremlin announced that 1,000 battle tanks had been withdrawn from Hungary as part of the Soviet program to withdraw 10,000 tanks and 56,000 personnel carriers from Eastern Europe. By May 5, it also had withdrawn 1,000 tanks from East Germany.

April 28, 1989

The United States sends mixed signals regarding its policies toward Japan.

Mixed signals in U.S. policy toward Japan emanated from Washington. The same day the United States and Japan agreed to cooperate in developing the FSX fighter aircraft, U.S. trade Representative Carla Hill threatened retaliation against Japanese imports if Tokyo did not drop restrictions on U.S. access to Japan's telecommunications and radio market. Hill's report also cited trade barriers to U.S. products in South Korea, Taiwan, Brazil, India, and the European Community. Japan, however, continued to have the greatest surplus in U.S. trade relations.

See January 12, 1989.

April 30, 1989

President Bush thanks Iran for releasing U.S. hostages held in Lebanon.

President Bush thanked Iran for assisting in the release of Frank Reed, who had been held hostage in Lebanon by the Iran-backed Hezbollah since 1986. The first information that Iran would assist in the hostage release came on February 22, when a *Tehran Times* editorial urged Lebanese Muslim groups to release its hostages. Subsequently, on April 22, both Reed and Robert Pohill were released by Islamic Jihad. Pohill was an American University of Beirut professor captured in January 1987. Bush indicated there was no deal with Iran for the hostage release.

See October 21, 1986.

May 4, 1989

Hungary dismantles its fence border with Austria.

Since October 18, 1988, when Hungary adopted a constitution to guarantee human rights, its government moved toward democracy. Now, in what became a significant change of policy for Eastern Europe, Hungary's government ordered its troops to dismantle the barbed wire fence that separated it from Austria. The decision opened the so-called iron curtain dividing Europe since the end of World War II.

For effect of this act on East Germany, see September 10, 1989.

May 4, 1989

Oliver North is found guilty of obstructing Congress in the Iran-Contra affair.

A U.S. federal court found Oliver North guilty of obstructing the congressional investigation of the Iran-Contra affair, which arose under President Reagan. In January 1989, Special Prosecutor Lawrence Walsh dropped the more serious charge of U.S. Marine Colonel Oliver North's illegally diverting $14 million to Nicaragua's Contra rebels because the Reagan administration refused to declassify materials Walsh requested that might prove North guilty.

Despite the scandal involving the Nicaraguan Contras during the 1980s, President Bush sought and received $49.9 million in "nonlethal" aid for the Contras, who were trying to overthrow the socialist regime of Daniel Ortega, even though Nicaragua was working with the United Nations to plan for democratic elections in 1990.

See June 25, 1986; April 7, 1990.

May 11, 1989

The United States sends more troops to Panama following a fraudulent election.

President Bush sent an additional 2,000 U.S. troops to Panama to bolster the 12,000 U.S. army personnel already there after a fraudulent election renewed the power of Panama's military leader, General Manuel Antonio Noriega. International observers overseeing the May 7 elections claimed that the Democratic Alliance's candidate, Guillermo Endara, won by a margin of 3-to-1 before government troops raided the vote-counting centers and Noriega's candidate, Carlos Duque, claimed victory. Because violence erupted after popular demonstrations Bush denounced the elections and sent more U.S. forces to Panama.

See December 20, 1989.

May 13, 1989

The United States and Iran settle small claims from the 1979 Iranian Revolution.

The United States and Iran signed an agreement to settle 2,000 small claims that resulted from the 1979 Iranian Revolution. The U.S. claims were brought to the Claims Tribunal of the International Court of Justice in The Hague. Iran agreed to pay the United States $105 million as a settlement.

May 14, 1989

Peronists win the presidency and control of Argentina's Congress.

In Argentine elections, Peronist candidates won the presidency and gained control of both houses of Congress. Replacing Raul Alfonsin, President Carlos Saul Menem planned to undertake a reform program designed to privatize state industries and end Argentina's high inflation rate.

May 25, 1989

The Soviet Congress of People's Deputies elects a new Supreme Soviet with Mikhail Gorbachev as its president.

The 2,250 members of the Congress of People's Deputies elected in March convened its first session in Moscow on May 25 (see March 26, 1989). During the two week session of the People's Deputies, some delegates made unprecedented public criticism of Soviet Chairman Mikhail Gorbachev, the Soviet Communist Party, and the KGB's operations as the secret service. Before adjourning on June 9, the People's Deputies elected a new Supreme Soviet with 542 members as a standing legislature and elected Gorbachev as the Supreme Soviet's President. In the People's Deputies election, Gorbachev gained 95% of the votes with some hard-line communists casting blank ballots because they opposed Gorbachev's reform program. Thus, blank ballots made the Deputies vote more democratic than the automatic 100% votes of the old Supreme Soviet but, as Garthoff indicates in *The Great Transition*, a "long step" away from a popular democratic vote for the presidency. The People's Deputies also elected Nikolai I. Ryzhkov as prime minister of the new Supreme Soviet.

May 29–30, 1989

NATO accepts U.S. proposals to reduce Europe's short-range missiles and U.S.-USSR conventional forces.

After Secretary of State James Baker visited European allies and Moscow, he realized the issue of conventional forces in Europe (CFE) was closely linked to short-range nuclear missile forces (SNF) that were not part of the 1987 intermediate-range nuclear forces (INF) treaty. On March 5, Baker was in Vienna when the negotiations on CFE began. The CFE talks involved members of NATO and the Warsaw Pact seeking to determine how many combat aircraft, tanks, armored personnel carriers, and artillery each side should retain for "purely defensive purposes." After the first round of CFE talks failed to reach an agreement, Baker returned to Washington where he persuaded President Bush to link CFE with SNF during NATO's May 29–30 sessions.

To prepare for future CFE negotiations, President Bush and other NATO leaders held a summit to develop a strategy for future talks with the Warsaw Pact. An immediate NATO concern was NATO plans to deploy America's newest Lance missiles in Germany. Although Chancellor Helmut Kohl had opposed deploying the new missiles in West Germany, he finally accepted a U.S. proposal for "partial reductions" in NATO's SNF as well as a 20% reduction of U.S. and Soviet troops in Europe. The 20% would be an initial CFE reduction for CFE negotiators' consideration. Any remaining U.S. Lance missiles in West Germany would be pulled out after the CFE agreement was finalized.

See December 8, 1987; November 17, 1990.

June 3, 1989

Iran selects Khamenei to replace the Ayatollah Khomeini.

Following the death of Iranian religious leader Ayatollah Khomeini, the Shiite theologians selected Hojatolislam Seyed Ali Khamenei to succeed him. On July 28, the Majlis (parliament) elected Hojatolislam Hashemi Rafsanjani as president.

June 3–4, 1989

Chinese troops kill hundreds of protesters in Tiananmen Square.

U.S. relations with China were severely tested after hundreds of Chinese demonstrators were killed in the "Tiananmen massacres." Protests against Chinese police who killed four bicyclists brought thousands of Chinese to Beijing's Tiananmen Square on June 3, where army troops and tanks assaulted the protesters, killing hundreds and wounding many more.

Student demonstrations had begun on April 15 following the death of Communist Party leader Hu Yaobang, who was considered a party reformer. Protests grew during the days leading to Hu's burial on April 22, and students presented their grievances to Premier Li Peng that included demands for more democratic politics and punishment of corrupt Communist Party officials. The students accepted the party's authority because Premier Li promised to continue Hu's reforms. Zhao Ziyang, who replaced Hu as party leader, was sympathetic to the students' reform proposals but other party leaders, including Deng Xiaoping—China's actual ruler—opposed political changes.

On May 15, Soviet Communist Party First Secretary Mikhail Gorbachev visited Beijing, and with television cameras and other world media reporting the visit, Chinese students publicized their cause by staging a hunger strike at Tiananmen Square. After Gorbachev departed, Deng dealt harshly with the students, declaring martial law and bringing in local army troops. The troops fraternized with demonstrators and many army officers signed a student letter against using violence to disperse demonstrators. By June 3, these local troops had not cleared the square of protesters and Premier Li brought army units from outside Beijing to replace them. The new

units led an assault to disperse the protesters, which took place after midnight on June 3 when foreign television cameras and reporters quickly transmitted the bloody events by satellite around the world, sending pictures of soldiers bayoneting civilians. During the next month, Deng continued persecuting dissidents and purged the party of all pro-democracy members, including party General Secretary Zhao Ziyang. The government executed 7 dissidents in Beijing, 17 in Janin, and 3 in Shanghi.

June 5, 1989

President Bush responds to the Tiananmen massacres with stringent measures.

In response to the Tiananmen massacres, President Bush took punitive actions, short of severing relations, to demonstrate U.S. disapproval of China's tactics. On June 5, he announced sanctions against China suspending all military sales and high-level contacts and asking the IMF and World Bank to postpone Chinese loan applications. He also declared that the U.S. embassy in Beijing was correct in giving refuge to Chinese dissident Fang Lizhi and his wife. Nevertheless, Bush arranged secret meetings of U.S. officials with the Chinese to prevent the complete breakdown of diplomatic and trade relations.

On the secret U.S. actions, see July 1, 1989.

June 5, 1989

President Bush and Pakistani Prime Minister Bhutto discuss Afghanistan.

President Bush met with Prime Minister Benazir Bhutto to discuss methods of achieving peace in Afghanistan as rebel factions continued the civil war there. In Washington, Bhutto also spoke before a joint session of Congress to assure its members that Pakistan's nuclear program was intended only for peaceful purposes.

See November 3, 1990.

June 19, 1989

Burma's military regime changes the country's name in English to Union of Myanmar.

June 27, 1989

European Community members all agree to join the European Monetary Union.

Meeting in Madrid, European Community (EC) ministers agreed their countries would join the European Monetary System in July 1990. Although British Prime Minister Margaret Thatcher was expected to oppose any movement toward EC unity, she helped formulate a compromise to broaden the European Monetary System during the next year to establish a central bank and common currency.

July 1, 1989

U.S. officials make a secret trip to Beijing to sustain contacts with Chinese leaders.

Despite China's massacre of protesters in Tiananmen Square on June 4, President Bush sent secret emissaries to Beijing for a day of clandestine talks. Believing contacts with Beijing were essential to retain some semblance of favorable trade and diplomatic relations despite widespread congressional opposition, Bush decided secret contacts were worth the risk and sent National Security Adviser Brent Scowcroft and Deputy Secretary of State Larry Eagleburger to Beijing. Previously, Bush wrote to Chinese leader Deng Xiaoping asking the Chinese to accept the secret dispatch of two U.S. envoys.

As Bush and Scowcroft explain in their book *A World Transformed* (1998), the Americans flew to Beijing to avoid a complete rupture in U.S. relations with China. Scowcroft carried a message to Deng Xiaoping that President Bush had to protest the massacres by imposing sanctions but did not want to destroy the good relations with China that existed previously. U.S. relations with China could revive if Deng stopped the arbitrary executions of dissidents and ended martial law. The secret visit was not disclosed to the U.S. public until December.

See December 9, 1989

July 1, 1989

Soviet leader Mikhail Gorbachev sees ethnic nationalism as a danger to the Soviet empire.

Gorbachev saw evidence of nationalism's danger in demonstrations held in the Soviet Republic of Georgia in February and April, in Georgia's autonomous province of Abkhazia during March, and in Soviet Uzbekistan in June. Gorbachev's television address failed to halt the rise of nationalism as it grew stronger in 1989.

Although Gorbachev complained again about "separatist" nationalism in a speech on September 19, words proved incapable of stopping the division among the Soviet republics. The local governments of Lithuania and Estonia passed laws to introduce free-market policies and on July 30, 1989, the Russian Republic under Boris Yeltsin formed the 300 members of its Congress of People's Deputies into an Inter-Regional Group of Deputies.

See August 17, 1989.

July 6, 1989

The United States accepts communist leader Hun Sen as part of the Cambodian government.

Before the summer of 1989, the United States refused to recognize Cambodia's government of President Heng Samrin and Foreign Minister Hun Sen because Vietnam backed that regime. On June 6, Secretary of State James Baker said he was willing to recognize the legitimacy of Heng Samrin's government as a "fact of life" especially because Vietnam was withdrawing its troops from Cambodia. Nevertheless, Baker said the United States would not allow any Cambodian government to have any Khmer Rouge leaders who were part of the Pol Pot regime that killed millions of Cambodians during the 1970s (see December 14, 1987).

Thus, Baker revised U.S. policy and supported negotiations between Hun and opposition leader Prince Norodom Sihanouk that began on May 2, 1989. By July, Sihanouk and Hun formed an alliance and international discussions regarding Cambodia moved to Paris on July 23. The Paris talks had delegates from 19 nations including the United States and the Soviet Union, but they could not resolve the disputes among Cambodia's main factions, largely because China insisted on giving the Khmer Rouge a role in a new government. The peace talks collapsed on August 28 while heavy fighting continued between the Khmer Rouge and Hun Sen's army.

See July 18, 1990.

July 7, 1989

Soviet leader Mikhail Gorbachev recognizes that communist nations have varied ways to solve their economic problems.

As Soviet leader in 1985, Gorbachev found ways to begin reforming the Soviet economy. On July 7, he suggested these reform ideas to the USSR's Warsaw Pact allies at their annual meeting in Bucharest, Romania. Gorbachev called for tolerance among communist leaders who had "independent solutions of national problems." The summit's final press release said there were "no universal models of socialism."

Some Warsaw Pact nations had already begun instituting reforms. On June 24, 1989, Hungary reformed the Communist Party's Central Committee by establishing a four-member presidium headed by reform advocate Rezso Nyers, who became party chairman. Other Presidium members were Party General Secretary Karóny Grósz, Premier Miklós Németh, and Minister of State Imre Poszgay. In Poland, the reformist Solidarity Union was making rapid headway by moving to invigorate Poland's private sector of the economy.

See July 18 and August 17, 1989.

July 13–19, 1989

President Bush offers economic aid to Poland and Hungary and attends the G-7 summit.

During an extensive European tour, President Bush's trip was highlighted by visits to Poland and Hungary. Because both nations had undertaken market-oriented economic reforms to improve trade relations with the Western powers, Bush promised the two nations financial aid from the United States and the World Bank.

On July 14, Bush attended the annual G-7 meeting in Paris, where there were celebrations for the 200th anniversary of the French Revolution. The G-7 members agreed to provide financial aid to Hungary and Poland but condemned China's military action against its pro-democracy demonstrators on June 3–4. They also called for restrictions on ozone-depleting chemicals and for international efforts to control drug traffic.

July 18, 1989

Poland's legislature elects Wojciech Jaruzelski president of a democratic government.

Since 1988, when Solidarity leader Lech Wałęsa ended strikes against the government, Poland had moved toward democracy. Beginning in January 1989, First Secretary of the Polish United Workers Party General Jaruzelski met with Wałęsa's Solidarity movement/

Helmut Kohl, George Bush, and François Mitterrand enjoy a joke at the G-7 meeting. George Bush Presidential Library

union and on April 5 agreed to abandon the existing unicameral legislature. The new parliament consisted of a Senate with 100 seats and a lower house (Sejm) with 460 seats. The United Workers (Communist) Party and its allies would have 65 percent of the Sejm seats with the remainder as well as all Senate seats filled by free elections. Elections were held on June 4 with runoffs conducted on June 18. Solidarity won 99 of the 100 Senate seats as well as all 161 opposition seats in the Sejm. The Communist Party had 294 Sejm seats reserved for them.

On July 18, a joint session of parliament elected Communist Party First Secretary Jaruzelski as president. Former Interior Minister Czesław Kiszczak was to be premier but could not form a coalition to govern.

See August 24, 1989.

July 23, 1989

Japan's ruling party loses its upper-house majority.

Japan's ruling Liberal Democratic Party lost its majority in the upper house of the Diet (parliament) but retained a majority in the more powerful lower house. The elections were a setback for Japan's longtime ruling party, coming in the wake of Prime Minister Naboru Takeshita's admission on April 11, 1989, that he had been involved in influence peddling. On August 9, Toshiki Kaifu was elected prime minister, although the upper-house majority voted for Takako Doi, leader of Japan's Socialist Party.

July 23, 1989

Mexico accepts IMF restrictions to obtain financial assistance.

Mexican President Carlos Salinas de Gortari accepted the U.S. "Brady Plan" to relieve Mexico's $53 billion of medium- and long-term debts. In exchange for its adoption of International Monetary Fund (IMF) principles requiring Mexico to privatize its state-owned enterprises and promote free trade with other nations, Mexico's 500 international creditors agreed either to reduce interest, reduce principal, or extend further credits. The July arrangements came after the IMF agreed on April 11 to provide a $3.64 billion loan to enable Mexico to repay $104 billion of its foreign obligations.

See March 10, 1989.

July 28, 1989

Israel captures Hezbollah's spiritual leader in Lebanon.

Israeli commandos captured Sheik Abdul Karim Obeid, the spiritual head of the Hezbollah Muslim militia. Israeli officials offered to release Obeid and 100 other Lebanese detainees in exchange for all Israeli and Western hostages held in Lebanon. Rejecting the offer, Hezbollah kidnapped and hanged U.S. Marine Colonel William R. Higgins on July 30 and threatened to but did not kill American hostage Joseph James Cicippio.

August 17, 1989

President of the Supreme Soviet Mikhail Gorbachev plans economic autonomy for all Soviet republics.

According to Mikhail Gorbachev's *Memoirs*, Gorbachev wanted to resolve Soviet problems in 1989 by democratic discussions and tolerance, but at the same time to warn the Soviet people about extremists who sought to destroy the Soviet Union's unity. After consulting with the Central Committee of the Communist Party of the Soviet Union (CPSU), Gorbachev issued a publication titled, "The nationalities policy of the Party under modern conditions" on August 17, 1989. The publication emphasized the need for a "radical renewal of nationality policy" that would make "meaningful political and economic" changes, expand the opportunities of all forms of national autonomy, and guarantee equal rights for all people without infringing on the "rights of citizens because of nationality." At the same time, Gorbachev warned that extremists might try to tear apart the Soviet Union as a "living organism." The Soviet Communist Federation must not allow extremists to "begin destroying what we have created."

In brief, Gorbachev and the Communist Central Committee offered some degree of autonomy for each of the 15 USSR republics, while keeping the Central Committee's control over foreign affairs, defense, and internal security. Gorbachev believed the August 17 document was "outstanding" in trying to resolve the nationality problem, but leaders of the Baltic Republics and other Soviet republics saw the Central Committee offer of some autonomy as a half-way measure that came too late to satisfy their local nationalism.

Previously, on November 16, 1988, Estonia's Supreme Soviet had amended the Republic of Estonia's constitution by adding a Declaration of Sovereignty. On November 18, 1989, the Supreme Soviet of the Soviet Union declared Estonia's action was unconstitutional, but Estonia's nationalists ignored that decree. By August 1989, Latvia and Lithuania had joined Estonia in issuing Declarations of Sovereignty that led toward independence. Leaders in the three Baltic republics also held a memorial remembrance of the 50th anniversary of the 1939 Nazi-Soviet pact that annexed the three Baltic states to the Soviet Union's sphere-of influence (see August 23, 1939). The celebration was designed to promote the independence movement in the three Baltic Republics.

See August 20, 1991.

August 24, 1989

Polish communists join with Solidarity members to form a coalition ministry.

Between June 18 and August 23, 1989, Communist party leader Czesław Kiszczak was unable to form a cabinet with enough votes in Poland's parliament (Sejm). To resolve this political situation, Soviet leader Gorbachev telephoned the Chairman of the Communists Polish United Worker's Party (PUWP), Mieczyslau Rakowski. During the call, Gorbachev advised Rakowski that because national reconciliation was the best way to proceed in Poland, Rakowski should have Kiszczak join a coalition government led by Tadeusz Mazowiecki, a Solidarity member proposed by Solidarity leader Lech Wałęsa. As Raymond Garthoff's *The Great Transition* explains, Solidarity originated as a trade union movement in Gdansk but in 1989 campaigned as a political party to encourage all Polish workers and peasants to join Solidarity and campaign for local candidates for parliament. These efforts enabled Solidarity to win 99 of the 100 seats in Poland's senate and all 161 opposition seats permitted in the Sejm, the lower house of parliament (see July 18, 1989).

After Rakowski received approval to follow Gorbachev's advice from the PUWP's Politburo, Solidarity's Mazowiecki formed a cabinet that was confirmed by Poland's Senate and Sejm on September 12. The 23-member cabinet had 11 Solidarity members, 11 members from the Communist Party and its allies, and one independent member.

August 25, 1989

The United States provides Colombia aid to combat drug trafficking.

President Bush announced Colombia would receive $65 million of emergency aid to help fight the Medellín drug cartel. The U.S. aid included small arms, helicopters, jeeps, and military advisers to assist Colombia's war on drugs. The U.S. aid was dwarfed by the $4 billion the drug lords collected from drug users in North America and Europe. Colombia's problems increased on August 16 when assassins killed Colombian Judge Carlos Ernesto Valencia, who had upheld arrest warrants of two drug lords: Pablo Escobar and José Gonzaleo Rodríguez Gacha. On August 18, the cartel assassinated presidential candidate Luis Carlos Galan. The next day, President Vigilio Barco Vargas reinstated the U.S. extradition treaty of 1979 and issued emergency measures to keep drug suspects incommunicado for a week. At the same time, Barco refused President Bush's offer to send U.S. army forces to aid the war on drugs.

See October 14, 1989.

September 5, 1989

The United States increases spending on the "drug war."

President Bush told a TV audience he would allocate $7.9 billion for the "war on drugs" in fiscal year 1990. The costs did not include the $65 million of recent emergency aid to Colombia but was to fight drug traffickers in Peru, Bolivia, and Colombia, the source of many drugs consumed in the United States.

September 9, 1989

Boris Yeltsin, a Soviet politician, begins a U.S. visit.

Yeltsin, a former Communist Party official who was elected mayor of Moscow on March 26, disagreed with many of Soviet leader Gorbachev's policies. Yeltsin visited the United States to explain his beliefs that Gorbachev's political and economic reforms were not moving ahead as fast as they should be. He met with President Bush at the White House and visited New York, Baltimore, Chicago, and other cities.

September 10, 1989

Hungary acts to open its borders to Western Europe.

On May 4, when Hungary began dismantling its fences along the border with Austria, Hungary told East Germany's leaders to work out a solution to the emigration problem because East Germans often vacationed in Hungary. During the next three months, the East German government did nothing to resolve the emigration problem. Subsequently, on September 10, Hungary's Foreign Minister Gyula Horn announced East Germans could leave Hungary in any way they wished.

Subsequently, during the next 36 hours an estimated 10,500 East Germans crossed Hungary's border with Austria before moving on to West Germany. Although East Germany protested, the Soviet Union did not. By October 1, about 30,000 East Germans took the Hungarian route to the West.

See September 30, 1989.

September 21, 1989

In a speech at the United Nations, President Bush emphasizes the need to regulate chemical weapons.

President Bush's speech to the U.N. General Assembly emphasized the need for the world organization to help prevent the spread of chemical weapons, a project designed to complement a January 7, 1989, meeting in Paris at which 149 nations, including the USSR, reaffirmed their adherence to the 1925 Geneva Protocol opposing chemical weapons.

September 21, 1989

The United States and the USSR agree that with six months' notice either side could end the ABM treaty.

Soviet Foreign Minister Sheveradnadze visited Washington to deliver a letter from Soviet leader Gorbachev, asking if Bush would agree that either country could stop observing the Anti-Ballistic Missile (ABM) treaty of 1972 by giving six months'

notice. In addition, Gorbachev said the Soviets would destroy their Krasnoyarsk radar station, which the Reagan administration said violated the treaty.

In part, Gorbachev offered these terms after learning from Soviet dissident physicist Andrei Sakharov that the Soviets were wasting money on their missile defense research (SDI) that, Sakharov said, resembled the French Maginot Line in the 1930s. Sakharov had first stated these opinions at a secret meeting of U.S. and Soviet scientists in Moscow in 1987. U.S. scientists, whom the Reagan administration ignored, concurred with Sakharov's opinions.

See February 28, 1987.

September 30, 1989

East Germans seek to leave for West Germany via Prague.

After Hungary opened its Austrian border for East Germans to cross, Czechoslovakia experienced problems because over 5,500 East Germans had taken refuge in West Germany's Prague embassy and asked to go to the West. East German authorities agreed that the East Germans at their Prague embassy could go by train to the West, a decision precipitating the flight of East Germans who boarded trains in Dresden coming from Prague en route to the West. In Dresden, East German police clashed with an estimated 10,000 Germans who tried to board the trains. Because the Berlin Wall thus could now be bypassed, a crisis arose in East Germany.

See October 6, 1989.

October 3, 1989

The United States and Mexico reduce tariffs on certain products.

On a visit to Washington, Mexican President Salinas and President Bush signed an agreement to reduce import tariffs in specified industrial sectors including textiles. Salinas addressed the U.S. Congress on October 4, accusing Americans of exploiting Mexican immigrants and migrant workers.

October 6, 1989

Soviet leader Gorbachev tells East Germans to reform their government.

As some of its citizens were fleeing to West Germany, East Germany celebrated the 40th anniversary of its founding with Soviet leader Mikhail Gorbachev as the celebration's key speaker. Although the East German Communist Party's Politburo hoped for Soviet backing in suppressing protesters, Gorbachev told them to solve their problems by adopting Soviet-style reforms. His advice precipitated larger demonstrations in East Germany's main cities, with the police resorting to violence to beat and arrest protesters.

Owing to protests, East German leader Eric Honecker decided to "retire" from the Socialist Unity (Communist) Party (SED) on October 18. State Security Chief Egon Krenz was appointed SED chairman but protests continued in Berlin, Leipzig, Dresden, and elsewhere.

October 9, 1989

The Soviet Union fails to end protests by recognizing workers' right to strike.

Hoping to end strikes by Siberian miners, the Supreme Soviet (parliament) passed legislation recognizing the worker's right to strike but restricted circumstances permitting a strike and prohibited strikes in transportation, communication, defense and power-supply sectors. These concessions failed to end the Siberian unrest. Instead, workers staged more protests, seeking to implement the few concessions Gorbachev, as chairman of the Supreme Soviet, offered in July 1989.

October 14, 1989

The extradition of drug traffickers to the United States causes problems in Colombia.

After Colombia extradited four accused drug traffickers to the United States, new violence broke out in its drug war. On October 17, Federal Judge Hector Jiménez Rodríguez, who ordered the drug lords extradited, was assassinated. On November 27, a Boeing 727 exploded after taking off on a flight from Bogotá to Cali, Colombia, and 107 persons were killed. According to the U.S. Drug Enforcement Agency (DEA), the aircraft explosion and a bomb explosion outside a government building killing 452 people were probably the work of drug dealers protesting the extradition of drug suspects to America.

October 18, 1989

South Korea asks the United States not to reduce its troop strength on the Korean peninsula.

During a six-day U.S. visit, South Korean's President Roh Tae Woo asked a joint session of Congress not to cutback American troop strength in South Korea. Despite his efforts to build better relations with North Korea, Roh also approved U.S. plans for South Korea's purchase of 120 advanced fighter jets. On December 20, Seoul announced McDonnell Douglas would be South Korea's partner in constructing these planes.

October 18, 1989

The Hungarian National Assembly ends the powers of the Communist Party and inaugurates the Republic of Hungary.

The changes in Hungary's government began in early October at a special Hungarian Socialist Workers (Communist) Party Congress, whose delegates voted 1,005 to 159 to change their name to the Hungarian Socialist Party with a new party platform. The congress adjourned on October 9 after abolishing the party's four-member presidium and its Central Committee. It formed a 24-member presidium and elected reformer Reszo Nyers as president. The congress also divested the party of most of its property holdings and abandoned all Workers' Militia and party factory cells.

When the National Assembly met on October 18, it voted to delete the Hungarian constitution's references to the Communist Party's leading role. The assembly also approved laws to allow political parties, codify civil and human rights, and form separate executive, legislative, and judicial units.

On October 23 at a rally celebrating the 33rd anniversary of the 1956 uprising against Soviet forces, Hungarian President Mátyás Szuros fulfilled the National Assembly's desire by declaring the "free Republic of Hungary" to replace the "People's Republic of Hungary." On November 16, a national referendum decided Hungary's president should be elected by parliament, not by popular vote. Hungary's first free elections for parliament was on March 28, 1990.

October 21, 1989

President Bush disrupts Nicaraguan plans for democratic elections.

By approving legislation granting $9 million aid to Nicaragua's Contra rebels, President Bush disrupted Nicaragua's plans for democratic elections scheduled for February 1990. In cooperation with the United Nations, presidents of five Central American countries (Guatemala, Honduras, El Salvador, Costa Rica, and Nicaragua) had agreed to close Contra bases in Honduras and relocate the rebels so Nicaragua could hold democratic elections.

On April 18, 1989, Nicaragua's socialist government of President Daniel Ortega approved laws for "free and fair" elections, and on September 2, the moderate Coalition National Opposition Union (UNO) named Violeta Barrios de Chamorro, owner of the opposition's *La Prensa* newspaper, as its presidential candidate.

These U.N. plans were ruptured after Bush approved aid to the Contras, who ambushed and killed 19 Nicaraguan soldiers. Because the Contras violated the U.N.-brokered cease-fire, Ortega said new military operations would continue against the Contras until the United States stopped financing them. On November 9, Ortega spoke with Contra representatives at a U.N. meeting but they were unable to agree on details about the demobilization and withdrawal of Contra rebels from Honduras before elections were held.

On December 12, the presidents of Guatemala, El Salvador, Honduras, and Nicaragua met in Costa Rica. They agreed to link the status of Nicaraguan Contra rebels with El Salvador's left-wing rebels and asked the United States to stop aiding the Contras. The linkage failed because an airplane carrying arms for Salvadoran rebels was shot down in eastern El Salvador. Apparently, the plane was shot down from Nicaragua.

On U.S. foreign aid, see November 20, 1989.

October 22, 1989

General Aoun rejects Lebanon's new constitution but agrees to peace talks.

Lebanon's parliament accepted a constitution drawn up at a meeting in Taif, Saudi Arabia. The document divided political power equally between Christians and Muslims. Previously, the Christians had greater authority than the Muslims, although the president would continue to be a Christian and the prime minister a Muslim. Because Syrian troops would oversee the new government, many observers believed Syria's army would play the leading role in Lebanon.

General Aoun, who led one Christian army, rejected the new constitution, a decision causing further bloodshed when Aoun's forces challenged the Syrians. On November 5, Aoun also rejected Rene Moawad, a Christian elected president by Lebanon's parliament. Aoun's supporters staged riots in Beirut on November 6, and President Moawad was assassinated on November 22. After parliament elected Christian Elias Hwari president, Aoun agreed to attend negotiations sponsored by Maronite Christian bishops and French officials.

November 6–7, 1989

The United States and eleven Asian nations meet to form a regional trade group.

The first Asia-Pacific Conference met in Canberra, Australia, to form a regional trade group. In addition to discussing their common economic interests, the delegates decided to invite China, Taiwan, and Hong Kong to the next meeting.

November 7, 1989

U.N. observer group is formed for Central America.

The U.N. Security Council unanimously approved the creation of a U.N. observer force in Central America. The group would monitor cease-fire accords in Nicaragua and elsewhere, demobilize rebel armies in the region, and work with the U.N. International Commission of Support and Verification.

See February 25, 1990.

November 9, 1989

The Berlin Wall falls.

Since its construction in 1961, the Berlin Wall had symbolized totalitarianism and the Iron Curtain that separated democratic Western Europe from the communist regime of the East. The Wall finally began to be torn down after East Germany's government announced that exit visas would be granted to all citizens wishing to leave the country at any border.

Among the many paintings and graffiti to adorn the remaining segments of the eastern side of the Berlin Wall was one commemorating the day it fell. Glenda F. Burns

This decision followed the resignation of East German Premier Willi Stoph and his entire cabinet on November 7, leading to changes in the Communist Party's Politburo that evicted 11 hard-liners and added 4 dissenters.

After several nights of Berlin celebrations between East and West Germans, Hans Modrow, Dresden's reform leader, was confirmed as premier by the Volkskammer (parliament) on November 13. Elections were called for December, and Modrow abolished the Ministry for State Security (Stasi), reforming it as the Office of National Security.

See December 8, 1989.

November 11, 1989

U.N.-supervised elections create Namibia's Constitutional Assembly.

In accordance with the Brazzaville protocol of 1988 (see December 13, 1988) that granted Namibia independence from South Africa, the South West Africa People's Organization (SWAPO), the former rebels, won 41 of 72 seats in the Constituent Assembly in U.N.-supervised elections. The assembly would draft a constitution for Namibia's government.

See March 21, 1990.

November 20, 1989

The U.S. budget provides foreign aid for new democracies and old military rulers.

President Bush signed legislation for foreign aid that gave economic assistance not only to new democracies in Europe but to authoritarian regimes in the Americas. This bill provided to Hungary and Poland, nations in transition from socialist to market economies. At the same time the bill assisted El Salvador's military regime in fighting left-wing guerrillas.

November 28, 1989

Prague demonstrations lead to power-sharing talks between Communists and the Civic Forum.

In Czechoslovakia, antigovernment demonstrations led to negotiations between the communist regime and Václav Hável's Civic Forum. Since January 15, when demonstrators were arrested or dispersed by police, more citizens in and outside Prague staged protests. In May, Hável was released from prison, where he was serving a nine-month sentence for disturbing the peace.

During the summer, protests grew larger and were staged on a regular basis. On October 28, 100,000 protesters filled Prague's streets, where riot police beat many demonstrators and arrested 355 people. On November 17, another round of antigovernment demonstrations preceded a meeting of opposition leaders, including Hável. The opposition decided to unite as the Civic Forum on November 19. Four days later, Alexander Dubček, the Czech leader during the 1968 Prague Spring, joined the protests, telling a Bratislava rally to back the pro-democracy opposition. Millions of workers throughout the nation showed support for democracy by staging a two-hour work stoppage on November 27.

Meanwhile, the Communist Party Central Committee instituted political changes enabling moderates to remove hard-liners from the party Politburo. The new Communist leader, Premier Ladislav Adamec, held discussions with Civic Forum leaders before opening power-sharing discussions on November 28. The next day, the Czech parliament changed the constitution by removing clauses that stated the Communist Party had a "leading role" in the government.

For further dramatic changes see December 28, 1989.

November 28, 1989

OPEC raises oil production but Iraq's delegate opposes the increase.

The decision by OPEC ministers to raise oil production from 18 million to 22 million barrels per day was the second production increase in 1989. On June 7, OPEC had raised production to provide a price of $18 per barrel. Iraq opposed both of OPEC's increases because President Saddam Hussein wanted OPEC to cut production and increase oil prices to $20 or $25 per barrel.

See March 28, 1990.

December 1–3, 1989

At Malta, President Bush and First Secretary Gorbachev discuss arms limitations.

Meeting near the island of Malta aboard the Soviet cruise ship *Maxim Gorky*, President Bush and Soviet leader Gorbachev discussed Europe's conventional forces as well as strategic arms reduction and tactical nuclear missiles. In addition, Bush told Gorbachev he would change the U.S. policy that had denied the Soviets most-favored-nation trade status since 1974 (see December 24, 1974) and would have a Soviet delegate observe GATT meetings. Above all, the Malta talks demonstrated that the Bush administrations supported Gorbachev's perestroika and the democratic values he promoted in Eastern Europe. After the Malta talks ended, Bush visited Brussels to brief NATO leaders on the discussions with Gorbachev and to consider methods for reuniting Germany.

December 1, 1989

President Bush orders U.S. jets to support the Philippine government against a coup.

At the request of Philippine President Corazon Aquino, President Bush ordered two F-4 jets to give air support to Philippine government forces and prevent further air raids by rebels who made a coup attempt against Aquino. Although the rebels gained control of Manila's financial district, where many foreigners were located, Aquino persuaded them to accept a cease-fire on December 6 after the Philippine Congress gave her emergency powers.

Bush and Gorbachev meet at Malta to discuss trade and arms control. George Bush Presidential Library

Rebels continued to occupy Cebu airport as 1989 ended.

See May 14, 1990.

December 6, 1989

Secretary of State Baker proposes a plan for Israeli-Palestinian talks.

After a year in which the United States tried to renew the peace process between Israel and Palestinians, Secretary Baker prepared a five-point plan called the Baker Plan. He proposed that foreign ministers from the United States, Israel, and Egypt meet to set guidelines for negotiations in Cairo between Israel and Palestinian, delegates regarding elections in the occupied territories. Egypt and Israel accepted the plan but Israel insisted that the Palestinian delegation could not include members of the Palestine Liberation Organization (PLO).

See March 15, 1990.

December 6, 1989

Jimmy Carter fails to achieve peace in the Sudan.

Since the overthrow of Sudanese President Gaafar al-Nimeiry in 1985, the Sudan had experienced civil war. Aided by Libyan leader Mu'mammar al-Gadhafi, Islamic fundamentalists took control but fought with Christian tribes who refused to convert to Islam. Combined with drought that caused starvation in parts of Africa, the war caused many Sudanese to depend on food airlifted to them by the United States, the Red Cross, and U.N. food agencies.

Although U.S. Deputy Secretary of State Kenneth L. Brown achieved a cease-fire in 1988, Sudanese President Sadiq al-Mahdi rejected a peace settlement. Conditions continued to deteriorate, and on June 30, 1989, Brigadier General Omar Hassan al-Bashir ousted al-Mahdi. The United States hoped al-Bashir would end the civil war between the government and the Sudanese People's Liberation Army (SPLA) rebels.

The United States and humanitarian aid groups believed al-Bashir's rule would be salutary because he wanted to end the war by holding a national referendum on whether or not the Sudan should abolish Islamic fundamentalist laws instituted by al-Mahdi. The Christians who formed the SPLA rebel group opposed these laws, and ending the war would enable humanitarian aid to be distributed without interference by groups fighting the civil war.

Although al-Bashir never held a referendum on Islamic law, he accepted a cease-fire and peace talks sponsored by former U.S. President Jimmy Carter. The negotiations began in Nairobi, Kenya on December 1. Following five days of talks with delegates from the Sudanese government and Christians in the south of the country, Carter announced that the talks were not successful. Carter believed the primary reason for failure was al-Bashir's insistence on applying Islamic law (Sharia) to all Sudanese including Christians. No dates were set to renew peace talks.

See April 6, 1985, and October 4, 1990.

December 8, 1989

East German socialists are divided on the issue of a united Germany.

The East German government planned reforms but the Socialist Unity (Communist) Party (SED) was ambivalent on the issue of a united Germany. After the East German parliament repealed the SED's "leading role" in the government on December 1, the SED's Central Committee expelled 12 members accused of bribery and corruption, including former President Eric Honecker and Premier Willi Stoph.

On December 9, the SED congress elected Gregor Gysi as chairman but voted to reject West German offers of reunification. Many members of the SED and Dresden's New Forum preferred to be separate from West Germany to devise their own path to socialism. The socialist plans were never fulfilled because demonstrations in Dresden and other cities demanded German unity as proposed by West German Chancellor Helmut Kohl.

See December 19, 1989.

December 9, 1989

High-level U.S. officials visit China and Japan.

To brief leaders of China and Japan on his Malta talks with Soviet leader Mikhail Gorbachev, President Bush sent National Security Adviser Brent Scowcroft and Deputy Secretary of State Lawrence Eagleburger to Tokyo and Beijing. In Beijing, they discussed the best means to improve U.S.-Chinese relations but achieved no immediate results. The Chinese claimed that their treatment of pro-democracy demonstrators in Tiananmen Square on June 4 was an internal matter. On October 31, when former President Richard Nixon visited China, Chinese leader Deng Xiaoping blamed the United States for encouraging the dissidents who caused the Tiananmen massacres. Nevertheless on December 19, Bush appeased China by waiving the June 1989 ban imposed on Export-Import Bank loans to firms doing business with China.

In Tokyo, Scowcroft and Eagleberger simply told Japan's foreign minister the details of Bush's arms control discussions with Gorbachev.

December 14, 1989

Pinochet's candidate loses the Chilean presidential election to Patricio Aylwin.

Aylwin won Chile's first multiparty presidential election since 1970 (see September 11, 1973). As the candidate of a 17-party Coalition for Democracy, Aylwin defeated Augusto Pinochet's former finance minister, Hernán Buchi. The multiparty elections were required by Chile's constitutional changes that Pinochet and the leaders of the Coalition for Democracy accepted in May 1989. Under the agreement, Pinochet would be army commander in chief for four years but would relinquish the presidency to Aylwin in March 1990.

See April 24, 1990.

December 19, 1989

With U.S. backing, West German Chancellor Kohl and East German Prime Minister Modrow agree on a process for German reunification.

As early as October 8, Secretary of State Baker told reporters that U.S. policy always supported Germany's peaceful reunification and that the fall of the Berlin Wall required specific ideas about how unity should be achieved. On November 28, Kohl outlined a 10-point plan for German unity, but Britain and France were skeptical about a united Germany. To clarify the U.S. position on German unity, President Bush and Secretary Baker decided on four points regarding unification: pursuing self-determination without preconceived ideas; unification in the context of Germany's commitment to NATO and the European Community; peaceful step-by-step procedures; and respecting borders as outlined in the Helsinki human rights agreements.

West Germany's leaders appreciated the U.S. position that Baker reiterated in a Berlin speech on December 12 and during a meeting with Modrow later that day. Baker informed President Bush that Modrow favored early reunification because East Germany needed West German economic assistance.

On December 19 Kohl and Modrow discussed future ties between East and West Germany. The first items they accepted were to open Berlin's Brandenberg Gate before Christmas 1989 and to establish cultural and economic ties in the next several months.

See February 12, 1990.

December 20, 1989

A U.S. invasion overthrows Panamanian President Noriega.

Following the fraudulent May 7 election, Panama experienced continuous difficulties after General Manuel Noriega annulled the presidential victory of Guillermo Endara. On October 3, Major Moisés Giroldi Vega led a coup that failed to overthrow Noriega. President Bush admitted that the United States knew about coup plans but denied that the U.S. aided dissidents who protested against Noriega's fraudulent election of May 7, 1989. The coup involved about 300 Panamanian soldiers, ten of whom, including Giroldi, were killed or executed. Following the coup, U.S. Senator Jesse Helms (R-N.C.) proposed a resolution authorizing U.S. forces to overthrow Noriega, but the Senate defeated it by a vote of 74 to 25.

On December 15, the Panamanian National Assembly named General Noriega "maximum leader" and declared that a state of war existed with the United States. After a U.S. soldier was killed in Panama City on December 16, President Bush mobilized American troops in Panama. Soon after midnight on December 20, a Panamanian judge administered to Endara the oath of presidential office before U.S. forces attacked. American troops seized Panama's airfields, power stations, and the headquarters of the Panamanian Defense Force, but Bush had to send 2,000 additional troops to Panama before order was restored on December 23. In a televised speech to Americans on December 20, Bush said he intervened to protect American citizens and uphold U.S. rights under the Panama Canal Treaty.

While Panama officially disbanded its army in favor of forming a public security force, Washington announced that 24 American and 139 Panamanian soldiers had been killed. Meanwhile, General Noriega eluded capture and took refuge in the residence of the Vatican nuncio, who would not turn him over until Noriega agreed.

See January 1, 1990.

December 20, 1989

Soviet leader Mikhail Gorbachev opposes Lithuanian independence.

Lithuania's Communist Party Congress withdrew from the Central Committee of the Communist Party of the USSR, indicating that Lithuania's government would declare an independent Lithuania. Soviet leader Gorbachev told Lithuanian officials he opposed secession because it would bring "discord, bloodshed and death." Gorbachev said he would visit Lithuania to talk with its party leaders.

See April 24, 1990.

December 22, 1989

The Romanian army joins protesters to overthrow President Ceauşescu.

In Bucharest, key Romanian army leaders joined crowds to attack the Communist Party's Central Committee building. During the attack, President Nicolae Ceauşescu and his wife tried to flee by helicopter but were captured. After a counterattack by army units loyal to Ceauşescu failed, dissident leader Ion Iliescu announced plans for a noncommunist government. A military field court martial ordered Ceauşescu to be executed on December 25 for the crimes of genocide and sending $1 billion abroad for his personal use. Iliescu was named interim president with elections slated for 1990.

See May 20, 1990.

December 27, 1989

Bulgaria abolishes the Communist Party's leading role in the life of the nation.

Following a protest movement by the environmentalist Eco-Glasnost group that began on November 3 and that led to the resignation of Communist Party General Secretary Todor Zhivkov, the Bulgarian government and the opposition Union of Democratic

Forces entered negotiations. On December 27, the government and nine opposition groups agreed to abolish the Communist Party's leading role in society, hold free elections, expel President Zhivkov from the Communist Party, and appoint Petar Mladenov party leader.

December 28, 1989

Elections in Czechoslovakia bring the end of the Communist government.

Following the November 28 meeting between Czechoslovakia's Communist Party leader Premier Ladislav Adamec and members of the Civic Forum, a dissident group led by Václav Hável, Adamec resigned his position (see November 28, 1989). On December 10, Marian Calfa became Czechoslovakia's premier, forming a cabinet of 10 communists and 11 non-communists. The final step ending the Communist Party's rule came on December 28, when the Czechoslovakian Federal Assembly elected Václav Hável president of Czechoslovakia and Alexander Dubček chairman of the Assembly. In 1968, Dubček had been replaced by the armed forces of the Soviet Union and Warsaw Pact because Dubček's government initiated reforms the Soviet's General Secretary Leonid Brezhnev opposed (see August 20, 1969). Hável was a writer and poet who often had been jailed by Czechoslovakia's Communist regime because of his persistent dissidence (see January 15, 1989).

After Dubček and Hável were elected to their new positions, they instituted reforms to confirm the Communist Party's loss of its leading role in the government. Among its first reforms, Czechoslovakia's Federal Assembly dropped the Marxist-Leninist curriculum from schools and approved elections for a new Federal Assembly to be held in 1990.

See June 9, 1990.

1990

January 1, 1990

Panama gains a new administrator for the canal; former Panamanian General Noriega is flown to Florida.

Acting in accord with the 1977 U.S.–Panama Canal Treaty, Fernando Manfredo Bernal became acting administrator of the canal. After the U.S. invasion in December, General Noriega fled to the papal mission. On January 3, by prior agreement, he left the mission to be arrested by U.S. Drug Enforcement Agency officers. The United States flew Noriega to Florida, where on May 4 he was arraigned on drug charges in a Miami district court. President Bush sought funds to aid Panama's recovery and Congress approved $420 million for Panama on May 24 as part of a foreign aid package that gave $355 million to Latin American nations and a $400 million loan guarantee to Israel.

See December 20, 1989.

January 23, 1990

The Yugoslav League of Communists is dissolved.

Disputes among the Yugoslav republics of Slovenia, Croatia, and Serbia increased in 1989 after Serbian President Slobodan Milošević enlarged Serb control over the "autonomous" provinces of Kosovo and Vojvodina. On September 17, 1989, Slovenia's Assembly adopted legislation giving it the right to secede from Yugoslavia if Serbia tried to gain control over Yugoslavia's six republics. In Croatia, Franjo Tudjman formed an anti-Serb party of Croatian nationalists (HDZ) to counter Milošević's propaganda appeals to the Serb minority in Croatia.

　　More frictions among these three republics arose during a convention of the Yugoslav League of Communists (YLC) because delegates from Slovenia and Croatia challenged Milošević's attempt to enact constitutional "reforms" to enhance the power of Yugoslavia's central government. Following disputes with Serbia's delegation about proposed constitutional changes, Slovenia's delegates seceded from the YLC and walked out of the convention. Although Milošević called on the convention to continue by forming a "new quorum," the Croatian delegation joined Slovenia in leaving the meetings. Unable to proceed, Convention Chairman Momir Bulatović called for a 15-minute break he later said "lasted throughout history." Yugoslavia's disintegration began although it was not completed until June 1991.

See March 24, 1989. and April 8, 1990.

February 2, 1990

South Africa legalizes the African National Congress and other parties.

South African President F.W. de Klerk launched changes in South Africa by legalizing the African National Congress (ANC), the South African Communist Party, and the Pan-African Congress. De Klerk also promised to free ANC leader Nelson Mandela, who had been in jail for 27 years. Mandela was freed on February 11. In May, the ANC and De Klerk's government began talks about releasing political prisoners and granting immunity to returned exiles. On August 6, the ANC called a cease-fire in its armed struggle with South Africa's government.

February 12, 1990

The reunification of Germany will be decided by two plus four (2+4) negotiations.

Since November 28, 1989, when West German Chancellor Helmut Kohl suggested ways to reunite Germany, U.S. Secretary of State Baker sought to foster Germany's reunification while reassuring the British, French, and Soviets that Germany would maintain its cooperation with other European nations. In January, Baker and other State Department personnel devised a plan to conduct talks between East and West Germany regarding Germany's internal political and economic relations. At the same time, the four powers (United States, France, Great Britain, USSR) occupying Germany after World War II would negotiate with East and West Germany regarding external relations with Germany's allies and neighbors. The four powers plan became known as the 2 + 4 plan.

　　Anticipating that the six nations could approve the 2 + 4 plan at a February conference in Ottawa, Canada, Baker contacted British, French, Soviet, East and West German and other European states to explain his proposal. In addition, West German Chancellor Helmut Kohl met with Soviet leader Mikhail Gorbachev in Moscow to assure the Soviets that Germany would remain part of the European Community and negotiate future borders with Poland. Subsequently, the 2 + 4 plan was finalized at the Ottawa Conference, where 23 members of NATO and the Warsaw Pact discussed Germany's future and control of conventional weapons in Europe. In announcing the plan, Baker said negotiations would begin after East German elections scheduled for March 18.

See March 18, 1990.

February 15, 1990

The United States and three South American countries agree to cooperate against drug traffickers.

President Bush and the presidents of Colombia, Bolivia, and Peru signed agreements to work together in combatting drug traffickers. Bush said the United States would work to control the consumption of and demand for drugs in the United States—a promise that was easy to make but difficult to keep.

On January 8, the United States had abandoned a plan for a naval blockade to control the drug traffic because Colombian President Virgilio Barco denounced it. On January 17, Medellín leaders offered to stop bombings and assassinations if the government agreed not to extradite suspected drug traffickers to the United States.

On Colombia see December 17, 1990; on Peru, see September 12, 1990.

February 25, 1990

The U.S. favorite wins Nicaraguan elections.

In Nicaraguan elections, the U.S.-favored candidate, Violeta Barrios de Chamorro, defeated the incumbent, President Daniel Ortega. Because the United States opposed Ortega's Sandinista National Liberation Front (FSLN), Washington was delighted that Chamorro was elected and that her National Opposition Union (UNO) gained control of 52 of the 90 seats in the National Assembly. The FSLN received only 38 seats. On March 13, President Bush assisted Chamorro by lifting U.S. economic sanctions and requesting $300 million emergency aid that Congress approved on May 24. The remaining issue was the demobilization of the U.S.-sponsored Contra rebels who continued to fight Nicaragua's government.

See March 23, 1990.

February 25–27, 1990

U.S. Deputy Secretary of State Lawrence Eagleburger urges the European community to solve Yugoslavia's problems.

When President Bush took office in 1989, his administration decided Yugoslavia was no longer the vital U.S. interest it had been during the Cold War. Reaching Belgrade in 1989, U.S. Ambassador Warren Zimmermann learned about Yugoslavia's recent political and economic problems and persuaded Deputy Secretary of State Lawrence Eagleburger to visit Belgrade.

From February 25 to 27, Eagleburger met with Yugoslav Prime Minister Ante Marcović, representatives of Yugoslavia's six republics, and leaders of opposition groups. After Marcović was elected prime minister in March 1989, he tried to establish free-market reforms needed to obtain IMF loans. Under IMF guidelines, the long-term benefits of reforms required short-term cuts in social welfare programs and workers' wages while state-owned industries were privatized. Slovenia, Serbia, and Croatia opposed the IMF reforms because they caused unemployment, less income for retired people and wage workers, and the loss of jobs in state-owned businesses. In addition, Serbia's President Slobadan Milošević wanted constitutional changes to centralize power in the federal government, but leaders of Slovenia and Croatia wanted each republic to control its own economy.

After leaving Belgrade, Eagleburger instructed U.S. ambassadors in Europe to call their host countries' attention to the danger of Yugoslavia's disintegration. Bush focused attention on uniting Germany and watching Mikhail Gorbachev's reforms in the Soviet Union, while the State Department hoped the European Community could deal with Yugoslavia's problems.

See March 23, 1989; January 23 and April 8, 1990.

March 7, 1990

President Bush denies that the United States set fire to a Libyan factory producing mustard gas.

After an ABC news broadcast revealed that Libya was producing mustard gas in a factory near Tripoli, the White House confirmed the accuracy of the report. A week later, the Libyan factory producing the gas was reported to have been burned down and Libya blamed CIA agents. Bush denied any U.S. role in setting the fire.

March 13–15, 1990

The Soviet Union's People's Congress repeals the Communist Party's monopoly of power.

The first step toward ending the Communist Party's monopoly of power was taken by the Plenum of the Central Committee of the Communist Party on February 7, when the members approved party First Secretary Gorbachev's proposal to end the party's monopoly of political power. The Plenum's decision was recommended to the Third Soviet Congress of People's Deputies at its March meeting. On March 14, the deputies voted 1,817 to 133 to repeal the constitutional guarantees of the Communist Party's monopoly. The Congress also created the office of executive president, electing Mikhail Gorbachev president. Popular elections would choose future presidents. On March 24, Gorbachev appointed a 16-member Presidential Council to assist him.

See June 3, 1990.

March 15, 1990

The Baker Plan disrupts Israel's coalition cabinet.

Although in December Israel agreed to proceed with the Baker Plan, events in early 1990 made it difficult to continue. On January 14, Prime Minister Yitzhak Shamir said Israel needed the occupied territories to house Soviet Jewish immigrants. On February 4, the terrorist Islamic Jihad for the Liberation of Palestine ambushed a bus in Egypt, killing 16 Israeli tourists.

On February 12, Ariel Sharon of the Likud Party resigned from the cabinet and 10 days later, the Labor Party threatened to leave the coalition unless Shamir accepted their interpretation of the Baker Plan requiring some type of Palestinian representation. These actions split Israel's cabinet because of differences about the U.S. peace plan between the Likud Party's Prime Minister Shamir and Labor's Finance Minister Shimon Peres. After Shamir removed Peres from office, all other Labor Party ministers resigned. Shamir had to form another coalition ministry.

See December 6, 1989, and June 8, 1990.

March 18, 1990

East German elections confirm the desire to reunite with West Germany.

In East German elections, the Alliance for Germany, which favored speedy reunification with West Germany, won 48.1% of the vote. Its rival, the Social Democrats, received only 21.8% and the former Communist Party, the Party of Democratic Socialism (SED), gained 16.3% of the votes. Following the election, the Alliance for Germany and the Social Democrats formed a "grand alliance" coalition government. On April 28, a European Community meeting approved a united Germany as a member, setting the stage for German reunification.

See May 2, 1990.

March 21, 1990

Secretary of State James Baker represents the United States at Namibia's presidential inauguration.

Baker represented the United States at the inauguration of Sam Nujoma as Namibia's first president. Namibia had received independence from South Africa in 1988.

See December 13, 1988.

March 23, 1990

Nicaragua and the Contras agree to a cease-fire, overseen by observers.

Sponsored by the United States and the United Nations, Nicaragua's Contra leaders met with Nicaraguan president-elect Chamorro. The Contras agreed to dismantle rebel camps in Honduras and accepted a cease-fire monitored by a multinational U.N. Observer Group. In turn, former President Daniel Ortega's Sandinista Party recognized Chamorro's right to control Nicaragua's army and security forces. Chamorro was sworn in as president on April 25. The Contras soon raised other questions about Chamorro's policies, and the rebels' disarmament was not ended until June 29, 1990.

March 27, 1990

U.S. Television MARTI begins broadcasting into Cuba.

An American-financed station, TV MARTI began trial broadcasts into Cuba, which decided not to jam the station's broadcasts. On August 26, President Bush said the TV station was successful in bringing music and news to Cubans and its operation would continue.

March 28, 1990

British and U.S. customs agents prevent nuclear detonators from reaching Iraq.

U.S. customs officers were on this case after Iraq ordered specially designed nuclear detonator-capacitors from CSI Technologies of San Marcos, California. When the detonators arrived at London's Heathrow airport on March 28, British police arrested the Iraqi Airway's manager and four other Iraqis who worked for the Iraqi Ministry of the Interior's explosives research division. The five Iraqis were arrested for smuggling atomic weapons parts into Iraq. President Saddam Hussein denied the detonators were for nuclear weapons, claiming they were for laser research.

The London incident was one of three in March 1990 that led Saddam Hussein to assert that the U.S. and Israel conspired against Iraq. The first was a report of the growing number of Jews emigrating from the USSR to Israel. The second was the assassination of a Canadian ballistics expert, Gerald Bull, in Brussels. Bull had developed a long-range artillery weapon for Iraq and was developing a new super gun for Iraq at the time of his murder.

See April 1, 1990.

April 1, 1990

Iraqi President Saddam Hussein threatens to destroy half of Israeli population with binary nerve gase.

Denouncing the United States and Britain, Hussein threatened to use binary nerve gas weapons to destroy half of Israel if it made a preemptive attack on Iraq as it did in 1981. Following the end of the Iraq-Iran war in 1988, Hussein tried to become the Arabs' primary leader against Israel and the Western powers, who, he said, assisted the "Zionists."

Although neither the Reagan nor the Bush administration immediately recognized Hussein's anti-Americanism, the U.S. Congress opposed a $350 million Export-Import Bank credit to Iraq that President Bush bypassed with an executive order in January 1990.

In February 1990, President Hussein told a meeting of Arab leaders to put Arab unity ahead of petro-dollars and to force the United States to remove its ships from the Persian Gulf. In March, Hussein was further incensed by three events involving Israel and the West. Together, these developments led to Hussein's April 1 tirade against Israel as part of a policy to be the great leader of all Arabs opposing Israel's military power.

See June 7, 1981; March 28 and July 27, 1990.

April 3, 1990

Mexico complains about the actions of American bounty hunters.

The bounty hunters captured a Mexican, Dr. Humberto Alvarez Machain, who was suspected of the 1985 torture and killing of a U.S. Drug Enforcement Agency officer. After the bounty hunters flew Machin to El Paso, Texas, U.S. drug officials arraigned him in a Los Angeles court on April 4. Mexico was alarmed by the U.S. action and ask the Bush administration to explain its legality. Although bounty hunters may legally perform such actions within the United States, these and other tactics in the war on drugs often damaged relations between the United States and Mexico.

April 5, 1990

U.S.-Japan trade negotiations achieve some success.

After two weeks of trade negotiations, Japan agreed to open its market to more imports of U.S. supercomputer products. It also agreed on future negotiations to eliminate any barriers to free trade.

April 7, 1990

A federal court convicts John Poindexter for obstructing justice in the Iran-Contra affair; Oliver North's conviction is suspended.

The federal court convicted President Reagan's former national security adviser, John M. Poindexter of obstructing justice and lying to Congress about the Iran-Contra affair. On June 11, he was sentenced to six months in prison. In contrast, on July 20, a federal appeals court suspended Oliver L. North's three felony convictions in the Iran-Contra affair because he had been given immunity by Congress.

On Iran-Contra, see November 26, 1986.

April 8, 1990

Yugoslavia's unity is threatened when Slovenian and Croatian nationalists win elections.

The first blow to the Yugoslav Federation of Socialist Republics came in January 1990, when the Slovenian and Croatian delegates walked out of the annual meeting of the Yugoslav League of Communists due to disputes with Serbian delegates regarding the future power of Yugoslavia's federal government (see January 23, 1990). Slovenian communists led by Milan Kuchan, and Croatian communists led by Franjo Tudjman wanted the Yugoslav Federation to allocate more authority in economic affairs to each of the Yugoslav Republics, while Serbian President Slobodan Milošević planned to enhance the central role of the Yugoslav presidency. These differences between Yugoslavia's largest and most prosperous republics precipitated the break-up of the Yugoslav League of Communists in January and led to the victories of Slovenian and Croatian nationalists who opposed Milošević's nationalistic program for a Greater Serbia.

In early April, before the Slovenian and Croatian election date, the pro-Serb Yugoslavian Defense Minister, Veljko Kadijevic, visited Slovenia and Croatia, where he openly threatened to retaliate against any group that questioned the territorial integrity of Yugoslavia. As Laura Silber and Allan Little's *Yugoslavia: Death of a Nation* concludes: General Kadijevic's threat backfired because Slovenian and, especially, Croatian voters resented the general's threat. One Croat Communist Party leader told Kadijeic the Slovenians and Croatians were not breaking Yugoslav apart but "It is Milošević and your refusal to resist him."

In April 8 elections for the Republic of Slovenia's Assembly and president, Slovenia's Communist Party leader Michael Kuchan won 60% of the votes, defeating Joze Pucnik, the nominee of the DEMOS coalition of seven parties that included the Christian Democrats and Greens (environmental) Party. Before the election Kuchan's followers changed the party name from Communist to the Party of Democratic Reform, while hard-line communists were on the ballot under the name of the Communist Party. In Slovenia's Assembly election, reformers in the DEMOS and the Party of Democratic Reform won 55% of the votes, the Communist Party 17%. Smaller parties won the remaining 28%.

On April 22, the Republic of Croatia's elections were won by members of the Croatian Democratic party (HDZ), a party established in February 1989 under the leadership of former General of the Yugoslav National Army Franjo Tudjman. HDZ's political campaign was based on Croatian nationalism and a pledge to make Croatia independent. In Croatia's elections, Tudjman was elected president with 66% of the votes, and after runoff elections on May 6 and 7, 1990, HDZ members won 205 of the 356 seats in Croatia's parliament (Sabor), the Communist Party won 73 seats, and eight smaller parties won the remaining 78 seats. Primarily, the HDZ victory was due to the Communist Party's support for Serbian nationalists who favored the Serb Republic's Slobodan Milošević. Both Tudjman and Kuchan opposed Milošević's plans for a Greater Serbia.

See October 1, 1990.

April 24, 1990

President Bush faces a crisis regarding Lithuania and the Soviet Union.

Because Bush favored self-determination for the Soviet republic of Lithuania, he faced a crisis after Lithuania tried to secede from the Soviet Union. In March 1990, when Lithuania's Supreme Soviet declared independence, Soviet President Gorbachev rejected their decision and, on April 19, placed an economic embargo against Lithuania that shut off its oil and natural gas from the USSR. President Bush favored Lithuanian self-determination but realized Gorbachev would not allow any Soviet republic to secede because other republics would follow.

In an agreement with British Prime Minister Margaret Thatcher, French President François Mitterrand, and German Chancellor Helmut Kohl, Bush proposed negotiations between Gorbachev and Lithuania's President Vytautas Landsbergis as the best way to accommodate both sides. The situation also benefited when on April 26 Mitterrand and Kohl sent

Landsbergis a letter urging Lithuania to suspend its declaration of independence and negotiate with the Soviets.

Amid this crisis and against Bush's wishes, the U.S. Senate led by Senator Jesse Helms (R-N.C.) passed legislation on May 1 to withhold trade benefits from Moscow. Although the Senate action upset the Soviets, the Franco-German appeal to Lithuania got Landsbergis's attention. During a summit meeting in June, Bush persuaded Gorbachev to negotiate with Lithuania as the best way to end the crisis. After discussions in Moscow between Gorbachev and Landsbergis, Lithuania suspended its independence declaration on June 29 and the Soviets reopened the oil and gas pipelines to Lithuania.

April 24, 1990

China and the Soviet Union sign a 10-year economic cooperation agreement.

During Premier Li Peng's visit to Moscow, China and the Soviet Union signed a 10-year agreement to cooperate in economic and scientific affairs. Li was the first Chinese leader to visit the USSR since 1964. Li Peng and General Secretary Mikhail Gorbachev also agreed to decrease the size of military forces along their mutual borders.

April 24, 1990

Chilean courts order an investigation of Letelier's assassination in Washington, D.C.

Acting at the request of Patricio Aylwin, who became president on March 11, Chile's Supreme Court ordered the military to review its investigation of the 1975 assassination of Orlando Letelier, Chile's former ambassador to the United States who was assassinated in Washington by a car bomb (see November 29, 1979). On May 12, Chile formed a commission to investigate the human rights violations of the military government of General Augusto Pinochet Ugarte and to determine what compensation Chile should pay the United States as compensation for the bombing that killed the American citizen Ronnie K. Moffett, who was riding in the car with Letelier.

See November 29, 1979, and March 4, 1991.

April 30, 1990

The United States and Panama agree to work together against drug traffickers.

President Bush and Panamanian President Guillermo Endara signed an agreement to combat drug traffickers who used Panama as a base. Bush also nominated Gilberto Guardia Frabega as administrator of the Panama Canal in accord with the 1977 Canal Treaty.

See September 7, 1977.

May 2, 1990

The 2+4 talks result in Germany's having a single currency.

During an initial series of talks between East and West Germans, the delegates finalized terms for ending the circulation of the East German currency and replacing it with the German mark, to become effective on July 1, 1990. Discussions on German political unity were also underway in "2+4" negotiations between the German states plus four allies from World War II.

See September 12, 1990.

May 14, 1990

The Philippine Islands face the problems of closing U.S. bases and defeating rebel groups.

Throughout 1990, Philippine President Corozon Aquino dealt with two demanding issues. First, to meet popular demands, she asked the United States to remove its navy and air force bases from the islands. Second, she ordered the Philippine army to defeat the rebel groups seeking to overthrow the government.

On April 10, President Bush appointed Assistant Secretary of Defense Richard L. Armitage to negotiate the future of U.S. bases in the Philippines. When Armitage arrived in May, he faced serious threats from protesters against American personnel. On May 1, the communist New People's Army staged protests during which they killed a U.S. Marine sergeant at Subic Bay naval base and two U.S. airmen at Clark Air Force Base. Following preliminary talks in May Armitage returned from September 19 to 22, but talks failed over disagreements about phasing out U.S. bases.

The Philippine army and police had to deal with militant soldiers and also the New People's Army. The most serious soldiers' rebellion began on October 4, when 200 rebels captured a Mindanao outpost to set up an independent state. After the Philippine air force bombed the rebel stronghold on October 10, most of the militant soldiers surrendered, including their leader, Colonel Alexander Noble.

The guerrillas proved more dangerous to Aquino. Although on August 29 she offered to negotiate a cease-fire, the rebels refused. The Philippine army faced the difficult task of trying to defeat the guerrilla New People's Army, whose members hid in mountains and jungles scattered throughout the islands.

See December 27, 1991.

May 20, 1990

Romanian acting president is elected in each landslide victory.

In Romanian multiparty elections, acting president Ion Iliescu was victorious when his National Salvation Front (Communists) received 85% of the vote and 67% of the seats in each house of Romania's bicameral parliament. Despite his election, many students opposed Iliescu, staging massive protests in Bucharest. To end the demonstrations on June 14, Iliescu brought in 10,000 coal miners from northern Romania who successfully beat the students into submission. Although the United States expressed disapproval of Iliescu's method and the European Community suspended economic relations with Romania, Iliescu was sworn in as president on June 20, promising a commitment to free markets, pluralism, and "traditional democracy."

May 29, 1990

Boris Yeltsin is elected president of the Russian Federation.

Campaigning on a platform of political and economic sovereignty for the Russian Federation, the largest of the republics in the USSR, Yeltsin defeated Alexsander V. Vlasov, who was the Soviet Communist Party's candidate. Yeltsin's victory was followed by further moves to gain the federation's independence. On June 19, a conference of the Russian Federation's Communist Party established a party organization separate from the Soviet Communist Party and elected Ivan K. Polozkov to head the Russian Federation's party organization. On August 10, the Russian Federation's parliamentary Presidium declared the federation's sovereignty over its natural resources.

Alarmed by these developments, Soviet President Mikhail Gorbachev sought a compromise on the authority of the central Soviet government's rights compared to those of the Russian Federation. Between August and December 1990, Gorbachev and Yeltsin discussed various plans for restructuring the political and economic power held by each entity. But they were unable to agree on a solution that would keep all Soviet republics in the Union.

See December 17, 1990.

May 30, 1990

The United States vetoes a U.N. resolution calling for U.N. observers to be stationed on the Israeli-occupied West Bank.

The U.N. Security Council resolution was designed to send U.N. observers to Palestinian land occupied by Israel in the Six-Day War (1967). Riots by the PLO *intifada* in the West Bank and Gaza erupted in bloody confrontations from May 20 to 22 after a discharged Israeli soldier killed seven Palestinian laborers near Tel Aviv. On May 25, PLO leader Yasser Arafat asked the United Nations Security Council (UNSC) to send UN observers to the West Bank and Gaza and to protect Palestinians from Israel's Defense Forces (IDF). The United States vetoed the resolution, claiming the UN observers would violate Israel's internal sovereignty.

See June 8, 1990.

June 3, 1990

Presidents Bush and Gorbachev provide a basis for future arms reduction treaties.

President Bush and Soviet President Gorbachev concluded a Washington, D.C., summit that had begun on May 30. During the sessions, they discussed a variety of issues before signing bilateral accords that provided a basis for further negotiations on reducing strategic nuclear weapons, ending the production of chemical weapons, and giving the Soviets most-favored-nation (MFN) trade status.

On August 2, at a meeting in Irkutsk, Siberia, Soviet Foreign Minister Eduard Shevardnadze and U.S. Secretary of State James Baker took another step to avoid nuclear war. Shevardnadze told Baker the Soviets would stop producing the SS-24 rail-mobile ICBMs. The Soviet Union's SS-24 was the counterpart of the United States' MX system, an

A meeting at Camp David (clockwise around table): President Bush, Vice President Quayle, Brent Scowcroft, Foreign Minister Eduard Shevardnadze, President Gorbachev, Marshal Sergei Akhromeyev, Peter Afanasenko (interpreter), James Baker. George Bush Presidential Library

ICBM missile carrying multiple warheads (MIRVs). When President Ronald Reagan's Strategic Defense Initiative was combined with the MX missile system, the United States would have a superior nuclear war-fighting capability to force an opponent to surrender. For the United States, President Carter enunciated a nuclear war-fighting strategy in Presidential Directive 59 of 1980 (see August 5, 1980).

The nuclear war-fighting strategy raised tensions between the Soviet Union and the United States during the 1980s, but by 1987 Soviet General Secretary Mikhail Gorbachev had ended Soviet concerns regarding SDI or other American missile defense systems (see February 28, 1987). Rather than rely on a missile defense system for the Soviet Union, Moscow was developing the Topol-M ICBM's with the ability to penetrate and destroy any nation's missile defenses.

Despite these Soviet perceptions of America's anti-missile defenses, the Bush administration continued to spend $3 billion to $4 billion per year on variations of Reagan's original Strategic Defense Initiative. In 1989, the Pentagon claimed technology known as Brilliant Pebbles would deploy a viable missile defense system within three years. Brilliant Pebbles consisted of several thousand small interceptors in space orbits above the earth. Each Pebble would carry computerized data that would locate an ICBM target on its mid-course trajectory from the Soviet Union and send a kill vehicle to ram and destroy the ICBM. By 1991, Brilliant Pebbles had failed several tests and the Pentagon had replaced

Brilliant Pebbles with a plan called Global Protection Against Limited Strikes (GPALS).

See September 17–23 -, 1991.

June 8, 1990

Israeli Prime Minister Shamir announces a new Israeli cabinet dominated by Likud Party members; U.S. Secretary of State Baker realizes his peace plan is now hopeless.

Following the March 15 crisis that ended the Likud-Labor coalition government, Prime Minister Shamir formed a Likud-dominated cabinet that excluded Labor Party members Shimon Peres and Yitzhak Rabin, on whom Secretary of State Baker depended to persuade Shamir to adopt his December 1989 peace plan.

The formation of Shamir's new cabinet, added to recent conflicts between Palestinians and Israelis, made it clear that Baker's proposals could not be revived. Although President Bush and Secretary Baker believed Shamir was responsible for the failure of the peace talks, Bush suspended the U.S. dialogue with the PLO after its leader, Yasser Arafat refused to condemn an attempted Palestinian raid on Israel on May 30, 1990. The United States had encouraged a dialogue between the Palestinians and Israel since 1988. As Baker's *Politics of Diplomacy* (1995) indicates, Shamir was as unreliable as Arafat in seeking peace. Despite U.S. opposition to Jewish settlements in occupied territory, Shamir continued building new settlements that precipitated conflicts with the PLO before and after the Iraqi invasion of Kuwait on August 2, 1990.

See December 14, 1988; May 30 and October 12, 1990.

June 9, 1990

Elections for Czechoslovakia's parliament are won by reformers.

In free elections, the alliance of President Václav Hável's Civic Forum and its Slovak Republic counterpart, Public Against Violence, won 170 of the 300 seats in the bicameral Federal Assembly. The other assembly seats were divided among the Communists (47 seats), the Christian Democratic Union (40 seats) and the separatist Slovak National Party (10 seats).

See December 10, 1990.

June 17, 1990

Bulgaria's former Communists win elections but protests continue.

In December 1989, protest demonstrations led to the overthrow of Bulgaria's Communist Party General Secretary Todor Zikov and the establishment of a coalition government to end the Communists' leading role in Bulgaria. The coalition government also called for free multiparty elections in 1990 and the Communist Party changed its name to the Socialist Party (see December 27, 1989). When the Bulgarian elections for parliament were held on June 17, 1990, the newly named Socialist Party of former communists gained a majority 211 of the 400 seats in parliament. The Union of Democratic Forces won 144 seats and smaller parties had the remaining 45 seats in parliament. On August 7, 1990, Bulgaria's parliament elected Socialist Party leader Andrei Lukanov as President and Socialist Zhelya Zhelan as Premier.

The June 17 elections did not end protest by opposition groups who complained Bulgaria's old communist's secret police controlled internal affairs and gave opposition groups no access to the state controlled media outlets of radio, television, and newspapers. Protests continued during the next four months before President Lukanov agreed to resign.

See December 7, 1990.

June 27, 1990

The United States lifts retaliatory tariffs on Brazilian products; President Bush proposes a hemispheric free-trade zone.

During the 1980s, the Reagan administration had a variety of disputes with Brazil about Brazil's restrictions on American imports before the United States levied tariffs on many Brazilian products. After President Bush took office, a series of talks with Brazil enabled U.S. Special Trade Representative Carla A. Hill to report that the United States would lift retaliatory tariffs on Brazil's products. Her announcement reflected Brazil's willingness to reduce tariffs on all foreign imports and to protect foreign intellectual property rights.

Also on June 27, President Bush proposed a U.S. initiative to create a Western Hemispheric free-trade zone. Bush's Enterprise for the Americas Initiative (EAI) would encourage Latin American economic growth by forgiving up to 50 percent of the Latin American debts owed the United States and creating a hemispheric free-trade zone. The EAI complemented Bush's movement toward a North American free trade agreement with Mexico and Canada.

See September 13, 1986.

June 29, 1990

The United States joins 92 other nations for Aid to Third World countries in reducing the amount of their ozone-depleting gases.

During a U.N. meeting in London, the United States joined with representatives of 92 other countries to find methods to end the production of chlorofluorocarbons (CFC) by the century's end and to help developing nations reduce their use of CFC. At a May 9 U.N. conference, the United States opposed direct aid to Third World nations but reversed this policy on June 15, when it agreed to spend $256 million to fund the project over three years.

July 5, 1990

By dissolving Kosovo's parliament, Serbia assumes direct control over the province.

In 1989, the Serb Republic took over Kosovo's seat on the Federation of Yugoslavia's eight-member presidency (see March 23, 1989). One year later, on March 24, 1990, the Serbian Ministry of Internal

Affairs took control of Kosovo's police force, expelling all Kosovo policemen who were ethnic Albanians. Finally, on July 5, 1990, the Serb Republic's National Assembly officially dissolved Kosovo's provincial parliament and assumed direct control of the province. This action was another step in Serb President Slobodan Milošević's call for a Greater Serbia. Despite these Serbian actions to suppress Kosovo's Albanian (Kosovars) who were 90% of the province of Kosovo's population, the Kosovars in the provincial parliament continued to oppose Serbian authority.

Three days before the Serb National Assembly voted to abolish Kosovo's parliament, Kosovo's provincial parliament voted on July 2 to declare Kosovo's independence of the Serb Republic. Throughout the period from July 1990 to 1998 (see March 5, 1998), the Kosovars adopted nonviolent methods to deal with Serbia's harassment of Kosovars. In 1990, the President of Kosovo's Association of Writers, Ibrahim Rugova, founded the Democratic League of Kosovo (DLK). With Rugova's leadership, Kosovars organized secret meetings of an Albanian Assembly to draw up a constitution for the Republic of Kosovo. By meeting secretly in private homes or deserted buildings, the Kosovars held a referendum to approve a constitution, elect a parliament, and choose Rugova as President of the Republic of Kosovo. In addition to the DLK, other Kosovar parties included the Christian Democrats, the Social Democrats, and the Liberal Party.

Because Serb President Milošević became involved in warfare with Croatia and Bosnia from 1990 to 1996, the unofficial Kosovo Republic was able to conduct many day-to-day affairs in the lives of Kosovars, including functions such as keeping hospitals and schools open for Kosovars. In addition, most Kosovars adopted Rugova's nonviolent methods as the best means for Rugova to seek international backing from Western Europeans and the United States in opposing Serbia's illegal take over of Kosovo province.

In 1990, the plight of Kosovars gained attention from the U.S. Ambassador to Yugoslavia Warren Zimmermann, and U.S. congressional leaders who sympathized with the Kosovars. United States Representative Joseph Dioguardi, a Democrat from New York and an Albanian-American, became concerned about Kosovo in 1988, and after losing his campaign for re-election in 1988, became a lobbyist in Washington who called attention to Serb violations of Albanian human rights. In particular, Dioguardi gained attention from Senators Robert Dole (R-Kans.), Alfonse D'Amoto (R-N.Y.), and Don Nickles (R-Okla.). In August, 1990, these three senators visited Belgrade to talk with leaders from each of Yugoslavia's republics before visiting Kosovo to meet Rugova and other Kosovar leaders.

According to Ambassador Zimmermann's memoir *Origins of a Catastrophe*, Dole, D'Amoto, and Nickles believed Kosovo should be independent from the Serbs, who used abusive methods against the Kosovars. On returning to Washington, Senator Nickles added an amendment to foreign aid legislation for fiscal year 1991. Supported by Dole and D'Amoto, the Nickles Amendment would cut U.S. economic assistance to Yugoslavia down to $5 million in May 1991 if Yugoslavia did not stop suppressing the Kosovars. Although the legislation passed Congress, both President Bush and Ambassador Zimmermann opposed the Nickles Amendment because it did not effect Milošević's Serb Republic, the real culprit. By May 1991, the Nickles Amendment was no longer relevant because the Yugoslav Federation collapsed in June 1991.

See October 1, 1990

July 5, 1990

Poland's austerity program disrupts its government.

On January 1, 1990, Poland adopted the advice of U.S. economists to implement austerity methods that included price increases, wage freezes, and currency deregulation. Because inflation increased while wages fell, the reforms caused widespread discontent. In May, members of Lech Wałęsa's Solidarity union won local elections in which the Communists received only 2% of the votes, a sign of popular dismay with the economic reforms. To relieve the discontent, on July 5 Premier Mazowiecki removed three former communists from his cabinet: the defense, interior, and transportation ministers. He also held meetings with Wałęsa to "preserve social peace" prior to the national elections scheduled for November.

See December 9, 1990.

July 8, 1990

The United States agrees to close its military bases in Greece.

On July 8, the United States and Greece signed an agreement to close two U.S. army bases near Athens, although the United States could maintain an air and naval base on the Greek island of Crete. The United States also reaffirmed its military aid to Greece and Turkey that favored Greece by a seven-to-ten ratio.

July 11, 1990

Meeting in Houston, Texas, the G-7 nations agree on three important issues.

President Bush hosted the four-day session of the seven leading industrial nations. The G-7 leaders agreed to study the possibility of giving the USSR economic aid to encourage a Soviet free-market economy; to pursue efforts to end Soviet agricultural subsides; and to accept President Bush's suggestion to delay decisions about limiting the reduction of "greenhouse gases" until 1992.

July 18, 1990

The United States ends recognition of Cambodia's rebel coalition.

During the year after U.S. Secretary of State James Baker changed policy to promote peace in Cambodia, Baker reversed his peace effort by withdrawing U.S. diplomatic recognition of Cambodia's rebel coalition and its right to U.N. membership. Baker announced this new effort because the Khmer Rouge boycotted the U.N.-sponsored talks in Tokyo and another round of intense fighting began.

Baker also offered to negotiate with Vietnam, and on September 29, Baker and Vietnamese Foreign Minister Nguyen Co Thach discussed Cambodia but found no solutions for peace. Although China was disappointed with Baker's decision to involve Vietnam in Cambodia, the United Nations Security Council (UNSC) agreed to provide an interim Cambodian government if the four Cambodian factions accepted a peace plan. The U.N. plan could not be implemented and Cambodia's fighting intensified near the end of 1990.

See July 6, 1989.

July 27, 1990

Increased OPEC oil prices do not satisfy Iraqi President Saddam Hussein.

In Geneva, the Organization of Petroleum Exporting Countries (OPEC) ministers failed to satisfy Iraq's demand for higher oil prices. They cut oil production 20% to yield a $21 per barrel price, but Iraq wanted the price at $25. After opposing OPEC's small price increase in May, Hussein claimed the Arab League had conspired to keep prices low. He also demanded that Iraq's Arab neighbors write off the $30 billion Iraqi debt and insisted that Kuwait stop "stealing oil from the disputed Rumalia oil field along their mutual" border.

To placate Iraq, Egyptian President Hosni Mubarak arranged a meeting between Iraq and Kuwait at Jedda, Saudi Arabia, but the talks broke down on August 1 because Iraq rejected Kuwait's compromise proposal. During the Jedda meetings, Iraq's Vice-President of the Revolutional Command Council Izzat Ibrahim demanded that Kuwait pay Iraq $14 billion because Kuwait violated the oil quota given to Kuwait by the Organization of Petroleum Exporting Countries (OPEC) during Iraq's war with Iran in the 1980s. Ibrahim also wanted Kuwait to give Iraq the Islands of Bubiyan and Warba that would provide Iraq with a better seaport on the Persian Gulf. Without directly rejecting Iraq's demands, Kuwait's Foreign Minister Sheikh Sabal al Ahmad proposed that Iraq lease the two Persian Gulf Islands from Kuwait. Sheikh Sabal's proposals were unsatisfactory to Izzat Ibrahim who asserted that Kuwait must accept all Iraqi demands or nothing. Although the Kuwait delegation asked permission to prepare other concession to Iraq, Ibrahim and the other members of Iraq's delegation refused to negotiate, packed their bags, and left Jedda.

See August 2, 1990.

July 29, 1990

Mongolia's reform Communist Party retains control of parliament.

In Mongolia's first multiparty election, the Communist Party was victorious, keeping 75% seats in the Great Hural (upper house) and 60% of the seats in the Small Hural (lower house). On March 14, the reformist chairman of the party's Politburo, Gombojavyn Ochirbat, promised to develop democracy and protect human rights. Parliament also amended Mongolia's constitution to end the Communists' power monopoly and allow direct elections.

July 30, 1990

U.S. Marines are sent to evacuate embassy personnel from Monrovia, Liberia.

In May 1990, rebels led by Yormie Johnson threatened Liberia's government, and on May 31, President Bush ordered 2,000 U.S. Marines to evacuate Americans in Liberia. In early July, Johnson's guerrillas again besieged Monrovia and threatened to take foreign hostages. Bush again sent the marines to Liberia, and on August 4, they rescued over 125 American and European diplomats.

August 2, 1990

Iraq invades Kuwait, easily conquering the small Arab state.

When news of Iraq's invasion of Kuwait reached Washington late in the evening of August 1, 1990, Iraqi forces had already conquered Kuwait City, three and one-half hours after crossing the border. The White House immediately issued a statement condemning Iraq's attack and President Bush ordered the U.S. Treasury Department to freeze all the financial assets of Iraq and Kuwait held in the United States.

The Bush administration also adopted the suggestion Soviet Foreign Minister Eduard Shevardnadze made to Secretary of State Baker in Siberia to have the United Nations issue a condemnation of Iraq's aggression and order Iraq to end its occupation of Kuwait (see August 2, 1990). United Nations support not only would avoid a Soviet veto of any unwarranted United Nations Security Council resolutions against Iraq but also justify international economic sanctions against Iraq until Baghdad withdrew its forces from Kuwait.

Between August 2 and November 29, 1990, the United Nations Security Council approved ten resolutions as part of a U.S.-led international coalition to evict Iraq from Kuwait. The first two of the ten resolutions were United Nations Security Council Resolution 660, which condemned Iraq's conquest of Kuwait, and Resolution 661, which levied economic sanctions on Iraq (see August 25, 1990).

Persian Gulf Region

In addition to seeking United Nations backing, the Bush administration consulted with NATO members and officials of Saudi Arabia, Jordan, Egypt, and other Middle East countries near Iraq to obtain their support in evicting Iraq from Kuwait. Most important of all these contacts was sending a team of United States military advisers to consult with Saudi Arabia's King Faud and Saudi Lieutenant General Prince Khalid Bin Sultan al-Saud, who worked with U.S. General Norman H. Schwarzkopf until the Iraqi conflict ended in March 1991. Headed by Defense Secretary Richard Cheney and Commander of United States Central Command for the Middle East General Schwarzkopf, these U.S. advisers gave King Faud specific intelligence data regarding Iraq's threat to countries such as Saudi Arabia, Qatar, and Jordan.

Despite Saddam Hussein's denunciation of U.S. policies between January and August 1990, Bush failed to perceive the Iraqi leader's rising anger during the week before the invasion. On July 25, U.S. Ambassador to Iraq, April Glaspie met with Hussein, who claimed Kuwait was a lackey of Washington and waged economic warfare on Iraq.

Glaspie tried to placate Hussein by saying she had insufficient time to prepare a response but the United States wanted Iraq's friendship. Glaspie told him problems could be handled by diplomacy although the United States had no security commitments with Kuwait. Glaspie's attitude was clarified in her recommendation to the State Department to relax its public criticism of Iraq. In response, Bush composed a letter for Glaspie to convey to Hussein that "in a spirit of friendship and candor," the United States would help find a peaceful solution to Iraq's problems with Kuwait. Some historians think Glaspie and Bush gave Hussein the impression that the United States would not oppose an Iraqi invasion of Kuwait.

See September 4, 1980, and August 6, 1990.

August 2, 1990

Secretary of State Baker and Soviet Foreign Minister Shevardnadze condemn Iraq's invasion of Kuwait.

In a fortuitous circumstance, U.S. Secretary of State Baker was meeting with Soviet Foreign Minister Eduard Shevardnadze in Irkutsk, Siberia when they learned about the invasion of Kuwait. The two ministers condemned Iraq's invasion in a mutal understanding that became the basis for U.S.-USSR cooperation in meeting Saddam Hussein's challenge and avoiding a Soviet veto in the U.N. Security Council. Shevardnadze's decision worried the Kremlin because some Soviet officials sympathetic to Iraq argued that the USSR had helped Iraq in the past. The Soviet Union had over 7,000 advisers in Baghdad.

See August 25, 1990.

August 6, 1990

Using UNSC resolutions against Iraq, President Bush orders U.S. forces to protect Saudi Arabia as a Desert Shield operation.

Adopting Soviet Foreign Minister Shevardnadze's suggestion to use the United Nations Security Council (UNSC) to force Iraq to leave Kuwait, President Bush consulted with European and Arab leaders. He also sent U.S. military advisers to determine whether Saudi King Fahd should request U.S. assistance. With King Fahd's approval, on August 6 Bush ordered U.S. forces to begin an operation known as Desert Shield. The United States immediately dis-

patched 2,300 paratroopers in addition to AWAC, B-52, and F-111 aircraft to provide an early defense for the Saudis prior to the arrival of an aircraft carrier task force and army ground forces. On August 8, Great Britain, Egypt, and other nations joined the multinational force to deter further Iraqi aggression and enforce U.N. economic sanctions against Iraq.

On August 8, Bush's televised broadcast informed Americans he accepted King Fahd's request for protection from Iraq's expansionism as a "wholly defensive operation." On August 10, Bush notified Congress about troops sent to defend Saudi Arabia without invoking the 1973 War Powers Act because "war is not imminent." Later, on October 1–2, the House and Senate voted to support the president's defensive actions toward Iraqi aggression.

August 25, 1990

The U.N. Security Council authorizes naval and air blockades of Iraq.

To enforce the economic sanction levied against Iraq on August 2, the Security Council approved resolution 665 by a vote of 13-0 (Cuba and Yemen abstaining). Resolution 665 authorized U.S. and allied ships blockading Iraq to use force if necessary to carry out the sanctions. The vote was delayed until August 25 because the Soviet Union thought Saddam Hussein would negotiate a settlement and leave Kuwait. On September 25, Resolution 670 extended the Iraqi embargo by ending air flights to and from Iraq.

On September 9, after Moscow realized Saddam Hussein intended to stay in Kuwait, Soviet President Mikhail Gorbachev met with Bush in Helsinki to declare U.S.-USSR solidarity in condemning Iraq's invasion and calling for Iraq's unconditional withdrawal from Kuwait. On October 15, Gorbachev received the Nobel Prize for his reforms leading to the end of the Cold War.

See October 19, 1990.

September 12, 1990

The 2 + 4 talks result in a final treaty for German reunification.

In Moscow, the final treaty resulting from six months of 2 + 4 talks was signed by representatives of the United States, the Soviet Union, Great Britain, France, West Germany, and East Germany, plus a representative from Poland. In addition to providing

President Bush meets with the Emir of Kuwait, Jabir Al-Ahmad Al Jabir Al-Sasbah, at the White House, September 28, 1990. George Bush Presidential Library

for the political reunification of Germany, the agreements included these key clauses: 1. Germany guaranteed the Oder and Neisse Rivers as its eastern border with Poland; 2. Soviet troops would leave East Germany by 1994, with the West German government paying the cost of their Soviet withdrawal; 3. Germany would be a member of NATO but with limits on the size of the German army (370,000), with no nuclear weapons in eastern German territory, and with Germany as a signatory of the Nuclear Non-Proliferation Treaty.

During the six months of talks on Germany's future, NATO adopted policies to show that the Warsaw Pact and NATO nations were not adversaries. The two blocs would reduce their front-line defenses and make use of nuclear weapons "a last resort," a phase modifying the "first-use" strategy of previous years. Finally, NATO invited Warsaw Pact leaders to establish a diplomatic liaison at NATO's Brussels headquarters.

September 12, 1990

Peru rejects U.S. plans to combat drug trafficking.

Contrary to Peru's agreement to help combat drug traffickers, newly elected President Alberto Fujimori rejected, on June 10, U.S. support for military efforts to combat drug traffic. The United States offered Peru $39.5 million for a counterinsurgency campaign to eliminate drug traffickers, but Fujimori hoped to use free-market incentives to stop farmers from growing coca, used producing cocaine.

September 18, 1990

The Salvadoran government and rebels fail to get a cease-fire; President Bush sends El Salvador more aid.

Having negotiated in Costa Rica since July 26, representatives of El Salvador and the Farabundo Marti para la Liberacion Nacional (FMLN) rebels failed to agree on a cease-fire by September 18. Rebel leaders announced a new "political offensive" to change the government, and fighting increased during the next two months. On December 7, Bush announced the United States would rush $8 million to assist the Salvadoran government.

See April 4, 1991.

September 20, 1990

East and West Germany reunite in accordance with the 2+4 talks.

German reunification was completed by a treaty signed on August 31 that the East and West German parliaments ratified on September 20. The ratified agreement was the Settlement with Respect to Germany signed in Moscow on September 12, 1990. German unity was solidified on October 14 when elections were held in five new states formed from the former East Germany. In elections for the united German Bundestag (lower house of parliament), Chancellor Helmut Kohl's Christian Democratic Union Party won a majority or plurality of votes in all states except Brandenburg, where Social Democrats won a plurality.

In line with the 2 plus 4 talks, East Germany withdrew from the Warsaw Pact on September 24. On November 9, Germany and the Soviet Union signed a nonaggression pact and friendship treaty, and on November 14 Germany and Poland signed a treaty making their current boundaries permanent along the Oder and Neisse River 5.

September 30, 1990

In Rwanda, Tutsi tribes try to overthrow the Hutu government.

Trouble between Rwanda's ruling Hutu majority and the Tutsi minority began in September 1990 when refugee Tutsi tribesmen tried to overthrow the Hutu. Rwandan President Juvenal Habyarimana requested assistance from Belgium and France, which sent 650 paratroopers to protect the government. On October 18, French President François Mitterrand persuaded Habyarimana to allow neutral nations to supervise a cease-fire and permit Tutsi exiles to return home. Mitterrand's proposal was not carried out because civil strife continued in Rwanda (see June 8, 1994).

October 1, 1990

Slovenia and Croatia take steps against Serb dominance of Yugoslavia.

On September 28, Slovenia, one of six Yugoslav republics, amended its constitution to make the republic's laws superior to Yugoslav laws. Slovenia also assumed control of its territorial defense forces.

In contrast to Slovenia, where few Serbs lived, Croatia's attempt to end Serb dominance was com-

plicated because by the large number of Serbs living in the northeast border region of Croatia known as the Krajina. On July 25, 1990, Milan Bobic, a Serb dentist who lived in Knin, the Krajina's largest city, began organizing Serb protests to gain autonomy from Croatia and, perhaps, become part of the Serb Republic. Bobic and many other Croatian Serbs were inspired by Slobodan Milošević's propaganda calling for a Greater Serbia. To verify that the people of Krajina desired autonomy, Bobic called for a referendum to be held in the Krajina on August 18, 1990. Two days before the referendum, Croatia's President Franjo Tudjman declared the Krajina referendum unconstitutional and ordered Croatian police to march on Knin and enforce Croatia's constitution by preventing the referendum from taking place. Croatia's Minister of the Interior also ordered three helicopters loaded with Croatian police reservists to back up the police objectives.

As Laura Silber and Allen Little's *Yugoslavia: Death of a Nation* explains, Tujdman's attempt to stop the referendum became a fiasco. After learning the police were on the way to Knin, Bobic telephoned Belgrade and asked Serb President Milošević for help against Croatia's police. Milošević immediately dispatched the Yugoslav National Army's (YNA) aircraft to fly across the Croatian border, frighten the Croatian police, and attack the helicopters if necessary. After the YNA's MiG fighter planes buzzed the helicopters to scare them away from Knin, the MiG pilot radioed the helicopters, telling the helicopter pilots to return directly to their bases or be shot down. The helicopter's turned homeward while the Croatian police stopped their march toward Knin and retreated to their home bases.

After the confrontation ended and despite President Tudjman's complaints against Milošević, the Krajina referendum was held with 99% of the Croatian Serbs voting in favor of autonomy for Krajina. Tudjman failed to suppress Serb nationalism but took action to revitalize Croatia's Territorial Defense Force (TDF) and to purge Serbia officers of the YNA stationed in Croatia. Compared to Croatians, the disproportionate number of Serbs in the TDF and the YNA were expelled from the services and Croatians were recruited to replace them. Tudjman was able to build a national Croatian army to prepare for Croatia's secession from the Yugoslav Federation and gain independence.

See June 25, 1991.

October 4, 1990

The United States cuts off food aid to the Sudan.

When Sudan's civil conflict broke out in 1985, the United States and other humanitarian aid groups airlifted food and medicine to starving Sudanese, especially in southern Sudan (see April 6, 1985). After Sudan's General Omar al-Bashir overthrew Sudan's President Sadeq al-Mahdi in 1989, al-Bashir rejected former United States President Jimmy Carter's peace proposal (see December 6, 1989). On April 24, 1990, Sudanese rebels in the Sudanese People's Liberation Army failed in their attempt to oust al-Basir. Next, in September, 1990, the United States' CIA informed the White House that al-Bashir's government was selling food and medicine supplied by the United States, the Red Cross, and the United Nations to other African nations and using the profits to purchase military equipment from Libya, Iraq, and Iran. Because of the CIA's information, the Bush administration announced on October 8 that the United States was joining other international humanitarian groups in cutting off food and medicine supplies they had been sending to Sudan until better methods were found to distribute those supplies to the starving Sudanese. The food deliveries resumed in 1991 (see March 18, 1991).

October 12, 1990

A U.N. resolution criticizes Israel for West Bank violence and calls for a U.N. fact-finding mission.

In a resolution introduced by Britain and supported by the United States, the Security Council criticized Israel for recent violence in the West Bank and Gaza and requested the U.N. secretary-general to investigate conditions on the West Bank. This resolution was a compromise with a Third World resolution recommending U.N. protection for Palestinians from the Israeli army. This compromise enabled the United States to maintain support from its Arab allies against Iraq in the conflict over Kuwait.

The Security Council decision followed an incident at Jerusalem's Temple Mount in which Israeli troops fired on a Palestinian crowd throwing rocks at Jews who gathered at the Wailing Wall. Israeli gunfire killed 21 Palestinians and injured about 150 others. After Israel rejected the U.N. investigation called for in the British resolution, the council adopted an October 24 resolution that deplored Israel's refusal to investigate the Temple Mount incident.

October 19, 1990

President Bush rejects a proposal to compromise with Iraq.

To placate hard-liners in the Soviet Foreign Ministry who criticized Foreign Minister Shevardnadze's cooperation with U.S. Secretary of State Baker on the Kuwait conflict, President Gorbachev sent former *Pravda* correspondent Yevgeny Primakov to Baghdad, Washington, and London in search of a diplomatic solution.

In Baghdad, Primakov discussed Saddam Hussein's August 12 proposal to combine a conference on Kuwait with a conference to settle all Arab-Israeli disputes. Primakov next came to Washington to tell Bush that Hussein was "flexible" in working out details of the Kuwait and Arab-Israeli meetings. But Bush refused to link the Kuwait issue with the Arab-Israeli conflict, telling Primakov to make sure Hussein understood Iraq must unconditionally leave Kuwait.

Finally, Primakov visited London to talk with Prime Minister Margaret Thatcher but learned Thatcher would not compromise. Thatcher lectured Primakov on Hussein's treachery, saying there was no option but war, not only to free Kuwait but also to destroy Iraq's military power. Primakov's failed "peace" effort did not end hard-line criticism of Shevardnadze in the Kremlin.

See November 8, 1990.

November 3, 1990

Pakistan's National Assembly elects Nawas Sharif as prime minister.

On August 6, Pakistani President Ghulam Ishaq Khan dismissed Prime Minister Benazir Bhutto, accusing her of "corruption and nepotism" and of ordering the army to control national television and telephones. In national elections on October 24, Bhutto's People's Party coalition received only 45 of

150 assembly seats compared with 105 seats for Sharif's Islamic Democratic Alliance. When the Assembly convened on November 3, Sharif was elected prime minister.

November 5, 1990

President Bush signs budget legislation for fiscal 1991 that includes tax increases.

Throughout 1990, the Democrat majority in Congress pushed for tax increases to reduce the budget deficit and lower the national debt, which grew to over $3 trillion under President Reagan. In October, President Bush approved legislation to keep the government running, but on November 5 he compromised with Congress. The final budget appropriations for 1991 raised the top income tax rate from 28% to 31% and increased excise taxes. Bush had hesitated to agree with the Democratic Members of Congress because his 1988 campaign slogan was "read my lips, no new taxes."

November 6, 1990

Democrats increase their majority in Congress.

In congressional elections, the Democrats increased by one seat their Senate majority—56 seats to the Republicans' 44. In the House, Democrats gained 8 seats, an advantage of 267 to 167.

November 8, 1990

President Bush moves to take the offensive against Iraq.

Two days after congressional elections, President Bush announced U.S. forces in the Middle East would be doubled to obtain "an adequate offensive military option." Bush's plan to increase troops began in October when the White House adopted rhetoric to condemn Saddam Hussein as a new "Hitler" who placed foreign hostages as human shields near military bases, terrorized the Kuwaiti population, looted Kuwaiti banks, and prepared to use chemical and nuclear weapons. Bush and Secretary of State James

George and Barbara Bush walk along the desert with General Schwarzkopf. George Bush Presidential Library

Baker also contacted friendly nations to ask their support in future action against Iraq.

Bush's increase of U.S. forces in the Persian Gulf led many members of Congress to be skeptical of his rhetoric against Hussein, and Senate hearings examined his decision.

For information on the Senate hearings see November 27,1990.

November 15, 1990

President Bush signs amendments to the 1970 Clean Air Act.

Prompted by Canada to review the 1970 Clean Air Act, which failed to deal with acid rain, Congress reviewed the 1970 legislation to determine proper regulations of acid rain and the regulations' effects on unemployed coal miners. The 1990 amendments regulated the amounts of sulfur dioxide and nitrogen oxide that public utilities could emit from smokestacks. In addition, the budget for fiscal 1991 provided funds for unemployed workers who lost their jobs because of the reduced amount of coal used by utilities, the principal industry emitting acid rain.

November 16, 1990

India's National Front Party takes control of parliament.

Although the opposing National Front Coalition gained a majority in both houses of parliament in March 1990, Prime Minister Singh lost a vote of confidence on November 7. Singh's Congress Party had been criticized in 1990 because of conflict with Pakistan in Kashmir. After losing the vote of confidence, Singh resigned and National Front leader Chandra Shekhar became prime minister.

November 17, 1990

The Treaty on Conventional Forces in Europe (CFE) is signed.

In Paris, leaders of NATO and Warsaw Pact nations signed the CFE Treaty. Resulting from meetings of the Commission of Security and Cooperation in Europe (CSCE), the pact limited each alliance to 20,000 battle tanks and artillery pieces, 30,000 armored combat vehicles, 6,800 combat aircraft, and 2,000 attack helicopters. Two days later, the CSCE members signed the Charter of Paris for a New Europe, declaring an end to

Europe's military and economic divisions and affirming democratic freedoms and human rights.

See June 14, 1991.

November 18, 1990

Saddam Hussein offers to release all foreign hostages in Iraq and Kuwait.

Hoping to divide the alliance opposing Iraq, Saddam Hussein offered to release foreign hostages in Iraq and Kuwait over a three-month period if no war began. Although President Bush rejected this ploy, Hussein released German hostages because, he said, Chancellor Helmut Kohl had made helpful remarks about peace. On December 4 without receiving U.S. or U.N. concessions, Hussein released the remaining Soviet hostages and approximately 3,000 Western hostages, including 163 Americans, the U.S. ambassador to Kuwait, and his four staff members. On December 11, the State Department said about 500 Americans chose to remain in Iraq or Kuwait.

November 27, 1990

The Senate Armed Forces Committee examines Iraqi economic sanctions.

Because of congressional opposition to President Bush's November 8 decision to increase troops in the Persian Gulf, the Senate Armed Services Committee under Chairman Sam Nunn (D-Ga.) conducted hearings on military action as compared to continuing economic sanctions. Appearing before the committee, Bush administration officials such as Defense Secretary Richard Cheney and Secretary of State James Baker argued that military action might be the only way to get Iraqi forces out of Kuwait. Opponents of Bush's policy, such as former Chairman of the Joint Chiefs of Staff Admiral William Crowe, did not deny the need to get Iraq out of Kuwait but contended that economic sanctions would achieve this goal if sufficient time were given for them to work. Nevertheless, Bush feared the coalition of Western and Arab countries might fall apart if sanctions took too long to compel Saddam Hussein to leave Kuwait. The debate on war or sanctions continued until the eve of war.

See January 12, 1991.

November 28, 1990

Britain's Conservative Party selects John Major as Prime Minister.

The Conservative Party was divided on the issue of Margaret Thatcher's policy toward economic unity with the European Community. Although a plurality of Conservative Party members favored Thatcher, she resigned on November 24, with Major replacing her.

November 28, 1990

Three Liberian factions accept a cease-fire and agree to hold peace talks.

Following rebel attacks on Liberia's government on July 30, 1990, the Economic Community of West Africa sent a peacekeeping force to resolve problems between two rebel groups and Liberia's government, whose President Doe was killed by Liberian rebels on September 7.

Under the auspices of the West African Community, delegates of the three factions met in Bamako, Mali on November 26 and two days later agreed to a cease-fire. After the cease-fire took effect on February 12, 1991, leaders of the three factions formed an interim government, but the cease-fire did not last.

November 29, 1990

The U.N. Security Council authorizes "all means necessary" to get Iraq out of Kuwait.

After President Bush ordered 20,000 additional U.S. troops to the Persian Gulf on November 8, his rhetoric emphasized Iraq's atrocities in Kuwait and Iraq's preparations for nuclear war. Visiting U.S. troops in Saudi Arabia on Thanksgiving Day, Bush said experts thought it would be years before Iraq had nuclear weapons but they "may be seriously underestimating the situation." Each day, Bush said, brought Iraq "one step closer" to having a nuclear arsenal to use.

As revealed in Khidhir Hamaz's *Saddam's Bombmaker* (2000), Iraq had tried since August 1990 to speed up the construction of a nuclear warhead small enough to mount on an Iraqi missile. But Iraqi scientists only completed a nuclear bomb too big to be carried by a missile, so Saddam Hussein ordered the nuclear experimental units hidden in case U.S.-led forces attacked. Iraq also planted thousands of chemical and biological weapons in southern Iraq near Basra, where bombs of an invader would release their contents in the air, a possible reason for the postwar Gulf War syndrome experienced by veterans of the 1991 war.

Without knowing Saddam's precise plans, Bush and Secretary of State Baker contacted over 20 heads of state and all Security Council members to seek

General Scowcroft, Bush with British Prime Minister John Major at Camp David. George Bush Presidential Library

approval for a deadline to attack Saddam Hussein. Baker's crucial task was to obtain wording satisfactory to Soviet Foreign Minister Sheverdnadze. Baker and Shevardnadze finally agreed the U.N. resolution should avoid the term "use of force," but after the resolution passed, Baker would call it an "authority to use force" as part of the U.N. record. Baker also accepted President Gorbachev's suggestion to call the interval before the January 15 deadline a "pause of goodwill" for diplomacy that might prevent war.

Having the diplomatic cards in place, the United States proposed Resolution 678, which Security Council members approved by 12 to 2, with Cuba and Yemen opposing while China abstained. The resolution authorized states "cooperating with the government of Kuwait" to use "all means necessary" to obtain Iraq's withdrawal from Kuwait and gave Iraq until January 15 to comply.

See November 30, 1990.

November 29, 1990

The U.S. embassy in Beirut, Lebanon, is reopened.

The U.S. embassy was shut down in February 1989 after intense fighting between Christians and Muslims endangered embassy personnel. After the Christian Phalangist leader Samir Geagea pledged allegiance to Lebanese President Elias Hwari on April 3, 1990, the Vatican obtained a cease-fire among the competing factions on May 17. On August 21, Lebanon's parliament approved constitutional changes giving Christians and Muslims equal representation in parliament. On September 21, President Hwari signed this document and proclaimed the "Second Lebanese Republic."

Only General Aoun's Christian army continued to fight against government forces. In September, the Lebanese army surrounded Aoun's forces, who defended their territory in Beirut until October 13, when Syrian jets bombed Aoun's headquarters, killing 750 people. Aoun resigned his command and took exile in the French embassy.

On October 25, Hwari announced that Christian, Druse, and Muslim Shiite militias had agreed to withdraw from Beirut, and the fundamentalist Hezbollah would also withdraw its forces. After all militias disarmed and Syria agreed to return its army to the Bekaa valley by early 1991, the United States reopened its

Beirut embassy. On December 4, all military forces had withdrawn from Beirut.

See February 14, 1989; May 22, 1991.

November 30, 1990

President Bush invites the Iraqi foreign minister to negotiate in Washington.

Following passage of U.N. resolution 678 on November 29, President Bush invited Iraqi Foreign Minister Tariq Aziz to Washington for negotiations and offered to send Secretary of State Baker to Baghdad for discussions. Although the offer disturbed U.S. allies because Bush did not contact them in advance, Bush simply planned to avoid war by telling Iraqi officials that the January 15 deadline for their unconditional withdrawal from Kuwait must be met. Subsequently, Washington and Baghdad made frequent attempts to schedule a time and place for meeting, with the United States insisting the date must be well before January 15. Baker finally met with Tariq Aziz.

See January 9, 1991.

November 30, 1990

President Bush again seeks to improve U.S.-Chinese relations.

President Bush met with Chinese Foreign Minister Qian Qichen at the White House in an effort to improve U.S. relations with China following the 1989 Tiananmen Square massacres. On June 25, the Chinese permitted dissident Fang Lizhi, who in 1989 had sought safety in the U.S. embassy in Beijing, to leave the country for London. At Secretary of State Baker's request, China abstained from the November 29 U.N. Resolution 678 on Iraq.

December 2, 1990

Reunited Germany holds its first general elections; Chancellor Kohl's alliance wins.

Reunited Germany's first general election was a victory for Chancellor Helmut Kohl's governing Christian Socialist Union (CSU)/Christian Democratic Union (CDU) coalition and his allied Free Democrats. East Germany's former communist party, renamed the Party of Democratic Socialism (PDS), won 17 of the 672 seats in the Bundestag (lower house) and East German Greens received 8 seats. German's Social Democratic Party remained the main opposition party.

December 3, 1990

President Bush begins a six-day visit to five Latin American states.

On the first stop of a tour of South America, President Bush addressed Brazil's Congress to praise President Fernando Collor de Mello, who, since his inauguration on March 15, had attracted international financial officials by beginning an economic austerity program. Collor's program reduced government spending and inflation, froze wages and prices for 30 days, and changed the currency from the cruzado to a cruzeiro. He also halted Brazil's secret nuclear weapons program and on November 28 joined with Argentine's President Menem to renounce the use of nuclear weapons.

After a brief visit to Uruguay, Bush met in Argentina with President Carlos Saul Menem on December 4. This meeting took place just two days after army forces loyal to the president put down an uprising of dissident troops who had seized army headquarters to demand the appointment of Colonel Mohammed Ali Seineldin as chief of staff. The loyalists regained control of all sites seized by the rebels, although 21 persons were killed in the conflict. After showing U.S. backing for Menem's government, Bush made short visits to Chile and Venezuela before returning home.

December 6, 1990

U.S. aircraft assist France in evacuating its citizens from Chad.

Washington and Paris had hoped Libyan dissidents would help Chad's President Hissene Habré defeat a rebel army backed by Libyan leader Mu'ammar al-Gadhafi. Instead, rebels led by General Idriss Deby captured Chad's capital, N' Djamena on December 2 and Habré fled into exile. At French request, U.S. planes airlifted 700 Libyan dissidents from Chad to Nigeria. The French also evacuated over 1,000 of their nationals from Chad.

December 7, 1990

Bulgaria moves toward a more democratic government.

Although Bulgaria's Communist Party was renamed the Socialist party and won Bulgaria's June elections, protests against Socialist Premier Lukanov broke out and led to his resignation in November. The Bulgarian parliament approved Ditmar Popov, a politically independent judge, as Bulgaria's premier. Popov organized a multiparty cabinet that included many Socialist Party members.

December 9, 1990

Poland's Communists lose in national elections.

Although Communist Premier Mazowiecki tried to alleviate Poland's social discontent in July 1990, his austerity policies were unpopular. They led to the presidential victory of the Solidarity Party's Lech Wałęsa who won 74% of the votes in a runoff election. On December 12, outgoing president Jaruzelski apologized for the "pain and injustice" the people suffered under the communists. Wałęsa was sworn in as president on December 22.

December 12, 1990

The Czechoslovak National Assembly specifies the powers of the country's two republics.

Because leaders of the Slovak Republic desired autonomy, President Václav Hável asked the National Assembly to define the federal powers related to authority of Slovakia. The assembly passed legislation that retained federal power over defense, foreign affairs, economic policy, and the protection of national minorities. The Czech and Slovak Republics held the remaining powers.

December 14–15, 1990

The European Community (EC) provides aid to the Soviets and asks Iraq to withdraw from Kuwait.

During a regularly scheduled session, EC leaders agreed to provide the USSR with $2.4 billion of aid.

They also called on Iraq to withdraw peacefully from Kuwait and proposed future talks to coordinate EC policies on foreign and security affairs.

December 16, 1990

In Haiti, Aristide's election as president brings democracy to the island.

Following the overthrow of President-for-Life Jean-Claude Duvalier (see February 7, 1986), various militants fought to gain power. The military regimes of General Namphy and General Avril (see April 9, 1989) were not satisfactory. Finally in July 1990, General Herard Abraham deposed Avril and sought U.S. advice about Haiti's elections scheduled for December 1990.

In the context of Haiti's political problems, Father Jean-Baptist Aristide rose in popularity. An advocate of Roman Catholic "liberation theology," Aristide ministered to the poor in a slum parish where he criticized Haiti's elite, who he said, claimed to be Christian while oppressing the lower class. After first rejecting a call to run for president, Aristide agreed to join a coalition led by the Lavalas Party, a reform coalition wishing to end corrupt military-dictatorial regimes and bring democracy to Haiti.

Although on December 5 militants attacked an Aristide campaign rally by detonating grenades that killed seven people, the event enhanced Aristide's popularity. Haiti's December elections were supervised by U.N. observers who reported that Aristide won 60 to 70% of the vote for president.

See February 7, 1986; November 29, 1987;
April 9, 1989; January 20, 1991.

December 17, 1990

Colombia refuses to extradite drug traffickers to the United States.

Although on May 27, 1990, Colombia elected as president César Gaviria Trujillo, a strong advocate of the war against drug lords as president, Gaviria knew he faced powerful opposition from the Medillín drug cartel. During the months preceding the May election, the Medellín claimed responsibility for killing two candidates: the Patriotic Party's nominee on March 22 and the first Liberal Party candidate of the April 19th Movement on April 26. As a result, Gaviria found it difficult to accept Colombia's February 15

agreement to cooperate when Washington sought to extradite several drug lords.

On August 11, Colombian police killed the Medellín's second-in-command, but on September 5 Gaviria offered not to extradite traffickers who surrendered, confessed in court, and turned their property over to the state, a decision he confirmed on December 17. The next day, drug lord Fabio Ochoa Vasquez turned himself in and was placed in a special jail.

December 17, 1990

The Soviet Congress of People's Deputies approves President Gorbachev's plan to revise the central authority; Eduard Shevardnadze resigns as foreign minister.

On December 17, President of the Supreme Soviet Mikhail Gorbachev sought to maintain Soviet unity by presenting a plan to the Congress of People's Deputies that consisted of 2,250 delegates from each Soviet republic who were elected in 1989 (see March 26, 1989 and May 25, 1989). Gorbachev was concerned about Soviet unity because throughout 1990, Soviet republics such as Lithuania (March 11), Estonia (March 11), Latvia (May 4), the Russian Federation (August 10), Armenia (August 5), and Ukraine (October 24) had proclaimed various degrees of independence from the Soviet Union.

On October 16, 1990 Gorbachev sought to meet the challenge of maintaining Soviet unity by offering his plan to the Supreme Soviet the standing legislative body consisting of 542 delegates elected by the People's Deputies in May 1989. Gorbachev's plan would restructure the economy and preserve the central government's authority over foreign policy, banking, taxes, and currency, but would also give each republic with autonomy in domestic affairs. The plan also called for a referendum to be held in each of Soviet republics to obtain the people's approval for maintaining Soviet unity. In October, the Supreme Soviet approved Gorbachev's plan although some hard-line communists such as the chief of the KGB's secret police Vladamir A. Kryuchkov opposed Gorbachev's plan as "Western economic involvement."

After obtaining the Supreme Soviet's approval, Gorbachev sought approval of his unity plan by the Congress of People's Deputies. After the Deputies convened on December 17, Gorbachev presented the plan approved by the Supreme Soviet, asking the delegates to assist Moscow in conducting the referendums in each of the republics. Before adjourning on December 24, the People's Deputies approved Gorbachev's reform plan and agreed to conduct the referendum. Also during the week of the congress, Soviet Foreign Minister Shevardnadze resigned. Although President Gorbachev said Shevardnadze simply needed a rest, President Bush and his advisers believed Shevardnadze was dismayed because hardline Communists such as Yevgeny Primakov had gained ascendancy in Moscow after Gorbachev placated them. This belief became reality when Primakov undertook efforts to help Saddam Hussein gain concessions from the United States in February 1991.

See February 22, 1991.
For results of the referendum see March 17, 1991

December 22, 1990

The United States agrees to dissolve its trust territories on Pacific Ocean islands.

The U.S. delegation to the United Nations concurred with a U.N. Security Council resolution dissolving all U.S. Trust Territories of the Pacific Islands except Palau island, which remained under a "free association" accord with the United States. These Pacific trusteeships were established following World War II.

See April 2, 1947, and October 13, 1980.

December 31, 1990

Israeli bombers hit PLO bases in southern Lebanon.

Although Israel realized it should avoid trouble in the Middle East to maintain President Bush's coalition against Iraq, Prime Minister Yitzhak Shamir wanted to keep the PLO from strengthening its position in south Lebanon. Hezbollah guerrillas continued to attack Israeli forces despite the peace among Lebanese factions. To retain Israel's position in south Lebanon, Shamir ordered Israeli fighter-bombers to attack Palestinian bases near Sidon, killing 12 persons. For similar reasons on December 29, Israeli troops put down demonstrations in the Gaza Strip that killed 4 Palestinians and wounded 125.

See November 29, 1990.

1991

January 5, 1991

Somalia's civil war requires the United States and Italy to rescue foreigners in Mogadishu.

American officials first became concerned about Somalia in 1978 because Soviet and Cuban forces assisted Ethiopia in defeating Somalia in a war caused by Somalia's claim to Ogadan province on the border with Ethiopia. Following the war, President Carter sent $7 million of food aid to Somalia. In 1982, President Reagan sent military aid to assist Somalia in another Ethiopian conflict, during which Cuban leader Fidel Castro sent 18,000 Cuban soldiers to help Ethiopia.

During the 1980s the Soviets and Cubans also helped rebel groups in Somalia seeking to overthrow the government of General Muhammad Siad Barre, who had taken power in 1969. By 1988, Barre was fighting various rebel forces. Rebels in northern Somalia such as the Somalia National Movement and the Somalia Democratic Salvation Front were

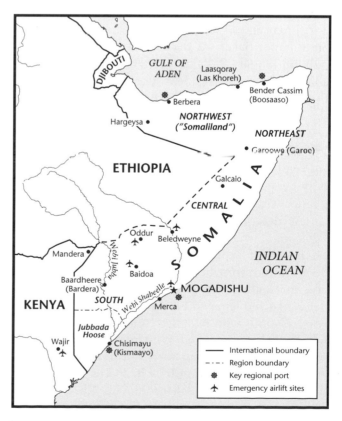

Somalia

well organized. In southern Somalia near Mogadishu, competing clans and subclans carried on their civil war, causing more trouble for Barre surrounding the capital by January 1991.

The fighting near Mogadishu prompted the United States and Italy to combine their forces in air and sea operations to rescue American, Soviet, Italian, and other foreigners in Mogadishu. U.N. groups providing food relief to Somalia also evacuated Mogadishu. To permit the safe rescue of foreign personnel, Somalia's warring factions accepted a temporary cease-fire while the evacuation took place. Following the rescue, civil war resumed, with the rebels overthrowing President Siad Barre on January 26. Intense fighting continued as two warlords, Mohammad Farah Aideed and Mohammad Ali Mahdi, competed for control of Somalia.

See March 8, 1978; July 12, 1982; April 24, 1992.

January 9, 1991

Secretary of State Baker fails to persuade Iraq to evacuate Kuwait.

Throughout December 1990, attempts to schedule negotiations between the United States and Iraq fell through. Finally on January 9, Iraqi Foreign Minister Tariq Aziz agreed to meet in Geneva with Secretary of State James Baker. At the first of two meetings with Aziz on January 9, Baker gave Aziz a copy of a letter addressed from President George Bush to Iraq's President Saddam Hussein. Baker asked Aziz to read the letter and respond to its contents. In part, Bush wrote: "We stand today at the brink of war between Iraq and the world. This is a war which (sic) began with your invasion of Kuwait; this is a war that can only be ended by Iraq's full and unconditional compliance with U.N. Security Council Resolution 687."

As described by Baker's memoir *The Politics of Diplomacy*, after reading the letter Aziz told Baker "it is full of expressions of threat" and "alien" to "communications between the heads of state." Aziz also threw the letter on a table, saying he would not deliver such a letter to President Hussein. During his conversations with Aziz that morning and again after lunch, Baker reiterated contents of Bush's letter, although using different words in trying to convince Aziz that Iraq must withdraw its forces from Kuwait. "If you do not leave," Baker told Aziz, "then we'll find ourselves at war" and "you will surely lose" because Iraq will face "devastatingly superior fire power."

Baker also warned Aziz that if Iraq should use chemical or biological weapons against our forces Americans will "demand vengeance." The United States, Baker said, has the means to eliminate the "current Iraqi regime."

Brushing off Baker's statement, Aziz said Iraq is not afraid of a war with America, describing a U.S. invasion of Iraq as simply an "alliance among the United States, Israel and former rulers of Kuwait." If the U.S. attacked, Aziz said, "Iraq will be justified in attacking Israel, an event that would rally all Arabs to the side of Iraq." Aziz not only refused to accept Bush's letter but refused to fear Baker's warnings about America's superior fire power. In a final attempt to avert war, U.N. Secretary General Javier Pérez de Cueller visited Saddam Hussein in Baghdad on January 12, where he too learned Hussein would not withdraw Iraqi forces from Kuwait.

See January 16, 1991.

January 12, 1991

Congress approves the use of military force against Iraq, if necessary.

Following two days of debate on whether the United States should attack Iraq or allow more time for economic sanctions to compel Iraq to withdraw its forces from Kuwait, Congress authorized the use of military force against Iraq if necessary. The Senate approved the resolution by 52 to 47; the House, by 250 to 183.

The vote for war was the closest since Congress approved James Madison's call for war against the British in 1812, but, unlike the Federalists in 1812, who continued opposing Madison, the Democrats in 1991 rallied behind President Bush. As Senator Sam Nunn (D-Ga.) said: "We may disagree in this chamber but when the vote is over . . . we are going to stand united."

See June 18, 1812.

January 16, 1991

Under U.S. direction, a multinational U.N. force launches the Gulf War.

Almost immediately after Iraq's deadline to leave Kuwait ended, the U.S.-led 28-nation multinational force attacked. On January 16 at 4:50 P.M. Eastern Standard Time (early morning of January 17 in Iraq), U.S. and allied aircraft began a 38-day blitz against Iraq. During this period, allied planes flew

Briefing on the progress of the ground war by General Powell—Secretary Cheney, Robert Gates, CIA, Secretary Baker, Governor Sununu, Vice President Quayle, General Scowcroft, Lawrence Eagleburger, and Marlin Fitzwater. George Bush Presidential Library

over 100,000 sorties while 284 U.S. navy Tomahawk missiles struck Iraq. The U.S. aircraft and Tomahawk missiles targeted Iraq's air defense system and communication centers, tried to find and destroy Iraq's nuclear and chemical-biological weapons, and sought out the launching pads for SCUD missiles. Air raids also struck targets near the Kuwaiti border, where Iraqi tanks and troops were preparing to engage the allied ground forces.

Allied planes dominated the air. Iraqi aircraft that initially sought combat were shot down, and Iraq's remaining combat planes sought sanctuary in Iran. On January 28, after some allied planes were lost, Iraq TV broadcast videos of seven airmen captured by Iraq (one American) and said the pilots would be dispersed to potential allied targets where they would risk death if those targets were bombed. Overall, the air raids succeeded but were not sufficient to end the war.

For a summary of the ground war, see February 28, 1991.

January 17, 1991

Iraq uses unorthodox tactics against U.N. forces.

Iraqi President Saddam Hussein responded to allied air attacks by a series of unorthodox retaliatory tactics.

On January 17, Iraq's SCUD missiles attacked Israel. Hussein hoped the SCUD attack would force Israel to retaliate, destroying the U.S. alliance with the Arab states. Israel did not strike back and the United States sent a Patriot antimissile system to help defend Israel from SCUDs. On January 20, Iraq began launching SCUDs targeted on military locations in Saudi Arabia. On February 24 a SCUD hit the U.S. barracks in Dhahran, killing 28 U.S. soldiers.

In a second unorthodox move, Iraq set fire to Kuwaiti oil wells, which generated oil spills from Kuwaiti facilities into the Persian Gulf. Iraq's only ground attack during the period of allied air raids was a surprise raid against the Saudi town of Khafji on January 29. The attack failed, and within 36 hours, armies of Saudi Arabia and Qatar, with assistance from U.S. Marines, drove out the Iraqi forces.

January 20, 1991

Haiti's parliamentary elections are won by Aristide's Lavalas coalition.

In runoff parliamentary elections, President-elect Jean-Baptiste Aristide's coalition gained control of Haiti's National Assembly. Despite an attempted coup on January 6 by Roger Lafontant's militants, the election was held as scheduled. Lafontant had sought to prevent Aristide's assuming office on February 7.

February 22, 1991

President Bush rejects peace proposals with Iraq sought by the Soviet Union.

After rejecting two peace proposals that Moscow had brokered with Iraq, President Bush informed Iraqi President Saddam Hussein that Iraq had until noon on February 23 to begin withdrawing from Kuwait or allied ground forces would attack. The Soviet peace effort began on February 12 when Politburo member Yevgeny Primakov visited Hussein and returned with proposals that Bush and other allied leaders called a "hoax." Iraqi Foreign Minister Tariq Aziz then flew to Moscow to make a second peace offer that President Gorbachev sent to Bush. Gorbachev said Iraq offered to withdraw unconditionally from Kuwait, but details of Iraq's message indicated Hussein would be absolved from all responsibility for invading Kuwait.

In turn, Bush rejected both offers and on February 22 informed Hussein that Iraq had 24 hours to demonstrate a desire for peace by withdrawing Iraqi forces from Kuwait; otherwise, a ground war would begin.

See February 28, 1991.

February 23, 1991

Despite Kenya's poor human rights record, President Bush sends Kenya military assistance.

In appreciation for Kenya's support in the war against Iraq, President Bush sent that country $5 million of military aid. Previously, U.S. military assistance had been withheld because of Kenya's many human rights violations.

Throughout 1991, Kenya's human rights problems festered, a situation leading private Kenyan lawyers to organize an opposition party led by former Vice President Oginga Odinga. After the police arrested the publisher of *Nairobi's Law Monthly*, 40 lawyers questioned President Daniel arap Moi's tactics and defended the publisher, Gitobu Imanyara. Kenya's human rights violations continued throughout 1992, with Moi being reelected president on December 29, 1992.

February 25, 1991

The Warsaw Pact's military and economic institutions are disbanded.

Meeting in Budapest with East Germany no longer a member, leaders of the six remaining Warsaw Pact countries agreed to disband their military structure by March 31, 1991. The members signed agreements that provided for Soviet troops to withdraw from Poland, Czechoslovakia, and Hungary by June 21, 1991.

On June 18, 1991, the Warsaw Pact disbanded its economic organization, COMECON, at a second Budapest meeting.

February 28, 1991

In a 100-hour ground war, Iraq's forces are evicted from Kuwait.

At 5 A.M. Kuwaiti time, within 100 hours after U.S. and allied armies began an offensive, Iraq's armies were defeated. President Bush announced a cease-fire and Iraq's Foreign Minister Aziz accepted previous U.N. resolutions regarding Iraq's withdrawal.

As Bush had warned, the U.S.-led ground assault began soon after the deadline on February 23. French, British, and U.S. forces struck along the Saudi-Iraqi border while Saudi, Egyptian, Syrian, and other Arab forces advanced into Kuwait with U.S. Marines paving the way through Iraqi obstacles on the road to Kuwait City. Because Iraq placed inexperienced soldiers in front-line trenches, many of these troops surrendered en masse. Elsewhere, some Iraqi elite Republican Guards engaged allied forces on Iraqi territory, but others withdrew to safe positions to prevent their destruction and allow them to enhance President Hussein's efforts to remain in power.

In the post-conflict analysis, critics said President Bush stopped the war a few hours too soon because allied forces had prepared to encircle two Republican Guard divisions near Basra. Bush's cease-fire order prevented the defeat of those units and left Saddam Hussein in power.

March 3, 1991

Iraqi military leaders sign official U.N. cease-fire terms.

U.S. General Norman Schwarzkopf, Saudi prince General Khalid bin Sultan, and other allied comman-

President Bush welcomes military personnel returning from the Persian Gulf. George Bush Presidential Library

ders met Iraqi commanders at Iraq's Safwan Air Base to sign a cease-fire. Under cease-fire terms of U.N. resolution 686 of March 2, Schwarzkopf did not negotiate with Iraq's generals, who simply accepted the U.N. terms. The agreement dealt with POW exchanges, avoiding future military incidents, and Iraq's acceptance of the final peace terms to be drawn up by the U.N. Security Council. In retrospect, Schwarzkopf said his major mistake was failing to stop Iraqi helicopter flights. This mistake proved crucial when Iraq used helicopters to savagely put down anti–Saddam Hussein uprisings after the war ended.

See March 6, 1991.

March 4, 1991

Chile reports on Pinochet's human rights violations.

In April 1990, Chilean President Patricio Aylwin Azócar formed a commission to investigate the human rights abuses that took place during the 17-year regime of General Augusto Pinochet Ugarte. On March 4, President Aylwin released the commission report that provided details about the murder, torture, and disappearance of over 2,000 Chileans by the military junta and secret police. Pinochet rejected the report and Chile's military leaders backed him. The complicity of Chile's government in the murder

of many citizens did not become public for 10 more years.

See December 21, 2000.

March 6, 1991

President Bush heralds the start of a "new world order."

In a "victory" speech to Congress after Iraq surrendered, Bush called for a "new world order" of justice and fair play to protect weak nations. Applied to the Middle East, Bush's program would stabilize the region by achieving peace between Arabs and Israel, sharing security measures, promoting economic development, and eliminating weapons of mass destruction. Despite Bush's optimism, his ideals proved difficult to fulfill because Iraqi leader Saddam Hussein remained in power and immediately used Iraqi forces against Iraqi Shiites and Kurds.

March 6, 1991

Iraqi Shiites and Kurds rebel but are defeated by Saddam Hussein's forces.

During the gulf conflict, President Bush often urged the Iraqi people to overthrow their leader, Saddam Hussein. In response, after Iraq surrendered, both Shiite and Kurdish dissidents staged uprisings in Iraq but received no American aid. In southern Iraq, a Shiite revolt captured the cities of Basra and Karbala, but Shiite leaders could not unite and Hussein's Republican Guard viciously suppressed the uprising. As many as 30,000 Shiites fled to camps in Saudi Arabia, and 2,000 Shiites who preferred to live in Iran were sent to Iran. In August 1992, President Bush joined with Britain, France, Saudi Arabia, and Kuwait to declare a no-fly zone at the 32nd parallel below which U.S. combat planes would shoot down any Iraqi planes venturing into the area. The decision resulted from Hussein's continued attacks on Shiites in the marshland areas of southern Iraq.

The Kurds' rebellion in the northwest was more complex. Initially, the Kurds captured the cities of Mosul and Kirkuk, but after defeating the southern Shiites, Republican Guard troops moved north where they used tanks, armored vehicles, artillery, and helicopters to drive the Kurds into the mountains bordering Turkey and Iran. Neither state welcomed the Kurds. Although U.S. planes shot down one Iraqi plane in the area, President Bush refused to change the cease-fire terms allowing Iraq to use helicopters (see March 3, 1991). On April 5, with over 1.3 million Kurdish refugees seeking protection, the U.N. Security Council condemned Iraq's repression, and the United States, Britain, and France sent aid to the refugees. Four days later, U.N. Resolution 688 created a "safe-zone" for Kurds north of the 36th parallel and authorized a 1,440-member observation team to oversee the zone. The United States, Britain, and France sent a combined force of 12,000 soldiers to the area to guarantee order and protect the Kurds.

See July 15, 1991.

March 17, 1991

A referendum shows most Soviet citizens prefer a united Soviet Union.

The results of a national referendum indicated that 77% of the voters wanted to preserve Soviet unity. President Gorbachev conducted the referendum after several republics held demonstrations to demand independence. The ballot was flawed because six republics boycotted the referendum: Estonia, Latvia, Lithuania, Georgia, Armenia, and Moldavia. In both the Ukraine and the Russian Federation, miners were on strike in opposition to Gorbachev's reforms because they disputed the central government's

power. Gorbachev's problems with the miners continued.

See August 19, 1991.

March 27, 1991

The United States withdraws medium-range missiles from Europe.

Acting in accordance with the 1987 Intermediate Range Nuclear Missile Treaty (INF) with the Soviet Union, the United States announced that its last medium-range nuclear missiles had been removed from the European continent.

See December 8, 1987.

March 30, 1991

The Gulf Cooperation Council (GCC) stops financial aid to Jordan and the PLO.

Made up of Saudi Arabia, Qatar, Bahrain, United Arab Emirates, and Kuwait, the GCC members voted to halt all financial aid to Jordan and the PLO because they had supported Iraq during the recent Gulf war.

March 31, 1991

The Sudan's president allows international groups to send food to starving Sudanese.

After corruption in the Sudan caused most international food shipments to be cut off in October 1990, reports of the Sudan's starving populace prompted its government to accept conditions for U.S. and U.N. agencies to distribute food to the starving. With warfare subsiding, relative peace enabled donor nations to send $8 million of food to the Sudan. But, fighting broke out again in early 1992.

April 4, 1991

The Salvadoran government and rebel forces accept reforms to end the civil war.

Following March 10 elections in which the governing National Republican Alliance (ARENA) won only a plurality of National Assembly seats, delegates of the government and rebel Farabundo Marti para la Liberacion Nacional (FMLN) met in Mexico City to agree on reforms to end the civil war.

On April 29, the National Assembly approved reforms that cut back the power of the military, created a nonmilitary police force, strengthened the judiciary, and instituted electoral reforms. Although the Mexico City reforms did not include a cease-fire, the two sides took steps to establish one.

See December 15, 1991.

April 5, 1991

Iraq accepts stringent cease-fire terms set by U.N. Security Council Resolution 687.

From the cease-fire of March 3 to early April, Security Council members debated various terms for Iraq. On April 3, the Council set terms contained in Resolution 687, and on April 5 Iraq's Revolutionary Command Council ratified the agreement. Because multinational forces remained in southern Iraq, President Hussein submitted, although he soon discovered ways to circumvent the cease-fire terms. Iraq not only accepted Resolution 687 but also resolutions made before the January conflict.

The resolution's principal terms were as follows: (1) U.N. inspection teams would oversee the destruction of Iraq's nuclear, chemical, and biological weapons as well as its missiles and launchers having a range over 90 miles; (2) Iraq could not import offensive weapons and dual-use technologies; (3) economic sanctions remained on Iraq until all the terms of Resolution 687 were fulfilled; (4) a U.N. committee would supervise Iraq's imports of food and medicine.

See April 18, 1991.

April 11, 1991

Panama agrees to help the United States investigate drug money laundering.

Although it had arrested General Noriega following its 1990 invasion, the United States was concerned that Panama's banks were laundering drug money. To investigate these practices, the United States and Panama signed the Mutual Legal Assistance Treaty allowing U.S. officials to investigate money laundering by examining Panama's bank records. The United States also gave Panama $80 million of financial assistance.

April 18, 1991

Saddam Hussein begins to deceive the United Nations about Iraq's weapons of mass destruction.

Iraq complied with cease-fire terms by giving U.N. weapons inspectors a list of its non-conventional weapons. On April 29 after inspectors checked the weapons list, the United States claimed Iraq had failed to include all its nuclear weapons. Iraq finally admitted to the International Atomic Energy Agency (IAEA) that it failed to account for all its weapons-grade nuclear materials. Thus, Iraq's pattern of deception began in dealing with U.N. inspectors.

See June 22, 1991

April 25, 1991

President Gorbachev and leaders of nine Soviet republics agree to cooperate.

Hoping to retain unity among the Soviet Union's republics, Soviet President Mikhail Gorbachev met with leaders of nine Soviet republics including Russia's Boris Yeltsin. During the meeting, Gorbachev persuaded the nine leaders to cooperate in restructuring the role of the Soviet Union's government. Under these agreements, the Soviet Union's constitution would be revised to give each republic a greater role in the Soviet Union's political decision making. In return, the nine republics' leaders agreed to honor the existing economic arrangements of the central government and enforce Soviet laws within their borders.

On June 17, negotiations between the Soviet central government and representatives of the nine republics finalized plans to revise the Soviet constitution in accordance with the April 25 agreements. Unfortunately for Gorbachev's plans to save the Soviet Union, Soviet communists opposing his plans tried to overthrow him.

See August 19, 1991.

May 7, 1991

U.N. peacekeepers arrive in Kuwait to oversee peace between Kuwait and Iraq.

Acting in accordance with a U.N. resolution of April 9, the 1,400-member U.N. peacekeeping force arrived in the demilitarized zone between Iraq and Kuwait. The peacekeepers replaced U.S. troops who had been in southern Iraq since the March 3 cease-fire agreement.

May 7, 1991

Five Latin American nations create a free-trade zone.

The presidents of Colombia, Peru, Ecuador, Venezuela, and Bolivia agreed to create a free-trade zone and common market. They set January 1, 1992, to begin negotiations to create a free trade zone and common market.

May 9, 1991

Gulf Cooperation Council (GCC) approves a U.S. role for defense preparations.

Although Pentagon planners wanted a larger role in all five GCC states, the GCC said each member state should reach separate arrangements with Washington. Only Kuwait wanted a direct U.S. role, and on September 4, the United States and Kuwait signed a "memorandum of understanding" permitting the United States to stockpile essential military equipment in Kuwait and conduct training and defense exercises with Kuwait's armed forces.

Qatar, Bahrain, and the United Arab Emirates did not make formal security agreements with Washington but generally allowed U.S. naval ships to use their seaports.

Saudi Arabia was the most vital state to the Pentagon because important U.S. aviation facilities were on Saudi territory. Saudi Arabia wanted U.S. weapon stockpiles and U.S. forces to remain "over the horizon" as they were before August 1990. Nevertheless, the Saudi's gave the U.S. navy access to their seaports and permitted the U.S. air force to have personnel protecting its aircraft facilities.

May 13, 1991

President Bush proposes an international ban on chemical weapons.

To encourage other nations to prepare a treaty prohibiting the use of chemical weapons, President Bush pledged that the United States would not use chemical weapons and asked other leaders to join him in drafting a treaty to ban them. If a treaty were approved, the United States would destroy its chemical weapons stockpile.

To prevent the spread of chemical weapons, Bush proposed restrictions on exporting chemicals needed to make chemical weapons. On May 30, 19 industrial nations agreed to restrict the export of these chemicals.

May 22, 1991

Lebanon recognizes Syria's right to maintain forces in the Bekaa Valley.

Lebanon and Syria signed a Treaty of Brotherhood, Cooperation and Coordination ratified by both nation's parliaments on September 26, 1991. The treaty was to solve Lebanon's security problems, although Israeli forces and pro-Israeli Lebanese forces controlled a "security zone" south of Lebanon's Litani River.

May 26, 1991

The United States sponsors peace talks between Ethiopia and Eritrea.

In London, U.S.-sponsored talks between Ethiopia's government and three rebel armies resulted in a cease-fire agreement. The accords allowed rebels in the People's Revolutionary Democratic Front, led by Meles Zenawi, to enter Addis Ababa. Zenawi disavowed any intention of installing a strict Marxist regime. On July 5, a meeting of 24 Ethiopian political and ethnic groups selected an 87-seat legislature as a transitional government, and on July 21, Zenawi was elected head of state for a two-year term.

In the province of Eritrea, a U.N.-sponsored referendum was to be held on independence, while a provisional government was led by Isaias Afwerki of the People's Liberation Front.

May 29, 1991

President Bush proposes to ban all weapons of mass destruction in the Middle East.

In a speech at the U.S. Air Force Academy, President Bush proposed to ban weapons of mass destruction and create a system to control conventional weapons in the Middle East. His basic suggestions for the Middle East were create a nuclear-free zone, ban surface-to-surface missiles, prohibit chemical and biological weapons, set up methods to regulate materials for unconventional weapons, and establish methods for arms exporters to notify other nations about arms exports.

Following his speech, Bush held meetings with the Big Five—the United States, France, Britain, China, and the Soviet Union—but they failed to agree on methods to freeze the transfer of conventional weapons in the Middle East. There were meetings of arms negotiators in Paris in July 1991, in London in October, and in Washington from February to May 1992. During the three meetings in 1991 and 1992, the delegates from the Big Five powers were unable to prevent future armament sales to Middle East nations. Although the Big Five delegates said they opposed an arms buildup in the Middle East, not one of the five delegates was willing to risk the loss of profits their armament manufacturers made by selling weapons to their Middle East customers. The United States was the biggest arms supplier, selling to Middle Eastern nations $32.2 billion of armaments during the period from August 1990 to August 1992.

May 31, 1991

Angola obtains a cease-fire based on proposals by U.S. Secretary of State Baker and Soviet Foreign Minister Shevardnadze.

Angola's cease-fire resulted from a U.S.-Soviet proposal of December 13, 1990. Secretary of State Baker and Soviet Foreign Minister Shevardnadze had presented the plan to representatives from Portugal, the Angolan government, and UNITA (National Union for the Total Independence of Angola) rebels to negotiate. The United States and USSR agreed they would end all arms shipments to Angola and UNITA. In addition, the 50,000 Cuban troops, supported by Moscow, left Angola before May 25. As a result, Angola's government and the UNITA rebels led by Jonas Savimbi accepted a cease-fire to end their 16-year war and prepare democratic elections in 1992.

Despite Baker's role in Angola's peace effort, the U.S. House of Representatives voted on June 11 to continue covert aid to UNITA, although it reduced the aid from $60 million to $20 million. On July 15, the Angolan government approved an amnesty for persons jailed for crimes against the state, and on September 29, Savimbi returned to Luanda to run for president.

See October 17, 1992.

June 8, 1991

The Organization of American States agrees to act against any military coup in the Western Hemisphere.

During the 21st Assembly of the Organization of American States (OAS), delegates agreed to take action against any regime that overthrew a legitimate government. The accord was designed to promote hemispheric democracy. The first OAS implementation of this decision followed a coup in Haiti.

See September 30, 1991.

June 14, 1991

After Secretary of State Baker and the Soviet Foreign Minister resolve problems, the CSCE members agree on limiting conventional weapons.

On June 14, members of the Commission on Security and Cooperation in Europe (CSCE) accepted amendments to the initial Conventional Forces in Europe (CFE) treaty. Because disputes arose about the size of Soviet armored personnel carriers and about reports that some Soviet military units moved beyond the Ural Mountains outside the treaty's Atlantic to Ural definition, U.S. Secretary Baker met with Soviet Foreign Minister Aleksandr Bessmertnykh on June 1 to solve the problems. After the United States and the Soviet Union agreed on the interpretation of these issues, NATO and Warsaw Pact members met to sign the final CFE agreement.

See November 17, 1990.

June 22, 1991

Secretary of State Baker visits Albania, whose communist regime is floundering.

Secretary of State Baker arrived in Tirana, Albania, where large crowds shouted "U.S.A.! U.S.A.!" Baker's car needed an hour to go four miles from the airport to downtown. He visited Albania to promote democracy in a country whose Stalinist regime had kept it isolated from the outside world since World War II.

Since February 6, 1991, Albanian students advocating reform had demonstrated against the Communist regime, but in an election on March 31, the Communist Party allegedly won 66% of the vote to keep control of the People's Assembly. Protesters led by Sali Berisha, a heart surgeon who became the leader of opposition to the Communist regime, claimed the elections were fraudulent, and their demonstrations escalated after Premier Fatos Nano appointed a cabinet excluding all opposition parties. Because of the unrest, the government resigned on June 4, and Nano appointed a nonpartisan interim government that scheduled elections for 1992. That government ended 47 years of despotic communist rule under Enver Hoxha and his successor, Ramiz Alia.

See March 22, 1992.

June 22, 1991

Iraqi soldiers disrupt U.N. inspectors trying to locate nuclear weapons.

Iraqi soldiers obstructed and fired warning shots at U.N. weapons inspectors who seized documents indicating Iraq's nuclear capacity was further along than previously believed. Iraqi forces also interfered with U.N. inspectors at a factory building for a week during which U.S. intelligence satellites detected trucks hauling materials away from the factory's rear door. The U.N. Security Council fixed a deadline for Iraq to comply with the inspectors' demands. On July 25, President Saddam Hussein allowed inspectors to "see and inspect whatever they will."

Saddam Hussein's deception in the June incident was duplicated in September 1991 when a joint team of United Nations Special Commission (UNSCOM) and International Atomic Energy Agency (IAEA) inspectors moved into a high-rise building in downtown Baghdad to find files about Iraq's atomic bomb program. On leaving the building, the inspectors were stopped by Iraqi troops in the parking lot, beginning a three-day confrontation. The crisis ended with a compromise that Iraq could inventory the documents before they were taken away. But, as Khidhir Hamaz's *Saddam's Bombmaker* (2000) explains, Iraq found a way to fool the inspectors. While inventorying the documents, Iraqi officials slipped them to Iraqi scientists who removed some documents or erased critical data to mislead inspectors when they were handed back. Thus, the inspectors took away tainted documents, leading UNSCOM and Washington to believe Iraq's nuclear weapons program was less advanced than it actually was. After defecting to the United States in 1996, Hamaz revealed information about the Iraqi deception. Hamaz's book also tells the story of his first attempt to defect in 1994 that was stymied by a CIA agent who refused to believe one of Iraq's top nuclear scientists, educated in America, would defect.

See February 5, 1992.

June 25, 1991

Despite Secretary of State Baker's objection, Slovenia and Croatia declare independence from Yugoslavia.

Four days after meeting with Secretary of State Baker in Belgrade, Slovene President Kuchan and Croatian President Tudjman declared the independence of their republics. Baker had urged them to maintain Yugoslav unity, but their efforts to obtain reforms failed and in 1990 the two republics voted for independence. Following a meeting with European Union representatives on June 28, Slovenia and Croatia suspended their independence declarations, but after they were attacked by the Yugoslav National Army (YNA), dominated by Serbia, each republic declared immediate independence on September 7. The next day the republic of Macedonia also declared its independence.

See September 25, 1991.

July 11, 1991

The United States lifts economic sanctions against South Africa.

Because President F.W. de Klerk's government had fulfilled five conditions set by Congress in its 1986 Anti-Apartheid Act, President Bush lifted U.S. economic sanctions against South Africa. After becoming president in September 1989, de Klerk took steady steps to end apartheid. He admitted black students to former all-white schools, freed Nelson Mandela and other black political prisoners, had parliament repeal laws to register citizens by categories based on race. De Klerk also negotiated with Mandela's African National Congress and agreed to have a convention prepare changes for South Africa's constitution. On December 20, 1991, the Convention for a Democratic South Africa opened in Johannesburg to prepare constitutional reforms.

See October 2, 1986; September 26, 1992.

July 15, 1991

U.S. and allied forces complete withdrawal from northern Iraq.

In April, U.S., British, and French forces had entered the "safe zone" of northern Iraq to protect Kurdish refugees. Now the allies withdrew their forces from Iraq but retained air force units based in Turkey to protect Kurds in the safe zone from Iraqi attacks. On September 23, the United States said allied ground troops and helicopters had left Turkey while air-strike forces protected the Kurds.

July 22, 1991

The United States and 13 Caribbean nations sign a trade cooperation pact.

President Bush's Enterprise for the Americas Initiative took its first step to develop a hemispheric free market by signing a trade accord with 13 Caribbean countries. The agreement created the U.S.-Caribbean Community Trade and Investment Council to foster commerce and reduce trade barriers. On August 22, Bush advanced the initiative further by forgiving $341 million of Bolivia's debt and canceling $217 million of Jamaica's debt.

July 31, 1991

Presidents Bush and Gorbachev sign a strategic arms reduction treaty (START I)

At the first post–Cold War summit in Moscow, Presidents Bush and Gorbachev signed START I, a treaty to be in effect for 15 years and be renewable. It limited each nation to 6,000 nuclear warheads and 1,600 intercontinental ballistic missile delivery systems. START was the first of a series of President Bush's efforts to reduce the number of nuclear weapons.

See September 17-23, 1991.

August 16, 1991

Saddam Hussein rejects a U.N. Security Council oil-for-food program.

Although President Bush wanted to link the U.N. OIL-FOR-FOOD PROGRAM to Hussein's fulfillment of the April cease-fire accords, reports of Iraq's starving and sick women and children impelled Bush and the Security Council to reach a compromise embodied in resolution 706. The resolution permitted Iraq to sell oil to buy food and medicine and begin paying reparations to Kuwait. Although the $1.6 billion of oil fell short of the $2.6 billion recommended by the U.N. relief agency, Saddam Hussein rejected the offer. Reports from Baghdad indicated Iraq's wealthy had revived their luxurious living but Hussein allowed less fortunate people to bear the burden of suffering by rejecting the oil-for-food program. Nevertheless, some critics blamed the United States for the suffering in Iraq because Washington insisted on economic sanctions until Hussein eliminated Iraqi weapons of mass destruction. Other observers blamed Hussein's refusal of oil-for-food programs and flaunting the U.N. weapons inspections required by the April 1991 agreement. His persistent refusal to accept oil-for-food programs continued until 1998.

August 19, 1991

A coup attempt fails to overthrow Soviet President Gorbachev.

During the year before the attempted coup against Soviet President Mikhail Gorbachev, the central authority of the Communist Party of the Soviet Union (CPSU) had lost much of its policy making power. In addition, Gorbachev's *glasnost* policy permitting freedom of speech led to criticism of the CPUS and of Gorbachev for weakening the Soviet military organization and accepting reductions in tactical and strategic missiles and in conventional forces stationed in Europe. Soviet Defense Minister Marshall Dimitry Yazov complained that Gorbachev did not recognize that the Western powers continued to regard the Soviet Union as the "enemy" while they encouraged Gorbachev to disarm the Soviet Union. Moreover, hard-line conservatives like Yazov believed Gorbachev permitted various Soviet Republics to gain influence that weakened Soviet relations with the Western world (see December 17, 1990). Finally, Yazov believed Gorbachev's acceptance of a second strategic arms reduction treaty with U.S. President George Bush in July 1991 was further evidence that Soviet power was withering away (see July 31, 1991).

Following his July meeting with Bush, Gorbachev left Moscow to relax for two weeks at his dacha in the Crimea, expecting to return to Moscow on August 19. One day before his scheduled return, Gorbachev was visited by a delegation from Moscow. The delegates were Gorbachev's Deputy on the Council of Defense Oleg Baklanov, Communist Party Secretary Oleg Shenin, Deputy Minister of Defense Valentin Varennikov, and Gorbachev's former Chief of Staff Valery Boldin. The delegates told Gorbachev that Communist Party leaders wanted a state of emergency declared, and asked him to sign the directive on the emergency or resign and turn his authority over to Vice President Gennady Yanayev. After Gorbachev refused to sign the directive or resign, the Moscow delegation cut off his ability to communicate with the outside world, leaving Gorbachev and his family with only a radio and television set to learn what was happening in Moscow. The delegates placed Gorbachev under house arrest with a small number of his bodyguards to protect him.

That night, August 18–19, Gorbachev heard Radio Moscow announce that Gorbachev's illness required him to remain in the Crimea, a lie of course, and that Gennady Yanayev had assumed Gorbachev's duties. Gennady's first act was to issue a Declaration of the State of Emergency in the Soviet Union and to transfer authority to a newly organized Council for the State of Emergency. The State Council members were Gennady, Prime Minister Valentine Pavlov, KGB secret service Chairman Vladimir Krychkov, Minister of the Interior Boris Pugo, Defense Minister Marshall Dmitry Yazov, Deputy Chairman of the Defense Council Oleg Baklov, Representative of the Industrial Sector Aleksander Tizyakov, and Representative of the Agricultural Sector Vasily Starodubtsev.

In Moscow, Russian President Boris Yeltsin rallied the resistance to Gennady and the Council for the State of Emergency. After declaring the Council for the State of Emergency unconstitutional, Yeltsin built a stronghold in the Soviet parliament building. From this fortress, Yeltsin made a televised speech that denounced the traitors and urged Muscovites and other Russians to demonstrate against Gennady's Council. In Moscow, Yeltsin joined 50,000 Russians who protested against the coup; in Leningrad, thousands of Russians demonstrated against Gennady.

Later, Gorbachev learned the coup leaders had failed to get key military officials to join their plot. After Yeltsin's televised speech, Soviet Marshall of Aviation Yevgeny Shaposhnikov opposed the State Council and was joined in condemning the Council's action by Chief Soviet Naval Officer Admiral Vladimir Cherrnavin, Commander of the Strategic Missile Forces Yury Maksimov, and Commander of the Soviet Airborne Troops Lieutenant General Pavel Grachen.

By the third day of the coup (August 21), State Council members had weakened their resolve. After Marshall Yazov resigned from the State Council, he told Deputy Chairman of the Defense Council Oleg Baklov to withdraw all Soviet troops from Moscow or resign from the State Council. On August 21, Yeltsin's success in resisting the State Council became clear when the State Council commandeered Soviet armed vehicles that failed to disperse protesting crowds in front of the Soviet parliament. After three men were killed by army gunfire, Soviet soldiers refused to attack fellow citizens and some army troops joined the protesters. Yeltsin's victory over the State Council was assured on August 22, when the KGB's special forces, the elite division of the Minister of the Interior's troops, and the Soviet army guarding Moscow's airport refused to move into the city and attack the demonstrators.

On August 22, a delegation from the Russian Federation's Supreme Soviet led by Russia's Vice President Alexsander Rutskoi flew to the Crimea to escort Gorbachev back to Moscow. Marshal Yazov and KGB Chief Krychkov asked Gorbachev to pardon them but they were arrested and imprisoned. With Gorbachev's approval, Russian police arrested the other members of the State Council including Gennady on charges of high treason. On August 24, Gorbachev resigned as the General Secretary of the Communist Party and disbanded the Central Committee of the Communist Party of the Soviet Union.

See December 8, 1991.

August 20, 1991

Three Soviet Baltic republics declare independence.

During the three-day coup in Moscow, the Soviet republics of Estonia, Latvia, and Lithuania affirmed their national independence and expropriated Communist Party property. Russian Federation President Boris Yeltsin quickly recognized the three nation's independence. On September 2, the United States and the European Union also recognized the Baltic nations' independence.

On September 6, the new Soviet State Council also approved the independence of the three Baltic states.

See September 16, 1991.

September 12–14, 1991

Secretary of State Baker visits Moscow and the newly independent Baltic states.

During a human rights conference in Moscow, Secretary of State Baker met with the new Soviet foreign minister, Boris Pankin, and military chief of staff General Vladimir Lobov. Among other matters, Baker and Pankin agreed to encourage peace in Afghanistan, announcing that the United States and the USSR would end military aid to both warring sides by the end of the year.

Baker also visited Estonia, Latvia, and Lithuania, promising the three nations a total of $14 million of U.S. assistance.

See January 1, 1992.

September 16, 1991

The Iran-Contra prosecutor drops charges against Oliver North.

Special Prosecutor Lawrence Walsh dropped all charges against Lt. Colonel Oliver North for his activity in the Iran-Contra affair because North had received immunity from Congress. On November 16, a federal court also dismissed five felony convictions that Walsh had obtained against National Security Adviser Admiral John Poindexter for his role in the same affair.

September 17–23, 1991

The U.N. General Assembly admits new members and hears President Bush introduce an arms control initiative.

The U.N. General Assembly's 46th session admitted seven new members: South Korea, North Korea, the Marshall Islands, Micronesia, Latvia, Lithuania, and Estonia.

On September 23, President Bush's address to the assembly was highlighted by an offer to unilaterally eliminate naval cruise missiles, tactical nuclear missiles, and 24,000 nuclear warheads including the multiple warheads carried by MX missiles for which the Pentagon never found suitable basing on railroad rails or hardened underground silos. Bush also invited Soviet President Gorbachev to join the United States in developing a new version of the SDI missile defense system, a plan known as Global Protection Against Limited Strikes (GPALS).

Since 1991, SDI research had changed from the complex Brilliant Pebbles missile defense system to GPALS, a system of only 1,000 Pebbles in space combined with 1,000 ground-based missiles at seven sites in the United States. GPLAS would allegedly protect the United States and other nations from attacks by "rogue nations" such as Iraq and North Korea as well as an accidental ICBM launch from the Soviet Union or China. Bush asked Gorbachev to join in developing GPALS because their joint venture would allow the termination of the 1972 ABM treaty.

On September 27, Bush implemented his promise to take all American bombers off alert. Although on October 3, Gorbachev ignored Bush's GPLAS proposal, his response exceeded Bush's initiative by announcing Soviet plans to unilaterally deactivate 503 intercontinental missiles and all short-range nuclear weapons from Soviet ships, submarines, and land-based naval aircraft. Gorbachev also ordered a ban on Soviet nuclear testing for one year. Although Bush's initiative exempted nuclear weapons on submarines, any deal with the Soviets became more complicated when the Soviet Union was divided into separate republics in December 1991.

See June 3, 1990; December 18, 1991.

September 25, 1991

The U.N. Security Council embargoes arms to Yugoslavia.

Although the embargo on military weapons was intended to end the war between Croatia and Serbia that began in July 1991, it was based on the unrealistic notion that Yugoslavia still existed and became an obstacle to nations wanting to help Bosnia and Herzegovina by sending arms after Serbian military forces attacked Bosnia in 1992. Unlike the Slovene, Croatian, and Serbian republics, Bosnia wanted Yugoslavia to reunite and was unprepared for war when Serbia's army attacked its capital, Sarajevo in 1992.

See April 6, 1992.

September 30, 1991

Haiti's democratically elected president is overthrown in a military coup.

Haiti's constitutionally elected government lasted only seven months after President Aristide was inaugurated in February 1991. Aristide's upper-class opposition grew because he tried to uproot Haiti's elite power base and eliminate corrupt practices by purging the army and police allied with the elite groups. Aristide appointed General Raoul Cedras to replace General Herard Abraham as army commander. As later investigations indicated, Cedras was a secret member of the Sécurité Intelligence Nationale (SIN), a CIA-funded group organized to maintain an authoritarian Haitian ruler. The September 30 coup was led by Cedras, who, before and after the coup, gave the CIA false reports about Aristide's mental health.

Because Aristide was democratically elected, President Bush suspended Haiti's economic aid and joined the OAS in refusing to recognize the Cedras regime. Aristide fled to exile, first in Venezuela, later to the U.S. mainland while Bush let the OAS negotiate for his return.

See also November 18, 1991.

October 4, 1991

The 1959 Antarctica treaty is extended for 50 years.

Meeting in Madrid, 24 nations extended the 1959 Antarctica treaty by levying a 50-year moratorium on mining and military activity and setting guidelines for scientific research.

See December 1, 1959.

October 11, 1991

Turkey's conflict with rebels extends into Iraq.

Because of escalated attacks by the Kurdish Workers Party (KPP), Turkish forces launched raids on Kurds in northern Iraq. Turkey claimed that the rebel Kurds hid in Iraq for protection. As the conflict continued, the United States faced a dilemma. It needed Turkish

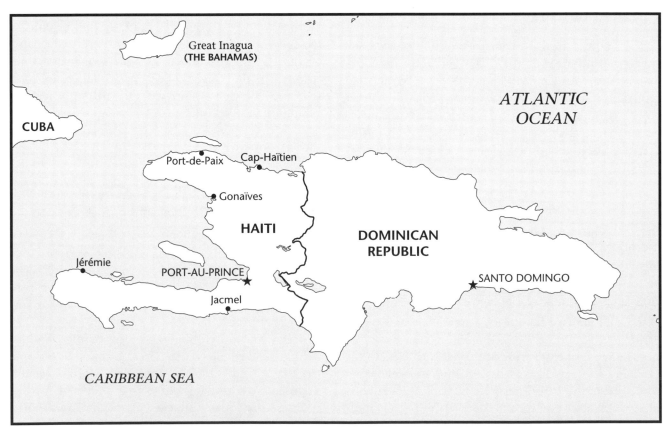

Haiti and the Dominican Republic

air bases to protect Iraq's Kurdish population but opposed Turkey's violations of human rights.

See June 26, 1992.

October 13, 1991

Bulgaria's democrats win elections against the Communist Party.

In national elections, Bulgaria's anticommunist Union of Democratic Forces (UDF) won 111 seats in parliament and joined with the Movement for Rights and Freedom's 24 seats to provide a majority in the 240-seat parliament. Although Bulgaria's government unveiled a new constitution on July 14, many Bulgarians were dissatisfied. On November 8, parliament elected UDF leader Filip Dimitrov as premier.

October 19, 1991

A Kosovar assembly proclaims independence for Kosovo from Serbia.

The semi-secret assembly proclaimed independence for Kosovo, a region of the Serbian Republic. Although Serbia abrogated Kosovo's autonomy in 1989, Serbian President Milošević permitted Kosovars to organize an assembly—which elected Ibrahim Rugova, who advocated nonviolent disobedience, president—because Serbia was waging war with Croatia. During the next four years Serbia ignored Rugova's bid for recognition of Kosovo's independence, but his efforts became the basis for Kosovo's claim to independence after the wars among Serbia, Croatia, and Bosnia and Herzegovina ended in November 1995.

October 21, 1991

Lebanese Shiites release three hostages.

The Shiite Islamic Jihad's intention to release many hostages became evident when they released American citizen Jesse Turner, the third hostage released in 1991. On August 8, British journalist John McCarthy was released, and on August 11, U.S. citizen Edward A. Tracy gained freedom. Later on November 18, Islamic Jihad released two more hostages: Terry Waite of Great Britain and the American Thomas M. Sutherland. The five were taken hostage at various times between 1985 and 1987. Observers linked their release to Israel's releasing 13 men and 2 women from

south Lebanon's Al Khiyam Prison, including Hezbollah leader Ali Fawaz

October 23, 1991

Cambodia's four factions sign a peace agreement.

A U.N. proposal succeeded when Cambodia's government and three rebel factions signed a Paris peace treaty providing for the United Nations to share power with four factions during a transition to democracy. The treaty named Prince Sihanouk provisional leader while rebels disarmed and the peace process moved toward democratic elections. Sihanouk returned after 13 years in exile to become president, but trouble began in Phnom Penh on November 28 when the Khmer Rouge's leader, Khieu Samphan, who was notorious for having killed many Cambodians, returned. He soon fled to Thailand after mobs nearly lynched him. On December 30, Cambodia's factions requested the immediate deployment of U.N. peacekeeping forces.

See April 1, 1992.

October 30, 1991

A Middle East peace conference convenes in Madrid.

Sponsored by the United States and the USSR, an ill-fated peace conference launched a process to end 40 years of conflict in the Middle East. Following the Gulf War, President Bush and Secretary of State Baker made concerted efforts to hold the meeting by convincing Syria, Lebanon, Jordan, the PLO, and Israel to attend. Israel agreed after Bush withheld a U.S. loan guarantee of $10 billion and Palestinians accepted Israel's condition that PLO delegates would initially be part of Jordan's delegation, without PLO leader Yasser Arafat attending.

When the Madrid meeting began, Baker had no fixed agenda, intending that face-to-face sessions would be a first step toward future bilateral talks. After the Madrid sessions adjourned, negotiations began in Washington in December 1991 but bogged down when the Israeli election campaign began in the spring of 1992.

See January 24, 1992.

November 5, 1991

China and Vietnam normalize diplomatic relations that had been perfunctory since a 1979 border conflict.

In 1979, China and Vietnam severed their diplomatic relations after Chinese forces invaded Vietnam's northern border, alleging that Vietnam was being punished for sending Vietnamese armed forces to fight the Khmer Rouge guerrilla movement led by Pol Pot. China's government supported the communist Khmer Rouge's attempt to gain control of Cambodia's government (see February 17, 1979). Throughout the 1980s, China and Vietnam continued political disputes that often ended in border clashes. Vietnam's decision to remove its armed forces from Cambodia (see July 6, 1989) enabled Chinese and Vietnamese delegates to negotiate the basis for renewing their peaceful relations. These negotiations brought about the formal renewal of diplomatic relations on November 5, 1991.

For the 1979 situation, see February 17, 1979.

November 5, 1991

The Senate confirms Robert M. Gates as CIA director.

On May 14, President Bush nominated Gates to replace William Webster to head the Central Intelligence Agency. Before approving the Gates nomination, the Senate investigated allegations that as former national security adviser, Gates had slanted intelligence estimates for political reasons.

November 8, 1991

NATO approves post–Cold War strategic concepts.

NATO leaders meeting in Brussels approved post–Cold War strategic concepts that their defense ministers had prepared in May. The new concepts ended the earlier doctrines of "forward defense" and "graduated response," while emphasizing collective planning for operations, NATO's primacy in European security, and keeping nuclear forces to a minimum. NATO also reaffirmed the role of the United States and Canada in the alliance and called for diplomatic and security contacts with the Soviet Union. Military plans provided for 70,000 NATO troops including a British-led rapid reaction force, six multinational defense forces, and one all-German force.

See May 22, 1992.

November 8, 1991

U.S. nuclear weapons are removed from South Korea; the two Koreas move toward reconciliation.

As part of his September 27 program to eliminate U.S. nuclear warheads, President Bush announced that the United States would remove all nuclear weapons from South Korea by April 1992. Because the United States was concerned about North Korea's nuclear complex at Yongbyon, the removal of U.S. nuclear weapons was designed to thwart North Korea's claim to need nuclear weapons as protection from South Korea. On November 8, South Korean President Roh Tae Woo announced his government would not store or possess nuclear weapons, and he asked North Korea to eliminate its existing nuclear weapons and abandon its program to produce new ones. While visiting Seoul on November 21, U.S. Secretary of Defense Richard Cheney said the United States would delay pulling more U.S. army personnel out of South Korea until North Korea clarified its activity regarding nuclear weapons.

After the U.S. began withdrawing its nuclear weapons from South Korea on November 29, the two Korean states moved toward better relations. On December 13, North and South Korea signed agreements regarding trade, reconciliation, nonaggression, and peaceful coexistence between the two nations. On December 26, North Korea said it would sign the International Atomic Energy Agency (IAEA) agreement and permit IAEA inspections of its research center at Yongbyon. On December 30, the two Koreas agreed to free their peninsula of nuclear weapons.

November 15–17, 1991

Secretary of State Baker visits China to discuss nuclear technology and human rights.

Secretary of State Baker visited Beijing to discuss nuclear weapons and China's human rights record. During Baker's visit, Chinese officials agreed to support a nuclear-free Korean peninsula; to ask the Chinese People's Congress to ratify the Nuclear Non-Proliferation Treaty; to "intend" to stop exporting medium-range missile technology to Pakistan and other states; and to continue discussions with U.S. representatives about improving China's human rights record. According to Baker's *Politics of Diplomacy* (1995), he thought China's concessions would prevent the U.S. Congress from removing China's most-favored-nation status.

See June 2, 1992.

November 18, 1991

President Bush orders the deportation of Haitian refugees; a federal court upholds his decision.

Bush ordered 1,800 refugees to be sent back to Haiti. A federal judge prohibited Bush's forced deportations, but an appeals court approved them on December 19. Although more refugees fled Haiti after the September 1991 military coup, Bush and his advisers were never pleased with Haitian President Aristide, who sought better wages and working conditions for Haitians working for U.S.-owned manufacturing companies. The restoration of Haiti's democracy was also delayed.

See September 30, 1991; February 24, 1992.

November 21, 1991

Congress approves the Nunn-Lugar program to help destroy Soviet nuclear weapons.

Senators Sam Nunn (D-Ga.) and Richard Lugar (R-Id.) proposed bipartisan legislation by which Congress authorized $400 million to defray the costs of destroying the former Soviet Union's nuclear, chemical, and biological weapons as required under treaties with the United States. Funds were also allocated to the Department of Defense to transport, store, and safeguard these weapons prior to their destruction. The legislation was intended to prevent these weapons falling into unfriendly hands.

On June 17, 1992, the United States and Russia signed an agreement for Russia to accept the Nunn-Lugar assistance. Later, other former Soviet republics agreed to accept similar U.S. aid: Belarus on October 22, 1992; Ukraine on October 23, 1993; Kazakhstan on December 13, 1993.

In subsequent years, Congress expanded the 1991 legislation to include defense conversion, joint military contacts, housing for military personnel, and environmental restoration at former Soviet military sites.

November 22, 1991

U.S. and Vietnamese seek to normalize relations.

The process leading to U.S.-Vietnamese talks began on April 9, 1991 when Washington outlined plans to end Vietnam's trade embargo and seek its cooperation in ending Cambodia's civil war. On April 25, the United States sent Vietnam $1 million of financial aid, and on October 23 Secretary of State Baker lifted some restrictions on trade with Vietnam and said American tourists could visit Vietnam. In turn, Vietnam allowed 60,000 Vietnamese refugees to return home from Hong Kong if Hong Kong officials would confirm that they were economic, not political, refugees.

December 4, 1991

The U.N. General Assembly elects Egyptian Boutros Boutros-Ghali as secretary-general to replace Javier Pérez de Cuellar.

December 8, 1991

Three former Soviet republics form the Commonwealth of Independent States (CIS).

Following the August 1991 attempt by hard-line Communist Party members to overthrow Soviet President Mikhail Gorbachev (see August 19, 1991), Gorbachev proposed that all republics in the Union of Soviet Socialist Republics should form a confederation. The confederation of republics would allow eaach republic to elect local officials responsible for conducting day-to-day domestic affairs while an all-Soviet State Committee dealt with foreign affairs, security issues, banking regulations, and essential economic matters such as maintaining the value of the rouble. The proposed confederation had some merits, but leaders of the republics rejected Gorbachev's plan, probably, as Gorbachev admits in his memoir, because the confederation plan was proposed in 1991, not 1989, after many republics already chose independence from any centralized authority.

Rather than accept Gorbachev's confederacy, the republics of Russia, Belarus, and Ukraine declared independence from the Soviet Union. On October 22, the Ukraine parliament created an independent army, navy, and air force. On November 1, the Russian Federation's Congress of People's Deputies gave President Boris Yeltsin power to end price controls on Russian products and to cut funds the Russian Federation's budget previously provided for Soviet foreign aid and for 70 Soviet ministries that no longer were relevant to Russia's needs. Two weeks later, Yeltsin asked Russian officials to assume control of Soviet Union's natural resources, such as coal and lumber, within the boundaries of the Russian Federation. Belarus and Ukraine followed Russia's lead regarding natural resources within their boundaries. By November 25, 1991, all Soviet republics had rejected Gorbachev's plans for a confederation.

On December 8, 1991, Russian President Yeltsin, Ukraine President Leonid Kravchuk, and Belarus President Stanislav Shushkevich met to form the Commonwealth of Independent States (CIS) and to issue invitations to former Soviet republics to join the CIS. By December 12, the parliaments of Russia, Ukraine, and Belarus ratified the agreement to form the CIS. Between December 8 and December 14, CIS membership was accepted by the republics of Kazakhstan, Kirghizia, Tajikistan, Turkmenistan, Uzbekistan, Armenia, Moldavia, and Azerbaijan. Only the Baltic republics of Estonia, Latvia, and Lithuania did not join the CIS.

See December 18, 1991.

December 10, 1991

The European Community (EC) plans to create a single currency and central bank.

Meeting in Maastricht, the Netherlands, EC leaders signed a treaty to pledge closer political unity by planning for a single currency and a central European bank by 1999. Only Britain refused to commit to a common currency, indicating it would decide later about what Maastricht measures to adopt.

December 15, 1991

The U.N. General Assembly votes 111 to 25 with 13 abstentions to revoke the 1975 resolution equating Zionism with racism.

In 1975, the United States and Israel tried to prevent the United National General Assembly from approving a resolution condemning Zionism as a form of racism. At that time, the General Assembly had many delegates from former colonial areas who persistently joined the Soviet Union in voting to criticize Israel or the United States (see November 15, 1975). By 1991, the end of the Cold War—combined with the United States' agreeing to nuclear arms reduction treaties—enabled the United States to gain sufficient votes in the General Assembly to revoke the 1975 resolution. (The United States did not have veto power in the General Assembly as it had in the U.N. Security Council.)

December 17, 1991

The European Community (EC) votes to recognize the independence of Croatia and Slovenia.

Despite opposition from former U.S. Secretary of State Cyrus Vance, and former General Secretary of NATO, Britain's Lord Carrington, EC members agreed to recognize the independence of Slovenia, Croatia, and other former Yugoslav republics that met "humanitarian standards." Although in September 1991 Vance and Carrington were appointed by the United Nations and the EC to negotiate with Croatia, Slovenia, and Serbia to resolve problems regarding the disintegration of Yugoslavia, Vance and Carrington ignored Yugoslav Premier Ante Marković's attempts to preserve Yugoslav unity.

On November 23, Vance persuaded Serbia and Croatia to accept a cease-fire monitored by a U.N. Protective Force (UNPROFOR). At the same time, Carrington prematurely believed Yugoslavia's factions had agreed to accept Vance's cease-fire between Croatia and Serbia. Carrington was premature because Serbian President Milošević refused to withdraw the Yugoslav National Army units from Croatia.

Both Carrington and Vance warned EC members not to recognize the independence of any former Yugoslav republic because it would damage the cease-fire and peace proposals. Nevertheless, an EU commission examined the situation and reported Yugoslav unity could not be restored and the EC should set standards to recognize former Yugoslav republics. The EC formally recognized the independence of Slovenia and Croatia on January 15. The EC also favored Macedonia's independence but delayed because Greece objected to the name "Macedonia," a Greek province associated with the ancient empire of Alexander the Great.

December 18, 1991

Eleven members of the CIS agree to respect the Soviet Union's international treaties, especially on arms control.

When Secretary of State Baker visited Moscow and several Central Asian cities between December 14 and 16, he wanted to ascertain that the new commonwealth republics would carry out the START I and CFE treaties made with the USSR. In Moscow, Russian President Boris Yeltsin assured Baker that Russia would control the use of nuclear weapons in consultation with other Commonwealth of Independent States (CIS) an assurance finalized on December 18 when leaders of 11 former Soviet republics met at Alma Atta, the capital of Kazakhstan. The leaders of Russia, Kazakhstan, Belarus, and Ukraine—the states having nuclear weapons or ICBM missiles on their soil—promised to fulfill the cuts in nuclear weapons agreed to by President Gorbachev and allow U.S. advisers to help dismantle their weapons.

December 25, 1991

Mikhail Gorbachev resigns as president of the Soviet Union.

After Gorbachev's televised speech, the Communist red flag was lowered from the Kremlin and replaced by Russia's white, blue, and red flag. On December 30, Commonwealth of Independent States (CIS) leaders agreed to control jointly the nuclear weapons previously under the control of the Soviet Union, but still had to decide how to handle their economic and military affairs. They also agreed to let Russia have the USSR's permanent seat on the U.N. Security Council.

December 25, 1991

Rebels endanger the elected president of the former Soviet republic of Georgia.

On May 26, 1991, Zviad Gamsakhurdia won Georgia's presidency in a multiparty election. Gamsakhurdia led

Post–Cold War, end of 1991

Georgia's independence movement in March 1991 but became a despotic ruler, and in September violence broke out in the capital city, Tbilisi. After 10,000 people rallied to demand his resignation, rebels seized the government broadcasting center on September 22. Gamsakhurdia called a state of emergency and loyal army troops fired on the rebels, killing four people. Peace talks failed on September 30 and sporadic violence took place from October to December. Opposition groups launched another offensive against the government on December 22, and the year ended with President Gamsakhurdia and his loyalists defending themselves in the parliament building.

See January 6, 1992.

December 27, 1991

The United States announces it will withdraw from all Philippine bases by the end of 1992.

After negotiations on bases in the Philippines reached an impasse on December 27, the Philippine government asked the United States to withdraw from Subic Naval Base and Clark Air Force Base by the end of 1992. The Bush administration agreed to honor the Philippine request.

1992

January 1, 1992

The United States and the former Soviet Union end military aid to Afghanistan; Moscow plans a peace agreement for the Afghans.

As agreed in September, the United States and the former USSR stopped all their military aid to the Afghan government and the Afghan mujahideen rebels. To promote peace in Afghanistan, Soviet Foreign Minister Pankin met with Afghan rebel leader Burhanuddin Rabbani to finalize a peace agreement on November 15, 1991. The accords provided for a transitional working group to transfer political power from President Najibullah's communist regime to a unified government. A U.N. mediator and the Islamic Conference Organization would oversee the peace process expected to begin by April 1992.

See September 12–14, 1991; April 28, 1992.

January 1–10, 1992

President Bush obtains few concessions from Japan to reduce the U.S. trade deficit.

Seeking some Japanese trade concessions, President Bush and U.S. business executives toured the Pacific Ocean area. Together with some members of Congress and U.S. automobile manufacturers, the Bush administration blamed Japan for the U.S. economic recession, which caused America workers to be laid off. Critics noted that U.S. exports to Japan steadily increased in recent years, while the U.S. trade deficit with Japan declined from $56 billion in 1987 to an estimated $44 billion in 1991. Japan did have barriers to many U.S. imports and during Bush's Tokyo visit Prime Minister Kiichi Miyazawa offered to facilitate the entry of some U.S. goods into the Japanese market.

Kiichi's few concessions disappointed the Big Three American automobile makers, who blamed Japanese trade restrictions for their inability to sell cars in Japan or compete with Japanese cars imported to the United States. Yet, as one critic said, U.S. automobile dealers sold few cars in Japan because U.S. models were not suited to Japan's left-hand drive highways. Typically, most TV reports avoided the complexities of trade relations, focusing instead on Bush's illness at a banquet, where he suffered from intestinal flu.

January 2, 1992

Serbia and Croatia accept U.N. cease-fire terms.

Former Secretary of State Cyrus Vance negotiated for the United Nations to obtain a Serbo-Croat cease-fire monitored by a U.N. peacekeeping force. On February 21, the U.N. Security Council approved a U.N. protective force (UNPROFOR) to oversee the cease-fire between Croatia and Serbia. When the first 1,200 peacekeepers arrived in Croatia on April 4, no "peace" existed. Despite the cease-fire, tensions continued between Serbs and Croats, who rejected peace proposals prepared by the EC's representative, Britain's Lord Carrington in November 1991. Although the Serbo-Croat cease-fire held until December 1994, Serbian forces soon began attacking Bosnia and Herzegovina.

See April 6, 1992.

January 6, 1992

The president of the former Soviet republic of Georgia loses to rebels.

After rebels trapped him in the parliament building on December 25, 1991, Georgian President Zviad Gamsakhurdia fled into exile, leaving rebels in charge. The rebel commanders formed a military governing council and named Tengiz Sigua to head a civilian government.

January 16, 1992

Peace treaty ends El Salvador's civil war.

Representatives of El Salvador's government and the rebel FMLN (Farabundo Marti National Liberation Front) signed a treaty to end the 12-year civil war. On January 24, El Salvador's legislature approved laws granting amnesty to the war's participants excepting those involved in the worst massacres.

The next day, Salvadoran courts sentenced two army officers to 30 years in prison for the 1989 murder of six Jesuit priests, their housekeeper, and her daughter. On December 8, 1992, El Salvador's army abolished the Atlacal Battalion, which human rights groups blamed for most of the massacres since 1981.

January 23, 1992

Fifty four nations agree to send food and medicine to former Soviet republics.

In planning for the January 23 meeting, U.S. Secretary of State James Baker began by dramatizing the need for a humanitarian aid conference known as Operation Provide Hope by first having U.S. air force aircraft airlift 38 million pounds of food and medicine to the former Soviet republics. Next, when the conference convened in Washington, D.C., President Bush announced the United States would provide $645 million of humanitarian aid to the newly independent states.

Representatives of 47 nations and 7 humanitarian organizations attended the conference, and each offered to send some form of humanitarian assistance to the former Soviet states. On January 30, British Prime Minister John Major gave Russia 280 million British pounds of export credits and investment insurance; on February 7, France donated $392 mil-

lion to allow Russia to import French grain and technical assistance. Other nations and groups offered various types of aid to the former Soviet republics during the next three months.

January 24, 1992

The United States fails to defuse a Middle East crisis and restore peace talks.

The crisis began on January 3 after Israel deported 12 Palestinians, a move the U.N. Security Council condemned on January 13. Because President Bush continued to link possible Israeli loan guarantees to Jewish West Bank settlements, peace talks could not be restored among Israel, Jordan, Syria, and the Palestinians. These talks convened several times in 1992 but were unsuccessful until the Israeli Labor Party replaced the Likud Party as a result of Israel's June 23 elections.

See August 11, 1992.

January 26, 1992

President Bush's proposed budget for 1993 cuts defense spending over five years.

In presenting a 1993 budget to Congress, President Bush included a post–Cold War cut in defense appropriations of $50 billion over the next five years. The proposed budget total of $1.5 trillion would result in a 1993 deficit of $268.7 billion, an amount higher than the record deficit of 1992. The final congressional defense budget signed in October 1992 allocated $253.8 billion.

January 31, 1992

The U.N. Security Council plans a greater U.N. role in collective security.

During a summit to discuss post–Cold War policies, the United Nations Security Council (UNSC) members accepted a greater U.N. role in maintaining peace. The Security Council also recognized nonmilitary causes of international instability and asked Secretary-General Boutros-Ghali to make recommendations regarding preventive diplomacy, peacemaking, and peacekeeping.

February 1, 1992

The CIS agrees to withdraw former Soviet troops from the three Baltic states.

The Commonwealth of Independent States (CIS) agreed to withdraw 100,000 former Soviet troops from the three Baltic states of Estonia, Latvia, and Lithuania. The agreement was not fulfilled in 1992 because Estonia and Latvia adopted laws limiting the civil rights of ethnic Russians living in their territory. The Baltic leaders also questioned their need to pay Russia to help finance the troop withdrawal. On October 29, Russia suspended its troop withdrawal.

February 5, 1992

The U.N. Security Council renews economic sanctions against Iraq.

Security Council members renewed economic sanctions against Iraq because President Saddam Hussein did not cooperate with U.N. teams monitoring destruction of Iraq's nonconventional weapons and missiles as required by the April 1991 cease-fire. Iraq continued obstructing inspection teams from February 26 to March 19 and again from July 5 to 27, 1992. Iraq's tactic was to delay inspections before promising to comply, then again refusing to cooperate. Iraq also continued to attack Shiites in southern Iraq.

See August 26, 1992.

February 11, 1992

Secretary of State Baker visits former Soviet republics to discuss their problems.

Following a February 1 meeting between President Bush and Russian President Yeltsin at Camp David, Secretary of State Baker agreed to visit Russia and other former Soviet republics to determine the situation regarding nuclear arms control and the need for food and medicine.

During the Camp David meetings, Yeltsin assured President Bush that Russia had full control of the former Soviet Union's nuclear weapons, including the nuclear weapons in Belarus, Ukraine, and Kazakhstan. Yeltsin also proposed a second arms reduction treaty (START II) with the United States to reduce nuclear warheads from the 10,000 warheads allowed under START I to about 2,500 warheads, especially by removing all multiple and independent retargetable vehicles (MIRVs) from all land based ICBMs and sea based SLBMs. Although he would negotiate reductions in ICBMs, President Bush told Yeltsin the United States would not accept reductions of SLBMs because they were part of the U.S. triad of bombers, ICBMs, and SLBMs with nuclear warheads designed to deter an enemy (see June 17, 1992).

On February 11, following the Camp David meeting, Secretary of State James Baker left Washington to visit seven former Soviet republics. From February 12 to 14, Baker made brief visits to talk with the leaders of Armenia, Azerbaijan, Turkmenistan, and Tajikistan before reaching Yekaterinberg, Kazakhstan, early on February 15. Secretary Baker was concerned about the Commonwealth of Independent States' (CIS) nuclear facilities and the future employment of hundreds of former Soviet nuclear scientists who had not been paid their salaries for the past two or three months. Baker's Kazakhstan host drove him from Yekaterinberg to the isolated and previously secret city of Chelyabinsk-70, where the Research Institute of Technical Physics was the center for developing and testing nuclear weapons. Known as the "Los Alamos" of Soviet nuclear technology, Chelyabinsk-70 was one of the four Commonwealth of Independent States' (CIS) nuclear facilities, the others being Belarus, Ukraine, and Russia. Meeting with 25 of the Institute's senior nuclear scientists, Baker asked how the United States and other Western nations could provide job security for them. One scientist told Baker there were many difficulties for them that were "tied to economics." He informed Baker that the nuclear scientists had many ideas for future products, such as developments in fiber optics or improvements in nuclear magnetic resonance, that could be valuable for peaceful purposes. Other scientists told Baker that Iranians and North Koreans had approached them about hiring them to help build nuclear weapons or long range ballistic missiles. To alleviate their concerns, Baker told them about his plan to organize a joint scientific center that would match the nuclear scientists with individuals prepared to invest money in research projects that would challenge their scientific abilities.

See June 17, 1992.

February 17, 1992

Iran and five former Soviet republics form an Islamic free market.

Iran hailed the beginning of an Islamic free market. After concluding a two-day meeting, the former Soviet Muslim republics of Azerbaijan, Turkmenistan, Tajikistan, Uzbekistan, and Kirghizia joined Turkey, Pakistan, and Iran in an Economic Cooperation Organization.

February 24, 1992

The Supreme Court upholds President Bush's decision to forcibly repatriate Haitians.

The Supreme Court upheld a December 1991 federal appeals court decision that the United States could forcibly repatriate Haitian refugees who fled their homes but could not prove political reasons for leaving. U.S. authorities claimed most Haitians fled for economic, not political, reasons.

On May 24, President Bush prevented all Haitian refugees from reaching the United States by ordering the Coast Guard to stop refugee boats leaving Haiti and returning them to Haiti, another decision the Supreme Court dismissed on August 1. U.S. human rights advocates took these cases to court because Bush's decisions on Haitians differed from U.S. policy toward Cuban refugees fleeing to the United States. Human rights lawyers claimed Haitians were refused political asylum in the United States because their heritage was African, a discrimination violating U.S. refugee law, an argument the Supreme Court rejected.
See January 27, 1993.

February 27, 1992

Germany and Czechoslovakia affirm their common borders.

German Chancellor Helmut Kohl and Czechoslovak President Václa Hável signed a friendship treaty to affirm their current border and pledged economic and cultural cooperation.

March 1, 1992

Saudi King Fahd codifies laws in a constitution.

Saudi Arabian King Fahd issued decrees to codify Saudi law in a written constitution to decentralize political power and protect individual rights. Fahd also established a 60-member Consultative Council with Justice Minister Ibrahim al-Jubayr as its speaker.

March 3, 1992

The U.N. Human Rights Commission votes 23 to 8 to condemn Cuba for human rights violations.

The Human Rights Commission's vote to condemn Cuba's violations of human rights was a sign that former communist nations in Eastern Europe were taking positions in the United Nations that differed from the Warsaw Pact's uniform acceptance of Moscow's positions before the Soviet Union collapsed in December 1991. The resolution to condemn Cuba for violating the human rights of its people was cosponsored by Poland and Czechoslovakia. Other Eastern European delegates on the Human Rights Commission who joined the United States and Western European delegates by voting to condemn Cuba were from Hungary and Bulgaria.

March 14, 1992

North and South Korea agree to inspect each other's nuclear sites.

North Korea agreed to the mutual inspection of each nation's nuclear arms sites by mid-June. On January 30, North Korea had signed the International Atomic Energy Agency (IAEA) inspection agreement, a condition the Bush administration linked to canceling the U.S.-South Korean military exercises. On May 7, the two countries agreed to unite Korean families who had been separated since 1953, and on July 28 they agreed in principle to establish land, sea, and air links and scientific cooperation.

March 17, 1992

The United Nations fails to stop war between Armenia and Azerbaijan.

As the Soviet Republic of Armenia and the Soviet Republic of Azerbaijan, the two countries had been fighting sporadically for more than four years. In 1988 Armenian Christians living in the Azerbaijan *oblast* (province) of Nagorno-Karabakh staged protests during which Azerbaijan police killed 32 Armenians in forcefully breaking up the demonstrations (see February 11, 1988). Following more large Armenian demonstrations in July 1988, the Soviet Union's

General Secretary Mikhail Gorbachev sent Soviet army units to the oblast to maintain order, but they were unable to prevent fighting between the Armenian Christians and Azerbaijani Muslims (see July 4, 1988).

Early in 1992, the United Nations sent former U.S. Secretary of State Cyrus Vance to seek a cease-fire and peace settlement between Armenia and Azerbaijan. By March 17, Vance admitted that neither side was willing to compromise on the future status of Nagorno-Karabakh. Soon after Vance left, Armenian forces launched an attack on Azerbaijan. By August 9, Azerbaijan's armed forces chased most Armenian Christian forces out of Nagorno-Karabakh. The potential of a complete victory for Azerbaijan led Armenian officials to ask the Commonwealth of Independent States (CIS) to intervene.

March 22, 1992

Sali Berisha becomes president of Albania by defeating his Communist opponent with 62% of the vote.

After Albania's Communist Party leader Enver Hoxha died in 1985, Ramiz Alia replaced him as party leader and president of Albania. Alia continued to serve until March 23, 1992. When students staged pro-democratic demonstrations in Albania, Alia offered to hold multiparty elections. On March 22, Sali Berisha defeated Alia in the election for president.

March 25, 1992

CSCE nations sign an "open skies" treaty.

At a meeting of the Commission on Security and Cooperation in Europe (CSCE), twenty five nations signed the "open skies" treaty, permitting reconnaissance flights over their territory. The treaty affected North America, Europe, and the former Soviet republics.

March 31, 1992

The U.N. Security Council votes to cut off all air traffic to Libya.

The council approved a resolution calling for all U.N. members to cut off air links and arms sales to Libya unless it extradited two terrorists suspected of bombing Pan Am flight 103 in 1988. Libya refused to extra-dite the suspects and U.N. sanctions became effective on April 15.

See December 21, 1988.

April 1, 1992

Under U.N. supervision, Cambodia forms a Supreme National Council.

After the civilian chief of a U.N. peacekeeping force arrived on March 15, a coalition of Cambodian parties formed a Supreme National Council. Its members signed two agreements with the United Nation's peacekeepers. The first was the Universal Declaration of Human Rights (see December 9, 1948); the second was an agreement to repatriate Cambodian exiles in Thailand. Refugees began returning from Thailand on March 30 but the United Nations had problems because the exiled Khmer Rouge refused to occupy camps in Cambodia designated for them by U.N. peacekeepers.

See November 30, 1992.

April 6, 1992

President Bush suspends U.S. aid to Peru.

On April 6, Bush said Peru took a step away from democracy because President Fujimori dissolved the National Assembly on April 5 and suspended parts of the constitution to defeat Shining Path rebels. An Organization of American States resolution also criticized Fujimori.

A year earlier on July 31, 1991, Bush reported that Peru's improved human rights record permitted $94 million of aid to help Peru fight the drug trade, on August 14, Congress froze funds for Peru because of abuses by Peru's security teams but on October 30 Bush released antinarcotics funds that Congress had frozen.

See November 22, 1992.

April 6, 1992

The European Community recognizes the independence of Bosnia and Herzegovina; the United States follows suit.

When war broke out between Serbs and Croats in the summer of 1991, Bosnia was unprepared for independence, hoping Yugoslav unity would be maintained. Bosnian President Alija Izetbegović preferred Yugoslav unity because Bosnia's population was a

Bosnia-Herzegovina, 1992

mixture of 44% Muslim, 31% Serb, 17% Croat, and 5.5% Bosnians who had intermarried and called themselves Bosniaks or Yugoslavs.

After the EC recognized the independence of Slovenia and Croatia in January 1992, Bosnia held a referendum on independence on February 29. Ninety-nine percent of those voting approved independence, but Bosnian Serbs boycotted the election. Because the Serb Republic's President Slobodan Milošević urged them to join a Greater Serbia, Bosnian Serbs led by Radovan Karadžić staged a referendum on independence from Bosnia in November 1991. Subsequently he established an independent Serbian Republic in January 1992, a move Washington and the EC condemned. Milošević assisted the Bosnian Serbs by sending Yugoslav National Army (YNA) equipment and officers to train Serb paramilitaries. The YNA also erected and manned artillery that began bombarding Sarajevo, the capital of Bosnia and Herzegovina, early in April 1992.

Despite Serb attacks on Bosnia's Muslims and Croats, the EC recognized Bosnia's independence on April 6. The next day, the United States recognized Bosnia's independence as well as the independence of Slovenia and Croatia. Although the American media paid slight attention to Balkan events, Secretary of State Baker waited for the results of Bosnia's February referendum because, he figured, delaying a decision on recognition might restrain Milošević—a belief based on former Secretary of State Cyrus Vance's inability to comprehend Milošević's deceptive tactics. Reports showed that the Serb Republic, and the YNA assisted–Bosnian Serbs, persistently lied to U.S. Ambassador Warren Zimmermann, claiming the conflict was a "purely Bosnian" affair.

See June 8, 1992.

April 9, 1992

A U.S. court convicts Noriega of drug trafficking.

A U.S. federal court convicted General Noriega, former president of Panama, on eight counts of drug trafficking and money laundering. He was sentenced to 40 years in prison.

On Noriega's arrest, see January 1, 1990.

April 24, 1992

A U.N. resolution authorizes observers to monitor a cease-fire in Somalia.

Since January 1991 when rebels overthrew the government of Said Barre, civil strife raged in Somalia. Hoping to end the struggle and humanitarian problems caused by the conflict, U.N. Resolution 751 dispatched 50 observers as a U.N. operation in Somalia (UNOSOM I) to monitor a U.N. cease-fire that Somalia's militant factions never observed. Although the U.N. observers lessened the dangers to nongovernment humanitarian groups who sent emergency food and medical aid, Somalia's problems multiplied in 1992.

See December 3, 1992.

April 26, 1992

Prior to Russia's joining the International Monetary Fund (IMF), the G-7 nations approve aid to Russia.

On January 2, Russian President Boris Yeltsin issued economic reforms to end state subsidies for most products and permit price increases. These free-market reforms were required to receive an IMF loan but brought complaints from many Communists, who proposed a vote of no confidence to remove Yeltsin as president. Yeltsin survived when the Russian Congress of People's Deputies rejected the noconfidence proposal by a vote of 447 to 412 with 70 abstentions. Although Russia's Congress declared conditional support for Yeltsin's reforms, IMF officials approved Yeltsin's reforms.

On April 1, President Bush and German Chancellor Helmut Kohl proposed an aid package to stabilize the rouble, making it convertible to Western currencies, provide export credits, and give financial assistance to the Russians. These events permitted the finance ministers of the seven major industrial nations (G-7) to endorse an aid package of $24 billion to Russia under IMF auspices. On June 1, Russia formally joined the IMF.

April 28, 1992

The Afghan Communist regime ends but the peace process is disrupted.

In 1989, President Bush rejected Soviet leader Mikhail Gorbachev's offer for both nations to embargo arms to Afghanistan. Because conflict escalated in Afghanistan, Secretary of State Baker changed U.S. policy and obtained a Soviet agreement for the two countries to cut off all military aid to both warring sides in Afghanistan. Military aid was cut off and the possibility of a new Afghan regime arose in 1992 because of a Soviet agreement with Afghan rebels.

In early April, U.N. mediator Benon V. Sevin supervised the transfer of power from Communist leader Najibullah to a six-member commission led by Ahmed Shah Massoud. Several Islamic nations gave diplomatic recognition to the new regime. In Washington, the State Department welcomed the new government, urging it to resolve all conflicts with militant factions. Although many militant factions accepted peace on May 25, hard-line guerrilla leaders and mercenaries previously paid by Najibullah rejected the new regime and fighting continued.

See February 23, 1989; January 1, 1992; September 27, 1996.

May 18, 1992

An American oil company agrees to invest in Kazakhstan oil fields.

The Chevron Oil Corporation and the government of Kazakhstan signed an agreement for Chevron to develop the Tengiz oil fields with an investment of $20 billion over 40 years.

May 18, 1992

Klaus Kinkel becomes German foreign minister.

German Chancellor Kohl chose Kinkel to replace Foreign Minister Hans-Dietrich Genscher following a split in the Free Democratic Party, a part of Kohl's parliamentary coalition.

May 19, 1992

Intense fighting breaks out in southern Lebanon.

A week of fighting began between Israeli-backed Lebanese forces and fundamentalist Muslims in southern Lebanon. The fighting ended on May 27 after Israel bombarded guerrilla bases, killing 24 persons in the worst of recent conflicts in Israel's "security zone."

May 20, 1992

A House of Representatives committee investigates the Bush administration's relations with an Atlanta bank.

The House Judiciary Committee decided to investigate the Bush administration's relations with Iraq before its August 1990 invasion of Kuwait, especially concerning a $5 billion bank loan and fraud case. The House investigators sought information about Atlanta, Georgia's branch of Italy's Banca Nazionale del Lavoro (BNL), which helped Iraq purchase armaments. On June 1, BNL bank manager Christopher P. Drogoul pleaded guilty in federal court of transferring bills of credit worth $4 billion from the Atlanta bank to an Iraqi account in the Rome branch of BNL, and the House Committee asked for a special prosecutor to investigate. U.S. Attorney General William Burr asked retired judge Frederick B. Lacey to examine the evidence, and on December 9, Lacey said there were "no grounds to pursue" the case.

May 21, 1992

British Prime Minister Major has problems with members of the Conservative Party over the Maastricht Treaty.

Soon after the British Conservative Party won a majority in Parliament on April 2, the House of Commons approved Prime Minister John Major's legislation to implement the 1991 European Community's Maastricht treaty. Later in 1992, controversy over the treaty developed among Conservative Party members, and on November 4, Major narrowly survived a key vote on the treaty in the House of Commons.

May 22, 1992

Three former Yugoslav republics are admitted to the United Nations.

On May 22, the U.N. General Assembly voted to admit Croatia, Slovenia, and Bosnia and Herzegovina as U.N. members but on May 30, the Security Council condemned the rump Yugoslavia of Serbia and Montenegro for providing military assistance to the Serb Republic, assistance that internationalized the war in Bosnia. The Council also levied economic sanctions on Serbia and Montenegro, including a trade embargo and freeze on the former Yugoslavia's foreign assets.

On April 27, the Republics of Serbia and Montenegro proclaimed a new Federal Republic of Yugoslavia to replace the former Yugoslav federation. The Belgrade ceremony celebrating the "new Yugoslavia" was boycotted by diplomats of the European powers, Canada, and the United States, who refused to recognize the "Serb-Montenegrin Yugoslavia." On September 22, 1992, the United Nations expelled the rump Yugoslavia because of Serbia's role in the Bosnian war.

May 22, 1992

Russia and Poland sign a friendship treaty.

Russian President Boris Yeltsin and Polish President Lech Wałęsa signed a Polish-Russian treaty of friendship. In addition, Yeltsin indicated 40,000 Soviet troops would leave Poland by November 5, 1992.

May 23, 1992

The United States and four CIS republics agree to comply with the START I treaty of 1991.

The United States and the four Commonwealth of Independent State (CIS) countries with nuclear arms signed the Lisbon Protocol to comply with the 1991 START I treaty negotiated with the Soviet Union. Since January, U.S. Secretary of State Baker had negotiated with leaders of the Ukraine, Kazakhstan, and Belarus, which joined Russia in agreeing to fulfill START I. In addition, all except Russia agreed to sign the Nuclear Non-Proliferation Treaty (NPT) as non nuclear states. One problem developed because on November 18, 1993, Ukraine's parliament approved Start I but refused to sign the treaty.

On Russia's START II, see June 17, 1992.

May 24, 1992

The Pentagon issues a defense policy guidance program for the post–Cold War era.

Following a review of U.S. strategic defense policies, the Department of Defense issued a Defense Policy Guidance paper that emphasized the U.S. commitment to collective military action. Notably, the May 24 guidance paper deleted a March 8 draft including phrases urging the United States to remain the world's only superpower by preventing competitor nations from challenging U.S. primacy in Western Europe and East Asia. These phrases raised extensive criticism, leading the Pentagon to delete them from the final Defense Policy Guidance.

Defense Secretary Richard Cheney was also concerned about updating the Pentagon's Single Integrated Operations Policy (SIOP) for using nuclear weapons. The seldom publicized SIOP had not been altered since October 1981 following President Reagan's announcement of a "launch on warning" nuclear strategy. During the next decade, the SIOP added more and more targets in the Soviet Union for U.S. nuclear warheads before Cheney ordered a reduction in targets from 40,000 to 10,000.

Significantly absent from the Pentagon's guidance report was mention of the SDI program. In March 1992, the Government Accounting Office (GAO) reported that neither GPALS nor Brilliant Pebbles was a viable antimissile defense. Although a single GPALS ground-based system might comply with the 1972 ABM treaty, the Senate Armed Services Committee learned that two GPALS tests failed and in July 1992, the committee found GPLAS could not be deployed by 1996, as scheduled.

See October 2, 1981; September 17, 1991.

June 2, 1992

President Bush extends China's most-favored-nation (MNF) trade status.

Despite disputes with Congress over China's trade status, President Bush extended China's MFN for another year. On February 21, Bush lifted sanctions blocking U.S. exports to China of high-tech material, but Congress passed legislation requiring China to stop sending nuclear arms to countries such as Iran and to improve its human rights record, a measure Bush vetoed on March 3. Subsequently, Congress took action against renewing China's MFN trade status.

See September 15, 1992.

June 8, 1992

The U.N. Security Council orders UNPROFOR to protect Sarajevo's airport.

UNPROFOR "peacekeepers" were sent to Croatia as part of former U.S. Secretary of State Cyrus Vance's cease-fire agreement between Croatia and Serbia. On June 8, UNPROFOR forces were sent to occupy and protect Sarajevo's airport that the Yugoslav National Army and Bosnian Serbs had surrounded to stop humanitarian aid from reaching the besieged city. Since April 5, superior Serb forces assisted by the YNA committed "ethnic cleansing" against Bosnia's Muslims and Croats by killing, torturing, and imprisoning males and raping many women, atrocities that were reported by the BBC and U.S. reporter Roy Gutman.

See January 2, 1992; July 3, 1992.

June 14, 1992

An environmental conference agrees to reduce greenhouse gases.

At the Rio de Janeiro Conference on Environment and Development, delegates of 178 countries agreed to promote economic development that would protect the earth's nonrenewable resources and signed a treaty to reduce emissions of carbon dioxide and greenhouse gases. During the meeting, U.S. delegates were criticized for refusing to support a treaty protecting endangered plants and animal species.

June 17, 1992

Presidents Bush and Yeltsin agree on the basis for START II.

At a two-day Washington meeting, Presidents Bush and Yeltsin agreed to draft a second strategic arms reduction treaty leaving each side one-half the number of nuclear warheads proposed under START I. By 2003, the United States would have 3,500 warheads, Russia 3,000. Bush and Yeltsin also agreed to cooperate in space operations, sign a friendship treaty, provide a global protection system, and allow U.S. businesses to avoid double taxation if they operated in Russia. Bush told Yeltsin that Russia would receive most-favored-nation trade status and a $610 million aid package, agreements Congress approved on August 6. On September 14, Russia opened its biological research buildings to let U.S. and British inspectors verify its adherence to the 1972 germ warfare treaty.

See January 3, 1993.

While Presidents Yeltsin and Bush discuss economic and arms control matters, they take time to pose with Barbara Bush, Ranger, and Millie. George Bush Presidential Library

June 24, 1992

A cease-fire in the former Soviet republic of Georgia proves to be temporary.

After Georgian President Eduard Shevardnadze and Russian President Boris Yeltsin met with Ossetian rebels, a cease-fire was achieved on June 24. Since January 6, the bloody conflict continued after opponents of President Zviad Gamaskhurdia captured the capital city of Tbilisi and formed a Military Council. On March 10, Georgia's council prevented a coup by the former president's loyalists before selecting former Soviet Foreign Minister Shevardnadze as interim president. The June 24 cease-fire proved temporary because on July 23, rebels outside Tbilisi declared independence. As war continued on November 2, Yeltsin sent Russian troops to disarm the rebels in the Ossetia and Ingushetia regions.

See July 27, 1993.

June 26, 1992

Turkey allows U.S. forces to protect Kurds in Iraq.

Because Kurdish tribes in Turkey fought to gain independence, Turkey's leaders were concerned about the status of Iraq's Kurds. Despite these concerns, Turkey's parliament agreed to a U.S. request for its rapid reaction force to remain in Turkey to protect Kurdish tribes in Iraq as it had done since April 1991.

See July 5, 1993.

June 29, 1992

Algeria's High Council names Ali Kafi as president.

The council named Kafi to replace President Mohamed Boudiaf, who was assassinated by Islamic Salvation Front (FIS) rebels who sought to overthrow the government. Boudiaf had been president since February 16, after Algeria's High Council canceled the January 12 elections the FIS expected to win. Fighting continued between government forces and the FIS.

See May 27, 1993.

July 2, 1992

NATO announces all U.S. tactical nuclear missiles have been withdrawn from Europe.

July 3, 1992

Bosnian Croats proclaim an independent state of Herzeg-Bosna.

Seeking to copy the Bosnian Serb claim of the Serbian Republic's independence, ethnic Croats in Bosnia proclaimed an independent Herzeg-Bosna. The Bosnian Croats' decision ended cooperation between Croats and Muslims who had been fighting Bosnian Serbs.

See April 6, 1992; April 19, 1993.

July 16, 1992

William Clinton and Ross Perot challenge George Bush for the U.S. Presidency.

At the Democrat party convention, William Clinton was nominated for president and Albert Gore for vice president. In July, independent candidate Ross Perot said he would not run for president, but on October 1 he entered the presidential race.

See August 20, 1992.

July 22, 1992

U.S. "war on drug's" policy is questioned after Colombian drug lord Escobar escapes from prison.

In June 1991 when Colombia's most dangerous drug lord, Pablo Escobar, surrendered, Colombian President Gaviria proclaimed a victory in restricting the drug trade. Escobar surrendered under Gaviria's policy prohibiting extradition for trial in the United States.

By January 1992, evidence showed that Escobar continued directing drug trafficking from a luxurious prison in Medellín, where his cell had carpets, a bathtub, and a boardroom style table. The drug lord's ability to order murders of rival drug lords and direct the cartel's drug trade persuaded President Gaviria to move Escobar to a distant, more secure prison. Not wanting to move, Escobar escaped during a battle between the army and the drug trafficker's paramilitary. Because evidence showed some politicians and Colombia's security forces aided Escobar's escape, Gaviria arrested the suspects but vowed to continue the policy of refusing to extradite drug traffickers who surrendered.

In Washington, D.C., Escobar's escape caused critics of the "war on drugs" to call for changes in U.N. policy. President Bush continued tactics followed for 20 years. Since 1989, the war on drugs budget doubled to $12 billion dollars, two-thirds expended on drug enforcement with the other third used for prevention, drug treatment, and education. With no significant decrease in U.S. drug use, the longest war in U.S. history was being lost but received little attention in the 1992 presidential campaign.

See December 2, 1993.

August 6, 1992

President Bush seeks humanitarian aid for Sarajevo but rejects air attacks against the Serbs.

Bush's policy on Serb aggression was to provide humanitarian aid to Sarajevo and to expect the United Nations and European Community to use UNPROFOR to protect food and medicine rushed to Sarajevo. As a 1996 Carnegie report indicated, UNPROFOR acted as a neutral between Serb aggressors and the Muslim/Croat victims, a position that dampened public pressure for a "robust" response to Serb atrocities. For example, on July 10 NATO and the EC sent warships to the Adriatic Sea to enforce the U.N. trade embargo on Yugoslavia, but EC officials told naval officers not to interfere in the war among Serbs, Muslims, and Croats in Bosnia.

In Washington, Bush refused to use U.S. air attacks against Serbs as recommended by U.S. Ambassador to Yugoslavia Warren Zimmermann. Bush did not intervene in the conflict because of the 1992 election campaign and the so-called Vietnam syndrome, which questioned involvement of U.S. forces in distant warfare. Despite journalist Roy Gutman's reports of Serb ethnic cleansing, Bush said the United States had no "vital" interests in the Balkans, but at his request Congress provided funds for humanitarian aid.

See August 27, 1992.

August 11, 1992

President Bush approves a $10 billion loan guarantee to Israel.

Bush offered Israel a $10 billion loan guarantee because Prime Minister Yitzhak Rabin suspended the allocation of land to Jewish settlers in Gaza and West Bank territories. Following Israel's June 23 elections, Rabin's Labor coalition replaced Shamir's Likud Party. Rabin's main problem was the narrow 62 parliament votes out of a total 120. The narrow margin made it difficult to conduct peace talks with the Palestinians, but Rabin was expected to be more conciliatory than the Likud Party. On October 5, Congress approved the loan guarantee. The loan guarantee plus Rabin's suspension of more Jewish settlements enabled peace talks to resume between Israel and the Palestinians. Nevertheless, Arab-Israeli conflict continued in the occupied territories and southern Lebanon even as peace talks were renewed.

See December 12, 1992.

August 20, 1992

The Republican Party nominates George Bush for a second term.

The Republican National Convention again nominated Bush for president and Dan Quayle for vice president. On August 13, Secretary of State Baker resigned to become Bush's chief of staff and campaign manager, being replaced by Lawrence Eagleburger as acting secretary.

August 26, 1992

A "no-fly zone" in southern Iraq is established to protect Shiites from Iraqi attacks.

After receiving approval from Britain, France, Saudi Arabia, and Kuwait, President Bush established a no-fly zone below the 32nd parallel in Iraq. In early 1992, Iraqi forces had mounted attacks to eradicate the southern Shiites who tried to overthrow Saddam Hussein. Designed to protect the Shiite population from Iraqi aircraft, pilots from U.S. aircraft carriers in the Persian Gulf flew daily sorties to shoot down any Iraqi aircraft threatening the Shiites. On December 31, 1992, an F-16 plane was the first to shoot down an Iraqi jet entering the no-fly zone of southern Iraq.

August 27, 1992

A U.N.-EC conference in London fails to end war in Bosnia.

During a London conference, representatives of the United Nations and the European Community were unable to end Bosnia's conflict. The U.N. and EC mediators met with Franjo Tudjman (Croatia), Slobodan Milošević (Yugoslavia), Radovan Karadžić (Serb republic), and Alija Izetbegović (Bosnia). The U.N. delegates specified that territory gained by force would not be recognized, but Milošević rejected this proposal. When the conference ended on August 27, Milošević and Karadžić appeared to accept an accord as a peace framework, but no steps were taken to implement the agreements.

See October 3, 1992.

August 30, 1992

The United States will purchase enriched Russian uranium.

To prevent Russia's high-grade enriched uranium from falling into "unfriendly hands," President Bush agreed to purchase up to 500 metric tons of it to prevent Russia from selling it to other nations. The uranium could make 30,000 nuclear bombs. The U.S. Department of Energy would transform the high-grade uranium into a lower-grade for use in U.S. nuclear power plants.

September 1, 1992

Nicaragua takes action allowing the United States to release economic aid.

In June 1992, Congress froze aid to Nicaragua. In order to receive the aid, Nicaragua's President Chamorro dismissed 12 police officers who allegedly had ties to the Sandinistas. After Chamorro complied, U.S. authorities found Nicaragua's human rights record had improved, releasing $140 million in economic aid.

September 3, 1992

Geneva conference delegates approve a chemical weapons convention.

On September 3, delegates to a Geneva disarmament conference agreed to a Chemical Weapons Convention (CWC) and forwarded it to the U.N. General Assembly. After the assembly approved the CWC, the United Nations held a meeting in Paris on January 13, 1993, where each nation's delegate could sign the CWC treaty. The agreement would become effective in 1995 in order to liquidate chemical weapons by 2005. The United States and Russia had the largest stockpiles of weapons such as mustard gas and nerve gases, but experts believed 23 other nations also possessed chemical weapons.

The United States signed the treaty, but Senate ratification was delayed for over four years.

See April 24, 1997.

September 4, 1992

The United States and the Netherlands end restrictions on each other's airline flights.

In an agreement hailed as the most liberal air treaty ever, the United States and the Netherlands eliminated restrictions on airline flights between the cities of the two nations. The treaty enabled KLM Royal Dutch airlines to conclude an agreement with U.S. Northwest Airline to schedule destinations to other U.S. and European cities. Because the European Community had planned to deregulate inter-European flights on January 1, 1993, other joint ventures between U.S. and European airlines were expected to take place.

September 15, 1992

Commercial trade problems continue between China and the United States.

Although President Bush extended China's most-favored-nation (MFN) trade status on June 2, Congress passed legislation on September 15 that conditioned China's MFN status on improving human rights, lowering trade barriers, and curbing nuclear and missile exports. After bilateral trade talks broke down in August 1992, Bush threatened to place 100% tariffs on Chinese imports, but on October 10 China agreed to lower some import barriers. Simon-U.S. trade issues continued after Deng Xiaoping opposed political reforms at the Communist Party congress on October 21.

See November 11, 1993.

September 16, 1992

Russia will withdraw its troops from Cuba.

Russia said it would withdraw its 1,500 troops from Cuba by mid-1993. Two months later, on November 11, the two nations signed agreements on trade relations and retained Russia's electronic intelligence-gathering facilities in Cuba.

September 21, 1992

The U.N. General Assembly admits twelve new members but rejects the new Yugoslav Federation. President Bush will support U.N. peacekeeping operations.

When the U.N. General Assembly convened, twelve new member states attended after being admitted between March 2 and May 22: Armenia, Azerbaijan, Kazakhstan, Kyrgyzstan, Moldova, Tajikistan, Turkmenistan, Uzbekistan, San Marino, Croatia, Slovenia, and Bosnia and Herzegovina. On September 22, the assembly voted against a proposal to have the Federal Republic of Yugoslavia (Serbia and Montenegro) occupy the former Yugoslav U.N. seat.

In addressing the assembly, President Bush said the United States would support a wide range of U.N. peacekeeping operations but did not mention the $733 million the United States owed in U.N. peacekeeping and membership fees.

September 26, 1992

South Africa forms a nonracial interim government.

South African President de Klerk and African National Congress President Nelson Mandela ended a stalemate over a nonracial constitution by creating an interim government. Although some black African groups opposed Mandela's talks and staged attacks on white Afrikaners, South Africa's parliament passed legislation approving an interim government including blacks in the cabinet. Nevertheless, the black radicals' Azanian People's Liberation Army, whose members opposed Mandela, continued to attack whites in South Africa.

October 2, 1992

The 1993 U.S. budget includes a ban on nuclear tests.

When President Bush signed budget authorizations for fiscal 1993, the $274 billion defense budget was $6.7 billion less than he requested. The budget legislation also included a measure banning U.S. nuclear tests. Because President Bush threatened to veto a bill prohibiting tests, Congress inserted a clause to ban tests in legislation authorizing funds for energy and water including $517 million for a super-colliding beam machine that Bush wanted to build in Texas. The congressional bill banned nuclear tests for nine months, after which a restricted number of tests could test safety measures for existing nuclear weapons until 1996. After September 1996, tests were banned unless another country conducted them.

October 2, 1992

The United States and South Korea sign a free-trade agreement.

President Bush and South Korean President Roh Tae Woo signed a trade agreement opening South Korea's market to U.S. goods. Bush also offered Roh financial aid to help expand South Korea's technological base.

October 2, 1992

The U.N. Security Council votes to allow U.N. members to seize Iraqi assets to pay for U.N. expenses.

The Security Council voted to allow its members to seize Iraqi foreign assets held in their banks and financial institutions. Valued between $500 million and $5 billion, the assets would pay for U.N.'s disarmament and relief efforts in Iraq and compensate victims of the 1990 Kuwait invasion.

October 3, 1992

The United States airlifts humanitarian supplies to Sarajevo.

On October 3, a U.S. United States air transport plane was one of the first aircraft to arrive at Sarajevo's airport, carrying over 200 tons of food and medicine for the besieged city. U.N. flights to Sarajevo were suspended on September 3 after a Serb ground-to-air

Admiral Leighton Smith, Commander IFOR visits the besieged city. Department of Defense

missile shot down an Italian plane, killing four of its crew. On September 14, the U.N. Security Council agreed to renew flights and added 6,000 troops to help UNPROFOR protect supplies from the besieging Serbs. Because presidents of the city needed to stockpile food and medicine to survive the harsh Balkan winter.

On October 3, the council also created a no-fly zone prohibiting all military aircraft from flying over Bosnia, a measure applying to Serbs as the only group with combat planes in Bosnia. But the Council did not authorize methods to enforce the no-fly provision because President Bush refused to commit troops to Bosnia and the Europeans feared the Serbs would retaliate against UNPROFOR if a Serb plane was shot down.

See May 6, 1993.

October 17, 1992

Angolan election returns are challenged by Jonas Savimbi.

In Angola's runoff elections for president, the Popular Movement's Jose Eduardo dos Santos defeated UNITA's Jonas Savimbi, who claimed election fraud. On November 26, fighting again broke out between the two groups, but on December 7, U.N. peace moni-

tors persuaded Santos and Savimbi to form a coalition government.

See May 19, 1993.

October 23, 1992

Vietnam cooperates in a search for American MIAS.

Vietnam provided U.S. Department of Defense investigators with documents, photographs, and personal effects of U.S. personnel from the Vietnam War. These data were to help the DOD determine what happened to 2,265 Americans listed as missing in action (MIA) from the Vietnam War. In response to Vietnam's cooperation, on December 14 the United States lifted its 17-year trade embargo on Vietnam, permitting American companies to do business with Vietnam.

November 3, 1992

William Clinton defeats George Bush in the presidential elections.

Clinton won the presidential election with 43% of the popular votes to 38% for Bush and 19% for Ross Perot. In the electoral college, Clinton won 370 to 168; Perot received no votes. The Democrats continued to control Congress, with 57 senators and a House margin of 258 to 176 plus one independent.

November 9, 1992

Touring both West and East, Russian president Yeltsin signs friendship agreements.

Visiting London on November 9, Russian President Boris Yeltsin met with British Prime Minister John Major to sign a friendship treaty. Later, Yeltsin flew to South Korea, where on November 18, Russian and South Korean officials signed a treaty of friendship. South Korea also resumed Russia's $3 billion in aid, suspended in December 1991, when the future of the Soviet Union was uncertain.

November 19, 1992

The U.N. Security Council places an arms embargo on Liberia, where 5 American nuns were killed in October.

In an attempt to end Liberia's rebellion, the Security Council approved an arms embargo and called for a cease-fire. On October 22, the rebel National Patriotic Front led by Charles Taylor had besieged the capital, Monrovia, which was defended by a 7,000-man peacekeeping force from the West African Economic Community. Although five American nuns were killed in October, 90 missionaries and most diplomats were evacuated. Attempting to end the conflict, the Security Council placed an arms embargo on Liberia.

November 20, 1992

GATT talks are stalled because of U.S. disputes with France over agricultural subsidies.

On November 20, France opposed a compromise on farm subsidies that the United States and European Community members accepted. France's obstruction delayed approval of the Uruguay round of the General Agreement on Tariffs and Trade (GATT) negotiations. Another year of negotiations was necessary before the United States and France agreed on agricultural subsidies.

See December 14, 1993.

November 22, 1992

President George Bush retracts his criticism of Peru's elections.

In April 1992, Peru's President Alberto Fujimori suspended Peru's constitution by claiming it was the best way to defeat the guerrilla rebellion of the Shining Path movement. In response to the suspension, the Bush administration denounced Fujimori's decision and suspended U.S. foreign aid to Peru (see April 6, 1992). Between April and October 1992, Peru's police and army captured the leader of the Shining Path and 10 of his cohorts. On October 10, 1992, the 11 Shining Path members were convicted of treason in trying to overthrow the government and sentenced to life in prison. In Peru's November 22 elections, candidates for parliament who supported Fujimori's April decision were elected. In light of events between April and November, the Bush administration stated that Peru's elections were free of fraud despite claims by opposition leaders who boycotted the election. Bush also retracted his previous criticism of Peru and released the U.S. foreign aid suspended in April.

November 23, 1992

Russian President Yeltsin and his critics compromise on economic reforms.

After the demise of the Union of Soviet Socialist Republics in December 1991 (see December 25, 1991), Russian President Boris Yeltsin inherited the Congress of People's Deputies, whose members were elected in 1989 (see May 25, 1989). Throughout the months from January to November 1992, hard-line communists whom Yeltsin referred to as "Stalinists" criticized President Yeltsin for weakening Russia by agreeing to withdraw from the Baltic states (see February 1, 1992), accepting strategic arms treaties that would eliminate many of the former Soviet Union's ICBMs (see May 23 and June 17, 1992), and withdrawing troops from Cuba that the Soviet Union used as a military base in the Western Hemisphere (September 9, 1992). To reduce Yeltsin's power and increase the Congress of People's Deputies' power, the "Stalinists" wanted to amend the constitution that was last approved by the Soviet Union in 1977.

On November 23, 1993, Yeltsin received enough votes from critics in the Congress of People's Deputies to achieve a compromise on his proposed legislation

November 30, 1992   **1225**

to create a free market economy and stabilize the rouble. Before the Congress of People's Deputies adjourned on December 1, 1992, the members voted to reject amendments to the 1977 constitution proposed by Yeltsin's critics. In addition, Yeltsin offered to draft a constitution for the Russian Federation that would replace the 1977 Soviet Constitution and hold a referendum on the new constitution in 1993.

See April 25, 1993

November 24, 1992

The United States returns its Philippine bases.

As previously announced, the United States turned Subic Bay Naval Base over to the Philippines, ending nearly 100 years of American possession. On November 6, the Philippines agreed to give U.S. ships and aircraft access to Subic Bay installations.

On the U.S. acquisition of bases, see March 23, 1901, and July 4, 1902.

November 25, 1992

Czechoslovakia's assembly approves the separation of the republics.

In March 1991, student demonstrators in Bratislava, Slovakia, urged the Slovakian government to declare independence from the Czechoslovakian Federation. Following the Bratislava demonstrations, members of Slovakia's parliament debated the independence question for over a year before Slovakia's parliament voted by a narrow margin to remain part of the Czechoslovakian Federation.

The question of separating the Czech Republic from the Slovak Republic did not disappear because nationalists on both sides continued to advocate separation. During elections in Czechoslovakia on February 5–6, 1992, the Czech's nationalist leader Vaclav Klaus became Prime Minister of the Czech Republic after his Civic Democratic Federation won a majority of seats in the Czech parliament. Likewise, Slovakia's nationalist leader Vladimer Meciar became Prime Minister of the Slovak Republic after his Slovak Movement for a Democratic Slovakia won a majority of seats in the Slovak parliament.

On August 26, 1992, Klaus and Meciar agreed on a plan to amend the Czechoslovakia Federation's Constitution. The amendments would enable Czechoslovakia to dissolve *without* holding a referendum such as Czechoslovakia's President Václav Havel

had advocated. On November 25, 1993, the Czechoslovakian Federal Assembly approved the constitutional amendments sponsored by Klaus and Meciar.

See January 1, 1993

November 26, 1992

Industrialized nations accept methods to stop ozone-depleting chemicals.

At a Copenhagen meeting, the world's major industrialized nations agreed on a quicker timetable to end production and use of ozone-depleting chlorofluorocarbons. On September 29, the U.S. National Aeronautics Space Agency reported that the ozone layer over the south polar area had grown to its largest size ever.

November 30, 1992

France and Germany say their military unit will not hinder NATO.

On May 22, 1992, France and Germany announced the formation of a 35,000-member military force. Intending the joint force to be a pillar of Western European defense forces, the French and Germans reassured NATO that if European security were threatened, the joint force would be under NATO's operational command. German Chancellor Kohl proposed the joint force to calm French fears about the status of a united Germany.

The creation of a Franco-German army was the first instance since 1949 of two Western European nations planning to act outside the Atlantic alliance. The 1999 Kosovo conflict revived additional European efforts to create armed forces separate from U.S. control.

November 30, 1992

U.N. fails to keep Cambodia's Khmer Rouge from disrupting the peace process.

Although in March 1992, U.N. peacekeepers seemed to make progress, on June 10 the Khmer Rouge refused to occupy camps under U.N. supervision. With the peace process stalled on November 30, the U.N. Security Council tried to punish the Khmer Rouge by prohibiting trade with rebel territory and excluding them from forthcoming elections. In

LIBRARY
UNIVERSITY OF ST. FRANCIS
JOLIET, ILLINOIS

response, on December 17 the Khmer seized 46 U.N. peacekeeping troops. Obviously, the U.N. was a peace-making group, not "peacekeepers."

See May 28, 1993.

December 3, 1992

President Bush tries to end Somalia's fighting by offering a U.S.-led humanitarian mission.

After United Nations Operations in Somalia (UNOSOM I) was established, U.N. attempts at "peacekeeping" and protecting humanitarian aid groups failed because violence escalated in Somalia. On July 27, the United Nations sent 500 "peacekeepers" to protect humanitarian aid distribution, and on August 17 Bush ordered air force planes to transport food and medicine to Somalia, where 25% of the population suffered from starvation.

American, U.N., and other aid groups distributing supplies were hampered because U.N. bureaucrats worked at cross-purposes and did not coordinate their activity with the U.N. secretary-general's special envoy, Mohamed Sahnoun, an official from the Organization of African States. U.N. bureaucrats opposed Sahnoun's meetings with militant clan leaders to arrange peace terms, although by mid-October, Sahnoun believed the clans were close to a peace agreement. Yet U.N. bureaucrats complained to

Secretary-General Boutros-Ghali because Sahnoun bypassed the proper channels to U.N. headquarters in New York.

To placate the bureaucrats, Boutros-Ghali replaced Sahnoun with a loyal U.N. bureaucrat İsmet Kittani. Thus, Sahnoun's peace attempts broke down and Mohammad Farah Aideed, the strongest clan leader in Mogadishu, denounced the United Nations as the enemy, promoting intense clan fighting in early November. The armed Somalia clansmen disrupted aid distributions more than before with gangs looting warehouses containing food and medical supplies, and attacking U.N. camps at Mogadishu's airport.

Although President Bush lost the November election to Bill Clinton, he decided the U.S. should assist Somalia, claiming it was a humanitarian intervention. Because militant Somalia clans disrupted the distribution of humanitarian aid, President Bush's offer of assistance was accepted by Boutros-Ghali. On December 3, United Nations Security Council (UNSC) Resolution 794 authorized a U.S.-led Unified Task Force (UNITAF) to "establish a secure environment for humanitarian aid operations in Somalia." Exactly why Bush made this decision is uncertain. Bush's *All the Best* (1999) includes his December 4 letter to Boutros-Ghali, that the U.S. mission is "to create secure conditions which will permit

President Bush visits U.S. forces in Somalia. Department of Defense

the feeding of the starving Somali people and allow the transfer of this security function to the UN." The letter also said the military mission was "to secure ports, airports and delivery routes, and to protect storage and distribution of humanitarian supplies and relief workers."

U.N. documents indicate that Boutros-Ghali asked Bush to have UNITAF disarm the Somalia factions to create a "secure environment." In contrast, Bush and General Colin Powell, chairman of the Joint Chiefs of Staff, avoided disarming the factions. The Joint Chiefs told Bush that U.S. forces should enter Somalia, secure an area for relief supplies in a short time, withdraw U.S. troops, and let the United Nations take over. Although the "quick exit" strategy avoided doubts about the "Vietnam syndrome," former Secretary of State Henry Kissinger commented that if the warlords listened to Bush, they would lay low, cooperate with the United States, and renew their fighting after the Americans left. Kissinger's comment proved to be correct. Moreover, Bush's special envoy, Robert Oakley, realized the UNITAF mission required diplomacy to prevent attacks by Somalia's militants. Oakley went to Somalia before U.S. Marines arrived, convincing clan leaders to restrain their fighting or be destroyed by U.S. forces.

See April 24 and December 11, 1992.

December 7, 1992

The German Bundestag (parliament) acts to keep refugees from entering Germany.

The Bundestag passed legislation making it difficult for refugees and asylum seekers to enter the country. The legislation reversed a long-standing policy of freely admitting refugees. The new laws came after right-wing gangs and thugs rioted and firebombed foreign residences in Berlin and Rostock. Showing that most Germans opposed such neo-Nazi activity, 350,000 Germans demonstrated in favor of tolerance in Berlin on November 8 and in Munich on December 6. Prior to parliament's action, Chancellor Kohl failed to persuade other European nations to accept more refugees. On November 27, Kohl also banned two neo-Nazi parties and ordered police to seize firearms from party members.

December 9, 1992

U.S.-led UNITAF forces arrive in Somalia; Oakley persuades militants not to fight Americans.

On December 9, the first of UNITAF's 37,000 troops (28,000 Americans) arrived in Somalia on the same day that President Bush's envoy, Robert Oakley arrived and convinced Mogadishu's two warlords, Mohammad Aideed and Ali Mahdi Mohammad not to interfere with UNITAF. With the two warlords' consent, U.S. Marines arrived on December 11 and without opposition took control of Mogadishu's airport. Because of Oakley's action, the marines had no difficulty in Mogadishu but at Somalia's southern port of Kismayo, Belgian forces had to fight militant clans. The Belgians had to be assisted by U.S. Quick Reaction Forces in December and during another round of Kismayo fighting from March 16 to 20.

See January 15, 1993.

December 11, 1992

U.S. forces join U.N. troops in Macedonia, keeping that state out of Bosnia's war.

Under U.N. Resolution 795, President Bush sent 500 U.S. troops to join a U.N. observer force in Macedonia to prevent Bosnia's conflict from spreading. Recognition of the independence of the Republic of Macedonia had been delayed in April 1992 because Greece objected to the name "Macedonia" for historic reasons. Later, Greece accepted the name "Former Yugoslav Republic of Macedonia."

December 12, 1992

An Arab-Israeli crisis arises because of two killings.

An Arab-Israeli crisis began after Israeli troops killed a 10-year-old Arab girl and Palestinians retaliated by killing an Israeli soldier. To punish the Palestinians, Prime Minister Rabin ordered the deportation of 415 Palestinians to Israeli's "security zone" in southern Lebanon. The crisis finally ended on February 1, 1993, when Israel permitted 101 deportees to return home, saying the others could return within a year.

December 15, 1992

El Salvador ceremonies celebrate the end of civil war.

With many of the world's leaders joining the ceremonies, El Salvador celebrated the end of its civil war. The peace was achieved after the government and Farabundo Marti para la Liberacion Nacional (FMLN) rebels signed an accord on January 16, 1992, to move toward a final peace. On January 23, El Salvador's legislature passed an amnesty for wartime violations and the government abolished the notorious Atlacatl Battalion, which had murdered six Jesuit priests and massacred over 1,000 civilians in 1989.

December 16, 1992

A U.N. peacekeeping mission sends 7,500 troops and civilians to monitor Mozambique's cease-fire and elections.

December 17, 1992

The United States, Canada, and Mexico sign a free-trade agreement.

Following lengthy consultations, negotiators from the three nations began preparing a final draft of the trade agreement on October 7. When the treaty was finalized on December 17, President Bush, Mexican President Carlos Salinas de Gortari, and Canadian Prime Minister Brian Mulroney signed the North American Free Trade Agreement (NAFTA).

In December, Democratic President-elect Bill Clinton expressed support for NAFTA but said he desired clauses about the environment and protection of worker standards, subjects causing disputes in 1993 when the U.S. Senate considered treaty ratification.

See November 20, 1993.

December 17, 1992

German Chancellor Kohl provides Russia with debt relief and housing funds.

Helmut Kohl provided Russia with $11.2 billion of debt relief and $318 million to build housing for former Soviet troops scheduled to leave eastern Germany by August 31, 1994.

December 24, 1992

President Bush pardons six Reagan officials involved in the Iran-Contra scandal.

During 1992, the most prominent official indicted by a federal grand jury was former Defense Secretary Caspar Weinberger. On October 10, special federal prosecutor Lawrence E. Walsh released excerpts from Weinberger's notes stating Vice President Bush knew about President Reagan's arms-for-hostage deal with Iran, although Bush continued to deny the allegation. On November 24, Weinberger pleaded not guilty in court but Bush's pardon avoided a trial.

1993

January 1, 1993

Czechoslovakia is divided into two separate nations.

In accordance with agreements made on November 25, 1992, Czechoslovakia was divided into the Czech and Slovak republics. On February 15, Václav Havel was elected president of the Czech Republic; Michael Kovac was elected president of Slovakia.

January 3, 1993

Presidents Bush and Yeltsin sign START II.

The second strategic arms reduction treaty (START II) was finalized and signed by Bush and Yeltsin. After the document was ratified by the two nations, START II would, within a decade, eliminate all land-based multiple nuclear warheads and reduce by one-third the current level of each nation's nuclear arsenals. At this time, START I needed to be ratified by all parties, including the former Soviet republics. On February 4, the Republic of Belarus ratified START I.

See October 24, 1993.

January 15, 1993

Somali leaders oppose a peace agreement; President Bush sends some soldiers home.

At a U.N.-sponsored conference, 14 Somali clan leaders could not achieve a peace agreement because Mohammad Aideed rejected all U.N. proposals. The conference obtained only one concession from Mogadishu's two major clans when warlords Aideed and Ali Mahdi agreed to move their artillery and

Russia's President Boris Yeltsin and President Bush sign START II treaty. George Bush Presidential Library

heavy weapons into storehouses outside the city. Before the conference adjourned, militants in Mogadishu harassed U.S. Marines, who had to use tanks and helicopters to attack Aideed's stronghold to capture a large weapons arsenal.

Despite continuing threats to Somalia's security, President Bush ordered 1,100 American soldiers to leave Somalia the day before he left office, a move symbolizing Bush's December promise to withdraw U.S. troops from Somalia before President Clinton's inauguration.

See March 27, 1993.

January 20, 1993

William Jefferson Clinton is inaugurated as president of the United States.

After Clinton's inauguration, he named as his foreign policy leaders Secretary of State Warren Christopher, Secretary of Defense Les Aspin, and National Security Adviser Anthony Lake. The U.S. ambassador to the United Nations was Madeleine Albright.

January 27, 1993

Haiti's premier refuses to allow U.N. human rights observers to visit the island.

Raoul Cedras, Haiti's military leader, rejected a U.N. plan to send human rights observers to Haiti. Since September 1991, when the military junta overthrew President Aristide, U.N. envoy Dante Caputo sought to restore the democratically elected president.

After the coup, President Bush levied mild economic sanctions on Haiti, but his policy focused on

President William Clinton. National Archives

preventing Haitian refugees from reaching the United States. President Clinton campaigned for president by promising more humane treatment for refugees, but after 352 Haitians landed in Florida in early January, Clinton changed his mind on January 14, deciding to temporarily continue Bush's forcible-repatriation of Haitians.

See February 24, 1992; June 21, 1993.

February 18, 1993

The United States restores normal diplomatic relations with New Zealand.

The United States restored diplomatic relations with New Zealand that were severed in 1985 because New Zealand did not allow U.S. nuclear-powered or nuclear-armed naval ships to dock in its seaports.

See February 4, 1985.

February 27, 1993

Muslim terrorists bomb New York City's World Trade Center.

A bomb explosion at New York City's World Trade Center killed six people. On March 6, Muhammad Al Salameh was arrested and on August 25, Muslim cleric Sheik Abdel Rahmen surrendered to federal authorities and was indicted on conspiracy charges. On May 4, 1994, a jury of the U.S. District Court for New York found four men guilty of bombing the World Trade Center. The men, who had ties to radical Muslim groups in Egypt and Afghanistan, were sentenced to a total of 240 years in prison.

February 28, 1993

U.S. Air Force planes drop food and medicine to Bosnian Muslims.

President Clinton ordered U.S. Air Force C-130s to drop food and medicine to Bosnian Muslims in towns besieged by Serb forces. Although the first parachutes went astray and were captured by Serbs, later air drops helped the Muslims and were continued whenever

more supplies were needed. The air drop was Clinton's first attempt to deal with the Bosnian war.

See May 1, 1993.

March 15, 1993

A U.N. report indicates the White House covered up El Salvador's massacres.

The U.N. Truth Commission's report on El Salvador's human rights violations revealed that Presidents Ronald Reagan and George Bush covered up the role of El Salvador's officials implicated in serious abuses, including massacres of women and children. The U.N. report and declassified documents obtained by the *New York Times* provided evidence that the White House kept the information from congressional committees to get approval for $6 billion of aid to Salvador during the 1980s.

The report stated El Salvador's police and "security forces" committed 85% of the abuses. Among examples of abuses were the Atlacatl Battalion's massacre of 700 women, children, and elderly men in 1981 and the head of the right-wing ARENA Party Roberto d'Aubuisson's role in assassinating Archbishop Oscar Arnulfo Romero and four American churchwomen. Some U.S. officials dismissed the Truth Commission report for assuming that the "Foreign Service is filled with liars." On March 20, El Salvador's National Assembly ignored the report by approving a sweeping amnesty for all participants in the 12-year civil war, an act denounced by El Salvador's religious leaders and moderate politicians.

See April 24, 1994.

March 27, 1993

The United Nations forms a national council to govern Somalia.

A first Addis Ababa meeting in January was sabotaged by Mohammad Farah Aideed, whom the United Nations would not recognize as Somalia's primary leader. At a second Addis Ababa conference, the United Nations persuaded Somalia's militants to accept a cease-fire and form a national council to govern the country. The conference began on March 13 but was disrupted when fighting broke out in Kismayo. During the Kismayo conflict, UNITAF made a crucial mistake by backing General Hersi Morgan's clan rather than clans allied with Mohammad Aideed. Although his clan won, Aideed

Support for Project "Restore Hope" is signaled by a U.S. aircraft carrier off the Somalia coast. Department of Defense

did not forget that the U.N. group favored his opponent.

After the Kismayo fight was resolved, the Addis Ababa delegates accepted the U.N. plan for a National Council. These plans proved inadequate because they provided no means for electing council members and enforcing the cease-fire accepted by clan leaders. While the leaders met at the Addis Ababa conference, humanitarian aid agencies met with Somalia's non-military groups including elderly clan leaders, women's organizations, and Islamic leaders. The donors pledged $130 million to provide agricultural rehabilitation, clinics, and job opportunities, but the pledges became irrelevant. After UNITAF left, Somalia's social order broke down.

See May 4, 1993.

April 2, 1993

President Clinton releases U.S. aid to Nicaragua.

President Clinton released $50 million in aid to Nicaragua that Congress withheld in June 1992 owing to Nicaragua's human rights violations. Although former Sandinista rebels still held key positions and President Chamorro had difficulty in gaining control over Sandinista and Contra rebels, Clinton said there was sufficient human rights progress to justify releasing the money.

See August 25, 1993.

April 4, 1993

The United States and Russia announce a partnership; financial aid is provided for Russia.

On April 4, Presidents Clinton and Yeltsin announced a "new democratic partnership." Clinton offered Russia $1.6 billion of credits and grants to purchase American grain. Russia received additional financial aid on April 15 when G-7 finance ministers provided a total of $28.4 billion to help Yeltsin reform Russia's economy by cutting inflation and increasing tax revenues.

See September 8, 1993.

April 8, 1993

Macedonia is admitted to the United Nations.

Macedonia was admitted as the 181st U.N. member under the name "Former Yugoslav Republic of Macedonia." Although Macedonia declared independence in 1991, its recognition by Western European nations and the United States was delayed because

Greece objected to the name "Macedonia," the same as a region of Greece that dated back to Alexander the Great.

April 19, 1993

War breaks out between Bosnian Croats and Bosnian Muslims.

After the Republic of Croatia assisted Bosnian Croats to form a "nation" called Herzeg-Bosna, war broke out after Bosnian Croat militia attacked the village of Ahmici, killing dozens of Muslim women, children, and elderly people and burning their homes. The Croats captured other Muslim villages before a Bosnian Muslim army turned them back at Tavnik. With international attention focused on Sarajevo, little attention was given to this conflict, which the Croat Republic's President Tudjman promoted much as Serbian President Slobodan Milošević aided the Serb Republic. The Croat-Muslim conflict helped Bosnian Serbs gain more territory until the Clinton administration helped end the conflict.

See February 28, 1994.

April 16, 1993

Srebrenica is declared a "safe area" by the U.N. Security Council.

Following a month long crisis with Serb forces in Bosnia, UN resolution 819 declared Srebrenica a "safe area" to be protected by UNPROFOR. The events leading to resolution 819 humiliated UNPROFOR, undermined the U.N. credibility, threatened to split NATO allies, and destroyed the Vance-Owen peace plan. Respect for UNPROFOR and the Security Council was lost because their attempt to remain neutral between Serb aggressors and Muslim victims led UNPROFOR officials to deceive the public about what happened at Srebrenica.

In February, an offensive by Serb forces sought to surround Srebrenica and compel 200,000 Muslims to seek refuge in Muslim territory as part of the Serbs' ethnic cleansing to create a Greater Serbia. Serb General Ratko Mladić had ordered a blockade to prevent humanitarian aid convoys from reaching Srebrenica. On March 11, UNPROFOR Commander and French General Phillipe Morillon defied Mladić and escorted a convoy of three vehicles to the city, where he observed the starving, dying, Muslim refu-

gees living in the streets. The Muslims wanted Morillon to stay in the city and protect them. The general told the inhabitants: "I will never abandon you." Morillon then went to Belgrade and told Milošević to end the Serb assault and allow supply convoys to reach Srebrenica.

The Serb assault did not end and one aid convoy reached the city, where, after the trucks unloaded, desperate women and children jumped on board asking to be taken away from Srebrenica. Mladić's army stopped a second aid convoy, saying no more convoys could be sent until Muslims in Srebrenica surrendered and were disarmed. While UNPROFOR negotiated with Mladić, Serbs continued bombarding the city. On April 12, a Serb bomb exploded in the city streets, killing 56 people including 14 children playing in a school yard, an attack U.N. human rights personnel could not ignore. British human rights official Larry Hollingworth dropped the façade of U.N. neutrality, telling reporters Mladić was to blame. Hollingworth did not know that rather than punish the Serbs, U.N. representatives would accept Mladić's demand to disarm the Muslims.

Despite pleas from U.S. officials for military intervention against the Serbs, NATO members with personnel in UNPROFOR preferred to negotiate with Mladić. After General Morillon met with Mladić at Sarajevo's airport, the United Nations accepted his terms allowing Serb forces to remain in positions that surrounded Srebrenica. After 140 Canadian troops reached the city, they helped evacuate the wounded and, as U.N. representatives had agreed, disarmed the Muslims.

Although Mladić said he achieved "surrender terms," UNPROFOR officials covered up their mistake in yielding to his demands. Rather than say they appeased Mladić, U.N. officials said they made a "disarmament agreement" and cease-fire with the Serbs. The disarmament was implemented although Muslims kept concealed small arms, but these arms did not match the Serbs' heavy artillery in place outside the city.

While Morillon negotiated with Mladić, in New York the Security Council passed resolution 819 to declare Srebrenica a "safe area." The term "safe area" was crafted in place of "safe haven," an international law term that meant refugees were immune from attack. To monitor the "safe area," the United Nations sent a small UNPROFOR contingent to stand between Serbs and Muslims until Srebrenica's final disaster on July 11, 1995. Because the United States and its NATO allies disagreed about a response to Mladić's demands, Muslims and Croats learned they could not depend on U.N. protection or on the U.N. or NATO members and soon rejected the Vance-Owen peace proposal.

See May 1, 1993.

April 25, 1993

A Russian referendum approves President Yeltsin's reform policies.

In Russia's national referendum, 53% approved President Boris Yeltsin's economic and social policies. Yeltsin had contended with the Congress of People's Deputies about his policies since March 13, when the deputies voted to cancel the referendum and limit his power. Supported by U.S. President Clinton's promise of economic aid, Yeltsin survived an impeachment vote by the deputies and felt Yeltsin confident of the people's favor. Yeltsin ignored the congress and conducted the April 25 referendum. Following the favorable referendum, Yeltsin organized a meeting of Russia's regional leaders to draft a new constitution that would abolish the Congress of Deputies that had been elected as a Soviet parliament before the Soviet Union split apart in 1991.

See April 4 and October 4, 1993.

May 1, 1993

President Clinton's "lift and strike" proposal for Bosnia is rejected by the U.N. Security Council and NATO.

Because Europeans feared their UNPROFOR troops would be endangered by NATO air attacks, they rejected Clinton's "lift and strike" proposal to bring peace to Bosnia. "Lift" meant the Security Council would allow Bosnian Muslims to obtain armaments by ending the U.N.'s September 1991 embargo on arms; "strike" meant NATO aircraft would aggressively enforce the no-fly zone over Bosnia to persuade Bosnian Serbs to accept peace terms.

After the Europeans rejected NATO air raids, U.S. Secretary of State Warren Christopher told an interviewer that the "intractable Bosnian plight could never be cured." During the remainder of 1993, U.S. policy in the Balkans permitted air drops of food, supported U.N. Resolution 819, making Srebrenica a "safe area," and U.N. Resolution 824 extending "safe areas" to the Bosnian towns of Tuzla, Zepa, Goražde and Bihać. On May 25, Clinton also favored the creation of a war crimes tribunal to try the former Yugoslavia officials.

See June 16, 1993.

May 4, 1993

UNITAF's Somalia mission is transferred to UNOSOM II.

The transition from UNITAF to UNOSOM II was completed after all but 5,000 U.S. troops left Somalia. According to former President Bush's December 1992 schedule, UNITAF was to end before Clinton's inauguration, but in early March, the schedule for a secure environment in Somalia had not been fulfilled, although Bush's envoy, Robert Oakley, told reporters "the problem of clan warfare which has taken Somalian lives is virtually gone."

Oakley's evaluation was proven wrong in mid-March when fighting broke out in Kismayo. Despite U.N. Secretary-General Boutros-Ghali's December request, UNITAF did not disarm militants and provided temporary security to only 40% of Somali territory near Mogadishu. Although UNITAF's mission was not fulfilled, Clinton insisted on withdrawing most U.S. troops by May 3.

To prepare for UNITAF's departure, the Security Council established UNOSOM II with 5,000 U.S. troops; 37,000 from Third World nations such as Bangladesh, Botswana, and Pakistan; 1,130 French; and 2,538 Italians. Germany sent 1,500 men who were engineers or technicians not trained for combat. Turkish General Cevik Bir headed UNOSOM II, and U.S. Admiral Jonathan Howe replaced Ismet Kittani as the envoy for Secretary-General Boutros-Ghali.

See June 4, 1993.

May 6, 1993

Paraguay's Colorado Party candidate wins a three-man race for president.

Juan Carlos Wasmosy of the ruling Colorado Party was elected president in Paraguay's first multiparty, direct elections for a civilian head of state. Wasmosy won 40% of the vote, Domingo Laino of the Authentic Radical Party won 32% and Guillermo Caballero Vargas of the National Encounter received 25%. On August 15, Wasmosy was sworn in as president.

May 19, 1993

President Clinton cooperates with the United Nations by recognizing Angola's new government.

President Clinton recognized Angola 17 years after it gained independence from Portugal. He changed the U.S. policy that financially aided Joseph Savimbi's UNITA rebels, whom Presidents Reagan and Bush had called anticommunist "freedom fighters." Savimbi had accepted a cease-fire in 1991, but after UNITA lost in Angola's September 1992 elections, he called them a fraud and resumed fighting. Because the United Nations backed Angola's government, Clinton's cooperation achieved some success. On December 4, after the U.N. Security Council banned sales of food and arms to UNITA, Savimbi accepted a U.N. cease-fire. In 1994, UNITA again broke the cease-fire.

May 28, 1993

President Clinton renews China's most-favored-nation (MFN) trade status.

President Clinton extended China's MFN trade status for one year but stated that a 1994 renewal depended on China's human rights record. Some congressional leaders criticized the renewal, saying Clinton put monetary interests of American corporations ahead of human rights considerations. Nevertheless, because of problems with China's sale of missile technology to Pakistan, Clinton imposed a few trade sanctions on China.

During 1993, China's economy faced "capitalist" problems after a flood of investment activity caused the inflation rate to soar. In March 1993, China's Communist Party Congress reelected Premier Li Peng and Communist Party General Secretary Jiang Zemin and adopted a constitution using the words "socialist market economy" to describe its capitalist-oriented economic reforms. In order to lower the inflation rate, China began an austerity program in the summer of 1993, and in November, the Communist Party's Central Committee made changes in China's banking system, increased taxes, and began regulating the number of foreign investments.

See August 25, 1993.

May 28, 1993

Cambodia elects a 120-seat assembly.

In U.N.-sponsored elections, Cambodia elected a constitutional assembly led by a coalition of Cambodian People's Party (CCP) with 51 seats and the royalist United National Front for an Independent, Neutral, Peaceful and Cooperative Cambodia Party's (FUNCINPEC) 58 seats. Returning from exile in China, Prince Norodom Sihanouk became head of state; the assembly coalition was led by the CCP's Hun Sen and the FUNCINPEC's Norodom Ranariddh—the son of Prince Sihanouk. Although the Khmer Rouge boycotted the election, its armed forces merged with the government's army on June 3. On September 17, the constituent assembly adopted a new constitution making Sihanouk a constitutional monarch. The U.N. role was completed except that the Khmer Rouge still controlled territory near the border with Thailand.

See July 7, 1994.

June 4, 1993

After Somalian warlord Aideed's forces attack U.N. forces, a hunt for Aideed begins.

Somalia's problems escalated after Aideed's forces ambushed Pakistan "peacekeepers" inspecting an ammunition depot, killing 24 Pakistanis. The Secretary General Boutros-Ghali's Special Representative to Somalia Admiral Howe had trouble with Aideed soon after the United Nations International Task Force (UNITAF) ended because the warlord wanted to control Mogadishu and disputed Howe's plans for a reconciliation conference among clans in central Somalia. Aideed boycotted the conference, urging Somalians to meet with him instead of Howe.

Soon after the conference adjourned, Howe and General Bir learned Aideed planned attacks against UNOSOM, and Howe ordered Pakistani troops to inspect Aideed's munitions depot. Howe's order unleashed Aideed's surprise attack on Pakistanis. The attack pinned down Pakistan forces until a U.S. Quick Reaction Force dispersed Aideed's militants. In addition to 24 Pakistani deaths, 56 UNOSOM II troops were wounded. Because Aideed's clansmen also attacked a U.N. food-distribution center elsewhere in Mogadishu, Howe believed the attacks were "calculated and premedi-

Clinton withdraws most U.S. forces, but a small amphibious ``Quick Reaction Team'' is offshore aboard U.S. ships. Department of Defense

tated.'' The U.N. peacekeeping effort focused on a hunt for Aideed, offering a $25,000 reward for information leading to his arrest. Because most Somalians sympathized with Aideed and the anti-U.N. propaganda spread by Radio Mogadishu, the U.N. reward was never given because the hunt for Aideed became a disaster.

See October 3, 1993.

June 16, 1993

All Bosnian groups oppose the Vance-Owen peace plan.

The Vance-Owen plan would divide Bosnia into 10 cantons with a weak central government. Bosnia's Muslims and Croats opposed the plan because they lost too much territory and feared the United Nations would not protect their areas; the Serbs rejected the plan because they got too little land. After Vance resigned from the U.N. negotiating team, the Norwegian Thorvald Stoltenberg replaced him. Stoltenberg and Lord Owen revived U.N. negotiations but the talks broke down.

See October 2, 1993.

June 21, 1993

The U.S. Supreme Court permits the forcible repatriation of Haitian refugees.

The Supreme Court ruled that a forcible repatriation of Haitian refugees without asylum hearings did not violate U.S. or international law. Human rights lawyers feared the Supreme Court's ruling would set a precedent for other countries to reinterpret the 1951 refugee treaty resulting from guilt about the treatment of Jewish refugees fleeing Nazi Germany. The U.N. high commissioner for refugees said the decision was "a major setback to international refugee law." Because many refugees were fleeing from conflicts in the Balkans, Somalia, Southeast Asia, and elsewhere, the Supreme Court's decision had widespread influence.

June 26, 1993

U.S. missiles attack Baghdad's intelligence building.

In the attack on Baghdad, 23 Tomahawk missiles were fired from U.S. naval warships in the Persian Gulf and Red Sea. Three Tomahawks missed their target and killed eight civilians in nearby homes, but the other 20 hit the headquarters of Iraq's intelligence services in downtown Baghdad.

After the raid, President Clinton asserted an attack was justified because an FBI investigation verified that Iraqi officials helped the six men who plotted to assassinate former President George Bush during his April 1993 Kuwait visit. Kuwait authorities captured the men and on June 4, 1994, five Iraqis and one Kuwaiti were sentenced to death for attempting to kill Bush.

July 3, 1993

President Clinton announces a new U.S. policy regarding nuclear testing.

After a review of U.S. nuclear testing operations, Clinton approved Presidential Decision Directive PPD-11, indicating that the United States would not conduct any nuclear tests before September 1994, a moratorium that would remain in effect unless another nation conducted nuclear tests. Clinton's PPD-11 was the middle way between moderates wanting to end nuclear tests and conservatives preferring to conduct tests to maintain U.S. nuclear superiority. Clinton's decision permitted Los Alamos to continue tests for safety and reliability as well as maintaining the intellectual ability of its scientists to design nuclear weapons.

See October 5, 1993.

July 3, 1993

A U.N. agreement with Haiti's junta promises Aristide's return as president.

Aristide's peaceful return from exile in the United States seemed imminent after General Cedras signed the Governor's Island Agreement mediated by U.N. envoy Daniel Caputo. Cedras had previously refused to talk with Caputo, but he agreed to talks on June 16 after U.S. Ambassador to the U.N. Madeleine Albright persuaded the Security Council to levy a worldwide arms and oil embargo on Haiti. With U.N. sanctions in place, Cedras met with Caputo, Aristide, and U.S. Secretary of State Christopher at Governor's Island, New York, from June 28 to July 3 where an agreement was signed. The agreement's key sections were that Haiti's legislature would reform the police and army under U.N. supervision; Aristide's exile groups could return home; coup leaders were granted amnesty but would leave Haiti before Aristide returned in October; and a 1,200-member U.N. peacekeeping force, including U.S. and Canadian army engineers and technicians, would rebuild Haiti's infrastructure.

See October 12, 1993.

July 5, 1993

Turkey selects a woman as premier.

Following parliamentary elections in Turkey, Tansu Ciller was the first woman to become Turkey's premier, replacing Suleyman Demirel. Demirel became president on June 16 following the death of Turgut Ozal. The United States was concerned about changes in Turkish politics because American and British aircraft used Turkish air bases to patrol the no-fly zone in northern Iraq.

July 27, 1993

The Republic of Georgia gets aid from Russia for a cease-fire in Abkhazia.

In March 1993, the Republic of Georgia's parliament asked the United Nations for help because Georgia claimed Russia aided ethnic Abkhazian rebels who wanted independence. During the next three months, Georgian President Shevardnadze persuaded Russian President Yeltsin to stop aiding the rebels and accept a friendship treaty with Georgia. Yeltsin also helped Georgia complete a cease-fire with the rebels on July 27.

On September 2, Georgia faced another rebellion in its Mingrelia region on the Black Sea. Georgian and Russian forces eventually defeated these rebels on November 7. While Georgia focused on Mingrelia, Abkhazian rebels again began fighting that continued until December 1, when U.N. mediators gained a cease-fire.

August 11, 1993

President Clinton selects General John Shalikasvili to replace Colin Powell as chairman of Joint Chiefs of Staff.

Previously, Shalikasvili served as commander of NATO forces in Europe.

August 17, 1993

The *New York Times* reports that 1984 tests on the SDI were rigged to appear successful.

In June 1984, the Reagan administration reported that tests on a Homing Overlay Experiment (HOE) were successful. The HOE tests had been hailed as having demonstrated that a bullet could hit a bullet in the same way that the Strategic Defense Initiative (SDI) would perform in space. In 1993, the *New York Times* reported interviews with four Reagan administration officials who revealed that the 1984 tests were rigged to demonstrate the possibility of successful SDI weapons to defend the country.

To substantiate these news reports, the Pentagon and the General Accounting Office (GAO) took 12 months to investigate the experiments. In July 1994, the GAO report indicated the four Reagan officials' 1993 claims were correct, although they did not have the precise facts about the experiments. During the first three 1983 tests, the interceptor missiles flew so far from the target that an explosion could not fool the Soviets. For the fourth test in 1984, Pentagon officials "enhanced" the target to double its normal size so the interceptor missile could easily find it. They also installed a small bomb on the target missile to explode as the interceptor defense missile flew past. Pentagon officials told investigators the explosion was designed to deceive the Soviet Union and force it to spend more money on a counterdefense system. The Pentagon's deception also deceived members of Congress, who approved more funding for the SDI.

The GAO report said the Pentagon's action was "secretive" but "not deceptive." When the GAO report appeared, Senator Sam Nunn (D-Ga.) said the Pentagon's action in 1983–1984 was "indefensible" in whatever terms the GAO applied.

See June 10, 1984.

August 18, 1993

The State Department adds the Sudan to its list of terrorist nations.

After leading a military coup, Omar Hassan al-Bashri persisted in attacks against Sudanese southern Christian tribes to convert them to Islamic fundamentalism. In February 1993, the U.N. Human Rights Commission condemned the Sudan for arbitrary arrests and terrorist activities, and in April international airlifts of food stopped because relief workers were frequently attacked.

The U.S. decision to name the Sudan a center of terrorist activity came after a June 25 report revealed that five of the eight terrorists plotting attacks in New York City had travel documents issued by the Khartoum regime. Combined with the Sudan's propagation of harsh Islamic laws against southern tribes, the travel documents seemed sufficient evidence that the Sudan was a terrorist center. Hassan al-Turabi was identified as the Sudanese mastermind of terrorism. Turabi headed the Nationalist Islamic Front Party, whose members held key post in Omar Bashir's government. According to reports from the U.S. Central Intelligence Agency (CIA), Turabi received Iranian funds in trying to overthrow the governments of Egypt, Algeria, Tunisia and Saudi Arabia.

See June 28, 1995.

August 25, 1993

The United Nations resolves conflicts between Nicaragua's Contras and Sandinistas.

A conflict broke out on July 21 when Sandinista soldiers seized a city in northern Nicaragua. After government troops regained the city, Contra rebels kidnapped 38 government officials and Sandinistas captured 34 conservative politicians, causing an impasse between the two factions. U.N. mediators stepped in and on August 25 persuaded both sides to release their hostages. President Chamorro promised to replace some government officials, and on September 2 she removed General Humberto Ortega Saavedra as defense minister.

See February 24, 1994.

August 25, 1993

The United States impose trade sanctions on Pakistan and China.

On July 19, the Clinton administration warned China that its export of missile technology to Pakistan violated U.S. laws, requiring the president to levy economic sanctions on both nations. The United States said China was violating the Missile Technology Control Regime by selling technology for Pakistan's missile M-11 with a range of 300 miles and the ability to carry a nuclear warhead. China argued that the Nuclear Non-Proliferation Treaty (NPT) did not cover the M-11 missile. Clinton disagreed, and when U.S. intelligence reported that China's technology had reached Pakistan, Clinton imposed punitive sanctions on the two countries. Pakistan's sanctions were described as "minor," but the sanctions on China involved an estimated $1 billion of U.S. high-technology sales that China had ordered. China condemned the U.S. sanctions and threatened to withdraw from the missile sales pact.

For U.S. problems with Pakistan, see November 11, 1993; for problems with China, see October 5, 1993.

September 8, 1993

The United States and Russia sign a military cooperation agreement.

U.S. Secretary of Defense Les Aspin and Russian Defense Minister Pavel Grachev signed a military cooperation agreement that included conducting joint U.S.-Russian peacekeeping exercises and having frequent meetings between U.S. and Russian defense officials.

September 13, 1993

The Oslo Accords are signed by Israel and the PLO.

In Washington, President Clinton presided over a meeting with Israeli Prime Minister Rabin and PLO Chairman Arafat, who signed accords concerning the West Bank and Gaza Strip, occupied by Israel in 1967. Although the Israeli-Arab peace negotiations began in Madrid in October 1991 and continued until early August 1993, they achieved no agreement. Meanwhile, secret talks in Oslo, Norway, were successful. Following exploratory talks with the Palestinians, Israeli Deputy Foreign Minister Yossi Beilin met with them to draft a declaration of principles for Palestinian self-government. Prime Minister Rabin approved the draft that resulted in the 1993 Oslo Accords.

On August 30, the Oslo Accords were made public to get the endorsement of Israel's parliament and the PLO Executive Committee, and to have Israel recognize the PLO as the sole Palestinian representative. U.S. mediators were not involved in these negotiations, but President Clinton supervised the signing because both parties realized the United States was needed to implement the accords after Rabin and Arafat worked out the details.

See October 30, 1991; October 1, 1993.

September 27, 1993

President Clinton asks the U.N. General Assembly to promote free trade and limit U.N. peacekeeping.

Addressing the General Assembly, President Clinton urged U.N. members to expand free-market democracies and end the proliferation of nuclear, chemical, and biological weapons. Clinton also emphasized that the United States was willing to help selected U.N. peacekeeping missions: "If the American people are to say yes to UN peacekeeping, the United Nations must know when to say no."

Secretary Christopher announces that Israeli's Prime Minister Rabin and PLO Chairman Arafat have signed accords concerning the West Bank and Gaza Strip occupied by Israel in 1967. White House

Another notable event at the U.N. sessions was the unsuccessful effort of Japan and Germany to become permanent Security Council members.

September 29, 1993

OPEC discontinues oil production quotas; oil prices fall.

On February 16, 1993, OPEC members agreed to continue oil production quotas designed to increase petroleum prices. Kuwait rejected its quota and increased production, a decision favoring American consumers. When OPEC met again on September 29, the delegates set an overall production quota of 24.5 million barrels per day but permitted each country to decide its own quota because Kuwait and other oil-exporting nations disliked fixed quotas. OPEC's decision led to declining oil prices in 1993.

See March 26, 1994.

September 30, 1993

The U.S. budget is completed for 1994.

In completing his budget for fiscal year 1994, Congress reduced President Clinton's proposal by $493 billion over four years. The budget included tax increases for the wealthy, for some Social Security recipients, for business corporations, and for gasoline but provided tax credits for small businesses and the poor. Congress also closed the supercollider project in Texas, appropriating $650 million to shut down the atom smasher; its projected cost had been $2 billion. Clinton hoped to save $108 billion over five years by cutting the number of federal workers.

For foreign aid, Congress appropriated $14.4 billion, only 1% of federal spending. The foreign aid included $2.5 billion for Russia and other former Soviet republics; $3 billion for Israel; and $2.1 billion for Egypt. In contrast, Clinton promised to help Central American nations move toward democracy but cut El Salvador's aid from $126 million to $45 million, Nicaragua's from $226 million to $10 million, and Honduras's from $50 million to $7.5 million.

After Defense Secretary Les Aspin made a complete review of defense spending, he reorganized the Strategic Defense Initiative office, renaming it the Ballistic Missile Defense Organization (BMDO), and redefined its mission as "theater high attitude area defense" (THAAD) to by-pass the limits fixed by the 1972 Anti-Ballistic Missile Treaty. Clinton repudiated Presidents Reagan and Bush's broad interpretation of the ABM pact. In line with Aspin's changes, Congress authorized Defense Department funds for THAAD to protect American and allied troops on the battlefield. The defense bill also funded the last five B-2 bombers and restricted the Department of Energy's development of nuclear warheads to testing and preserving the "core intellectual and technical competencies" in nuclear weapons.

October 1, 1993

Donors pledge $3 billion to implement the Israeli-PLO Oslo accords.

Assuming the chief role in backing the September 13 accords, President Clinton invited donors to a White House meeting where they pledged $2 billion to help the PLO implement the Israeli-PLO Oslo agreement. For the United States, Clinton pledged $250 million over a two-year period because the United States had given Israel and Egypt more than $5 billion annually since 1979 in conjunction with the Camp David Accords.

See December 12, 1993.
See August 25, and November 2, 1993.

October 2, 1993

President Clinton favors a U.N. peace plan rejected by the Bosnian Muslims.

In a September 1993 meeting, Clinton advised Bosnian President Alija Izetbegović to accept Lord Owen's peace plan although it gave the Serbs more land than the Muslims. Clinton was willing to appease Serb aggressors by awarding them more land, but on October 2 Bosnia's Muslim-dominated assembly and President Izetbegović rejected the Owen plan. As prepared by Owen and Thorvald Stoltenberg, who replaced Cyrus Vance, the plan divided Bosnia-Herzegovina into three ethnic states, but the Muslim population of 44% received only 30% of the land. Although the Serbs had to relinquish 25% of the area controlled by their army, they were given more land than either the Muslims or the Croats. In addition Izetbegović said the plan provided no way to enforce its decisions

In rejecting the Owen-Stoltenberg plan, the Muslims knew there were risks involved, especially because humanitarian supplies for isolated Muslim cities were needed during the coming winter. For the Muslims, the good news was a victory by their army against Bosnian Croats, who would have had a separate state under the Owens-Stoltenberg plan.

See December 1, 1994.

October 3, 1993

A Somali disaster leads President Clinton to withdraw American troops.

On October 3, the Somalian warlord Aideed's militants attacked the U.S. Delta and Army Rangers and shot down two U.S. Blackhawk helicopters, killing 18 and wounding 78 other Americans. The attack ended UNOSOM's hunt for Aideed that began in June (see June 4, 1993) and in August brought in 400 elite U.S. Delta and Ranger forces after four Americans were killed in an ambush. Although the Delta-Ranger soldiers arrested many Somalians and a few of Aideed's officers, they never captured Aideed.

On October 3, the Rangers' commander learned that Aideed's officers would meet in a two-story house near Mogadishu's Olympic Hotel. Because the house was located within an Aideed stronghold, the raid was risky but the U.S. commander expected to capture two of Aideed's top leaders. The Delta-Ranger forces attacked the house and captured 24 militants before large numbers of Aideed's forces counterattacked and surrounded the U.S. troops. The U.S. assault forces were stranded throughout the night, but early the next day, a U.S. Quick Reaction Force and UNOSOM troops dispersed the militants, killing over 500 Somalians. Nevertheless, Somali civilians celebrated their victory by dragging the wounded U.S. Chief Warrant Officer Michael Durant through the streets while television cameras relayed the event around the world.

On October 6, Clinton ordered U.S. commanders to stop hunting for Aideed and prepare a withdrawal from Somalia. The U.S. exit was completed on March 25, 1994, with 50 marines staying to protect U.S. diplomats in Somalia. After admitting that the U.N. had erred in focusing on the hunt for Aideed, Clinton sent Robert Oakley to help the UNOSOM II reconcile differences among Somalia's clans. The U.N. Security Council suspended Aideed's arrest warrant, but Aideed refused to compromise with any U.N. peace proposal. Between November 1994 and March 1995, the remaining UNOSOM troops left Somalia while militant factions continued to fight for control.

October 4, 1993

Russian President Yeltsin evicts the Congress of People's Deputies.

Under the obsolete 1977 Constitution of the Union of Soviet Socialist Republics, members of the Congress of People's Deputies had been elected to the Soviet parliament before the Soviet Union came to an end in December 1991 (see December 25, 1991). Throughout 1992 and the first nine months of 1993, the Congress of People's Deputies had thwarted Russian President Boris Yeltsin's attempts to reform Russia's economic and political institutions (see April 25, 1993). Facing an uprising provoked by hard-line communist members of the Congress of People's Deputies, Yeltsin decided to preempt the Deputies' plan by ordering Russian police and Russian military units to depose all members of the Congress of People's Deputies. The police also dispersed hard-line communists who demonstrated outside the building where Congress met. During two days of violence, the Russian army shelled the White House building where Congress met and arrested 160 dissenters. The violence caused the death of 187 people. After deposing the Congress of People's Deputies, Yeltsin announced that elections for a new Russian parliament and a referendum to approve a new Russian constitution would be held in December 1993 (see December 12, 1993).

Notably, Yeltsin's decision to depose members of the Congress of People's Deputies was backed by President Bill Clinton and the European members of the NATO alliance.

See December 12, 1993.

October 5, 1993

China violates the world moratorium on nuclear tests.

Despite President Clinton's plea to Chinese Premier Li Peng, China conducted nuclear underground tests on October 5. China's tests violated an informal global agreement against nuclear tests with the White House, which believed these tests would lead to more tests by other nuclear powers such as France, Russia, and Great Britain. After learning about China's tests, Clinton ordered the U.S. Department of Energy to prepare for possible U.S. tests in 1994.

In part, China ignored Clinton's plea because the United States had recently levied sanctions on China and U.S. naval vessels had harassed the Chinese ship *Yen Hi* headed for the Middle East. A CIA report claimed the *Yen Hi* was carrying chemical weapons to Iran. Consequently, U.S. naval vessels followed the *Yen Hi* from the South China Sea to the Persian Gulf, where Saudi Arabia cooperated with the United States in inspecting the Chinese ship. On September 6, the inspector's report showed that the CIA had been mistaken. The United States was embarrassed by the event, while China insisted it should be compensated for the disruption of the *Yen Hi*'s voyage.

In light of deteriorating U.S.-Chinese relations, China ignored an October 1 warning from Secretary of State Warren Christopher that nuclear tests would risk the loss of China's most-favored-nation trade status. The Clinton administration's policy of warnings, threats, and economic sanctions proved ineffective and would soon be changed.

October 5, 1993

After China conducts nuclear test, the United States considers resuming its nuclear testing.

Prior to China's nuclear tests on October 5, the United States and other nuclear powers such as France, Britain, and Russia believed China had also agreed to a moratorium on nuclear testing. In July 1985, China and the United States had signed a pact to cooperate in developing nuclear power (see July 23, 1985). Six days later, the Soviet Union and the United States agreed on a moratorium on nuclear testing (see July 29, 1985). Between 1985 and 1992, the United States and the Soviet Union conducted some nuclear tests to determine the best means to verify nuclear tests (see November 20, 1987). Furthermore, these cooperative agreements did not become formal treaties to ban or regulate nuclear testing. On July 3, 1993, President Bill Clinton announced the U.S. would obey a moratorium on nuclear testing as long as no other country conducted nuclear tests.

Thus, after China's 1993 nuclear test, the Clinton administration said the United States would consider resuming nuclear testing in 1994 after consulting with Russia, Britain, and France. China's test revived the question of the need for a formal international treaty to ban or regulate all nuclear testing. Since 1985, all

discussions about nuclear testing avoided the signing of a formal treaty.

See September 5, 1995.

October 12, 1993

President Clinton orders noncombat troops not to land in Haiti.

President Clinton ordered U.S. and Canadian noncombatants aboard the USS *Harlan County* not to land in Haiti. Haiti's military junta did not fulfill the terms of the Governor's Island agreement requiring them to end violence and pave the way for President Aristide's peaceful return in October 1993. In September, violence broke out among militants opposing the Governor's Island agreement, and the Haitian Army General Cedras made no attempt to suppress it.

Thus when the *Harlan County* arrived on October 11 near Port-au-Prince, armed mobs blocked the streets near the landing dock, threatening to kill Haitians who supported Aristide. As a result, Clinton called off the landing and Aristide did not return. Many Americans misunderstood these events because U.S. media reports failed to emphasize that Americans and Canadians on the *Harlan County* were engineers and technicians, not combat forces.

See July 3, 1993; July 31, 1994.

October 22, 1993

NATO adopts a "partnership for peace" for former Warsaw Pact countries.

NATO defense ministers adopted a "partnership for peace" program to prepare former Warsaw Pact countries for NATO membership. The United States suggested the "partnership for peace" process because Russia feared having a NATO military force near its borders. On January 10, 1994, NATO leaders met in Brussels and approved the Partnership for Peace plan.

October 24, 1993

The United States helps Ukraine eliminate its nuclear weapons.

The United States pledged $300 million of economic and technical aid to Ukraine after President Leonid Kravchuk promised to eliminate Ukraine's nuclear arsenal. Although on June 7 Kravchuk told U.S.

Defense Secretary Aspin that Ukraine would store its nuclear warheads under international supervision, Kravchuk took direct control of Ukraine's government on September 23 and complained that the United States and European members of NATO did not give sufficient economic aid to his country. After U.S. Secretary of State Christopher visited Kravchuk on October 3 and pledged $300 million of aid, Ukraine agreed to dismantle all its nuclear weapons. Ukraine would deactivate half of its nuclear warheads by the end of 1993 and the others in 1994, a promise Kravchuk repeated when visiting President Clinton on January 12, 1994.

See March 4, 1994.

October 29, 1993

North Korea prevents U.S. plans for a nuclear-free Korean peninsula.

North Korea continued to thwart U.S. efforts to make the Korean peninsula a nuclear-free zone. Although pledging on July 19 to open its Yongbyon nuclear facilities to inspection, North Korea stopped International Atomic Energy Agency (IAEA) inspectors from visiting those facilities on October 29. The United States offered to pay the costs of converting Yongbyon's facilities into peaceful purposes, but this and other incentives were rejected by President Kim Il Sung. Later, in December 1993, Kim refused to give the IAEA access to its facilities. The IAEA reported it could not assure North Korea intended only peaceful uses for its nuclear materials.

See February 15, 1994.

November 1, 1993

The European Union's Maastricht Treaty takes effect.

The 1991 Maastricht Treaty came into force after all EU members ratified it. Germany was the last to approve the measure in October 1993.

November 2, 1993

U.S.-Chinese military leaders end two days of discussions.

Beginning in mid-September, the Clinton administration reviewed its Chinese policies and President Clinton decided to write to General Secretary Ziang Zemin, informing the Chinese that the United States wanted to promote a "strong, stable and prosperous China" and seek dialogues for better relations. The first substantive result of Clinton's effort took place on November 1 and 2, when high-ranking U.S. and Chinese military officials met in Beijing to discuss mutual concerns.

Although no major agreements resulted from the meetings, both sides agreed that important dialogues had begun and would continue. On November 2, China demonstrated the importance of the event by screening the press conference on state television, which featured U.S. Assistant Secretary of State Charles W. Freeman and China's Central Military Commissioner Liu Huaqing. Freeman said the United States was pleased to resume high-level contacts after four years. The dialogues, he said, were important to prevent misinterpretations of each side's perspective on problems. Likewise, Liu said the two days of talks were a "good beginning" and future contacts would continue. The U.S. and Chinese delegates had agreed to more professional exchanges regarding peacekeeping missions and problems involved in converting defense industries to civilian use. They also admitted they had candid disagreements about China's sale of military technology to Pakistan and U.S. sales of weapons to Taiwan.

See November 19, 1993.

November 11, 1993

The United States and Pakistan disagree about Pakistan's nuclear program.

Negotiators from the United States and Pakistan could not resolve their differences over Pakistan's nuclear weapons program. After Benazir Bhutto's People's Party gained control of Pakistan's parliament in October 6 elections, Prime Minister Bhutto pushed Pakistan's M-11 nuclear missile program despite U.S. economic sanctions imposed on Pakistan and China. Bhutto wanted a successful nuclear program since Pakistan claimed India would soon be able to test nuclear weapons soon.

See August 25, 1993; August 9, 1994.

November 16, 1993

Hezbollah rebels try to disrupt the Israeli-PLO peace accords.

Because Hezbollah rebels in Lebanon opposed peace between the PLO and Israel, the rebels' heavy artillery fired on Israeli forces south of the Litani River. In July 1993, Israel staged a seven-day raid on the rebels' camps before Prime Minister Rabin declared a cease-fire. After the November attack ended the cease-fire, Rabin believed Syria helped Hezbollah and radical factions in Lebanon who opposed PLO leader Arafat's accord with Israel. Nevertheless, Rabin hoped negotiations with Syria could solve problems in Lebanon and in Israel's occupation of the Golan Heights.

See January 16, 1994.

November 19, 1993

President Clinton meets Chinese leader Ziang Zemin in Seattle.

During the Asian-Pacific Economic Conference in Seattle, Washington, Clinton held a scheduled one-hour meeting with General Secretary Ziang Zemin, the first meeting of U.S and Chinese leaders since 1989. Although U.S.-Chinese relations had deteriorated during the first nine months of the Clinton administration, the president decided to improve them. First, there was a dialogue between U.S. and Chinese military leaders. Next, on November 18 Secretary of State Warren Christopher informed China's Foreign Minister Qian Qichen that the United States approved the sale of a high-tech super-computer to China as well as components for China's nuclear power plants, including generators China had ordered from General Electric Company. The supercomputer sale had been delayed because of U.S. sanctions levied against China. Clinton approved these sales as a gesture of goodwill before he met with Ziang Zemin in Seattle.

Clinton's session with the Chinese leader resulted in no significant agreements regarding differences with China on human rights, technology sales to Pakistan and Chinese trade restrictions. According to Clinton's Deputy Assistant Bowman Cutter, Ziang Zemin lectured Clinton for 15 minutes on not interfering in China's internal affairs (e.g., human rights). In response, Clinton said Americans were concerned about Chinese violations of human rights but that issue would not dominate U.S. relations with China. Generally, Clinton's meeting with China's leader resulted in better relations with China.

See August 25 and November 2, 1993; May 24, 1994.

November 20, 1993

Congress approves the North American Free Trade Agreement (NAFTA).

The Senate agreed to the NAFTA Treaty three days after approval by the House of Representatives. Beginning on January 8, 1993, when President-elect

President Clinton at the Asia-Pacific Economic Conference meeting in Seattle, Washington. White House

Clinton met with Mexican President Carlos Salinas de Gortari, the United States, Canada, and Mexico held frequent discussions about NAFTA amendments regarding labor costs, the environment, and human rights. On August 13, the three nations accepted changes involving labor relations and the environment that enabled Clinton to campaign for congressional approval. Supported by former U.S. Presidents Bush, Carter, and Ford, Clinton worked hard for NAFTA's approval. Clinton's biggest deal with House members was with Florida representatives, who received protection for the state's citrus fruits and vegetables. Among other deals, Clinton pleased great Plains states by limiting Canada's exports of durham wheat and Louisiana's sugar beet growers by limiting sugar imports. Leaders of U.S. labor unions worried about losing jobs to foreign workers, but Clinton did almost nothing to help them. The president hoped to repair relations with labor unions before the 1996 elections.

November 20, 1993

President Clinton hosts an Asian-Pacific Cooperation Conference.

President Clinton hosted a meeting of the Asian-Pacific Economic Cooperation group founded in 1990. During the week of November 20, Clinton described visions of future world trade that previous presidents had avoided. He said that the realities of global interdependence meant that creating a job for one worker in Seattle may require creating six jobs in Jakarta, Indonesia. Clinton proposed a Pacific Ocean free-trade zone.

See November 15, 1994.

November 23, 1993

Problems with North Korea are discussed by Presidents Clinton and South Korean Kim Young Sam.

Clinton and Kim Young Sam met to discuss common problems with North Korea. Kim was touring the United States to meet possible business investors before coming to Washington. He and Clinton discussed ways to persuade North Korean leader Kim Il Sung to permit inspections of nuclear sites and to discuss peaceful relations with South Korea.

See February 15, 1994.

November 23, 1993

Washington repeals sanctions levied against South Africa.

The United States repealed economic sanctions on South Africa because South African President F. W. de Klerk and African National Congress President Nelson Mandela took enormous strides toward ending apartheid and giving black people the same political rights as whites. Although some violence occurred between militant white supremacists and black radicals of the Inkatha Freedom Party, 20 different political parties drafted a multiracial constitution on August 20. On September 7, South Africa's white National Party agreed to share power with blacks on a transitional multiracial council to oversee April 1994 elections. On September 24, Mandela addressed the U.N. General Assembly, asking the international community to lift all economic sanctions from South Africa. On the same day, the U.S. Senate voted unanimously to repeal sanctions and President Clinton signed the measure on November 23.

See April 26, 1994.

November 29, 1993

Iraq allows U.N. inspectors to install surveillance cameras.

Iraq agreed to let U.N. inspectors place surveillance cameras in its military installations for long-term U.N. monitoring of Iraq's potential for manufacturing weapons of mass destruction. On June 10, Iraqi President Saddam Hussein resisted placing cameras at military sites, but chief U.N. inspector Rolf Ekeus and Iraqi Foreign Minister Tariq Aziz finally agreed cameras could be installed after technical details were worked out. Hussein approved these details on November 29, hoping the U.N. Security Council would lift economic sanctions levied against Iraq at the end of the 1991 war.

See April 14, 1994.

December 2, 1993

Colombian police kill a drug lord; President Clinton's antidrug program is not implemented.

Colombian police killed Pablo Escobar Gaviria, the notorious drug lord, after arresting or eliminating other drug traffickers. Nevertheless, the cocaine business was too profitable to vanish, and new drug lords took over by using bribes instead of bullets to keep cocaine flowing to the United States and other countries where there was a demand for drugs.

Although American prisons were filled with minor drug dealers, the demand for drugs never diminished. After becoming president, Clinton laid plans to emphasize drug rehabilitation and prevention but in 1993 did nothing to implement an antidrug policy.

December 2, 1993

Bosnian peace talks break down again.

Britain's Lord David Owen and Norway's Thorvald Stoltenberg revived peace talks on November 29, but they lasted only four days before adjourning. The talks focused on how much land Bosnian Serbs and Bosnian Muslims would occupy. The Serbs continued to reject proposals to relinquish land they had captured.

See February 9, 1994.

December 12, 1993

Rabin and Arafat delay transferring authority over Jericho and the Gaza Strip.

Although the transfer deadline was December 13, PLO leader Arafat recognized that the PLO could not guarantee the safety of Jewish settlers in Jericho and the Gaza Strip. On October 29, five members of Arafat's al-Fatah were arrested by Israeli police for killing Jewish settlers and on November 24 West Bank riots broke out and Israeli police wounded 37 Palestinians while dispersing demonstrators. Because Arafat understood Israeli Prime Minister Rabin's concern about transferring Jericho and the Gaza Strip, Rabin made a goodwill gesture by allowing the last 400 Palestinians deported in December 1992 to return to their homes.

See January 16, 1994.

December 12, 1993

Russians approve a new constitution but parties opposing President Yeltsin win elections.

In national elections, Russians approved a new constitution. Nationalists and former Communist depu-

ties won 35% of the votes for parliament. With President Clinton's backing, President Yeltsin focused on the approval of a new constitution to increase the Russian president's powers to issue decrees, veto legislation, and appoint government ministers. In early December, Clinton provided $2.5 billion in aid to Russia including funds to help Russia implement the START II nuclear reduction treaty. Clinton also praised Yeltsin for approving a Russian military doctrine based on a defensive posture that considered no nation an enemy of Russia.

See March 4, 1994.

December 12, 1993

Eduardo Frei is elected president of Chile.

The center-left coalition candidate Eduardo Frei was elected president of Chile with 58% of the votes. He defeated the right-wing candidate Arturo Alessandri. Frei replaced Patricio Alywn as president of Chile.

December 13, 1993

The United States and Kazakhstan agree on funds to dismantle nuclear weapons.

The United States and Kazakhstan signed an agreement for the United States to provide $84 million in economic aid to help Kazakhstan dismantle its nuclear arsenal. Kazakhstan would also sign the Nuclear Non-Proliferation Treaty to permit the International Atomic Energy Agency to inspect its nuclear facilities.

December 14, 1993

The Uruguay round of GATT is completed.

On December 14, the United States and the European Community (EC) reached a compromise that concluded the Uruguay round of GATT, begun in 1986. The key issue of agricultural subsidies between France and the United States was resolved by reducing agricultural tariffs by 3% in industrial nations and by 24% in developing nations. On average, the United States and the EC would reduce tariffs by 50% while other countries would decrease their tariffs by lower percentages.

See September 15, 1986; December 5, 1988; December 1, 1994.

December 15, 1993

Britain and Ireland agree on peace terms for Northern Ireland.

After Britain and Ireland agreed on peace negotiations in Northern Ireland, British Prime Minister Major offered the Irish Republican Army a role in the peace talks if it would stop its violence for three months.

See October 4, 1994.

1994

January 1, 1994

Mexican rebels seize Chiapas.

The Zapatista National Liberation Army (EZLN) seized four towns in the southeastern state of CHIAPAS, declaring war on the federal government. The government deployed heavily armed forces to recapture the town, forcing the guerrillas to flee to wooded mountain areas. On January 12, the two sides accepted a cease-fire to begin discussions about political reforms to give more representation in the Mexican government to people from southeastern states. On March 12, the government released 38 EZLN prisoners and promised EZLN delegates to create public works projects in Chiapas that would benefit the impoverished region. Other reforms were announced the next summer.

See August 21, 1994.

January 16, 1994

President Clinton and Syrian leader Assad discuss peace terms for the Golan Heights.

President Clinton met with President Hafiz al-Assad to discuss peace terms between Israel and Syria. Assad said he would negotiate on Israel's return of the Golan Heights but gave no specific terms. Assad also wanted to resolve the issue of Israeli troops in south Lebanon.

For four day in May 1994, Secretary of State Christopher engaged in shuttle diplomacy between Tel Aviv and Damascus but could not resolve the issues of the Golan Heights and Israeli troops in Lebanon.

See October 26, 1994.

January 28, 1994

President Clinton tries to clarify policies on U.S. peacekeeping missions.

President Clinton announced a policy for U.S. participation in international peacekeeping. The president would support peacekeeping for humanitarian or military purposes under three conditions: if the situation was urgent, if other countries joined, and if American troops were under U.S. command. Because critics said the president's 1993 foreign policy was inconsistent, Clinton's advisers hoped a policy statement would explain his approach to foreign affairs. In fact, Clinton's January 28 statements were ambiguous enough to perpetuate inconsistent foreign policies.

February 3, 1994

The United States ends its 19-year embargo on trade with Vietnam.

President Clinton ended the 19-year U.S. trade embargo on Vietnam that followed North Vietnam's conquest of Saigon (April 29, 1975). The president rewarded Vietnam for assistance in locating remains of U.S. soldiers who were missing in action after the war. Moreover, American investors' desire to do business in Vietnam was an important reason for the announcement.

See July 11, 1995.

February 9, 1994

Bosnian Serbs are given 10 days to remove their artillery from near Sarajevo or be bombed.

NATO gave the Bosnian Serbs 10 days to give UNPROFOR control of their heavy artillery surrounding Sarajevo or be bombed by NATO aircraft. At NATO's January 11 meeting in Brussels, NATO refused to warn Serbs about bombarding Sarajevo because Britain and France opposed President Clinton's request for an immediate air strike against the Serbs.

In February, after Serb mortar shells struck a Sarajevo marketplace and killed 69 Muslims, France joined Clinton in advocating NATO bombing to force Serbs to move artillery away from the city. Because British Prime Minister John Major objected to NATO's bombing, the United States and France compromised by giving the Serbs a 10-day ultimatum. Major and British General Sir Michael Rose, who commanded UNPROFOR troops near Sarajevo, used the 10 days to negotiate with Russia and Bosnia's Serbs.

British negotiations gave Serb President Radovan Karadžić a virtual victory. Karadžić lied to Rose, who accepted Karadžić's fallacious claim that Muslims, not Serbs, had bombed Sarajevo's market. Rose also accepted Karadžić's proposal to deploy UNPROFOR troops along a line partitioning Sarajevo between Serbs and Muslims, an important Serb objective. While Rose negotiated concessions acceptable to Karadžić, Major visited Moscow and accepted President Yeltsin's offer to deploy 400 Russian soldiers to observe Serb artillery in places that U.N. forces could not inspect.

The U.N. claim to be "neutral" between the two factions had in reality benefited Serb aggressors. With sympathetic Russians "observing" their activity, Serbs could bombard Sarajevo whenever they wished.

See February 28, 1994.

February 15, 1994

North Korea approves inspections of its nuclear sites, averting possible U.S. economic sanctions.

On February 4, the United States, Britain, France, and Russia ask China to persuade North Korea to permit the International Atomic Energy Agency (IAEA) to inspect its nuclear weapons sites. The four nations threatened economic sanctions against North Korea if it refused an inspection. On February 15, Kim Il Sung averted economic sanctions by permitting IAEA inspections of seven nuclear sites to determine if North Korea violated the Nuclear Non-Proliferation Treaty by using high-grade plutonium to develop nuclear weapons.

Two weeks later, the IAEA began inspections, but on March 15 North Korea blocked them by interfering with tests to reveal how much weapons-grade plutonium was produced. Because North Korea did not comply with the IAEA inspections, President Clinton cancelled talks with its officials and considered asking for U.N. economic sanctions against the regime.

See August 10, 1994.

February 22, 1994

A CIA officer is arrested for selling data to the Soviet Union and Russia.

Aldrich Ames, a CIA counterintelligence officer, was arrested for selling secret information to the Soviet Union and Russia. After the Federal Bureau of Investigation arrested Ames, they portrayed him as the worst traitor in FBI history. Before letting the FBI investigate Ames, the CIA bureaucracy botched the job of discovering Ames's espionage, which began in 1985. Ames betrayed 11 Russians, 9 of them Soviet agents of the KGB or GRUS who worked for the United States. Not only were 10 of these agents executed in 1986 but Ames's illegal activity also damaged the CIA's entire espionage system. On April 26, Ames pleaded guilty and was sentenced to life in prison. His wife, Rosario, pleaded guilty to lesser charges and was sentenced to prison for six years. The CIA's reputation was damaged and many Americans wondered whether espionage was vital to the nation's security.

February 24, 1994

The last Contra rebels disarm.

The Contras fought Nicaragua's Sandinista government during the 1980s as part of the "freedom fighters" supported by President Reagan, and they were implicated in the Iran-Contra scandal.

See September 1, 1984.

February 28, 1994

NATO aircraft shoot down four Bosnian Serb aircraft; Croats and Muslims form a federation.

NATO fighter aircraft shot down four Bosnian Serb ground attack planes violating the U.N. no-fly zone over Bihać. The action was NATO's first combat attack in 45 years. The NATO attack became a precedent for future attacks on Serbs violating no-fly or safe-area zones on April 10, May 24, August 5, and November 21, 1994.

The February 28 attack came a week after NATO withdrew its threat to bomb the Bosnian Serbs who moved their artillery far enough from Sarajevo to permit supplies to reach the city. The Serbs' constant threat to Sarajevo also inspired Bosnia's Muslims and Croats to unite against the Serbs. On February 23, Bosnia's Croats and Muslims signed a cease-fire mediated by the United States as well as a

Washington Framework Agreement as the basis for a joint constitution. This Framework Agreement was finalized in Washington on March 18, when Croat and Muslim leaders signed the constitution to unite them in a loose federation. U.S. mediation ended a Croat-Muslim war and united both groups against the Serbs. Representatives of the Republic of Croatia attended the Washington meeting to sign trade agreements. The new federation army also cooperated in fighting the Bosnian Serbs.

See April 10, 1994.

March 4, 1994

The United States doubles aid to Ukraine for its reforms and nuclear disarmament.

By allocating $700 million to Ukraine, President Clinton doubled the amount given in 1993. The aid was contingent on Ukraine's continuing economic reforms and total nuclear disarmament. Having already transferred 60 tactical nuclear warheads to Russia for dismantling, Ukraine's remaining 1,540 warheads were to be transferred by the end of 1994. From March 17 to 23, U.S. Defense Secretary William Perry inspected the dismantling of nuclear warheads in Ukraine, Kazakhstan, Belarus, and Russia.

March 26, 1994

OPEC retains its current oil quotas.

Although oil prices had fallen and some OPEC members wanted production to increase, OPEC decided to maintain the overall production ceiling established in 1993.

April 10, 1994

NATO bombing of Serb forces causes dissent among UNPROFOR leaders in Bosnia.

On April 10, U.N. monitors in the "safe area" of Goražde appealed for help after Serbs began an offensive near Goražde on March 29 and escalated artillery fire on the city in April. To provide help, UNPROFOR commander Rose ordered two U.S. Air Force F-16 aircraft under NATO command to bomb Serb artillery and tanks near Goražde. On April 11, when the Serb attacks continued, Rose had two U.S. Marine F/A-8 Hornets drop three more bombs.

These minor NATO raids caused dissent between NATO and U.N. officials. Yasushi Akashi, the U.N.

Secretary General's Special Representative in Bosnia, opposed NATO raids because they were not "neutral" toward the Serbs, a perspective allowing Serb General Mladić to break promises and launch offensive attacks whenever he wished. Despite the two NATO raids, Mladić's forces captured the strategic heights overlooking Goražde and could take over the city whenever they desired. As in the Bihać crisis of 1993, President Clinton urged NATO to bypass the United Nations and protect the "safe area" but Clinton refused to send American troops as part of UNPROFOR until peace terms were accepted.

See May 13, 1994.

April 14, 1994

U.S. Air Force planes mistakenly shoot down a U.S. helicopter.

Two Air Force F-15 planes mistakenly shot down two U.S. army helicopters carrying U.N. officials on a humanitarian mission to help Kurdish tribes in northern Iraq. In the helicopter crash, 26 U.N. aid officials and workers were killed, including 15 Americans.

In part, this event was linked to tensions raised on March 18 when Iraq sent Republican Guard units to the northern border of the Kurdish no-fly zone. Observers assumed President Saddam Hussein was demonstrating anger toward the United Nations for refusing to abolish economic sanctions levied on Iraq in 1991.

In August 1994, the U.S. air force charged the combat pilots with negligent homicide pending an investigation to decide if a court-martial should be held. The air force also charged five crew members of an AWAC radar plane with dereliction of duty for not informing the combat pilots that a U.S. helicopter was in the area. On June 20, 1995, a court-martial exonerated Air Force Captain Jim Wang, who had been charged with negligence for shooting down the helicopter.

See October 16, 1994.

April 24, 1994

El Salvador's ruling party keeps control of the National Assembly.

In El Salvador's runoff elections, Armando Calderón Sol of the ruling Nationalist Republic Alliance (Arena) was elected president and his right-wing coalition kept control of the National Assembly. The leftist

Farabundo Marti National Liberation Front and two other leftist parties received 22 seats in the 84-seat assembly.

April 26, 1994

The African National Congress Party wins control of South Africa's government.

On April 26, the day South Africa's new constitution and bill of rights went into effect, South Africa's polling places opened. When voting ended on April 29, the election resulted in a landslide victory for Nelson Mandela's African National Congress Party. Mandela was inaugurated president on May 10, 1994.

April 30, 1994

President Clinton ends restriction on arms sales to Taiwan.

President Clinton ended limits on selling armaments and aircraft to Taiwan, a restriction made 12 years earlier when President Reagan signed an agreement with the People's Republic of China regarding relations with Taiwan.

On September 8, the new arms policy was followed by a State Department announcement that U.S. policy toward Taiwan "is committed to maintaining commercial, cultural and other contacts" with the people of Taiwan. Beijing denounced this statement of U.S. policy. Although China and Taiwan signed an accord on August 8 to resolve their disputes on fishing rights and patrol boats in the Straits of Taiwan, China still claimed that Taiwan was an integral part of China.

See August 16, 1982.

May 4, 1994

Israel renews talks with Palestinians, delayed because of the Hebron massacres.

PLO-Israeli negotiations broke off in February after a Jewish settler in Hebron entered a mosque and used an automatic rifle to kill 29 and wound 150 Palestinian worshippers. Although the Israeli government reported that the settler, Baruch Goldstein, acted alone, Palestinians and Israeli police clashed in Hebron, during which 10 Palestinians and 1 Israeli were killed. President Clinton denounced Goldstein's action and urged the PLO and Israel to renew their peace talks despite the gross act of a murderer.

Negotiations resumed after Israel took measures to disarm violence-prone Jewish settlers and outlaw the anti-Arab Kach and Kahane Chai groups as terrorists. Although the Palestinian Hamas group continued harassing Israeli police and soldiers, on April 12 Israeli and Palestinian negotiators agreed on terms for the deployment of Palestine police and the release of 500 Palestinian prisoners held by Israel.

On May 4, Israeli Prime Minister Rabin and Palestine National Authority (PNA) Chairman Arafat agreed on methods to establish the PNA in the Gaza Strip and Jericho. On July 1, Arafat crossed the border from Egypt to Gaza to establish PNA headquarters. On July 5, Arafat visited Jericho, where he appointed 12 members of a PNA Council.

See November 8, 1994.

May 13, 1994

The five-member Contact Group offers plans for peace and a cease-fire in Bosnia.

Diplomats from the United States, Russia, Britain, France, and Germany issued a peace proposal for Bosnia, asking combatants to accept a cease-fire while discussing the plan. Known as the Contact Group, foreign ministers of these five nations offered to give the Federation of Bosnia and Croatia 51% and Bosnian Serbs 49% of Bosnia and Herzegovina's land. Although the Serbs made up 32% of Bosnia's population before the war, they controlled 70% of the land and would need to withdraw from 21% of those holdings. A cease-fire was signed on June 8 but provided no enforcement methods except by UNPROFOR troops in Bosnia.

See August 4, 1994.

May 14, 1994

Abkhazia and Georgia sign a second cease-fire in Moscow.

On January 13, 1994, U.N. mediators obtained a cease-fire between the Republic of Georgia and the secessionist region of Abkhazia, but the cease-fire fell through. On February 23, Georgian President Shevardnadze and Russian President Yeltsin agreed that former Soviet military bases in Georgia would be under Russian control because Georgia had joined the Commonwealth of Independent States (CIS) in

October 1993. As a result, Russian troops joined the Georgian army to fight the rebels, a decision that persuaded the rebels to negotiate in Moscow, where delegates from Georgia and the secessionist-minded Abkhazians signed a cease-fire. Under its terms, 3,000 CIS troops would deploy as peacekeepers along the Inguri River separating Abkhazia from Georgia proper.

May 24, 1994

The United States and Japan reach a basis for bilateral trade negotiations.

Although trade talks with Japan collapsed in February, on May 24 Japan agreed to interpret its open-market program by both "qualitative and quantitative" standards, and the United States agreed not to insist on specific numerical access for its import guarantees. By October 1, 1994, Japan agreed to open its markets to foreign competition in insurance, flat glass, and telecommunications and medical equipment.

See June 28, 1995.

May 26, 1994

President Clinton renews China's most-favored-nation trade status.

In announcing the renewal of China's MFN, Clinton indicated that the United States would no longer link trade relations to China's human rights progress. U.S. human rights advocates criticized Clinton's new position. Despite China's human rights violations, Clinton argued that by maintaining trade relations the United States had leverage regarding various U.S.-Chinese problems.

See June 2, 1995.

June 8, 1994

President Clinton agrees to help the U.N. humanitarian mission in Rwanda.

President Clinton's decision regarding Rwanda was made when the killing of Hutus and Tutsi was in progress. On April 6, 1994, the airplane carrying Rwanda President Juvenal Habyarimanna was shot down, killing everyone on board. No one knew who shot the plane down but Habyarimanna's death signaled twelve weeks of Hutus and Tutsi being killed in Rwanda and neighboring Burundi. After the plane crash, the ruling Hutu government blamed the Tutsi for shooting down the plane. To punish Tutsi for killing the president, ruling Hutu militiamen and the Presidential Guard set up roadblocks around Kigali, the nation's capital, and began murdering all Tutsi who passed along the roadway. Soon after the plane crash, other Hutu not only killed Tutsi but also hunted down and killed moderate Hutu who opposed President Habyarimanna. Other Hutu militia captured 10 Belgian soldiers who protected some Tutsi. After capturing them, the Hutu took the Belgians to a camp outside Kigali where they tortured and killed the soldiers before mutilating their dead bodies. Other Hutu gangs detained Tutsi women and children before hacking them to death. Hutu gangs also attacked Tutsi families, especially killing Tutsi men and boys.

The Rwanda conflict led Belgium to remove its soldiers from Rwanda. The U.N. Assistance Mission to Rwanda also left. In contrast, France helped Tutsi by sending arms and ammunition to the Tutsi Rwanda Patriots Front. Skilled fighters when they had the necessary equipment, the Tutsi rebels fought their way toward Kigali, killing any Hutu they found. By mid-June 1994, the Rwanda Patriots Front captured Kigali while other Tutsi swept through Rwanda, killing any Hutu who had not already fled for refuge to Zaire, Burundi, or Tanzania.

With the thousands of killings and tens of thousands of people seeking refuge, President Clinton changed his mind on June 8, saying the United States would support the U.N. mission because Rwanda's conflict had reached genocidal proportions. Under a U.N. resolution Clinton sent armored personnel carriers to Rwanda, but all U.N. troops were from France and African states sent by the Organization of African Unity. After French-led forces obtained a cease-fire in July, Clinton sent 200 American soldiers to open Rwanda's airport for aircraft bringing food and medical supplies needed to combat a cholera epidemic. He sent another 2,000 Americans to Goma, Zaire, whose airport was the main entry point for U.N. refugee supplies.

See April 18, 1995.

June 23, 1994

The U.N. General Assembly readmits South Africa.

South Africa was readmitted to the General Assembly after being suspended for 20 years because of its apartheid policy. The U.N. action followed Nelson

Mandela's election as president of South Africa on May 10. Mandela replaced F.W. de Klerk, who had negotiated with Mandela and the African National Congress in preparing a South African constitution and bill of rights that became effective on April 26, 1994.

July 7, 1994

Cambodia's assembly outlaws the Khmer Rouge.

On March 25, 1994, Cambodia's army had captured Pailin, the headquarters of the Khmer Rouge guerrilla movement formed during the 1970s by Pol Pot who had recently died. But one month later (April 24), the Khmer regained control of Pailin. Because the Khmer Rouge refused the cease-fire and peace terms that the United Nations Mission to Cambodia offered, Cambodia's National Assembly voted on July 7, 1994 to outlaw the Khmer Rouge.

July 10, 1994

In Belarus, Aleksandr Lukashenko wins the presidential election by a wide margin.

A former Soviet republic, Belarus prepared a constitution in 1991 to create a democratic government. By 1994, many politicians used their position to depress the economy by siphoning government funds into Swiss bank accounts. The corruption was first exposed on January 26, 1994, when the Belarus House of Representatives voted to dismiss Prime Minister Stanislaus Shushkevich on charges of corruption. Although the Belarus prime minister retained his office, the corruption charges paved the way for Aleksandr Lukashenko to be elected.

In the first round of presidential elections, Lukashenko won 45% of the vote, but in the runoff election he received over 80%. The new president had pledged to remove all corrupt officials. Immediately after his election, he abolished the free press and took charge of other communications media, claiming dissent impeded his ability to deal with corruption. Subsequently, he renationalized the banking system, saying bank officials robbed the people. Lukashenko gradually re-created a communist-style dictatorship in Belarus.

See November 24, 1996.

July 25, 1994

Israel and Jordan agree to end their state of war.

In Washington, Jordanian King Hussein and Israeli Prime Minister Rabin signed a declaration to end their state of war, which began in 1948. Presiding over the signing, President Clinton said the United States would help Jordan ease its $7 billion debt and continue supporting Israel's security requirements. King Hussein also spoke to a joint session of the U.S. Congress, saying Jordan was "ready to open a new era of our relations with Israel." Rabin told Congress he was "a soldier in the army of peace." On August 3, when Israel's Knesset (parliament) voted in favor of the Washington Declaration, members of the Likud Party joined with Rabin's Labor Party in endorsing the Declaration.

See October 26, 1994.

July 31, 1994

The U.N. Security Council approves a resolution for U.S.-led forces to intervene in Haiti.

The U.N. Security Council approved Resolution 940 for the U.S.-led multinational force to intervene in Haiti and restore Jean-Bertrad Aristide as Haiti's president. The vote was unanimous, with Brazil and China abstaining.

The council action resulted from cooperation with President Clinton that began on May 6, 1994, in tightening an embargo on Haiti to relieve the problem of Haitian refugees and persuade Haiti's military junta to restore democracy. After Aristide's overthrow in September 1991, Haitians continued seeking asylum in the United States because the junta terrorized them. As investigative reporters disclosed, the terror was not only from the Tontons Macoutes, who preferred the Duvalier family that ruled Haiti until 1986 when Jean-Claude Duvalier was overthrown as President of Haiti (see February 7, 1986), but also from the CIA-backed Front for the Advancement and Progress in Haiti (FRAPH). In December 1993, FRAPH members attacked Port-au Prince's largest slum area, Cite Soleil, inhabited by many Aristide supporters. FRAPH members killed at least 70 residents and burned down 1,000 shacks, leaving 10,000 people homeless.

Jordan's King Hussein meets with Secretary of State Warren Christopher, with President Clinton in background, in Washington, D.C. White House

After Haiti's current leader Colonel Raoul Cedras ignored the U.N. resolution, on June 8 Clinton canceled U.S. commercial air flights to Haiti and froze all Haitian bank accounts in the United States. To support Clinton, Canada and France canceled Haitian air flights—the former hurt the most as Paris was a favorite destination for Haiti's wealthy. These steps set the stage for U.S.-led multinational intervention in Haiti.

See September 19, 1994.

August 4, 1994

Yugoslavia severs economic and political ties to the Bosnian Serbs.

After the Contact Group achieved a cease-fire in Bosnia on June 8, delegates from the Bosnian Federation (Croats and Muslims) and Bosnian Serbs were given a map showing the 51-49 division of territory. Muslim President Izetbegović accepted the plan because the 51% provided better terms for the federation than the 1993 Vance-Owen plan. To the contrary, Bosnian Serb President Karadžić insisted on changes, telling the Contact Group, "There won't be a single Serb who would accept this." Although

Russia's Foreign Minister, Vitaly Churkin was a member of the Contact Group, Karadžić called the plan an "American *diktat*."

Karadžić was wrong about "all Serbs" because Serbian President Slobodan Milošević wanted Karadžić to accept the proposal. On August 3, Karadžić formally rejected the plan unless a referendum in the Serbian Republic approved it. The next day, Milošević announced Yugoslavia would sever all economic and political ties with the Serbian Republic. Milošević also permitted international inspectors to be stationed on Yugoslavia's border with Bosnia-Herzegovina to see that fuel and military supplies did not cross into Bosnia. Immediately after, Karadžić ended the cease-fire by ordering Boznian Serb forces to attack Muslims and Croats and to cut off natural gas, electricity, and water intended for Sarajevo.

Because of Milošević's cooperation, the Contact Group asked the U.N. Security Council to lift some economic sanctions from Yugoslavia. The Contact Group tightened sanctions on the Serbian Republic and barred its leaders from political contacts outside of Serbia and foreign travel.

See May 13 and November 22, 1994.

August 9, 1994

The United States refuses to deliver fighter aircraft to Pakistan.

President Clinton announced the United States would not sell Pakistan the 38 F-16 fighter planes as previously scheduled. The State Department said Pakistan continued developing nuclear weapons and would not negotiate with India on peaceful solutions to their Kashmir dispute. Pakistan claimed its nuclear weapons and ballistic missiles were intended to deter an attack by India.

See March 8, 1995.

August 10, 1994

The United States reaches an agreement with North Korea to inspect its nuclear facilities.

Although in March 1994, President Clinton threatened to ask the U.N. Security Council to place economic sanctions on North Korea, he decided first to pursue new high-level talks with Kim Il Sung, and negotiators reached a tentative agreement for another International Atomic Energy Agency (IAEA) inspection of North Korea's nuclear facilities. Discussions broke down in April, but on June 15, former President Carter visited Kim Il Sung, who agreed to renew discussions. Owing to Kim Il Sung's death on July 8, talks were delayed until his son and successor, Kim Jong Il, selected delegates to negotiate the August 10 pact. Under the agreement, North Korea would permit IAEA inspections and retain membership in the Nuclear Non-Proliferation Treaty. The United States would give North Korea financial and technical assistance to build two light-water nuclear reactors for peaceful uses and provide security guarantees against a nuclear attack on North Korea.

On August 15, South Korean President Kim Young Sam announced his country would give North Korea financial and technical assistance. In October, North Korea accepted a 10-year timetable to transform its nuclear facilities into peaceful uses and to permit international inspections of them.

See December 17, 1994.

August 21, 1994

Election confirms the continued rule of Mexico's PRI.

The U.S. House of Representatives became involved in Mexico's election by approving a House resolution to send selected American observers to monitor Mexico's August 1994 election. Many members of the House who voted for the North American Free Trade Agreement (NAFTA) in 1993 (see November 30, 1993) wanted to ascertain the value of Mexico's election reforms. The observers' concerns were whether or not the reforms allowed Mexican political parties opposing the reigning PRI Party to have adequate access to the public media during the election campaign and if they found any corrupt practices at the ballot boxes on election day. After Zedillo was elected president and the PRI retained control of Mexico's Senate and Chamber of Deputies, the observers sent by the U.S. House reported the elections were fair and free. However, news reports indicated the PRI's antipoverty program subsidized schools for poor children and distributed checks to small farmers to persuade many working-class people to vote for the PRI. Rebels in Chiapas province complained that the elections were fraudulent, but after discussions with PRI officials, the rebels accepted the governor elected for Chiapas.

See January 31, 1995.

September 9, 1994

The United States and Cuba agree on the number of Cubans to enter the United States.

Havana agreed that in exchange for the U.S. admitting a minimum of 20,000 Cubans each year, Cuba would prevent its citizens from fleeing by sea to the United States. In addition, 30,000 Cubans held by the United States in Guántanamo or Panama could remain where they were or return to Cuba but could not go to the U.S. mainland.

Prior to the agreement on August 19, Clinton ordered the Coast Guard to detain at Guantánamo's naval base over 2,000 Cubans who had fled on rafts and small boats seeking refuge in the United States.

Clinton also stopped payments that Cuban Americans sent to relatives in Cuba. The president's tough new policies resulted in talks with Castro's government and the September 9 agreement ended previous U.S. policy that allowed all Cuban refugees to take residence in the U.S. excepting undesirable Cubans. Clinton's action was influenced by U.S. policy on Haiti's refugees, who were seldom allowed to become residents.

See May 2, 1995.

September 19, 1994

General Cedras cooperates with U.S.-led forces arriving in Haiti.

American soldiers arriving in Haiti met no resistance because Haitian General Raol Cedras cooperated with the U.S.-led multinational force. Following President Clinton's announcement on September 14 that U.S. forces were ready to invade Haiti to restore President Jean-Bertrand Aristide, Cedras negotiated with three envoys: former President Jimmy Carter, retired General Colin Powell, and Senator Sam Nunn (D-Ga.). Clinton gave Cedras 48 hours to accept surrender terms or be attacked. At the last moment, Cedras and Haitian Army Chief of Staff Philippe Biamby accepted the pact offered by the three U.S. envoys. Haiti's acting President Emile Jonassaint signed an agreement requiring Cedras and Biamby to resign and leave Haiti. After the landing of multinational forces, Haiti prepared for Aristide's return on October 15.

The night of September 18–19, U.S. Marines and paratroop units took control of the Port-au-Prince docking facilities and airport before the other soldiers arrived from the United States, other Western Hemisphere nations, and France who joined with U.N. civilian personnel to restore Aristide as Haiti's democratically elected president.

Although crowds of Haitians cheered when U.S. forces arrived, Haitians favoring Aristide's return continued to be abused or killed because Haiti's notorious Police Chief Michael François rejected President Jonassaint's agreement. To combat the abuses, President Clinton ordered U.S. troops to use their weapons against any Haitians who used "unreasonable force" against local citizens. This enabled marines to confiscate weapons of Haitian police units and crack down on François, who fled to the Dominican Republic. The marines' worst conflict was at Haitian's second largest city, Cap-Haitien, where 10 militants opposing Aristide were killed. The multinational force secured Haiti's principal areas by October 15 and Aristide returned to complete his term of office, which would expire in early 1996.

See October 15, 1994.

September 20, 1994

After President Clinton's U.N. speech asks for strong measures to help Sarajevo, he meets Russian President Yeltsin to discuss nuclear weapons.

President Clinton's speech to the U.N. General Assembly warned about the dangers of the Serb siege of Sarajevo and called for U.N. peacekeeping measures to include the use of force when necessary. His message on Bosnia had little influence because he refused to support U.N. "peacekeeping" operations, except for sending food and medicine to Sarajevo, and deploying U.S. aircraft as part of NATO's mission to patrol no-fly zones. During the same assembly session, Russian President Boris Yeltsin emphasized the need to restrict the production of nuclear weapons and to ban nuclear testing.

Following their assembly speeches, Presidents Clinton and Yeltsin met in Washington, D.C., for two days and signed a "partnership for economic progress" regarding U.S. trade and investments in Russia that could total $1 billion. Clinton and Yeltsin also discussed ways to speed up implementation of the START II, signed on January 3, 1993.

See November 22, 1994.

September 30, 1994

The U.S. budget for fiscal 1995 includes $243 billion for military activities.

For fiscal year 1995, Congress appropriated $243.7 billion for all military activities. Congress approved the Department of Defense funds proposed by the Clinton administration that cut Pentagon funds from $1.7 to $1.4 billion. Clinton's plan kept President Bush's basic strategy for armed forces capable of winning two regional wars at one time. It cut Pentagon funds in each branch of the armed services by $1.7 billion to $1.4 billion over five years, a plan approved by both Secretary of Defense Les Aspin and Chairman of the Joint Chiefs General Colin Powell. The budget also appropriated $13.8 billion for foreign aid and $27.7 billion for the State, Commerce, and Treasury Departments.

The budget also added $2.7 billion to the Ballistic Missile Defense Office (BMDO), which was expected to receive a total of $50 billion by 2010.

October 4, 1994

President Clinton tries to revive peace talks between Britain and the Irish Republican Army (IRA).

By having IRA leader Gerry Adams meet with State Department officials, President Clinton hoped to revive peace talks between Adams and Britain. On August 31, the IRA announced a cease-fire in Northern Ireland, but British Prime Minister Major said negotiations would begin only if the IRA accepted a permanent cease-fire. On October 4, Clinton praised the IRA's cease-fire as a "promise of peace for all the people of Ireland." Clinton also abolished the 20-year U.S. ban on contacts with Sinn Fein, the IRA's political wing. Clinton's decisions permitted Sinn Fein leader Adams to enter the United States to discuss Ireland's future with the State Department. Following Adams's visit, he accepted Britain's cease-fire terms, and on December 9 British and IRA delegates opened peace talks.

See March 16, 1995.

October 15, 1994

Haitian President Aristide returns but lacks the power he had before the 1991 coup.

As scheduled by the September 18 agreement, President Aristide returned to Port-au-Prince but realized he lacked the authority he had before the coup of 1991. U.S. Defense Department officials had rejected Aristide's demand to disarm all Haiti's army as well as the militant Tontons Macoutes and CIA-supported Front for the Advancement and Progress of Haiti (FRAPH), whose members hid in jungles and mountains to terrorize Haitians who favored Aristide.

In November 1994, Aristide reduced the size of Haiti's army and over 5,000 soldiers lost their jobs; many had difficulty finding employment on an island with high rates of unemployment. The veterans also lost their severance pay and army pensions because the former Haitian leader Raol Cedras transferred the army's funds to foreign banks before destroying Ministry of Defense records. In December 1994 after

unemployed soldiers rioted, the United States and the United Nations appropriated funds to train soldiers for other jobs, but future employment opportunities remained scarce. Aristide also faced financial problems after international bankers withheld funds they had promised because Haiti lacked the domestic security bankers required.

See June 25, 1995.

October 16, 1994

Following extensive U.N. and U.S. actions, Saddam Hussein withdraws Iraqi soldiers from the Kuwait borders.

Iraqi President Hussein had caused trouble with the United Nations and United States throughout 1994. On March 18, Iraq relocated Republican Guard troops to within 20 miles of Kuwait's border. On July 18, after the U.N. Security Council rejected Iraq's demand to abolish economic sanctions, Hussein deployed more troops near the Iraqi city of Basra, 40 miles from Kuwait.

On October 12, after President Clinton learned Iraq had sent 20,000 Republican Guards toward Basra, he ordered U.S. navy and marine forces to move to the Persian Gulf. At the same time, Secretary of State Christopher met with members of the Gulf Cooperation Council (GCC) to gain support for the U.S. decision. The GCC offered to pay the cost of the U.S. deployment. On October 15, the Security Council condemned Iraq's deployment and told it to remove its troops from the Basra region. With the 1991 alliance rallying against Iraq, President Hussein surrendered the next day by moving the Republican Guards back to bases near Baghdad. On November 14, the Security Council refused to lift Iraq's sanctions.

See February 23, 1996.

October 26, 1994

President Clinton oversees the signing of an Israeli-Jordanian peace.

Clinton's first stop on a Middle East tour was in Tel Aviv, Israel, where he witnessed Israeli and Jordanian leaders sign a peace treaty evolved from the Israel-Jordan-Washington Declaration. The treaty resolved territorial disputes, delineated water rights, and renewed full diplomatic relations between these neighbors.

After the treaty signing, Clinton continued his tour of the Middle East to demonstrate the U.S. commitment to peace in the region. In Jordan he discussed a regional economic plan with King Hussein, flew to Damascus to encourage Syria to negotiate with Israel regarding the Golan Heights, gave a talk to U.S. forces in Kuwait, and met with King Fahd of Saudi Arabia. While Clinton sought peace on his tour, the radical Islamic Hamas protested on the West Bank and in Lebanon.

See July 25 and November 8, 1994.

November 8, 1994

In midterm elections, Republicans gain control of both houses of Congress.

The Republican Party gained control of Congress for the first time since 1954. Their victory in the House of Representatives was most significant because they had had a Senate majority several times since the 1950s. As a result of the elections, Newt Gingrich (R-Ga.) became speaker of the House in January 1995, obtaining this post because former Republican minority leader Robert Michel retired from Congress after 40 years. Michel excelled as a consensus builder, but Gingrich and other Republic candidates campaigned on the controversial "Contract with America." The "contract" sought term limits and a balanced budget amendment but advocated isolationist foreign policies including an enhanced defense for the United States—meaning a SDI system that would violate the 1972 ABM treaty. Such a system would repudiate Defense Secretary Aspin's theater defense system and resemble those proposed by Presidents Reagan and Bush.

See September 30, 1993.

November 8, 1994

Israeli Prime Minister Rabin and PNA leader Arafat try to restrict protests of Islamic militants.

Following violence committed by a terrorist Hamas brigade that killed 21 Israeli civilians in October, Rabin agreed to help Yasser Arafat's Palestine National Authority (PNA) strengthen its position to overcome violence by Hamas and other Islamic militants. Rabin expanded PNA authority over education, health, social welfare, tourism, and taxation in the West Bank and Gaza Strip and issued 90,000 permits to Palestinians for jobs in Israel.

In return for Rabin's aid, Arafat agreed to deal severely with Hamas and other Islamic radicals who attacked Israeli police or committed violence in the West Bank or Gaza. On November 18, PNA police opened fire on Hamas demonstrators in Gaza City, killing 13 and wounding about 150. Each side blamed the other for the violence but Arafat placated Hamas by freeing 31 militants from prison. Rabin also sent more Israeli forces to protect Jewish settlements in Gaza and the West Bank.

On October 14, Norway announced that Rabin, Arafat, and Israeli Foreign Minister Shimon Peres were awarded the Nobel Peace Prize, an event overshadowed by violence in Israel and the West Bank.

See September 28, 1995.

November 15, 1994

During an Asian-Pacific meeting the United States and Indonesia quarrel over human rights.

An Asian Pacific Economic Cooperation Forum meeting in Jakarta was highlighted by a public dispute between U.S. and Indonesian delegates who quarreled over Indonesia's human rights violations, especially in East Timor. Other issues at the meeting were less controversial, and the delegates agreed to establish free-trade conditions among members by 2020.

November 21, 1994

NATO's limited bombing campaign fails to stop Bosnian Serb aggression.

NATO aircraft bombed Serb-controlled air bases in Croatia to alleviate the Serb army's siege of Bihać. Although in August, Yugoslavia stopped shipments of fuel and military supplies to Bosnian Serbs, the Yugoslav Army secretly helped Bosnian Serb General Ratko Mladić's army launch an offensive against the Bosnian Muslim-Croat Federation. Under Mladić, Serb forces regained territory lost to the Muslims and Croats in October before attacking Bihać, a city the U.N. had designated as a "safe area" in 1993. After Serbs used an air base in Croatia's Krajina region to send combat planes against Bihać, the U.N. Security Council condemned the attack on November 11, warning the Serbs to withdraw from the "safe area." The Serbs ignored the warning and on November 19 the council approved NATO's bombing of the Serbs' base in Croatia.

After Serb planes bombed Bihać for two more days, 50 NATO aircraft from the United States, Britain, France, and the Netherlands raided the Serbs' air base, destroying a runway and antiaircraft installations. Nevertheless, Mladić's artillery continued shelling Bihać and on November 23 NATO planes attacked Serb surface-to-air missile sites.

To counteract the NATO air raids, Mladić's army took 300 UNPROFOR troops hostage as human shields around Serb military installations. Mladić's move brought an end to NATO's attacks because Britain and France objected. Although, U.S. President Clinton wanted to continue the air raids, the Europeans were upset because he refused to have U.S. ground troops join UNPROFOR. On November 28, Clinton stopped talking about bombing the Serbs, accepting French and British views to preserve NATO unity. Having defied NATO and the United Nations, the Bosnian Serbs continued attacking Bihać.

See December 1, 1994.

November 22, 1994

President Clinton praises Ukrainian President Kuchma for reforms and abolishing nuclear weapons.

During a White House meeting, Clinton praised President Leonid Kuchma for Ukraine's free-market reforms and willingness to eliminate nuclear weapons as part of the strategic arms reduction treaties (START I and START II). Clinton also informed Kuchma that the United States would provide Ukraine with an additional $200 million in aid. After Kuchma returned home, Ukraine's Parliament voted to make the nation nuclear free and to carry out both START I and START II.

November 23, 1994

U.S. transfers uranium from Kazakhstan to U.S. facilities.

The United States completed the transfer of over 1,300 pounds of weapons-grade uranium from a nuclear plant in Kazakhstan to U.S. storage facilities. Called Project Sapphire, the operation was secret because U.S. officials believed the uranium was vulnerable to theft by terrorists or black marketeers.

December 1, 1994

The Senate ratifies the World Trade Treaty.

The U.S. Senate ratified the GATT world trade treaty by a vote of 76 to 24 after the House approved it on November 29. Signed in 1993 after years of negotiation, the GATT agreement among 124 nations also created the World Trade Organization (WTO).

December 1, 1994

During a NATO meeting, the United States seeks to separate Bosnian problems from NATO unity issues.

U.S. Secretary of State Christopher opened a session of the North Atlantic Council in Brussels by "delinking" the U.N. problems in Bosnia from other important NATO issues, including the partnership for peace program with Eastern European countries desiring to join NATO. In November, the United States differed with its NATO allies about bombing Bihać, a city in northwestern Bosnia, and on Clinton's November 10 decision to stop enforcing Bosnia's arms embargo. (On Bihać, see December 24, 1994.)

Pushing aside NATO's internal disagreements, Christopher emphasized the enlargement of NATO membership. NATO's "partnership" program invited states such as Poland, Hungary, the Czech Republic, and Slovenia to become NATO members in 1999. Christopher expected Russia's foreign minister to sign the "partnership" agreement but Russia refused to sign on December 1. In March 1995, Russian President Yeltsin signed the partnership plan.

See September 28, 1995.

December 9, 1994

President Yeltsin orders "all measures available" to disarm Chechen rebels.

From 1991 to 1994, Moscow opposed Chechnya's efforts to become a sovereign partner in a greater Russian federation rather than its status as an autonomous republic. Led by Jokar Dudayev, who called himself "president," Chechnya acted as an independent state with its principal income coming from smuggling and other criminal activity. Chechnya's principal value to Russia was the possession of a pipeline carrying oil to Russia from the Caspian Sea.

In 1994, Yeltsin sought to overthrow Dudayev by having Doker Zavgaev, the local Communist Party leader, oust Dudayev. This attempt failed and in November Russian generals persuaded Yeltsin the army could easily take control of Chechnya as the Americans had gained control of Haiti, an irrelevant analogy. Yeltsin accepted their recommendation and on December 9, ordering Russian forces to seal Chechnya's borders and airspace, he set a deadline of December 17 for Dudayev to disarm his army and recognize Russian sovereignty. Dudayev did not respond and Russian jets began bombing the capital city, Grozny. On December 27, the Russian army invaded Chechnya.

See January 20, 1995.

December 10, 1994

Western Hemisphere nations will negotiate a free-trade zone.

Hoping to expand the North American Free-Trade Area, President Clinton conducted a summit of 33 Western Hemispheric nations. Clinton called the meeting the start of a "true partnership for prosperity." The delegates agreed to develop a free-trade zone that could become effective in 2005.

December 17, 1994

North Korea shoots down an American helicopter that crossed the 38th parallel.

A North Korean surface-to-air missile shot down a U.S. OH-58 helicopter that strayed across the border. The aircraft crash killed one American pilot and injured another. The United States insisted that North Korea acknowledge that the pilot simply made a mistake in crossing the border and no espionage was involved. Although North Korea returned the dead pilot's body on December 22, the U.S. State Department sent a negotiator to obtain the release of the injured pilot on December 30. Clinton administration officials handled the situation carefully because they wanted to maintain cooperation in the pending deal to inspect North Korea's nuclear facilities.

See January 21, 1995.

December 24, 1994

Former President Jimmy Carter obtains a cease-fire in the Bihać crisis with Bosnian Serbs.

Carter obtained a cease-fire agreement to end the Bihać crisis (see December 1, 1994) between Serbs and the Bosnian Federation of Muslims and Croats. Carter was not an official U.S. agent but had simply accepted Bosnian Serb President Karadžić's invitation to come to Bosnia—a means of saving Karadžić from dealing with U.N. or NATO officials. Carter's negotiations began on December 18, and on December 24, Bosnian leaders signed a cease-fire and agreed to U.N. negotiations based on the Contact Group's 51/49 territorial division. The U.N. mediators extended the seven-day cease-fire to four months, providing time for peace negotiations. Critics of these decisions said the cease-fire gave the Serbs four winter months to regroup for new assaults on Bosnian Croats and Muslims.

The cease-fire signed on December 24, 1994 saved the city of Bihać for the Bosnian Croatians and Bosnian Muslims. Later in December 1994, the Republic of Croatia's President Franjo Tudjman ordered the Croatian army to launch an attack against Croatian Serbs in the Krajina. The Croatian invasion violated the January 1992 cease-fire agreement (see January 2, 1992). But, of course, the Croatian Serbs had already violated the cease-fire when Croatian Serbs flew combat aircraft they received from the Republic of Serbia from an airbase in the Krajina to attack Bosnia Croats and Bosnia Muslims in Bihać in 1994 (see November 24, 1994).

See March 20, 1995.

1995

January 20, 1995

President Yeltsin declares a Russian victory in Chechnya.

On December 27, 1994, the Russians launched an attack on Chechnya to defeat rebels who fought for independence from the Russian Federation. Although the United Nations Security Council denounced the attack, Russia's army continued fighting until it conquered Chechnya's capital city of Grozny, enabling

Russian President Boris Yeltsin to declare victory in Chechnya on January 20, 1995.

See April 5, 1995.

January 21, 1995

The United States eases its trade embargo levied on North Korea in 1950.

The U.S. trade embargo on North Korea was eased for the first time since it was levied during the Korean War in 1950. The U.S. action permitted phone calls to, and travelers could use credit cards in, North Korea. On January 9, North Korea ended its ban on trade and financial transactions with the United States as part of the 1994 nuclear deal. In Washington, Defense Secretary William Perry told the Senate Foreign Relations Committee that in 1994 the Pentagon considered bombing North Korea's nuclear facilities but decided instead tightening economic sanctions was a better way to achieve agreement. Secretary of State Christopher assured the committee that South Korea and Japan would pay most of the $4.5 billion cost to rebuild North Korea's nuclear reactors for peaceful use.

See June 13, 1995.

January 31, 1995

The United States prevents Mexican banks from failing.

The United States provided Mexico with a $20 billion aid program to prevent its banks from collapsing. Mexico's financial problems became evident after President Ernesto Zedillo Ponce de Leon devalued the peso on January 3. U.S. President Clinton could not persuade Congress to approve aid to stabilize Mexico's economy. Nevertheless, on February 1 the U.S. Treasury Department provided $20 million of loans and loan guarantees to prevent Mexico from defaulting on loan payments.

During February, the United States and other nations provided an international loan package of $50 billion to rescue Mexico's economy. In return for the international aid, Mexico adopted a stabilization program on March 10 that caused hardships for Mexicans who lost their jobs and experienced cuts in welfare benefits. Because Zedillo was elected president only in December 1994, most economists blamed the policies of former president Carlos Salinas de Gortari, who borrowed excessively and overextended Mexico's short-term investments.

February 23, 1995

France accuses five Americans of espionage.

France accused five Americans of political and economic espionage. The five included the departing CIA station chief in the Paris embassy and his deputy. Because France was having a presidential campaign, the spy story was leaked to newspapers rather than handled by the usual diplomatic practices of allowing accused Americans to leave quietly. French officials told U.S. Ambassador Pamela Harriman that the CIA chief and his colleagues stole information regarding French policy on the Uruguay round of global trade talks, including French attempts to prevent Hollywood movies from being imported.

February 28, 1995

China makes concessions regarding U.S. copyrights.

China agreed to protect the copyrights of American intellectual properties such as movies, compact discs, and computer software—products Chinese companies had copied to sell cheaply in Asian markets. This was the major concession China made during trade talks that began on February 5.

See June 16, 1995.

March 8, 1995

A CIA report shows the White House knew about Serb atrocities since the summer of 1992.

A CIA report provided evidence that Bosnian Serbs were consistently the worst perpetrators of Bosnia's ethnic cleansing after war broke out in 1992. Leaked to *New York Times* journalists, the CIA report indicated that since the summer of 1992, Presidents Bush and Clinton had access to information about Serbs committing 90% of all Balkan atrocities. Between July and September 1992, CIA data included photographs of Serbs killing 3,000 Muslims in northern Bosnia and a list of detention camps where Serbs committed war crimes against prisoners. The CIA data was vital evidence for prosecuting Serbs for war crimes at the Hague International Tribunal for War Crimes in the Former Yugoslavia. CIA data also exposed the mistaken notion of U.N. officials that Serbs and Muslims were equally culpable for war crimes, a claim that some U.N. officials adopted to justify being "neutral" rather than punish Serb aggressors.

March 14, 1995

Under pressure from the president and Congress, Conoco cancels an oil deal with Iran.

Conoco Oil Corporation canceled its $1 billion contract to develop Iran's offshore oil fields in the Persian Gulf. After Conoco announced it received the contract on March 7, both President Clinton and congressional leaders protested the deal. The U.S. government took steps to keep American companies from dealing with Iran because it maintained that it assisted terrorists such as the Islamic Hamas in Lebanon and Israel.

See May 1, 1995.

March 16, 1995

President Clinton meets with the leader of Sinn Fein.

President Clinton met in Washington with Gerry Adams, the leader of Sinn Fein, the political wing of the Irish Republican Army (IRA). Following Adams's visit to the State Department in 1994, Adams and British representatives began negotiating peace and on February 22, 1995, proposed a cross-border council of Irish Protestants and Irish Catholics. The council would formulate a political solution to end the conflict in Northern Ireland.

On March 14, British Prime Minister John Major announced some British troops would leave the North to speed up the peace process. To advance peace, President Clinton told Adams the United States would do anything possible to end Ireland's civil conflict but said the IRA should disarm, as Britain had requested. Nevertheless, the peace process was blocked on July 3, 1995, when violence broke out for the first time in ten months.

March 18, 1995

Two Americans are killed in Pakistan.

Gunmen killed two Americans and a Pakistani in Karachi. Pakistani officials said they would track down the killers. The incident was one of a series of recent violence in Karachi. On March 10, a bomb exploded in a mosque, killing 11 people and wounding 22.

See April 16, 1995.

March 20, 1995

Bosnia's cease-fire is broken by the Bosnian Federation's army.

Bosnia's Muslim army ended the December 1994 truce by attacking Serb positions at Travnik. About the same time, Bosnian Croats took the offensive against Serbs near Bihać, forcing Serbs to fight on two fronts. In April, Croatia also launched attacks against Serbs in the Krajina, to regain territory Serbs occupied between July and December 1991.

Both the Bosnian Federation and the Croat Republic had secretly obtained heavy artillery and better weapons from countries such as Egypt and Iran to bypass the U.N. arms embargo. With these weapons and more troops able to fight, Muslims and Croats gradually won back territory the Serbs had taken in northwestern Bosnia. While Serbs struggled to defend the northwest, Bosnian Serb General Ratko Mladić drew attention away from those troubles by attacking Srebrenica, a Muslim city in eastern Bosnia that the Serbs had surrounded in 1993.

See July 11, 1995.

March 20, 1995

A Japanese terrorist cult release nerve gas in a Tokyo subway.

A terrorist religious cult in Japan released a deadly nerve gas in a Tokyo subway, causing the death of eight people. About 4,700 other persons were treated at Tokyo hospitals. On March 22, Japanese police raided the cult's office to arrest the occupants, charging them with complicity in the subway attack. On May 18, police seized the cult guru, Shoko Ashara, and 40 of his followers who organized the nerve gas attack.

March 25, 1995

President Clinton vows to dismiss any CIA agent withholding data on a 1992 killing in Guatemala.

President Clinton said CIA officials who withheld information about the death of the journalist Efrain Bamaca Velasques in Guatemala would be dismissed. Jennifer Harbun, Velasques's common-law wife, believed the CIA was involved in her husband's disappearance after being captured following a shoot-out between Guatemala's army and Mayan guerrillas on March 12, 1992. In November 1994, the CIA told Harbun that no information was available on her husband's disappearance or possible death.

Harbun, a Harvard-educated lawyer, began a three-year campaign in Washington and Guatemala to discover what happened to Velasques. On March 23, 1995, Robert G. Torricelli (D-N.J.), a member of the House Intelligence Committee, disclosed that the CIA knew one of its agents was involved in the capture, torture, and killing of Valesques and another American in Guatemala City. President Clinton reviewed the case and ordered the CIA to fire anyone who withheld information. Yet Guatemalan historians noted that even without CIA prompting, violence by Guatemala's army against Mayan Indians had been perpetrated in various forms since 1620 when Mayans resisted slavery imposed on them by the Spanish, led by Hernán Cortés. In addition, historians noted the CIA had been involved in Guatemala since 1954. Clinton did not fulfill his promise to dismiss those CIA agents.

See June 9, 1954; March 17, 1997.

March 31, 1995

President Clinton joins Haiti's ceremony giving the United Nations responsibility for Haiti's future.

President Clinton participated in ceremonies during which the United Nations assumed responsibility for Haiti's return to democracy. American combat troops withdrew from Haiti, but the United States deployed 500 Haitian police rookies trained at Fort Leonard Wood, Missouri's International Criminal Investigation Training School. Although police experts believed one year of education was needed to train competent police, the rookies had only four months of training. Moreover, Haitian President Aristide was not pleased with the rookies, claiming they were infiltrated with members of the Front for Advancement and Progress in Haiti (FRAPH) and other terrorist groups the CIA had supported since 1989. During the next year, Aristide's claim was backed by reports of sadistic methods used by police

"rookies" who caused the deaths of 46 people in their custody.

See December 17, 1995.

April 5, 1995

President Yeltsin halts the Russian army's fight against Chechnen rebels.

Russian President Boris Yeltsin ordered the army to stop fighting in Chechnya because it interfered with Russia's 50th anniversary celebration of victory over Germany in World War II. Because of Russia's economic hardships since the Cold War ended, many Russians looked forward to celebrating the victory over Germany. In Chechnya, rebels continued fighting while the Russian army used artillery to bombard mountain areas where rebels continued guerrilla warfare.

See July 30, 1995.

April 5, 1995

A U.N. conference in Berlin agrees to negotiate limits on greenhouse gases.

Although U.S. delegates to the Berlin conference on world climate changes felt little urgency to act because pollution seemed unimportant to most Americans, other delegates agreed to negotiate limits on emission of greenhouse gases. German Chancellor Helmut Kohl urged delegates to reduce greenhouse gases by 1997.

April 16, 1995

Pakistani Prime Minister Benazir Bhutto is unable to obtain a multibillion dollar U.S. loan.

Prime Minister Bhutto visited Washington to persuade President Clinton and Congress to provide her country with multibillion-dollar loans that had been withheld since 1990. Pakistan had not received aid because congressional legislation prohibited the loans unless the president certified Pakistan had no nuclear weapons program. Bhutto denied Pakistan had a nuclear program although admitted that Pakistan had plutonium required for weapons and advised Iran on how to begin a nuclear program. Both Presidents Bush and Clinton refused to certify the absence of a nuclear program because the CIA said Pakistan had a secret program—a fact validated in 1998 when Pakistan detonated a nuclear bomb.

April 17, 1995

President Clinton signs an order to declassify all 25-year-old records after 1999.

President Clinton signed Executive Order 12598 stating that after 1999 all classified government documents 25 or more years old would be released to the public unless a special panel exempted certain sensitive materials. This order supplemented a 1991 order by President George Bush mandating fewer declassification exemptions for 30-year old documents. Historians and other scholars were dismayed by the government's overclassification of records and hoped the United States would begin to classify only sensitive documents rather than documents that might embarrass bureaucrats.

See June 26, 1997.

April 18, 1995

Fighting in Rwanda escalates between Hutu and Tutsi tribes.

Rwanda's army tried to shut down Hutu refugee camps, but the Hutu refugees refused to leave because they feared Tutsi warriors would kill them in response to Kwanda's soldiers opened fire and, according to U.N. observers, slaughtered 2,000 people. Since 1994, Rwanda and neighboring Burundi had experienced fighting between the Tutsi minority and the Hutu majority.

See June 8, 1994.

May 1, 1995

The United States imposes a trade embargo on Iran.

President Clinton ordered a trade embargo on Iran for assisting terrorist groups and trying to build nuclear weapons. Iran denied it was manufacturing nuclear weapons but refused to sign the nuclear Non-Proliferation Treaty. The CIA and other Western intelligence agencies reported Iran was developing long-range ballistic missiles as well as nuclear weapons.

Clinton's principal reason for the embargo, however, was to stop American oil companies from buying Iranian oil and reselling it on the international market. In 1994, U.S. companies bought 20% of Iran's oil, totaling $2 billion.

May 2, 1995

President Clinton and Cuban leader Castro amend their 1994 agreement on Cuban refugees.

Following secret high-level talks, Clinton and Fidel Castro amended the agreement of September 9, 1994. Under the new pact, the United States would admit 21,000 Cuban refugees being held at the U.S. naval base at Guantánamo Bay. More significant for Cuban Americans, the United States would return to Cuba all Cubans trying to reach Florida by boat. The new agreement retained the 1994 arrangement permitting 20,000 Cubans to migrate legally to the United States each year.

May 8, 1995

President Clinton's tour of Europe extends from the Normandy beaches to Moscow.

In February 1995 the U.N. Security Council sent a non-military mission to persuade Rwanda and Burundi to make changes in their governments that would end the internecine warfare between Tutsi and Hutu as well ending the military activities of the armies of Rwanda and Burundi. To achieve new governments that could end the conflicts, the U.N. mission hoped to find some moderate individuals willing to be candidates for government position in the two countries. The leaders of Burundi claimed the U.N. mission was neo-colonization by Europeans. In rebuttal to those claims, the U.N. High Commissioner for Refugees Sadako Ogata told news reporters that neither the U.N. nor non-government humanitarian organizations could resolve conflicts in Rwanda, Burundi, or other African countries. The people and leaders of those countries must accept their share of responsibility for controlling what happens in their homeland.

During early 1995, the U.N. Security Council refused to send any more U.N.-sponsored troops to the area although 200,000 refugees remained in camps in Zaire and Rwanda. A U.N. repatriation program for refugees also failed because the Hutus feared Tutsi reprisals if they returned home.

May 11, 1995

U.N. conference delegates make the nuclear Non-Proliferation Treaty permanent.

At a U.N. conference in Mexico City, delegates representing 174 nations agreed to make the nuclear Non-Proliferation Treaty (NPT) permanent. During the conference, four countries that did not have nuclear weapons challenged the right of five major nuclear powers to restrict them from having nuclear weapons. The five nuclear powers—United States, Russia, China, Britain, and France—pledged to negotiate the reduction or elimination of their weapons and to share information on peaceful uses of nuclear technology with other countries. The five countries refusing to sign the NPT were suspected of having nuclear warheads: India, Israel, Iran, Pakistan, and Syria.

For U.S. policy, the permanent extension of the NPT complemented President Clinton's presidential directive PDD-11, which sought to use the NPT to restrict expansion of nuclear weapons to other nations. U.S. policy continued searching for ways to halt the nuclear warheads and delivery programs of nations not signing the NPT. To prevent terrorists from securing nuclear weapons, Assistant Secretary of Defense for Nuclear Security Ashton Carter visited Russia and China to discuss these issues.

See July 3, 1993.

June 2, 1995

President Clinton renews China's most-favored-nation (MNF) status.

The president renewed China's MFN status despite a January 30 State Department report that China had not improved its human rights record. In 1994, Clinton said he would not link human rights with trade. Thus, Secretary of State Warren Christopher advised the president to renew China's MNF status rather than make such a linkage. By mid-June 1995, new tensions developed between Washington and Beijing.

See June 16, 1995.

Secretary of State Christopher visits with Chinese Foreign Minister Quian. White House

June 13, 1995

The U.S. and North Korea agree on ways to implement their 1994 nuclear agreement.

In February 1995, North Korea's rejection of U.S. proposals for South Korea to supply North Korea with two nuclear reactors for peaceful uses caused negotiations to break down. After the talks broke down, North Korean officials threatened to refuel the nation's nuclear reactor's capacity to produce nuclear weapons. To avoid a complete split in relations, North Korea agreed to resume negotiations with the United States in April. Two months later, negotiations resulted in the June 13, 1995 agreements. The United States agreed that North Korea could choose between South Korea's nuclear reactors or American nuclear reactors. Whatever choice North Korea made, South Korea would have a central role in constructing the nuclear reactors. In addition, President Clinton assured South Korea's President Kim Young Sam that American forces would remain stationed in South Korea as long as both countries thought they were necessary.

See December 16, 1995.

June 16, 1995

China recalls its ambassador from the United States.

In early May 1995, a pro-Taiwanese lobbying effort persuaded the U.S. Congress to vote almost unanimously to give Taiwan's President Lee Teng-hui a visa to receive Cornell University's alumni award. President Clinton granted the visa because he feared Congress might revise the 1979 Taiwan Act to allow Lee or other Taiwanese presidents to visit America, contrary to the wishes of the People's Republic of China. To reassure Beijing about American policy on Taiwan, Clinton announced on May 22 that Lee's visa was an exception to previous United States policy that recognized the agreement on visits by Taiwanese presidents made by President Richard Nixon during his visit to China in 1972 (see February 17, 1972). China was not placated by Clinton's May 22 announcement and recalled its ambassador from Washington on June 15, 1995. By September, China and the U.S. had renewed diplomatic relations.

See September 27, 1995.

June 25, 1995

Haitian elections jeopardize Haiti's loans from the International Monetary Fund.

In the June 25 elections, Lavalas Party members again won a majority of seats in Haiti's National Assembly. Two teams of observers monitored the elections. One team with only a few volunteer members was led by Robert Pastor of the Carter Center in Atlanta, Georgia. The Organization of American States (OAS) sent a larger team able to monitor all of Haiti's balloting stations.

After the election, Pastor's team reported the elections were a "step away from democracy" because Lavalas Party members controlled the election councils that supervised the election and appeared to have manipulated ballots to insure a Lavalas victory. In contrast to Pastor's report, the OAS team said the elections were as democratic as could be expected. The OAS team also rejected a request from political parties opposing Lavalas to void the election because of fraudulent practices at the balloting stations.

The election results were critical because the Lavalas Party opposed privatization of Haiti's state-owned enterprises. Founded by former Haitian President Jean-Bertrand Aristide, the Lavalas Party favored Aristide's belief that downtrodden Haitians should benefit from the higher wages paid by Haiti's state-owned enterprises after Aristide's return to Haiti in 1994 (see October 15, 1994). Since 1994, the Lavalas Party's control of a majority of Assembly votes enabled members to reject legislation to privatize Haiti's state-owned businesses as required by the International Monetary Fund (IMF). Because the IMF had withdrawn loans to repair Haiti's infrastructure, Haiti's economy stagnated and many Haitians sought refuge in the United States, the only realistic haven after the Dominican Republic closed its borders with Haiti on Hispaniola.

See December 17, 1995.

June 28, 1995

Japan and the United States agree on automobile trade terms between their nations.

After trade talks between Japan and the United States broke down on May 5, President Clinton decided to levy 100% tariffs on Japanese luxury cars such as Toyota's Lexus and Nissan's Infinite. Japan's U.S.

auto sales made up 55% of the $66 billion U.S. trade gap with Japan, but Japan refused to import U.S. automobile parts. Although Tokyo threatened to take the issue of 100% tariffs to the World Trade Organization, it first agreed to resume talks broken off in May 1995.

Following intensive discussions between U.S. Trade Representative Mickey Kantor and Japan's Trade Representative Ryutar Hashimoto, the two agreed on automobile trade terms. The accord enabled Clinton to cancel the 100% tariffs on luxury cars and slightly expanded U.S. parts sales in Japan. The agreement was not a victory but Kantor's realistic assessment was related not only to Japan's worst economic recession since the 1930s but also to the U.S.-Japanese Mutual Security Treaty agreement that was first signed in 1951 (see September 20, 1951) and reconfirmed in 1969 (see November 21, 1969). The Mutual Security Treaty assured Japan's cooperation with United States policies in the Far East, policies including American forces on Okinawa and air bases in Japan.

June 28, 1995

Egyptian and Sudanese forces clash along their borders.

Egypt and the Sudan had a long history of tensions after the British made them separate states in 1956. The current border tension grew from the Sudan's sponsoring of terrorism to expand Islamic fundamentalism into Egypt, Algeria, and Saudi Arabia. Egyptian President Hosni Mubarak had joined the United States in calling on the Sudanese to overthrow Sudan's government, headed by General al-Bashri, thereby increasing tensions between the two nations. The June 28 clash wounded three Egyptians and three Sudanese. This event added another dimension to al-Bashri's five-year-old war against southern Christians who refused to convert to Islam, and many Christians starved despite efforts of international agencies to air-lift food to starving Sudanese.

See January 1, 1956.

July 11, 1995

The United States extends full diplomatic recognition to Vietnam.

President Clinton announced the United States would extend full diplomatic recognition to Vietnam, 20 years after the last Americans left South Vietnam at the end of the Vietnam war. On January 28, 1995, the United States signed an agreement to purchase a building in Hanoi for the U.S. mission. In extending recognition on July 11, Clinton told reporters it was "time to bind up our wounds" with Vietnam. Although a few critics opposed recognizing Vietnam, many supported Clinton's decision, including investors hoping to profit from trade relations with Vietnam, as other nations were doing.

July 11, 1995

Bosnian Serb atrocities at Srebrenica lead to U.S. intervention.

Bosnian Serb atrocities at Srebrenica, a Muslim town in eastern Bosnia, became a turning point in the Bosnian war because President Clinton and NATO members agreed to take strong action in August 1995. The U.N. Security Council had designated Srebrenica a "safe area" in 1993 after the Serbs made the city vulnerable to attacks by capturing the surrounding hills. When fighting broke out again during the spring of 1995, Serb forces stopped U.N. supply convoys from reaching Srebrenica and bombarded the city. Although Dutch UNPROFOR troops protecting the safe area asked for help, Yasushi Akashi, a U.N. Special Representative in Bosnia, refused, vetoing NATO's offer to bomb Serb forces attacking Srebrenica. As in prior ventures, President Clinton urged NATO to bomb Serb military sites, but after two air raids on May 25–26, Britain and France opposed additional strikes because Serbs captured UNPROFOR soldiers to use as human shields around ammunition dumps and military installations.

French President Jacques Chirac, after replacing François Mitterrand as president on May 7, planned to make France a major player in European politics for the first time since French President Charles DeGaulle died in 1970. Along with many other French politicians, Chirac believed that after DeGaulle died, his presidential successors Valery Giscard d'Estaing, George Pompidou, and François Mitterrand played minor roles in Europe, a situation Chirac's election on May 7, 1995 would correct. Chirac had opposed NATO raids against the Serbians on May 25–26, 1995, but he wanted UNPROFOR to re-deploy widely scattered troops from each safe area to defensible positions. Then soldiers could move forward and shoot if necessary to open supply routes that the Serbs obstructed. After President Clinton refused Chirac's request for U.S. helicopter gunships to protect U.N. forces, British Prime Minister John Major adopted Chirac's plan by sending 1,500 British soldiers with tanks and heavy artillery, while France sent 4,000 troops with helicopter gunships.

Before U.N. forces fulfilled Chirac's deployment plan, Bosnian Serb General Ratko Mladić launched a final assault against Srebrenica that resulted in the worst massacre of Bosnia's three-year war. After U.N. officials rejected a second Dutch UNPROFOR request for assistance, Serb forces shoved the Dutch aside, took over Srebrenica, and rounded up 25,000 Muslims who had no way to defend themselves. The Serbs tortured and killed thousands of men and boys while women and girls were raped and forced to flee by bus or foot to nearby communities. Some U.N. officials refused to believe the horrors of the Serbs' ethnic cleansing until U.S. Ambassador Madeleine Albright displayed U.S. satellite and U-2 photos showing Serbs slaughtering Muslim civilians. After destroying Srebrenica, Mladić's forces attacked U.N. safe areas at Žepa and Goražde.

Before Serbs could complete other massacres, Clinton and NATO overrode the neutral stance of U.N. Special Representative Akashi, who was sent back to New York. U.S.-led NATO forces soon brought peace to Bosnia.

See August 28, 1995.

July 11, 1995

The CIA and NSA release secret "Venona" files on Soviet documents from the 1940s.

During public ceremonies at CIA headquarters in Langley, Virginia, directors of the Central Intelligence Agency, the Federal Bureau of Investigation, and the National Security Agency (NSA) revealed the declassification of a first batch of the Venona Project's files on Soviet intelligence activity in the United States during 1944 and 1945. After intercepting the Soviet messages, U.S. intelligence agents decoded the Soviet documents and translated into English so that American officials could learn about Soviet espionage activity. The decoding and translating process continued until 1981, with the contents classified as "top secret" and placed in NSA archives in Maryland.

The NSA and CIA decided to declassify and release Venona documents after President Clinton established a Commission on Protecting and Reducing Government Secrecy chaired by Senator Daniel P. Moynihan (D-N.Y.). During a May 1995 session, Moynihan learned about the Venona documents and asked CIA Director John Deutsch to find out if secrecy was essential. Moynihan's request resulted in the July 11 ceremony, in which the NSA released 49 messages from Soviet espionage showing the truth of the 1951 charges that U.S. citizens Julius and Ethel Rosenberg had given classified information about U.S. construction of atomic bombs to Soviet agents.

Following the July 15 ceremony, the NSA declassified other documents between 1995 and 1997 totaling over 29,000 messages involving more than 5,000 pages of text. Many of these documents were written in an abbreviated, telegraphic style and contained covered names of individuals whose alleged espionage helped the Soviets learn about U.S. secrets.

In 1956, Alan H. Belmont, the FBI's number-three officer, had reviewed Venona documents to determine if they could be used to prosecute any American for espionage. He concluded the Venona documents would be defective as evidence in any law court because most material was hearsay, full of gaps, and used Russian idioms that could be interpreted in various ways. In addition, an individual's real name was never clearly identified as an actual name. When the FBI released Belmont's evaluation of Venona documents in January 1999, the U.S. news media largely ignored it.

See April 5, 1951.

July 30, 1995

The Russian government and Chechen rebels sign an accord to end their conflict.

Russia and Chechen rebels signed a "partial accord" to end their conflict. When war began in December 1994, President Clinton called it an internal Russian affair, but in March he joined other Western leaders and the U.N. Security Council to protest the continued fighting. NATO asked President Yeltsin to stop the war because it violated agreements on Conventional Forces in Europe (CFE). The CFE prohibited a nation from moving 9,000 troops or 250 tanks without first notifying CFE nations about the troop movement.

By April 5, Russian troops controlled the Chechen capital of Grozny and Yeltsin had halted the Russian attacks, saying warfare interfered with Russia's 50th anniversary celebration over Germany in World War II. Chechnya's President, Jokar Dudayev, refused to surrender and fought Russian forces besieging Chechnya's southern city of Budyonnovsk until a cease-fire was accepted on June 24. The cease-fire led to the July 30 "partial accords," but the two sides still argued about Chechnya's future. Although the peace talks made little progress, the accords gave the rebels time to regroup and recruit more fighters. In November, rebels renewed their attacks on Russia's forces, first in small villages and later, on December 19, in intensive combat at the Chechnyan city of Gudermes.

See January 18, 1996.

August 5, 1995

Colombia captures two drug lords; President Clinton calls it a "Final blow."

A White House spokesman claimed Colombia's capture of the two drug lords was the "final blow" at the world's largest drug cartel. Despite the capture of drug lords, the U.S. war on drugs continued because other drug traffickers found ways to meet Americans' demand for drugs. The drug problem was also one of money and bribes by traffickers paid to various officials who were assigned to end Colombia's drug production. On June 5, a Florida court indicted a former U.S. prosecutor for protecting Cali drug cartel members from arrest.

See March 1, 1996.

August 5, 1995

Warren Christopher visits Cambodia to atone for U.S. actions in the 1970s.

When leaving for Cambodia, as the first U.S. Secretary of State to visit there in 40 years, Christopher told reporters he wanted to atone for the U.S. role in Cambodia's misery experienced after President Richard Nixon secretly bombed Cambodia in 1970. In Phnom Penh, Christopher urged Cambodians to develop democratic institutions, although Prime Minister Norodom Ranariddh said Western-style democracy had no place in his efforts to revive the nation's economy. Foreign observers believed

Cambodia had verged on civil war for two years since a U.N. Transitional Authority left the country.

See March 18, 1970; May 28, 1993.

August 28, 1995

NATO air raids on Bosnian Serbs lead to a peace conference.

NATO aircraft launched air raids on the Bosnian Serbs, whose artillery shelling had recently killed 37 people in Sarajevo. NATO's attack fulfilled President Clinton policy of August 2 to exert U.S. leadership in ending Bosnia's war. Clinton acted in cooperation with NATO after Secretary of State Christopher received approval from NATO leaders who were shocked by Serb atrocities at Srebrenica. Clinton also accepted Assistant Secretary of State Richard Holbrooke's advice to avoid criticizing Croatian President Tudjman, whose army had attacked Serbs in eastern Slavonia to regain Croatian land the Serbs had conquered in 1991. Although the Croatian attack on August 4 seemed to widen the war, it eliminated conflict between Tujdman and Yugoslavia's President Slobodan Milošević who had forsaken his dream of a Greater Serbia.

In August, Holbrooke led a U.S. negotiating team to Sarajevo to discuss cease-fire and peace terms with Tudjman, Milošević, and the three Bosnian factions. The combination of Holbrooke's diplomacy and NATO air raids succeeded. During September, Holbrooke led negotiations in Geneva while NATO conducted intensive daily air raids against Bosnian Serb military installations from September 5 until

Secretary of State Christopher witnesses the raising of the flag over the U.S. embassy in Hanoi. White House

September 21. At Geneva, Holbrooke persuaded the Bosnian Muslim, Croat, and Serb delegates to accept a cease-fire on October 12 and peace talks based on the five-member Contact Group's plan for a 49/51 land division to begin on November 1 in Dayton, Ohio.

See November 21, 1995.

September 5, 1995

French nuclear tests raise protests from the major powers.

France detonated a nuclear bomb at Mururoa Atoll in the South Pacific Ocean despite protests from the United States, other major powers, and environmental organizations. French President Chirac defied world opinion while riots erupted in Tahiti, part of the Polynesian island group where the tests took place.

Although the major nuclear powers had informally banned nuclear tests for three years, international negotiators in Geneva failed to formalize a test ban agreement. During the Geneva sessions, President Clinton's delegate offered to ban all nuclear tests including small-scale-tests, but the five major powers disagreed on the terms of a no-test treaty. President Chirac said France would accept a total ban on tests after completing its scheduled tests in the Pacific.

September 27, 1995

China takes steps to improve relations with the United States.

American-Chinese relations grew tense in June after China objected to Taiwanese president Lee Teng-hui's visit to the United States. Later, on August 2 China accused two U.S. air force officers of spying while they observed Chinese military exercises.

The first Chinese effort to improve relations came in late August. After Hillary Rodham Clinton, the wife of the U.S. president, made plans to attend the U.N. Woman's Conference in China, China permitted Harry Wu, a Chinese dissident, to fly home to the United States two days after finding him guilty of stealing state secrets. More crucial, on September 27 China canceled the sale of two nuclear reactors to Iran, reversing its policy of helping Iran obtain nuclear weapons.

September 28, 1995

Israel Prime Minister Yitzhak Rabin and Palestinian leader Yassar Arafat agree to transfer more West Bank towns to the Palestine National Authority.

Between November 1994 and September 1995, frequent violence was perpetrated by Islamic Hamas members who opposed the peace process undertaken by Rabin and Arafat in accordance with agreements worked out at Oslo, Norway (see September 13, 1993). On April 10, 1995, the Palestine National Authority (PNA) police arrested 300 Hamas militants in the Gaza Strip and on August 23, Israeli police arrested 12 Hamas members charged with igniting a bomb in Ramallah that wounded 100 people.

Despite the violence, Israeli Prime Minister Yitzhak Rabin and PNA leader Arafat met in Washington ceremonies known as Oslo II to reaffirm their commitment to peace. The September 28 agreement provided for an elected Palestinian Council and for instructions to transfer more West Bank areas to the PNA. These steps toward peace followed 1993 agreements giving the PNA control over Jericho and the Gaza Strip.

See November 4, 1995.

September 28, 1995

NATO lays plans to admit new members despite Russian objections.

NATO approved plans to add new members but could not convince Russia that the plans were meant to extend European security, not renew tensions between East and West. NATO agreed on the final steps by which Partners for Peace members would become NATO members. On October 22, Russia's opposition to NATO expansion surfaced when President Boris Yeltsin told the U.N. General Assembly he would take a strong stand against NATO's eastward expansion.

President Clinton favored expansion to promote democracy in central and eastern Europe and to guarantee a future U.S. role in European security. Critics of Clinton's policy contended NATO's expansion would be expensive and commit the United States to defend nations not vital to its interests. Critics also argued that NATO expansion could foster Russian nationalism.

See December 6, 1995.

October 1, 1995

A U.S. court finds 10 Islamic fundamentalists guilty of conspiracy.

A New York federal court found Egyptian Shiek Omar Abdel Rahman and nine of his followers guilty of conspiring to destroy the United Nations building and other New York City landmarks. The conspirators were also involved in bombing New York City's World Trade Center in 1993.

October 2, 1995

Congress opposes a law to fight terrorism in the United States.

On April 27, President Clinton proposed legislation to fight domestic terrorist activity. The president asked congress to provide for 100 FBI agents to investigate terrorism and allow members of the armed forces to investigate crimes regarding chemical, biological, or nuclear weapons. The proposal was not approved because congressional opposition was led by a combination of conservative Republicans and liberal Democrats who claimed the proposal gave the FBI too much authority.

See April 24, 1996.

November 4, 1995

Israeli Prime Minister Rabin is assassinated.

Yigal Amir, a Jewish student of Orthodox theology, assassinated Yitzhak Rabin because, he claimed, Jewish law permitted killing anyone who gave Jewish land to an enemy, as Rabin had done for Palestinians. Following a period of mourning, Shimon Peres was elected prime minister and promised to fulfill the Oslo Accords of 1993 and 1995. Peres took his first step on November 13 when he directed the last Israeli soldiers to leave the West Bank city of Jenin and allowed PNA police to take charge as required by the Oslo II agreement.

See December 28, 1995.

November 11, 1995

The U.S. ambassador leaves Nigeria after the government executes its critics.

Nigeria executed Ken Saro-Wiwa and eight others charged with killing four chiefs of the Ogoni tribes in northern Nigeria, where rebels opposed the government. Saro-Wiwa was executed despite protests from the United States, Britain, and other nations. He was an environmentalist and author whose "crime" was to criticize Nigeria's dictatorial rulers. Following the execution, the United States withdrew its ambassador and the World Bank canceled a $100 million loan to Nigeria.

See July 8, 1998.

November 13, 1995

President Clinton and Congress reach an impasse over the 1996 budget.

The confrontation between Clinton and Congress over the 1996 budget reached an impasse after the president vetoed legislation to extend government activity. On September 27, Clinton and Congress averted a federal shutdown by appropriating funds for six more weeks. The six weeks lapsed in November, but Congress and the White House had not compromised their budget differences. On November 14, the Treasury Department prevented a government shutdown by using trust funds to meet payments due on November 15 and 30, the precise tactic Congress had wanted to restrict in the bill Clinton vetoed on November 13.

The November budget crisis was not resolved until April 1996. All government offices closed six days early in December before the White House and Congress agreed on stopgap measures to keep the offices open. Stopgap agreements continued until April 1996, when the two sides agreed on a budget for the final five months of fiscal year 1996.

November 14, 1995

An explosion kills five Americans in Saudi Arabia.

Five Americans were killed and 40 Americans and Saudis were wounded in an explosion at the U.S. Military Training Center in Dhahran, Saudi Arabia. For 20 years, the center had taught the Saudi National Guard how to operate and maintain military equipment supplied to their country. Two Saudi groups claimed responsibility for the bombing. One was the Tigers of the Gulf, the other the Islamic Movement for Changes, which previously sent faxes to foreign embassies in Riyadh to criticize King Fahd's family and threaten to evict Western forces from Saudi Arabia if they did not leave by June 1995.

See May 31, 1996.

November 21, 1995

The Dayton Accords provide for peace in Bosnia and Herzegovina.

After three weeks of intensive, secret negotiations in Dayton, Ohio, the presidents of Yugoslavia, Croatia, and the Federation of Bosnia initialed a peace agreement to be signed in final form at Paris on December 14. In accordance with agreements signed by the Srpska Republic's President Karadžić, Yugoslav President Milošević represented the Bosnian Serbs. A Bosnian Serb delegation attended the meetings but did not directly participate in the negotiations.

Guided by U.S. Assistant Secretary of State for European Affairs Richard Holbrooke, who was assisted by U.S. Army General Wesley Clark, the presidents of Yugoslavia, Croatia, and the newly established Bosnian-Croat Federation (see February 28, 1994) initialed a peace agreement on November 21, 1995. During three weeks of intensive, secret negotiations in Dayton, Ohio, Milošević and the Croatian Republic's President Franjo Tudjman dominated the discussions. The Bosnia-Croat Federation's President Alija Izetbegović let Bosnia's Prime Minister Haris Silajdžić speak for the Bosnian-Croat Federation. As arranged previously, Milošević also represented Karadžić, although three Srpska Republic delegates attended the Dayton meetings as observers. When the accords were signed on November 21, the Srpska Republic delegates refused to approve the peace terms accepted by Milošević. After meeting with Milošević in Belgrade on November 23, Srpska President Radovan Karadžić signed the Dayton Accords.

Based on the Contact Group's 49/51 plan, the Bosnia-Croat Federation would occupy 51% of the former Republic of Bosnia and Herzegovina, the Srpska Republic would occupy 49%. The Dayton Accords provided a constitution for the new Federation of Bosnia and Herzegovina that had two entities, the Bosnia-Croat Federation and the Srpska Republic. The constitution provided that the Federation would have a three-member presidency representing, one member from each of the three ethnic groups to conduct foreign policy, formulate an annual budget and appoint a Council of Ministers consisting of one-third Serbs, one-third Croats, and one-third Muslims. Under the constitution a bicameral parliament had one house whose members consisted of two-thirds Croats and Muslims and one-third Serbs elected by democratic means. The second house of parliament would have 14 Serbs and 28

President Clinton, Secretary of State Christopher, and the presidents of Yugoslavia, Croatia, and the Federation of Bosnia initial the peace agreement. White House

Muslim and Croat delegates selected by the assembly of each entity. The first elections to be held within nine months of the December 1995 signing of the Accords in Paris would be supervised by a commission appointed by the Organization of Security and Cooperation in Europe (OSCE). Each of the two entities' citizens eligible to vote would vote in their municipalities based on the 1991 elections unless they petitioned to vote elsewhere.

The accords contained other political and military annexes to establish a multiethnic Bosnia, but three issues were controversial. First, Serbs in Sarajevo did not want to be under Muslim control, especially in the suburb of Pale where the current Srpska Republic's government had its headquarters. Milošević believed Bosnian Serbs could adjust to the two-entity government in which two-thirds of the government were Muslims and Croats, especially after Silajdžić promised Bosnia's Serbs would be treated as equals. Nevertheless, the Dayton agreement on Sarajevo did not satisfy those Bosnian Serbs who wished to become part of Milošević's Yugoslav Federation (see February 17, 1996).

Second, the future status of the city of Brčko was resolved by a compromise that proved to be difficult to implement because in 1991 Brčko's population was evenly divided between Serbs, Muslims, and Croats. Brčko was located in the Posavina corridor, a narrow strip of land bridging eastern and western parts of the Srpska Republic. When war began in 1992, Serb and Yugoslav army forces, and paramilitary gangs captured Brčko and began their brutal ethnic cleansing campaign against Croats and Muslims (see June 8, 1992). Although the Dayton accords permitted all refugees and displaced persons to return to their former homes, Brčko was a special case because the population had been evenly divided before armies and paramilitary gangs from the Republic of Serbia invaded Brčko in 1992. Thus, Brčko's political future depended on improving the relations between Serbs and returning Muslim refugees. To achieve a multiethnic city, the Dayton accords provided that Brčko's municipal government would be decided through binding arbitration by three arbitrators: one Muslim, one Serb, and a third selected by the other two. If the Muslim and Serb arbitrators could not agree on a third person, the International Court of Justice at The Hague would appoint the third arbitrator.

President Clinton and his national security team were pleased by the Dayton Accords, but the president found it difficult to persuade Congress to approve his deployment of 20,000 American soldiers as part of the NATO Implementation Force in Bosnia.

See December 14, 1995; February 17, 1996.

December 14, 1995

Dayton Accords are signed in Paris on December 14; France to participate in part of IFOR.

President Chirac agreed French troops would be part of NATO's Implementation Force (IFOR) joining NATO forces deploying in Bosnia after the Dayton Accords had been formally signed in Paris on December 14. Although historians prefer the term "Dayton Accords," the French called them "Paris Accords," a term designed to enhance French prestige.

See February 17, 1996.

December 14, 1995

Congress qualifies its approval of deploying U.S. troops in Bosnia.

Reluctantly and with qualifications, the U.S. Senate and House of Representatives approved deploying 20,000 U.S. troops in Bosnia. After the Dayton Accords were initialed in November, President Clinton visited Europe to cement the cooperation of NATO, whose member's supplied 40,000 of the 60,000 troops implementing the accords. The Europeans were pleased with peace in the Balkans but Clinton faced serious problems with Congress. As commander in chief, Clinton could send troops without congressional approval but preferred the backing of Congress.

Both congressional and public opinion had zigzagged as much as Clinton regarding the Balkan wars. As late as June 1995 when Serbs held UNPROFOR soldiers hostage as human shields, American opinion opposed intervention because a six-day search had been required to rescue Scott O'Grady, whose F-16 plane was shot down near Bihać by the Serbs. In mid-July, public opinion shifted, wanting Clinton to "do something" after television showed the Serb massacres of Muslims at Srebrenica.

After Holbrooke's diplomacy helped gain the October cease-fire and NATO planned for 60,000 peacekeepers, the House of Representatives voted on November 2 to deny funds for U.S. operations in Bosnia. Speaker of the House Newt Gingrich (R-

Senator John McCain and Major General William Nash discuss compliance of the Bosnian peace settlement. Department of Defense

Ga.) refused to withdraw the resolution despite appeals from Holbrooke and President Clinton.

In part, Clinton was to blame for the House resolution because he never spoke strongly, consistently, and clearly about Bosnian policy. Finally, in a nationally televised address on November 21, the president said a Balkan peace was in the national interest. Clinton's address did not convince most Americans who were uncertain about or opposed to U.S. involvement.

With an uncertain public, Clinton was fortunate to have the support of three influential Senators. Robert Dole (R-Kans.) and John McCain (R-Ariz.) joined with Robert Kerrey (D-Mass.) to offer a resolution supporting the president. Their bipartisan resolution passed the Senate by a vote of 69 to 30. Nevertheless, to obtain Senate approval, Clinton issued a statement that U.S. troops would withdraw after one year and he would arm Bosnia's Muslims to defend themselves if the Serbs did not comply with the Dayton Accords.

The House was less cooperative. Following lengthy debates during which Gingrich's followers denounced Clinton, the key vote was on a resolution to confirm the November 2 resolution withholding funds to support forces in Bosnia. The final vote took place on December 13, when enough moderate Republicans joined Democrats in defeating another proposal to withhold funds for U.S.

troops in Bosnia by a vote of 210 to 218. Funds were not cut off but the House never voted to back Clinton.

See February 17, 1996.

December 16, 1995

The U.S. and North Korea sign an agreement on nuclear reactors.

The United States and North Korea signed an agreement reached on June 13, 1995, to have South Korea construct nuclear reactors in North Korea. By December, the North Korean people faced famine conditions because heavy rains and floods destroyed almost all of the fall harvest. U.N. humanitarian aid groups and the Red Cross sought more food to prevent a winter famine.

See May 17, 1996.

December 16, 1995

Russian elections approve a new constitution but President Yeltsin's opponents control parliament.

The Communist Party and its allies won one-third of the parliamentary seats but the new constitution was approved. To pass the constitution, President Yeltsin, in the hospital allegedly due to a bad cold, left his hospital bed to make a televised appeal asking

Russians to approve the constitution but defeat Communist Party nominees who would throw Russia back to an earlier era. The elections gave left-wing extremists control of parliament, but the constitution gave Yeltsin greater authority to deal with corruption, veto legislation, and reform the economy. A presidential election was scheduled for July 1996.

See March 13, 1996.

December 17, 1995

René Preval is elected president of Haiti.

Preval was chosen president by 80% of the votes cast. Preval became the Lavalas Party nominee because the constitution restricted former President Aristide to a five-year term. Despite a low voter turnout, the election guaranteed a peaceful and democratic transition to power.

December 28, 1995

Israel and Syria renew peace talks in Washington.

On December 16, Secretary of State Christopher announced that Israel and Syria would resume peace negotiations in Washington that were stalled in June 1995 because of disputes about Israel's withdrawal from the Golan Heights. Following Prime Minister Rabin's assassination in November, Prime Minister Peres told Christopher he was willing to resume talks with Syria. Christopher met in Damascus with Syrian President Hafiz al-Assad before flying to Tel Aviv to confirm that Israeli delegates could begin negotiations at the Wye Conference Center near Washington, D.C. on December 28 for a two-day preliminary discussion.

Additional talks were held in early January and late February 1996 but were suspended in March because Hezbollah guerrillas in south Lebanon staged rocket attacks against Israel and its Lebanese allies. By April 3, President Assad had placed Syria on a war alert owing to the frequent violence in both Lebanon and the disputed West Bank territory occupied by Israel.

See April 26, 1996.

1996

January 14, 1996

A Mexican drug lord is expelled to Houston, where he pleads guilty to drug trafficking charges.

Having arrested Juan García Abrego on drug charges, Mexican police transferred him to U.S. authorities in Texas who had indicted him in 1995 for drug trafficking. García Abrego's arrest was hailed as a sign of Mexican cooperation with the Federal Bureau of Investigation, but *New York Times* reporter Sam Dillon disclosed that García Abrego was no longer a powerful drug lord. Mexican political leaders had abandoned him in favor of new drug lords connected to Colombia's drug cartels. When García Abrego was arrested, he inhabited a small cottage outside Monterrey, Mexico, no longer living his lavish lifestyle of the 1980s as head of a $4 billion cocaine industry.

Although the FBI listed him among its "ten most wanted" with a $5 million award in March 1995, the listing belied the fact that García Abrego had lost influence in Mexico City after Ernesto Zedillo became president in December 1994. Without protection from Mexican officials connected with the drug trade, he was subject to the arrest on January 14. As Dillon reported, the former drug lord's arrest represented deceit rather than victory over the Mexican drug traffickers.

January 18, 1996

Russian forces counterattack to free hostages held by Chechen rebels.

The July 30 Chechnya cease-fire fell apart in November 1995 when rebels attacked Russian forces. The rebel offensive captured 200 Russians whom they held as hostages to compel a Russian withdrawal. But in January, a Russian counterattack defeated the rebels and freed most of the hostages. Although President Yeltsin played down the war in Chechnya, the Russian army captured a rebel stronghold in February 29 before Yeltsin declared the war was over.

See March 13, 1996.

January 26, 1996

The U.S. Senate ratifies START II, which Presidents Bush and Yeltsin signed in 1993.

Three years after George Bush and Boris Yeltsin signed the second Strategic Arms Reduction Treaty (START II), the U.S. Senate approved it. Under the treaty terms, both sides would reduce deployed nuclear warheads to 3,000 and eliminate all multiwarhead and "heavy" intercontinental ballistic missiles by January 1, 2003. Start II would become effective after START I did. Although the parliaments of Belarus and Ukraine had ratified START I, Russia's Duma (parliament) had not approved it.

February 17, 1996

At a "Dayton II" meeting in Rome, Tudjman, Milošević, and Izetbegović confirm their adherence to the November 1995 accords.

Although the NATO-led Implementation Force (IFOR) easily divided Bosnia's Serb, Croat, and Muslim forces into zones designated by the Dayton Accords, IFOR problems in Bosnia and Herzegovina arose between Serbs and Muslims in Sarajevo and between Croats and Muslims in Mostar. To ensure that NATO and the other European groups involved had the full cooperation of the Serbs, Croats, and Muslims, Assistant Secretary of State for European Affairs Richard Holbrooke convened "Dayton II" in Rome.

During the Rome sessions, Yugoslav President Milošević, Croatian President Tudjman, and the Bosnian Federation President Izetbegović signed documents to affirm vital parts of the Dayton Accords: (1) Mostar and Sarajevo remained under the control of the Bosnian-Croat Federation; (2) each faction's prisoners of war would be exchanged by April; (3) all refugees would be allowed to return to their homes; (4) all war criminals would be prosecuted by the Hague Tribunal for the Former Yugoslavia.

These four agreements were partly carried out in 1996. Most prisoners were exchanged by April, but conflicts among Serbs, Croats, and Muslims did not end in Sarajevo and Mostar. Yet, IFOR's most difficult problem was the return of refugees to their former homes.

See April 3, 1996.

February 23, 1996

Two Iraqi defectors who returned home are killed by their family members.

In August 1995, Iraqi Generals Saddam Kamel al-Majid and his brother Hussein Kamel al-Majid defected to Jordan with their wives, who were the daughters of Iraqi President Saddam Hussein. In Jordan, the two generals called for the overthrow of Hussein and offered U.N. inspectors valuable data about Iraq's weapons of mass destruction. To preempt disclosure of these data, the Iraqi president gave the inspectors the same information. Although the generals were first accepted by the exile community hoping to oust Hussein, the exile leaders of the Iraq National Congress refused to accept them as heirs to Hussein or to lead a new Iraqi government.

Dismayed by the reaction of the Iraqi exiles, the brothers decided to return to Iraq. They received the consent of Iraq's Revolutionary Command members, who said they would be forgiven. On February 20, the brothers and their families returned to Baghdad. Two days later, the Iraqi News Agency reported that the two generals' wives had divorced them. Two hours later, Iraqi television reported that the two brothers had been slain by members of their family to remove the stains on the family honor.

See August 7, 1996.

March 1, 1996

President Clinton decertifies Colombia's cooperation in the drug war.

Under congressional legislation requiring the president to certify what nations cooperated with the United States in ending drug traffic, Clinton decertified Colombia because its cooperation weakened during 1995. The United States was pleased with Colombia's drug prosecutor, who convicted six of the seven Cali drug cartel leaders and helped eradicate a record cocoa crop in 1995. Yet the State Department indicated Colombian President Ernesto Samper received drug money to finance his 1994 election campaign and refused to extradite four drug lords captured by Colombian police.

Two later events seemed to verify the U.S. claim of Samper's connection with drug lords. In July, Colombia released the Medellín drug cartel leader, Jorge Luis Ochoa, after serving only five and one-half-years in prison but refused to extradite him to the United States. Second, two of Samper's associates were convicted of using drug money to finance his 1994 presidential campaign.

Although Colombia was decertified, U.S. legislation allowed the Clinton administration to continue funding Colombia's drug prosecutions, an amount making up most of the aid sent to Colombia. This legislation assisted American businesspeople and investors in Colombia who relied on bank credit from the U.S. Export-Import Bank or Overseas Private Investment Corporation.

March 1, 1996

A presidential espionage commission recommends smaller intelligence agencies.

Because members of Congress raised questions about financing 13 separate U.S. intelligence agencies, President Clinton established a special commission to study intelligence needs for the post–Cold War era. The commission proposed to shrink the number of intelligence groups but to retain the basic structure intact, giving the CIA authority to manage the future agencies. In addition, the commission suggested that Clinton ask Congress to reveal the total size of the budget for secret intelligence, a step the president took on April 24, 1996.

The need for better management of the agencies was evident in 1996 because on four occasions Americans were arrested for giving classified documents to foreign countries. On March 24, Robert Lipka, an employee of the National Security Agency (NSA), was charged with spying for the Soviet Union during the 1960s. Lipka had eluded detection until 1993 when his ex-wife told the FBI about his activities. After an FBI agent posing as a Russian intelligence officer solicited Lipka's willingness to spy again, Lipka was arrested.

Later in 1995, Robert King, Harold J. Nicholson, and Earl Edward Pitts were also arrested for spying. On September 25, King was arrested for using his position as a U.S. naval intelligence officer to deliver classified data to South Korea. On November 17, Nicholson became the highest-ranking CIA official to be charged with spying for Russia. And on December 19, FBI agent Pitts was arrested after he was found to have spied for Moscow for more than 13 years.

March 7, 1996

In Gaza, PNA leader Arafat claims the PNA's democracy is hindered by Israeli restrictions.

Arafat proclaimed a "new democracy" at the first meeting of the 88-member Palestine Legislative Council in Gaza. The council was elected in January 1996 in accordance with the 1995 Oslo II agreement. Foreign diplomats, an honor guard, and an Egyptian military band attended the meeting, but Arafat's problems with Israel persisted. To end Islamic terrorist influence in Gaza and the West Bank, Israel restricted all outside trade with the Palestinians, causing shortages of food and fuel in the "new democracy."

See March 13, 1996.

March 7, 1996

Chinese-Taiwan missile crisis disrupts Sino-American relations.

On February 4, President Clinton became aware that China began military exercises after naval intelligence reported that 10,000 troops, missiles, and heavy equipment moved into the Fujian province adjacent to Taiwan. Immediately, U.S. Undersecretary of State, told Chinese Vice Foreign Minister Li Zhaoxing that the U.S.-Taiwan Relations act directed the president "to resist any resort to force" against Taiwan. In response, Li claimed Taiwan's status was China's internal affair; no nation should interfere.

On March 7, a U.S. air force reconnaissance plane reported that three Chinese missiles had splashed into the ocean near Taiwan, one going directly over the capital city of Taipei before landing 19 miles offshore. That evening several of the president's security advisers met for a scheduled dinner with a senior Chinese security officer, Liu Huaqin. During the dinner, Defense Secretary William Perry referred to Taiwan, telling Liu the missiles fired that day employed a tactic that was reckless and there could be "grave consequences" should Chinese weapons strike Taiwan— diplomatic code words for a U.S. military response.

On March 9, Chairman of the Joint Chiefs of Staff General John Shalikashvili briefed Clinton's security advisers on the question of China's intentions. After explaining China's present military exercises, Shalikashvili ruled out a full-scale Chinese invasion of Taiwan because China had insufficient amphibious ships. China's intentions were unknown unless the Chinese simply meant to intimidate Taiwan prior to

Members of Clinton's foreign policy team meet in the Cabinet Room. From left: Coit Blacker, Samuel Berger, John Deutch, Anthony Lake, Warren Christopher, Strobe Talbott, James Collins. White House

the March 23 Taiwanese elections. Later that day, Clinton approved Defense Secretary Perry's proposal to send the aircraft carrier USS *Nimitz* to join its sister carrier the USS *Independence* near Taiwan.

Subsequently on March 12, Chinese officials told U.S. embassy officials in Beijing that the missiles fired were not intended to hit Taiwan. By March 25, China's military exercises were completed and the crisis ended. In April, Clinton boarded the *Independence* to congratulate the officers and crew for showing "our power to the world without firing a bullet." The president then ordered a review of U.S. policy on China. In July, he adopted a policy to seek a "strategic partnership" with China but the Taiwan issue remained.

See October 29, 1997.

March 12, 1996

President Clinton signs the Helms-Burton Act to restrict trade of other nations with Cuba.

The Helms-Burton Act was not considered in 1995 because of Clinton's veto threat. The bill was revived on February 24, 1996 after Cuban antiaircraft shot down two civilian airplanes, killing four passengers. Brothers to the Rescue, an anti-Castro group of Cubans who lived in Miami, Florida owned the aircraft. The Brother's aircraft was flying along Cuba's coastline to drop anti-Castro pamphlets that would be

carried by the wind to land near Havana. According to U.S. Secretary of State Warren Christopher, the Brother's airplane was unarmed and flying in international water when the Cuban antiaircraft shot it down. Because the plane did not threaten Cuban security, Christopher said Cuba violated international law by destroying the aircraft.

After this incident, President Clinton decided to punish Cuba by supporting the Helms-Burton Act that Congress had already approved (see January 1, 1997).

Many foreign governments objected to the Helms-Burton Act because it would restrict their trade and investments in Cuba. It sought to damage Cuba's economy by punishing foreign merchants and investors using property confiscated by Cuba's government after the 1959 revolution. The new law also codified U.S. embargoes against Cuba, meaning a Cuban embargo could be lifted only if the Congress consented.

Although Helms-Burton punished foreigners who invested in Cuba, U.S. Trade Representative Mickey Kantor claimed the legislation was consistent with the North American Free Trade Agreement and other world trade pacts. The United States had embargoed Cuban trade since 1961 and the Helms-Burton Act required other nations to join the embargo. The bill allowed American citizens to sue foreign individuals or foreign investors who managed, leased, possessed, used, or held an interest in property confiscated by the Cuban government from American citizens. Canada, Mexico, the European Union, Russia, and 14 Caribbean nations objected to the legislation, demanding to know how it affected their relations with Cuba.

See June 4, 1959; January 1, 1997.

March 13, 1996

President Clinton and Egyptian President Mubarak sponsor a conference to condemn terrorism.

At Sharm al-Shiek, Egypt, 27 national leaders condemned suicide-bombing attacks against Israel and agreed to cooperate in fighting terrorism. In addition to Clinton and 14 Arab leaders, the one-day session was attended by Russian President Boris Yeltsin, French President Jacques Chirac, and British Prime Minister John Major. Another outcome of the Sharm al-Shiek meeting was Canada's agreement to give the Palestine National Authority (PNA) detecting devices to help police locate explosives, a method to prevent potential bombers from attacking Israel. Securing the cooperation of these leaders was a major achievement and Clinton hoped to boost the candidacy of Israeli Prime Minister Yitzhak Peres and his Labor Party members in the May 31 elections.

The United States also made plans to help Israel defend its borders. On April 29, Clinton announced the United States would assist Israel in building a defense shield against the ballistic missiles and small size-rockets that Hezbollah's fundamentalist Islamic group used to bomb Israeli territory along the Israeli-Lebanese border.

Clinton was disappointed that Syrian President Hafiz al-Assad rejected an invitation to attend. Since February 16, the Hezbollah had raided Israeli military installations and villages on Lebanon's border. On March 20, Clinton asked Assad to control the Hezbollah attacks but Assad refused.

See April 24, 1996.

March 13, 1996

President Yeltsin orders an end to the war in Chechnya.

With Russia's presidential elections scheduled for June 16, 1996, Boris Yeltsin wanted to end the unpopular Chechnya war. Russian opinion polls showed that Communist Party candidate Gennadi Zyuganov could win the election in June, and Yeltsin wanted favorable conditions to help him defeat Zyuganov. In addition to playing down the Chechnya conflict, Yeltsin used his control of the media to report stories opposing Zyuganov to assure Yeltsin's election victory.

See July 3, 1996.

March 12, 1996

Taiwanese President Lee is reelected.

Since June 1995 when President Lee Teng-hui visited the United States, Chinese relations with Taiwan had been tense. After China fired missiles toward Taiwan, the United States sent navy carrier groups to monitor Chinese military exercises, but the Chinese said the missile test was not the prelude to an invasion.

Apparently China sought to intimidate Taiwan, whose presidential election was held on March 23. If so, the Taiwanese rebuked Beijing, giving President Lee a second term in a landslide victory. Although he advocated Taiwan's independence from China, Lee complied with U.S. requests to avert a confrontation by softening his demands for independence.

See March 7, 1996.

April 3, 1996

The death of U.S. Secretary of Commerce Ron Brown in a plane crash over Croatia draws attention to the rebuilding of Bosnia.

The November 1995 Dayton Accords gave the European Union (EU) primary responsibility for reconstructing Bosnia's economy but did not commit funds for this purpose. In December 1995, the World Bank surveyed the Bosnian economy whose infrastructure had been destroyed after three years of war. The EU appointed former Swedish Prime Minister Carl Bildt to direct the reconstruction, but in March Bildt warned that the job could not be completed by the December 20, 1996, deadline Clinton had requested.

As secretary of commerce, Brown played a key role in arranging U.S. investment funds to help Bosnia. The crash killed him, the aircraft's crew, and 35 passengers, who were executives of American businesses, construction firms, and engineering groups.

Despite the tragedy, the EU and World Bank held a scheduled conference in Brussels on April 10 to

The headquarters of the European Union Parliament and Council at Strasburg.
Lester Brune

determine priorities for a three-year building program expected to cost $5 billion. President Clinton appointed Trade Representative Mickey Kantor as secretary of commerce to oversee U.S. investments in Bosnia. At Brussels, the EU solicited donor pledges for the first year of the program. Among the first donations, the United States pledged $281.7 million; Japan, $285 million; the EU, $373 million; and the World Bank, $350 million. After Americans questioned the right of Bosnian Serb aggressors to obtain financial aid, the delegates agreed aid was intended for all Bosnian groups complying with the Dayton Accords.

See June 14, 1996.

April 14, 1996

American troops evacuate hundreds of U.S. and foreign citizens from Liberia.

After experiencing civil conflict since 1989, Liberia's three factions agreed to a cease-fire and established an interim government on March 7, 1994. The three factions were a rebel guerrilla band in Sierra Leone, a faction led by Liberian interim President Amos Sawyer, and a faction led by Charles Taylor, who had begun a rebellion against Liberia's President Samuel K. Dove in December 1989. The March 7 cease-fire in Liberia ended in April when factions resumed their struggle for power. Because most of the U.S. embassy had been evacuated previously, on April 15 U.S. Marines from naval ships evacuated hundreds of foreigners endangered in Liberia.

Although on April 26, U.N. mediators persuaded the three factions to pledge a cease-fire, fighting continued through most of the summer. On August 18, the West African Economic Community joined U.N. peacekeeping forces to obtain a cease-fire.

See July 19, 1997.

April 17, 1996

President Clinton and Japanese Prime Minister Hashimoto affirm the need for U.S. bases in Okinawa and other East Asian areas.

President Clinton visited Tokyo at a time when questions were arising about American bases in Okinawa. On March 7, three U.S. servicemen were convicted for raping an Okinawa woman and some Japanese wanted U.S. forces to leave the island.

To resolve the situation, Prime Minister Ryutaro Hashimoto and President Clinton announced that a U.S. military presence was essential to both nations. In line with Clinton's policy, U.S. Defense Secretary William Perry announced on March 5 that the United States would relinquish 20% of the land for its base in Okinawa and take steps to reduce U.S. military activity on Okinawa.

April 22, 1996

The United States, Brazil, and the OAS prevent the overthrow of Paraguayan President Wasmosy.

Following his election in 1993, Juan Carlos Wasmosy discovered he had been betrayed by Army Commander General Lino César Oviedo, who had helped him win the election but now tried to override the president's authority over the armed forces. On April 22, Wasmosy told General Oviedo to resign as army commander but Oviedo refused, threatening to rally the army to overthrow Wasmosy.

Before firing Oviedo, Wasmosy told his plan to U.S. Ambassador Robert Service, Argentinian Ambassador Nestor Ahuad, and Brazilian Ambassador Marcio d'Oliveira Dias. After Oviedo refused to resign, these ambassadors urged Wasmosy to hold firm and not resign as president. The U.S. embassy in Asunción issued a statement condemning Oviedo's action as unconstitutional and contrary to democratic norms accepted by Western Hemisphere countries. The United States also asked the Organization of American States (OAS) to condemn Oviedo's action at its next Washington meeting.

After Oviedo talked with the three ambassadors, they told newspaper reporters that the OAS opposed any interruption in Paraguay's democratic process. If Oviedo did not resign, Paraguay would be isolated.

Although most of Paraguay's politicians backed Wasmosy, the president feared that an army attack on the presidential palace would cost the lives of many citizens. To delay an attack, Wasmosy agreed to move to the U.S. embassy. The U.S. State Department also asked all foreign ministries in Europe and Latin America to send messages of support for Wasmosy. The foreign approval was aided by demonstrations in the streets of Asunción, where crowds favored the president. Workers, labor union leaders, and even political opposition parties backed Wasmosy.

On April 24, Wasmosy delivered a speech saying Oviedo must resign because it was the will of the Paraguayan people. Soon after, Oviedo resigned because Paraguay's air force, navy, and all but a few army battalions expressed support for Wasmosy. The military coup was prevented by immediate foreign support for the government. Some political analysts contrasted Paraguay's success with the failure of the United States and other nations to support Haiti's President Aristide in 1991.

See September 30, 1991.

April 24, 1996

President Clinton signs antiterrorism legislation.

In the wake of the April 1995 bombing of an Oklahoma City federal building and terrorist attacks in New York City, Congress passed legislation aimed at stopping terrorist attacks and curbing numerous court appeals by death-row inmates. Clinton signed a law that, among other items, gave special deportation courts the power to conceal evidence from suspects and authorized funds for counterterrorist measures. On September 30, 1996, Clinton signed an Omnibus Appropriation Bill providing $1.1 billion to implement the antiterrorist legislation.

April 26, 1996

Secretary of State Warren Christopher obtains a cease-fire on the Lebanon-Israeli border.

After a lull in the 1995 attacks and retaliations between Israel's Defense Forces (IDF) and the Iranian-backed Hezbollah (Party of God) fundamentalist Shiites stationed in south Lebanon, each side began intensified attacks in February 1996. These attacks escalated in April after Hezbollah rockets struck Israeli outposts in southern Lebanon. Israeli Air Force (IAF) jets retaliated by bombing Hezbollah strongholds in Beirut and southern Lebanon while Israel's Navy blockaded the seaports of Beirut, Tyre, and Sidon and naval guns shelled Lebanon's coastline where Hezbollah camps were located.

The series of U.S.-sponsored peace talks between Syria and Israel at the Wye Conference Center near Washington (see December 28, 1995) were suspended in February after the Lebanese attacks began. Military raids by both sides continued throughout March, causing civilians in Israel and Lebanon to flee their border homes to seek refuge elsewhere. To stem these attacks, Israeli Prime Minister Shimon Peres ordered the IDF to begin daily attacks known as Operation Grapes of Wrath against Lebanon's Hezbollah after warning Lebanese civilians they were in danger of being hit. Operation Grapes of Wrath began on

April 11 and did not end until a cease-fire agreement was reached on April 26, 1996.

The intensified Israel attacks persuaded many European officials to seek terms for a cease-fire. During these 15 days, cease-fire proposals were made by foreign ministers from France, Germany, Italy, Russia, Iran, Iraq, and Egypt, as well as the Chairman of the European Union. French Foreign Minister Herve de Charette played a significant role by obtaining cease-fire terms favored by Syria's President Hafiz al-Assad and Lebanon's President Elias Hwrawi. Israel's Prime Minister Peres rejected the proposals of De Charette and other foreign ministers saying they confused the situation.

On April 19, President Clinton sent Christopher and the Special U.S. Representative Dennis Ross to the Middle East to negotiate between Syria, Lebanon, and Israel. Christopher's efforts obtained a cease-fire satisfactory to Peres and Assad but its signing was delayed for two days because de Charette tried to persuade Syria's President Assad to first take control of Hezbollah's military action in Lebanon. On April 25, Christopher finally witnessed the signing of the cease-fire agreement by Peres in Jerusalem and by Assad in Damascus. The agreement included French officials in a group to monitor the cease-fire. Christopher explained the agreement's terms to de Charette, who agreed France would join the monitoring group. The cease-fire became effective on April 27 at 4 o'clock in the morning local time.

To monitor the cease-fire, delegates from France, the United States, Israel, Syria, and Lebanon would make up a monitoring team to replace U.N. monitors on July 12, 1996. The U.S. State Department claimed U.N. monitors should be removed from Lebanon because U.N. Secretary General Boutros Boutros-Ghali allegedly manipulated reports against Israel to get Arab and other non-aligned nation's support his second term campaign as the U.N. Secretary General.

See December 28, 1995. Regarding the monitors see July 9, 1996.

April 27, 1996

The U.N. Security Council imposes economic sanctions on the Sudan.

Although Sudanese President Omar Ahmad al-Bashir was reelected on March 11, international observers said the election was fraudulent because opposition parties were banned and elections were held only 12 days after being announced. In addition, on February 13, U.N. authorities reported the Sudan's refusal to extradite three men suspected of an attempted assassination of Egyptian President Mubarak in June 1995.

On April 4, after asking the U.N. Security Council to impose sanctions on the Sudan, the United States expelled the Sudan's U.N. diplomat, Ahmed Yousef Mohamed, for supplying information to Islamic terrorists plotting the 1994 bombing of the U.N. and other New York buildings.

Because the Security Council was divided on its Sudanese policy, the economic sanctions approved on April 27 were milder than the United States wanted. The sanctions never harmed the Sudanese economy which depended on aid from Libya, Iran, and Iraq, three nations also having U.N. sanctions levied against them.

May 6, 1996

A new constitution transforms South Africa from white supremacy to democracy.

South Africa's Constitutional Assembly approved the final draft of a constitution to establish democracy with no basis in race. Former President F.W. de Klerk realized Nelson Mandela's African National Congress would control the new parliament and resigned from South Africa's transitional council on May 9. De Klerk worked with Mandela to end South Africa's apartheid policy of white supremacy.

May 10, 1996

India's governing party is defeated in parliamentary elections.

Since 1947, India's Congress Party had been in power all but four years. In the May 10 elections, Congress received 25% of parliament's seats, with a plurality going to the right-wing Hindu Nationalist Party. On May 15, that party chose Atal Bihari Vajpayee as prime minister, but his Hindu nationalism alienated both Muslims and people favoring India's secular tradition. Realizing he could not get a vote of confidence, Vajpayee resigned after 13 days. In June, regional parties joined with the National Front–Left Front Alliance to organize a 13-party coalition with a government headed by H. D. Gowda. The son of a lower-caste farmer, Gowda became a millionaire from property investments and supervising road contracts. On June 12, Gowda's government received a vote of confidence from India's lower house of parliament.

See April 21, 1997.

May 17, 1996

South Korea's guards force North Koreans to leave the demilitarized zone (DMZ).

On April 5, 1996, North Korea's army began military exercises on the DMZ, hauling in mortar and machine guns pointing toward South Korea. This activity defied the 1953 agreement ending the Korean War, which allowed only a few soldiers carrying side arms to be near the center of the DMZ. Although South Korean President Kim Young Sam denounced these activities, U.S. officials thought they were meant only to annoy South Korea and demonstrate President Kim Young Sam could act as forcefully as his father following the death of North Korean President Kim Il Sung.

The April exercises became an incursion on May 17 when seven North Korean soldiers crossed the center before South Korean guards fired shots over their heads to chase them away. Tensions continued on the border and became serious four months later.

See September 18, 1996.

May 31, 1996

Saudi Arabia executes four men who bombed the U.S. barracks in Riyadh.

In March 1996, Saudi police arrested four suspects who confessed to bombing the Riyadh apartment complex in November 1995. According to Saudi law, they were beheaded on May 31.

A week before the execution, the U.S. embassy in Riyadh received an anonymous phone call that a Saudi militant group would retaliate if the four men were executed. Although the Saudi government convicted the four men without allowing the U.S. Federal Bureau of Investigation or the CIA to interrogate them, the militants wanted Washington to remove all U.S. military personnel from Saudi Arabia.

See June 25, 1996.

June 12, 1996

Former U.S. Senator George J. Mitchell heads Northern Ireland's peace talks.

Although Protestant critics claimed that Mitchell, a Roman Catholic, would be prejudiced against them, the senator's defenders said his fairness and integrity made him suitable for the discussions designed to end 30 years of conflict in Northern Ireland.

Mitchell faced a daunting task in Northern Ireland. Although a cease-fire was declared on September 1, 1994, it held only because British authorities feared more killings if they officially ended the cease-fire. Before Mitchell was named to head the peace talks, widespread but small-scale terrorist attacks continued by both Protestant and Roman Catholic militants. On June 16, soon after the peace talks were scheduled to begin, the Irish Republican Army (IRA) exploded a bomb in Manchester, England, wounding 200 people. Mitchell and the British did not achieve a cease-fire during 1996.

On December 1, President Clinton visited Northern Ireland, where he was cheered by thousands. Clinton called for a cease-fire and peace talks, but the IRA and militant Protestants continued the violence.

See October 5–6, 1968; June 25, 1997.

June 14, 1996

Balkan leaders sign an arms control agreement.

As required by the 1995 Dayton Accords, a Balkan arms control treaty was signed in Florence, Italy, on June 14. Negotiated under the auspices of the Organization for Security and Cooperation in Europe (OSCE), the treaty was approved by representatives from Yugoslavia, Croatia, the Bosnian Federation of Croats and Muslims, and the Srpska Republic where Bosnian Serbs lived. In Bosnia, the federation was allocated two weapons for every one allowed the Bosnian Serbs. The arms treaty also provided for weapons cuts for Yugoslavia and Croatia. Under the treaty, signatories would allow international experts to monitor the weapons that each possessed or destroyed under treaty terms.

One year later, the OSCE issued an optimistic report about the destruction of arms by each signatory. In reality, the arms agreement was being violated because tensions continued throughout the region.

See September 14, 1996.

June 25, 1996

Nineteen Americans are killed when a bomb destroys apartments in Dhahran, Saudi Arabia.

At 10 P.M. on June 25, a Mercedes-Benz fuel truck parked about 100 feet from the Khobar Towers apartments in Dhahran, the residence of U.S. air force personnel. When the truck exploded, the blast destroyed an entire section of the apartment complex, killing 19 Americans and wounding 450, of which 148 suffered serious injuries. The Dhahran attack resembled the bombing of the U.S. apartment complex in Riyadh in November 1995. Following that incident, the CIA and other bomb experts calculated that a 200-pound bomb was the largest Saudi militants were capable of making, an assumption proven wrong on July 25.

After the November attack, experts believed a 100-foot barricade in Dhahran was better than the 80-foot barricade at Riyadh, although some consultants wanted a barricade of 400 feet from the Khobar Towers. The 400-foot barricade was not erected, but new protection at Dhahran included more concrete barricades, a serpentine barrier, a metal antitank device, observation posts on top of the building, and a "Great Voice" that would go off loudly to warn of an emergency. None of these was effective on July 25. Suspects were spotted leaving the building but eluded capture.

See November 23, 1996.

June 27, 1996

Congress refuses to revoke China's MFN status.

Under prior legislation, President Clinton renewed China's most-favored-nation status on May 10, 1996. To defeat the MFN action, Congress discussed a joint resolution repealing the president's action. After the House rejected a proposal to repeal China's MFN status, the Senate did not take action.

In early 1996, Clinton had trouble with China's threat to attack Taiwan. China also refused to protect Americans from international copyright violations by Chinese citizens, but Beijing was also reported to have sold nuclear technology to Pakistan. On May 10, Clinton accepted China's denial of helping Pakistan's nuclear program, while Beijing promised to prevent copyright infringements.

June 29, 1996

Turkey's anti-Israel Welfare Party leads a new coalition government.

Most American experts on Turkey were surprised that the State Department accepted the new coalition because the Welfare (Refah) Party was an Islamic fundamentalist group similar to that ruling Iran after its 1979 revolution. Prime Minister Necmettin Erbakan's coalition included Tansu Ciller's Motherland Party. Ciller had previously opposed the Islamic fundamentalists but apparently thought her position as both deputy prime minister and foreign minister would moderate Erbakan's anti-Western attitudes.

U.S. support for Turkey's new government was demonstrated in August when U.S. Ambassador to the United Nations Madeleine Albright met Erbakan and gained approval for renewing Operation Provide Comfort's mandate, which had expired on December 31, 1996. This U.S.-British operation began in April 1991 to protect Kurds in northern Iraq.

In other respects, Erbakan's coalition aroused U.S. concern when, in October, Prime Minister Erbakan ignored U.S. warnings by signing trade agreements with Libya, Iran, and Iraq, nations on whom the United States had imposed economic sanctions.

See February 28, 1997.

July 3, 1996

Boris Yeltsin is reelected president of Russia.

Although Yeltsin's followers in the Duma (parliament) had not fared well against Communist and ultranationalists in the December 1995 elections, Yeltsin's chance for winning were revived by having also sought the services of an American consulting firm to provide instructions about polling, television ads, and a campaign to focus on Russians' fears of social disorder and class warfare if Communists and ultranationalists came to power.

On June 19, in the first round of voting for 10 candidates, Yeltsin received 35% of the vote; Communist Party nominee Gennadi Zyuganov, 32%; Independent Party candidate General Alexsandr Lebed received 20%; and seven other candidates divided the remaining 13%. Because General Lebed was idolized for his heroic actions during the Afghanistan war, Yeltsin appointed Lebed as Russia's National Security chief on June 30. Lebed announced his support for Yeltsin in the runoff election; thereby helping Yeltsin win the election. On July 3, Yeltsin defeated Zyuganov by a margin of 13%. Yet Yeltsin's campaign took a heavy toll on his health. By September, Yeltsin faced heart surgery while National Security Chief Lebed quarreled with Prime Minister Victor Chermomyrdin and the armed forces Chief of Staff Anatoly Chubais about the proper policy for ending Russia's conflict with Chechnya.

July 9, 1996

President Clinton's meeting with Israeli Prime Minister Netanyahu has no salutary results.

Although the Likud Party's right-wing coalition won Israel's May 31 elections, Prime Minister Benjamin Netanyahu did not form a ministry until June 18. Three weeks later, Netanyahu visited the United States to talk with Clinton, address a joint session of Congress, and meet with key politicians in Washington. His session with President Clinton failed to resolve their differences because Clinton preferred the peace process with Palestine promoted by former Israeli Prime Minister Peres. Netanyahu reversed the policies that Israeli leaders had advanced since the Oslo Accords were signed.

In particular, Netanyahu ended the freeze on Jewish West Bank settlements, proclaimed that Israel must have sovereignty over Jerusalem, and delayed the withdrawal of the Israeli Defense Force (IDF) from Hebron, as scheduled by former Prime Ministers Peres and Rabin. The Likud Party's hardline attitude soon broke into open conflict between the IDF and Palestinians.

See September 13, 1993; September 24, 1996.

August 5, 1996

The United States levies economic sanctions on countries doing business with Libya and Iran.

Despite objections from France, Italy, and Belgium, Congress and President Clinton approved sanctions on foreigners who invested at least $40 million in one year in Iran or in Libya's oil industries. In the case of Libya, the legislation backed a U.N. Security Council resolution calling for sanctions on Libya for refusing to extradite two bombing suspects. Allegedly, the two were involved in bombing a Pan American plane over Scotland, killing 270 people in December 1988.

See December 21, 1988.

August 7, 1996

The U.N. Security Council approves Iraq's sale of oil for food after Iraq accepts U.N. inspection devices.

Since September 1991, Iraqi president Saddam Hussein had rejected Security Council plans for an oil-for-food program to provide food and medicine for Iraqi people by selling Iraq's petroleum. During these years, the news media usually accepted Hussein's propaganda about the suffering of Iraq's women and children because of U.N. sanctions. In contrast, the U.S. State Department contended that Hussein should be blamed for the suffering because he used Iraq's financial assets to build lavish palaces, import antitank weapons from Bulgaria, and T-72 tanks from Russia and China. According to Richard Butler, head of the U.N. Special Commission inspecting Iraq's weapons, Hussein also used millions of dollars to rebuild a chemical weapons factory and two missile facilities destroyed during the 1991 war in the Gulf.

By early 1996, Iraq seemed ready to accept an oil-for-food program. The only obstacle was its approval of monitoring devices that the U.N. Special Commission (UNSCOM) would install in "sensitive" buildings where Iraq might try to produce weapons of mass destruction. In late July, Iraq agreed UNSCOM could install the devices, and, with U.S. approval, the Security Council permitted Iraq to sell $2 billion of oil and purchase food and medicine for Iraq's people.

See September 14, 1996.

August 9, 1996

Chechen rebels retake Grozny while Boris Yeltsin is inaugurated president for a second term.

Although in May 1996, Yeltsin arbitrarily declared that the war in Chechnya was over, fighting persisted. In April 1996, Chechen President Jokar Dudayev was assassinated and in July rebels launched an offensive giving them control of Grozny, the capital, by August

9, the same day Yeltsin was inaugurated as president of Russia. In the hope of ending the conflict, Yeltsin asked National Security Chief Alexsander Lebed to obtain a cease-fire.

See August 23, 1996.

August 12, 1996

Somali warlord Aideed dies and is replaced by his son, Hussein Aideed.

After all U.N. forces were removed from Somalia in 1995, conflict continued among various factions, especially near the capital, Mogadishu. Mohammad Farah Aideed remained as Mogadishu's strongest warlord but constantly had to defend the city's airport from sub-clan leaders fighting to seize the humanitarian supplies arriving from donor nations. In July 1996, Osman Hassan Ali (Atto) challenged Aideed by launching attacks on the airport. In repelling Atto's force, Aideed was wounded and died during surgery. His death intensified fighting in Somalia until Hussein Mohammad Aideed returned from the United States to lead his father's clan and sub-clans against other Somalian warlords and their clans. Hussein's mother had taken him to the United States during the 1980s, where he became a U.S. citizen and served with the U.S. Marines in Somalia in 1993. Now, he returned home to replace his father in the competition among Somalia's clans.

August 20, 1996

India vetoes the international test ban treaty.

Despite pleas from the United States and other nuclear powers, India refused to join a treaty to end nuclear testing. Although critics at Geneva blamed President Clinton for not pressuring other powers to obtain India's approval, India's negotiator, Arundhati Ghose, said India would never sign a test ban treaty until all nuclear powers pledged to destroy their own nuclear weapons facilities. Although undeclared nuclear powers Israel and Pakistan were ready to sign the treaty, India refused.

After the agreement faltered, Australia sponsored a nuclear test ban treaty before the U.N. General Assembly. On September 7, the assembly adopted the agreement but India refused to sign. In addition to India, Iran and Libya also rejected the test ban treaty.

August 23, 1996

Russia's peace treaty with Chechnya requires the withdrawal of most Russian forces.

After rebel forces recaptured Grozny on August 9, Russia's National Security Adviser, Aleksandr Lebed negotiated a cease-fire and peace agreement with rebel leader Aslan Maskhadov. Yet peace depended on negotiations to determine Chechnya's future relations with Russia.

Soon after Lebed completed the negotiations, about policy in Chechnya, President Yeltsin sought to resolve problems between his two principal officials: Lebed and Viktor Chernomyrdin. On September 10, Yeltsin showed preference for Chernomyrdin by giving him control of national security and law enforcement. Lebed was unhappy with the arrangement and Yeltsin dismissed him on October 17.

See November 23, 1996.

September 14, 1996

Bosnia's national elections are held; local elections are delayed.

In compliance with the 1995 Dayton Accords, the Organization of Security and Cooperation in Europe (OSCE) supervised national elections in Bosnia but delayed local and municipal elections because few refugees had returned to their former homes. The absentee ballots of refugees could easily be verified in national elections, but refugees would be unable to participate in campaigns for local elections.

Before conducting elections, the OSCE had to resolve several problems. On June 25, it reported that Bosnian conditions permitted "fair and free" national elections to be held, but Bosnian Federation President Izetbegović complained because the Serbian Republic's nominees were war criminals indicted by the Hague Tribunal. Under the Dayton Accords, NATO's IFOR was supposed to arrest war criminals, but such arrests had low priority for IFOR. In particular, IFOR did not arrest the Serbian Republic's President Radovan Karadžić and Army General Ratko Mladić, who controlled Bosnian Serb politics.

To satisfy Izetbegović, the five-member Contact Group of the United States, Russia, Great Britain,

France, and Germany met in London on July 10 and demanded Karadžić and Mladić resign. To carry out this demand, Richard Holbrooke and Russia's Contact Group member visited Belgrade and obtained Milošević's cooperation because he had represented the Serbian Republic at the Dayton conference. Milošević persuaded Karadžić to resign as president and head of the Serbs' Social Democrat Party (SDS). Although Mladić refused to resign, Biljana Plašvić replaced Karadžić as president, a change Izetbegović accepted as sufficient to hold elections.

With two-thirds of eligible voters participating, the OSCE reported that results confirmed Bosnia and Herzegovina's three ethnic divisions. Elected for the three-member presidency were the Serbs' Momčilo Krajisnik, the Croats' Kresimir Zubak, and the Muslims' Alija Izetbegović, who won a plurality of votes to become chairman of the presidency. In parliament, the Bosnian Federation won the expected two-to-one number of seats compared with the Serbs. In each ethnic group, hard-line nationalists won all but 7 of the 42 House of Representative seats. On September 19, the OSCE certified the election results and Bosnia's new government began to operate. The first meeting of the parliament of Bosnia and Herzegovina was on January 3, 1997.

On the Serbian Republic, see November 27, 1996.

September 14, 1996

The Iraqi army helps one Kurdish faction.

Iraqi armed forces joined Kurdish leader Massoud Barzani's forces to attack Kurds loyal to Kurdish leader Jalal Talaban. Since 1991, U.S. Presidents Bush and Clinton tried to unify Kurdish factions but hatred between Barzani and Talaban divided the Kurds. CIA agents believed the two leaders had healed relations but overlooked the fact that Barzani still cooperated with Iraqi President Saddam Hussein.

On August 17, fighting broke out between Barzani's Kurdistan Democratic Party (KDP) and Talaban's Patriotic Union of Kurdistan (PUK), but the White House ignored these events until August 31, when Iraqi forces helped the KDP. To assist Barzani, Hussein sent 40,000 Iraqi Republican Guardsmen to attack a PUK enclave at Arbil. After Iraqi troops entered the city, Barzani loyalists helped Hussein's secret police (mukabarat) find many PUK

members who were subsequently tortured and killed. Iraqi forces also destroyed the PUK's television, radio, and military installations.

President Clinton reacted slowly to Iraq's attack but on September 2 ordered U.S. aircraft in Turkey to launch missiles against northern Iraq, destroying some of Iraq's military equipment and forcing the Republican Guard to withdraw from Arbil on September 14. President Hussein had achieved his main goal of preventing Kurdish unity. Despite Barzani's treachery, Assistant Secretary of State Robert Pelletreau met with him on October 31 and reported that the KDP agreed to a cease-fire with the PUK. Barzani also offered to reconcile differences with Taliban to restore Kurdish unity.

See November 25, 1996.

September 18, 1996

Clinton's Korean policy is challenged at the demilitarized zone (DMZ).

Since 1994, North Korea's food supply had depended on humanitarian aid from the United States government and other American humanitarian aid groups. Except for United States donors, United Nations officials for the World Food Program reported they could not meet their minimum goal for North Korea of $12.5 million in food donations from all other nations combined. The U.N. officials estimated that 85% to 90% of all North Koreans suffered from deficient food as calculated by North Korea's official rations per-person per-day of less than 450 calories (in the United States dieticians say the minimum input of calories should be 2000 per day).

According to Walter R. Mead of the World Policy Institute in New York, most foreign donors viewed North Korea as "paranoid, rabid weasels, deaf to counsels of moderation" and ready to strike out in "vicious, unpredictable directions at any time." Although Mead's visit to North Korea persuaded him that this view was not accurate, the foreign impression seemed to be confirmed on September 18, 1996 when North Korean soldiers arrived by submarine near the 1953 demilitarized zone. South Korean troops found them and engaged the North Koreans in a fire-fight. The shoot-out killed 20 North Koreans and four South Koreans, including one civilian. Later, South Korean officials believed some North Korean deaths were either victims of mass suicide or of execution by their superior officers. The submarine incursion was the latest in a series of North Korean escapades near the border (see May 17, 1996).

Despite tensions between North and South Korea, the United States continued sending humanitarian aid to North Korea. During the fall of 1996, North Korea's government finalized plans for a conference with foreign investors in which North Korean businessmen could solicit foreign partners to participate in the free enterprise zone North Korea planned for a northeast sector of the country. In addition, North Korea permitted Americans to search for the remains of U.S. soldiers missing-in-action since the 1950–1953 Korean War, and to remove fuel rods from North Korea's nuclear plants as part of the 1994 Geneva Agreement (see August 10, 1994).

In contrast to these favorable relations between North Korea and the outside world, North Korean policies disappointed both the United States and South Korea. On September 20 the International Atomic Energy Agency (IAEA) condemned North Korea for not admitting international monitors to inspect its nuclear facilities. North Korea also refused to begin peace talks with South Korea as required by the 1994 Geneva agreements. Due to North Korea's perplexing policy of promoting good relations in some instances and demoting relations in others, U.S. relations with South Korea during the Clinton administration were difficult to assess.

September 24, 1996

Israel's opening of a Jerusalem tunnel leads to violence between Israelis and Palestinians.

In line with Prime Minister Netanyahu's effort to place all Jerusalem under Jewish authority, Israeli workers under a heavy police guard began a surprise predawn excavation of a disputed ancient tunnel that ran along the Al Aqsa mosque, an Islamic holy site near the Jewish Wailing Wall.

The surprise opening of the tunnel inaugurated protests by Palestinians that led to the greatest violence in the West Bank since 1993. For the first time, Israeli soldiers clashed with police of the Palestine National Authority (PNA) not only in Jerusalem but also in Ramallah, Nablus, Bethlehem, Hebron, and Gaza City. Over a period of four days, a Paris-based Human Rights Watch calculated that 15 Israeli sol-

diers and 86 Palestinians were killed, including 16 Palestinian children.

The violence raged until early October, when U.S. mediator Dennis Ross persuaded Israel and the Palestinians to negotiate their differences. Ross focused on the Hebron issue but achieved no results during 1996. Netanyahu wanted to modify prior agreements on Hebron, but PNA leader Arafat refused to reopen issues that Israel had accepted in the Oslo I and Oslo II agreements.

See January 14, 1997.

September 27, 1996

Afghan Taliban rebels capture Kabul and impose strict Islamic law; U.S. policy is uncertain.

The 1992 U.N. efforts failed to bring peace to Afghanistan because Islamic mujahideen guerrilla factions continued fighting (see April 28, 1992). In mid–1994, Pakistan severed its assistance to all Afghan factions except for the new Taliban ("seekers of knowledge"). Pakistan backed the Taliban not only because many Islamic scholars taught schools in Pakistan but

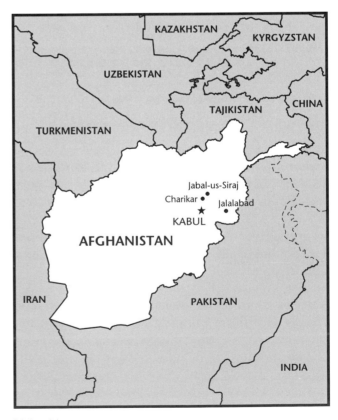

Afghanistan

also because India supported warlords fighting against the Taliban in northern Afghanistan.

In particular, Amir Mullah Muhammad Omar, a former mujahideen leader, studied the Koran in a Pakistan refugee camp when he began organizing the Taliban in 1994. Omar soon enrolled former Muslim guerrillas discontent with the internecine fighting among the mujahideen factions that had plundered Afghanistan since 1992. The Taliban's initial attack on a mujahideen encampment in 1994 led to the discovery of 800 truckloads of arms and ammunition hidden in a cave. The discovery provided the Taliban with enough weapons to gain command over other villages. The Taliban's early success led Pakistan to provide them with more weapons as well as food and other essential commodities.

After enlisting other soldiers, especially from fellow ethnic Pushtuns, the Taliban had gained control of Kabul, as well as 20 of Afghanistan's 32 provinces, by September 27, 1996. In capturing Kabul, they chased out Ahmad Shah Masud, a warlord who led the northern faction. Masud's guerrillas continued the struggle in Afghanistan's 12 northern provinces. Upon capturing Kabul, the Taliban soldiers killed many Afghan leaders who had joined Soviet forces during the Soviet Union's intervention between 1979 and 1989 (see January 15, 1989). The Taliban also attacked the U.N. compound, where they brutally killed former President Muhammad Najibullah before hanging his body in Kabul's main square. Najibullah had been in the U.N. building since 1992. Yet the capture of Kabul did not end the conflict because armies of Masud and guerrillas loyal to other warlords held out in northern Afghanistan.

In Kabul, Omar and eight other Taliban mullahs made up the governing council that instituted fundamentalist Islamic law codes that restricted women from working outside the home; stoned couples to death for committing adultery; and outlawed movies, music, and chess. Because of the Taliban's severe punishments based on ancient taboos and strict regulation of women, no United Nations member gave diplomatic recognition to the Taliban government.

Having had no diplomatic representation in Kabul since 1989, the United States was uncertain how to deal with the Taliban regime. Intensive fighting continued in northern Afghanistan and president Clinton's advisers were divided on what policy to pursue. Among them Robin Raphel, the State Department specialist on Afghanistan, thought that

by "engaging" the Taliban the United States could help the new regime moderate its policies and end the country's opium production of 2,500 tons of raw opium each year. Other advisers disagreed, arguing that the Taliban not only assisted opium farmers but also harbored terrorists such as Osama bin Laden, a member of a wealthy family in Saudi Arabia.

See April 28, 1992.

September 30, 1996

President Clinton signs the budget appropriation bill for fiscal year 1997.

On September 28, the White House and Congress compromised on the 1997 budget appropriations that became official on September 30. The compromise gave the president his desired spending priorities and allowed Congress to cut the budget by $30 billion compared with the 1996 budget. In national security affairs, State Department funds were decreased compared with 1996 authorizations. The Department of Defense received $1.6 trillion, including funds for missile defense known as "three plus three." Under this project, the Ballistic Missile Defense Organization (BMDO) would have three years to design and test a THAAD (Theater High Altitude Area Defense) system. If viable, another three years were allowed to deploy the THAAD, that is, by 2003. The proposed system would construct 20 ground-based interceptors capable of blocking the few missiles that might be launched by rogue states such as North Korea, Iraq, or Iran or accidentally launched by China or Russia.

On two other budget matters, Congress gave the president power to use a line-item veto, although opponents of this veto took the law to court to decide its constitutionality. Also, in a close vote requiring a two-thirds' majority, the Senate vote of 64 to 35 failed to approve a constitutional amendment requiring a balanced budget.

October 17, 1996

Crisis in Zaire, Rwanda, and Burundi; the United States, Britain, and France differ on causes.

A Rwanda crisis begun in 1994 erupted again on October 17 when Tutsi tribes in eastern Zaire rebelled against Zaire's army near Uvira. The Tutsi tribes living in a wealthy mining region rebelled after the Zaire governor ordered them to move from their homes in six days. Armed and trained by Rwanda, the Tutsi rebels captured the cities of Uvira and Bukavu, precipitating violence in Gama, where a second Tutsi tribe attacked other Zaire army units located near a Hutu refugee camp. Fighting also broke out on Zaire's border with Burundi, whose Tutsi regime sent an army to attack both Zaire and Hutu forces. Although the United Nations had supplied food aid to the refugees since 1994, the conflict doubled the number of refugees to one million.

In New York, U.N. Security Council decisions on Zaire were delayed because France backed Zaire's leader, Mobutu Sese Seke, who lived in a luxurious hotel in Berne, Switzerland, while Zaire's underfed and underpaid soldiers lived by looting homes in regions they controlled. Britain, backed by the United States, sympathized with Rwanda, whose leaders had to contend with internecine fighting between Tutsi and Hutu tribes. On November 15, the Security Council approved a Canadian-led force to protect U.N. aid sent to refugees in Rwanda and Zaire. These measures did not end the fighting.

November 5, 1996

Pakistani Prime Minister Bhutto is dismissed by President Leghari.

Describing Prime Minister Benazir Bhutto as incompetent, corrupt, and in violation of the constitution, President Farooq Leghari placed Bhutto under house arrest. Two days later, a caretaker government freed Bhutto and announced new parliamentary elections. When the elections were held on February 4, 1997, Bhutto's People's Party lost in a landslide victory for the Pakistan Muslim League led by Imran Khan.

November 6, 1996

President Clinton is reelected but Republicans retain control of Congress.

Clinton's popular vote exceeded his 1992 margin of victory, with Robert Dole losing by 8% of the vote. Ross Perot of the Reform Party received 8% of the total vote, an amount sufficient for the Reform Party to obtain federal funds for a Reform Party candidate in 2000. In the electoral college, Clinton received 479 votes to Dole's 159.

Clinton's victory did not allow Democrats to regain control of Congress. In the House of Representatives, Democrats gained 9 seats to reduce the Republican margin to 19 members. In the Senate, the Republicans gained 2 seats, giving them a margin of 11 seats.

November 23, 1996

FBI Director Louis Freeh and Saudi officials discuss the July bombing of Khobar apartments.

Since the July bombing that killed 19 Americans, Saudi Arabian officials had interrogated 40 suspects as conspirators. The Saudis believed Iran was involved in the conspiracy because some suspects were Shiites trained at Hezbollah camps in Lebanon and used false passports to visit Iran or Syria. Among the suspects were leaders of the Saudi Hezbollah and a Shiite bomb maker. The Saudis wanted the United States to retaliate against Iran, but Freeh believed there was insufficient evidence to justify an attack.

November 23, 1996

President Yeltsin orders all Russian troops to leave Chechnya.

After the cease-fire of August 23, Chechnya remained calm. Although the agreement permitted two Russian army brigades to stay in Chechnya, the rebels seeking independence from Russia demanded that all Russian forces withdraw before discussions began on Chechnya's future. Consequently, Yeltsin ordered all Russian troops to withdraw by January 27, 1997, when an election was scheduled for Chechnya's new president and legislature. A few Russian soldiers remained as part of a joint Russian-Chechen force to guard key buildings and Grozny's airport.

November 24, 1996

President Clinton meets with China's president but cannot resolve the trade-gap favoring the Chinese.

After visiting several Southeast Asian countries, Clinton met in the Philippines with Chinese President Ziang Zemin. During the session, Clinton's main effort was to persuade the Chinese president to join the World Trade Organization (WTO). As a WTO member, China would need to provide free access to its markets but, in turn, would be shielded from unilateral trade tariffs other nations could impose.

Although international analysts claimed China's politicians debated joining the WTO, its president offered no concessions to Clinton that helped close the trade gap favoring China.

November 24, 1996

A referendum in Belarus approves a tyrannical government.

After Belarus President Lukashenko was elected, there were persistent disputes between the president and the parliament's democratically elected House of Representatives. House leaders especially were upset when Lukashenko approved an agreement with Russia to form a "union state" as the prelude to the union of the two countries.

Although the International Monetary Fund withdrew a $300 million standby loan to Belarus, parliament continued to quarrel with Lukashenko regarding a new constitution that the president prepared for the November 24 referendum. Lukashenko finally silenced House opposition leaders by having his body guards beat and drag them out of the parliament building. Next, the president deployed the militia's armored personnel carriers around the parliament building. The deputies blockaded themselves inside the building, but Lukashenko replaced all of them with his handpicked supporters.

With the parliamentary deputies silenced, Lukashenko held the referendum that the Belarus voters approved. The new constitution gave Lukashenko complete power to govern Belarus. According to Matthew Brzezinski's "Back in the U.S.S.R.," *New York Times Magazine*, December 17, 2000, the popular vote supported Lukashenko's action because it invoked memories of the KGB keeping order. Belarus's most prosperous era was as an industrial economy under the old Soviet regime.

See July 10, 1994; March 24, 1997.

November 25, 1996

The U.N. Security Council authorizes an Iraqi oil-for-food program.

Although the council approved an oil-for-food program in August, Iraq's September attack on Kurds delayed implementing the program. During the next three months, U.N. Secretary-General Boutros-Ghali negotiated a new program that the council approved on November 25. Because Iraqi president Saddam Hussein complained that the oil-for-food program interfered in Iraq's internal affairs, the new program established a U.N. Office of Iraq Programs to supervise the oil-for-food program by using Iraq's own bureaucracy for oil sales or food and medical purchasing.

In 1997, U.N. Secretary General Boutros Boutros-Ghali appointed Benon V. Sevan to head the Office of Iraq Programs. Sevan soon saw inherent problems because he dealt with an Iraqi network of bureaucrats who hampered efficient sales of oil and purchases of food. Sevan was also dismayed because the program received less publicity than Iraqi televised pictures of Iraq's suffering women and children. Sevan told one reporter, "When you show on television a child malnourished with hollow eyes, it's a very strong statement. Yet, we have been very poor in showing all that we have done in order to take care of little children."

November 27, 1996

The Serbian Republic's President Plavsić forces General Mladić to resign.

After Biljana Plavsić replaced Radovan Karadžić as president in August 1996, Western leaders did not realize she was moderate compared with radical Serbs in the SDS Party. In November, Plavsić took the first step to moderate her government by ordering Mladić to resign as armed forces commander. Initially, Mladić ignored Plavsić's order, but he resigned after she appointed General Pero Colić as commander on November 27.

December 11, 1996

NATO makes plans to admit Eastern European nations and approves 30,000 troops for Bosnia for 18 months.

Despite Russian objections to NATO's eastward expansion, NATO approved plans to admit Poland, Hungary, and the Czech Republic during a July 1997 summit meeting. To allay Russian fears about Poland, a future NATO member on its border, NATO pledged that nuclear weapons would not be moved to Eastern Europe and offered security talks with Russia. Following talks between Secretary of State Christopher and Russian Prime Minister Yevgeny Primakov, Russia agreed to negotiate a security treaty

Secretary of State Christopher visits U.S. forces in Bosnia. Department of Defense

but still expressed its opposition to NATO's expansion.

In addition to discussing relations with Eastern Europe, NATO decided to leave 30,000 troops in Bosnia and Herzegovina as a Stabilization Force (SFOR) to replace the 50,000 there in 1996 as an Implementation Force (IFOR).

One NATO "nonaction" concerned France's offer to rejoin NATO's integrated forces in Europe, from which President Charles de Gaulle withdrew in the 1960s. Following his election as president in 1995, Jacques Chirac wanted to make France a major player in Europe's political and military affairs. To achieve this, Chirac cooperated with NATO in Bosnia and offered to rejoin NATO's military forces if the United States permitted a European (read French) naval officer to head NATO's Mediterranean operations in Naples, where an American admiral was commander. Clinton refused to yield this important position and France did not rejoin NATO's military forces.

See February 6, 1966.

December 12, 1996,

France announces its aircraft will not protect Kurds in Iraq after December 31, 1996.

Ever protective of France's status as a great power, President Chirac again challenged U.S. primacy by opposing U.S. air raids when Iraqi forces attacked Kurds. France also opposed U.N. economic sanctions on Iraq that the United States had promoted. Thus, President Clinton was not surprised when Chirac withdrew French aircraft that had assisted British and American aircraft in protecting Iraq's Kurds since 1991.

See September 14, 1996.

December 17, 1996

Kofi Annan is elected secretary-general of the United Nations.

On January 1, 1997, Annan would replace Boutros Boutros-Ghali, who lost reelection because of a U.S. veto. The State Department was dissatisfied with many of Boutros-Ghali's decisions, making it no secret it would veto a second term. The first vote favored Boutros-Ghali by 14 to 1, a decision that the United States vetoed. The United States then proposed Annan's candidacy. On December 4, Boutros-Ghali suspended his candidacy after four African nations accepted Annan. France persisted in backing Boutros-Ghali but finally dropped its veto of Annan. Thus, on December 17, the Security Council unanimously accepted Annan as secretary-general.

1997

January 3, 1997

President Clinton delays enforcement of the Helms-Burton Act on Cuban investments.

After signing the Helms-Burton Act on March 12, 1996, Clinton used escape clauses in the law to waive implementation of the legislation for six months. He continued to employ this waiver on January 3 and July 16, 1997. Senator Jesse Helms (R-N.C.) complained that Clinton had indefinitely suspended the act's key provision and thus prevented lawsuits by Americans against foreign companies violating the act. At the end of 1996, the only foreign companies facing lawsuits by American citizens were the Sherritt International Corporation of Canada and Groupo Damon of Mexico.

Stuart Eisenstein, President Clinton's special envoy in charge of placating U.S. allies who opposed the legislation, indicated that European and Western Hemisphere nations were pressuring Castro to reform his human rights record and promote democracy. For example, on December 4, 1996, the European Union (EU) passed a resolution asking Cuba to improve human rights and political freedom. On February 12, 1997, the EU postponed its October 2, 1996, complaint to the World Trade Organization (WTO) after the WTO formed a three-member panel to arbitrate the issue. On February 20, U.S. officials said the WTO was "not competent" to judge this foreign policy matter, refusing to attend the panel's meetings.

Subsequently, Clinton's representatives emphasized U.S. loyalty to the WTO, claiming their position was "that matters relating to national security and foreign policy should simply not be considered at the WTO, but rather at the U.N. or NATO."

January 14, 1997

Israel agrees to withdraw forces from Hebron.

Following Benjamin Netanyahu's election as Israeli prime minister in May 1996, violence surfaced on the West Bank, owing in part to Israel's refusal to withdraw from the West Bank city of Hebron as required by the Oslo II agreements. During November and December 1996, U.S. mediator Dennis Ross conducted a series of talks with Israeli and Palestinian leaders that culminated in an agreement on Hebron. Under it, Israel would give up 80% of Hebron, leaving an enclave of 450 Jewish settlers protected by the Israeli military pending a final settlement. By late 1998, Israel agreed to pull out of all West Bank regions except Jewish settlements and a few military bases. Although Israeli nationalists denounced the agreement, the Israeli cabinet and parliament approved it by January 17. The Palestine National Council had approved the accords on January 16.

See March 7, 1997.

January 20, 1997

President Clinton is inaugurated for a second term; he names new cabinet members.

After taking the oath of office, Clinton made an address in which he emphasized the need for bipartisanship between the White House and the Republican majority in Congress but offered no new initiatives. During the next week, the Senate confirmed Clinton's nomination of Madeleine Albright as secretary of state and William Cohen, a Republican, as Secretary of Defense. Albright was the first woman to head the State Department.

For the National Security Adviser, see March 17, 1997.

Madeleine Albright—the first woman secretary of state—with President Clinton. White House

January 27, 1997

Chechnya elects its chief of staff as president.

After Russia and Chechnya agreed on peace terms on August 23, they made plans for elections (see November 23, 1996). With foreign and Russian observers in agreement that Chechnya's election was "fair and democratic," Aslan Maskhadov was elected president. Maskhadov had led the Chechen rebels in trying to win independence from Russia between 1994 and 1996.

February 4, 1997

Serbian President Milošević permits the opposition to take municipal offices.

Since Serbia's November 1996 municipal and local elections, protesters had filled the streets of Belgrade because Milošević refused to validate victories of three opposition parties that formed the Zajendo (Together) coalition to win elections in Belgrade and other Serbian cities. In response, Together's supporters staged anti-Milošević demonstrations of 20,000 to 40,000 people every day. These protests aroused international criticism of Milošević by most European governments and the United States.

Milošević finally relented on February 4, 1997. The protests stopped, Zoran Djindjic of the Together Party became Belgrade's mayor, and other Together members controlled Belgrade's City Council and the city councils of 13 Serbian cities. Milošević retained his position as Serbia's president but faced more trouble from opposition groups.

See October 20, 1997.

February 11, 1997

In Ecuador, an interim president replaces Abdala Bucaram.

President Bucaram was elected in 1996, supported mainly by the poorer, rural segments of the population. Yet his austerity program caused increased utility costs that mainly hurt the poor. This led to outbreaks of protest against the government. On February 5, Bucaram ordered the armed forces to break up a general strike that had paralyzed the country. The next day, Congress voted 44 to 34 to remove Bucaram, who had a reputation among Congress members for "mental incapacity."

Although Bucaram refused to leave office, on February 11, Congress named Fabian Alarcon as interim president until a presidential election could be conducted.

February 19, 1997

Chinese leader Deng Xiaoping dies; Ziang Zemin becomes China's leader.

Deng's role in China's 1949 Communist revolution went back to the 1930s when he participated in the Long March of 1933–1934. Although he was purged during the 1960s Cultural Revolution, Deng was rehabilitated in 1970. After Mao Tse-Tung died in 1976, Deng solidified his power in 1978 and began China's move to a free market economy. He opposed political liberalization and ordered the army to crush the Tiananmen Square demonstrators in 1989.

By coincidence, Secretary of State Madeleine Albright was visiting China in February. She met with Ziang Zemin and reported good relations would continue under him.

See June 27, 1997.

February 28, 1997

Mexico arrests officials linked to drug cartel; President Clinton certifies Mexico's cooperation but not Colombia's.

President Clinton's annual report to Congress certified Mexico's cooperation in the drug war, making it eligible for military and economic aid. In contrast, Clinton again refused to certify Colombia because the Central Intelligence Agency (CIA) said President Semper had connections with drug lords.

On February 18, Mexico announced that the head of its National Institute to Combat Drugs, Jesus Gutiérrez Rebollo, was arrested for accepting gifts and money from drug cartel leader Amado Carrillo Fuentes. During the next week, 36 officers of the anti-drug institute were dismissed for similar offenses. Although these events enabled Clinton to certify Mexican cooperation against the drug trade, observers on the ground in Mexico and Colombia believe the drug trade continued to expand in both countries.

See March 1, 1996.

February 28, 1997

Turkey's National Security Council warns Prime Minister Erbakan that Turkey is a secular state.

After Necmettin Erbakan's Welfare Party formed a coalition government with Prime Minister Tansu Ciller's Motherland Party in 1996, Erbakan's government ignored economic problems and took steps toward his ultimate goal of transforming Turkey's secular state into a fundamentalist Islamic nation. Erbakan's party only won 21.4% of the vote in 1996 but received Ciller's help by squashing corruption charges she faced in parliament.

On February 14, 1997, thousands of demonstrators flooded the streets of Ankara in opposition to Erbakan's attempt to establish Islamic rule. Many protesters, mostly disputing fundamentalist laws against women's rights, carried signs reading "Down With Sharia [religious law]."

Turkish military leaders also opposed Erbakan's religious policies. After its regular meeting on February 27, the National Security Council of military and civilian representatives issued a communiqué on February 28. The report stated that the council had decided that "no steps away from the contemporary values of the Turkish Republic" would be tolerated. Separatists groups, it said, were weakening Turkish democracy and "blurring the distinction between the secular and the anti-secular." The council expressed concern that Turkey's efforts to join the European Union would be stymied if there were "speculation which may lead to suspicion about our democracy and damage Turkey's image and prestige abroad."

Turkish military leaders who supported the secular state created in 1923 by Kemal Atatürk, undoubtedly influenced the council report. During February 1997, senior Turkish military officers expressed their dismay with Erbakan's leaning toward Iran, Libya, and Syria and his anti-Israeli policies. In one incident, the army sent tanks onto the streets of a town near Ankara where Iran's ambassador to Turkey had made a fiery speech favoring Islamic fundamentalism. Later, army leaders forced Iran's ambassador to leave Turkey. Second, during a visit to Washington, Turkish General Cevic Bir made a speech asserting that Iran was a terrorist nation trying to subvert Turkey. Finally, during the last week of February, General Ismail Hakki Karadayi, commander in chief of Turkey's armed forces, made a three-day visit to Israel to emphasize the close military relations developing between Turkey and Israel.

U.S. State Department officers also became alarmed by Erbakan's foreign policies. After trying to accommodate him in 1996, these officials now objected to his anti-Israeli and pro-Iranian, -Libyan, and -Syrian policies. Yet, as Alan Makovsky told the Foreign Policy Research Institute (*Backchannel*, December 1996) President Clinton failed to develop a coherent policy taking into account Turkey's value to the United States.

See June 18, 1997.

March 3, 1997

A former CIA official pleads guilty of spying for Russia.

Harold Nicholson pleaded guilty in a federal court of spying for Russia between 1994 and 1996, saying he was paid $180,000 to provide classified top-secret information. After being arrested, Nicholson cooperated by explaining what data he gave the Russians. He was sentenced to prison for 23 years and 7 months.

March 4, 1997

Because of a scandal, South Korean President Kim appoints a new premier.

Following the indictment of 10 businessmen and politicians for corruption involving the Hambo Steel Industry, President Kim Young Sam apologized for his government after naming Koh Kun as the new premier and replacing eight cabinet members.

See August 7, 1997.

March 7, 1997

The United States vetoes the U.N. Security Council's condemnation of Israel for East Jerusalem settlements.

The ink was hardly dry on the January Hebron protocols before Israeli Prime Minister Netanyahu announced on February 19 that Israel would build 30,000 Jewish housing units in Har Homa, a section of East Jerusalem seen by Arabs as Arab territory since the 1967 war. The announcement of this housing project precipitated Palestinian protests and general strikes in the West Bank, Gaza, and Jerusalem.

Although on March 3 President Clinton met with Palestinian leader Yasser Arafat and criticized Israel's decision, on March 7 and again on March 21, U.S. vetoes killed an otherwise unanimous Security Council resolution calling on Israel to abandon the housing project. Israel claimed the Palestinians would also benefit from the project, which was to include new roads, sewage, and water systems for East Jerusalem. Actually, most evidence indicated Netanyahu's policy would increase the Jewish population of East Jerusalem and eventually encircle the city with a large Jewish population to prevent East Jerusalem from becoming the capital of a Palestinian state. In February, Netanyahu announced that Har Homa was the "beginning of the battle for Jerusalem."

For more than a year before the Har Homa project was announced, the Israeli minister of the interior had speeded up the process of evicting Palestinians from East Jerusalem by taking away identity cards issued to Palestinians living in Jerusalem after the 1967 war. Without the identity cards, the Palestinians had to move out of Jerusalem. Two human rights groups called the Israeli practice "quiet deportation," and in March 1997 Arafat told foreign diplomats that the tactic was an "ethnic cleansing" campaign.

According to the *Washington Post* (May 5, 1997) reporter Barton Gellman, Israel's Interior Ministry ordered 105 Palestinians with U.S. passports or green cards to leave their Jerusalem homes. Kathy Riley, chief U.S. consular official in Jerusalem, had met five times with the Interior Ministry to ask "Why have you changed this all of a sudden? For 30 years you haven't had this policy. Why are you now implementing this?" But Riley's protests were fruitless.

On March 18, despite international opposition, Israeli construction workers, guarded by 1,000 Israeli soldiers, began clearing land for Har Homa housing units in East Jerusalem. Moreover, peace talks between Israel and the Palestinian National Authority scheduled to begin in March 1997 were canceled. The U.S. State Department tried to revive these negotiations but failed for eight months.

See June 6, 1967; January 14, 1997; November 6, 1997.

March 17, 1997

George Tenet is nominated to head the CIA.

Anthony Lake was President Clinton's national security adviser from 1993 to 1996, when in January 1997 Clinton appointed him as CIA director. During the Senate hearings on the nomination, Lake's critics disclosed that he should have known more about China's attempts to influence U.S. elections and that his stock holdings in oil companies might prejudice his advice to the president. Although Lake sold the stock, the Justice Department concluded he had violated the conflict-of-interest law and fined him $5,000. After Lake withdrew his nomination, Clinton appointed George Tenet, who had been acting director since December 1996.

During the Senate hearings on his appointment, Tenet's involvement in a cover-up of CIA mistakes in Guatemala was revealed. Tenet had fired Richard Nuccio from his CIA position after Nuccio told the House Intelligence Committee about CIA connections to the death of the Mayan resistance leader Efrain Bamaca. Despite Nuccio's testimony about Tenet, the Senate approved Tenet's appointment. In 1995, President Clinton said he would fire any CIA agent who withheld data about Guatemala. Evidently, Clinton forgot about his 1995 promise when Tenet was appointed. A former unnamed State Department colleague of Nuccio told a reporter: "This [Clinton] administration is not willing to protect people [like Nuccio]. It's afraid of the CIA."

See March 25, 1995.

March 21, 1997

Presidents Clinton and Yeltsin foresee new NATO relations and fewer nuclear warheads.

President Clinton and Russian President Boris Yeltsin held a two-day summit in Helsinki, Finland, to discuss NATO's expansion and a third nuclear warheads reduction treaty. Clinton told Yeltsin NATO would promise not to deploy nuclear weapons in former Warsaw Pact states. Clinton also would support Russia's membership in the World Trade Organization. Yeltsin promised to submit the second Strategic Arms Reduction Treaty (START II) to parliament for ratification and agreed to undertake negotiations on START III to reduce more long-range nuclear warheads.

See May 27, 1997.

March 24, 1997

Belarus expels a U.S. diplomat; the State Department retaliates in kind.

Following a series of antigovernment protests in early March, the Belarus government expelled a member of the U.S. embassy staff, Serge Alexandrov, for allegedly participating in the demonstrations. The next day, the U.S. State Department expelled Belarus diplomat Vladimir Gramyka for the "unwarranted" expelling of Alexandrov.

The antigovernment demonstrators opposed Belarus President Lukashenko's meeting with Russian President Boris Yeltsin to plan the formation of a "union state." The Yeltsin-Lukashenko meeting ended the same day Alexandrov was expelled. During the Belarus-Russian negotiations, Yeltsin and Lukashenko agreed to form a supranational body to oversee the "union state," although Yeltsin did not accept a fully merged state with impoverished Belarus. After three years of planning a socialist state, Lukashenko had failed to revitalize the Belarus economy.

See September 7, 1997.

April 11, 1997

Angola's unity government is completed under President Dos Santos.

On November 20, 1994, Angola's government and the rebel National Union for the Total Independence for Angola (UNITA) signed a peace accord mediated by the United Nations. The accord provided for Angola's government to share power with UNITA to end the 19-year civil war. UNITA's leader, Jonas Savimbi, refused to attend the treaty signing, claiming that government police might kill him. Although tensions continued between the government and UNITA, the U.N. officials supervised the writing of Angola's new constitution leading to the April 11 elections in which Jose Eduardo dos Santos won the presidency.

See January 17, 1999.

April 15, 1997

The U.N. Security Council authorizes European nations to be peacekeepers in Albania.

Albanians had experienced corrupt governments since 1991, when student demonstrations led to the resignation of its Communist Party regime (see June 22, 1991). In 1992, Sali Berisha was elected president in a multiparty election (see February 22, 1992). For four years, the work of Berisha's government went unquestioned.

On February 17, 1997, the Albanian government's investments in the Gjallico pyramid scheme lost almost all of its private investor's money when the scheme collapsed. Albania's market values dropped fast in January 1997. On February 1, Albania's Prime Minister Aleksander Mekia told investors the decline in value of the project should give investors about 60% of their original investment. By February 4, Mekia's estimate of 60% return was proven wrong because most investors received little or no money from the government. The next day, protests against Mekia's government began in Tirana, the capital of Albania. The protests gradually turned into riots, causing Mekia to declare a state of national emergency before resigning from office.

Between February 5 and April, Albanian protests turned into large scale riots by gangs who looted banks, stores, and military warehouses, where they stole 40,000 guns plus ammunition and other military equipment. During March, an estimated 40,000 Albanians fled by boats across the Adriatic Sea, seeking protection in Italy. The Italian government opposed the arrival of Albanians, turning back as many boatloads of refugees as possible.

To end the anarchy in Albania, the United Nations Security Council approved requests from Italy and other European nations to send troops to restore a stable government in Albania. The first 1,200 European troops under an Italian commander reached Albania on April 15, 1997. Eventually a total of 6,000 troops from Italy, France, and Spain arrived in Albania.

See July 6, 1997.

April 21, 1997

In India after a no-confidence vote on Gowda's government, Gujral becomes prime minister.

After India's Congress party lost parliamentary election in 1996, H.D. Deve Gowda formed a United Front coalition having several members of the Congress Party in the cabinet (see May 10, 1996). On April 11, 1997, Prime Minister Gowda lost a vote of confidence in parliament because Congress Party members opposed what they called Gowda's inefficient leadership. On April 21, Congress Party members joined a new coalition headed by Hindu National Party leader Inder K. Gujral who became prime minister.

April 22, 1997

Peruvian commandos free hostages held by rebels at the Japanese embassy.

Following a 126-day standoff at Japan's embassy in Lima, commandos stormed the embassy building to free 72 hostages held by adherents of the Tupac Amaru Revolutionary Movement (MRTA), better known as the Shining Path. The attack was approved by President Alberto Fujimori who had waged a long campaign to eliminate the MRTA and other leftist guerrillas. In the attack, all 14 rebels and two commandos were killed. One hostage struck by a bullet died from a heart attack.

April 24, 1997

The Senate ratifies the Chemical Weapons Convention, its implementation laws are delayed.

With support from former Senator Robert Dole (R-Kans.) and retired General Colin Powell, President Clinton overcame the opposition of many congressional Republicans who thought the treaty could not be enforced. The U.S. Chemical Manufacturer's Association also urged treaty ratification because it would suffer "considerable economic loss" if the United States did not become an original party to the treaty. The Chemical Weapons Convention was scheduled to become effective on April 29, 1997 because necessary 120 nations already ratified the treaty.

In the final Senate vote, all 45 Democrats and 29 Republicans approved the treaty, with 7 votes more than the necessary two-thirds. The United States was the 75th country to approve the treaty, by which signatories would destroy all their chemical weapons stocks by 2007.

Ratification did not complete U.S. participation in the treaty because Congress had to approve legislation to implement the treaty. In May 1997, the Senate Foreign Relations Committee recommended legislation to insert restrictions on U.N. inspections of U.S. facilities. These clauses in the U.S. Chemical Weapons Implementation Act would undermine the Chemical Weapons Convention because other nations could order similar restrictions. An example of the Implementation Act's restrictions was a clause allowing the president to thwart international inspections if they "pose a threat" to the national interest. Another section titled "Not Subject to Judicial Review" included clauses that empowered the Federal Bureau of Investigation to designate an agent to accompany each inspection team and permitted the president to object to any particular individual serving on an inspection team.

See October 20, 1998.

April 24, 1997

Bulgaria's parliament chooses Ivan Kostov as prime minister.

In January 1997 thousands of Bulgarians had gathered in Sofia to protest the unreconstructed Communist leaders and an inflation rate of 310%, which raised the price of bread and energy while wages did not increase. Inspired by Serbian demonstrations that began in November 1996, Bulgarian workers, students, and civil servants were striking, and marching for change.

In reaction to these complaints, elections on April 19 gave the United Democratic Force (UDF) coalition 137 of 240 parliamentary seats. The prior majority Socialist (former Communist) Party won 58 seats. Kostov, an economist, became Bulgaria's prime minister.

May 1, 1997

Britain's Labour Party wins elections for Parliament.

After 18 years of Conservative Party rule, the Labour Party won 418 of 659 seats in the House of Commons, making Tony Blair prime minister. The Conservatives were divided regarding British participation in the Euro currency. In contrast, Blair moved the Labour Party toward the political center, abandoning its socialist identity.

See June 25, 1997.

May 6, 1997

President Clinton begins a five-day tour of Central America with a visit to Mexico.

Accompanied by his wife, Hillary, and eight cabinet members, Clinton visited Mexico City to sign with Mexican President Ernesto Zedillo Ponce de Leon accords on trade, the environment, and border problems. Most important was an agreement for a mutual effort to combat drug trafficking. In Costa Rica, Clinton met with seven Caribbean nation leaders to assure them that tougher U.S. immigration laws would not cause more to return to their native homelands. Finally, on May 10, he attended the Barbados summit of 15 Caribbean leaders to discuss economic relations.

On the Mexican election, see July 6, 1997.

May 7, 1997

The Hague International Tribunal convicts a Bosnian Serb of war crimes.

Although in 1996 a Croat pleaded guilty to the crime of ethnic cleansing in Bosnia, Dušan Tadić pleaded not guilty before the International Tribunal for War Crimes in the Former Yugoslavian Federation. Tadić's trial was the first for war crimes since World War II. He was convicted of torturing and killing 31 Muslim prisoners in 1992.

A controversial trial issue was the prosecutor's effort to show the crime was not committed during a civil war within one nation but in an international war between Serbia and Bosnia. Two of the three Hague judges ruled that the prosecution did not offer sufficient evidence to prove it was an international conflict.

May 18, 1997

General Kabila's rebels overthrow Zairean President Mobutu.

Rebels from the Alliance for the Liberation of Congo-Zaire, led by the former nightclub owner Laurent Kabila, began in October 1996 while President Mobutu Sese Seko recovered from prostate surgery in France. Mobutu, who had ruled Zaire since 1965, siphoned off Zaire's wealth to purchase luxuries for his personal use and expensive homes in Europe (see November 25, 1965). When the civil war began, Mobutu hired British mercenaries to join Zaire's underpaid army in repelling the rebels. Yet on March 15, Kabila's forces captured Zaire's second-largest city, Kisangani, and advanced on Kinshasa the capital. Mobutu and Kabila met on May 4. During their meeting, Kabila offered nominal power to Mobutu in a government in which Kabila would be the dominant political authority. Mobutu refused.

As Kabila's forces entered Kinshasa on May 16, Mobutu fled to exile in Togo before dying from cancer on September 7, 1997. On May 18, the rebels established control over Kinshasa. On May 29, Kabila was sworn in as president and changed Zaire's name to Democratic Republic of the Congo. He promised a new constitution and elections in two years.

See November 25, 1965; February 17, 1999.

May 23, 1997

Muhammad Khatami, a moderate cleric, is elected president of Iran.

Although most conservative clerics opposed Khatami, his predecessor, Hojatolislam Ali Akbar Hashemi Rafsanjani, backed his moderate program. During the election campaign, Khatami's support came from women, young people, and leftists because he proposed to improve economic ties with the West, saying better relations with the United States required Americans to change their attitude toward Iran.

May 27, 1997

NATO members plus Russian President Yeltsin sign the Founding Act in Paris.

Yeltsin was skeptical about NATO expansion, but on May 14, 1997, he accepted a treaty with NATO permitting its expansion into Eastern Europe. After the final details of the treaty were worked out, President Clinton, leaders of 15 other NATO states, and Yeltsin met to sign the Founding Act on Mutual Relations, Cooperation and Security. This accord established a NATO-Russia Permanent Joint Council to discuss security issues without, according to U.S. officials, limiting NATO's authority to station troops or weapons wherever the alliance wished.

The accord was obtained after negotiations with Russia included nonbinding agreements not to deploy nuclear weapons or substantial numbers of foreign troops on territory of new NATO member states. In turn, Yeltsin promised to remove Russia's nuclear warheads targeted on Western Europe.

See July 8, 1997.

May 31, 1997

Russia and Ukraine sign a friendship treaty.

Because of persistent friction following the demise of the Soviet Union in December 1991, Russia and Ukraine sought to end their disputes by approving a friendship treaty on May 31, 1997. In addition to providing for political and economic cooperation, the treaty recognized Ukraine's territorial integrity including Moscow's previous claim to Sevastopol, the Soviet Black Sea fleet base. Ukraine agreed that Russia could operate its Black Sea fleet from Ukrainian territory.

Russian President Yeltsin sought the friendship treaty to counteract NATO's expansion into Eastern Europe. There were rumors that Ukraine might seek NATO membership, but Ukrainian President Leonid Kuchman claimed his country was not interested in joining NATO.

June 1, 1997

French elections result in a defeat for President Chirac's center-right coalition.

After two years as president, Jacques Chirac called new elections, hoping to win a mandate to continue tough economic reforms to prepare France for membership in the European common currency in 1999. His tough economic measures became unpopular as unemployment reached 12.8% in 1997. Thus, in the second round of elections on June 1, a left-wing coalition won the majority in the National Assembly. On June 3, Socialist Party leader Lionel Jospin became premier. During the campaign, Jospin claimed

France should not have to reduce its budget deficit to meet the Maastricht Treaty requirements for France to join the European monetary unit.

The European Union's Maastricht Treaty of December 1991 required members' budget deficits to be no more than 3% of the gross domestic product by the end of the year. To meet this level, Jospin promised not to cut government welfare payments or otherwise reduce the budget.

June 11, 1997

Jean Chrétien's Liberal Party retains control of the Canadian Parliament.

Although the Liberal Party lost 19 seats in elections for Parliament, it retained a slim majority of 155 seats in the 301-member parliament. Chrétien's government had introduced tough reforms to erase Canada's budget deficit, but it created many new jobs and cut inflation to 2%.

Canada continued to experience internal discord over the status of Quebec province. On September 14, 1997, a meeting in Calgary of leaders of Canadian provinces and territories proposed a unity program to affirm the equality of all provinces and identified Quebec's federal government as a guarantor of Quebec society's "unique character." Critics opposing the Calgary accords claimed there was no validity to the idea of Quebec's "unique character."

June 18, 1997

Turkish Prime Minister Erbakan resigns after losing a parliamentary majority.

Since February 1997, Prime Minister Erbakan's cabinet had been under attack for trying to create an Islamic state. After Erbakan resigned on June 18, President Suleyman Demirel approved a new government headed by Mesut Yilmaz of the Motherland Party. Yilmaz had replaced Tansu Ciller, who allied with Erbakan in 1996.

See February 28, 1997.

June 22, 1997

The G-7 becomes the G-8; Russia is admitted to the group of major industrial states.

The meeting of industrial states in Denver, Colorado, opened on June 19, with Russia admitted as the eighth member. When the meeting ended on June 22, Russia was also admitted to the Paris Club of creditors that helped developing countries manage their debts. In its final press release, the G-8 expressed opposition to human cloning, urged China to respect democracy in Hong Kong, and urged the Democratic Republic of the Congo (former Zaire) to embrace democracy and respect human rights.

June 25, 1997

British Prime Minister Blair announces a new plan for Northern Ireland.

Tony Blair modified earlier British policy regarding peace in Northern Ireland. He announced that Sinn Fein, the political arm of the Irish Republican Army, could join peace negotiations on Northern Ireland provided the IRA surrendered its weapons and declared a cease-fire.

On July 19, the IRA declared a cease-fire. Unfortunately, on July 23, the largest Protestant pro-union parties rejected plans calling for the "parallel decommissioning" of arms held by the Protestants and Catholics.

See April 10, 1998.

June 26, 1997

Historians' panel criticizes CIA secrecy about its 30-year-old operations.

The Advisory Committee on Historical and Diplomatic Documentation was appointed by the State Department after a volume of the department's *History of United States Foreign Relations* on Iran failed to mention CIA involvement in overthrowing Prime Minister Mossadegh on August 19, 1953. The committee report said recent volumes of the foreign relations series "stand in never-never land" and the Advisory Committee was contemplating a recommendation to stop future publications because of the deficiencies.

While recognizing that the CIA had recently released data on Guatemala and British Guiana, the report said that by September 30, 1996, only partial records of CIA actions were declassified among the 30- or more year-old documents. Although the CIA said it could not release sensitive materials, the historians replied that they did not seek sensitive data. The committee believed all basic CIA materials covering the 30-year policy could be declassified "without fear of hurting living people or damaging current policy."

Regarding Guatemala, the CIA released only 1,400 pages of 180,000 from the CIA "secret archives."

The historians' claims were bolstered by a May 26, 1997, report of Daniel Patrick Moynihan's (D-N.Y.) Senate Committee on Protecting and Reducing Government Secrecy. The committee found the U.S. government bureaucracy continued to have as many as 400,000 new secrets at the top-secret level. Protecting these secrets cost taxpayers $5 billion per year. Moynihan said the committee wanted to deregulate most government secrecy and "develop a competing culture of openness." Bureaucrats must be given power to disclose information rather than keep it secret.

June 27, 1997

Secretary of State Albright begins a visit to Vietnam.

Greeted at the Hanoi airport by U.S. Ambassador Pete Peterson, Secretary of State Albright was also welcomed by Vietnamese Foreign Minister Nguyen Manh Can. Since 1995, when Secretary of State Warren Christopher raised the U.S. flag at the U.S. embassy in Hanoi, the State Department and Vietnam's Foreign Ministry had pursued efforts to account for the 1,584 Americans still listed as missing in action from the Vietnam War. Albright's other concern was to normalize U.S. economic relations with Vietnam by completing a trade agreement. Washington submitted the draft of a trade agreement but Vietnam did not immediately respond.

June 27, 1997

Congress renews China's most-favored-nation (MFN) trade status.

The House of Representatives approved the renewal of China's trade status despite opposition groups who opposed the legislation. In May, President Clinton proposed the renewal of China's trade status but had to contend with the opposition of congressional Democrats such as Minority Leader Richard Gephardt, who strongly opposed China's MFN status because of its religious discrimination and poor human rights record.

Although China had promised to stop its nuclear weapons tests and refrain from selling nuclear technology to other nations, the CIA reported in October 1996 that China had helped Pakistan build plants at two locations to make missile components similar to China's M-11 rockets. Apparently, the CIA was unable to obtain photos of the Pakistani plants, suspecting the construction was hidden when U.S. spy satellites passed over the area (Pakistani officials knew when the U.S. satellites passed by).

See October 29, 1997.

June 30–July 1, 1997

Hong Kong returns to Chinese rule; Secretary of State Albright affirms good U.S. relations.

In Hong Kong, a ceremony turned the British crown colony over to China. The British ruled Hong Kong for 150 years before the Union Jack was lowered then replaced by China's red flag. Attending the ceremony was Secretary Albright, British Prime Minister Tony Blair, and other foreign dignitaries.

During her Hong Kong visit, Secretary Albright met with Chinese Foreign Minister Qian Qichen. Albright told Qian that the United States reaffirmed its good relations with China but also reproved China for sending 4,000 troops to Hong Kong that morning and for its decision to replace Hong Kong's elected City Council with the provisional City Council. Albright said the United States wanted China to be a responsible partner in the international system.

See August 29, 1842; October 29, 1997.

July 6, 1997

Mexico's ruling party fails to win a majority in the Chamber of Deputies.

For the first time since 1929, Mexico's Institutional Revolutionary Party (PRI) failed to win a majority of the Chamber of Deputies. The loss was attributed to widespread political corruption and an economic crisis. The PRI won a plurality of the 500 deputies and retained a majority in the Senate. The other Chamber of Deputies seats were divided between the National Action Party (PNA) with 122 seats and the left-wing Democratic Revolutionary Party (PRD) with 125. The PRD candidate, Cuauhtemoc Cardenas Solorzano, won Mexico City's first-ever mayoral election. The PNA won six elections for provincial governors.

July 6, 1997

Cambodian Prime Minister Hun Sen overthrows Prince Norodom Ranariddh.

On July 5, Cambodia appeared ready to accept a deal with the Khmer Rouge rebel leaders, who offered to end the civil war and join the Cambodian army. The agreement never went into effect because Hun Sen removed his co-prime minister, Ranariddh, from office while he was in Paris.

Following elections in 1993, Hun Sen and Ranariddh were named co-prime ministers, but after U.N. peacekeepers left Cambodia, the two became rivals. During the same time, Pol Pot's Khmer Rouge began to fall apart, and in 1996 a group of Khmer commanders contacted the government regarding negotiations to end the civil war. In February 1997, 10 officials visited the dissident commanders, but Pol Pot loyalists ambushed and killed them.

On May 16, Tep Kunnal, a senior Khmer political officer, met with government military delegates to seek reconciliation and a permanent cease-fire. These talks continued at Anlong Veng, and on June 1 Ranariddh met secretly with Khieu Samphan, the nominal Khmer head of state, but soon after the Khmer peace group fought with Pol Pot loyalists. On June 19, with government troops helping the Khmer peace group, Pol Pot was captured and his few remaining loyalists fled to the jungles. On June 21, the peace negotiators met to complete details of an agreement.

After the final cease-fire and peace agreements were ready, Khieu Samphan prepared a surrender ceremony with a press conference for July 6 to announce the peace settlement. But the July 6 ceremony was canceled because of Hun Sen's coup in Phnom Penh.

Although Hun Sen had daily briefings about the peace talks, he became concerned for two reasons. First, Prince Ranariddh became the chief peace negotiator after June 2. Second, the peace agreement permitted Khmer members to form a National United Front political party and join Ranariddh's coalition, which opposed Hun Sen. Fearing he would lose power, Hun Sen launched the coup on July 5 by sending tanks and armored vehicles into Phnom Penh. He also ordered his followers to execute or arrest their enemies. Because of the coup, tourists and foreign businessmen fled from Cambodia. Ranariddh escaped to Paris.

From Paris, Ranariddh urged the United Nations and the United States to help restore his authority but both refused. The United States suspended $35 million of aid to Cambodia. In Phnom Penh, Hun Sen replaced Ranariddh with Toam Chay, a member of a weak opposition party.

July 6, 1997

In Albanian elections, Socialists defeat President Berisha's party.

In elections supervised by European peacekeepers, the former Communist Party won a majority in parliament and elected party leader Rexhep Mejdani as president. On July 24, Mejdani named Fatos Nano premier. Nano immediately stated that the government could not reimburse people who had lost money on the pyramid scheme (see April 15, 1997).

July 8, 1997

Three Eastern European nations are invited to join NATO.

During a NATO meeting in Brussels, Hungary, Poland, and the Czech Republic were invited to become members of NATO. Although Russia reluctantly approved the expansion of NATO, Foreign Minister Yevgeny Primakov thought the expansion was a "big mistake." The admission of new members required amendments to the 1949 NATO treaty. Thus, the U.S. Senate had to ratify the changes.

See April 30, 1998.

July 10, 1997

With U.S. aid, the British seize indicted Bosnian Serb war criminals.

With logistical support from American soldiers, a British unit under NATO command captured one Serb who was indicted by the Hague War Crimes Tribunal. A second indicted Serb resisted arrest and was shot and killed by British soldiers. One British officer was wounded in the incident. They captured a Serb, Milan Kovacević, who was sent to The Hague to await trail on charges of genocide committed by Serbs against Bosnian Muslims in 1992.

July 19, 1997

Liberia elects Charles Taylor president; observers find the election fair and free.

Following a seven-year civil war that cost 150,000 lives, Liberia held a peaceful election on July 19. The election resulted from the Nigerian-led peacemaking mission of the Organization of African Unity (OAU). The OAU agreement led rival factions to comply with agreements by which they turned in thousands of weapons in January 1997. Taylor, who won the election, led one of the warring factions accepting the peace agreement. International observers who monitored the election agreed that it was fair and free.

August 5, 1997

President Clinton signs budget legislation for fiscal year 1998.

Unlike November 1995, when disagreements between Clinton and Congress reached an impasse on the budget, the White House and Capitol Hill agreed on May 2 on a budget for 1998 as part of a five-year attempt to balance budgets by 2002. In part, their cooperation resulted from a strong economy that decreased the deficit spending of previous budgets. A bipartisan effort to finalize the spending and revenue bills continued until July 30, when Congress approved both pieces of legislation.

As agreed in May, the 1998 budget would begin moving to the fully balanced budget by 2002. The spending bill cut Medicare costs by $115 billion through lower payments to health care providers and eliminated $10 billion in Medicaid by reducing payments to hospitals treating poor people. At the same time, $23 billion went for state grants to provide health care for uninsured children. Many Democrats disliked the Medicare/Medicaid cuts but approved the education and environmental expenditures.

August 7, 1997

The United States, China, and the two Koreas hold peace talks; North Korea begins a nuclear project.

On February 19, 1997, North Korea agreed to attend a meeting on proposals to settle issues remaining from the Korean War of 1950–1953. As a result, on August 7, representatives of the United States, China, and the two Koreas concluded a two-day session that considered ways to formulate a permanent peace treaty. A second round of peace negotiations began on December 9, 1997.

In part, North Korea was ready to establish better relations because of famine conditions requiring food aid from the United States, South Korea, and other U.N. donors. The United States renewed emergency food aid in February, and in July President Clinton sent another $27 million worth of grain.

In addition on August 19, North Korea launched the $5 billion nuclear energy project agreed to in 1994. With U.S. and South Korean assistance, North Korea began building two light-water nuclear reactors near Kumho. In return, North Korea agreed in 1994 to halt its nuclear arms program.

See August 10, 1994.

August 20, 1997

President Clinton's Bosnian policy assists Serb moderates to control Banja Luka.

After the Srpska (Bosnia Serb) Republic's President Biljana Plavsić removed General Ratko Mladić as army commander, President Clinton decided the United States must play a direct role in having the Stabilization Force (SFOR) get Serb cooperation in implementing the Dayton Accords. Clinton appointed Assistant Secretary of State Robert Gelbard as his special representative on Bosnia and General Wesley Clark as NATO commander. He also sent additional State Department personnel, U.S. special observer forces, and CIA officials to Bosnia to aid SFOR. In accord with these decisions, the United States, backed Plavsić in her disputes with former Srpska President Radovan Karadžić, an indicted war criminal.

Clinton's policy of aiding Plavsić was evident on August 20 when U.S. army helicopters supported British and Czech forces in seizing thousands of grenades, rifles, rocket launchers, and weapons stored at the Banja Luka police station. Because Serb police and army personnel loyal to Karadžić opposed Plavsić's moderate policies, Plavsić feared the police intended to overthrow her government. SFOR's action allowed her to appoint loyal police and army officers.

Other SFOR measures to aid Plavsić began on August 28 when U.S. peacekeepers occupied the Brčko police station despite protests from Serbs. SFOR also evicted a Serb telephone-tapping squad allowing Karadžić loyalists to monitor calls in Banja Luka and imposed SFOR control over a special police force protecting Karadžić at his Pale headquarters. With U.S. support, Plavsić called for Srpska Republic elections.

See November 27, 1996; November 23, 1997.

September 7, 1997

U.S. financier George Soros closes his foundation in Belarus.

After Aleksandr Lukashenko was elected president in 1994, he moved toward censoring the news media while closing down many independent newspapers. The Soros Foundation's objective was to promote a free press and political pluralism. But after June 1994, it experienced increasing problems with Lukashenko's regime. In May 1997, Belarus fined the foundation $3 million for allegedly violating laws on currency exchange. This action began more harassment of the foundation, finally convincing Soros to close it.

See July 10, 1994; June 22, 1998.

September 17, 1997

President Clinton announces the United States will not sign the land mine treaty in December.

Advised by the Joint Chiefs of Staff, who opposed the current treaty draft, President Clinton told a press conference there was a legitimate national security need to reject the land mine treaty. U.S. military leaders calculated that giving up antipersonnel mines permitted an enemy to clear a column through an antitank minefield in 10 rather than 30 minutes, a difference of 20 minutes that would cost many American lives. For example, an attack in Korea by 1 million North Korean troops unimpeded by land mines would quickly overrun the demilitarized zone on the way to Seoul, only 20 miles away.

In 1996, Joint Chiefs Chairman John Shalikashvili persuaded Clinton to ban the use of "dumb mines" that lay beneath the surface for many years before victims ignited them. These plans enabled the United States to produce "smart mines" that self-destructed after a set period of time. Yet humanitarian groups wanted all land mines to be banned, claiming it was unrealistic to expect countries with dumb mines to give them up if the United States had smart mines.

For the land mine treaty signing, see December 3, 1997.

September 24, 1997

Algerian rebel leaders order their followers to stop combat operations.

For the past six weeks, both rebels and Algerian security forces had killed an estimated 425 people, the worst carnage being 85 killed on the outskirts of Algiers and 98 killed near the village of Rais. Hoping to end the slaughter, the principal fundamentalist Islamic group called for a truce by ordering its supporters to stop fighting at least temporarily.

September 26, 1997

NATO-Russia Joint Council begins operating; the United States and Russia sign arms control pacts.

Secretary of State Madeleine Albright and Russian Foreign Minister Yevgeny Primakov joined NATO members in launching the new partnership agreed to in the Foundation Act (see May 27, 1997). Albright and Primakov called this a new era of cooperation between former Cold War foes, but both acknowledged that NATO and Russia must learn to trust each other as NATO expanded toward the Russian border. In addition, Albright said NATO would open an information center in Moscow and welcome Russian military representatives to NATO headquarters in Brussels.

During the same Brussels meetings, Albright and Primakov signed two nuclear missile agreements. One pact extended the period for cuts in long-range nuclear missiles to 2007 and the other called for deactivation of their banned missiles by 2003. The extensions allowed Russia to spread the costs of replacing banned missiles over a longer period. Primakov also agreed to push Russia's legislature to ratify START II.

In another agreement, Primakov allowed the United States to exempt its theater high-altitude area defense (THAAD) system, but no other faster upper-tier systems from the 1972 ABM treaty. The agreement infuriated Senator Jesse Helms (R-N.C.) because it would prohibit navy and air force antimissile systems as well as extensive ground-based antimissile systems. As a result, Senate Republicans blocked Clinton from submitting the treaty with Russia for ratification.

See May 27, 1997.

October 16, 1997

President Clinton conducts a "town meeting" in Argentina after visiting three South American nations.

While touring Argentina, Clinton used a method he popularized by holding a town meeting in Buenos Aires. Facing a mostly youthful audience, the president fielded questions about drugs, immigration, and free-trade policies of the United States. The same day, his wife, Hillary Rodham Clinton, called for better opportunities for women and more access to family planning programs.

Before visiting Argentina, Clinton toured Venezuela and Brazil. In Caracas, he praised President Rafael Caldera for permitting private investments in nationalized industries and called for lower trade barriers in North and South America. In Brazil, he emphasized the need for the United States and Brazil to reduce the greenhouse gases causing global warming.

October 20, 1997

President Milošević loses elections in Serbia and Montenegro.

Slobodan Milošcvić's trouble began in June 1997. Because he was not eligible for a third term as president of Serbia, he manipulated a clause of the Yugoslav constitution allowing him to become Yugoslav president after resigning as President of Serbia. Thus, after he resigned as Serbia's president, he had the Yugoslav parliament elect him Yugoslav president. Milošević's final maneuver was to name a loyal follower, Milan Milutinović, president of Serbia.

Milošević's plans appeared on course until October 20, when elections were being held in the Yugoslav Federation, as well as the Republic of Serbia and the Republic of Montenegro. The elections failed to elect Milošević's candidates in all three of these political units. In Serbia, Milutinović lost to Radical Party leader Vojislav Seselj. To rectify this loss, Milošević had the Serbian supreme court invalidate the October election, claiming that fewer than 50% of the electorate voted. On December 6, new elections were held but no candidate won 50% of the vote. In runoff elections on December 23, Milutinović was declared winner but his opponent, Seselj, claimed that less than 50% had voted, a claim that the supreme court rejected.

Milošević's manipulation saved the day in Serbia but he could not control elections in Montenegro. On October 20, Milošević's loyalist Momir Bulatović lost to Milo Djukanović, who advocated Montenegro's independence from Yugoslavia. Without Montenegro, Milošević would lose all claims to be president of a Yugoslav Federation as successor to the Yugoslavia that existed before 1990. Djukanović's election also allowed him to control Montenegro's seats in the Yugoslav parliament, enough to seek favorable economic concessions or move toward independence.

See November 23, 1997.

October 27, 1997

Treasury Secretary Robert Rubin says the economy is strong despite the Asian crisis.

Between October 20 and 24, world equity prices in currencies declined sharply. To assuage American concerns about a crisis that affected Mexico, Argentina, and Brazil, Secretary Rubin told reporters the fundamentals of the U.S. economy were strong. The Asian crisis continued into 1998, affecting Americans with investments in Asia and requiring

Chinese President Ziang Zemin. National Archives

the World Bank and International Monetary Funds to make loans to countries hardest hit, especially South Korea, Thailand, and Malaysia and Indonesia.

October 29, 1997

Chinese president Ziang Zemin visits President Clinton.

Ziang began a nine-day visit to the United States on October 26 when he arrived in Hawaii. He visited Williamsburg, Virginia, on October 27 before coming to Washington, D.C. Following Ziang's talks with Clinton, the two announced China would buy 50 jet aircraft from Boeing. Clinton said because China agreed on October 17 to stop giving Iran nuclear energy assistance, the United States would no longer ban the sale of nuclear technology to China. Finally, responding to hundreds of Americans protesting outside the White House against China's human rights record, Ziang defended China's human rights policy, which Clinton had also criticized.

November 6, 1997

Israeli-Palestine talks end with no significant results.

Four days of discussions with U.S. mediators in Washington obtained only a few insignificant results regarding technical details of the Oslo II agreements. The negotiations ended a year of disputes between Israel and the Palestine National Authority. After Israel decided to construct Jewish housing units at Har Homan in East Jerusalem, a round of violence took place among Palestinians, the Israeli Defense Force (IDF), and Jews living in West Bank settlements. The clashes included a July 30 Palestinian suicide bomb which exploded in a Jewish market, killing 13 and wounding 170 Israelis, as well as the IDF's destruction of 10 Palestinian buildings including an East Jerusalem building housing a clinic for elderly and disabled people funded by $30 million from Canada and Switzerland.

While ordering Palestinian buildings destroyed, Prime Minister Netanyahu approved the construction of 3000 housing units for Jewish settlements at the West Bank village of Efrat. Despite U.S. attempts to have Israel stop building more Jewish homes on the West Bank, Netanyahu claimed they were for the "natural growth" of the Jewish population, but Israel's government made generous grants and offered tax breaks to lure Israelis to move to the settlements. Netanyahu did not mention that the Arab population's "natural growth" was greater than Jewish growth.

Although both Israel and the Palestine National Authority sent delegates to negotiate in Washington, the November talks did not end the disputes.

See March 7, 1997; October 23, 1998.

November 10, 1997

President Clinton bypasses U.N. authorization and threatens to bomb Iraq.

Clinton's threat to Iraq followed President Saddam Hussein's obstruction of the United Nations Special Commission (UNSCOM) inspectors of Iraq's weapons of mass destruction (WMD). On October 27, the Iraqi parliament voted to turn back U.N. inspectors until the Security Council set a timetable to end U.N. economic sanctions imposed after the 1990–1991 war. Two days later, Iraq ordered all U.S. inspectors on UNSCOM to leave the country within seven days, claiming they were spies.

In response, UNSCOM's executive officer, Richard Butler, an Australian who replaced Rolf Ekeus in the summer of 1997, suspended inspections unless Americans could participate.

In New York, the Security Council rejected any strong action against Hussein because France, Russia, and China preferred to end inspections and U.N. economic sanctions placed on Iraq in 1991. On November 10, President Clinton objected to the council's failure to act and threatened Iraq with a U.S. military response if it did not cooperate with UNSCOM inspectors. In addition, Clinton sent U.S. reconnaissance aircraft to resume surveillance of Iraq, dispatched four F-16 combat aircraft and five KD-135 tanker airplanes to the Incirlik airbase in Turkey, and sent the aircraft carrier USS *Nimitz* to the Persian Gulf.

Clinton's threatened attack was delayed when Iraq appeared ready to yield. On November 20, Russian Foreign Minister Yevgeny Primakov, an old friend of President Hussein, worked out an agreement with Iraq allowing UNSCOM inspectors to return, including Americans.

President Clinton adopted a wait-and-see policy and Hussein's promises soon evaporated. On December 12, Hussein again prohibited UNSCOM from inspecting "sensitive sites," claiming they were

essential to Iraq's sovereignty. On January 13, 1998, Hussein again obstructed U.S. inspectors by claiming UNSCOM Team 222 leader Scott Ritter was an American spy and demanding that diplomats from France, Russia, and China accompany UNSCOM inspectors visiting "sensitive sites."

Despite Iraq's obstructions, the Security Council extended Iraq's oil-for-food program, permitting Iraq to sell $2 billion of oil for six more months, a plan finalized with Iraq on December 27, 1997. Yet tensions between UNSCOM and Iraq intensified in 1998.

See February 22, 1998.

November 10, 1997

Defense Secretary Cohen approves Defense Department reforms; President Clinton signs new strategic weapons guidelines.

Secretary of Defense William S. Cohen took steps to reform his department, although the Quadrennial Defense Review of May 15, 1997, had proposed few changes. The May review asked for moderate cuts in uniformed personnel and military units but preserved all major military procurement programs.

During the summer of 1997, Cohen set up a task force of outside military experts in addition to an internal Pentagon committee to work on possible changes in the department. After merging the ideas of these two groups, Cohen announced on November 10 that his office personnel of 3,000 would be cut to 2,000 with comparable reductions in personnel of the Joint Chiefs of Staff offices and supporting defense agencies. His plan also realigned several offices to eliminate 2 of the 11 assistant secretary positions and slashed 28,000 of the 141,000 civilian jobs in the Defense Department.

Although Cohen expected to save $6.4 billion between fiscal 1999 and 2003, he said the changes were not simply to save money but focused on the department's post–Cold War concerns, including the spread of nuclear weapons and terrorism. The restructuring changed how the Pentagon prepared for major wars more than how it conducted business. His reforms maintained a military force of 1.4 million but transformed the department's management practices by subjecting more jobs to competitive bidding. The most difficult change would be persuading Congress to close more U.S. military bases to save billions of dollars that could be spent on military procurement. Congress had rejected the Pentagon's last attempt to close bases that Cohen believed were not needed.

Perhaps more important to U.S. defense policy, just before Thanksgiving, President Clinton signed new guidelines regarding preparations for possible nuclear war. The guidelines abandoned the concept of fighting and winning a protracted nuclear war adopted by the Reagan administration, an idea most experts claimed was a war no one would win. The new guidelines focused on deterring nuclear, chemical, or biological warfare attacks on the United States and its allies. General Eugene E. Harbiger, commander of the U.S. Strategic Command, said that rather than talk about prevailing in a protracted nuclear war, "there's a more realistic approach now."

Yet the new guidelines raised questions about how nuclear threats could deter a rouge nation, such as North Korea, from launching a terrorist strike, or how to deter an unknown enemy.

See May 29, 1982.

November 23, 1997

Election of the Srpska Republic's parliament has mixed success for U.S.-backed President Plavsić.

In June 1997, Srpska Republic President Plavsić called for new elections and denounced the corrupt practices of former President Radovan Karadžić, who retained a larger following in the eastern section of the Srpska republic. Supported by U.S. advisers in Bosnia, Plavsić dismissed the Srpska parliament dominated by Karadžić's loyalists, expecting elections would give moderate Serbs a majority. After radical Serbs protested and expelled Plavsić from Karadžić's Social Democratic Party, Plavsić followed U.S. advice by asking Yugoslav President Milošević to convene a meeting between Plavsić and Karadžić regarding elections. At a September meeting in Belgrade, Plavsić and Karadžić agreed to hold parliamentary elections in November followed by December elections in which both President Plavsić and Momcilo Krajišnik, the Serb representative on Bosnia's presidency, would seek reelection.

Two changes were made in the Belgrade agreements. First, Karadžić violated a promise to open Bosnian Serb television and radio broadcasts to Plavsić's political moderates. To fulfill Karadžić's promise, SFOR troops raided four key TV transmission stations and turned control over to Plavsić's officials.

Second, after the Organization for Security and Cooperation in Europe (OSCE) objected to monitoring two crucial votes in a short time, the election for the Srpska president was postponed until January 1998.

Despite SFOR's assistance, the November 22–23 parliamentary elections had mixed results. Karadžić lost his parliamentary majority after his Social Democratic Party won 24 seats and the allied Radical Party won 15 seats, giving 39 seats total in an 85-seat parliament. Plavsić's People's National Alliance won 15 seats, and Muslim-Croat refugee absentee ballots gained 16 seats. Two small parties won four seats, leaving the nine seats of the Socialist Party as a potential balance of power for control of the government.

See December 18, 1997.

December 3, 1997

One hundred and twenty one nations sign the land mine treaty; the United States refuses to sign.

Meeting in Ottawa, Canada, representatives of 121 nations signed the Land mine treaty banning the manufacture and use of land mines. As announced by President Clinton (see September 17, 1997), the United States did not sign the treaty, especially because it wanted to have land mines along South Korea's border with North Korea, where a 1953 truce still prevailed. The treaty provided for the destruction of land mine stockpiles within four years and the clearing of all land mines in the signatories territories within 10 years. The treaty would go into effect six months after 40 nations ratified it. By August 1998, 40 nations had ratified the treaty, making it effective in March 1999.

December 11, 1997

One hundred and fifty nations prepare a treaty to limit greenhouse gases like carbon dioxide.

Meeting in Kyoto, Japan, since December 1, 150 nations prepared a treaty to limit the world's greenhouse gases that came principally from fossil fuels (coal) and crude oil. The gases were believed to trap energy in the earth's atmosphere and cause rising temperatures harmful to humans, plants, and wildlife. The leading issue at Tokyo was how much to reduce the gases in industrial nations, with the United States emitting most of the world's gases, as compared with the few gases emitted in developing nations.

The final Tokyo protocol provided that by 2012 industrial nations would reduce their gases to 6–8% below 1990 levels. Developing countries were free to reduce emissions as they wished, without a quota. To make necessary reductions in greenhouse gases, the United States would have to shift its energy consumption to renewable sources such as solar or wind power.

In the United States, lobbyists for the fossil fuel industries persuaded members of Congress who understood little about climatology that the Kyoto Protocol "isn't global and won't work." Consequently, the Clinton administration was unable to persuade the Senate to ratify the treaty.

December 11, 1997

The Organization of Islamic Conference condemns terrorism.

After three days of discussions in Tehran, the Islamic Conference adopted a declaration condemning terrorism as incompatible with Islam. The declaration referred particularly to the murder of 58 foreign tourists in Luxor, Egypt, on November 17, 1997. In this incident, six Islamic fundamentalists whose gunfire was responsible for the tourists' deaths were hunted down by Egyptian police and killed in the hills near Luxor.

During the conference, Iran's supreme religious leader, Ayatollah Sayyed Ali Khamenei, criticized U.S. efforts to dominate Middle East peace efforts and Western civilization in general. In contrast, Iranian President Muhammad Khatami expressed his willingness to broaden contacts with the West and reestablish a dialogue with the "great People of the United States."

December 18, 1997

President Clinton indicates U.S. troops will remain in Bosnia indefinitely.

Because the NATO-led peacekeepers made significant progress after arriving in Bosnia in December 1995, the initial December 1996 deadline was extended to June 30, 1998. During a press conference on December 18, Clinton admitted his mistake in setting deadlines for withdrawing NATO forces. Rather, he said, an indefinite time was better because it was difficult to know when all Bosnian refugees would be able to return to their homes and when a stable government for Bosnia could be established.

In 1995, the United States sent 27,000 soldiers as part of the NATO force, but by the end of 1997 only 8,000 Americans remained in Bosnia. On December 22, Clinton, his wife, former Senator Robert Dole (R-Kans.), and 11 other members of Congress visited

President Clinton visits with U.S. forces in Bosnia. Department of Defense

Sarajevo and other Bosnian towns to survey conditions in Bosnia.

See March 5, 1998.

December 18, 1997

Kim Dae Jung, a former dissident, is elected president of South Korea.

Kim won the presidential election by receiving 40.4% of the vote, edging out Lee Hoi Chang's 38.6%, with a third candidate getting 22%. The presidential campaign took place during Asia's financial crisis, with all candidates agreeing to fulfill reforms set by the International Monetary Fund.

Kim first ran for president in 1972. After losing the election he was arrested for his dissenting views and sentenced to death in 1980. The death sentence was commuted to life in prison, but Kim was released in 1982, going in exile to the United States. Five years later, he returned to Korea, where he was an unsuccessful presidential candidate in 1987 and 1992.

See October 27, 1997; February 25, 1998.

December 29, 1997

President Clinton approves Iran's opening a gas pipeline from Turkmenistan.

The Clinton administration decided in July 1997 to approve a natural gas pipeline extending from Turkmenistan to Tehran and eventually across northern Iran to Turkey. On December 29 the first part of the pipeline was opened from Turkmenistan to Tehran in ceremonies featuring the leaders of both countries.

President Clinton approved the pipeline because Iran would pay all construction costs until it reached Turkey. In addition, Turkmenistan's oil and natural gas fields were blocked from going through Russia in 1993 because Moscow wanted to reassert its dominance in the region of former Central Asian Soviet republics, now free countries since 1990. Moscow's action left Turkmenistan without means to export its oil and gas until it made the pipeline deal with Iran. Moreover, because Iran would pay the initial costs of constructing the pipeline, the agreement was exempted from U.S. opposition under the Iran-Libya Sanctions Act signed by Clinton on August 5, 1996. This legislation required the president to impose economic sanctions on any foreign nation investing more than $20 million in one year in either Iran or Libya.

The Iran-Turkmenistan pipeline route was one of several proposed to deliver Turkmenistan's energy resources to Western Europe, the United States, and the Far East. Both Royal Dutch Shell and an investment consortium led by France's Total Oil Company were considering routes from the Caspian Sea region to the Black Sea or via Afghanistan to Pakistan and the Arabian Sea. A route directly south through Iran to the Persian Gulf was the least expensive one, but the Clinton administration vetoed such proposals unless U.S. relations improved with Iran.

1998

January 21, 1998

The media report a story about President Clinton's relations with a White House intern.

On January 21, the news media reported that President Clinton had had sexual relations with Monica Lewinsky, an unpaid White House intern. These allegations surfaced after Lewinsky filed an affidavit in the case of Paula Jones, who charged that Clinton made sexual advances toward her in 1991 when he was governor of Arkansas. In her affidavit, Lewinsky denied having sexual relations with the president, but on January 12, Linda Tripp, Lewinsky's so-called "friend", gave Kenneth Starr tape recordings of her telephone conversations with Lewinsky about sexual relations with Clinton.

Starr, an independent counsel investigating the Whitewater scandal in Arkansas, received approval from a three-judge panel to expand the investigation to include Lewinsky's possible obstruction of justice in the Jones case. Starr's actions were revealed by news reports on January 21, becoming a widely reported scandal that by October 8, 1998, led the House of Representatives to impeach the president.

Clinton's domestic problems intensified through 1998, and while denied by his White House advisers, probably affected his foreign policy decisions as well.

See October 8, 1998.

January 27, 1998

President Clinton's State of the Union address praises 1999's balanced budget and supports action in Iraq and Bosnia.

Clinton hailed the fact that his 1999 budget would be balanced and have surpluses for the first time in 30 years, but he said the surplus income should be used to make Social Security secure. In foreign affairs, he emphasized that Iraq must not be allowed to rebuild weapons of mass destruction and asked Congress to continue supporting U.S. troops in Bosnia as part of NATO's peacekeeping mission.

February 13, 1998

Nigerian troops overthrow Sierra Leone's military rulers.

A military junta led by Lt. Colonel Johnny Paul Koromah had ousted Sierra Leone's democratically elected government in 1997. Although Koromah promised the West African alliance of peacekeepers he would return a civilian government to power, he never fulfilled that commitment. On February 5, Nigerian-led peacekeeping forces attacked the junta's headquarters, capturing it on February 12 when Koromah surrendered. Over 100 people were killed in the week of fighting.

February 22, 1998

Avoiding an attack on Iraq, U.N. Secretary-General Annan makes a dubious compromise with Saddam Hussein.

After promising to open Iraq to UNSCOM inspectors, Iraq again prevented inspections of its "sensitive sites" on December 12, 1997. A few inspections took place until January 12, when Iraq accused American Scott Ritter's team of spying and ordered the team to leave Iraq. Although a group of French and Russians visiting Iraq were impressed with President Saddam Hussein's cooperation, the United States and Britain contended that UNSCOM teams were more experienced in dealing with Iraq and knew what questions to ask. The French and Russians had become supportive of Iraq and minimized the need to inspect sensitive sites.

Subsequently, the United States and Britain again threatened to bomb Iraq to force Hussein's cooperation with UNSCOM. To give Iraq one last chance, President Clinton and Prime Minister Tony Blair agreed that Kofi Annan could visit Baghdad to talk with Hussein. Thus, on February 22 Annan announced Iraq would "fully" cooperate with UNSCOM. Reluctantly, the United States and Britain accepted Annan's compromise despite the fact that it created new obstacles for UNSCOM

inspectors. In particular, UNSCOM could visit sensitive sites only if accompanied by diplomats from France, Russia, and China.

Despite these obstacles, Annan's success probably satisfied many Americans who had demonstrated against the U.S. bombing of Iraq. Early in February, hundreds of protesters demonstrated in New York's Times Square, and demonstrations also took place at a forum at Ohio State University. During the forum, hecklers shouted so loudly they drowned out Secretary of State Albright and Defense Secretary Cohen, who tried to explain why Iraq must be forced to allow UNSCOM inspections.

The demonstrations in Ohio, New York, and elsewhere may have been related to the fact that television pictures showed the suffering of Iraq's women and children staged by Hussein in Baghdad but never showed Hussein's expenditures on luxurious palaces and military weapons. Nor did TV show the work of the U.N. and other relief agencies in southern Iraq, an area Hussein declared off-limits to international television cameras. Secretary Albright often showed the UNSC satellite pictures of Iraq's palaces and arms shipment but television never transmitted them. (See also February 23, 1999 for U.N. report on Hussein's tactics.)

As groups of Americans protested the war, Saddam Hussein constructed an expensive vacation resort 85 miles south of Baghdad, which remained a secret until May 8, 1999, when Iraq's state television broadcast Saddam receiving the city's key. The new city was named Saddamiat al-Tharthar, was situated on the artificial Lake Tharthar, and had a gateway with a 30-foot high bronze statue of Saddam, another sign of Saddam's extravagant spending while most Iraqis suffered from deprivation. International television did not broadcast the ceremony, although the *New York Times* printed the Associated Press's May 8 report on page 7.

From March to September 1998, the Clinton administration hoped to placate those nations who opposed the bombing of Iraq by working with the Security Council and Arab leaders to get Hussein's full cooperation. Clinton urged Australia's Richard Butler, Executive Officer of UNSCOM, to avoid intrusive inspections and "go slow" on surprise "challenge" inspections, while building a definitive case against Iraq's failure to provide full information about its weapons of mass destruction.

On August 4, Clinton's cautious approach raised problems when Hussein again interfered with a UNSCOM inspection team led by Scott Ritter. On August 7, Butler decided to withdraw UNSCOM to protest Clinton's go-slow policy. Soon after, Ritter resigned from UNSCOM and complained to the Senate Committee on Foreign Affairs that Clinton was not aggressive enough against Iraq, a complaint denied by Secretary of State Albright and Butler. Republican Party members on the committee backed Ritter, citing his courage in reporting Clinton's alleged weakness. By September, there were more problems with Iraq.

See November 10, 1997; October 31, 1998.

February 25, 1998

Kim Dae Jung is inaugurated as president of South Korea.

Two months after his election, Kim was sworn in as the nation's first president from an opposition party. Although South Korea faced serious financial problems in 1997, international creditors agreed on January 28 to renegotiate $24 billion of short-term foreign currency loans with South Korean banks. In Kim's inaugural address, he asked for parliamentary support from the majority Grand National Party and expressed his willingness to discuss future peace plans with North Korean leader Kim Jong Il.

See December 18, 1997; June 9, 1998.

March 5, 1998

Serb attacks in Kosovo lead Clinton to impose sanctions on Yugoslavia.

In 1992, the Yugoslavia Federation of Socialist Republics broke up. The Republics of Serbia and Montenegro claimed to be the Federal Republic of Yugoslavia, although the United Nations General Assembly refused to have their delegate occupy the seat of the former Yugoslavia (see September 21, 1992). Despite the U.N. Assembly's action, the autonomous province of Kosovo remained part of the Republic of Serbia after Serbia revoked its autonomy as a province (see March 23, 1989).

From 1989 to 1998, the Republic of Serbia's President Slobodan Milošević took dictatorial control of Kosovo, ordering Serb police to arrest ethnic Albanians in Kosovo, known as Kosovars, and to kill any who resisted arrest. The police especially tar-geted Kosovar intellectuals, political leaders, and business managers, whose positions were taken over by ethnic Serbs. The Serbs did permit Kosovo's unofficial president, Ibrahim Rugova, to fulfill his executive duties in Kosovo because Rugova advocated nonviolent methods to resist Serb violations of human rights. Between 1989 and 1993 an estimated 368,000 Kosovars who opposed Rugova's nonviolent tactics chose exile in Switzerland, Germany, or the United States. Most of the Kosovars remaining in their homeland accepted Rugova's nonviolent methods as a way to gain international backing for Kosovo's plight.

The 1995 Dayton Accords gave peace to Bosnia but offered no changes in Kosovo (see November 21, 1995). Lacking any international support for Rugova's nonviolent tactics, Kosovars began organizing the Kosovo Liberation Army (KLA) to defeat the Serbs in Kosovo and win independence from the Serb Republic. According to the former U.S. Ambassador Warren Zimmermann and the British reporter for the *London Times* Tim Judah, Milošević's officials in control of Yugoslavia's radios, television stations, and newspapers proclaimed that KLA members were thugs and "Mafia-like narcotic traffickers." In reality, most Kosovars the KLA recruited were ordinary men who decided nonviolence did not work and took up arms to defend their villages from Serbian depredations.

When exiles in Zurich, Switzerland, and Germany began organizing the KLA they received financing assistance from exiled Kosovars including those in the United States. Most KLA members had little conventional military training but learned to fight guerrilla-style warfare in Kosovo's forests and mountains. Although Albania harbored some KLA forces, the collapse of Albania's government in 1997 enabled the KLA to buy Albanian arms cheaply (see April 15, 1997). In May 1997 Kosovar exiles told reporters in Zurich, Switzerland, the KLA was responsible for two acts of violence in January 1997: the assassination of the Serbian rector of Pristina University, Radivoje Papovic, and the detonation of a bomb near Pristina University that killed two Serbs and two Kosovars. In September 1997 small student protests began in Pristina, growing in size until they reached collectively 20,000 students and other Kosovars on September 30. These protests did not cease until October 1, 1997, after Serbian police beat many students and detained their leaders.

On February 28, 1998, protests turned into open warfare between Serbs and Kosovars after Serbian police ambushed a KLA contingent, and the ensuing fire-fight left two Serbs dead. Serb police then turned on two nearby households, where they killed 26 Kosovars.

Between March 1 and 10, Serbian police and para-militaries using helicopter gunships, tanks, armored vehicles, and combat aircraft attacked the cities of Likoshani and Prekas, killing 77 Kosovars and destroying all the homes. These unrestricted attacks on civilians were beyond the standards for antiguerrilla warfare defined by the United Nations and other international bodies.

On March 5, President Clinton responded to the Serbs' attacks by imposing mild sanctions such as stopping the expansion of Yugoslav consular personnel in the United States. Later in April the United States, Japan, and the European Union froze Yugoslav foreign assets and prohibited further investments in Yugoslavia. Secretary of State Albright tried to get the six-member Contact Group—United States, Britain, France, Germany, Italy, and Russia—to form a united front against the Serbs, but France, Italy, and Russia rejected strong action. On April 1, the U.N. Security Council imposed an arms embargo on both the KLA and Yugoslavia just two weeks after Russia sent Serbia a shipment of tanks, attack helicopters, and heavy artillery. Effective action by the United States, the Contact Group, and NATO did not take place until October.

See March 23, 1989; October 12, 1998.

March 17, 1998

Chinese Premier Li Peng is replaced by Vice Premier Zhu Rongii.

Li Peng had served the legal limit of 10 years as premier. As Vice Premier in charge of China's economic policy, Zhu Rongii, the new premier, succeeded in cutting back China's inflation rate during 1997.

March 23, 1998

President Clinton begins an 11-day visit to Africa.

The trip took the president and his wife to Ghana, Uganda, Rwanda, South Africa, Botswana, and Senegal. Clinton drew the television spotlight on Africa to emphasize the continent's need for more trade and investments by Western financial interests. He also offered regrets for American participation in slavery, U.S. support for African dictators during the Cold War, U.S. failure to intervene in the 1994 genocide in Rwanda, and U.S. complicity in South African apartheid.

President Clinton and President Jerry John Rawlings of Ghana address the people on a stage in Accra, Ghana, with their wives Hillary Rodham Clinton and Nana Kohadu Agyeman Rawlings. Clinton Presidental Materials Project

Clinton was the first U.S. president to visit South Africa, where, during a press conference, President Nelson Mandela responded to U.S. critics by saying his continued ties with Cuba, Iran, and Libya were because those countries helped the African National Congress overthrow South Africa's white domination.

March 27, 1998

Russian President Boris Yeltsin appoints Sergey Kiriyenko as premier.

On March 27, 1998, President Yeltsin delivered a televised address to tell the Russian people he had asked all Russia's cabinet members to resign, except Foreign Minister Yevgeny Primakov. Yeltsin said he wanted younger people to "bring more energy and efficiency" into Russia's cabinet. Premier Victor Chernomyrdin was dismissed and replaced by 35-year old Sergei Kiriyenko, who had been Russia's Minister of Energy. Yeltsin indicated Kiriyenko would take necessary measures to improve Russia's program to privatize Russia's state-owned indus-

tries, but Yeltsin expected few changes would take place in other policies.

See September 1, 1998.

April 8, 1998

The International Monetary Fund lets Indonesia renew food and fuel subsidies.

Indonesian President Suharto had failed to implement all previous IMF requirements for an aid package of $40 billion. During early 1998, Indonesia's people began suffering from starvation and malaria due to drought and extensive brushfires. To solve these problems, the IMF worked out an agreement with Suharto to send part of the funds and permit the government to subsidize the costs of food and fuel.

See May 21, 1998.

April 10, 1998

Britain and Ireland reach an accord to bring peace to Northern Ireland.

Former U.S. Senator George Mitchell (D-Me.) as chairman of the negotiating teams assisted the com-

Indonesia

pletion of accords to end a civil conflict that had cost 3,248 lives during the past 29 years. Participants in the peace talks included British Prime Minister Tony Blair, Irish President Bertie Ahern, David Trimble the Northern Protestant Party leader, John Hume the Social Democratic Party [Catholic] leader, and Gerry Adams, a northern Irish Catholic and the head of Sinn Fein, the political arm of the Irish Republican Army (IRA).

Under the agreement, Britain would continue ruling Northern Ireland but a new provincial assembly would have jurisdiction over local issues. The provincial assembly would also work with Ireland's government on a new North-South Ministerial Council. A third new organ, the Council of the Isles, would deal with mutual interests of Britain and Ireland. The accord would have to be approved in a referendum of the people of Northern Ireland and by the parliament of Ireland and Britain.

By the end of April, the Northern Protestant Party and Ireland's parliament had approved the accords. The Irish Republican Army created a problem on April 30 by refusing to surrender its arms, as required by the accords.

On May 22, referenda were held in Ireland and Northern Ireland. In Ireland, 94% of voters approved the accords; in Northern Ireland, 71% approved. Despite these votes for peace in both parts of Ireland, the various paramilitary groups had not yet disarmed as the accords required.

See September 10, 1998.

April 19, 1998

Thirty four Western Hemispheric nations agree to negotiate a free-trade zone.

President Clinton met with 33 other Western Hemispheric leaders at the second Summit of the Americas in Santiago, Chile. Clinton told the delegates that he would ask the U.S. Congress to restore the "fast-track" trade authority Congress denied the president in 1997. The fast-track authority meant Congress could not add amendments to a trade agreement negotiated by the executive branch.

In concluding their summit on April 19, the hemispheric leaders said that negotiations would begin in 1998 to create a free-trade zone able to operate by 2005. The leaders also agreed to undertake new efforts to combat drug trafficking.

April 30, 1998

The U.S. Senate ratifies amendments for three new nations to join NATO.

Three former Warsaw Pact nations—the Czech Republic, Poland, and Hungary—had been invited to join NATO in 1997 but their membership required amendments to the 1949 NATO treaty.

The U.S. Senate approved these amendments by a vote of 80 to 19. The United States was the fifth NATO country to approve the amendments; eventually all 15 NATO members approved them.

See July 8, 1997.

April 30, 1998

The Defense Department approves a deal to develop a national missile defense system.

Secretary of Defense Cohen announced that the Pentagon had awarded $1.6 billion to the Boeing Aircraft Company for design, development, and testing of a limited national defense system. The basic contract was for three years to find out whether a defense system was viable. In 2000, the president would determine whether performance tests were successful. If the development and tests of the system appeared successful, Boeing could receive about $5 billion to make the final tests and to deploy a limited system. The defense system would consist of ground-based interceptor missiles, space-based satellites for missile-launch detection and interceptor guidance, and a battle management command, control, and communication system.

Since President Reagan first proposed a national missile defense system in 1983, the United States had spent nearly $50 billion to achieve it, but missile intercept tests had been failures.

May 1, 1998

Before a U.N. war crimes tribunal former Rwandan Premier Kambanda pleads guilty to genocide.

Former Premier Jean Kambanda was the first Rwandan convicted by the U.N. International Tribunal on War Crimes in Rwanda, whose proceedings were conducted in Tanzania. A rebel Hutu tribal leader, Kambanda was charged with chairing meetings to plan the massacres of thousands of Tutsis before installing a regional Hutu government.

A week earlier on April 24, Rwanda executed 22 people convicted of genocide. During a three-month period in 1994, the Hutu regime killed about 500,000 Tutsis and moderate Hutus. Two Roman Catholic priests were among the 22 convicted and executed. The priests had organized Hutu tribesmen to kill 2,000 Tutsis seeking refuge in a church in the town of Kivumu. In Rwanda, about 125,000 suspects awaited trial for war crimes.

See June 8, 1994.

May 11, 1998

Joseph Estrada is elected president of the Philippine Islands.

Vice President Estrada, a populist and former film actor, was elected president in national elections. In the legislature, candidates from President Fidel Ramos's Lakas Party continued to have a majority in the lower house. Ramos was ineligible for a second term.

May 15, 1998

The Group of Eight (G-8) major powers focus their attention on Asian problems.

Holding their annual meeting in Birmingham, England, the group included Russia as a formal member for the first time. During its sessions, the G-8 members condemned India's nuclear testing program and called for India to sign the Nuclear Non-Proliferation Treaty (NPT). The G-8 asked Pakistan to cancel plans for its nuclear tests.

The G-8 members also discussed Asia's financial crisis that began with Thailand's banking system in the summer of 1997. To inform G-8 members about Asia's current financial condition, World Bank vice president for East Asia and the Pacific Jean-Michael Severino reported Southeast Asian governments had taken positive steps to cushion their financial problems. They cut their budget deficits and placed price controls on consumer goods to avoid inflation. In addition, Southeast Asian political officials were learning how the global free market functions and educating their citizens in economics and business. Moreover, many Southeast Asian nations are moving toward democratic governments, especially in Thailand where a new 1997 constitution enabled the government to remove corrupt officials from office.

See May 28, 1998.

May 18, 1998

President Clinton gives a permanent waiver of the 1996 Helms-Burton Act.

Following negotiations between the United States and the European Union (EU), Clinton and the EU leaders met in London to sign the final draft of an agreement regarding the Helms-Burton Act. Under the agreement, Clinton gave a permanent waiver of Helms-Burton to EU members, a waiver he had previously given every six months. In exchange, the 15 EU nations would join the United States in creating a global registry of property confiscated by Cuba and other governments such as Libya and Iran that would then be off-limits to investors. EU members also agreed not to upgrade their political and economic relations with Cuba unless Cuba improved its human rights conduct and moved to establish democracy.

Despite many advantages for the United States under the London accords, Senate Majority Leader Jesse Helms (R-N.C.) criticized them for being "too small a loaf," saying there should be an act of Congress before the London accords became effective.

See March 12, 1996; January 3, 1997.

May 21, 1998

Indonesian President Suharto resigns under the threat of impeachment.

After student demonstrations in March 1998, Indonesia was calm until May 4, when the government announced cuts in subsidies for gasoline by 71%, on diesel fuel by 58%, and on electricity by 20%. Then Suharto made a new deal with the International Monetary Fund (IMF) in April that permitted subsidies on food and household fuel but required them to be cut for other products.

The subsidy reductions inflamed many throughout the country and violent demonstrations erupted again. Between May 12 and 15, an estimated 500 died from building fires or police bullets. On May 15, Suharto returned from a visit to Egypt and restored the subsidies. By the time he acted, thousands of students had occupied the parliament building while soldiers gathered as observers. After dissidents rejected Suharto's offer to change cabinet members and conduct early elections, the speaker of parliament announced that impeachment proceedings would begin in two days unless Suharto resigned.

Suharto resigned on May 21 and the Indonesian People's Consultative Assembly named Vice President Bacharuddin Jusuf (B.J.) Habibie president. A protégé of Suharto, Habibie appointed a cabinet retaining 15 of Suharto's appointees. Among those replaced was Suharto's son-in-law, Prabowo Subianto, who commanded an elite armed forces unit. On May 22, Indonesian troops removed 2,000 students from the parliament building and Habibie ordered the release of two jailed dissident leaders.

Although Habibie announced that new elections would be held before 2003, more demonstrations began in November 1998, paving the way for elections in 1999.

May 28, 1998

The United States imposes sanctions on Pakistan and India because of their nuclear tests.

During May 1998, India and Pakistan conducted successful nuclear weapons tests. India's five underground tests were made on May 11 and 13. Indian Prime Minister Atal Bihari Vajpayee wrote to President Clinton that tests were necessary because India was concerned about China's military aid to Pakistan. Nevertheless on May 13, Clinton announced that the United States was placing economic sanctions on India as required by the 1994 Nuclear Proliferation Prevention Act (NPPA).

Fifteen days later, Pakistan conducted five successful underground tests and, as with India, the United States and other signatory nations of the NPPA levied sanction on Pakistan. The sanctions had an immediate impact on both countries. The Karachi stock exchange dropped 40% in value between May 13 and June 1, and the World Bank delayed a $206 million loan to India. While urging the two nations to settle their grievances over Kashmir, the Western powers continued to withhold loans from them.

See July 14, 1998.

June 9, 1998

President Clinton meets with South Korean President Kim Dae Jung.

While on a nine-day tour of the United States, President Kim met with Clinton in the White House. Both were eager to obtain better relations

President Kim Dae Jung of South Korea meets with President Clinton at the White House. Clinton Presidential Materials Project

with North Korea, calling for Western investments and other incentives to help open up North Korea.

June 21, 1998

Colombian Conservative Party candidate Pastrana is elected president.

In a final runoff after May 31 elections left no candidate with a majority, Andrés Pastrana Arango was elected by a narrow margin over the Liberal Party's Horacio Serpa Uribe. Pastrana's presidential campaign emphasized his desire to hold cease-fire talks with left-wing rebels, cut the budget deficit, and lower the value-added tax. The Clinton administration hoped Pastrana would cooperate by controlling Colombia's drug trade so Colombia could again be certified to receive U.S. financial assistance. In 1997, the Clinton administration had been unable to certify Colombia because Colombia had not cooperated in the U.S. war on drugs.

See February 28, 1997.

June 22, 1998

Ambassadors from the United States, Japan, and the European Union leave Belarus.

Because Belarus President Aleksandr Lukashenko threatened to take over homes on Ambassador's

Row in Minsk, the U.S., Japanese, and EU ambassadors joined in withdrawing from the country to protest Lukashenko's action. Reports circulated that Lukashenko wanted to have Minsk's entire diplomatic compound for his own offices and living quarters.

After the recall of the most important ambassadors from his country, Lukashenko backtracked after the various ambassadors refused to move their apartment's furnishings. In addition, the U.S. State Department asserted that the residences of ambassadors were inviolable property under international standards of diplomatic immunity.

Subsequently on December 28, Lukashenko withdrew his threats and announced that the ambassadors could return to their residences in early 1999.

See December 26, 1998.

June 25, 1998

President Clinton arrives in China to meet with President Ziang Zemin.

Although evidence indicated that Chinese officials had illegally contributed $28,000 through John Chung, a California businessman, to back the Democrats during the 1996 election campaign, President Clinton did not want to further isolate China by canceling his visit.

After arriving in China, Clinton visited Tiananmen Square, the site of the 1989 massacre of pro-democracy groups (see June 3–4, 1989). On June 27 after meeting with Ziang Zemin, Clinton and Ziang held a joint news conference broadcast live over Chinese television. In their comments, Clinton criticized the 1989 crackdown while Ziang defended it for assuring China's current political stability. Ziang denied that China gave financial aid to the Democratic Party in 1996 and said he was willing to meet with the Dali Lama if Tibet's spiritual leader would recognize Tibet and Taiwan as parts of Chinese territory. Both leaders promised not to sell India or Pakistan missiles capable of delivering nuclear weapons.

Finally, Ziang Zemin said China would sign the International Convention on Civil and Political Rights, a promise indicating China might stop prosecuting its dissidents. But before 1998 ended, Western optimism about China's human rights progress fell. In December, China not only arrested five members of a new China Democracy Party but also conducted its usual swift trials to sentence three leading dissidents to 10 years in prison. The three dissenters were Wang Youcai, Xu Wenli, and Qin Yong. As reported by *New York Times* reporter Elizabeth Rosenthal, following the dissidents' imprisonment, Ziang Zemin proclaimed that challenges to Communist rule would be "annihilated in the early stages."

Before leaving China on June 30, Clinton spoke at Beijing University and visited Shanghai, where he answered questions from callers on a radio talk show.

See November 22, 1998.

June 25, 1998

The Supreme Court invalidates the line-item veto.

After Congress passed the line-item veto legislation in 1997, President Clinton used the veto power to cross out 43 items in the legislation Congress had authorized. Although the Republicans' 1994 "contract with America" called for the line-item veto, many Republicans feared a veto under Democratic President Clinton.

Thus, the legislation's constitutionality was tested by a group of Republicans who asked a federal court to rule on the bill. The federal court decision upheld the line-item veto legislation but Republicans appealed to the U.S. Supreme Court. Thus, on June 25, the Supreme Court ruled that the line-item veto was unconstitutional. In a 6-to-3 ruling, Justice John Paul Stevens wrote the majority opinion, that the law was unconstitutional because the president's only two options were to sign or veto an entire congressional authorization bill.

July 8, 1998

Nigeria forms a provisional government following the death of General Abaca.

Following the deaths of two Nigerian leaders within one month, General Abdul Salam Abubakr formed a provisional government as a transition to civilian rule. On June 8, General Sani Abaca died after ruling as a military dictator since 1993, when the military overthrew and imprisoned elected president Moshood Abiola. During his rule, Abaca plundered Nigeria of most of it income from oil exports. Since 1996, reports from the Berlin-based Transparency International monitoring corruption ranked Nigeria as the world's most corrupt country to do business.

On June 9, General Abubakr became the junta's leader but promised a transition to democracy by releasing Abiola from prison. After being freed, Abiola collapsed while meeting with U.S. diplomats to discuss Nigeria's political future. Several hours later, Abiola died from a heart attack. Although an autopsy by Western pathologists confirmed that his death was due to heart disease, Abiola's Yoruba clansmen suspected foul play, staging violent protests that killed 45 people before the Yoruba accepted Abubakr's call for ending the bloodshed.

On July 15, Abubakr began another transition to democracy by canceling regional elections planned by the junta and dissolving the political parties that had backed Abaca's dictatorship. Abubakr freed all political prisoners and said new political parties could form to nominate candidates for 1999 elections. He also promised to pay $630 million owed to international oil companies who refined Nigeria's oil.

July 12, 1998

Japan's ruling party loses its majority in the Upper House of the Diet.

Although Japan's Liberal Democratic Party (LDP) won only 44 of the 126 seats at stake in the House of Councillors, the Party retained a plurality in that house as well as a majority in the lower house of the Diet. Nevertheless, LDP Prime Minister Ryutaro Hashimoto resigned on July 13 because the nation's economy remained in a recession. On July 24, Foreign Minister Keizo Obuchi was elected president of the LDP and became prime minister on July 30. Obuchi had served as a member of the Diet since 1963.

July 14, 1998

Congress eases sanctions on India and Pakistan.

President Clinton had levied sanctions on India and Pakistan in May but Congress agreed in a voice vote to let U.S. farmers sell $40 million of wheat to Pakistan or India, both nations being major purchasers of U.S. wheat. The next day, the Senate passed a bill permitting the president to waive any sanctions on the two countries required under the 1994 Nuclear Proliferation Prevention Act. Later, on November 6, the Clinton administration lifted all sanctions from India and Pakistan after they announced a moratorium on nuclear testing. Clinton's decision enabled India and Pakistan to receive loans from the World Bank and International Monetary Fund.

See May 28, 1998.

July 17, 1998

The International Criminal Court for War Criminals adopted at U.N. Rome conference.

Following a year of negotiations, delegates from more than 100 U.N. member states met in Rome and adopted a treaty to create an international court to try suspects for war crimes, genocide, and crimes against humanity.

The United States made strong objections to the treaty text adopted on July 17. Early in 1998, U.S. negotiators had urged modifications to clarify the conditions for a suspect to be arrested, but delegates from many small countries claimed the U.S. proposals would reduce the possibilities of anyone being tried for violations of human rights. In addition to the United States, France and China opposed the International Criminal Court.

See December 31, 2000.

July 26, 1998

In flawed Cambodian elections, Hun Sen's party forms a majority in the national assembly.

Cambodia's elections were held despite the June 25 preelection reports of observer teams of the U.S.-based National Democratic Institute and the International Republican Institute that the elections were fatally flawed during the campaign period. These two teams reported on hundreds of murders, intimidation, and beatings of people supporting opposition parties during the campaign. Hun Sen's party monopolized media information on television and radio. Hun Sen also financed a $550,000 five-month publicity campaign led by former Reagan administration lawyer Bretton Sciaroni.

Under these conditions, Hun Sen's Cambodian People's Party won only 41% of the vote but increased their seats in the 122-seat National Assembly from 59 to 64 by using a new method to allocate seats. Prince Norodom Ranariddh's Funcinpec Party received 43 seats. In spite of the flawed campaign U.N. observer teams and the two U.S. observer groups approved the elections as a "successful experiment in national self-determination."

As Tina Rosenberg explains ("Hun Sen Stages an Election" (*New York Times Magazine*, August 30, 1998), although the United States, the United Nations, and the European Union invested millions of dollars in Cambodia during the 1990s, the international groups were happy to leave Cambodia with a façade of democracy. On July 30, Hun Sen encouraged Cambodian democracy by asking Ranariddh and Sam Rainsy of the third-place party to join a coalition government. (Pol Pot, the notorious Khmer Rouge leader, died on April 15, 1998.)

See December 5, 1998.

August 20, 1998

President Clinton retaliates against terrorists who bomb U.S. embassies in Africa.

On August 7, bombs exploded at the U.S. embassies in Nairobi, Kenya, and Dar es Salaam, Tanzania. The next day, Israel sent 170 soldiers trained in rescue operations but only a few people were brought out alive from the building. Eventually, the death toll in Nairobi was 213, including 12 Americans, while 540 others were hospitalized. In Dar es Salaam, 11 people died and 70 were wounded. On August 15, Pakistan arrested a suspect who confessed that Osama bin Laden, the wealthy son of a Saudi Arabian businessman, led the operation that included many militant Muslims intent on bombing U.S. targets around the world.

On August 20, after U.S. intelligence agents reported that bin Laden had masterminded many assaults against Americans, President Clinton ordered U.S. naval ships to take action against him. In the Red Sea and Arabian Sea the U.S. navy fired Tomahawk cruise missiles at bin Laden's terrorist training camps in Afghanistan and at the Al Shifa Pharmaceutical Industries factory in Khartoum, Sudan, where officials believed components of chemical weapons were manufactured. Although the CIA claimed Sudan produced chemical weapons components, other reports indicated there was no evidence for this claim, and the White House discontinued references to it in 1999.

Clinton announced these strikes in a televised address from the White House. The president said the United States had strong evidence that bin Laden was responsible for the African embassy bombings and that Afghanistan and Sudan harbored terrorists. On August 27–28, Muhammad Rashed Daoud al-Owhali and Muhammad Saddiq Odeh, two suspects in the bombings, were brought to New York City and arraigned on charges of murder at the Nairobi embassy.

By the end of 1998, a New York grand jury had indicted Osama bin Laden on charges of conspiracy to kill Americans since 1989, not only in Kenya and Tanzania but also during the 1993 conflict in Somalia, and five other men for the bombing of the U.S. Tanzanian embassy. None of the six were in custody.

August 28, 1998

Libya agrees to turn over bombing suspects to a Special Court in the Netherlands for trial.

Following the 1988 bombing of a Boeing 747 with many Americans among the 259 passengers flying over Scotland, U.S. President-elect George Bush promised to punish those responsible (see December 21, 1988). Initially, Syria and Iran were suspected of ordering the attack, but by 1991, investigations by the United States Federal Bureau of Investigation (FBI) and Interpol investigators from Britain, France, Italy, and Germany showed that two of Libya's intelligence agents were responsible. After the U.N. Security Council levied sanctions against Libya, its leader Mu'mmar al-Gadhafi, seemed ready to turn the suspects over for trial. Following negotiations with the United States and Britain, Gadhafi agreed to turn the suspects over for trial in the Netherlands before a panel of Scottish judges.

See December 21, 1988; November 25, 2000.

August 31, 1998

North Korea successfully fires a long-range ballistic missile.

A powerful two-stage ballistic missile was fired from a secret base in North Korea that flew high over Japan before landing in the Pacific Ocean. North Korea's Taepo Dong-1 missile had a range of up to 1,240 miles, carrying a payload of 500 pounds. The range would permit the missile to hit Taiwan and the Philippines as well as Japan, South Korea, and southern China. Moreover, North Korea could sell these missiles to clients such as Iraq, Iran, and Libya, other rouge states. Because Kim received international humanitarian aid to feed the people, he had money to spend on weapons.

Some pundits believed Kim Jong Il fired the missile to impress U.S. and South Korean delegates who renewed peace talks with North Korea in New York City the same day. These talks were another effort to finalize peace terms for the 1950–1953 Korean War.

September 1, 1998

President Clinton and Russian President Yeltsin cannot resolve nuclear issues; Clinton learns more about Russia's financial crisis.

When President Clinton arrived in Moscow, Russia had been in the midst of a financial crisis since early August. The crisis began with a decline in oil prices, a major Russian export, and in reaction to the effects of Asia's financial problems. Attempting to alleviate Russian business concerns, President Yeltsin dismissed Premier Sergey Kiriyenko and returned Viktor Chernomyrdin as premier. On August 27, the new premier halted all trading in currencies because the rouble continued to depreciate. On September 11, Yeltsin appointed Foreign Minister Yevgeny Primakov to replace Chernomyrdin. But these cabinet changes did not solve Russia's financial problems.

On reaching Moscow, President Clinton offered Yeltsin little concrete help except to promise aid if Russia retained its free-market reforms. Principally, Clinton wanted to discuss how Russia's parliament could be persuaded to ratify the second Strategic Arms Reduction Treaty (START II).

See March 27, 1998.

September 10, 1998

After President Clinton's visit to Ireland, the IRA leader Gerry Adams meets Protestant leader David Trimble.

Peace seemed to arrive in Ireland when an agreement negotiated by former U.S. Senator George Mitchell (D-Me.) was announced (see April 10, 1998). On September 1, President Clinton traveled to Northern Ireland, where he met with Gerry Adams, leader of Sinn Fein, the political organization of the Irish Republican Army (IRA). Adams told Clinton Northern Ireland's violence was "a thing of the past," despite the bombing on August 8, 1998, for which the IRA accepted responsibility. On September 8, the IRA declared it would accept the cease-fire required by April 10, 1998, agreement.

After visiting Adams, Clinton met with members of the Northern Ireland Assembly and with the relatives of 29 victims killed in the August bombing, the worst incident of violence since April 1998. On September 12, after Clinton left Northern Ireland, Adams met with the Ulster Union's Protestant leader David Trimble to discuss ways to maintain the April peace accords.

See April 10, 1998; February 16, 1999.

September 12, 1998

CIA data on Chile reveals that President Nixon plotted Allende's overthrow.

Declassified documents requested by the independent National Security archive indicated that President Nixon ordered the overthrow of Chilean President Salvador Allende. According to the documents, Nixon ordered action against Allende soon after Ambassador Edward Korry, a conservative Republican, reported that Allende's election victory would lead to a communist takeover of Chile. Nixon told CIA Director Richard Helms that the CIA could use $10 million or more to "save Chile" from Allende, preferably before he was inaugurated as president. The CIA sent guns and ammunition to seek aid from Chile's army in ousting Allende and provided a story for *Time* magazine that criticized Allende and called for an invasion of Chile.

Because the CIA could not quickly arrange for a Chilean military leader to stage a coup before Allende's 1970 inauguration, the CIA's efforts continued for three years before there was a successful coup on September 11, 1973. During the coup, Allende allegedly committed suicide as Chile's armed forces entered his office. After the coup, Chile was led by a junta led by General Augusto Pinochet.

See September 11, 1973; April 24, 1990;
November 30, 2000.

September 27, 1998

German elections end Helmut Kohl's 16 years as chancellor.

In parliamentary elections, Gerhard Schröder's Social Democratic Party's 298 members of parliament had a plurality of votes. By forming a majority coalition with Green Party representatives, Schröder became Germany's chancellor. Kohl not only lost his own seat in parliament, but his Christian Democrats won only 35% of the popular vote. During the election campaign, Schröder emphasized the need for a change of government to help fight Germany's high unemployment rate and cut the high taxes levied to help reunify Germany after 1989.

October 4, 1998

Brazilian President Cardoso is reelected by a narrow margin.

President Fernando Henrique Cardoso was reelected by 50.9% of the vote, barely enough to avoid a runoff election. Following his reelection, Cardoso took bold steps to end Brazil's financial crisis, which began in 1997. On October 28, Cardoso proposed to raise revenue by $1 billion in tax increases and $7 billion in spending cuts to achieve a surplus in the federal budget. These changes were essential for Brazil to obtain loans of $42 billion or more from various international groups.

See January 13, 1999.

October 8, 1998

The House of Representatives votes to hold impeachment hearings on President Clinton.

The House vote approved an October 5 recommendation from the Judiciary Committee considering possible hearings. The committee based its finding on 4,600 documents it received from independent counsel Kenneth Starr regarding conversations between Starr and Monica Lewinsky and taped recordings made by Linda Tripp, a Pentagon employee, of her phone conversations with Lewinsky. The House vote favoring impeachment hearings was 258 to 176, with 31 Democrats voting yes.

See January 21, 1998; February 12, 1999.

October 8, 1998

Iran retaliates against Afghans for killing 11 Iranian diplomats.

On September 10, Afghanistan's Taliban admitted their soldiers were guilty of the August 1998 killing of 11 Iranian diplomats. For Iran, the admission of guilt was insufficient and 270,000 Iranian army troops mobilized along the border with Afghanistan, vowing to avenge the deaths. Although U.N. Secretary-General Kofi Annan tried to mediate the dispute, conflict broke out along the border and Tehran announced that its troops had inflicted "heavy casualties" on the Afghan rebels. The Iran-Afghanistan dispute was between two fundamentalist Muslim groups. The Taliban represented Sunni teachings; Iran represented Shiite teachings: two divergent but absolutist interpretations of the Koran and Prophet Mohammad's "hadith" as a way of life.

October 12, 1998

Assistant Secretary of State Richard Holbrooke persuades Milošević to accept a cease-fire in Kosovo.

The escalation of fighting since late February 1998 between Serbs and Kosovars escalated with the United States and its Western allies uncertain how to end the war and the refugee crisis, which had over 200,000 Kosovars from their homes. The Serb offensive also inspired more Kosovar exiles to return and join the Kosovo Liberation Army (KLA). During June, NATO made contingency plans to bomb Serbia and staged military exercises along Kosovo's borders with Albania and Macedonia. NATO especially wanted to prevent the conflict from expanding into those two countries.

After the exercises, NATO military leaders wanted to issue Milošević a final warning to remove all Serb forces from Kosovo, but France wanted the U.N. Security Council to authorize any threat of force, and Russian President Boris Yeltsin forestalled the threat by inviting Milošević to Moscow to discuss the situation. After the meeting, Yeltsin praised Milošević for offering concessions, but after NATO leaders studied the details, they rejected the terms. U.S. Secretary of State Albright told a congressional committee that Milošević refused NATO's most essential demand that Serb forces in Kosovo must be reduced to pre-March 1998 levels. Holbrooke also met with Milošević and KLA leaders but saw no real basis for a cease-fire or peace agreement.

Fighting continued in Kosovo, with the largest battle fought to control Padesh on a highway where the KLA imported arms from Albania. After four days of struggle with many casualties on both sides, the Serbs gained control of Padesh.

By September, many humanitarian aid groups were leaving Kosovo not only because the Serbs interfered with delivery of food and medical aid but also because Serb police killed three workers helping the Mother Theresa relief group. The U.N. relief agency said Serbs near Pec surrounded 40,000 refugees and prevented the agency from delivering food and tents for shelter.

Hoping to end the crisis, the Security Council passed Resolution 1199 to demand a Serb cease-fire but only after dropping a warning to avoid a Russian veto. Milošević ignored the resolution, prompting U.S. Secretary of Defense William Cohen and British Foreign Minister Robin Cook to assert that NATO did not need U.N. approval to act against Serbia.

President Clinton was hesitant to deal with Milošević because he faced impeachment hearings in the House of Representatives. On October 2, Clinton announced a "near ultimatum" giving Milošević two weeks to pull Yugoslav troops and Serb police out of Kosovo, end the Serb blockade of humanitarian workers, and schedule peace talks. Clinton also told Holbrooke to ask Milošević to accept U.N. reoslution 1199.

The combination of Resolution 1199, NATO threats, and Holbrooke's mission prevented air attacks in October 1998. On October 12, one day before NATO authorized attacks to begin, Milošević agreed to a cease-fire. The outcome of Holbrooke's talks with Milošević was unusual because, as Holbrooke later explained, neither Yugoslavia, the Serb Republic, nor the Kosovars signed any formal agreements. Rather, both sides accepted a cease-fire enabling NATO to suspend air attacks after unilateral steps were taken by the Yugoslav government. The so-called October accords of 1998 were embodied in an 11-point process approved by the Yugoslav and Serbian parliaments. In addition, Yugoslavia made agreements with NATO military commanders and with the Organization for Security and Cooperation in Europe (OSCE). The OSCE would send 2,000 or more unarmed observers as a Kosovo Verification Mission (KVM).

The three most important of the 11 points that Yugoslavia accepted were 1) to reach a just solution with Kosovo; 2) to recognize the sovereignty and boundaries of Yugoslavia; 3) to hold democratic, free, and fair elections in Kosovo.

Milošević soon broke his agreements and the conflict was renewed.

See March 5, 1998; January 15, 1999.

October 15, 1998

President Clinton and Congress agree on budget terms for fiscal 1999.

The Republican-controlled Congress and the White House agreed on the final parts of the $1.7 trillion budget. The Republicans wanted the budget to include a tax cut because a big surplus was expected in 1999. The Republicans agreed not to cut taxes after Clinton insisted the surplus should protect Social Security. Nevertheless, the president accepted the Republicans' desire to make the largest peacetime increase in military spending since Ronald Reagan's 1985 budget.

In the final budget authorization, the Department of Defense received $280 billion, including $1 billion for maintenance, $4.8 billion for updating aging weaponry, $1.9 billion for U.S. forces in Bosnia, and $1 million for a missile defense system. Congress also added $4.5 billion for pet projects that the department did not request. The State Department received $20 billion for department operations and foreign aid. Congress also approved $18 billion for the International Monetary Fund, whose funds were depleted by the recent financial crisis in Asia and Russia.

October 20, 1998

Congressional legislation implements the chemical weapons convention (CWC).

Having ratified the CWC in 1997, Congress delayed legislation for implementing it because of arguments about inspections of U.S. facilities. On October 20, Congress approved the CWC Implementation Act as part of an omnibus appropriation bill, the House voting 333-95 and the Senate 65-29. President Clinton signed the legislation on October 21, 1998.

The final step for U.S. implementation was for the State and Commerce Departments to agree on the role of each department in establishing regulations for implementation. This step was finalized on July 21, 1999. On-site inspections of U.S. chemical industries began in May 2000.

October 23, 1998

With U.S. guidance, Netanyahu and Arafat sign the Wye accords.

After Israel turned Hebron over to the Palestine National Authority (PNA), the land-for-peace exchanges stalled because Israel Prime Minister Netanyahu wanted to decrease PNA land especially in East Jerusalem. Throughout the next 18 months U.S. State Department officials held extensive discussions with Israeli and Palestinian representatives. Finally, both sides met at Wye Plantation near Washington, D.C., on October 15. After three days of unsuccessful talks Netanyahu and Palestinian leader Arafat joined President Clinton and Jordan's King Hussein to finalize and sign the Wye accords on October 23. The agreement lists "reciprocal responsibilities" for each side plus a timetable detailing each step to be taken. The accords required Israel to turn over about 13% more West Bank land currently under its control, while the PNA would combat terrorist organizations as well as repeal clauses in the Palestine Liberation Organizations Charter that called for Israel's destruction. In addition, the U.S. Central Intelligence Agency would monitor the accords with technical intelligence-gathering methods.

Unfortunately, the Wye accords proved difficult to fulfill because both Netanyahu and Arafat faced stiff opposition when they returned home.

See January 14 and March 7, 1997; December 21, 1998.

October 23, 1998

Declassified reports reveal that the CIA knew about human rights abuses in Honduras in the 1980s.

On October 23, a CIA inspector general's report was declassified, revealing field dispatches and agency reports to Congress that played down human rights abuses by members of the Honduran army. On the more positive side, CIA agents were not present at Honduran torture sessions, as some previous news reports had alleged.

October 26, 1998

Peru and Ecuador sign a peace treaty to end decades of conflict.

Because of persistent border conflicts, Peruvian President Alberto Fujimori and Ecuadoran President Jamil Mahaud Witt agreed that four guarantor nations—the United States, Brazil, Argentina, and Chile—would decide on the border, allowing Ecuador access to the Amazon River and two seaports in Peru.

October 31, 1998

Iraq ends all UNSCOM inspections, demanding an end to all U.N. economic sanctions.

Despite President Saddam Hussein's promise to cooperate "fully" with UNSCOM inspections, Iraq again challenged UNSCOM's right to continue their work unless the United Nations dropped economic sanctions levied against Iraq in 1991. With the American Scott Ritter no longer on inspection teams, Hussein also demanded the removal of Australia's Richard Butler as executive director of UNSCOM. Hussein wanted someone from France or Russia to take charge of UNSCOM and agree to end all inspections.

Because the U.N. Security Council delayed its response to Iraq's latest demands, the Clinton administration prepared for a military response and requested a strong U.N. response against Iraq's failure to comply with previous promises. Although France, Russia, China, and most Arab states supported Clinton's request for strong action, Secretary-General Annan interfered by writing a letter to Hussein on November 14, asking Hussein to cooperate with UNSCOM. Hussein agreed. Although skeptical that Hussein would fulfill his promises, Clinton and British Prime Minister Blair accepted Annan's action but assumed that if Iraq again interfered with UNSCOM, Iraq would be punished by a military attack.

See December 16, 1998.

October 31, 1998

The United States and Israel sign a "strategic cooperation" agreement.

In announcing a strategic cooperation pact, President Clinton and Prime Minister Netanyahu issued a joint statement saying they were concerned about Iran's development of medium- and long-range missiles and weapons of mass destruction. In July, Iran had successfully tested the Shahab-3 missile with an 800-mile range while a newer Shahab-4 missile being developed had a range of 1,200 miles. In addition, both Syria and Iraq had Scud missiles able to hit Israel.

The United States had cooperated with Israel in the successful testing of an Arrow-2 missile defense system. Under the new arrangement, the two nations would have greater cooperation through a Joint Strategic Planning Committee.

See December 21, 1998.

November 22, 1998

China's President Zemin signs a strategic partnership with Russian President Yeltsin.

Following an October 1998 visit to China of Russian Defense Minister Igor Sergeyev, Chinese President Ziang Zemin went to Moscow for discussions that China's New China News Agency described as ending decades of hostility with Russia to forge a "strategic partnership." Previously, the two nations had collaborated in opposing American policy toward Kosovo and Iraq, as well as criticizing U.S. plans for a theater missile defense system.

Despite U.S.-Chinese policy differences, the United States was China's most lucrative market, worth about $60 million annually.

During his Moscow visit, Zemin met with President Yeltsin and Foreign Minister Yevgeny Primakov. The New China News Agency reported Zemin offered Russia food and cash to help Russia's financial difficulties. The offer included China's continued purchase of Russian military equipment to transform China into a "first-class military power." Since 1995, China had spent about $1 billion annually to purchase Russian submarines and fighter jets.

Whatever "strategic partnership" might develop between China and Russia, Western intelligence sources believed China's armed forces were no immediate threat to the U.S. military. The most serious China-U.S. problem regarded Taiwan's status.

December 2, 1998

NATO troops arrest Serb General Radislav Kristić.

U.S. troops, who were part of NATO forces in Bosnia, arrested a high-ranking Serb official, General Kristić under a sealed indictment issued by the Hague War Crimes Court of the Former Yugoslavia. Kristić was charged with participating in the killing of nearly 7,000 people in Srebrenica in the summer of 1995.

NATO's Stabilization Force (SFOR) had become more aggressive in arresting indicted war criminals. On January 9, 1999, French forces under NATO killed a Bosnian Serb, Dragan Gagova, who fled when French soldiers tried to arrest him.

December 5, 1998

The last Khmer Rouge forces surrender in Cambodia.

Following the formation of a coalition government in the summer of 1998, the number of Khmer Rouge rebels continued to decline. On December 5, the surrender of nearly 1,000 rebels appeared to be the last of the Khmer Rouge. With the help of a consortium of private aid donors, Cambodia gradually rebuilt its fragile political stability and was admitted to the Association of Southeast Asian Nations (ASEAN) on April 30, 1999.

See July 26, 1998.

December 16, 1998

U.S. and British aircraft bomb Iraq for not cooperating with UNSCOM.

Following President Saddam Hussein's offer to cooperate with UN inspectors, UNSCOM teams returned to Iraq on November 18. Almost immediately, Iraq placed restrictions on what buildings UNSCOM could enter and what documents they received. For three weeks, UNSCOM Commander Richard Butler tallied places where Iraq refused to cooperate before issuing a report to the U.N. Security Council on December 15.

Being briefed in advance about Butler's report, President Clinton and Prime Minister Blair decided to make a surprise attack on Iraq the day after Butler reported. Saying previous Council threats against Iraq justified their decision, the United States and Britain launched the raids quickly as the best way to succeed against Iraq's military targets. Called Operation

A foreign policy meeting regarding Iraq. Seated around the table, left to right: unidentified military person, George Tenet, unidentified, Secretary Albright, Sandy Berger, Secretary William Cohen (Defense Department), General Henry Shelton, Donald Kerrick, Leon Fuerth, President Clinton, John Podesta. Clinton Presidential Materials Project

Desert Fox, the bombing began the evening of December 16 and continued until December 18, the first day of Islam's holy month of Ramadan.

Although initial reports were skeptical about Desert Fox's success, analyst William M. Arkin's "Desert Fox's Real Mission" (*Washington Post National Weekly*, January 25, 1999) reported that the bombing weakened Iraq's command and control centers, air defense systems, and production of weapons of mass destruction. Assisted by British and American intelligence plus UNSCOM inspection reports, all 49 of Desert Fox's bombs hit Iraq's military strongholds, transportation agencies, the Basra oil refinery complex, palaces, and Baath Party headquarters. Nevertheless, Arkin calculated that Iraq could rebuild these facilities within a year.

See October 31, 1998; January 6, 1999.

December 19, 1998

A CIA analyst is found guilty of selling U.S. secrets to the KGB.

In another CIA debâcle, David Sheldon Boone, a former National Security analyst, was sentenced to 30 years in prison after pleading guilty to selling top-secret documents to the KGB (Soviet secret police), including descriptions of U.S. nuclear targets in Russia. After being indicted, Boone admitted he gave Moscow a list of the U.S. intelligence collection

system and documents on Europe's tactical nuclear weapon targets for the Soviet bloc after 1987.

See March 3, 1997.

December 21, 1998

Israeli Prime Minister Netanyahu's coalition will not support the Wye accords.

Soon after Netanyahu and Palestinian leader Arafat returned to the Middle East from signing the Wye accords, they faced groups opposing the Wye accords. To quiet Israeli opposition, Netanyahu waited until Arafat arrested Hamas radicals who planned the suicide bombing of an Israeli bus that killed an Israeli guard. On November 20, the Israel Government approved withdrawing Israeli troops from 13% of West Bank territory, the first stage of the Wye agreements. In approving the withdrawal, Netanyahu's cabinet added many conditions related to future withdrawals.

Although President Clinton and Secretary of State Albright visited the Middle East from December 12 to 15 to promote the Wye accords, their efforts were unsuccessful. On December 21, Netanyahu's parliamentary coalition collapsed and parliament voted to dissolve the government, a decision requiring new Israeli elections in 1999.

See October 23, 1998; May 17, 1999.

December 26, 1998

Russian President Yeltsin agrees to closer ties with Belarus.

Russia and Belarus took another step toward closer political and economic ties, just short of the political merger that President Yeltsin opposed. In particular, they agreed to unify their currencies. After Belarus gained independence in 1992, President Aleksandr Lukashenko, to demonstrate Belarus's prosperity, allowed state-owned banks to issue so much currency the printing press ran day and night. On August 12, 1998, *New York Times* reporter Michael Wines indicated people in Belarus called the currency "bunnies" who breed devalued money.

1999

January 1, 1999

The Euro, the new European currency, becomes effective for the stock and bond market.

Eleven European Union (EU) nations participating in the shared currency introduced the Euro for each of the states (see accompanying chart). Great Britain was the only major EU nation refusing to join the currency union. In addition, Denmark, Greece, and Sweden did not join. Nevertheless, leaders of France and Germany hailed the Euro as a symbol of a common identity for "Euroland."

EURO RATES	
1.95583	German marks
6.55957	French francs
40.3399	Italian lire
166.386	Spanish pesetas
2.20371	Dutch guilders
40.3399	Belgian francs
13.7603	Austrian schillings
200.482	Portuguese escudos
5.94573	Finnish markka
0.787564	Irish pounds
40.3400	Luxembourg francs

In contrast to praise from participating members, skeptics on the stock and bond exchange markets were wary of the Euro's viability. Both France and Germany were in the midst of an economic downturn and the extensive expenses of social entitlements for their people made them vulnerable to competition in the global economy dominated by the United States.

The first sign of Germany's need to change costly social entitlements came on March 10, 1999. Chancellor Gerhard Schröder wanted to create more jobs without cutting welfare payments while raising workers' wages. Schröder realized German business could not compete with other countries if wages and welfare benefits increased production costs for German business. With Germany continuing to absorb the expenses of its 1990 reunification, Schröder had to forgo plans to increase wages to maintain welfare payments.

See May 2, 1990.

January 6, 1999

The United States admits it used spies in Iraq; the United States and Britain still attack Iraqi "no-fly zones."

The United States admitted using spies posing as UNSCOM inspectors to install devices to monitor Iraqi security communications. Britain and Israel admitted helping the United States interpret the communications.

Although UNSCOM's future remained uncertain following the December bombing of Iraq by American and British aircraft, U.S. and British aircraft continued to shoot down or destroy Iraqi aircraft or anti-aircraft batteries operating in the "no-fly zones" established after 1991. By May 1, 1999, U.S. and British pilots also destroyed 70 Iraqi tanks, some located as close as 30 miles to Baghdad.

In November 1998, the U.S. Congress passed the Iraq Liberation Act, allocating $97 million to prepare an Iraqi rebellion against President Saddam Hussein. But Iraqi exile groups were weak and divided among several leaders who did not want to act without U.S. military forces to back them up.

January 13, 1999

Brazil devalues its currency to meet IMF demands for a $41 billion loan.

Brazilian President Fernando Henrique Cardoso had struggled to balance the federal government's budget since late 1998 (see October 4, 1998). To adjust Brazil's economic status, Cardoso devalued Brazil's currency—the *real*—to eliminate the budget deficits and make Brazil eligible for $42 billion worth of loans from various international financial agencies, especially the International Monetary Fund (IMF).

On February 4, Brazil and the IMF announced an agreement permitting part of the $42 billion loan to reach Brazil. President Cardoso said Brazil would privatize more of its industries.

January 15, 1999

Serb massacres of Kosovars at Racak prove the October 1998 accords a failure.

Although Serbs and Kosovars had had minor skirmishes since November 1998, the Organization of Security and Cooperation in Europe (OSCE) monitors were shocked to discover 45 mutilated Kosovar bodies on a hillside near Racak on January 15. During November 1998, heavy snow prevented Serb-Kosovar clashes but allowed about one-third of the 300,00 Kosovar refugees to return and start rebuilding homes burned by Serb paramilitaries.

Yugoslav President Milošević proved troublesome to U.N., OSCE, and NATO officials throughout the winter of 1998–1999. In November, he refused visas to U.N. investigators who under the October agreements were allowed to search for war crimes in Kosovo. Even worse, Milošević announced he would not agree to the Contact Group's (CG) peace proposals as promised in October. Instead on November 18, Milošević conducted a Serbian Conference of hand-picked delegates from his political party including some selected from Kosovo's Muslims, Turks and obscure "national communities" such as Goranies, Egyptians, and Romanies. He did not invite any Kosovar leader such as the moderate Ibrahim Rugova. The conference drew up what Milošević called a framework for "self-governance" in Kosovo. In contrast, he persistently rejected or refused to discuss peace proposals of CG negotiators Christopher Hill and the European Union's Wolfgang Petritsch.

Defying international attempts at making peace, Milošević ordered the Yugoslav National Army (YNA) to launch an attack on Christmas Eve 1998. In a four-day battle with Kosovar defenders at Podujevo, Serbs attacked both civilians and armed rebels. Unarmed OSCE monitors finally negotiated a cease-fire on December 29, but early in January the Serbs launched an offensive that caused the January 15 massacre of 45 people at Racak.

On January 21 an OSCE monitor's report recited the details of Serb barbarism at Racak, indicating civilian men, women, and children were victims. Contrary to Serb claims, the report indicated the peo-ple killed were not in KLA uniforms but were "humble peasants" in ordinary clothes. Examples of OSCE findings include: "One adult male killed outside his house. The top of his head had been removed and was found 15 feet from his place of death," or "One adult male shot and his head decapitated," or "One adult woman shot in the back of the head."

On January 17, UN Secretary-General Annan, OSCE, and NATO leaders condemned the massacres, saying Milošević was personally responsible for the attack. Milošević's response was to refuse visas to U.N. war crimes investigators from the Hague War Crimes Tribunal. He also ordered the YNA to renew attacks in mountains near Racak. Before January ended, OSCE monitors reported on "grisly" massacres at Rakovina and Rogovo.

Western leaders had no plans for dealing with Serb violations of the 1998 October accords. On January 19, NATO Generals Wesley Clark and Klaus Neumann visited Milošević to display a portfolio of color photographs of Racak's massacred victims, including a dead child holding a pacifier. Milošević shouted at Naumann: "This was not a massacre. It was staged. The [Albanian] people were terrorists."

NATO and CG leaders agreed with Secretary of State Albright that direct negotiations between the two sides were essential. After the English and French foreign ministers, Robin Cook and Hubert Vedrine, respectively, accepted Albright's suggestion for NATO to use a threat of air attacks to obtain direct negotiations, Secretary Albright visited Moscow. France also sent an aircraft carrier to the Adriatic Sea and 40 fighter planes to NATO's Italian air base to be ready for an attack if necessary. On January 26, Albright issued a joint statement with Russian Foreign Minister Igor Ivanov to demand that Yugoslavia comply with the 1998 accords and engage in negotiations for a settlement "providing substantial autonomy for Kosovo."

In the context of a mutual agreement by leaders of the United Nations, NATO, the OSCE and the CG, Yugoslavia and the Kosovars were invited to send delegates to Rambouillet, near Paris, on February 6, 1999. On January 30, NATO supported the "invitation" with a warning that air strikes would be authorized against Yugoslavia if the CG's negotiations were not successful.

See February 23, 1999.

January 17, 1999

U.N. Secretary-General Annan says the peace process has collapsed in Angola.

In 1994, a U.N. mediator persuaded rebels in Angola to sign a peace agreement with the government. Although National Union for the Total Independence of Angola (UNITA) rebels shared power with the new government, Jonas Samvimbi, the UNITA leader, was not satisfied with UNITA's role. Subsequently, rebels attacked government forces and by early 1999 large-scale warfare began.

On January 21, the U.N. Security Council voted to continue peacekeeping in Angola, but on February 26 the council accepted President Jose Eduardo dos Santos's request to pull out U.N. peacekeepers.

See April 11, 1997.

February 7, 1999

Jordanian King Hussein dies; Crown Prince Abdullah becomes king.

For the last six months of 1998, King Hussein was being treated for cancer at Minnesota's Mayo Clinic. After returning home on January 19, 1999, he prepared a letter explaining that his son Abdullah should be his successor rather than Abdullah's brother Hassan. The king accused Hassan of meddling in the policies of Jordan's army and foreign ministry. As a result, Abdullah II ascended the throne on February 7. The next day, President Clinton and three former U.S. presidents—Gerald Ford, Jimmy Carter, and George Bush—joined with many other international leaders to attend King Hussein's funeral in Aman, Jordan.

February 12, 1999

President Clinton is acquitted of impeachment charges.

On December 19, 1998, the House of Representatives approved two articles of impeachment against Clinton. On January 7, the Republican-controlled Senate began hearings on the two articles, with 13 House managers presenting the case against the president.

After hearing evidence from the House managers, the Senate acquitted Clinton of both charges. The charge of perjury before a grand jury failed with only 45 votes in favor; the article of obstruction of justice received 50 votes, 17 votes short of the two-thirds required to convict.

February 16, 1999

Northern Ireland's legislature approves the structure for an executive government.

Taking a major step in implementing the 1998 peace agreement, the legislature of Northern Ireland voted 77 to 29 to structure an executive office. The executive government would include 10 departments to form a cabinet, with cabinet positions for two members of the Sinn Fein, the political arm of the Provisional Irish Republican Army (IRA).

See April 10, 1998; May 29, 2000.

February 17, 1999

Congo rebels launch an offensive against the government.

Following General Laurent Kabila's 1997 victory over the government of Mobutu Sese Seko other rebel groups in the area refused to surrender although Kabila promised "democratic" elections in the Republic of the Congo—Kabila's new name for the former Zaire.

Before elections were held, rebels led by Ernest Wamba dia Wamba renewed warfare against Kabila.

See May 18, 1997; July 10, 1999.

February 23, 1999

A U.N. report blames President Saddam Hussein for the suffering of Iraq's population.

The U.N. report contrasted with U.S. media reports that blamed U.N. sanctions for the suffering of Iraq's women and children (see February 22, 1998). The report from Secretary-General Kofi Annan's office evaluated the effect of Iraq's oil-for-food programs from late 1996 to the end of 1998. The report showed that about 50% of the $540 million Iraq earned from oil sales either disappeared into Iraq's bureaucracy or was diverted for other purposes by Iraq's government. For the remaining 50%, Iraq's bureaucrats failed to contract for essential medicine needed by clinics or for food nutrients given to women and children. In addition much food remained in Baghdad, having been withheld from the Iraqi people, who suffered from illness and malnutrition.

February 23, 1999

Talks between Serbs and Kosovars adjourn until March 15, 1999.

Peace negotiations that began at Rambouillet, France, on February 6 were extended from the original completion date of February 14 to February 23 in the hope of concluding a peace agreement. The talks were completely successful by February 23, and the Contact Group (CG) decided to adjourn until March 15, expecting delegates from the two sides to consider all options and return to conclude a peace arrangement.

During the Rambouillet talks, the CG used the unusual tactic of "enforced negotiations," expecting the two sides to readily accept the CG proposal based on the 11-point October accords and various suggestions from the two sides gathered by the CG's Christopher Hill, Wolfgang Petritsch, and Boris Mayorski. The three essential parts of the CG proposal were a cease-fire, some degree of autonomy for

President Jacques Chirac meets with Secretary Albright and President Clinton in the Oval Office regarding the crisis with the Serbs. Clinton Presidential Materials Project

Kosovo, and the removal of the Yugoslav army and Serb secret police and paramilitary units from Kosovo. A fourth point regarded the use of NATO forces to implement a peace agreement because it was obvious that unarmed OSCE monitors must be replaced by armed peacekeepers such as NATO sent to Bosnia in 1996.

Despite the CG's optimism for a quick solution, there were no breakthroughs at Rambouillet. President Clinton's role in the negotiations was limited until February 12, when the Senate voted against his impeachment. In mid-February, Clinton clarified U.S. policy, indicating the United States would send 4,000 Americans as part of a 20,000 NATO peacekeeping force and approved NATO's plans for air attacks if Yugoslavia did not accept a peace agreement. On February 18, the United States sent 51 heavy bombers to Europe to let Serbian President Milošević know a NATO air attack was possible.

Both houses of Congress showed support for Clinton's decisions. The House approved using air attacks early in March by a vote of 219 to 191, and on March 23, the Senate voted 58 to 41.

Although the Kosovar delegation was anxious to finalize the CG peace proposals, Serbia sent only minor officials who never engaged in meaningful talks. To obtain Serbia's perspective, Christopher Hill flew to Belgrade to talk with Milošević, returning to France to add several concessions to meet Milošević's demands in a revised CG plan. Even with these concessions, the Serb delegates rejected the CG proposals. On February 18, Secretary Albright returned to France, and after reviewing the talks, suggested the sessions should adjourn until March 15.

See March 23, 1999.

February 23, 1999

Rebel leader Abdullah Ocalan is extradited from Kenya to Turkey.

Ocalan, the leader of the rebel Kurdish Worker's Party (PKK), had fled from Syria to Italy in 1998 before arriving in Kenya, where Nairobi police arrested him for extradition to Turkey. In Ankara, the Turkish government wanted to try Ocalan for human rights violations as leader of the PKK. The PKK had waged a war for independence in southeastern Turkey for 15 years during which they killed 30,000 people by the time Ocalan was captured.

After reaching Turkey, Ocalan was charged with murder. During his trial, he spoke in favor of peace if the Turkish government would allow the Kurdish people to speak freely in their own language, to have a Kurdish television station, and to have Turkey acknowledge a Kurdish ethnic identity. Nevertheless, Ocalan was convicted of murder and sentenced to death.

Ocalan's lawyers filed appeals to overturn the death sentence, but on November 26, 1999, the five appeals court judges unanimously upheld the death sentence.

See February 9, 2000.

February 27, 1999

Eritrea accepts the Organization of African Unity's peace plan to end its war with Ethiopia.

Following border conflicts with Ethiopia during which Eritrea seized Ethiopian territory in 1998, the Organization of African Unity (OAU) offered a peace plan. Although Ethiopia accepted the plan for a cease-fire and talks about the future status of their border, Eritrea did not agree until February 27.

See May 12, 2000.

March 7, 1999

Bosnian Serbs protest a U.N. ruling on the status of Brčko.

The U.N. team headed by Robert Brown ruled that Brčko should be a multiethnic city with representation from Bosnian Croats and Muslim refugees as well as the existing Bosnian Serb population. The 1995 Dayton Accords called for binding arbitration to determine Brčko's status. Brčko had been a multiethnic city before Yugoslavia's National Army and paramilitaries invaded it in 1992.

From 1996 to 1998, the arbitration required by the Dayton Accords failed to resolve Brčko's status because the Bosnian Serb delegate rejected any solution that allowed Bosnian Croats or Muslims to return to their homes. After Brown's team called for a multiethnic city, the Srpska (Bosnian Serb) Republic's parliament voted 57 to 15 to declare that the U.N. report violated the Srpska constitution. The parliament's action was followed by its attempt to remove the republic's prime minister, Milorad Dodik, from office.

Because the Srpska parliament overstepped the authority granted by NATO's Stabilization Force (SFOR), Spanish diplomat Carlos Westendorf, who headed the Office of High U.N. Representative in Bosnia, removed Nikola Poplasen as the Srpska Republic's president. Westendorf acted because Poplasen often abused the authority of the assembly by ignoring its legislation. Westendorf also reinstated Dodick as prime minister. In April after the crisis subsided, Westendorf established an Expert Commission from members of the Srpska parliament to meet regularly with the Office of High Representative. (See March 8, 2000.)

Shortly after the Brčko crisis, a tragedy occurred in a village near Tuzla, the headquarters of U.S. SFOR troops. On May 6, 15 to 20 Serbs attacked four U.S. soldiers. One Serb used a club to hit an American from behind. As he fell, the American drew a weapon and shot the attacker. Although the shot killed the vice president of the local Serbian Radical Party, the U.S. soldier was exonerated by a U.S. military court martial because he shot in self defense.

March 21, 1999

U.S.-European Union (EU) trade dispute: the United States adds beef to banana war.

The U.S.-EU trade dispute began on December 22, 1998, when the United States threatened to place 100% tariffs on a list of EU goods because the EU discriminated against banana imports from Central America, from which two American businesses exported bananas: Chiquita Brands International and Dole Food Company. The United States claimed the EU did not comply with the ruling of a World Trade Organization (WTO) panel that EU imports gave unfair advantages to bananas from former European colonies.

In February 1999, after appealing to the WTO to punish the EU for continuing to favor former colonies in banana imports, the United States levied 100% tariffs on EU luxury imports such as Belgian chocolates, French designer handbags, and Scottish cashmere sweaters. On April 7, a WTO appeals panel said U.S. banana exporters had been damaged by the EU discriminatory practices, requiring the EU to pay $191 million to the U.S. companies.

The banana wars were settled but on March 21, the United States also disputed the EU's right to ban the importation of cattle treated with growth hormones and issued a list of EU products on which 100% tariffs would be levied provisionally. Although the EU could not prove that beef with hormones was harmful to humans, the EU offered to import more beef without hormone treatments, a deal the U.S. Department of Agriculture accepted on April 29.

Yet the Clinton administration's trade representative, Charlene Barshefsky, wanted to demonstrate the EU could not ignore a WTO ruling that allowed hormone beef to be sold abroad. On June 4, Canada agreed to join the United States in asking a WTO arbitration committee to rule on the EU ban on hormone-treated beef. Although French farmers strongly rejected the importation of hormone-treated beef, on July 13 the EU Executive Committee accepted a WTO decision that the United States and Canada should be paid $125 million in damages because of the banning of their meat. Generally, trade experts believed the issues raised by beef and bananas were part of a series of complaints from other WTO countries to determine future decisions of the WTO.

March 23, 1999

Serbian President Milošević rejects all offers for peace; NATO prepares to bomb Serbia.

Although both Serb and Kosovar delegates convened in Paris at France's International Conference Center on March 15, the Serb delegates refused to sign a peace agreement that Kosovars had signed. Most Kosovar delegates were ready to sign on February 23, but during the next two weeks the leading Kosovar delegate, Hashim Thaci, persuaded all KLA local commanders to see the advantages of having NATO on their side. In addition, with no official role, former U.S. Senator Robert Dole (R-Kans.) met Kosovar leaders in Macedonia to tell them that the United States supported autonomy for Kosovo.

The Serb delegates said on February 23 that some items in the proposals submitted by the Contact Group with representatives from the United States, Britain, France, Germany, and Russia had to be clarified, but many observers and some Organization for Security and Cooperation in Europe (OSCE) monitors thought Milošević wanted time to prepare the Yugoslav National Army (YNA) and Serbian paramilitary units for a spring offensive. As early as February 22, the OSCE reported Serb police harassed and beat unarmed monitors during a conflict near Pristina. Later at Bukos, Serb police detained 21 monitors for

20 hours until the Serb Police captured the city. Although on February 2 CIA Director George Tenet told a Senate Armed Services committee about Serbia's Operation Horseshoe, a plan to launch a military offensive in Kosovo in March, NATO leaders believed that, as in October 1998, Milošević would wait until the last minute to sign a peace plan. But NATO miscalculated. By the end of February, between 30,000 and 40,000 YNA troops plus secret police and paramilitary groups massed on Kosovo's borders accompanied by heavy artillery, M-85 tanks, and armored personnel vehicles. On March 4, British Major General John Drewienkiewicz, the commander of the OSCE monitors in Kosovo, told *New York Times* reporter Carlotta Gall that Serb attacks would soon begin in Kosovo. Soon after OSCE monitors began leaving Kosovo on March 1, a few Serb attacks began and about 2,000 Kosovar refugees fled from villages on Kosovo's border with Serbia to Macedonia. As the last OSCE monitors left on March 20, Kosovo's Serbs cheered while Serb secret police began ethnic cleansings of Kosovars at least four days before NATO began bombing.

When Yugoslav and Kosovar delegates returned to Paris on March 15, the Kosovars were ready to sign, but the Serb delegation gave the Contact Group a completely revised proposal, asking to begin a new round of talks. The CG representatives voted unanimously against the Serb response, saying only technical adjustments could be made to the February 23 proposal. On March 18, the Kosovars signed the peace agreement but the Serbs refused. The next day, the CG meetings adjourned, indicating they would resume only if Serbs were ready to sign the agreement. They also warned Belgrade that any Serb military attacks would have the gravest consequences.

The Serbs did not relent even though several U.S. and European efforts tried to persuade Milošević to avoid an all-out war. Early in March, both German Foreign Minister Joshka Fischer and U.S. Assistant Secretary of State for European Affairs Richard Holbrooke visited Milošević without success. On March 22, President Clinton still hoped to avoid war, sending Holbrooke back to see whether Milošević would relent. Milošević refused to conduct serious talks with Holbrooke, whose visit reassured reluctant NATO members such as France, Italy, and Greece that Milošević chose war, not peace. After consulting with all NATO leaders, NATO Secretary-General Javier Solana authorized air strikes against

Yugoslavia on March 23. NATO's bombing started the next day.

See June 10, 1999.

March 24, 1999

Paraguay's president Raul Cubas Grau faces impeachment but chooses exile.

Paraguay's lower house of Congress voted to begin impeachment procedures against Cubas for refusing a Supreme Court order to arrest General Lino Cesar Oviedo who had been sentenced to prison for planning a coup against a former president. The lower house decision came the day after Paraguay's Vice President Luis Maria Argana and his driver were killed by four men who used grenades and guns to attack Argana's automobile.

Rather than face impeachment hearings, Cubas fled to Brazil where he received political asylum. President of Paraguay's Senate Luis Angel Gonzales Macci became President of Paraguay.

March 24, 1999

Arrest of former Chilean president Pinochet is upheld by the House of Lords.

Great Britain's House of Lords approved Pinochet's arrest. Spain's government had asked Britain to arrest Pinochet for extradition on charges of murder, torture, and kidnapping.

See March 12, 2000.

March 29, 1999

Pentagon's test of THAAD fails to hit its target.

Initially, the Pentagon claimed the March 29 test of the Theater High Altitude Area Defense (THAAD) was successful but news reporters soon discovered that THAAD's "kill-vehicle" missed the target just as it had six other times since 1996.

As William J. Broad (*New York Times*, April 18, 1999) indicates, the Pentagon based its claim on the fact that radar instruments tracked the target, something radar had done for over fifty years. In contrast, THAAD failed two crucial tests; it was unable to use infrared seekers to locate the target from the heat of a mock warhead and it also failed to hit the mock target in outer space.

Since Ronald Reagan's 1983 dream of Star Wars, a variety of Pentagon missile defense experiments failed to hit targets in space at a cost of $50 to $60 billion. During the 1990s, the Pentagon's Ballistic Missile Defense Office (BMDO) changed to a scaled-down version of a National Missile Defense System (NMDS) of which THAAD was the latest version.

Despite these costly experiments, President Clinton became a proponent of a national missile defense system (NMDS) in 1998. Clinton changed his opposition to NMDS after an independent panel of experts led by Republican Donald Rumsfeld reported that North Korea or Iran had the potential to hit the United States with a missile within five years after North Korea tested an intermediate-range missile. (See August 31, 1998.)

Thus in 1999, Clinton provided the BMDO with a $10.5 billion fund over six years to test and deploy a NMDS by 2003. Observers believed Clinton had political, not strategic, reasons for offering BMDO funds as a way to keep Republicans from calling Democrats pacifists during future election campaigns. Clinton accepted NMDS even though Russia and China objected to any type of NMDS because it violated the 1972 ABM treaty. Russian and Chinese leaders warned that U.S. NMDS preparations violated the ABM treaty and would permit them to increase their intercontinental ballistic missile system and stop reducing the number of their nuclear warheads, as required by START I and START II arms control treaties.

See August 31, 1998; September 30, 1999.

April 9, 1999

During NATO's bombing, Bosnian Serbs cause no significant disturbances.

In rejecting the Rambouillet agreements, Serbian President Milošević miscalculated in believing the conflict would spill over into Bosnia, where NATO's Stabilization Forces (SFOR) were peacekeepers. On March 1 SFOR disbanded the Bosnian Serbs 311th Infantry Brigade after it was caught smuggling weapons, including antitank and 18 SA-7 air defense systems. When the bombing began, Milošević ordered Bosnian Serbs to begin guerrilla war against NATO, but the Srpska (Bosnian Serb) Republic's Chief of Staff Momir Talić told SFOR Commander General Mike Willcocks he had refused Milošević's order.

Early in April, Milošević sent two Yugoslav MiG-29 jets into eastern Bosnia, but NATO planes immediately shot them down. This aborted Milošević's efforts to spread the war into Bosnia.

April 9, 1999

U.S.-Chinese tensions mount when trade talks between President Clinton and Premier Zhu Rongji fail.

Both before and after Premier Zhu Rongji visited the United States, tension between the two countries increased.

On March 5, the United States claimed China used data stolen from U.S. government laboratories to miniaturize its nuclear warheads. When China's prime minister met with President Clinton at the White House, Zhu denied China had stolen any U.S. secrets.

During his visit, Zhu hoped to resolve differences about trade negotiations. During the initial talks on April 8, Zhu offered trade concessions to open Chinese markets to agriculture, telecommunication, banking and other U.S. industries. Clinton approved the concessions and concurred with China's desire to join the World Trade Organization (WTO) in the near future.

Following the first meeting, Clinton changed his mind. Secretary of Commerce William Daley said the White House wanted a "bulletproof deal" because Democrats in Congress supporting U.S. labor unions would join with conservative Republicans who opposed a deal with China because, allegedly, it had stolen U.S. secrets and repressed human rights. Thus, a U.S.-China trade deal failed although Clinton told Zhu that China would be able to join the WTO within a year if Zhu offered a few more concessions.

See September 11, 1999.

May 7, 1999

U.S. aircraft mistakenly bomb the Chinese embassy in Belgrade.

Shortly after the Chinese trade deal failed (see April 9, 1999), U.S.-Chinese relations soured on May 7 when U.S. aircraft mistakenly bombed China's embassy in Belgrade, killing three Chinese diplomats. The U.S. bombing was part of the NATO bombing of Yugoslavia. (See March 23, 1999.) An investigation disclosed the bombing error occurred because the CIA used outdated maps of Belgrade to recommend targets to the U.S. air force. China rejected this excuse

and massive anti-American demonstrations began throughout China.

May 2, 1999

Panama elects Mireya Elisea Moscoso as its president.

In a three-way election for president, Moscoso won 45% of the vote, becoming Panama's first woman president. She was the widow of former President Arnulfo Arias, whose political party she headed since 1991.

May 15, 1999

Russia's Duma (parliament) fails to impeach President Boris Yeltsin.

Three days after Yeltsin removed Yevgeny Primakov as premier, the Duma voted on five articles of impeachment that could have removed Yeltsin as president. In the final vote, all five articles were rejected by parliament. The principal charge against Yeltsin was that he started the war against Chechnya in 1994. On May 19, parliament confirmed Sergey Stepashin to replace Primakov.

May 17, 1999

Israeli Prime Minister Netanyahu loses his reelection bid to Ehud Barak.

During the election campaign, Barak led a Center-Left Israel coalition that defeated Benjamin Netanyahu's Likud coalition. Barak's coalition won 56% of the vote to the Likud's 44%. In the 120-member Knesset (parliament), One Israel won 26 seats, the Likud won 19, and Shas (an ultrareligious party) won 17 seats. To form a cabinet, Barak put together seven center-left parties that totaled 75% of Knesset members. Barak became prime minister on July 6.

See July 18, 1999.

May 29, 1999

Nigeria inaugurates a democratically elected president: Olusegun Obasanjo.

On February 27, Obasanjo was elected president as part of a three-step process established under a provisional government led by General Abdulsalami Abubakar. In December 1998, the first step was an election for municipal government during which three parties emerged as the strongest. The People's Democratic Party, a centrist group led by Obasanjo, received 60% of the votes cast. The right-wing All People's Party of former General Abacha's faction and an Alliance for Democracy from the Yoruba clan shared the other 40%.

On January 8, Nigerians elected governors and state legislators, with Obasanjo's party obtaining a majority of seats for senators and representatives in the National Assembly. The third and final step took place on February 27 with Obansanjo's election. His inaguration was celebrated on May 29. The new government had to resolve serious problems that had divided Nigerians for many years.

See July 8, 1998.

June 10, 1999

After 78 days of bombing, Yugoslavia accepts NATO's cease-fire and peace terms.

Although Yugoslav President Slobodan Milošević surrendered on June 10, the Republic of Serbia's paramilitary units nearly achieved the ethnic cleansing of Albanians in Kosovo (Kosovars). The Serbians had killed thousands of Kosovars and forced hundreds of thousands more to take refuge. According to the United Nations High Commission for Refugees, an estimated 848,100 Kosovars sought refuge in Macedonia, Albania, and Montenegro, or were airlifted to other European countries. In addition another estimated 20,000 Kosovars sought refuge by hiding in Kosovo's hills during the spring of 1999.

When NATO's air raids began on March 24, NATO leaders expected Milošević to surrender in three or four days, but the Yugoslav National Army (YNA) and Serb paramilitary units continued attacks on Kosovars that began in January at Racak (see January 15, 1999). The NATO raids did not stop the YNA and paramilitary units from rounding up Kosovars and raping their women before putting them on crowded buses or trains headed for the borders of Macedonia and Albania as refugees.

While the Serbs terrorized Kosovars, NATO escalated its bombing raids on May 3 as pressure to persuade Milošević to surrender and stop the Serbs' savage treatment of Kosovars. During NATO's air raids, television cameras focused on the plight of Kosovars fleeing to safety in Macedonia and Albania; the pictures verified the Serbs' treatment of Kosovars who were not connected to the Kosovo

Liberation Army that fought Serbian forces during 1998 (see March 5, 1998).

The negotiations resulting in Milošević's surrender began on April 24 when Russian President Boris Yeltsin sent his Special Representative Viktor Chernomyrdin to negotiate with Milošević in Belgrade. Initially, Milošević refused to negotiate unless NATO stopped its air raids; NATO leaders rejected the proposal. Negotiations stalled between May 7 and June 3 because a U.S. bomber mistakenly hit the Chinese embassy in Belgrade, and later because the International Tribunal for the War Crimes in the Former Yugoslavia indicted Milošević for crimes against humanity.

Following this period of canceled talks, Chernomyrdin and former Finnish President Martti Ahtisaari met with Milošević on June 3. After two meetings with Chernomyrdin and Ahtisarri, Milošević accepted their peace plan but demanded that rather than NATO forces an unarmed U.N. mission should monitor the agreements. In response, NATO intensified its air attacks while the U.S. State Department's Special Envoy Strobe Talbott met in Bonn, Germany with Chernomyrdin, Ahtisarri, and Russian Foreign Minister Igor Ivanov to formulate a list of non-negotiable demands Milošević must accept. On June 10, Chernomyrdin and Ahtisarri returned to Belgrade where they read the non-negotiable cease-fire and peace terms to Milošević. After consulting with Yugoslavia's parliament members, Milošević accepted the peace terms on June 11. The same day, Milošević told Serbian television audiences that The Republic of Serbia would remain as sovereign over Kosovo. He did not mention that NATO forces would deploy in Kosovo.

See July 15, 1999.

July 4, 1999

After talks with President Clinton, Pakistani Prime Minister Nawaz Sharif promises a cease-fire in Kashmir.

On July 4, 1999, Pakistan's Prime Minister Nawaz Sharif met in Washington, D.C. with President Clinton to discuss the conflict in Kashmir between India's Hindu population and Pakistani's Muslims. During May 1999, the war in Kashmir intensified after India's army discovered that Pakistani troops had crossed the border into a part of Kashmir that was awarded to India following previous border disputes between the neighboring states. During their July 4 talks Nawas promised Clinton that Pakistan would withdraw its forces from Kashmir as soon as possible. Although there was another Pakistani incursion into Kashmir on July 6, after Nawas arrived home Pakistani forces began leaving Kashmir. By July 26, 1999, India's New Delhi officials reported that Pakistani troops had completed their withdrawal from Kashmir.

See March 19, 2000.

July 10, 1999

The Congo and five other nations sign a cease-fire to end civil war.

On January 5, Tutsi and Hutu rebels in the eastern part of the Democratic Republic of the Congo renewed fighting. The civil strife appeared about to end on July 10 when six nations signed a cease-fire. Although most fighting was in the Congo, a multinational agreement was essential because Angola, Namibia, and Zimbabwe helped Congo's government while Rwanda assisted the Hutu and Uganda assisted Tutsi. The rebel groups signed the accords on August 31.

See March 12, 2000.

July 15, 1999

Bernard Kouchner arrives in Kosovo as head of the U.N. mission (UNMIK).

U.N. Secretary-General Kofi Annan chose French Health Minister Kouchner as civilian head of the U.N. Mission in Kosovo (UNMIK). Kouchner was responsible for establishing a civilian government in Kosovo to make it a self-governing province. Following the arrival of NATO's Kosovo Forces (KFOR) in June 1999, Kosovo's Albanians (Kosovars) and Serbs continued to fight each other. By the time Kouchner arrived, KFOR had arrested 180 Kosovars and 20 Serbs for murder, arson, or looting.

To help UNMIK rebuild Kosovo, nearly 100 countries and international agencies and organizations pledged $2.1 billion, including $500 million by the United States. These pledges were made on July 28, but when Kosovar refugees returned home faster than expected, UNMIK had inadequate funds from donor nations. According to reports, U.S. bureaucrats did not begin signing letters of intent with contractors until late August, and European bureaucrats delayed

longer due to vacations scheduled in July and August. As a result, a few Kosovars rebuilt their burned out homes, but most of the 800,000 returned refugees had to use tents or temporary housing supplied by UNMIK for the winter of 1999–2000.

Kouchner and the UNMIK staff turned former Kosovo Liberation Army members into the Kosovo Protection Corps and began training other groups to perform police work with KFOR. Kouchner also announced that a UNMIK-Kosovo Council would be formed in January to share responsibility in forming a multiethnic entity and make plans for Kosovo elections.

July 18, 1999

Israeli Prime Minister Barak meets with President Clinton to set a deadline for Middle East Peace.

Eherd Barak became prime minister in July and immediately sought to achieve final peace agreements with Palestinians and Syria. Before visiting President Clinton in Washington, D.C., Barak met with Egyptian President Hosni Mubarak on July 9, with Palestinian leader Yasser Arafat on July 11, and with Jordan's King Abdullah II on July 13. Barak then visited Clinton at Camp David from July 15 to 18. Before leaving the United States, Barak set September 2000 as a deadline for a final settlement with the Palestine National Authority (PNA) and a peace agreement with Syria regarding the Golan Heights.

See September 4, 1999.

July 22, 1999

China outlaws Falun Gong, a religious sect.

Although Falun Gong (Buddhist Law) stressed religious and moral values with no apparent political agenda, China's government declared the sect was illegal and on July 23 detained thousands of Falun Gong members and seized their publications.

August 3, 1999

Indonesian elections are won by a party opposed to President Habibie.

Owing to allegations of fraud in the June elections, B.J. Habibie delayed announcing the results until August 3. In Indonesia's first free election in 44 years, the opposition Indonesian Democratic Party of Struggle won 34% of the vote and Habibie's Golkar Party 34%. The other 23.6% was divided among 46 other parties.

See September 4, 1999.

August 5, 1999

Montenegro wants equality with Serbia in a Yugoslav commonwealth.

In 1997, Montenegro's relations worsened with Serbia after Milo Djukanović was elected president of Montenegro on a platform advocating independence from the Yugoslav Federation. After opposing Yugoslav President Slobodan Milošević's policies in Kosovo, Montenegro, the smaller of Yugoslavia's two republics, sought equal status with Serbia by advocating changing Yugoslavia into a commonwealth of equal states. Milošević opposed any changes in Yugoslavia, including Kosovo as a province controlled by Serbia.

See October 20, 1997.

August 10, 1999

Tensions multiply after India's military shoot down a Pakistani aircraft.

A crisis arose after an Indian plane shot down a Pakistan aircraft, killing all 16 aboard. India claimed Pakistan's plane was six miles across India's border, an assertion Pakistan denied. On August 11, Pakistan retaliated by firing a missile at two Indian planes near the crash site.

See October 7, 1999.

August 23, 1999

Berlin again becomes the capital of a united Germany.

For the first time since World War II ended in 1945, Berlin became Germany's capital city. Although the Germans had previously voted to make Berlin their capital, the process was not complete until August 23, 1999, when Chancellor Gerhard Schröder and the German Bundestag (parliament) moved their offices to Berlin.

September 4, 1999

East Timor votes for independence from Indonesia; the United Nations intervenes after civil conflict begins.

The official U.N. report on East Timor's August 30 elections indicated that 78.5% of voters favored independence rather than having greater autonomy within Indonesia. Reacting against the vote, the pro-Indonesian militias went on a rampage, destroying property and killing people. While 400,000 fled into West Timor's jungles for refuge, reports indicated Indonesia's army assisted the Indonesian militias in East Timor.

On September 12, Indonesian President B.J. Habibie agreed that U.N. peacekeepers could enter East Timor. On September 15, the U.N. Security Council voted unanimously to deploy a force of 8,000 peacemakers including 4,000 Australians and 200 American support troops. On September 20, the first 2,500 members of the International Force for East Timor (INTERFET) arrived and two days later raided a militia headquarters to arrest six militant leaders. On October 31, Indonesia's army completed its withdrawal from East Timor, leaving it under the authority of the United Nations to assist the transition to a self-governing state.

September 4, 1999

Israelis Prime Minister Barak and Palestinian leader Arafat agree on a peace plan.

Following U.S. President Bill Clinton's meeting with Ehud Barak, Israeli and Palestinian negotiators dealt with issues arising from the 1998 Wye agreements concerning the exchange of prisoners and the territory Israel would transfer to the Palestine National Authority (PNA). After agreements on the prisoners and land exchange were finalized, the treaty known as Wye II was formally signed at Sharm al-Sheikh, Egypt, by Barak and Yasser Arafat. Egyptian President Mubarak, Jordan's King Abdullah II, as well as representatives of the European Union (EU), Norway, and Japan attended the ceremony. On September 8 the EU gave Arafat a letter of assurances to support the Wye II agreement and reaffirm the EU's backing for the unqualified right of Palestinians to national self-determination.

The Wye II agreement set a timetable for releasing 350 Palestinian prisoners from Israeli jails.

Nevertheless, Wye II was troublesome because radical Palestinians, such as Hamas, believed the 1998 Wye I agreement allowed the release of 750 prisoners. Although their belief was incorrect, Hamas caused problems for Arafat and the PNA.

Regarding land transfers, Barak had agreed to transfer more West Bank land to the PNA by early 2000, but Wye II made significant changes in the 1998 accords. (See October 23, 1998.) Between October 1998 and July 1999, during which time Barak became prime minister, former Prime Minister Netanyahu violated the 1998 Wye Accords by establishing 42 new Jewish settlements on the West Bank. Despite Arafat's protests, Barak gave up only one of five uninhabited settlements planned by Netanyahu.

As the *Journal of Palestinian Studies'* "Peace Monitor" explains, 32 of the 42 new settlements had only a handful of people living there although Israel's housing director expected their population to grow larger in a few years. In addition, many of the new settlements were designed as barriers to separate Palestinian cities where the 1998 agreement transferred land to the PNA. Media reports on the land transfers made Barak appear courageous for yielding one settlement but Arafat made a major concession in accepting just one settlement rather than the 32 having few settlers.

See November 2, 1999.

September 11, 1999

President Clinton and Chinese President Ziang agree on China's WTO membership.

Meeting privately during an Asia-Pacific conference in New Zealand, Clinton and Ziang Zemin agreed that their countries recent tensions were behind them. Clinton agreed to push for China's membership in the World Trade Organization (WTO).

See September 17, 1999; November 15, 1999.

September 17, 1999

President Clinton lifts sanctions on North Korea after it stops missile tests.

Less than a week after North Korea agreed to stop its long-range missile tests, Clinton lifted some economic sanctions on North Korea, thus allowing imports of U.S. consumer products and investments by U.S. companies. Sanctions were imposed after North Korea tested ballistic missiles.

See August 31, 1998; June 14, 2000.

September 30, 1999

The Pentagon performs the first successful limited test on THAAD kill vehicle.

Following many test failures on the Theater High Altitude Area Defense (THAAD), the Pentagon's experiment with an exoatmospheric (outer space) kill vehicle succeeded on September 30. The Pentagon hailed the success as bringing THAAD close to realization, although the test's last-stage "kill vehicle" was not integrated with THAAD's other major components. Future tests needed to combine the kill vehicle with an interceptor defense, the radar location system, and THAAD's computer network. In addition, final tests had to demonstrate that decoys around enemy nuclear warheads would not deceive THAAD. Most of all, THAAD had to show that its kill vehicle would hit the target 100% of the time. Any nuclear warhead THAAD missed could cause vast damage in America.

In November 1999, the Defense Department's independent panel of experts led by retired U.S. Army General Larry Welch reported that THAAD's testing was behind schedule and required the Pentagon to change its deadline for deployment from 2003 to 2005. Although President Clinton was scheduled to decide about deployment in 2000, the best THAAD's tests might achieve was to make deployment "feasible" but not "ready to deploy."

See July 8, 2000.

September 30, 1999

A nuclear accident occurs at a Japanese nuclear fuel plant 70 miles from Tokyo.

After workers mistakenly poured seven times the prescribed amount of uranium into a nitric acid purification tank, high levels of radiation were released into the air. In Japan's worst nuclear accident, more than 50 people were exposed to radiation and 300,000 in the area were told to remain in their homes.

October 5, 1999

Russian Prime Minister Vladimir Putin says Russian policy is to destroy all Chechen terrorists.

Russia's problems in Chechnya were renewed on August 10 when Islamic militants in the neighboring region of Dagestan declared independence. To overcome the rebels, the Russian army attacked them while aircraft bombed Chechen rebel bases. On August 25, Russia claimed that the militants had been driven out of Chechnya but refused to surrender. During September, Moscow had experienced a series of explosions that President Yeltsin blamed on Islamic "terrorists" from Dagestan.

After the rebels downed a Russian plane on October 4, Russian forces invaded the area beginning with air raids against rebel bases. With more Russian soldiers dying in Chechnya, Prime Minister Vladimir Putin said terrorists were trying to oust Chechen President Aslan Maskhadov. On October 5, Putin said Russian forces would destroy all "terrorists" as intense fighting began in Chechnya.

See February 21, 2000.

October 7, 1999

In Indian elections, Hindu nationalists increase their majority in parliament.

Prime Minister Atal Behari Vajpayee's Bharatiya Janata Party maintained its majority in parliament. Vajpayee promised to restart the peace process with Pakistan despite problems earlier in 1999.

See August 10, 1999.

October 12, 1999

Pakistan's army overthrows Prime Minister Nawaz Sharif.

Soon after Sharif dismissed the head of the army, General Pervez Musharraf, the army ousted Sharif. Most Pakistanis viewed Sharif as corrupt and incompetent, but his attempt to control the army caused his overthrow. After arresting Sharif and other government leaders, Musharraf imposed martial law, suspended the constitution, and dissolved parliament.

See April 2, 2000.

October 13, 1999

The U.S. Senate refuses to ratify the Comprehensive Test Ban Treaty calling for ending all nuclear testing.

President Clinton had signed the test ban treaty in 1996 (see August 20, 1996) but did not send it to the Senate for ratification until 1999. For the first time since the Treaty of Versailles and the League of Nations in 1919–1920, when Republicans opposed Democrat President Woodrow Wilson's treaty, a Republican majority in the Senate rejected the test ban treaty by a vote of 51 to 48. The Republicans claimed the treaty was unverifiable and would not stop other nations from testing nuclear weapons.

Although the treaty would not become effective until ratified by 44 nations with nuclear capability—26 had approved so far—Clinton pledged to abide by the treaty's provisions.

October 20, 1999

The Indonesian assembly elects Abdurrahman Wahid as president.

After President Jusuf Habibie withdrew from the election, Megawati Sukarnoputri, former leader Sukarno's daughter, was favored to win the election. Nevertheless, Indonesia's People's Consultative Assembly selected Wahid by a vote of 373 to 313. The same day, the assembly approved East Timor's independence

See September 4, 1999.

October 24, 1999

In Argentina Rua Peronists lose the presidential election.

Former Buenos Aires Mayor Fernando de la Rue defeated the Peronists' candidate, Eduardo Duhalde. In recent years, Carlos Saul Menem's Peronists had governed Argentina.

October 27, 1999

The Armenian prime minister and seven others are killed by five gunmen.

The five assassins entered the parliament building in Yerevan, where they killed Prime Minister Vasgen Sarkissian and seven other government officials. The gunmen also took 40 hostages, whom they released on

October 28 after negotiations with Armenian President Robert Kocharian. Later three of the gunmen were arrested and charged with the murder of seven people. On November 3, Kocharian appointed Aram Sarkissian, the brother of Vasgen, as the new prime minister.

November 2, 1999

Israel and the Palestinians agree to talks on a final settlement.

Meeting in Oslo, Norway, with U.S. President Clinton during ceremonies honoring the fourth anniversary of the death of Israeli Prime Minister Rabin, Israeli Prime Minister Barak and Palestinian leader Arafat agree to begin talks on a final settlement of the peace process.

See December 6, 1999.

November 15, 1999

China and the United States accept terms for China to join the World Trade Organization.

Although U.S. tensions with China escalated in early 1999, the two nations set their differences aside and renewed negotiations in the fall of 1999. On November 15 the two countries agreed to open the way for China's membership in the WTO, even though China still had to negotiate with the European Union and other countries. Under the November 15 agreement, China allowed foreigners to sell directly to the Chinese market and foreign car makers could sell to Chinese buyers. On average, China would reduce its tariffs from 22.1% to 17%. At the same time, the United States would reduce quotas on Chinese textile imports and end them entirely by 2005.

See September 11, 1999; May 24, 2000.

November 14, 1991

President Clinton and Republicans agree on tactics to save the U.S. U.N. General Assembly vote.

Unless it paid "back dues" to the United Nations, the United States could not vote in the U.N. General Assembly. This situation had arisen because the Republican majority in the House of Representatives had opposed expenditures on U.N. funds to promote abortion rights. To compromise on the issue, the White House and Republican House leaders agreed on paying the U.S. back dues of $926 million over three years, while separate legislation would place a one-year ban on U.S. support for international organizations promoting abortion.

See January 19, 2001.

November 18, 1999

President Bill Clinton visits southeastern European countries and attends OSCE summit.

President Clinton's tour of southeastern Europe began on November 16 in Ankara, Turkey. After visiting the site of a November 12 earthquake, Clinton addressed Turkey's Grand National Assembly. He told the Assembly that all Americans felt sorry for the 675 Turkish lives lost by the earthquake and appreciated Turkey's permission for U.S. and British aircraft to use Turkish bases to monitor Iraqi military activity during the years since the 1991 war to liberate Kuwait.

On November 18, Clinton went to Istanbul, Turkey for a conference of the Organization for Security and Cooperation in Europe (OSCE). The summit meeting of 54 leaders of OSCE members began with some OSCE members criticizing Russian President Boris Yeltsin for Russia's human rights violations in the war against Chechnya. The main conference agenda was to revise a 1990 conventional forces in Europe (CFE) agreement (see November 17, 1990). On November 19, the OSCE members unanimously approved a CFE agreement to reduce by one half the number of tanks, artillery, and combat vehicles allowed in 1990.

On November 19, Clinton and Yeltsin met privately to discuss Chechnya where Islamic terrorists recently killed 300 Russian soldiers in an ambush. Following their meeting, Yeltsin told a press conference that despite critics of Russia's policies, Russia was "obliged to put an end to the cancer of terrorism in Chechnya." Clinton told reporters that he urged Yeltsin to "seek a peaceful resolution" in Chechnya by negotiating with Chechens willing to seek peace but not to negotiate with terrorists.

After the OSCE conference adjourned on November 20, Clinton visited Athens, Greece. On November 17, about 10,000 Greeks opposing Clinton's visit protested against Americans bombing Serbians, who, like most Greeks, were Orthodox Christians, in early 1999 (see March 23, 1999). On arriving in Athens, Clinton was guarded by police who kept protesters away from his motorcade. As host for a dinner with Greek government officials at the U.S. Embassy, Clinton sought to calm Greek anger against Americans. In a brief speech, Clinton said "If some engage us in passionate debate, it is well to remember how hard both our countries have fought for their right to do just that."

From Athens, Clinton went to Sofia, Bulgaria where he received a warm welcome. During a speech at Nevsky Square in Sofia, Clinton expressed the gratitude of Americans for Bulgarian support during NATO's bombing of Yugoslavia. Bulgaria had granted NATO permission to fly over its territory whenever necessary.

On November 23, Clinton visited Kosovo. At the headquarters for U.S. soldiers operating as part of NATO's Kosovo Force (KFOR), Clinton's spoke to U.S. troops and Kosovars living near the KFOR encampment. He praised KFOR for performing their tasks in excellent fashion and asked Kosovars to forgive Serbs for past behavior as the best way to reconcile their differences. Clinton also visited Pristina where he met with Kosovar and Serb political leaders in Kosovo.

See November 17, 1990.

November 25, 1999

The rescue of a five-year-old Cuban boy begins an international dispute.

On November 23, a boat carrying Cuban refugees sank off Florida's coast and 10 people drowned. Three others including five-year-old Elian Gonzáles, survived in inner tubes and were rescued by the U.S. Coast Guard on November 25. Because Elian's mother drowned, the U.S. Immigration and Naturalization Service (INS) released him to relatives living in Florida. On November 28, Cuba's Foreign Ministry said Juan Miguel Gonzáles, who was divorced from Elian's mother, claimed that the boy was kidnapped and demanded his return to Cuba. On December 5, Cuban leader Fidel Castro supported the father's claim, a decision making Elian's future an international dispute. Although the INS agreed the boy should be returned, Cuban exiles in Florida wanted him to remain in Florida and pursued legal action to keep him in the United States.

See June 28, 2000.

December 1, 1999

The World Trade Organization (WTO) is hampered by discord inside and riots outside its meetings.

Meeting in Seattle, Washington, the WTO achieved no satisfactory conclusions because of heated arguments among the 135 delegations and because of riots in the streets of Seattle. Although the WTO wanted to prepare an agenda for a ninth round of negotiations, President Clinton's address urged the delegates to beware of trade decisions that harmed the environment or discriminated against workers' right to a living wage. Clinton's address precipitated a heated debate among conference delegates.

While delegates debated Clinton's proposals, crowds demonstrated against the WTO's neglect of human and environmental rights. Most protesters were not violent but a small group received most of the attention from television cameras. Seattle's police were not prepared for the extensive violence and some used tear gas and rubber bullets against the peaceful demonstrators.

See April 16, 2000.

December 2, 1999

Parliament transfers British power to Northern Ireland.

In accordance with previous British agreements to bring peace to Northern Ireland, the British Parliament completed legislation for transferring power to Northern Ireland. On December 2, the official transfer took place the same day as two other essential events. First, the British signed a treaty in Dublin in which Ireland renounced its claim to Northern Ireland. Second, the Irish Republican Army (IRA) appointed its representatives to an International Committee on Decommissioning to negotiate the disarming of the IRA.

See May 29, 2000.

December 6, 1999

Secretary of State Albright's visit to the Middle East begins a month of peace talks.

Although President Clinton's Oslo meeting with Israeli Prime Minister Eherd Barak and Palestine National Authority leader Yasser Arafat paved the way for December peace talks, Secretary of State

Albright first visited Saudi King Faud on December 6 to explain U.S. efforts at seeking peace. (See November 2, 1999.) On December 7, she visited Damascus, where President Hafiz al-Assad agreed to negotiate with Israel. On December 8, Albright met separately with Israeli Prime Minister Barak and with Palestinian leader Arafat to explain the U.S. peace proposals.

Owing to these endeavors, on December 15–16, Barak and Syrian Foreign Minister Farouk al-Shara began negotiations in Washington. The talks focused on the future status of the Golan Heights, which Israel seized in June 1967. (See January 10, 2000.)

On December 21–22, Barak and Arafat held negotiations in Ramallah on the West Bank, the first time an Israeli Prime Minister held talks in a Palestinian-controlled city.

See November 2, 1999; February 3, 2000.

December 14, 1999

Acting under the 1977 treaty, the United States cedes the Panama Canal to Panama.

During a ceremony, former president Jimmy Carter headed the U.S. delegation to transfer the canal's operation to Panama.

See September 7, 1977; January 1, 2000.

December 14, 1999

U.S. border officials arrest an alleged terrorist at Port Angeles, Washington.

Three days after the State Department warned Americans outside the United States to beware of terrorist attacks at millennium celebrations, customs officials at the U.S.-Canadian border in the state of Washington arrested an alleged terrorist. The officials detained Ahmed Ressam, an Algerian, after finding liquid explosives, gun powder, and timing devices in his car—enough material to destroy a large building. On December 22, Ressam was indicted, and a few days later an alleged coconspirator was arrested.

The December arrests succeeded in stopping terrorist attacks, but generally U.S. expenses for counter-terrorist activity have increased rapidly since 1996. Yet according to a Stimson Center report, U.S. authorities have seldom fulfilled promises to provide sufficient training for local police, firefighters, and hospitals.

December 20, 1999

China takes over Macao from Portugal.

In 1557 Portugal established Macao, which comprises the peninsula of Macao and the two small islands of Taipa and Colôane off the southern coast of China. After Portugal and China agreed to create a Macao Special Administrative Region, Chinese troops were able to enter Macao following ceremonies heralding the change of regimes. Under the Administrative Region, Macao maintained its market-oriented economic system and continued to permit gambling, which was illegal in China.

December 31, 1999

Russian president Yeltsin resigns and selects Vladimir Putin as acting president.

In a televised address on New Year's Eve, Boris Yeltsin announced his resignation as president and the appointment of Prime Minister Vladimir Putin as acting president. Yeltsin asserted that "new politicians . . . new personalities" should lead Russia in the new millennium. Putin became prime minister in August 1999 and vigorously pursued the Chechnya war.

On December 19, the Communist Party won 25% of the seats, but the Duma's pro-government bloc of seats would support acting-President Putin's decision regarding Russia's conflict with Chechen rebels.

See March 26, 2000.

December 31, 1999

After plane is hijacked, India agrees to release three Taliban prisoners.

On December 24, an Air India jet leaving Nepal was hijacked with 189 people aboard. The hijackers forced the pilot to fly the plane from one location to another. Finally the plane landed in Afghanistan, and was surrounded by Taliban militia. Taliban officials said the hijackers demanded that India release a Muslim cleric and several Kashmir guerrillas from prison. On December 31, India released three prisoners in exchange for the plane's hostages.

2 0 0 0

January 1, 2000

Panama gains full control of the canal from the United States.

Thirteen ships passed through the Panama Canal, for the first time under Panamanian authority, to cross the 50-mile Panama isthmus. At noon on January 1, U.S. control of the canal reverted to Panama after 85 years under U.S. control.

The United States had acquired the right to construct and control the Panama Canal in 1903. (See November 18, 1903.) In 1977, U.S. President Jimmy Carter and Panama's Chief of Government General Omar Torrijos signed a treaty to return the canal's ownership to Panama on December 31, 1999. (See September 7, 1977.) Former President Carter headed the U.S. delegation to transfer the canal to Panamanian control.

January 10, 2000

Eight days of Israeli-Syrian peace talks achieve no results.

As agreed on December 16, 1999, Israeli and Syrian negotiators met in Shepherdstown, West Virginia, to discuss the future status of the Golan Heights. Despite protracted discussions about when and how the Golan Heights could be returned to Syria's control without jeopardizing Israel's security, the two sides could not agree. President Clinton attended some of the meetings and helped draft an Israel-Syria Peace Treaty to clarify each side's perspective, but the session ended on January 10 with no significant results.

January 22, 2000

Ecuadoran President Mahuad Witt seeks exile; Vice President Noboa assumes the presidency.

With masses of protesters pouring into the presidential palace on January 21, President Jamil Mahuad Witt fled and a three-man junta took charge. The next day, acting Defense Minister General Carlos Mendoza dissolved the junta and yielded the presidency to Vice President Gustavo Noboa Bejarano.

Mahuad had been criticized by Indian groups and military leaders for trying to end Ecuador's 60% infla-

tion rate by replacing the country's currency—the sucre—with the U.S. dollar. On March 9, Noboa successfully changed the currency to the dollar to stabilize the economy. After changing the currency, Ecuador became eligible for $2 billion from the International Monetary Fund.

January 27, 2000

President Clinton's state of the union message affirms that the country has never been in better shape.

The week before President Clinton's address, unemployment was at a low 4%, and the Dow Jones average of industrial stock was at 11722.98, an average gain that was among the ten best averages during the decade; Clinton's proclamation that the country was "never in better shape" reflected these figures. Regarding U.S. foreign policy, the president urged Congress to remove the remaining U.S. trade barriers and establish "normal trade" relations with China.

February 3, 2000

Despite warnings from the EU, Austria installs a right-wing government.

On January 1, the European Union's (EU) chairman Antônio Guterres of Portugal, warned Austria not to form a government that included Joerg Haider's extreme right-wing Freedom Party. The party opposed immigration of non-German speakers, and his speeches used pro-Nazi language, stating that the Nazi Waffen SS units of World War II deserved "honor and respect."

Despite the EU warnings, Austrian President Thomas Klestil approved a coalition government led by Chancellor Wolfgang Schussel that included the Freedom Party's Susanne Riess-Passer as vice chancellor. Haider remained as head of the Freedom Party.

Immediately after Klestil approved Schussel's cabinet, the United States and Israel recalled their ambassadors from Vienna. The EU froze all bilateral ministerial contacts with its Austrian member. Schussel's response was to assert that outsiders could not change Austrian politics.

See September 12, 2000.

February, 7, 2000

President Clinton proposes a budget for 2001 with a $184 billion surplus.

President Clinton's budget for fiscal 2001 estimated that there would be revenue of $2.019 trillion and an outlay of $1.835 trillion, leaving a surplus of $184 billion, the highest surplus ever. It included tax cuts for low-income people and the use of a Social Security surplus of $160 billion to reduce the $5.7 trillion national debt. Clinton proposed spending $300 billion for the Defense Department, more than the combined defense budgets of all NATO allies and six times more than that of Russia or China.

See December 16, 2000.

February 7, 2000

A pro-Western candidate is elected president of Croatia: Stipe Mesic.

On December 10, 1999, Croatian President Franjo Tudjman died of cancer. Tudjman had been president since 1991, when Croatia seceded from Yugoslavia. Thereafter, he became a virtual dictator. Unlike Yugoslav President Slobodan Milošević, Tudjman usually cooperated with NATO peacekeepers in Bosnia following the 1995 Dayton Accords.

After Tudjman's death, Croatia held a democratic election in January 2000 and a runoff election on February 7. In the runoff election, Mesic received 56% of the vote. Although a former Communist, Mesic said he was committed to Western-style democracy.

See June 25, 1991; August 28, 2000.

February 9, 2000

The Kurdish Workers Party (PKK) announces it will abandon violence to be independent.

In renouncing violence, the PKK followed the advice of its leader, Abdullah Ocalan, whom the Turkish government imprisoned in 1999.

See February 23, 1999.

February 10, 2000

Afghan hijackers release hostages after negotiations with British police.

On February 6, hijackers took control of an Afghan passenger jet after it took off from Kabul's airport. With 180 hostages aboard, the plane flew to Uzbekistan, Kazakhstan, then Moscow, where 30 hostages were released in exchange for food and fuel. Finally it flew to London and landed at Stansted airport on February 7. British police negotiated with the hijackers, who released all remaining hostages on February 10. British officials said 13 men being charged with the hijacking were opposed to

Croatian President Franjo Tudjman discusses problems with U.S. Admiral Leighton Smith in Zagreb, Croatia. Department of Defense

Afghanistan's Taliban regime. In addition, 69 hostages asked England to grant them political asylum.

February 18, 2000

Iranian moderates win a majority in parliamentary elections.

The parliamentary elections gave moderates supporting reform-minded President Muhammad Khatami a victory over religious conservatives. Election returns showed moderates would have 141 of the 195 seats in the Majlis (parliament). The conservatives would have 44 and the independents 10. The moderates hoped to improve ties with Western nations through judicial reforms and independent news reports. Unfortunately, Khatami's efforts were blocked by Islamic fundamentalists controlling Iran's legislation.

See March 13, 2000.

February 21, 2000

Russia declares victory in Chechnya after capturing Grozny.

Russia's war against Chechen rebels resumed in August 1999 and intensified during the next four months. On December 25, the army launched an offensive to capture Grozny, the Chechen capital. Rebel forces strongly resisted artillery and air raid attacks that their small armaments could not match.

On January 1, Vladimir Putin became Russia's acting president and was determined to destroy all rebel forces. After the army captured Grozny on February 6, the air force bombed rebel strongholds in mountain areas. On February 26, Putin indicated that guerrilla forces in southern mountain enclaves would be attacked by Russia's armed forces until Chechnya was totally "liberated." For Russia, defeating all the rebels became a long-term effort owing to Chechnya's mountainous southern terrain.

See October 5 and December 31, 1999; March 26, 2000.

March 1, 2000

The State Department certifies Mexico and Colombia as cooperating in the drug war.

Usually Colombia was the country whose drug war cooperation was not certified. Although its cocaine production increased in 1999, Colombian President

Andrés Pastrana was cooperating with the United States in the war on drugs.

Mexican officials also cooperated with Washington, but U.S. border patrols continued to fight losing battles in trying to prevent cocaine and other illegal drugs from reaching the thriving U.S. market.

See July 2 and August 30, 2000.

March 5, 2000

Israel to pull out of Lebanon.

Prime Minister Barak and Palestinian leader Arafat conclude talks on land transfers. In accordance with Prime Minister Barak's recommendation, Israel's cabinet voted to pull its armed forces out of southern Lebanon by July 2000, whether or not President Clinton could persuade Syrian President Hafiz al-Assad to renew Israeli-Syrian talks. Clinton visited Assad on March 26 but Syria refused to talk with Barak.

On March 8, Barak met with Arafat and agreed to turn 6.1% more land over to Palestine National Authority (PNA) control on March 21. The March meeting came after Israel missed a deadline for handing over West Bank land to the PNA, owing to differences about what land would be transferred to the PNA, a subject Barak and Arafat clarified on March 8.

See May 15, 2000.

March 12, 2000

Chile's Socialist president is installed; Pinochet comes home.

In a run-off election for president on January 16, Socialist candidate Ricardo Lagos Escobar defeated Joaquin Lavin, a former aide to Chile's General Augusto Pinochet. Lagos, who was inaugurated on March 12, pledged to show the world Chile was a democratic country where the armed forces were subservient to the authorities elected by the people.

General Pinochet returned home on March 4 after having been detained in England since October 1998 at the request of Spanish authorities. On January 14 British Home Secretary Jack Straw said Pinochet was too ill to stand trial for extradition to Spain and agreed Pinochet could return to Chile. Lagos was the first Socialist president since 1973, when a junta led by Pinochet overthrew Salvador Allende.

See September 11, 1973; June 5, 2000.

March 12, 2000

The United Nations sends peacekeepers to the Democratic Republic of the Congo.

The U.N. Security Council agreed to send 500 observers and 5,000 troops to supervise a cease-fire in the Congo. A 1999 cease-fire and peace agreement had broken down and warfare erupted in January 2000. For nearly two years the civil strife in the Congo resulted in complete confusion. Angola, Namibia, and Zimbabwe aided the government of Congolese President Laurent Kabila but were opposed by three different rebel groups assisted by Uganda, Rwanda, and Burundi.

Although President Kabila asked the Security Council for assistance, Kabila changed his policy in April 2000 by launching a military offensive against the rebels. Initially, Congo's army scored victories, but a rebel counteroffensive in August defeated the army and captured tons of new weapons. Subsequently, the opposing sides were again stalemated. Angolan and Zimbabwean forces retained control of regions around the capital city, Kinshasha, while rebels aided by Uganda and Rwanda kept control of eastern Congo.

See July 10, 1999; January 18, 2001.

March 13, 2000

The Clinton administration eases Iran's sanctions after moderates win a majority in parliament.

After Iranian moderates won a majority in parliament in February, the Clinton administration undertook to show that the United States was interested in mending relations with Iran. Consequently, on March 13 the United States announced that it would lift sanctions on nonenergy imports from Iran such as carpets, caviar, and pistachio nuts. Yet U.S. oil contracts with Iran were still void.

March 14, 2000

U.S. Defense Secretary Cohen visits Vietnam.

Secretary of Defense William Cohen's Vietnam trip was highlighted by his visit to an excavation site at Dong Phu, where U.S. forensic experts were assisted by Vietnamese in searching for the remains of an American listed as missing in action during the 1960s war. Cohen visited Dong Phu, where a U.S. aircraft was allegedly shot down while workers at the site sifted through dirt, looking for aircraft wire, metal pieces, or human remains. Vietnam's cooperation in this excavation process began in 1995 after the Clinton administration ended an embargo on trade with Vietnam that was imposed 20 years ago.

See November 16, 2000.

March 15, 2000

U.S. troops thwart Albanian raids from Kosovo into southern Serbia.

The eastern borders of Kosovo province have mountains that peak before descending into the Republic of Serbia's Presova valley where the ethnic majority is Albanian. After the Kosovars (ethnic Albanians in Kosovo) appeared successful against the Serbs in June 1999, Albanians in the Presova Valley organized the Liberation Army of Presova, Medvedja, and Bujanovac (UCPMB) to gain independence from the Serb Republic or, at least, become part of an independent Kosovo.

In January 2000, UCPMB rebels attacked Serb police and villages near the demilitarized zone in southern Serbia. Because of the UCPMB attack, U.S. Secretary of State Madeleine Albright met with NATO leaders and decided that U.S. KFOR soldiers should not only try to stop future UCPMB attacks but also should prevent the Kosovo Liberation Army from assisting the UCPMB. On March 15, about 350 Americans troops raided UCPMB strongholds on the border with southern Serbia. The Americans seized mortars, grenades, firearms, and ammunition while arresting nine Kosovars. The UCPMB did not end its attacks and nine months later KFOR again tried to halt UNPMB attacks in southern Serbia.

See December 17, 2000.

March 18, 2000

Taiwanese elect an opponent of the Nationalist Party.

For the first time since Nationalist leader Chiang Kai-shek fled from Communist forces on the Chinese mainland in 1949, the Nationalist Party candidate lost to Chen Shui-bian, the former mayor of Taipei. Chen won 39% of the vote to Nationalist candidate Lien Chan's 23%. Independent candidate James Soong received 38%.

Although Chen had always supported Taiwanese independence from mainland China, he said he would not declare independence unless China attacked Taiwan. On March 21, Chinese Premier Zhu Rongji declared he would not negotiate with Chen. In Washington on April 15, U.S. Defense Secretary William Cohen asserted that Taiwan had sufficient forces to defend itself, even though Taiwan needed more modern weapons than the United States would supply. On April 17, the Clinton administration agreed to sell Taiwan a radar system, air-to-ground missiles, and antitank missiles.

March 19, 2000

President Clinton begins a tour of Bangladesh, India, and Pakistan.

The first leg of President Clinton's tour of south Asia began on March 19 in Dhaka, the capital of Bangladesh. First, Clinton visited a nearby village to observe the poverty of one of the world's poorest countries. Next, he talked with Prime Minister Sheikh Hasina Wazed to report that Bangladesh would receive $200 million from the U.S. to purchase food, improve schools, and forgive debts owed to the United States.

On March 20 Clinton flew to New Delhi to meet with India's Prime Minister Atal Bihari Vajpayee. The day before Clinton arrived Muslim guerrillas based in Pakistan had attacked and killed 36 Hindus and Sikhs living in India's province of Kashmir. For more than a year, Indian and Pakistan forces were at war in Kashmir, where Pakistani Islamic groups sought to win Kashmir's independence from India (see July 4, 1999). In his visit with Vajpayee, Clinton asked the Prime Minister to work with Pakistan to obtain a cease-fire in Kashmir. Vajpayee said he was willing to negotiate cease-fire and peace terms if Pakistan agreed.

Clinton's last stop was in Islamabad, where he met with Pakistan's President and Army General Pervez Musharraf, who had led the military coup to oust Prime Minister Nawaz Sharif in October 1999 (see October 12, 1999). Unlike Sharif, Musharraf wanted to assist Pakistan's Islamic militants, who planned to liberate Kashmir from India. Clinton tried to persuade Musharraf to accept India's offer to negotiate a cease-fire.

After Clinton returned to Washington, Pakistan and India agreed to a cease-fire in Kashmir. The cease-fire failed to stop frequent Islamic militant raids into Kashmir. For example, on January 17, 2001, Islamic militants attacked a heavily guarded airport at Sringar, Kashmir, causing the death of 11 people including 6 militants. Nevertheless, India's Prime Minister Vajrayee announced that India would continue to observe the cease-fire.

March 26, 2000

Vladimir Putin is elected Russian president; the United States asks for an end to the war in Chechnya.

Acting President Putin was elected to a full term in Russia, avoiding a runoff election by winning 53% of the vote. Although Gennad Zyuganov, the Communist Party candidate, was expected to win enough votes to require a runoff election, he received only 30% of the votes cast, with the remainder going to a variety of candidates. Putin won even though Chechen rebels continued to hold out in Chechnya's southern mountains.

When President Clinton phoned Putin to offer congratulations on his election, he urged Putin to negotiate an end to the Chechen war. At a U.N. Human Rights Conference in early March, the Clinton administration refrained from supporting resolutions criticizing Russia's human rights violations in Chechnya. Nevertheless, on March 27 a U.S. State Department spokesperson said that until a political solution ended the conflict, "we will have a serious and profound disagreement" with Russia.

See June 3, and July 8, 2000.

March 29, 2000

OPEC approves an increase in oil production, which helps lower U.S. gasoline prices.

In the last six months, U.S. oil prices became the highest since the 1991 Gulf War. To assist the U.S. and Europe in lowering oil prices, OPEC met in Vienna for its biennial meeting, where members agreed to increase oil production. OPEC's increased output was too small to prevent a large increase in U.S. gasoline prices. States in midwestern U.S. were especially hard hit by price increases from $1.37 per gallon in January to $2.13 on June 9.

April 5, 2000

Yoshiro Mori becomes Japanese prime minister; Japan begins talks with North Korea.

On April 1, Premier Keizo Obuchi suffered a stroke and went into a coma. On April 5, Mori was chosen leader of the Liberal Democratic Party, and the Diet (parliament) elected him prime minister.

Also on April 5, Japanese officials began negotiations with North Korea. Following two days of discussions in Pyongyang, North Korea, the talks broke down because North Korea wanted Japan to apologize and pay reparations for its occupation of Korea from 1910 to 1945, but Japan refused.

April 6, 2000

Former Pakistani Prime Minister Sharif is sentenced to life in prison.

After a military coup overthrew Nawaz Sharif in 1999, he had been tried for hijacking and terrorism and sentenced to life in prison. The judge had acquitted six others, including Sharif's brother. Sharif's case stemmed from his attempt to prevent a commercial airliner from landing. The passengers on the plane included General Pervez Musharraf, who led Sharif's overthrow that day.

See October 12, 1999.

April 8, 2000

A CIA officer is dismissed for mistakenly targeting China's embassy in Belgrade.

Following a yearlong investigation on the bombing of China's embassy (see April 9, 1999), CIA Director George Tenet announced one CIA officer was dismissed and six other agents were reprimanded.

April 14, 2000

Russia ratifies SALT II; one week later it ratifies the Comprehensive Test Ban Treaty.

In January 1993, U.S. President Bush and Russian President Yeltsin signed the second Strategic Arms Reduction treaty (START II), ratified by the U.S. Senate in 1996. On President Putin's recommendation, the Russian Duma (parliament) approved the treaty by a vote of 228 to 131. Under the treaty, both countries would reduce their nuclear warheads to 3,500, half the number of current warheads, by 2007.

One week later, the Duma ratified the Comprehensive Test Ban Treaty. Although 150 countries had ratified the treaty, all 44 countries with a known nuclear capability had to approve the treaty before it became effective. Among 15 countries not ratifying the treaty was the United States; the Senate refused to ratify the treaty in 1999.

See October 13, 1999.

April 16, 2000

IMF and World Bank members reach agreement despite crowds of protesters.

The International Monetary Fund (IMF) and the World Bank held their spring meeting in Washington, D.C. Although protesters claimed that IMF policies harmed the poor and the environment, the meeting continued without difficulty. On April 16, the IMF promised to renew emphasis on debt relief to poor countries. The next day, the World Bank agreed to accelerate debt relief, spend more funds to fight the global threat of AIDS, and urge industrial nations to increase market access to the exports of poor nations.

See September 30, 2000.

May 12, 2000

Ethiopia and Eritrea resume fighting when Ethiopia launches an offensive.

After peace negotiations failed on May 5, Ethiopian forces renewed a two-year-old border conflict by attacking Eritrea to reclaim border areas it had previously lost. After regaining its former territory, Ethiopia declared the war was over on May 31. Eritrea refused to end the war and fighting continued until June 18, when the foreign ministers of the two countries signed a cease-fire agreement in Algiers. Under the cease-fire terms, Ethiopia's forces had to withdraw to their May 6, 1998, positions. In addition, a 15.5-mile buffer zone was established in Eritrea's territory until a final peace settlement could be arranged.

May 15, 2000

Despite West Bank fighting, Israel approves the transfer of villages.

The issue of Israeli withdrawal from Lebanon was resolved March 5, but on April 11, problems arose concerning several villages on the West Bank that Israel was scheduled to turn over to the Palestine National Authority (PNA). Israel set three conditions for the PNA to fulfill before it would recognize Palestine as a separate state: Palestinians must be demilitarized; no Palestinians had the right to return from foreign refugee camps such as those in Lebanon; and most Jewish settlers would remain in West Bank settlements. After meeting with U.S. President Clinton on May 1 in Washington, D.C., PNA leader Arafat asserted that the Israeli terms were unacceptable but might be negotiated.

On May 2 and 3, negotiations between Israeli Prime Minister Barak and Arafat broke down because Arafat insisted on the right of Palestinians to return home. Despite renewed violence in the West Bank town of Ramallah on May 15, Barak persuaded Israel's cabinet and parliament to approve the transfer of three West Bank villages to the PNA. Barak expected to meet with Arafat in early June, but the death of Syrian President Hafiz al-Assad intervened.

See March 5 and June 10, 2000.

May 16, 2000

The Dominican Republic's presidential election is won by opposition leader Hipolito Mejia.

In contrast to Haiti's problems, the Dominican Republic's election went smoothly. Mejia won fewer than a majority of votes, but the ruling party's candidate conceded the presidential election to Mejia rather than have a runoff election.

See April 28, 1965; May 22, 2000.

May 22, 2000

Haiti's legislative elections are won by the Lavalas Party.

Although Haiti's legislative and municipal elections were delayed for a month, Jean-Bertrand Aristide's Lavalas Party won 80% of the legislature's seats. The International Observers Coalition of Independent Observers (IOCIO) reported that large numbers of Haitians voted in the elections that were fair and free despite isolated incidents of intimidation at a few voter bureaus.

Although Haiti was the most poverty stricken nation in the Western Hemisphere, American news reports tended to focus on Port-au-Prince, the capital city, where wealthy and middle class people lived. In Port-au-Prince, well-to-do individuals joined opposition parties in boycotting the elections. In the rural areas where IOCIO teams monitored elections in eight provincial regions, voter turnout was large. Among the poor in rural regions, the Lavalas party continued to be popular.

Despite favorable reports on the elections by IOCIO and the Organization of American States (OAS), most European nations and U.S. officials with few observers in Haiti did not accept the election results. These groups depended on news reports by opposing groups in Port-au-Prince, where elite French-speaking Haitians rejected the social programs of Aristide and President René Preval to help the poor.

The U.S. State Department urged Haiti's Election Commission to make an "honest" count of the ballots, even though the United States had rejected Haiti's request for funds to assist the election process. On June 2, the commission reported that Lavalas won a majority of seats in the Senate.

See November 26, 2000.

May 24, 2000

The House approves permanent trade relations with China.

Following a yearlong debate about granting China permanent "normal trade relations" rather than making relations depend on an annual review, the House of Representatives voted 237 to 197 in favor of permanent relations with China. The House approval cleared the way for China to join the World Trade Organization.

The vote on China's trade was delayed in the Senate because a few senators were concerned about China's human rights record and its delivery of nuclear weapons to Pakistan. On September 19, the Senate approved the trade bill by a vote of 83 to 15.

May 24, 2000

Israeli troops complete their withdrawal from Lebanon.

The Israeli troop withdrawal came before the July 1 schedule. In the weeks before their withdrawal, violence increased between Israeli forces, their south Lebanese Christian allies, and Lebanon's Hezbollah guerrillas. On May 4, Hezbollah fired rockets into Israeli territory and Israel retaliated with jet attacks on power stations near Beirut and Tripoli and suspected Hezbollah ammunition depots. When Israeli troops withdrew, at least 2,000 south Lebanese Christian soldiers and their families sought refuge in Israel.

See September 3, 2000.

May 28, 2000

Peruvian President Fujimori is reelected in a controversial election.

In the April 9 elections, President Alberto Fujimori failed to win a majority of votes and faced a runoff election against Alejandro Toledo on May 28. Charging that the April elections were fraudulent, Toledo's supporters asked for a delay in the runoff until international observers had time to guarantee a fair and free election.

By a vote of 3 to 2, Peru's National Election Commission rejected the request for a delay and Toledo withdrew from the election. Official election results gave Fujimori 51% of the vote and Toledo 18%. All the rest were defaced or blank. On May 28, 80,000 people in Lima protested Fujimori's election.

May 29, 2000

Northern Ireland's government resumes power suspended by Britain.

On February 1, the Irish Republican Army (IRA) failed to disarm as required by the peace agreement in 1998 (see April 10, 1998). As a result, the British government suspended the power-sharing arrangement begun in December. On February 10, the IRA said it was committed to disarmament but Britain should first remove some of its installations in Northern Ireland. The British said the IRA proposal was a step in the right direction, but they would not

agree to remove installations at that time. Angry about this decision, the IRA pulled out of all negotiations.

On May 5, British Prime Minister Tony Blair and Irish President Bertie Ahern dropped the demand that paramilitary groups disarm provided they put their weapons "beyond use." The Ulster Unionists and the IRA accepted the plan for the IRA to put their weapons beyond use provided that the IRA would permit inspections of its arms caches.

The Northern Ireland Assembly resumed its power sharing agreement on May 29, but in July the Protestants and Catholics could not agree on a chief executive and the Northern Ireland Assembly had to shut down. To resolve the problem, Blair and Ahern sent the former U.S. Senator George Mitchell, who was chairman of the original agreements in 1998 (see April 10, 1998).

See December 13, 2000.

May 29, 2000

The United Nations says all hostages have been freed in Sierra Leone; war continues there.

Early in May, rebels seized 500 U.N. peacekeepers trying to enforce a 1999 cease-fire agreement. The rebels refused to disarm as the accords required and detained peacekeepers outside Freetown, the capital. On May 8, British troops arrived in Freetown and evacuated foreign nationals. On May 17, after pro-government troops seized rebel leader Foday Sankoh, most fighting ended in Freetown. On May 29, the United Nations reported that all hostages had been freed.

The hostage release did not end the civil war. Although Britain left 200 soldiers to train and equip government soldiers to fight the rebel Revolutionary United Forces (RUF), British officers refused to stay under U.N. commanders, who insisted that "peacekeepers" remain neutral between warring parties, the same tactic that had failed in the Balkans. Jordan and India sent well-trained troops to Sierra Leone, but they were scheduled to leave on December 31, 2000.

Senior State Department officials criticized the absence of U.S. efforts to assist the United Nations in Sierra Leone. They claimed the Clinton administration offered meager efforts in response to Africa's problems because President Clinton would not risk the loss of American lives in Africa following the 1993 débâcle in Somalia. Congress had limited U.S.

aid to West Africa, but on May 26, 2000 Clinton gave $20 million to the United Nations to support operations in Sierra Leone.

By the end of 2000 the U.N. mission was weakened, and Sierra Leone's conflict spilled into the neighboring states of Guinea and Liberia.

June 3, 2000

President Clinton arrives in Moscow, a visit highlighting his European tour.

President Clinton's European tour began on May 30 in Portugal, where he met President Jorge Sampaio and held discussions with European officials about U.S.-EU trade. From June 1 to 3, he visited Berlin for the first time since its restoration as Germany's capital. In Berlin, Clinton met with Chancellor Gerhard Schröder and attended a meeting of 13 world leaders who pledged to find a common solution to global problems such as the spread of infectious diseases and to end wild swings in financial markets.

From June 3 to 5, he visited Moscow and Ukraine. In Moscow, Clinton met with President Vladimir Putin for the first time. His talks with

President Clinton walks with President Vladimir Putin in the Kremlin. Clinton Presidential Materials Project

Putin concerned trade relations, economic problems, and the U.S. missile defense system. Clinton urged Putin to negotiate a revision of the 1972 Anti-Ballistic Missile Treaty (ABM), but Putin opposed any revision that would destabilize existing arms control agreements. While Putin recognized the potential danger from rogue states, he believed it could be handled by cooperation between the United States and European nations. The one successful result of the Moscow meeting was a U.S.-Russian agreement to reduce their stockpiles of plutonium used for nuclear warheads.

In Ukraine, Clinton met with President Leonid Kuchma, who announced that the Chernobyl plant, the site of the world's worst nuclear accident, would be closed by December 15, 2000.

June 5, 2000

Chile's Court of Appeals ends Pinochet's immunity from prosecution.

After he returned from England, Augusto Pinochet Ugarta resumed the senatorial post that made him immune from prosecution for any crimes (see March 12, 2000). To change this, Chile's Court of Appeals voted 13 to 9 to revoke Pinochet's right to be a senator. On August 8, Chile's Supreme Court upheld the lower court's decision, enabling prosecutors to indict him.

See January 8 and March 12, 2000.

June 10, 2000

Syrian President Hafiz al-Assad dies; his son succeeds him.

Assad had ruled Syria since a military coup in 1970. Immediately after his death, his Baath Socialist Party backed his son Bashar al-Assad as heir to the presidency. Parliament approved a constitutional amendment lowering the minimum age for president to 34, Bashar's age. On June 27, parliament named Bashar as the sole presidential candidate to be voted on in a July 10 referendum, which gave him a 97% favorable vote. After the referendum, the new president told parliament his top priority was to regain the Golan Heights from Israel.

June 14, 2000

The Presidents of North and South Korea agree to work for unification.

During a two-day summit in Pyongyong, North Korea, Presidents Kim Jong Il of North Korea and Kim Dae Jung of South Korea pledged to continue working toward the unification of Korea. In addition, they agreed that members of separated families could visit one another and arranged the repatriation of prisoners. Kim Dae Jung also promised to increase economic aid to North Korea.

Both Chinese and American leaders were pleased by the summit's success. On June 19, the Clinton administration lifted a few economic sanctions levied against North Korea but also indicated that the United States had no plans to withdraw its 37,000 troops from South Korea, a presence that Kim said was vital to regional security.

Between August 15 and 18, members of 200 Korean families separated since 1953 were reunited, half from the North and half from the South. In the first group, elderly parents and middle-aged children were selected to visit one another. Other reunions were planned for the future. On September 2, South Korea repatriated 63 spies and guerrillas from North Korea who, although released from prison, had remained in South Korea.

June 28, 2000

The U.S. Supreme Court allows a six-year-old boy to return to Cuba.

After seven months of legal wrangling in U.S. courts, Elian González flew back to Cuba with his father and other relatives who had joined him in a private home near Washington, D.C. (see November 25, 1999). The essential Supreme Court ruling was that the Immigration and Naturalization Service was not required to provide the asylum hearing his Miami relatives requested. Because the Supreme Court ruling was the first of its kind, it set a precedent for future immigration policies.

July 2, 2000

Mexico's PRI candidate loses the presidential election to the National Party's Vicente Fox.

For the first time in 71 years, Mexico's Institutional Revolutionary Party (PRI) lost to the National Action Party (PAN) by a vote of 43% to 36%. A third candidate from the Democratic Revolutionary Party (PRD) polled 16.5%. Fox promised to end the pervasive political corruption in Mexico and create jobs by stimulating the economy.

In voting for the Chamber of Deputies and Senate, the two opposition parties would have won a majority if they had cooperated. In the 500-member chamber, the PNA won 208 seats and the PRD 15, while the PRI won 209 seats. In the 128-member Senate, the PNA won 60 seats, the PRD 15, and the PRI 46.

July 8, 2000

Plans for a missile defense system are set back when a test fails to hit the target.

For the second time in 2000, a test of the National Missile Defense system failed. The Defense Department's aim to perfect a system to deploy by 2005 received another setback. Both on January 24 and on July 8, the kill vehicle designed to intercept and destroy an incoming warhead failed to separate from the booster rocket. Although critics noted that a missile defense intended for rogue nations was redundant because the United States had sufficient ICBMs with nuclear warheads to overwhelm a rogue nation, and was opposed by Russians, Chinese, and Europeans, President Clinton had yielded to Republican members in Congress in spending billions of dollars for a missile defense that might never work.

See September 1, 2000.

July 8, 2000

As unrest in Chechnya continues, President Putin gives a stern state of the union speech.

On July 2, two suicide bombings by Chechen rebels killed 555 Russian soldiers and wounded 84. Against this background of incessant violence, President Vladimir Putin stated that only a strong central government could protect Russia's political, civil, and economic freedoms. He said a free mass media was essential to democracy, expressed concern about corruption, and referred to plans to overcome a weak economy as well as Russia's falling birth rate.

July 21, 2000

G-8 meeting in Okinawa produces few agreements; President Putin says North Korea will forgo nuclear weapons production.

President Clinton met with seven other leaders of the G-8 states in an annual meeting. During the sessions, G-8 members pledged to cut world poverty in half by 2015 and reduce the number of AIDS cases by 25% before 2010 but offered no specific methods to achieve these goals.

Russian President Vladimir Putin reported that during a recent meeting, North Korean President Kim Jong Il said he was willing to end North Korea's nuclear weapons program if other countries helped North Korean scientists launch a space satellite.

July 25, 2000

Israeli Prime Minister Barak and Palestinian leader Arafat fail to reach a peace agreement at Camp David meetings.

On July 5, President Clinton called for an Israeli-Palestinian summit at Camp David to begin on July 11. Clinton wanted Palestine National Authority (PNA) Chairman Yasser Arafat and Israeli Prime Minister Ehud Barak to reach a final settlement on their disputes regarding an independent Palestine and the occupied West Bank territory, but both men had separate constituents back home who might oppose any concession made. The PNA had set September 13 as a deadline to declare independence with or without a final Israeli agreement.

Barak barely survived a confidence vote in Israel's parliament on July 10 and faced disputes in parliament concerning a replacement for President Ezer Weizman, who had resigned (see July 31, 2000). Nevertheless, Barak arrived at Camp David on July 11 to begin negotiations.

The two major issues that Clinton tried to mediate were whether Israel would be sovereign over Jerusalem or whether the PNA could make East Jerusalem the capital of a Palestinian state, and the right of Palestinian refugees to return to their previous homes.

The Camp David talks ended on July 25 after being extended while Clinton attended the G-8 summit in Okinawa. Over this two-week period, Clinton proposed several ways to resolve questions about Jerusalem and the refugees, but no agreements were reached. Neither Barak nor Arafat would compromise his demands for Jerusalem.

See September 10, 2000.

July 30, 2000

Venezuelan President Hugo Chavas Frias is reelected.

Frias was reelected with 59% of the votes cast. In parliamentary elections, the Frias coalition of parties

Israeli Prime Minister Ehud Barak and Palestinian leader Yasir Arafat with President Clinton at Camp David. White House

fell short of the two-thirds majority that would permit the president to promulgate new laws with virtually no debate.

July 31, 2000

Israel's parliament elects Moshe Katsav as president to replace Ezer Weizman.

On July 10, Israeli President Ezer Weizman resigned after Israel's attorney general found he had acted improperly by accepting $300,000 from a French businessman. Replacing Weizman caused political problems for Prime Minister Barak, who favored Shimon Peres, a former prime minister, while the Likud Party members of parliament challenged Peres by nominating Katsav. Subsequently, after two votes in parliament, Katsav was elected by a 63–57 vote. The election of Katsav made it difficult for Barak to make any concessions on a final settlement with the Palestine National Authority (PNA) leader Yasser Arafat because, while Peres had approved reasonable concessions with Arafat (see July 25, 2000), Katsav opposed any final settlement with the PNA.

See July 25, 2000.

August 2, 2000

Republicans nominate George W. Bush for president; 12 days later, Democrats name Al Gore.

Following primary elections begun in January, it was certain by April that George W. Bush and Vice President Al Gore would be the nominees of their respective parties. On July 25, Bush chose former Defense Secretary Richard Cheney for vice president; on August 7, Gore selected Senator Joseph Libermann (D-Conn.). The Republican ticket became Bush-Cheney on August 2; the Democrats chose Gore and Liberman on August 16 and 17.

Meanwhile, the Reform Party was in disarray. From August 10 to 12, the party's convention split apart, with Pat Buchanan claiming a majority of votes cast by email but he was challenged by John Hagelin. Because Ross Perot's Reform Party received more than 5% of the vote in 1992 and 1996, the Federal Elections Commission had to decide who should receive $12.6 million in federal funds. On September 12, the commission voted 5 to 1 in favor of Buchanan as the official Reform Party candidate.

August 12, 2000

The Russian submarine Kursk sinks; 116 crew members perish.

The *Kursk* sank to the bottom of the Barents Sea. Although not carrying nuclear weapons, the *Kursk* was powered by nuclear reactors. It fell from its cruising level of 60 feet below the surface to the seabed level of 350 feet. Russian authorities did not make the sinking public until August 14 and refused offers of help from other nations until August 16. On August 21, Norwegian divers reached the sub to open all the hatches, reporting that the entire vessel was flooded and all 116 members of the crew were dead. Russian officials said there was an internal explosion before the *Kursk* sank.

August 25, 2000

President Clinton begins a visit to Nigeria, Tanzania, and Egypt.

In Nigeria, Clinton talked with President Olsegun Obasanjo and addressed Nigeria's National Assembly. With Obasanjo, Clinton discussed the cost of Nigeria's oil, the AIDS epidemic, debt restructuring, and diamond smuggling. In Tanzania, Clinton expected to witness the signing of a cease-fire agreement among Burundi's warring Hutu and Tutsi tribes, but they refused to sign a peace accord. In Egypt, Clinton met with President Mubarak to discuss possibilities of achieving a peace settlement between Israel and the Palestinians.

August 25, 2000

Somalia elects a president, hoping to have a united government.

Since 1991, Somalia had no functioning central government owing to fighting among clans and subclans. The United States had tried but failed to end the civil war in 1993.

Following lengthy negotiations in Djibouti between businessmen and clan leaders, a provisional parliament was formed on August 13. Next, a transitional constitution was drafted, and, on August 15, parliament elected Abdikassim Salad Hassan as Somalia's president.

The new government still had to disarm the militant clans surrounding Mogadishu, the capital.

See December 3, 1992; January 14, 2001.

August 28, 2000

Croatia investigates Tudjman's trail of corrupt activities.

After his election as Croatia's president in February, Stipe Mesic began investigating the vast corruption created by deceased President Tudjman from 1990 to 1999. Mesic's investigation discovered that Tudjman's son Stjepan and daughter Nevenka Kosutic had obtained trust funds and companies under Croatia's privatization program. Investigators discovered many documents and audiotapes of conversations between Tudjman and his aides and confidants. Mesic gave the tapes to Croatian media outlets whose transcriptions provided Croatians with data, sometimes entertaining, about Tudjman's inner circle.

Yet the documents and tapes did not provide sufficient evidence for prosecutors to take legal action against Tudjman's individual associates. Economists estimated that billions of dollars were stolen, but tracing the movement of those funds in dummy corporations and secret holdings sent abroad required much time and effort and might never be located. Meanwhile, Mesic lacked sufficient funds to pay thousands of state workers, and many formerly profitable companies were on the brink of bankruptcy. Mesic wanted to clean up Croatia's financial problems to receive benefits from joining the European Union, but this would require Croatia to recoup some of the billions of dollars lost during Tudjman's rule.

See February 7, 2000.

August 30, 2000

President Clinton visits Colombian President Andrés Pastrana in Cartagena.

After Congress approved a grant of $1.3 billion to Colombia, Clinton met with Pastrana to clarify that U.S. funds were to eradicate the drug empire but not primarily to help Pastrana defeat Colombian rebels. Although millions of U.S. dollars would provide military equipment and training for Colombia's army, Clinton claimed U.S. funds were for "fighting drugs, not war."

U.S. critics said the U.S. war on drugs had been waged for over 30 years without success. The day before Clinton arrived, Pastrana told reporters the curtailment of international drug trafficking depended on reducing the demand for drugs in the United States and other countries. Such statements were not new, but in the United States it was more popular for Congress to authorize funds for the drug war than to control drug traffic by legalizing or severely penalizing individual drug users as much as drug dealers. Many Americans using illegal drugs were celebrities in the entertainment business or socialites.

September 1, 2000

President Clinton postpones a decision on constructing a missile defense system.

Although Defense Secretary William Cohen wanted to move ahead on constructing the National Missile Defense System, President Clinton chose to postpone a final decision because two of three interceptor tests had failed since January 2000. Clinton's decision meant the president elected in November 2000 would make the final decision on a missile shield.

See January 18, 2001.

September 3, 2000

In the second round of Lebanese elections, Syria's control is weakened.

Lebanon conducted its first election since Israel withdrew its troops from southern Lebanon, in May 2000. Two rounds of elections were held, on August 27 and September 3. When the votes were tallied, candidates associated with Syria no longer controlled Lebanon's government. One reason for Syria's weakened control over candidates was related to the death of Syrian President Hafiz al-Assad, whose son Bashar seemed less restrictive.

The election for 128 seats in parliament gave the majority to former Prime Minister Rafiq Hariri, who opposed the Syrian-backed party of Emile Lahoud. Lebanon's problems escalated when conflict broke out between Palestinians and Israelis in September and continued into 2001. Many Palestinians lived in Lebanese refugee camps, and the violence ended opportunities for Israel and Syria to make peace arrangements regarding Israel's occupation of the Golan Heights.

See May 24, June 10 and September 28, 2000.

September 8, 2000

The U.N. Millennium summit ends in New York City.

Beginning on September 2, leaders of 150 countries attended special sessions of the United Nations. The sessions focused on a broad range of topics including the income gap between rich and poor nations and the use of children under 18 years of age in armed conflict. During a chance encounter, President Clinton shook hands with Fidel Castro, the first handshake by a sitting U.S. president with the Cuban leader since he came to power in 1959.

In Clinton's U.N. speech, the president emphasized the need for help in bringing peace to the Middle East. In contrast, Russian President Vladimir Putin called for an international conference to examine the militarization of space, an indirect reference to U.S. plans for a national missile defense system opposed by Russia and many European nations.

See September 1, 2000.

September 10, 2000

The Palestinian Central Council votes to delay declaring Palestinian statehood.

During the U.N. Millennium meetings in New York, President Clinton met separately with the leaders of Israel and Palestine, persuading Yasser Arafat not to declare Palestinian statehood on September 13, as he had planned to do. After returning home, Arafat consulted with his Palestine Central Council, whose members agreed to delay a declaration of statehood. If Arafat or the Council had declared that Palestine was a state, Israeli Prime Minister Ehud Barak would have had little chance to resume talks on a final peace settlement with Palestinians.

See September 28, 2000.

September 10, 2000

Federal charges against scientist Wen Ho Lee collapse; Lee is freed from prison.

Early in 1999, Secretary of Energy Bill Richardson fired Lee for the alleged transfer of nuclear technology to China during the 1980s, after an unidentified source gave the CIA a document showing that Chinese scientists had made a nuclear warhead similar to U.S. warheads.

FBI investigators believed Lee was guilty. On December 10, 1999, Lee was arrested after being indicted for spying. A nuclear physicist at the Los Alamos National Laboratories, Lee was charged on 59 felony counts with removing classified information from the laboratories. Lee was imprisoned, denied bail, and put in solitary confinement.

On August 12, 2000, Lee's lawyers obtained a court hearing to obtain bail. During the hearing, FBI agent Robert Messemer admitted giving false testimony at the December bail hearings that was crucial to establishing Lee's guilt. On September 10, the government dropped 58 of the 59 charges against Lee, who plead guilty to one count of improperly gathering and retaining national security data. Lee also agreed to provide information on seven missing computer tapes. In November 2000, the FBI held several interviews with Lee regarding the lost tapes, but the attorney general's office refused to comment on the talks.

When U.S. District Judge James Parker sentenced Lee to "time served" since December 1999, Parker said the government had "embarrassed our entire nation" by exaggerating the case and imprisoning Lee in harsh conditions.

September 12, 2000

The European Union (EU) lifts sanction on Austria; the United States keeps limited sanctions.

After Austria's ruling coalition included members of the pro-Nazi Freedom Party, the EU and the United States imposed economic and diplomatic sanctions on Austria to protest against the influence of Nazi concepts in the Austrian government. On September 12, EU members agreed to lift those sanctions, but the U.S. State Department said limited U.S. diplomatic sanctions would remain against Austria.

See February 3, 2000.

September 24, 2000

Vojislav Kostunica wins Yugoslav presidency; Slobodan Milošević seeks a runoff election.

On September 24, Yugoslavia held presidential elections in which Yugoslav President Milošević's opponent, Kostunica, appeared to be the winner, with more than 51% of the votes cast. On September 26, the Milošević-dominated Election Commission reported that a run off election would be held on

October 8, claiming Kostunica had received only 48.96%, while Milošević had received the second highest percentage of 28.62%. The opposition argued that Milošević's commission had subverted the election results and refused to participate in a runoff.

Following NATO's 1999 bombing of Serbia, young Serbs who obtained information from the World Wide Web indicating that Milošević was to blame for their suffering had formed an underground network of opposition parties called Otpor that included workers, police, and soldiers, to plan Milošević's downfall. U.S. State Department officials had assisted Otpor and had met opposition leaders in Montenegro and Vienna, where they had urged Otpor to unite all anti-Milošević's groups to support one presidential candidate. Otpor had selected the constitutional lawyer Kostunica as their candidate and its network of opposition parties had gotten out the votes for Kostunica. After Yugoslavia's Election Commission called for a runoff election, Otpor members challenged the need for having a second election.

See October 6, 2000.

September 28, 2000

Violence breaks out in Jerusalem after Ariel Sharon visits the Temple Mount.

Amid attempts of Israeli Prime Minister Barak and Palestinian leader Arafat to reach a final peace settlement, Sharon's visit to the Temple Mount touched off intense violence between the Israeli Defense Force (IDF) and a Palestinian *intifada* uprising. The visit of Sharon, a member of the Likud Party opposing Barak, to a place sacred to Jews and Muslims increased Palestinian fears that Israel sought to evict all Palestinians from East Jerusalem.

On September 28, Sharon's visit with a group of legislators incited Palestinian youth to throw rocks at them. On September 29, some Palestinians threw stones at Jewish worshippers at the Western Wailing Wall near the Temple Mount. In retaliation, the IDF used excessive force against Palestinians, killing four and wounding 200 Muslims. On September 30, Israeli security forces killed 12 more Palestinians, an event causing more riots. The conflict spread to East Jerusalem, the cities on the West Bank, the Gaza Strip, and Israel proper. As a result of the violence, Israeli-Palestinian Peace talks were delayed.

See October 16, 2000.

September 30, 2000

The Taliban capture a site in northern Afghanistan.

Afghanistan's ruling Taliban militia captured a strategic site in the northern Farkhar River gorge. According to the Taliban official news agency, they took over the site after six generals formerly under an opposition leader's command switched sides to join Taliban forces. Because of the Taliban's recent military conquests north of Kabul, Russian President Putin was concerned about the security along Russia's southern border with Afghanistan. Putin sent a contingent of Russian army troops to establish stability along the border with Afghanistan.

September 30, 2000

The World Bank-IMF conference in Prague agrees to relieve poor nations' debts.

Following extensive protests in Prague on September 24, the first day of the Conference, officials of the International Monetary Fund (IMF) and the World Bank joined with the finance ministers of member nations to decide on methods to relieve the debts of poor nations and reform their World Bank and IMF loan restrictions.

Since the 1980s, the World Bank and the IMF had strictly regulated how debtor nations used loans they received. To obtain a loan, the recipient had to adopt austerity programs, privatize state-owned industries, and institute free-trade principles. Especially during the 1990s, these financial restrictions caused poor nations to face bankruptcy while wages of their low-income workers were reduced. At the same time, these wealthy individuals in nations sent billions of dollars to overseas banks. These circumstances caused massive protests in Prague by demonstrators advocating "fair" (not just free) trade, attention to environmental problems, and debt relief. In addition, some anarchists engaged in violent acts against all capitalists. Protests had previously disrupted financial conferences in Seattle (1999) and Washington, D.C. (April 2000).

Because of these previous disruptions, Prague delegates, including U.S. Secretary of the Treasury Lawrence H. Summers and Federal Reserve Chairman Alan Greenspan, offered proposals to reform restrictions on World Bank and IMF loans, especially changes to help raise the living standards of poorer nations.

When the Prague sessions concluded on September 30, the global financiers agreed to three essential reforms to help raise the living standards of poor nations. First, the IMF and World Bank would make grants of aid in addition to loans. These grants would be given to poor nations to improve living standards in such areas as education, fighting the AIDS pandemic, and establishing medical clinics for the poor.

Second, the rich nations would be more generous in forgiving the debts of poor nations and provide funds to help them pay off their loans and increase workers wages.

Third, wealthy nations, especially the G-8 industrial nations including the United States, agreed to open their markets to imports from poor nations. For example, the European Union would end subsidies to agricultural products of its member nations so farmers of poor nations would have a "fair" market for their products. The United States would have to repeal legislation protecting products such as textiles and sugar from foreign imports.

In cooperation with the United Nations, officials of the IMF and the World Bank worked with the office of U.N. Secretary-General Annan to prepare a list of remedies for helping poor nations improve their living standards. The U.N. report, released on February 1, 2001, listed 87 ways to help poor nations not only by forgiving debts but by offering more private investment and promoting commercial exports of poor nations to offset declines in foreign trade. The report noted that leaders of poor nations shared responsibility for their nation's poverty, especially because of corruption.

October 6, 2000

Massive protests in Belgrade force Milošević to concede the presidential election to Kostunica.

After Yugoslavia's September presidential election, a young underground student group called Otpor (resistance) led a coalition of 18 opposition groups in rejecting the runoff elections scheduled for October 8 (see September 24, 2000). Beginning on October 2, Otpor's network organized massive protests to force Slobodan Milošević to concede the election to Otpor's candidate, Vojislav Kostunica. Otpor

protests included roadblocks and strikes that virtually shut down activity in Serbia. Even the government's weather station stopped its forecasts until Milošević conceded. On October 3 and 4, strikes outside Belgrade such as those at mines in Kolubara found strikers joined by other workers and local police to hold back Serb security police sent by Milošević to break up the strikes.

Otpor's largest rally was on Thursday, October 5, when people from all parts of Serbia came to Belgrade to get rid of Milošević. To the surprise of foreign observers and Milošević, thousands of Serbs, including police, army soldiers, and security police came to Belgrade and occupied the Yugoslav parliament building, the central state broadcasting stations, and Belgrade police offices. Finally, in an October 6 televised speech, Milošević conceded the election to Kostunica. The same day, Milošević left Belgrade, going to his palace in Bor near the Romanian border.

Most Montenegrin Serbs had boycotted September's elections because they wanted independence from the Yugoslav Federation. In Kosovo, a few Serbs voted, but the large Kosovar population boycotted the election. Because Serbs were the overwhelming majority in Yugoslavia, the votes of Montenegrins and Kosovo's Serbs would not have changed the outcome other than to add to Kostunica's majority of 51%. Owing to these circumstances, Milošević's defeat at the ballot box and Otpor's rally of Serbs in the Republic of Serbia was evidence that Serbs united in overthrowing their despotic leader.

Most Americans knew little about Kostunica, but according to the British freelance reporter Timothy Garton Ash, Kostunica was a "moderate nationalist" Serb who detested the British and Americans for bombing Serbia in 1999 and did not believe Milošević ordered atrocities against Muslims in Bosnia and Kosovo. As a constitutional lawyer, Kostunica favored the rule of law, and believed in democratic elections and in negotiations to resolve problems such as those between the Republic of Serbia and the Republic of Montenegro. His immediate need was to gain support from the Serb Republic's president and legislature. The September 24 election was for president of the Yugoslav Federation, of which the Serb Republic was the dominating entity.

See September 24 and December 23, 2000.

October 12, 2000

The U.S. destroyer USS *Cole* is hit by a bomb off the coast of Yemen.

Two suicide terrorists drove a small boat into the U.S. warship carrying a bomb that tore an 80-foot by 40-foot hole in the side of the ship while it was stopping briefly for fuel in the port of Aden, Yemen, killing 17 American sailors. The ship's crew prevented the ship from sinking by controlling the internal flooding.

Yemen denounced the attack as a "premeditated criminal attack." The U.S. Federal Bureau of Investigation and navy investigators rushed to Yemen to determine what happened. The Saudi millionaire Osama bin Laden was the primary suspect for masterminding the bombing, just as he planned the bombings of two U.S. embassies in August 1998.

On November 12, Yemeni officials detained two suspects who admitted their roles in the bombing plot. One man said he purchased the boat used in the bombing after receiving a phone call from an unidentified person in the United Arab Republic who instructed him to buy the boat. He claimed to know nothing about the boat after taking it to a shack near Aden's harbor. Similarly, a woman admitted buying the car used to carry the boat to the shack near the harbor but knew nothing about what happened to the car after taking it to the shack. Probably, the network of Osama bin Laden's terrorists planned the attack on the *Cole*, giving individuals a role in the plot but keeping them ignorant of one another's roles in the bombing.

Following inspections, the *Cole* was piggybacked on a Norwegian heavy-lift ship and taken to the United States for repairs. An Arleigh Burke class destroyer, the *Cole* was built to survive a bomb attack; the navy expected to use it again.

In November, Yemeni President Ali Abdallah Salih told reporter Lally Weymouth (*Washington Post*, December 18, 2000) about a failed terrorist attack in January 2000. Terrorists planned to destroy the USS *Sullivans* in January 2000 in Aden harbor, but their boat sank when it was filled with explosives.

See January 14, 2001.

October 16, 2000

A summit meeting in Egypt seeks to end the violence between Israel and the Palestinians.

After more than two weeks of intensive violence, leaders of the United States, Egypt, Israel, the Palestinians, and Jordan joined U.N. Secretary-General Kofi Annan in a meeting at Sharm el-Sheik, Egypt, to attempt to end the conflict. On October 4, U.S. Secretary of State Albright met with Israeli Prime Minister Barak and Palestinian leader Arafat but achieved no results. Although on October 5, Barak and Arafat told their commanders to pull their troops back from the fighting, the violence continued with Palestinians destroying a Jewish holy site and the Israeli Defense Force retaliating. By October 12, the conflict approached open warfare with Palestinians killing Israeli soldiers and Israeli police firing guns and antitank rockets at Palestinians, while IDF helicopter gunships fired rockets to kill *intifada* at Ramallah and Gaza City.

When the summit ended on October 17, Barak and Arafat agreed to a cease-fire. Israel would reopen the Gaza City airport and pull back troops. Arafat would try to stop riots and other incidents after jailing Palestinian troublemakers. But the agreements failed to end the violence.

See January 20, 2001.

October 18, 2000

Congress eases sanction on the sale of food to Cuba.

Relaxing over 40 years of economic sanctions against Cuba, Congress approved legislation advocated by U.S. agricultural lobbyists to allow the sale of U.S. farm products to Cuba. Because the legislation did not permit U.S. government credits on private financing of the sales, it would be difficult, maybe impossible, for Cuba to purchase these products.

October 20, 2000

In court testimony, Osama bin Laden is linked to U.S. embassy bombings in Africa.

In New York's Federal District Court, Ali Mohamed, a former U.S. army sergeant, pleaded guilty to five charges in connection with the 1998 bombing of U.S. embassies in Kenya and Tanzania. Mohamed trained bodyguards for the Saudi millionaire bin Laden in the Sudan before scouting potential bombing targets in Nairobi. He said after showing bin Laden pictures and diagrams of the Nairobi embassy that bin Laden pointed to where a truck loaded with explosives could approach the building. Mohamed told the court that the purpose of the bombing was to retaliate for U.S. involvement in Somalia in 1992–1993.

Mohamed's guilty plea was the first step toward New York trials of four men suspected of the embassy bombings. Ali became the major prosecution witness in trials that began on February 5, 2001. In the February trial, defendants who pleaded not guilty were Mohamed Rashed Daoud al'Owali, who admitted driving the truck carrying the bomb to the Nairobi embassy; Khalfan Khamis Mohamed, who rode in a truck carrying the bomb to the Tanzanian embassy; Mohammed Saddiq Odeh, who planned the attacks for bin Laden's Al Qaeda terrorist group but was in Kenya when the bomb exploded; and Wadhi El-Hage, who was bin Laden's personal secretary and set up front companies in Kenya to aid the bombers.

In addition to the former U.S. army sergeant, Jamal Ahmed al-Fadl was an important witness. Before 1993, Al-Fadl was one of bin Laden's trusted lieutenants in charge of Al Qaeda's finances until he was caught taking $110,000 in kickbacks from the group's funds and fled to the U.S. embassy in Pakistan. In secret U.S. proceedings, he pleaded guilty to terrorist conspiracy and faced 15 years in prison. The FBI placed him in a witness protection program lest bin Laden have him assassinated.

During the trial, the U.S. government flew in more than 100 witnesses from six different countries. The indictments against the four suspects included a series of events involving Al Qaeda during the 1990s, including bin Laden's involvement in Somalia in 1993 when 17 U.S. Marines were killed.

October 28, 2000

Kosovo's election results favor Rugova's moderates.

In elections for municipal advisory councils, moderates affiliated with Ibrahim Rugova's Democratic League of Kosovo (LDK) won a landslide victory over Hashim Thaci's radical Democratic Party of Kosovo (PDK), the political section of the Kosovo Liberation Army (KLA). On November 7, when the Organization of Security and Cooperation in Europe (OSCE) announced final results, the LDK won control of 21 of 30 advisory councils; the PDK won control of 6 councils. Bernard Kouchner, head of the U.N. mission in Kosovo, appointed Serbs to control three other councils. Although Kosovo Serbs boycotted the election, Kouchner desired their representation in cities where Serbs were a majority.

Rugova's LDK remained popular among Kosovars but both Thaci and Rugova wanted Kosovo to be independent from the Serb Republic. In general, Kosovars made no distinction between the nationalism of Yugoslavia's new president, Vojislav Kostunica, and that of Slobodan Milošević. As Kostunica told the reporter Timothy Garton Ash, Kostunica refuses to believe Serbs committed atrocities in Bosnia or Kosovo.

October 28, 2000

Panel of experts indicates some Gulf War veterans were exposed to nerve gas.

Previously, the Defense Department asserted that there was no evidence that Gulf War veterans were infected by poison gas during the 1991 war with Iraq. Nevertheless, the Pentagon appointed an independent panel of experts under the chairmanship of former Senator Warren Rudman (R-N.H.) to review evidence on the Persian Gulf War. On October 28, Rudman's committee reported that half the veterans with postwar illness probably were infected by low levels of Sarin nerve gas. The report was based on better details about the weather in 1991 and more precise information on the location of U.S. troops. Nearly 30,000 veterans would receive letters informing them of their exposure to nerve gas; an equal number were not exposed.

November 7, 2000

Final U.S. presidential election results are stymied because of Florida's inconclusive returns.

Although Democratic Party nominee Al Gore led the nationwide popular vote, Electoral College results depended on the outcome of Florida's recounting of votes. Florida's vote count was challenged by Democrats in voting precincts where punch-hole cards were discarded by election judges because chads of paper hung between possible slots intended for particular candidates. After several election precincts began hand recounts, Republicans asked Florida courts to disallow them.

Disputes about the Florida recounts continued until December 12, when the U.S. Supreme Court by a 5-to-4 vote ended all recounts and gave Florida's Electoral College votes to Republican George W. Bush. The Court's decision was controversial because federal courts, especially the Supreme Court, had never before interfered with vote counts in any state's election, and the five justices favoring Bush were Republican appointees.

The elections for Congress were as divided between Republicans and Democrats as the presidential election. Congressional elections gave the Republicans a slim majority of six seats in the House of Representatives but created a 50-50 tie in the Senate, which could be broken by Republican Vice President Richard Cheney.

November 11, 2000

Bosnia's nationalist parties dominate election results.

Bosnia's elections failed to change the domination of the three major nationalist parties. Both before and after the 1995 Dayton Accords became effective, Bosnia's ethnic-based nationalist parties controlled political and economic power in their sections of Bosnia and Herzegovina. Except for one Muslim-Croat multiethnic Social Democrat Party that won nine seats in parliament, ethnic-based nationalist parties were elected in the November elections. Moreover, in the presidential election, the Bosnian Serb nationalist candidate, Mirka Sarovic, defeated moderate Serb Milorad Dodic. Sarovic's Social Democratic Party was formed by indicted war criminal Radovan Karadžić.

In the November 11 elections, parliament seats received are listed below.

Muslim-Croat FederationBosnian Serbs (Srpska)
Social Democrats (multiethnic): 9
Serb Social Democrats: 6
Bosnia-Herzegovina Party: 4
Minor parties: 8
Democratic Action (Muslim): 8
Croat Democratic Union (HDZ): 5
Other parties: 2

The constitution of Bosnia and Herzegovina allocates 28 seats to the Muslim-Croat Federation and 14 seats to the Srpska (Serbian) Republic.

November 11, 2000

A Haitian court sentences 37 officials for killing dissident Haitians in 1991–1994.

The 37 former Haitian army and police officers were tried in absentia in a trial that began on September 29. Army Commander Raul Cedras and 36 other army and police officers were tried for premeditated murder during the coup against President Aristide in September 1991 and for later killing many of Aristide's followers. The court sentenced the men to life in prison, but under Haiti's constitution they could have another trial if they surrendered. The court also assessed the defendants $43 million in civil damages for their destructive activities from 1991 to 1994, when U.N. peacekeepers replaced Cedras's junta. Among leaders convicted were Cedras and his confidant Philippe Biamby, Michel François, and Emmanuel Constant.

See November 26, 2000.

November 11, 2000

Angola celebrates independence day while civil war continues.

Celebrating 25 years of independence from Portugal, Angola's President Jose Eduardo dos Santos blamed UNITA rebels for rejecting peace proposals made in October 2000. Although rebel forces had weakened during the past year, they remained defiant of the government and controlled 10% of the country.

Angolans continued to suffer from civil war, poverty, and corruption. The World Food Program and other humanitarian aid groups struggled to import food to feed 1 million impoverished people and reported that 500 children die every day from malnutrition, disease, and land mines. Angola's government exported 1 million barrels of oil each day but spent about 40% of its revenues on the army and only 5% on health, education, and social services. The remaining 55% was siphoned off by corrupt politicians.

Although dos Santos promised to open oil accounts for inspection by the International Monetary Fund, the IMF still had to assess how Angola's extensive political bureaucracy handled the oil income and other government revenues.

November 13, 2000

The White House releases documents on Chile from the 1970s.

As part of the Clinton administration's Special Chile Declassification project, a White House spokesperson said documents released would allow the public to judge how U.S. secret action between 1973 and 1990 undercut the cause of democracy and human rights in Chile.

Over the past two years, 24,000 documents on Chile were declassified, including secret cables, memorandums, and cable messages to clarify the involvement of U.S. agencies during the 1970s when a military junta ruled Chile. In particular, the November 13 documents contained information on President Richard Nixon's opposition to Salvador Allende's election as president in 1970. In a declassified document for November 6, 1970, Nixon told selected cabinet members to "do everything we can to hurt [Allende] and bring him down." At that time, Nixon knew from a CIA cable from Chile in October 1970 that "You have asked us to provoke chaos in Chile." The CIA predicted the carnage would be "considerable and prolonged" in a civil war with at least 10,000 casualties if a military coup tried to overthrow Allende.

In fact thousands of Chileans were murdered after General Augusto Pinochet's junta overthrew Allende in 1973.

See September 11, 1973; December 21, 2000.

November 14, 2000

The United States continues Iran's economic sanctions for another year.

During 2000, the United States lifted bans on Iran's exports of luxury goods, but on November 14 the Clinton administration extended economic sanctions for another year. Iranian President Muhammad Khatami made several overtures to improve relations that broke off in 1979, but President Clinton did little in response. The ban on luxuries had slight effect and was offset by U.S. federal court decisions to compensate American hostages taken in Lebanon by terrorists affiliated with Iran. The men winning court judgments were Terry Anderson, David Jacobsen, Joseph Cicippio, Frank Reed, and William R. Higgins, whom Islamic Jihad terrorists killed in Lebanon.

Under congressional legislation approved in October 2000, American courts granted these five men and their families over $161 million in compensation. Other cases were pending against Iran in U.S. courts. If these cases were won, they could add up to $213 million without including punitive damages awarded by the courts. Iran refused to recognize U.S. court decisions.

See October 21, 1986; February 17, 1988; March 13, 2000.

November 16, 2000

President Clinton and 50 U.S. business leaders begin a visit to Vietnam.

President Clinton's plane landed at Hanoi's airport late in the evening of November 16 with formal welcoming ceremonies scheduled for the next morning. Yet as the president's limousine drove to the hotel, thousands of Vietnamese gathered along the highway and in front of the hotel, many of them shouting "uncle Bill, uncle Bill," a sign of respect for a famous dignitary.

The next morning a formal welcome from Vietnamese President Tran Duc Luong was held in the courtyard of a French-built palace in Hanoi. Afterward, Clinton visited an excavation site outside Hanoi where a U.S. Air Force F-105-D Thunderbird was shot down over a rice paddy 33 years ago during the Vietnam War. Lt. Colonel Lawrence G. Evert piloted the plane. Evert's two sons accompanied Clinton, hoping to find traces of their father's remains. The Americans and Vietnamese excavating the site had found some parts of an airplane and a small number of human remains. All the aircraft parts and human remains would be sent to Hawaii to determine if the plane was the Thunderbird flown by Colonel Evert and conduct DNA tests to determine whether they matched Evert's blood samples.

President Clinton and President Tran Duc Luong witness Ambassador Pete Peterson and Chu Tuan Nha, Minister of Science, Technology, and the Environment, signing an agreement. Clinton Presidential Materials Project

China also accompanied 50 U.S. business leaders from major U.S. corporations. Many U.S.-made products such as Coca-Cola were already popular in Vietnam, and the potential for new business ventures awaited U.S. investors. Although most of Vietnam's government remained in the hands of "old socialists" who refused to privatize many Vietnamese companies.

November 20, 2000

From Tokyo, Peruvian President Fujimori faxes his resignation to Peru.

Alberto Fujimori's authoritarian regime ended on November 20 with a simple fax sent from Japan saying he resigned. Fujimori's troubles began in May 2000 when he was reelected president despite charges of fraud by international monitors. Following the monitors report, Fujimori's inauguration ceremonies were marked by riots in Lima.

These riots were relatively mild compared with the protests on September 14 when a tape on television showed the president's chief adviser and director of the National Intelligence Agency, Vladimir Montesinos, giving a bribe to an opposition congressman. Later, the president's opponents revealed that unidentified sources had more tapes to further implicate Fujimori as well as Montesinos.

Fujimori asked Montesinos to resign and announced he would leave the presidency after elec-

tions in 2001. Montesinos refused to resign and Fujimori asked a respected lawyer, José Ugaz, to investigate Montesinos's activities. Within days, Ugaz announced that his investigation would implicate the president as well as the spy chief.

On November 12 after Peru's minister of justice, Alberto Bustamante, refused to fire Ugaz, Fujimori showed Bustamante a suitcases full of videotapes, Montesinos's bank accounts in the Cayman Islands, and other documents seized in police raids on Montesinos's property. Fujimori asked Bustamante to give the new evidence to Ugaz. The next day, Fujimori flew to Brunei for a scheduled conference before flying on to Tokyo, where he sent the fax on November 20.

In early November, Montesinos fled into hiding and at the end of the year was a "most wanted" criminal in Latin America, having been charged with corruption, election fraud, drug trafficking, money laundering, and bribery.

See May 28, 2000.

November 24, 2000

Global warming treaty talks reach an impasse.

Delegates at The Hague conference expected to finalize a treaty to prevent global warming called the Kyoto Protocol (see December 11, 1997), but two weeks of negotiations proved unsuccessful. The failure to achieve a final treaty was due to differences between Americans and Europeans on the best way to decrease the emission of greenhouse gases. During the last night of the conference, British Deputy Prime Minister John Prescott and U.S. negotiator Frank E. Loy reached a compromise, but delegates from European countries rejected their proposal.

During the conference, major issues were disputed between two environmentalist groups. Idealists wanted the United States to yield its position to promote a treaty, but environmental groups who worked closely with industries on pollution problems defended the U.S. decision to focus on building a political consensus to satisfy all industrial and farming interests. Before the conference adjourned, the delegates from 170 nations agreed to schedule another session at Marrakech, Morocco, in October 2001.

November 25, 2000

The prosecution rests its case in the trial on the bombing of a U.S. plane over Scotland.

Beginning on May 3, 2000, two Libyans were tried for bombing a Pan American plane over Lockerbie, Scotland (see December 18, 1988). After Libyan President Mu'ammar al-Gadhafi agreed to turn over two suspects, the men were taken to the Netherlands for trial before a panel of three Scottish judges (see August 27, 1998). During the trial, the prosecutors' case against Lamen Khaifa Fhimah was damaged because a star prosecution witness could not positively identify Fhimah as the man who put a rigged suitcase on the airplane that flew from Malta to Frankfurt, Germany, where the suitcase was placed on the Pan American flight by Abdel Basset Ali Megrahi. The prosecution rested its case on November 25, 2000. In January 31, 2001, the Scottish judges found Megrahi guilty and sentenced him to life in prison. Fhimah was found not guilty and was set free by the court.

See August 28, 1998.

November 26, 2000

Lavalas Party candidate Aristide is elected president of Haiti.

Jean-Bertrand Aristide had been Haiti's president from 1991 to 1995 but was not eligible for a second term until the 2000 election.

René Preval was Haiti's current president, but Aristide's Lavalas Family Party gained control of the National Assembly in 1996 and stymied Preval's efforts to privatize Haiti's state-owned companies. Although Aristide's opponents claimed the election was rigged and withdrew from the presidential race, the International Observers Coalition of Independent Observers (IOCIO) believed Aristide's popularity made him victorious, whatever fraud or intimidation may have taken place.

During the six years after U.S.-led peacekeepers returned Aristide to power, Haiti's economy never revived and Haiti continued to have the lowest living standards in the Western Hemisphere. Haiti became a cocaine center for Colombian drug cartels to bypass U.S. Coast Guard ships searching for drug traffickers on the way to Florida. Owing to the existing drug traffic and Preval's inability to end Haiti's corruption or meet the economic requisites for loans from the World Bank and the IMF, the United States sided with Haiti's opposition politicians and, as during the May elections, refused to validate Haiti's elections.

Hoping to help Haiti solve its social and economic difficulties, President Clinton sent a delegation to meet with President Preval and President-elect Aristide to agree on steps Aristide should take to obtain better relations with the United States and the international community. Led by Special Envoy Anthony Lake and U.S. State Department Coordinator on Haiti Don Steinberg, the U.S. delegates persuaded Aristide to sign an agreement on measures to improve Haiti's relations with the Organization of American States, the World Bank, and the International Monetary Fund. Signed by Aristide on January 5, 2001, the agreement contained six items for Aristide and the National Assembly to enact. First, Haiti should have a runoff election for 10 Senate seats awarded to Aristide's Lavalas candidates in May 2000. Second, opposition parties should be allowed to join Aristide's government. Third, a new election council should be formed in consultation with opposition leaders. Fourth, a semipermanent Organization of American States (OAS) Commission should oversee Haiti's political talks between the government and opposition groups. Fifth, international agencies would be permitted to monitor Haiti's human rights progress. Sixth, Haiti must undertake a dialogue with World Bank and IMF officials to enable it to obtain the $600 million being withheld for economic reconstruction. In addition, Aristide promised envoy Lake that he would move to cooperate with U.S. authorities in trying to abolish the cocaine traffic between Colombia and Florida.

Aristide was inaugurated in January 2001.

See May 22, 2000.

November 30, 2000

The Indonesian military tries to defeat separatists in two provinces.

After Abdurraham Wahid became president of Indonesia in 1999, parliament approved independence for East Timor. During the next year, the Indonesian province of Aceh on Sumatra and West Irian in the western part of New Guinea renewed their efforts to secede from Indonesia. To counter the separatist movement, on November 30 Wahid spoke to a television audience to explain why Indonesia must not tolerate the secession of any province. The same day, Wahid ordered 1,000 army troops and riot police to break up an independence rally in Djajapura, the capital of West Irian province.

The West Irian secessionists were relative newcomers in their attempt to become independent. In contrast, the Free Aceh Movement has tried to become independent since 1976. The province has rich oil and gas resources. Up to 5,000 secessionists were killed in the 1990s. During August 2000, violence intensified in Aceh, breaking a cease-fire between Aceh and Indonesia's government that was accepted in May 2000. Negotiations in Geneva since June 2 have been unsuccessful.

In addition to the violence, thousands rallied in Aceh on November 11, advocating a referendum on independence to be supervised by the United Nations. Indonesia has declared it does not want the United Nations to interfere in its internal affairs.

See October 20, 1999.

December 1, 2000

Vincente Fox is inaugurated as president of Mexico.

Fox was elected president of Mexico in July, winning a victory over the candidate of the Institutional Revolutionary Party (PRI) (see July 2, 2000). Fox and his National Action Party (PNA) brought hope to end corruption in Mexico and permit the country to obtain full benefits of the six-year-old North American Free Trade Act. In his inaugural address, Fox stated that the U.S. demand for illegal drugs has made Mexico a haven for drug traffickers and promised to take strong measures against them. In addition, Fox said he wanted to expand the benefits of NAFTA by opening U.S. borders for the importation of Mexican products as well as Mexican workers seeking jobs in the United States.

Fox's speech focused most attention on improving Mexico's relations with Canada and the United States but also gave attention to the Zapatista Liberation Army in southern Mexico. After his election in July, Fox submitted a series of legislative bills to Mexico's Congress to meet demands of the Zapatistas.

December 9, 2000

Russian President Putin pardons an American sentenced for espionage.

Upon the recommendation of Russia's Pardons Commission, President Vladimir Putin freed U.S. businessman Edmond Pope, who, on December 7, had been sentenced to 20 years in prison for espionage. Russia's Federal Security Service—the successor to the KGB (Soviet Secret Service)—claimed Pope illegally obtained blueprints of high-speed underwater torpedoes. The Pardons Commission urged Putin to pardon Pope because of the "cruel" 20-year sentence, as well as Pope's cancer, which was in remission before his arrest in April but had returned by December. The Pardon's Commission chairman, Anatoly Pristavkin, said that "based on the principles of humanism and mercy, we believe Mr. Pope is a sick man, who should be allowed to go free." Although President Clinton had tried to intercede with Putin on Pope's behalf, the commission's decision enabled Russia's president to free Pope.

December 10, 2000

An international treaty bans 12 toxic chemicals.

During a U.N.-sponsored conference in Johannesburg, South Africa, delegations from 122 countries accepted a treaty to ban 12 highly toxic chemicals.

Production and use of 9 of the 12 chemicals will be banned after the treaty takes effect, probably four or five years after signing ceremonies set for Stockholm, Sweden, in May 2001. In the treaty, delegates agreed that the Global Environment Fund would distribute $150 million annually to developing nations that need money to offset their costs of using cleaner alternative chemicals.

December 11, 2000

Ion Iliescu regains the presidency of Romania.

Romanian President Iliescu received 70% of the vote to 30% for the right-wing nationalist extremist, Corneliu Vadim Tudor. Iliescu received less than the 50% necessary in the November 26 election but easily defeated Tudor in the runoff election because he received the support of the other four candidates. Since 1990, Romania's standard of living had dropped so low that 40% of the population had less than $35 per month income. Iliescu pledged to adopt economic reforms that would permit Romania eventually to gain the benefits of membership in the European Union.

December 13, 2000

President Clinton visits Ireland hoping to restart the stalled peace process.

After a May agreement to disarm the Irish Republican Army (IRA) permitted the British to renew the power-sharing agreement between Protestants and Catholics in Northern Ireland, disgruntled IRA members continued terrorist attacks against Protestants. In October, former U.S. Senator George Mitchell (D-Me.) returned as a mediator to hold secret discussions between the IRA's political wing Sinn Fein and the Ulster Unionists. Disarming the IRA was the main dispute, but Mitchell failed to solve the problem.

Thus, in Clinton's last visit as president, he obtained only an informal agreement between IRA leaders and the British to do whatever possible to counteract terrorism and resolve the disarmament dispute that lingered into 2001.

See May 29, 2000.

December 16, 2000

The United States completes budget legislation for fiscal 2001.

Although the Defense Department's budget for fiscal 2001 was finalized in August 2000, Congress and the White House disagreed about domestic spending, including funds for foreign aid and the State Department. From September 30 to December 16, Congress and President Clinton agreed on a series of stopgap spending measures to keep the government running. When Congress returned after the November elections, it compromised with the White House on a final 2001 budget.

For fiscal year 2001, the Defense Department received $377 billion, including a pay raise for service personnel, foreign military aid, and various weapons. The State Department received $8 billion, the same as in 2000, while appropriations for foreign aid increased from $12 billion to $13 billion. The total budget for 2001 was $1.8 trillion.

December 17, 2000

A U.S.-Russian joint patrol seals Kosovo's border with southern Serbia.

The joint U.S.-Russian action was part of NATO's Kosovo Forces (KFOR) attempt to shut off the border to the demilitarized zone in southern Serbia, where guerrilla forces of the Liberation Army of Presovo, Medvedja, and Bujanovac (UCPMB) first launched an attack in January 2000.

On November 21, approximately 100 UCPBM rebels entered the demilitarized zone between Kosovo and southern Serbia (see March 15, 2000) and killed four Serbian policemen. Yugoslav President Vojislav Kostunica immediately ordered the Yugoslavia National Army (YNA) to send soldiers and army tanks to the area and asked KFOR to seal off the border region between Kosovo and the Republic of Serbia. KFOR sealed off the borders and on December 17, a combined American-Russian KFOR team used explosives to blow up a road where the UCPBM received supplies and armaments from Kosovars.

KFOR continued attempts to stop UCPBM guerrilla attacks in southern Serbia, but the UCPBM members took advantages of hiding in mountain areas of the region. During January 2001, Kostunica proposed ways for Serbian police to deal with the UCPBM but NATO Secretary General George Robertson warned Yugoslavia's president not to engage in military action against the Albanians in the Presova Valley of southern Serbia. Rather than military action, Robertson told Kostunica to recognize Albanian rights to political equality with Serbs in the Federation of Yugoslavia.

In response, Serbia's Vice President Nebojsa Cović offered a proposal to NATO in February 2001. Cović's plan would return Albanians in southern Serbia to positions that Milošević had stripped away from them in 1992. The plan called for the phased withdrawal of Yugoslav troops and secret police in the region. Albanian leaders rejected Cović's plan because it offered no autonomy or self-government in a region where Albanians were the majority. The Albanians agreed to negotiate but Cović said they must quickly agree to some plan.

Late in January 2001, Kosovar Albanians attacked a village in northern Macedonia, a country and former Yugoslav republic, where many Albanians lived. Fearing that a group called the National Liberation Army aspired to create a Greater Kosovo of Albanians in northern Macedonia and southern Serbia, Macedonian President Boris Trajkovski asked NATO peacekeepers in Kosovo to take more action to protect Macedonia's borders.

See March 18, 2000.

December 18, 2000

A U.S. report anticipates terrorist threats during the next 15 years.

A National Intelligence Report from the CIA, FBI, and NSA titled "Global Threats: 2015, A Dialogue About the Future With Experts" was issued on December 18. The report indicated that the threat of attacks against the United States by missiles with nuclear, chemical, or biological weapons would continue to grow during the next 15 years. Although pessimistic regarding the greater lethality of weapons of mass destruction, the report also said the United States would remain "unparalleled" in its economic, technological, military, and diplomatic influence up to 2015. The report went beyond the secret intelligence available to the National Intelligence Council (NIC) by holding a series of conferences at universities, corporations, and think tanks to get input from experts outside the government.

Among the scenarios identified as "unlikely but possible" were a geostrategic alliance among Russia, China, and India to offset U.S. dominance; a breakup of the U.S.-European alliance over disputes about economic and security plans; and the formation of an international terrorist coalition against the United States.

Regarding the terrorist threat, the report believed attacks by short- or medium-range missiles were more likely than intercontinental ballistic missiles. Moreover, short-range missiles might be smuggled into the United States or neighboring states to launch attacks on U.S. cities.

The NIC report together with other U.S. counter-terrorist programs focused especially on Osama bin Laden and other terrorist attacks around the world since 1981, most of them devised in the Middle East.

December 21, 2000

After examining former President Pinochet's illness, Chile's Supreme Court charges him with murder.

After Chile's Supreme Court stripped Augusto Pinochet Ugarto of senatorial immunity, the court dropped homicide and kidnapping charges against him. But the court ordered Judge Juan Guzmán to interrogate Pinochet possibly to bring new indictments for the execution of political prisoners following the 1973 coup by Pinochet's military junta.

After Pinochet's medical examination on January 23 found him suffering from a form of arteriosclerosis, Judge Guzmán interrogated Pinochet and found him able to stand trial. On January 29, Guzmán charged Pinochet with crimes he committed or ordered the secret police to commit between 1973 and 1990. Guzmán also placed Pinochet under house arrest pending a future trial.

Although some loyalists continued to support Pinochet, the army chief Ricardo Izurieta admitted in 2000 that the armed forces share responsibility for the disappearance of dissidents during Pinochet's regime. On January 7, 2001, Chile's armed forces revealed the location of 49 victims' bodies and admitted that 151 more bodies might never be found, having been dropped from airplanes into the Andean mountain range or dumped in the ocean.

See September 11, 1973; June 5, 2000.

December 23, 2000

Pro-democracy candidates win parliamentary elections in Serbia.

The 18-party coalition Democratic Opposition in Serbia won 176 of the 250 seats in parliamentary elections in Serbia, the more powerful republic of the Yugoslav Federation. Former Yugoslav President

Milošević's Socialist Party won 73 seats, and the Ultranationalist Socialist People's Party won 37 seats. When Serbia's new parliament met in January 2001, Kostunica's ally, Zoran Djindjić, was elected prime minister of Serbia.

Once in control of both Yugoslavia and Serbia, Kostunica and Djindjić replaced Milošević's loyalists who occupied high positions in the army and secret police. By the end of January, Kostunica had purged the Yugoslav army of Milošević's loyal generals, some of whom were indicted for war crimes by the International Tribunal for the former Yugoslavia at The Hague, the Netherlands. Nevertheless, neither Kostunica nor Djindjić was willing to extradite Milošević or other Serbs for a war crimes trial at The Hague tribunal. On January 23, 2001, Carla del Ponte of Switzerland, The Hague's chief prosecutor, met with Kostunica, who refused to acknowledge that Serbs committed war crimes but allowed that Milošević should be tried by Serbia for corruption in Serbia.

Meanwhile, Djindjić and his 17-member cabinet were sworn into office on January 25, 2001. They immediately fired the Serbia's security chief, Rade Marković, and two of his assistants involved in the ethnic cleansing in Bosnia and Kosovo. Djindjić also purged judges beholden to Milošević.

December 28, 2000

President Clinton calls off his visit to North Korea.

Since October 2000, the White House hoped to arrange a meeting in Pyongyong between Clinton and North Korean President Kim Jong Il. North Korean General Jo Myong Rok visited Washington in early October for discussions with Secretary of State Albright. Two weeks later, Albright visited Pyongyong to discuss pending issues with President Kim that might be finalized before Clinton left office. Albright sought to solve differences regarding North Korea's missile weapons program, its support of international terrorism, the military ties between North and South Korea, and a possible U.S. liaison office in Pyongyong.

Although U.S. and North Korean negotiators sought to reach agreement between October and December, their attempts failed. Thus, on December 28, Clinton canceled his visit. In announcing the cancellation, the president stated he discussed the nego-

tiations with president-elect George W. Bush, who, Clinton claimed, could consummate satisfactory deals with North Korea after January 20, 2001. One crucial item for the United States regarding North Korea was whether or not it remained one of the rogue nations for whom the U.S. missile defense system was intended.

December 31, 2000

President Clinton signs a treaty for a permanent international war crimes tribunal.

In announcing the signing of a treaty for a permanent war crimes tribunal, Clinton stated that before ratification, the U.S. Senate would need to add amendments relative to U.S. participation. The president said he signed the treaty because it fulfilled the American tradition of justice and individual accountability dating back to U.S. support for the Nuremberg War Crimes Tribunal.

President-elect George W. Bush said he would never send the treaty to the Senate for ratification. U.S. critics of the treaty feared Americans would have to face the tribunal for frivolous charges such as those connected to U.S. bombing of Serbia in the 1999 conflict.

See October 1, 1946.

2001

January 1, 2001

Taiwan ends its ban on direct trade to the Chinese mainland.

After 50 years of conflict with mainland China, Taiwan's government ended its ban on direct shipping and trade with the mainland. Previously, thousands of Taiwanese had traveled to China indirectly through Hong Kong or Macao. Beijing's leaders had urged Taiwan to end its ban on air travel, mail service, and shipping, but the Taiwanese feared this would lead to China's dominance over Taiwan's islands of Quemoy and Matsu. By 2000, Taiwanese businesspeople wanted the ban lifted to make their trade and investments easier to manage. Taiwan's government compromised by lifting the ban on shipping but not on air travel and mail service.

January 7, 2001

John Kufuor, Ghana's opposition leader, is elected president.

John Rawlings, Ghana's leader, changed his dictatorship into a democracy and free-market economy during the 1990s but was not eligible for a third term as president. His party nominated Vice President John Atta Mills for president. In the December 30 elections, Mills lost to the New Patriotic Party nominee, John Kufuor, who was inaugurated president on January 7. Kufuor's party also won 99 of the 200 seats in Ghana's parliament; Rawling's party won 92 seats. With opposition groups having nine seats, the Patriotic Party could select a prime minister.

January 8, 2001

President Clinton approves trade negotiations with three nations.

Between October and November 2000, the Clinton administration arranged bilateral trade deals with Jordan and Singapore but more complex trade talks were essential between the United States and Chile. Because Congress had rejected the president's "fast track" method of making trade agreements, the Clinton administration began making bilateral trade deals. On October 24, while visiting the Middle East about the Israeli-Palestinian peace process, Clinton announced a free-trade agreement with Jordan. On November 16, he announced that the United States and Singapore would begin bilateral trade talks.

Chile viewed the United States as its number one trade partner, and on November 29 Clinton said bilateral negotiations would begin with Chile on January 8, 2001. President Clinton expected starting discussions with Chile before January 20; the next administration could finalize an agreement. While Chile was not a partner in the North American Free Trade Agreement (NAFTA), the U.S. deal would give Chile similar trading rights. Chile previously had made trade pacts with Canada and Mexico.

January 10, 2001

Iraq is reported to produce chemical and biological weapons.

The U.S. Defense Department issued a report that Iraq had begun producing chemical and biological weapons of mass destruction similar to those made before the 1991 Persian Gulf War.

Based primarily on U.S. satellite photographs, the report said Iraq rebuilt factories destroyed by bombs dropped from British and U.S. aircraft in December 1998. The rebuilt factories gave evidence of producing toxic weapons that Iraq used against Iran and the Kurds in northern Iraq during the Iran-Iraq war (see November 26, 1984). From 1991 to 1998, the United Nations sent teams of inspectors to verify that Iraq had eliminated its weapons of mass destruction (WMD), but since 1998, Iraq had rejected all U.N. Security Council proposals for renewing these inspections as required by the April 1991 peace agreement.

President Saddam Hussein remained defiant of the United States and the Security Council. On January 20, one hour before George W. Bush's inauguration, an Iraqi surface-to-air missile fired on an American jet patrolling the no-fly zone. The jet immediately fired missiles that destroyed an Iraqi antiaircraft battery and a radar site. Such incidents between U.S. or British aircraft and Iraqi ground weapons had occurred frequently for the past two years, but this particular Iraqi attack sent a message to the son of George Bush, who had ordered the U.S.-led international forces to begin attacking Iraq on January 16, ten years before.

If Iraq's effort was symbolic, President George W. Bush soon demonstrated his agreement with the Clinton administration's Iraqi policies. On February 16, 2001, U.S. and British aircraft launched bombing raids on WMD facilities near Baghdad, that resembled those of December 1998. As in 1998, the Americans and British were criticized by France, Russia, and China. Arab nations such as Egypt criticized the attacks because they feared a larger war in the Middle East following Ariel Sharon's election as prime minister of Israel.

Iraq had established better relations with France, Russia, China and other nations who wanted to end U.N. economic sanctions against Iraq and who helped Iraq obtain conventional weapons. Moreover, Iraqi profits from the U.N.'s oil-for-food program and from the sale of oil smuggled through Turkey, Syria, and Jordan abetted President Hussein's ability to rebuild Iraq's WMD.

The Israeli-Palestinian conflict that escalated after September 24, 2000, also benefited Iraq's relations with other Arab nations, especially Egypt, Jordan, and Syria. In a televised address celebrating Iraq's survival and reconstruction since 1991, Hussein urged all Arabs to take up arms against the "Zionists" and liberate Palestinian land "from the river to the sea," an allusion to Israel's total destruction.

See November 26, 1984; January 20, 2001.

January 14, 2001

UNMIK leader Kouchner is replaced in Kosovo by Hans Haekkerup.

Bernard Kouchner headed the U.N. Mission in Kosovo (UNMIK) since its beginning. In his final message, he urged the people of Kosovo to continue moving toward self-government and asked all ethnic groups to participate in Kosovo elections for an assembly during the summer of 2001. Although Serbs in Kosovo boycotted the October advisory council elections, Kouchner gained some respect from Serb leaders for treating them as equals to members of other ethnic groups. Despite the efforts of UNMIK and NATO's Kosovo forces, sporadic violence continued, especially in Mitrovica and southern Serbia. Kouchner's last words to a television audience were "Stop the killings, my friends, stop the violence."

See July 15, 1999.

January 14, 2001

The U.N. Security Council prepares for another mission to Somalia.

Members of the Security Council asked Secretary-General Annan to prepare plans for a "peace-building" mission to Somalia. Since 1991, Somalia had struggled unsuccessfully to establish a central government. The U.S.-led mission in December 1992, to bring peace to Somalia failed and the Security Council withdrew the last of its peacekeeping troops in 1995. Somalia's hopes rose for returning to a peaceful and central government in August 2000 when a provisional government was established (see August 25, 2000).

During the last four months of 2000, a semblance of stability returned but Somali Prime Minister Al Khalif Galaydh sought U.N. help in demobilizing 20,000 militiamen who threatened the new regime's security. In addition, Galaydh asked for funds to rebuild Somalia's infrastructure, including electric grids and oil pipelines from an old refinery. U.S. Ambassador to the United Nations, Richard Holbrooke supported Somalia's request for assistance, and following Annan's report, the Security Council was expected to approve a Somali mission.

January 14, 2001

Yemen prepares to try three men for bombing the USS *Cole*; the FBI opposes the trial.

Following the October 2000 bombing of the USS *Cole*, Yemeni police arrested eight suspects in addition to three men they planned to try in absentia. Although the three were key figures in the bombing, Yemeni police and the FBI agreed the men had fled to camps in Afghanistan to be protected by Osama bin Laden. Omar al-Harazi, one of the three men, telephoned Yemen's leader Jamal al Badawi from the United Arab Emirates to give instructions for attacking the *Cole*. Al-Harazi was to be tried in absentia, but the FBI did not want the suspects to be tried until it was confirmed that they were not in Yemen.

See October 12, 2000.

January 17, 2001

OPEC cuts oil production by 5%.

During an unusually cold American winter with heating prices tripling, OPEC members meeting in Vienna agreed to curtail production by 5%, a decrease expected to raise oil prices by up to $40 per barrel. OPEC increased oil production by less than 3% in October 2000 about the same time the Clinton administration released 30 million barrels of oil from the U.S. strategic reserve. Neither of these increases had a significant effect on American prices, and OPEC's January cut in production increased U.S. gas prices more in 2001.

January 18, 2001

Secretary of State–designate Colin Powell favors a missile defense system.

In testimony before the Senate Foreign Relations Committee regarding his appointment as secretary of state, retired General Colin Powell said he favored deployment of the national missile defense system (NMDS). Because most of the NMDS tests had failed in 2000, President Clinton left a final decision on deployment to the next president. Powell's views concurred with those of President-elect George W. Bush and Defense Secretary–designate Donald Rumsfeld.

The Bush administration's approval of NMDS corresponded with congressional Republicans' views. The Republicans had pushed Clinton to accept billions of dollars for a NMDS in order to fulfill President Ronald Reagan's dream of a missile defense. Critics of NMDS believed Republican leaders were returning to isolationist policies in vogue after World War I but found wanting after 1945. Because the new Bush administration favored deploying NMDS despite objections from its NATO allies, a unilateral decision appeared likely.

Because the NMDS decision was a critical factor in U.S. relations with Europe, Russia, China, North Korea, and even Canada, Secretary of Defense Rumsfeld went to Munich, Germany, on February 4 to offer European friends and allies help in building their own missile defenses. The Europeans remained skeptical because Rumsfeld refused to provide details about President's Bush's security policies beyond saying they were under review by the new administration.

On February 5, Sergey B. Ivanov, Russian President Putin's national security assistant, told the Munich audience that restraining so-called rogue nations could be done more effectively by joint political efforts such as recent peaceful results with North Korea. In addition on February 20, Putin told NATO Secretary-General Lord Robertson that Russia and NATO might make a joint effort to develop a mobile antimissile system against future threats.

On February 6, Russian Defense Minister Igor D. Sergeyev told the Interfax news agency that Russia would not respond to U.S. missile defense plans by deploying more new missiles but by developing technologies to penetrate any missile shield. Sergeyev, the former commander of Russia's strategic rocket forces, said Russia had devised programs during the 1980s to counter Ronald Reagan's "Star Wars" defense system. These programs were dropped when the Cold War ended but the Russian Federation resumed an ICBM missile system that could overwhelm any U.S. missile defense plan, an ICBM system known as Topol-M.

On February 22, 2001, North Korea expressed dissatisfaction with the Bush administration's "hardline" stance on NMDS, saying it might resume testing its long-range missiles. In September 2000, North Korea promised the Clinton administration to suspend missile testing. Clinton's attempt to achieve a permanent deal with President Kim Jong Il ended when time ran out. Clinton advised the new administration that a deal with North Korea was close, but Secretary of State Powell did not immediately pick up on that negotiating offer.

Although President Bush and his national security appointees seemed anxious to deploy an NMDS, most experts indicated an NMDS was not likely to be ready for deployment as a mini-system until 2006 under the best circumstances.

See September 1 and December 28, 2000.

January 18, 2001

Congo President Kabila is killed; diplomats seek solutions for Congo's problems.

Following the assassination of Congo President Laurent Kabila, his son Joseph Kabila met with diplomats from the United States, Britain, France, China, Russia, Belgium, and Tunisia. Kamel Marjane of Tunisia headed the U.N. peacekeeping mission to the Congo.

Neither the diplomats nor most Congolese knew much about Joseph Kabila, who seldom visited the Congo, where his father overthrew Mobutu Sese Seko in 1997. Joseph Kabila, asked the U.N. Security Council to fulfill all its previous resolutions designed to bring a cease-fire and peace to the Congo. He also asked Marjane to complete deployment of the 5,000 peacekeepers under the U.N. mission to the Congo.

In early February 2001, Secretary of State Colin Powell met with two leaders affiliated with Congo's warfare. Powell urged Rwandan President Paul Kagan to stop the human rights violations of Rwandan troops and offered Kabila $10 million of humanitarian aid. Powell did not indicate whether or not the United States would provide additional funds for the U.N. mission to the Congo.

See May 18, 1997.

January 19, 2001

Having reduced U.S. payments to the United Nations, Ambassador Holbrooke heads a Security Council session on AIDS.

Throughout his four years as U.S. ambassador to the United Nations, Richard Holbrooke successfully demonstrated the benefits of U.N. membership to Republican Senator Jesse Helms (R-N.C.), who often opposed U.N. activity. Holbrooke arranged for Helms to speak before the U.N. Security Council and to meet with U.N. Secretary-General Kofi Annan. As a result of these meetings and discussions with other U.N. proponents, Helms better understood how various U.N. agencies helped the world's economic and social problems.

Helms was most concerned about U.S. funds allocated to various U.N. activities, especially U.S. costs compared with other G-7 nations, who had lower payments. To reduce these costs, Holbrooke and his U.N. budget negotiator, Donald Hays, made contacts with the 187 other U.N. members and arranged a review of each nation's assessments during 2000. Subsequently, at the December 2000 meeting of the U.N. General Assembly, member nations agreed to cut U.S. costs for administration from 25% to 22% and peacekeeping assessments from 31% to 26%. At the December meeting, Japan's share was also cut, but South Korea, Singapore, Brazil and the 15-member European Union's shares increased. On February 6, Congress authorized a payment of $582 million in dues owed to the United Nations to fulfill the Holbrooke agreement.

On January 19, Holbrooke's last day as U.S. ambassador, the Security Council carried out his request to initiate discussions of the AIDS pandemic. Holbrooke told the council that AIDS is "the most dangerous problem in the world today, the biggest health problem in 600 years."

January 19, 2001

Philippine President Estrada resigns; Vice President Macapagal-Arroyo becomes president.

In the Philippine Islands, People Power II (see February 25, 1986) persuaded President Joseph Estrada to resign, making Vice President Gloria Macapagal-Arroyo president. As with President Ferdinand Marcos's downfall (see February 25, 1986), thousands of Filipino citizens began massive demonstrations against Estrada on January 16, after Estrada's fellow party members in the Philippine Senate suppressed evidence regarding the millions of dollars Estrada allegedly received from gamblers, evidence vital to the president's impeachment trial.

On November 11, new reports disclosed Estrada's involvement in gambling rackets. On November 13, the Philippine House of Representatives began pre-

paring articles of impeachment against Estrada for a trial to be held in January 2001.

Three days after the Manila protests began, Philippine Armed Forces Chief of Staff General Angelo Reyes and Defense Secretary Orlando Mercado advised Estrada that the military was withdrawing support from the president. Estrada then resigned and sought exile in Australia. On the night of January 19–20, Arroyo was sworn in as president

January 20, 2001

Israeli Prime Minister Barak and Palestinian leader Arafat will meet and try to stop violence in the West Bank and Gaza.

Violence began in the West Bank and Gaza Strip cities in September after Ariel Sharon, the hawkish Likud Party leader, visited the Jerusalem plaza where a Muslim mosque was located (see September 28, 2000). Despite frequent attempts by President Clinton to mediate a final settlement between Barak and Arafat, Clinton failed to get an agreement regarding the key issues of Palestinian rights in East Jerusalem and the right of Palestinian refugees to return to their homes. A last-ditch effort to finalize an agreement was attempted at Taba, Egypt, on January 21 but the effort failed. On February 6, 2001, Barak lost the Israeli elections to Sharon. Many Israelis believed Sharon's "tough stance" against Palestinians is the best way to silence the radical *intifada* members who Arafat cannot control.

January 20, 2001

George W. Bush is inaugurated as president of the United States.

President Bush's inaugural address emphasized his efforts to unify the nation. "I will work," he said, "to build a single nation of justice and opportunity." With regard to national security issues, Bush said his objective was to build U.S. defense capability "beyond challenge, lest weakness invite challenge." He also would "confront weapons of mass destruction, so that a new century is spared new horrors."

In December, President-elect Bush's first appointment was retired General Colin Powell as secretary of state. Together with Vice President Dick Cheney, Powell was on former President George Bush's national security staff during the 1991 Persian Gulf War. For defense secretary, Bush named Donald

Rumsfeld, who served in that position under President Gerald Ford from 1974 to 1976. The new national security adviser, Condoleezza Rice was the least-experienced member of Bush's national security team, but she was Bush's adviser on foreign policy during the 2000 presidental campaign.

Select Bibliography

Reference Guides

Bemis, Samuel Flagg, ed. *The American Secretaries of State and Their Diplomacy.* 10 vols. New York: Knopf, 1928.

———— and Robert Ferrell, eds. *The American Secretaries of State and Their Diplomacy.* New series. 20 vols. New York: Cooper Square, 1963–1980 covering secretaries from Frank B. Kellogg (1928) to Cyrus Vance (1977–1980).

Bevans, Charles I., comp. *Treaties and Other International Agreements of the United States of America, 1776–1949.* 12 vols. Washington, D.C.: GPO, 1968.

Burns, Richard Dean, ed. *Guide to American Foreign Relations Since 1700.* Santa Barbara, Calif.: Clio, 1983.

———— ed. *Encyclopedia of Arms Control and Disarmament.* 3 vols. New York: Scribner, 1993.

DeConde, Alexander, Richard Dean Burns, Fredrik Logevall, and Louise Ketz, eds. *Encyclopedia of American Foreign Policy.* 2d ed. New York: Scribner, 2002.

Haines, Gerald K., and J. Samuel Walker, eds. *American Foreign Relations: A Historiographical Review.* Westport, Conn.: Greenwood Press, 1981.

Hodson, H.V., and Verena Hoffman, eds. *The Annual Register, a Record of World Events.* London: Longman, 1758–Continuous.

Langer, William L., ed. *An Encyclopedia of World History.* 4th ed. Boston: Houghton Mifflin, 1968.

Miller, David Hunter, ed. *Treaties and Other International Acts of the United States, 1776–1863.* 8 vols. Washington, D.C.: GPO, 1931–1948.

Morris, Richard B. *Encyclopedia of American History.* rev. ed. New York: Harper and Brothers, 1965.

Public Papers of the Presidents of the United States, 33 vols. Washington, D.C.: GPO, 1961–1974.

U.S. Department of State. *Department of State Bulletin.* Washington, D.C.: GPO, 1939–1989.

————. *Foreign Policy Bulletin.* Washington, D.C.: GPO, 1990–.

————. *Foreign Relations of the United States.* Washington, D.C.: GPO, 1861–. Continuous. Regular publications usually about 30 years after the events.

The United States in World Affairs, 1931–1967. New York: Simon and Schuster, 1932–1970.

United States Treaties and other International Agreements. Washington, D.C.: GPO, 1952–. Vols. 1–35 cover to 1984.

General Works

Bailey, Thomas A. *America Faces Russia: Russian-American Relations from Early Times to Our Day.* Ithaca, N.Y.: Cornell University Press, 1950.

Bemis, Samuel Flagg. *The Latin American Policy of the United States.* New York: Harcourt, Brace, 1943.

Blumenthal, Henry. *France and the United States: Their Diplomatic Relations, 1789–1914.* Chapel Hill: University of North Carolina Press, 1970.

Bryson, Thomas A. *American Diplomatic Relations with the Middle East, 1784–1975: A Survey.* Metuchen, N.J.: Scarecrow Press, 1977.

Callahan, James M. *American Foreign Policy in Mexican Relations.* New York: Macmillan, 1932.

Dulles, Foster R. *China and America: The Story of Their Relations Since 1784.* Princeton, N.J.: Princeton University Press, 1946.

Fairbank, John K., Edwin O. Reischauer, and Albert M. Craig. *East Asia: Tradition and Transformation.* Boston: Houghton Mifflin, 1973.

Foner, Philip S. *A History of Cuba and Its Relations with the United States.* 2 vols. New York: International Publishers, 1962–1963.

Griswold, Alfred W. *The Far Eastern Policy of the United States.* New York: Harcourt, Brace, 1938.

LaFeber, Walter. *The Panama Canal: The Crisis in Historical Perspective.* New York: Oxford University Press, 1978.

Langley, Lester D. *The Cuban Policy of the United States (1776–1962).* New York: Wiley, 1968.

Logan, Rayford W. *The Diplomatic Relations of the United States with Haiti, 1776–1891.* Chapel Hill: University of North Carolina Press, 1941.

Peterson, Harold F. *Argentina and the United States, 1810–1960.* Albany: State University of New York Press, 1962.

Tansill, Charles C. *The United States and Santo Domingo, 1798–1873.* Baltimore, Johns Hopkins Press, 1938.

Tulchin, Joseph. *Argentina and the United States: A Conflicted Relationship.* Boston: Twayne, 1990.

Williams, William A. *American-Russian Relations, 1781–1947.* New York: Holt, Rinehart and Winston, 1952.

Special Topics

Alterman, Eric. *Who Speaks for America? Why Democracy Matters in Foreign Policy.* Ithaca, N.Y.: Cornell University Press, 1998.

Bolling, Landrum with Craig Smith. *Private Foreign Aid: U.S. Philanthropy for Relief and Development.* Boulder, Colo.: Westview Press, 1982.

Bundy, McGeorge. *Danger and Survival: Choices About the Bomb in the First Fifty Years.* New York: Random House, 1988.

Dangerfield, Royden J. *In Defense of the Senate: A Study in Treaty Making.* Norman: University of Oklahoma Press, 1933.

Frey, Linda S., and Marsha L. Frey. *The History of Diplomatic Immunity.* Columbus: Ohio State University Press, 1999.

Johnson, Robert. *Thence Round Cape Horn: The Story of United States Naval Forces on Pacific Stations, 1818–1923.* Annapolis, Md.: U.S. Naval Institute, 1963.

Logan, John A., Jr. *No Transfer.* New Haven, Conn.: Yale University Press, 1961.

Ninkovich, Frank. *Modernity and Power: A History of the Domino Theory in the Twentieth Century.* Chicago: University of Chicago Press, 1994.

Paullin, Charles O. *American Voyages to the Orient, 1690–1865: An Account of Merchant and Naval Activities in China, Japan, and the Various Pacific Islands.* Annapolis, Md.: Naval Institute Press, 1971.

Paullin, Charles O. *Diplomatic Negotiations of American Naval officers, 1778–1883.* Baltimore: Johns Hopkins Press, 1912.

Prados, John. *Presidents' Secret Wars: CIA and Pentagon Covert Operations from World War II through the Persian Gulf.* Chicago: Ivan R. Dee, 1996.

Prins, Gwyn, ed. *Understanding Unilateralism in American Foreign Relations.* London: Royal Institute of International Affairs, 2000.

Schmitz, David F. *Thank God They're on Our Side: The United States and Right-Wing Dictatorships, 1921–1965.* Chapel Hill: University of North Carolina Press, 1999.

Sherry, Michael S. *The Rise of American Air Power: The Creation of Armageddon.* New Haven, Conn.: Yale University Press, 1987.

Smith, Tony. *America's Mission: The United States and the Worldwide Struggle for Democracy in the Twentieth Century.* Princeton, N.J.: Princeton University Press, 1994.

Tesón, Fernando R. *Humanitarian Intervention: An Inquiry into Law and Morality.* Dobbs Ferry, N.Y.: Transnational, 1988.

Wallerstein, Mitchel B. *Food for War—Food for Peace: United States Food Aid in a Global Context.* Cambridge, Mass.: MIT Press, 1980.

Weigley, Russell R. *History of the United States Army.* New York: Macmillan, 1967.

Wriston, Henry M. *Executive Agents in American Foreign Relations.* Baltimore: Johns Hopkins Press, 1929.

From 1607 to 1828

Personalities

Ammon, Harry. *James Monroe: The Quest for National Identity.* New York: McGraw-Hill, 1971.

Bemis, Samuel. *John Quincy Adams and the Foundations of American Foreign Policy.* New York: Knopf, 1949.

Clarfield, Gerald H. *Timothy Pickering and American Diplomacy, 1775–1800.* Columbia: University of Missouri Press, 1969.

Dangerfield, George. *Chancellor Robert R. Livingston of New York, 1746–1813.* New York: Harcourt, Brace, 1960.

Feiling, John. *John Adams: A Life.* Knoxville: University of Tennessee Press, 1992.

Hill, Peter P. *William Vans Murray, Federalist Diplomat: The Shaping of Peace with France, 1797–1801.* Syracuse, N.Y.: Syracuse University Press, 1971.

Hutson, James H. *John Adams and the Diplomacy of the American Revolution.* Lexington: University of Kentucky Press, 1980.

Ketcham, Ralph. *James Madison: A Biography.* New York: Macmillan, 1971.

Lycan, Gilbert L. *Alexander Hamilton and American Foreign Policy: A Design for Greatness.* Norman: University of Oklahoma Press, 1970.

Peterson, Merrill D. *Thomas Jefferson and the New Nation: A Biography.* New York: Oxford University Press, 1970.

Powell, John H. *Richard Rush: Republican Diplomat, 1780–1859.* Philadephia: University of Pennsylvannia Press, 1942.

Remini, Robert V. *Andrew Jackson and the Course of American Empire, 1767–1821.* New York: Harper & Row, 1977.

Stourzh, Gerald. *Benjamin Franklin and American Foreign Policy.* Chicago: University of Chicago Press, 1954.

Van Deusen, Glyndon G. *The Life of Henry Clay.* Boston: Little, Brown, 1937.

Walters, Raymond, Jr. *Albert Gallatin: Jeffersonian Financier and Diplomat.* New York: Macmillan, 1957.

American Revolution to 1789

Andrews, Charles M. *The Colonial Background of the American Revolution.* New Haven, Conn.: Yale University Press, 1931.

Bemis, Samuel F. *Diplomacy of the American Revolution.* Bloomington: Indiana University Press, 1955; reprint of 1935 edition.

Dickerson, Oliver M. *The Navigation Acts and the American Revolution.* Philadelphia: University of Pennsylvania Press, 1951.

Draper, Theodore. *The American Revolution.* New York: Times Books/Random House, 1996.

Gipson, Lawrence H. *The British Empire before the American Revolution.* 15 vols. New York: Knopf, 1939–1958.

———. *The Coming of the Revolution, 1763–1775.* New York: Harper, 1954.

Jensen, Merrill. *The New Nation: A History of the United States During the Confederation, 1781–1789.* New York: Knopf, 1950.

Kammen, Michael G. *Empire and Interest: The American Colonies and the Politics of Mercantilism.* Philadelphia: Lippincott, 1970.

Lint, Gregg. "The American Revolution and the Law of Nations, 1776–1789." *Diplomatic History* 1 (1977): 20–34.

Madariaga, Isabel de. *Britain, Russia and Armed Neutrality of 1789.* New Haven, Conn.: Yale University Press, 1962.

Morris, Richard B. *The Peacemakers: The Great Powers and American Independence.* New York: Harper and Row, 1965.

Savelle, Max. *The Origins of American Diplomacy: The International History of Anglo-America, 1492–1763.* New York: Macmillan, 1967.

——— *Seeds of Liberty: The Genesis of the American Mind.* New York: Knopf, 1948.

Stinchcombe, William C. *The American Revolution and the French Alliance.* Syracuse, N.Y.: Syracuse University Press, 1969.

From 1789 to 1828

Adams, Henry. *History of the United States during the Administrations of Jefferson and Madison.* 9 vols. New York: Scribner, 1889–1891.

Allen, Gardner W. *Our Navy and the Barbary Corsairs.* Cambridge, Mass.: Harvard University Press, 1905.

Bemis, Samuel F. *Pinckney's Treaty: A Study of America's Advantage from Europe's Distress.* Baltimore: Johns Hopkins Press, 1962.

Bolkhovitinov, Nikolai N. *The Beginnings of Russian-American Relations, 1775–1815.* Trans. Elena Levin. Cambridge, Mass.: Harvard University Press, 1976.

Burt, Alfred L. *The United States, Great Britain, and British North America from the Revolution to the Establishment of Peace after the War of 1812.* New Haven, Conn.: Yale University Press, 1940.

Combs, Jerald. *The Jay Treaty: Political Battleground of the Founding Fathers.* Berkeley: University of California Press, 1970.

De Conde, Alexander. *Entangling Alliance: Politics and Diplomacy under George Washington.* Durham, N.C.: Duke University Press, 1958.

———. *The Quasi-War: The Politics and Diplomacy of the Undeclared War with France.* New York: Scribner, 1966.

———. *This Affair of Louisiana.* New York: Scribner, 1976.

Hickey, Donald R. *The War of 1812: A Forgotten Conflict.* Urbana: University of Illinois Press, 1989.

Horsman, Reginald. *The Causes of the War of 1812.* Philadelphia: University of Pennsylvania Press, 1962.

Irwin, R.W. *The Diplomatic Relations of the United States with the Barbary Powers, 1776–1816.* Chapel Hill: University of North Carolina Press, 1931.

Perkins, Bradford. *Castlereagh and Adams: England and the United States, 1812–1823.* Berkeley: University of California Press, 1964.

———. *The First Rapprochement: England and the United States, 1795–1805.* Philadelphia: University of Pennsylvania Press, 1955.

———. *Prologue to War: England and the United States, 1805–1812.* Berkeley: University of California Press, 1961.

Pratt, James W. *Expansionists of 1812.* New York: Macmillan, 1925.

Rippy, J. Fred. *Rivalry of the United States and Great Britain Over Latin America, 1808–1830.* Baltimore: Johns Hopkins Press, 1929.

Ritcheson, Charles R. *Aftermath of Revolution: British Policy Toward the United States, 1783–1795.* Dallas, Tex.: Southern Methodist University Press, 1969.

Van Alstyne, Richard W. *Our Rising American Empire.* New York: Oxford University Press, 1960.

Whitaker, Arthur P. *The Spanish American Frontier, 1783–1795.* Lincoln: University of Nebraska Press, 1927.

———. *The United States and the Independence of Latin America.* Baltimore: Johns Hopkins Press, 1941.

Special Topics

Gilbert, Felix. *To the Farewell Address.* Princeton, N.J.: Princeton University Press, 1961.

Perkins, Dexter. *The Monroe Doctrine, 1823–1826.* Cambridge, Mass.: Harvard University Press, 1927.

From 1829 to 1896

General

Blumenthal, Henry. *A Reappraisal of Franco-American Relations, 1830–1871.* Chapel Hill: University of North Carolina Press, 1959.

Treat, Payson J. *Diplomatic Relations between the United States and Japan, 1853–1895.* 2 vols. Stanford, Calif.: Stanford University Press, 1932.

Personalities

Bartlett, Irving H. *Daniel Webster.* New York: Norton, 1978.

Brown, Charles H. *Agents of Manifest Destiny: The Lives and Times of the Filibusters.* Chapel Hill: University of North Carolina Press, 1980.

Cooling, Benjamin Franklin. *Benjamin Franklin Tracy: Father of the Modern American Fighting Navy.* Hamden, Conn.: Shoe String Press, 1973.

Donald, David Herbert. *Lincoln.* New York: Simon and Schuster, 1995.

Ferris, N.B. *Desperate Diplomacy: William H. Seward's Foreign Policy, 1861.* Knoxville: University of Tennessee Press, 1976.

Oeste, George I. *John Randolph Clay: America's First Career Diplomat* [1836–1860s]. Philadelphia: University of Pennsylvania Press, 1966.

Paolino, Ernest N. *The Foundations of the American Empire: William Henry Seward and U.S. Foreign Policy.* Ithaca, N.Y.: Cornell University Press, 1973.

Parton, Dorothy R. *The Diplomatic Career of Joel Roberts Poinsett.* Washington, D.C.: Catholic University of America Press, 1934.

Randall, James G. *Lincoln the President.* 4 vols. New York: Dodd, Mead, 1945–1955.

Sellers, Charles G. *James K. Polk: Continentalist, 1834–1846.* Princeton, N.J.: Princeton University Press, 1966.

Smith, Elbert B. *The Presidency of James Buchanan.* Lawrence: University Press of Kansas, 1975.

Tyler, Alice F. *The Foreign Policy of James G. Blaine.* Minneapolis: University of Minnesota Press, 1927.

Van Deusen, Glyndon G. *William Henry Seward.* New York: Oxford University Press, 1967.

Woodford, Frank B. *Lewis Cass: The Last Jeffersonian.* New Brunswick, N.J.: Rutgers University Press, 1950.

To the Civil War

Adams, Ephraim D. *Great Britain and the American Civil War.* 2 vols. New York: Longmans, Green, 1925.

Binkley, William C. *The Texas Revolution.* Baton Rouge: University of Louisiana Press, 1952.

Corey, Albert B. *The Crisis of 1830–1842 in Canadian-American Relations.* New Haven, Conn.: Carnegie Endowment for International Peace, 1941.

Fowler, William M., Jr. *Under Two Flags: The American Navy in the Civil War.* New York: Norton, 1990.

Graebner, Norman A. *Empire on the Pacific—A Study in American Continental Expansion.* New York: Ronald, 1955.

Jones, Howard. *To the Webster-Ashburton Treaty: A Study in Anglo-American Relations, 1783–1843.* Chapel Hill: University of North Carolina Press, 1977.

Jones, Wilbur D. *The American Problem in British Diplomacy, 1841–1860.* Athens: University of Georgia Press, 1974.

Latourette, Kenneth S. *The History of Early Relations Between the United States and China, 1784–1844.* New Haven, Conn.: Yale University Press, 1917.

McLemore, Robert A. *Franco-American Diplomatic Relations, 1816–1836.* Baton Rouge: University of Louisiana Press, 1941.

Merk, Frederick. *The Oregon Question: Essays in Anglo-American Diplomacy and Politics.* Cambridge, Mass.: Harvard University Press, 1967.

Pletcher, David M. *The Diplomacy of Annexation: Texas, Oregon, and the Mexican War.* Columbia: University of Missouri Press, 1973.

Schott, Joseph L. *Rails Across Panama: The Story of the Building of the Panama Railroad, 1849–1855*. Indianapolis, Ind.: Bobbs-Merrill, 1967.

Sowle, Patrick. "A Reappraisal of Seward's Memorandum of April 1, 1861, to Lincoln." *Journal of Southern History* 33 (1967): 234–239.

Spencer, Donald S. *Louis Kossuth and Young America: A Study of Sectionalism and Foreign Policy, 1848–1852*. Columbia: University of Missouri Press, 1977.

Thomas, Benjamin P. *Russo-American Relations: 1815–1867*. Baltimore: Johns Hopkins Press, 1930.

Warren, Gordon H. *Fountain of Discontent: The Trent Affair and Freedom of the Seas*. Boston: Northeastern University Press, 1981.

Post–Civil War

Jensen, Ronald J. *The Alaska Purchase and Russian-American Relations*. Seattle: University of Washington Press, 1975.

LaFeber, Walter. *The New Empire: An Interpretation of American Expansion, 1860–1898*. Ithaca, N.Y.: Cornell University Press, 1963.

Linn, Brian M. *The United States Army and Counterinsurgency in the Philippine War, 1899–1902*. Chapel Hill: University of North Carolina Press, 1989.

Perkins, Dexter. *The Monroe Doctrine, 1867–1907*. Baltimore: Johns Hopkins Press, 1937.

Pletcher, David M. *The Awkward Years: American Foreign Relations Under Garfield and Arthur*. Columbia: University of Missouri Press, 1961.

Smith, Goldwin. *The Treaty of Washington, 1871*. Ithaca, N.Y.: Cornell University Press, 1941.

Special Topics

Dennett, Tyler. *Americans in Eastern Asia*. New York: Macmillan, 1922.

Du Bois, W.E.B. *The Suppression of the African Slave Trade to the United States of America, 1638–1870*. New York: Longmans, Green, 1896.

Goebel, Julius. *The Struggle for the Falklands*. New Haven, Conn.: Yale University Press, 1927.

Johnson, Erwin. *For China Stations: The U.S. Navy in Asian Waters, 1800–1898*. Annapolis, Md.: Naval Institute Press, 1979.

Miller, Stuart C. *The Unwelcome Immigrant: The American Image of the Chinese, 1785–1882*. Berkeley: University of California Press, 1969.

Tate, Merze. *The United States and the Hawaiian Kingdom: A Political History*. New Haven, Conn.: Yale University Press, 1965.

Weinburg, Albert K. *Manifest Destiny*. Baltimore: Johns Hopkins Press, 1935.

From 1897 to 1944

Personalities

Ambrosius, Lloyd E. *Wilsonian Statecraft: Theory and Practice of Liberal Internationalism During World War I*. Wilmington, Del.: Scholarly Resources, 1991.

Bailey, Thomas A. *Woodrow Wilson and the Great Betrayal*. New York: Macmillan, 1944.

Beale, Howard K. *Theodore Roosevelt and the Rise of America to World Power.* Baltimore: Johns Hopkins Press, 1956.

Bix, Herbert P. *Hirohito and the Making of Modern Japan.* New York: Harper Collins, 2000.

Burner, David. *Herbert Hoover: A Public Life.* New York: Knopf, 1979.

Carpenter, John A. *Ulysses S. Grant.* New York: Twayne, 1970.

Clymer, Kenton J. *John Hay: The Gentleman as Diplomat.* Ann Arbor: University of Michigan Press, 1975.

Cronon, E. David. *Josephus Daniels in Mexico.* Madison: University of Wisconsin Press, 1960.

Dallek, Robert. *Franklin D. Roosevelt and American Foreign Policy, 1932–1945.* New York: Oxford University Press, 1979.

Eggert, Gerald G. *Richard Olney: Evolution of a Statesman.* University Park: Pennsylvania State University Press, 1974.

Link, Arthur S. *Wilson.* 6 vols. to date. Princeton, N.J.: Princeton University Press, 1947–1960.

Morgan, H.W. *William McKinley and His America.* Syracuse, N.Y.: Syracuse University Press, 1963.

Nevins, Allan. *Hamilton Fish: The Inner History of the Grant Administration.* New York: Dodd, Mead, 1936.

Pratt, Julius W. *Cordell Hull, 1933–1944.* 2 vols. New York: Cooper Square, 1964.

Pusey, Merlo J. *Charles Evans Hughes.* 2 vols. New York: Macmillan, 1951.

Stimson, Henry L., and McGeorge Bundy. *On Active Service in Peace and War.* New York: Harper, 1949.

Tyler, Alice Flet. *The Foreign Policy of James G. Blaine.* Minneapolis: University of Minnesota Press, 1927.

To World War I

Blount, Philip. *The American Occupation of the Philippine Islands.* New York: G.P. Putnam's, 1912.

Braisted, William R. *The United States Navy in the Pacific, 1897–1909.* Austin: University of Texas Press, 1958.

Callcott, William H. *The Caribbean Policy of the United States, 1890–1920.* Baltimore: Johns Hopkins Press, 1942.

Campbell, Alex E. *Great Britain and the United States, 1895–1903.* London: Longmans, 1960.

Campbell, Charles S., Jr. *Anglo-American Understanding, 1898–1903.* Baltimore: Johns Hopkins Press, 1957.

Denis, Alfred L.P. *Adventures in American Diplomacy, 1896–1906.* New York: Dalton, 1928.

DeNovo, John A. "A Railroad for Turkey: The Chester Project, 1908–1913." *Business History Review* 33 (1959):300–329.

Foner, Philip S. *The Spanish-Cuban-American War and the Birth of American Imperialism, 1895–1902.* 2 vols. New York: Monthly Review Press, 1972.

Grenville, John A.S., and George B. Young, *Politics, Strategy and American Diplomacy: Studies in Foreign Policy, 1872–1917.* New Haven, Conn.: Yale University Press, 1966.

Healy, David F. *U.S. Expansionism: The Imperialist Urge in the 1890's.* Madison: University of Wisconsin Press, 1970.

————. *The United States in Cuba, 1898–1902.* Madison: University of Wisconsin Press, 1963.

Linn, Brian McAllister. *The Philippine War, 1899–1902.* Lawrence: University Press of Kansas, 2000.

Mayer, Arno. *Politics and Diplomacy at Peacemaking: Containment and Counterrevolution at Versailles, 1918–1919.* New York: Knopf, 1967.

McCullough, David. *The Path Between the Seas: The Creation of the Panama Canal, 1870–1914.* New York: Simon and Schuster, 1977.

Morgan, H. Wayne. *America's Road to Empire: The War with Spain and Overseas Expansion.* New York: Wiley, 1965.

Parrini, Carl B. *Heir to Empire: United States Economic Diplomacy, 1916–1923.* Pittsburgh: University of Pittsburgh Press, 1969.

Perkins, Bradford. *The Great Rapprochement: England and the United States, 1895–1914.* New York: Atheneum, 1968.

Preston, Diana. *The Boxer Rebellion.* New York: Walker, 2000.

Tansill, Charles C. *Canadian-American Relations, 1875–1911.* New Haven, Conn.: Yale University Press, 1943.

Varg, Paul A. *The Making of a Myth: The United States and China, 1897–1912.* East Lansing: Michigan State University Press, 1968.

Vevier, Charles. *The United States and China, 1906–1913.* New Brunswick, N.J.: Rutgers University Press, 1955.

Interwar Years and World War II

Adler, Selig. *The Uncertain Giant, 1921–1940: American Foreign Policy before the War.* New York: Macmillan, 1965.

Browder, R.P. *The Origins of Soviet-American Diplomacy.* Princeton, N.J.: Princeton University Press, 1953.

Conn, Stetson, and Byron Fairchild. *The Framework of Hemisphere Defense.* Washington, D.C.: Office of the Chief of Military History, Department of the Army, 1960.

Divine, Robert A. *The Illusion of Neutrality.* Chicago: University of Chicago Press, 1962.

Ferrell, Robert H. *American Diplomacy in the Great Depression.* New Haven, Conn.: Yale University Press, 1957.

Frank, Richard B. *Downfall: The End of the Imperial Japanese Empire.* New York: Random House, 1999.

George, Margaret. *The Warped Vision: British Foreign Policy 1933–39.* Pittsburgh: University of Pittsburgh Press, 1965.

Kennan, George F. *Russia and the West under Lenin and Stalin.* Boston: Little, Brown, 1960.

————. *Soviet-American Relations, 1917–1920.* 2 vols. Princeton, N.J.: Princeton University Press, 1956–1958.

Kennedy, David M. *Freedom from Fear: The American People in Depression and War, 1929 to 1945.* New York: Oxford University Press, 1999.

Langer, William L., and S. E. Gleason. *The Challenge to Isolation, 1937–1940.* New York: Harper & Row, 1952.

————. *The Undeclared War, 1940–1941.* New York: Harper & Row, 1953.

Morison, Samuel E. *The Rising Sun in the Pacific, 1931–April 1942*. Vol. 3 of the *History of United States Naval Operations in World War II*. Boston: Little, Brown, 1948.

Moulton, Harold C., and Leo Pasvolsky. *War Debts and World Prosperity*. Washington, D.C.: Brookings Institution, 1932.

Smith, Robert F. *The United States and Revolutionary Nationalism in Mexico, 1916–1932*. Chicago: University of Chicago Press, 1972.

Sprout, Margaret, and Harold Sprout. *Toward a New Order of Sea Power*. Princeton, N.J.: Princeton University Press, 1940.

Thomas, Hugh. *The Spanish Civil War*. New York: Harper & Row, 1961.

Weissman, Benjamin M. *Herbert Hoover and Famine Relief to Soviet Russia, 1921–1923*. Stanford, Calif.: Hoover Institution Press, 1974.

Wetzler, Peter. *Hirohito and War: Imperial Tradition and Military War Making*. Honolulu: University of Hawaii Press, 1998.

Special Topics

Brune, Lester H. *The Origins of American Security Policy: Sea Power, Air Power and Foreign Policy, 1900–1941*. Manhattan, Kans.: Military Affairs/Aerospace Historian Publishing, 1981

Calhoun, Frederick S. *Uses of Force and Wilsonian Foreign Policy*. Kent, Ohio: Kent State University Press, 1993.

Daniels, Roger. *The Politics of Prejudice: The Anti-Japanese Movement in California and the Struggle for Japanese Exclusion*. Berkeley: University of California Press, 1962.

Holt, W. Stull. *Treaties Defeated by the Senate*. Baltimore: Johns Hopkins Press, 1933.

Maga, Tim. *Judgment at Tokyo: The Japanese War Crimes Trials*. Lexington: University of Kentucky Press, 2001.

Miller, Edward S. *War Plan Orange: The U.S. Strategy to Defeat Japan, 1897 to 1945*. Annapolis: Md: Naval Institute Press, 1991.

From 1945 to 1980

Personalities

Ambrose, Stephen E. *Eisenhower: Soldier and President*. New York: Simon and Schuster, 1990.

Bird, Kai. *The Chairman: John J. McCloy, the Making of the American Establishment*. New York: Simon and Schuster, 1992.

Brzezinski, Zbigniew. *Power and Principle: Memoirs of the National Security Adviser, 1977–1981*. New York: Farrar, Straus & Giroux, 1985.

Bundy, William. *A Tangled Web: The Making of Foreign Policy in the Nixon Presidency*. New York: Hill and Wang, 1998.

Carter, Jimmy. *Keeping the Faith: Memoirs of a President*. New York: Bantam, 1982.

Cohen, Warren I., and Nancy Bernkopf Tucker, eds. *Lyndon Johnson Confronts the World*. New York: Cambridge University Press, 1994.

Dobrynin, Anatoly. *In Confidence: Moscow's Ambassador to America's Six Cold War Presidents.* New York: Times Books, 1995.

Donovan, Robert J. *Conflict and Crisis: The Presidency of Harry S. Truman, 1945–1948.* New York: Norton, 1977.

———. *Tumultuous Years: The Presidency of Harry S. Truman 1949–1953.* New York: Norton, 1982.

Fink, Gary M., and Hugh David Graham, eds. *The Carter Presidency: Policy Choices in the Post–New Deal Era.* Lawrence: University Press of Kansas, 1998.

Guhin, Michael. *John Foster Dulles.* New York: Columbia University Press, 1972.

Halberstam, David. *The Best and the Brightest.* New York: Random House, 1972.

Haynes, Richard. *The Awesome Power: Harry S. Truman as Commander in Chief.* Baton Rouge: Louisiana State University Press, 1973.

Isaacson, Walter, and Evan Thomas. *The Wise Men: Six Friends and the World They Made.* New York: Simon and Schuster, 1986 (John McCloy, Charles Bohlen, Dean Acheson, Robert Lovett, Averell Harriman, George Kennan).

Kalb, Marvin, and Bernard Kalb. *Kissinger.* Boston: Little, Brown, 1974.

Kaufman, Robert G. *Henry M. Jackson: A Life in Politics.* Seattle: University of Washington Press, 1990.

Kearns, Dorothy. *Lyndon Johnson and the American Dream.* New York: Harper and Row, 1976.

Kennan, George F. *Memoirs.* 2 vols. Boston: Little, Brown, 1967, 1972.

Kennedy, Robert. *Thirteen Days: A Memoir of the Cuban Missile Crisis.* New York: Norton, 1969.

Khrushchev, Nikita. *Khrushchev Remembers: The Glasnost Tapes,* Boston: Little, Brown, 1990.

Kissinger, Henry. *White House Years.* Boston: Little, Brown, 1979.

———.*Years of Upheaval.* Boston: Little, Brown, 1982.

———. *Years of Renewal.* New York: Simon and Schuster, 1999.

May, Ernest R., and Philip D. Zelikow. *The Kennedy Tapes.* Cambridge, Mass.: Harvard University Press, 1997.

Messer, Robert L. *The End of an Alliance: James F. Byrnes, Roosevelt, Truman, and the Origins of the Cold War.* Chapel Hill: University of North Carolina Press, 1982.

Ognibene, Peter J. *Scoop: The Life and Politics of Henry M. Jackson.* New York: Stein & Day, 1975.

Saikal, Amin. *The Rise and Fall of the Shah.* Princeton, N.J.: Princeton University Press, 1980.

Schandler, Herbert. *The Unmaking of the President: Lyndon Johnson and Vietnam.* Princeton, N.J.: Princeton University Press, 1977.

Schlesinger, Arthur M. *A Thousand Days: John F. Kennedy in the White House.* Boston: Houghton Mifflin, 1965.

Schulzinger, Robert D. *Henry Kissinger: Doctor of Diplomacy.* New York: Columbia University Press, 1989.

Strong, Robert A. *Working the World: Jimmy Carter and the Making of American Foreign Policy.* Baton Rouge: Louisiana State University Press, 2000.

Vance, Cyrus. *Hard Choices: Critical Years in America's Foreign Policy.* New York: Simon and Schuster, 1983.

Walton, Richard J. *Cold War and Counter-Revolution: The Foreign Policy of John F. Kennedy.* New York: Viking, 1972.

Origins of the Cold War to 1960

Aldrich, Richard J., ed. *British Intelligence, Strategy and the Cold War, 1945–1951.* New York: Routledge, 1992.

Alexander, Charles. *Holding the Line: The Eisenhower Era, 1952–1961.* Bloomington: Indiana University Press, 1975.

Alperovitz, Gar. *Atomic Diplomacy: Hiroshima and Potsdam. The Use of the Atomic Bomb and the American Confrontation.* New York: Vintage, 1967.

Appleman, Roy E. *Disaster in Korea: The Chinese Confront MacArthur, 1950.* College Station: Texas A&M University Press, 1990.

Cullather, Nick. *Secret History: The CIA's Classified History of Its Operations in Guatemala, 1952–1954.* Stanford, Calif.: Stanford University Press, 2000.

Cumings, Bruce. *The Origins of the Korean War, 1947 to 1950.* 2 vols. Princeton, N.J.: Princeton University Press, 1990.

Dowers, John. *Embracing Defeat* [Japan]. New York: New Press, 1999.

Feis, Herbert. *Contest over Japan, 1945–1952.* New York: Norton, 1967.

Gaddis, John Lewis. *The United States and the Origins of the Cold War, 1941–1947.* New York: Columbia University Press, 1972.

Goncharov, Sergei N., John W. Lewis, and Xue Litai. *Uncertain Partners: Stalin, Mao and the Korean War.* Stanford, Calif.: Stanford University Press, 1993.

Hammer, Ellen J. *The Struggle for Indochina, 1940–1955: Vietnam and the French Experience.* Rev. ed. Stanford, Calif.: Stanford University Press, 1956.

Hwang, In K. "Korea's Unification Struggle." In Lester H. Brune, ed. *The Korean War: Handbook of the Literature and Research.* Westport, Conn.: Greenwood, 1996.

Ulam, Adam B. *The Rivals: America and Russia Since World War II.* New York: Viking, 1971.

Wittner, Lawrence S. *Cold War America: From Hiroshima to Watergate.* New York: Praeger, 1974.

From 1960 to 1980

Berman, Larry. *No Peace, No Honor: Nixon, Kissinger, and Betrayal in Vietnam.* New York: Free Press, 2001.

Beschloss, Michael P. *The Crisis Years: Kennedy and Khrushchev, 1960–1963.* New York, Harper Collins, 1991.

Brune, Lester H. *The Cuba-Caribbean Missile Crisis of October 1962.* Claremont, Calif.: Regina, 1996.

Burr, William. "New Sources on the Berlin Crisis, 1958–1962," *Cold War International History Project Bulletin* 2 (Fall 1992):21–24, 32.

Cahn, Anne Hessing. *Killing Détente: The Right Attacks the CIA.* University Park: Pennsylvania State University, 1998.

Divine, Robert A., ed. *The Cuban Missile Crisis.* Chicago: Quadrangle, 1971.

Garthoff, Raymond. *Détente and Confrontation: American Soviet Relations from Nixon to Reagan.* Rev. ed. Washington, D.C.: Brookings Institution, 1994.

Gelb, Leslie H. *The Irony of Vietnam: The System Worked.* Washington, D.C.: Brookings Institution, 1979.

Goodman, Allan. *The Lost Peace: America's Search for a Negotiated Settlement of the Vietnam War.* Stanford, Calif.: Hoover Institution, 1978.

Herring, George C. *America's Longest War: The United States and Vietnam, 1950–1975*. New York: Wiley, 1979.

Higgins, Trumbull. *The Perfect Failure: Kennedy, Eisenhower, and the CIA at the Bay of Pigs*. New York: Norton, 1987.

Kiernan, Ben. *The Pol Pot Regime: Race, Power, and Genocide in Cambodia Under the Khmer Rouge, 1975–1979*. New Haven, Conn.: Yale University Press.

Lewy, Guenter. *America in Vietnam*. New York: Oxford University Press, 1978.

Moise, Edwin E. *Tonkin Gulf and the Escalation of the Vietnam War*. Chapel Hill, University of North Carolina Press, 1996.

Nathan, James A., ed. *The Cuban Missile Crisis Revisited*. New York: St. Martin's, 1992.

Nelson, Keith. *The Making of Détente: Soviet-American Relations in the Shadow of Vietnam*. Baltimore: Johns Hopkins Press, 1995.

Porter, Gareth. *A Peace Denied: The United States, Vietnam and the Paris Agreement*. Bloomington: Indiana University Press, 1975.

Richter, James G. *Khrushchev's Double Bind: International Pressures and International Coalition Politics*. Baltimore: Johns Hopkins Press, 1994.

Schwab, George, and Henry Friedlander, eds. *Détente in Historical Perspective*. 2d ed. New York: Cyrco, 1978.

Shawcross, William. *Sideshow: Kissinger, Nixon and the Destruction of Cambodia*. New York: Simon and Schuster, 1979.

Sick, Gary. *All Fall Down: America's Tragic Encounter with Iran*. New York: Random House, 1985.

Smith, Gaddis. *Morality, Reason and Power: American Diplomacy in the Carter Years*. New York: Hill & Wang, 1986.

Stevenson, William, and Monika Jensen-Stevenson. *Kiss the Boys Goodbye: How the United States Betrayed Its Own POW's in Vietnam*. New York: Plume, 1991.

Szulc, Tad. *The Illusion of Peace: Foreign Policy in the Nixon-Kissinger Years*. New York: Viking, 1978.

U.S. Department of Defense. *The Pentagon Papers: The Defense Department History of United States Decision Making on Vietnam: The Senator Gravel Edition*. 5 vols. Boston: Beacon Press, 1971–1972.

Arms Control and Defense Policy

Aliano, Richard. *American Defense Policy from Eisenhower to Kennedy: The Politics of Changing Military Requirements, 1957–1961*. Athens: Ohio University Press, 1975.

Divine, Robert. *Blowing in the Wind: The Nuclear Test Ban Debate, 1954–1960*. New York: Oxford University Press, 1978.

Herken, Gregg. *The Winning Weapon: The Atomic Bomb in the Cold War, 1945–1950*. New York: Knopf, 1980.

Holloway, David. *Stalin and the Bomb: The Soviet Union and Atomic Energy, 1939–1956*. New Haven, Conn.: Yale University Press, 1996.

Moulton, Harland B. *From Superiority to Parity: The United States and the Strategic Arms Race, 1961–1971*. Westport, Conn.: Greenwood Press, 1973.

Newhouse, John. *Cold Dawn: The Story of SALT*. New York: Harper and Row, 1973.

Smith, Gerald C. *Doubletalk: The Story of the First Strategic Arms Limitation Talks.* New York: Doubleday, 1980.

Talbott, Strobe. *Endgame: The Inside Story of SALT II.* New York: Harper and Row, 1979.

Willrich, Mason, and John B. Rhinelander, eds. *SALT: The Moscow Agreements and Beyond.* New York: Free Press, 1974.

Special Topics

Anderson, Irvine H. *Aramco, the United States, and Saudi Arabia: A Study of the Dynamics of Foreign Oil Policy, 1933–1950.* Princeton, N.J.: Princeton University Press, 1981.

Bonsal, Philip Wilson. *Cuba, Castro and the United States.* Pittsburgh: University of Pittsburgh Press, 1971.

Chang, Gordon H. *Friends and Enemies: The United States, China, and the Soviet Union, 1948 to 1972.* Stanford, Calif.: Stanford University Press.

Cold War International History Project. *Bulletins* and other Publications. Washington, D.C.: Woodrow Wilson Center, Spring, 1992 to the present.

Djilas, Aleksa. *The Contested Country: Yugoslav Unity and the Communist Revolution.* Cambridge, Mass.: Harvard University Press, 1996.

Gilbert, Martin, and Richard Gott. *The Appeasers.* Boston: Houghton Mifflin, 1963.

Kolko, Joyce, and Gabriel Kolko. *The Limits of Power: The World and United States Foreign Policy, 1945–1954.* New York: Harper and Row, 1972.

Mower, A. Glenn, Jr. *The United States, the United Nations, and Human Rights: The Eleanor Roosevelt and Jimmy Carter Eras.* Westport, Conn.: Greenwood Press, 1979.

Perez, Louis A., Jr. *Cuba and the United States: Ties of Singular Intimacy.* Athens: University of Georgia Press, 1990.

1981 to 2001

Personalities

Baker, James, A., III. *The Politics of Diplomacy: Revolution, War and Peace.* New York: Putnam, 1995.

Bell, Coral. *The Reagan Paradox: U.S. Foreign Policy in the 1980s.* New Brunswick, N.J.: Rutgers University Press, 1989.

Bonner, Raymond. *Waltzing with a Dictator: The Marcoses and the Making of American Foreign Policy.* New York: Macmillan, 1987.

Boyer, Paul, ed. *Reagan as President: Contemporary Views of the Man, His Politics and His Policies.* Chicago: Ivan R. Dee, 1990.

Bush, George. *All the Best, George Bush: My Life in Letters and Other Writings.* New York: Simon and Schuster, 2000.

Bush, George, and Brent Scowcroft. *A World Transformed.* New York: Knopf, 1998.

Callahan, David. *Dangerous Capabilities: Paul Nitze and the Cold War.* New York: Harper Collins, 1990.

Cannon, Lou. *President Reagan: The Role of a Lifetime.* New York: Putnam, 1991.

Christopher, Warren. *In the Stream of History: Shaping Foreign Policy for the New Era.* Stanford, Calif.: Stanford University Press, 1998.

Crowe, Admiral William J. *The Line of Fire: From Washington to the Gulf: The Politics and Battles of the New Military.* New York: Simon and Schuster, 1993.

Doder, Dusko, and Louise Branson. *Gorbachev: Heretic in the Kremlin.* New York: Viking, 1990.

Dobrynin, Anatoly. *In Confidence: Moscow's Ambassador to America's Six Cold War Presidents* [1962–1986]. New York: Times Books, 1995.

Gates, Robert M. *From the Shadows: The Ultimate Insider's Story of Five Presidents and How They Won the Cold War.* New York: Simon and Schuster, 1996.

Gorbachev, Mikhail. *Perestroika: New Thinking for Our Country and the World.* New York: Bessie/Harper and Row, 1987.

———— *Memoirs.* New York: Doubleday, 1995.

Haig, Alexander M., Jr. *Caveat: Realism, Reagan and Foreign Policy.* New York: Macmillan, 1984.

Hart, Alan. *Arafat: A Political Biography.* Bloomington: University of Indiana Press, 1989.

Herzstein, Robert. *Waldheim: The Missing Years.* New York: Arbor House, 1988.

McFarlane, Robert C., with Zofia Smardz. *Special Trust.* New York: Cadell & Davies, 1994.

Matlock, Jack. *Autopsy on an Empire: The American Ambassador's Account of the Collapse of the Soviet Union.* New York: Random House, 1995.

Medvedev, Zhores A. *Gorbachev.* New York; Norton, 1986.

Nitze, Paul H. *From Hiroshima to Glasnost, at the Center of Decisions: A Memoir.* New York: Grove Weidenfeld, 1989.

Okawara, Yoshio. *To Avoid Isolation: An Ambassador's View of U.S.-Japanese Relations.* Columbia: University of South Carolina Press, 1989.

Powell, Colin, with Joseph E. Persico. *My American Journey.* New York: Random House, 1995.

Shultz, George. *Turmoil and Triumph: My Years as Secretary of State.* New York: Scribner, 1993.

Talbott, Strobe. *Master of the Game: Paul Nitze and the Nuclear Peace.* New York: Knopf, 1988.

Tobin, Jeffrey. *A Vast Conspiracy* [Clinton's impeachment]. New York, Random House, 2000.

Weinberger, Caspar. *Fighting for Peace: Seven Critical Years in the Pentagon.* New York: Warner, 1990.

Zimmerman, Warren. *Origins of a Catastrophe*[Yugoslavia]. New York: Random House, 1996.

End of the Cold War

Beschloss, Michael R., and Strobe Talbott. *At the Highest Level: The Inside Story of the End of the Cold War.* Boston: Little, Brown, 1993.

Carrere d'Encausse, Helene. *The End of the Soviet Empire: The Triumph of the Nations.* New York: Basic Books, 1993.

English, Robert D. *Russia and the Idea of the West: Gorbachev, Intellectuals and the End of the Cold War.* New York: Columbia University Press, 2000.

Garthoff, Raymond. *The Great Transition: American-Soviet Relations and the End of the Cold War.* Washington, D.C.: Brookings Institution, 1993.

Hogan, Michael, ed. *The End of the Cold War.* New York: Cambridge University Press, 1992.

LeBow, Richard, and Janice Gross Stein. *We All Lost the Cold War.* Princeton, N.J.: Princeton University Press, 1994.

Rowen, Henry S., and Charles Wolf, Jr., eds. *The Impoverished Superpower: Perestroika and the Soviet Military Burden.* San Francisco, Calif.: Institute for Contemporary Studies, 1990.

Shelton, Judy. *The Coming Soviet Crash: Gorbachev's Desperate Pursuit of Credit in Western Financial Markets.* New York: Free Press, 1988.

The Americas

Adkin, Mark. *Urgent Fury: The Battle for Grenada.* Lexington, Mass.: D.C. Heath, 1989.

Andreas, Peter. *Border Games: Policing the U.S.-Mexican Divide.* Ithaca, N.Y.: Cornell University Press, 2000.

Armstrong, Robert, and Janet Shenk. *El Salvador: The Face of Revolution.* Boston: South End Press, 1983.

Arnson, Cynthia. *Crossroads: Congress, the Reagan Administration, and Central America.* New York: Pantheon, 1989.

Avirgan, Tony, and Martha Honey. *La Penca: On Trial in Costa Rica: The CIA vs. the Press.* San Pedro, Costa Rica: Editorial Porvenir, 1988.

Beck, Robert J. *The Grenada Invasion.* Boulder, Colo.: Westview Press, 1993.

Booth, John A., and Mitchell A. Seligson. *Elections and Democracy in Central America.* Chapel Hill: University of North Carolina Press, 2d ed. 1989.

Burrowes, Reynold A. *Revolution and Rescue in Grenada.* Westport, Conn.: Greenwood, 1988.

Byrne, Hugh. *El Salvador's Civil War.* Boulder, Colo.: Lynne Rienner, 1996.

Cameron, Maxwell A., and Brian W. Tomlin. *The Making of NAFTA: How the Deal Was Done.* Ithaca, N.Y.: Cornell University Press, 2000.

Charlton, Michael. *The Little Platoon: Diplomacy and the Falklands Dispute.* Oxford: Basil Blackwell, 1989.

Cockbury, Leslie. *Out of Control: The Story of the Reagan Administration's Secret War in Nicaragua.* New York: Atlantic Monthly Press, 1987.

Cohen, William S., and George J. Mitchell. *Men of Zeal: A Candid Inside Story of the Iran-Contra Hearings.* New York: Viking, 1988.

Dinges, John. *Our Man in Panama: How General Noriega Used the United States and Made Millions in Drugs and Arms.* New York: Random House, 1990.

Farmer, Paul. *The Uses of Haiti.* Monroe, Me.: Common Courage Press, 1994.

Fass, Simon M. *Political Economy in Haiti: The Drama of Survival.* New Brunswick, N.J.: Transaction Books, 1988.

Gutman, Roy. *Banana Diplomacy: The Making of American Foreign Policy, 1981–1987.* New York: Simon and Schuster, 1988.

Hamilton, Nora, et al., eds. *Crisis in Central America Regional Dynamics and U.S. Policy in the 1980's.* Boulder, Colo.: Westview Press, 1988.

Johnson, Victor C. "Congress and Contra Aid, 1986–1987." In Abraham F. Lowenthan, ed. *Latin America and the Caribbean Contemporary Record, Vol. 6.* New York: Holmes and Meier, 1989.

Kempe, Frederick. *Divorcing the Dictator: America's Bungled Affair with Noriega.* New York: Putnam, 1990.

Kornbluh, Peter. *Nicaragua: Reagan's Wars Against the Sandinistas. The Price of Intervention*. Washington, D.C.: Institute for Policy Studies, 1987.

LaFeber, Walter. *Inevitable Revolutions: The United States in Central America*. New York: Norton, 1984.

Lake, Anthony. *Somoza Falling*. Boston: Houghton Mifflin, 1989.

Ledeen, Michael A. *Perilous Statecraft: An Insider's Account of the Iran-Contra Affair*. New York: Scribner, 1988.

Leiken, Robert S., ed. *Central America: Anatomy of a Conflict*. New York: Carnegie Endowment for International Peace/Pergamon, 1984.

Marshall, Jonathan, et al. *The Iran-Contra Connection: Secret Teams and Covert Operations in the Reagan Era*. Boston: South End Press, 1987.

Martz, John D. *United States Policy in Latin America: A Quarter Century of Crisis and Challenge, 1961–1986*. Lincoln: University of Nebraska Press, 1988.

Middlebrook, Martin. *The Fight for the "Malvinas": The Argentine Forces in the Falkland War*. New York: Viking, 1989.

Morley, Morris H. *Washington, Somoza and the Sandinistas: State and Regime in U.S. Policy Toward Nicaragua, 1969–1981*. New York: Cambridge University Press, 1994.

Nicholls, David. *From Dessalines to Duvalier: Race, Color and National Independence in Haiti*. New York: Cambridge University Press, 1997.

Pastor, Robert A. *Condemned to Repetition: The United States and Nicaragua*. Princeton, N.J.: Princeton University Press, 1987.

Perera, Victor. *Unfinished Conquest: The Guatemala Tragedy*. Berkley: University of California Press, 1993.

Pezzullo, Lawrence, and Ralph Pezzullo. *At the Fall of Somoza*. Pittsburgh: University of Pittsburgh Press, 1994.

Report of the President's National Bipartisan Commission on Central America [Kissinger Report]. New York: Macmillan, 1984.

Shacochis, Bob. *The Immaculate Invasion* [Haiti]. New York: Viking, 1999.

Sklar, Holly. *Washington's War on Nicaragua*. Boston: South End Press, 1988.

Soviet-Cuban Connection in Central America and the Caribbean. Washington, D.C.: Department of State and Department of Defense, March 1985.

Stotzky, Irwin P. *Silencing the Guns in Haiti: The Promise of Deliberative Democracy*. Chicago: University of Chicago Press, 1997.

U.S. Congress. *Joint Hearings on the Iran-Contra Investigation*. 2 vols. Washington, D.C.: GPO, 1987–1988.

U.S. Congress, Senate Select Committee on Intelligence. *Report on Preliminary Inquiry on Secret Military Assistance to Iran and the Nicaraguan Opposition*. Washington, D.C.: GPO, January 1987.

U.S. Department of State, and the Department of Defense. *Grenada: A Preliminary Report*. Washington, D.C.: GPO, 1983.

U.S. Department of State. *Lessons of Grenada*. Washington, D.C.: GPO, 1986.

United Nations. *Les Nations Unies et Haiti, 1990–1996*. New York: United Nations Blue Book series XI, 1996.

Valenta, Jiri, and Esperanza Duran, eds. *Conflict in Nicaragua*. Boston: Allen and Unwin, 1987.

———. and Hebert J. Ellison, eds. *Grenada and Soviet/Cuban Policy*. Boulder, Colo.: Westview Press, 1986.

Valenzuela, Arturo. *The Collective Defense of Democracy: Lessons from the Paraguayan Crisis of 1996*. New York: Carnegie Corporation, 1999.

Walker, Thomas W., ed. *Reagan Versus the Sandinistas: The Undeclared War on Nicaragua*. Boulder, Colo.: Westview Press, 1987.

Wilentz, Amy. *The Rainy Season: Haiti Since Duvalier*. New York: Simon and Schuster, 1988.

Womack, John, Jr. *Rebellions in Chiapas: An Historical Reader* [Mexico]. New York: New Press, 1994.

Wucker, Michele. *Why the Cocks Fight: Dominicans, Haitians, and the Struggle for Hispaniola*. New York: Hill and Wang, 1999.

Africa

Coker, Christopher. *The United States and South Africa, 1968–1985: Constructive Engagement and Its Critics*. Durham, N.C.: Duke University Press, 1986.

Hirsch, John L., and Robert B. Oakley. *Somalia and Operations Restore Hope: Reflections on Peacemaking and Peacekeeping*. Washington D.C.: United States Institute for Peace, 1995.

Lefebvre, Jeffrey A. *Arms for the Horn: U.S. Policy in Ethiopia and Somalia, 1953–1991*. Pittsburgh: University of Pittsburgh Press, 1993.

Legum, Colin. *The Battlefronts of South Africa*. New York: Africana Publishing House, 1988.

Lyons, Terrence, and Ahmed Y. Samatar. *Somalia: State Collapse, Multilateral Intervention, and Strategies for Political Reconstruction*. Washington, D.C.: Brookings Institution, 1995.

Melvem, Linda. *Rwanda: A People Betrayed: The Role of the West in Rwanda's Genocide*. London: Zed Books, 2000.

Oakley, Robert B. and John L. Hirsh. *Somalia and Operation Restore Hope*. Washington, D.C.: U.S. Institute of Peace, 1995.

Prunier, Gerard. *The Rwanda Crisis: History of a Genocide*. New York: Columbia University Press, 1997.

Sahoun, Mohamed. *Somalia: The Missed Opportunities*. Washington, D.C.: United States Institute for Peace, 1994.

United Nations. *The United Nations and Somalia, 1992–1996*. New York: United Nations Blue Book series VIII, 1996.

Wright, John. *Libya, Chad and the Central Sahara*. New York: Barnes & Noble, 1989.

Asia

Brook, Timothy. *Quelling the People: The Military Suppression of the Beijing Democracy Movement*. New York: Oxford University Press, 1992.

Burton, Sandra. *Impossible Dream: The Marcoses, the Aquinos and the Unfinished Revolution*. New York: Warner Books, 1989.

Garver, John W. *Foreign Relations of the People's Republic of China*. Englewood Cliffs, N.J.: Prentice-Hall, 1993.

Grinker, Roy Richard. *Korea and Its Future: Unification and Unfinished War*. New York: St. Martin's Press, 2000.

Jardin, Matthew. *East Timor: Genocide in Paradise*. Monroe, M.E.: Common Courage Press, 1999.

Lampton, David M. *Same Bed, Different Dreams: U.S.-China Relations, 1989–2000*. Berkeley, Calif.: University of California Press, 2001.

Rashid, Ahmed. *Taliban: Militant Islam, Oil and Fundamentalism in Central Asia.* New Haven, Conn.: Yale University Press, 2000.

Rostow, W.W. *The United States and the Regional Organization of Asia and the Pacific, 1965–1985.* Austin: University of Texas Press, 1986.

Schofield, Victoria. *Kashmir in Conflict: India, Pakistan and the Unfinished War.* New York: St. Martin's Press, 2000.

Wirsing, Robert G. *India, Pakistan and the Kashmir Dispute.* New York: St. Martin's Press, 1994.

Wood, Christopher. *The End of Japan Inc.: And How the New Japan Will Look.* New York: Simon and Schuster, 1994.

Wurfel, David. *Filipino Politics: Development and Decay.* Ithaca, N.Y.: Cornell University Press, 1988.

The Balkans

Biberaj, Elez. *Albania in Transition: The Rocky Road to Democracy.* Boulder, Colo.: Westview Press, 1998.

Bowden, Mark. *Blackhawk Down* [Somalia]. New York: Atlantic Monthly, Press, 1999.

Cohen, Lenard J. *Broken Bonds: Yugoslavia's Disintegration and Balkan Politics in Transition.* 2d ed. Boulder, Colo.: Westview Press, 1995.

Daalder, Ivo. *Getting to Dayton: The Making of America's Bosnia Policy.* Washington, D.C.: Brookings, 2000.

Danner, Mark. "The U.S. and the Yugoslavia Catastrophe," series of articles, *New York Review of Books* (November 20, 1997): 56–64; (December 4, 1997): 55–65; (February 4, 1998): 34–41; (February 19, 1998): 41–45; (March 26, 1998): 40–52; (April 23, 1998): 59–65.

Donia, Robert, and John Fine Jr. *Bosnia and Herzegovina: A Tradition Betrayed.* New York: Columbia University Press, 1994.

Doder, Dusko, and Louise Branson. *Milosevic: Protrait of a Tyrant.* New York: Free Press, 1999.

Gall, Charlotte. "Signs That Kosovo Conflict Crosses Macedonia's Border," *New York Times* on the Web (February 25, 2001).

Gutman, Roy. *A Witness to Genocide.* [Bosnia]. New York: Macmillan, 1993.

Holbrooke, Richard. *To End a War* [Bosnia]. New York: Random House, 1998.

Judah, Tim. *Kosovo: War and Revenge.* New Haven, Conn.: Yale University Press, 2000.

———. *The Serbs: History, Myth and the Destruction of Yugoslavia.* New Haven, Conn.: Yale University Press, 1997.

Malcolm, Noel. *Kosovo: A Short History.* Updated ed. New York: New York University Press, 1999.

Rohde, David. *Endgame: The Betrayal and Fall of Srebrenica.* New York: Farrar, Straus and Giroux, 1997.

Silber, Laura, and Allan Little. *Yugoslavia: Death of a Nation.* New York: Penguin, 1996.

Tindemans, Leo., et. al. *Unfinished Peace: Report of the International Commission on the Balkans.* Washington, D.C.: Carnegie Endowment for International Peace, 1996.

Weller, Marc. *The Crisis in Kosovo: 1998–1999* [Documents and analysis]. Cambridge: Cambridge University Press, 1999.

Woodward, Susan. *Balkan Tragedy: Chaos and Dissolution after the Cold War.* Washington, D.C.: Brookings, 1995.

Europe, Soviet Union, and United States

Bialer, Seweryn. *The Soviet Paradox: External Expansion, Internal Decline.* New York: Knopf, 1986.

Blinken, Anthony S. *Ally Versus Ally: America, Europe, and the Siberian Pipeline Crisis.* New York: Praeger, 1987.

Bradsher, Henry. *Afghanistan Communism and Soviet Intervention.* Cambridge, Mass.: Harvard University Press, 1999.

Calleo, David P. *Beyond American Hegemony: The Future of the Western Alliance.* New York: Basic Books, 1987.

Cohen, Stephen F. *Failed Crusade: American Tragedy of Post-Communist Russia.* New York: Norton, 2000.

Collins, Joseph J. *The Soviet Invasion of Afghanistan: A Study in the Use of Force in Soviet Foreign Policy.* Lexington, Mass.: Lexington Books, 1986.

Gall, Charlotte, and Tomas de Waal. *Chechnya: Calamity in the Caucasus.* New York: New York University Press, 1998.

Hough, Jerry F. *Russia and the West: Gorbachev and the Politics of Reform.* New York: Simon and Schuster, 1987.

Jaffee, Josef. *The Limited Partnership: Europe, the United States, and the Burdens of Alliance.* Cambridge, Mass.: Ballinger, 1987.

Jentleson, Bruce W. *Pipeline Politics: The Complex Political Economy of East-West Energy.* Ithaca, N.Y.: Cornell University Press, 1986.

Kugler, Richard L. *Commitment to Purpose: How Alliance Partnership Won the Cold War* [NATO]. Santa Monica, Calif.: Rand, 1994.

Laquer, Walter, and Robert Hunter. *European Peace Movements and the Future of the Western Alliance.* New Brunswick, N.J.: Transaction Books, 1985.

McGwire, Michael. *Military Objectives in Soviet Foreign Policy.* Washington, D.C.: Brookings, 1987.

Michta, Andrew A., ed. *America's New Allies: Poland, Hungary and the Czech Republic.* Seattle: University of Washington Press, 1999.

Oberdorfer, Don. *The Turn: From the Cold War to a New Era: The United States and the Soviet Union, 1983–1990.* New York: Poseidon Press, 1991.

Padoa-Schioppa, Tommso. *The Road to Monetary Union in Europe: The Emperor, the Kings, and the Genie.* New York: Oxford University Press, 1994.

Rady, Martyn. *Romania in Turmoil.* London: I.B. Tauris, 1992.

Smith, Steven K., and Douglas A. Wertman. *U.S.-West European Relations During the Reagan Years.* New York: St. Martin's Press, 1992.

Szabo, Stephen F. *The Diplomacy of German Unification.* New York: St. Martin's Press, 1995.

Tucker, Robert C. *Political Culture and Leadership in Soviet Russia: From Lenin to Gorbachev.* New York: Norton, 1987.

Wheaton, Bernard, and Zdenek Kavan. *The Velvet Revolution: Czechoslovakia, 1988–1991.* Boulder, Colo.: Westview Press, 1992.

Whelan, Joseph G. *The Moscow Summit, 1988.* Boulder, Colo.: Westview, 1990.

Zelikow, Philip, and Condoleeza Rice. *Germany Unified and Europe Transformed.* Cambridge, Mass.: Harvard University Press, 1995.

Middle East

Aronson, Geoffrey. *Creating Facts: Israel, Palestinians and the West Bank.* Washington, D.C.: Institute for Palestine Studies, 1987.

Beilin, Yossi. *Touching Peace: From the Oslo Accords to a Final Agreement.* Trans. by Philip Simpson. London: Weidenfeld and Nicolson, 1999.

Brune, Lester H. *America and the Iraqi Crisis of 1990–1992.* Claremont, Calif.: Regina Books, 1993.

————. *Kosovo Intervention and United States Policy.* On internet at 1stBooks.com.

Butler, Richard. *The Greatest Threat: Iraq, Weapons of Mass Destruction, and the Crisis of Global Society.* New York: Public Affairs Press, 2000.

Chubin, Shahram. *Iran's National Security Policy.* Washington, D.C.: Brookings, 1994.

Cockburn, Andrew, and Patrick Cockburn. *Out of the Ashes: The Resurrection of Saddam Hussein.* New York: Harper Collins, 2000.

Crystal, Jill. *Oil and Politics in the Gulf.* New York: Cambridge University Press, 1990.

Frank, Benis M. *U.S. Marines in Lebanon, 1982–1984.* Washington, D.C.: History and Museums Division, U.S. Marine Corps, 1987.

Freedman, Lawrence, and Efraim Karsh. *The Gulf Conflict, 1990–1991.* Princeton, N.J.: Princeton University Press, 1993.

Friedlander, Melvin A. *Sadat and Begin: The Domestic Politics of Peacemaking.* Boulder, Colo.: Westview Press, 1983.

Friedman, Thomas L. *From Beirut to Jerusalem.* New York: Farrar, Straus and Giroux, 1989.

Gabriel, Richard A. *Operation Peace for Galilee: The Israeli-PLO War in Lebanon.* New York: Hill & Wang, 1984.

Graham-Brown, Sarah. *Sanctioning Saddam: The Politics of Intervention in Iraq.* New York: St. Martin's Press, 1999.

Hammel, Eric. *The Root: The Marines in Beirut, August 1982–February 1984.* San Diego, Calif.: Harcourt Brace Jovanovich, 1985.

Hawaz, Khidir, with Jeff Stein. *Saddam's Bombmaker: The Terrifying Inside Story of the Iraqi Nuclear and Biological Weapons Agenda.* New York: Lisa Drew/Scribner, 2000.

Hiro, Dilip. *The Longest War: The Iran-Iraq Military Conflict.* New York: Routledge, 1987.

Hof, Frederic C. *Galilee Divided: The Israel-Lebanon Frontier, 1916–1984.* Boulder, Colo.: Westview Press, 1985.

Kahan Commission. *The Beirut Massacre. The Complete Kahan Commission Report.* New York: Karz-Cohl, 1983.

Keddie, Nikki, and Eric Hooglund, eds. *The Iranian Revolution and the Islamic Republic.* Syracuse, N.Y.: Syracuse University Press, 1986.

Khalidi, Rashid. *Under Siege. PLO Decision Making During the 1982 War.* New York: Columbia University Press, 1986.

Lockman, Zachary, and Joel Beinin, eds. *Intifada: The Palestinian Uprising Against Israeli Occupation.* Boston: South End Press, 1989.

Long, David E. *The United States and Saudi Arabia: Ambivalent Allies.* Boulder, Colo.: Westview Press, 1985.

Rubenberg, Cheryl A. *Israel and the American National Interest.* Champaign: University of Illinois Press, 1986.

Safran, Nadav. *Saudi Arabia: The Ceaseless Quest for Security*. Cambridge, Mass.: Belknap/Harvard University Press, 1985.

Salem, Elie. *Violence and Diplomacy in Lebanon, 1982–1988*. New York: St. Martin's Press, 1995.

Schiff, Ze'ev, and Ehud Ya'ari. *Intifada: The Palestinian Uprising—Israel's Third Front*. New York: Simon and Schuster, 1990.

Wright, Robin. *The Last Great Revolution: Turmoil and Transformation in Iran*. New York: Knopf, 2000.

Arms and Arms Control

Adelman, Kenneth. *The Great Universal Embrace: Arms Summitry—A Skeptic's Account*. New York: Simon and Schuster, 1989.

Alibel, Ken, and Stephen Handelman. *Biohazard: The Chilling True Story of the Largest Covert Biological Weapons Program in History—Told from the Inside by the Man Who Ran It*. New York: Random House, 1999.

Ball, Desmond, and Jeffrey Richelson. *Strategic Nuclear Targeting*. Ithaca, N.Y.: Cornell University Press, 1986.

Broad, William J. *Star Warriors: A Penetrating Look into the Lives of the Young Scientists Behind our Space Age Weaponry*. New York: Simon and Schuster, 1986.

———. *Teller's War: The Top Secret Story behind the Star Wars Deception*. New York: Simon and Schuster, 1992.

Center for Defense Information. *U.S.-Soviet Military Facts* 18, no. 5 (1988): entire issue.

Cockburn, Andrew. *The Threat: Inside the Soviet Military Machine*. New York: Random House, 1983.

Croll, Mike. *The History of Landmines*. London: Leo Company, 1998.

Daalder, Ivo H. *The SDI Challenge to Europe*. Cambridge, Mass.: Ballinger, 1987.

Douglass, Joseph D., Jr., and Neil C. Livingstone. *America the Vulnerable: The Threat of Chemical/Biological Warfare*. Lexington, Mass.: Lexington Books, 1987.

Emerson, Steve. *Secret Warriors: Inside the Covert Operations of the Reagan Era*. New York: Putnam, 1988.

Evans, Grant. *The Yellow Rainmakers*. New York: Verso, 1983.

Farrell, Theo. *Weapons Without a Cause: The Politics of Weapons Acquisition in the United States*. New York: Macmillan / St. Martin's, 1997.

Fitzgerald, Frances. *Way Out There in The Blue: Reagan, Star Wars and the End of the Cold War*. New York: Simon and Schuster, 2000.

Friedberg, Aaron L. *In the Shadow of the Garrison State: America's Anti-Statism and Its Cold War Grand Strategy*. Princeton, N.J.: Princeton University Press, 2000.

Gervasi, Tom. *The Myth of Soviet Military Supremacy*. New York: Harper & Row, 1986.

Green, William C., and Theodore Karasik, eds. *Gorbachev and His Generals: The Reform of Soviet Military Doctrine*. Boulder, Colo.: Westview Press, 1990.

Guillemin, Jeanne. *Anthrax: The Investigation of a Deadly Outbreak*. Berkeley: University of California Press, 1999.

Halloran, Bernard F. *Essays on Arms Control and National Security*. Washington, D.C.: United States Arms Control and Disarmament Agency, 1987.

Harris, Elisa D. "Sverdlovsk and Yellow Rain: Two Cases of Noncompliance?" *International Security* 2: 4 (1987): pp. 41–95.

Hoover, Robert A. *The MX Controversy: A Guide to Issues and References.* Claremont, Calif.: Regina Books, 1982.

Kan, Hideki. "The Reagan Administration and the Expansion of the Military-Industrial Complex." *Journal of American and Canadian Studies* 3 (Spring 1987): 166–178.

Krepon, Michael. *Arms Control in the Reagan Era.* Lanham, Md: University Press of America, 1987.

Odom, William E. *America's Military Revolution: Strategy and Structure after the Cold War.* Washington, D.C.: American University Press, 1993.

———. *The Collapse of the Soviet Military.* New Haven, Conn.: Yale University Press, 1998.

McDonald, John W., Jr., and Diane Bendahmane. *U.S. Bases Overseas Negotiations with Spain, Greece and the Philippines.* Boulder, Colo.: Westview Press, 1990.

Mendel, Richard A. *The Defense Game: An Insider Explores the Astonishing Realities of America's Defense Establishment.* New York: Harper and Row, 1986.

Nunn, Sam. *Reports of a Task Force: U.S–Russia–NIS Cooperations to Prevent Deadly Conflict* [on Nunn-Lugar aid to former Soviet republics]. New York: Carnegie Corporation, 1999.

Pugh, Michael. *The ANZUS Crisis, Nuclear Visiting and Deterrence.* New York: Cambridge University Press, 1989.

President's Commission on Defense Management, Final Report. *A Quest for Excellence* [Report of Packard Commission].Washington, D.C.: GPO, 1986.

Sagan, Carl. "Nuclear War and Climate Catastrophe: Some Policy Implications." *Foreign Affairs* 62 (Winter 1983–1984): 257–291. Ibid., 65 (Fall 1986: pp. 163–168).

Scheer, Robert. *With Enough Shovels: Reagan, Bush and Nuclear War.* New York: Random House, 1982.

Scovill, Herbert, Jr, *MX: Prescription for Disaster.* Cambridge, Mass.: MIT Press, 1981.

Shimko, Keith L. *Images and Arms Control: Perceptions of the Soviet Union in the Reagan Administration.* Ann Arbor: University of Michigan Press, 1991.

Snyder, William P., and James Brown. *Defense Policies in the Reagan Administration.* Washington, D.C.: National Defense University, 1988.

Stares, Paul B. *The Militarization of Space: U.S. Policy, 1945–1984.* Ithaca, N.Y.: Cornell University Press, 1985.

———. *Space and National Security.* Washington, D.C.: Brookings Institution, 1987.

Talbott, Strobe. *Deadly Gambits: The Reagan Administration and the Stalemate in Nuclear Arms Control.* New York: Knopf, 1984.

Waller, Douglas C. *Congress and the Nuclear Freeze* [1982–1983]. Amhurst, Mass.: University of Massachusetts Press, 1987.

Waller, Douglas C., et al. *The Strategic Defense Initiative: Progress and Challenges.* Claremont, Calif.: Regina Books, 1987.

Wise, David. *Cassidy's Run: The Secret War over Nerve Gas.* New York: Random House, 1997.

Spies and Terrorism

Barron, John. *Breaking the Ring: The Bizarre Case of the Walker Family Ring.* Boston: Houghton Mifflin, 1987.

Carsese, Antonio. *Terrorism, Politics and Law: The Achille Lauro Affair.* Princeton, N.J.: Princeton University Press, 1989.

Duffy, Brian, and Steven Emerson. *The Fall of Pan Am 103: Inside the Lockerbie Investigation.* New York: Putnam, 1990.

Hayes, John Earl, and Harvey Klehr. *Venona: Decoding Soviet Espionage.* New Haven, Conn.: Yale University Press, 1999.

Hersh, Seymour M. *The Target Is Destroyed: What Really Happened to Flight 007 and What America Knew About It.* New York: Random House, 1986.

Kwitny, Jonathan. *The Crimes of Patriots: A True Tale of Dope, Dirty Money and the CIA.* New York: Norton, 1987.

Maas, Peter. *Killer Spy: The Inside Story of the FBI's Pursuit and Capture of Aldrich Ames, America's Deadliest Spy.* New York: Warner Books, 1995.

Weiner, Tim, David Johnson, and Neil A. Lewis. *Betrayal: The Story of Aldrich Ames: An American Spy.* New York: Random House, 1995.

Wise, David. *Nightmover* [on spy Aldrich Ames]. New York: Harpers Collins, 1995.

Woodward, Bob. *Veil: The Secret Wars of the CIA, 1981–1987.* New York: Simon and Schuster, 1987.

Special Topics

Blumenthal, Sidney, and Thomas Byrne Edsall, eds. *The Reagan Legacy.* New York: Pantheon, 1988.

Brandt Commission. *Common Crisis, North-South: Co-operation for World Recovery.* Cambridge: MIT Press, 1983.

Boutros-Ghali, Boutros. *Unvanquished: A US-UN Saga.* New York: Random House, 1999.

Brune, Lester H. *The United States and Post–Cold War Intervention in Somalia, Haiti, and Bosnia.* Claremont, Calif.: Regina Books, 1999.

Cahn, Anne Hessing. *Killing Détente: The Right Attacks the CIA.* University Park: Pennsylvania State University Press, 1998.

Damrosch, Lori Fisler, ed. *Enforcing Restraint.* New York: Council on Foreign Relations, 1993.

David, Steven R., and Peter Digeser. *The United States and the Law of the Sea Treaty.* Baltimore: Johns Hopkins University Press, 1990.

Destler, I.M., Leslie H. Gelb, and Anthony Lake. *Our Own Worst Enemy: The Unmaking of American Foreign Policy.* New York: Simon and Schuster, 1985.

Drew, Elizabeth. *On the Edge: The Clinton Presidency.* New York: Simon and Schuster, 1994.

———. *Showdown: The Struggle between the Gingrich Congress and the White House.* New York: Simon and Schuster, 1996.

Ehrlich, Paul, and Anne Ehrlich. *Betrayal of Science and Reason: How Anti-Environmental Rhetoric Threatens Our Future.* Washington, D.C.: Island Press, 1996.

Garthoff, Raymond. *Détente and Confrontation: American-Soviet Relations from Nixon to Reagan.* Washington, D.C.: Brookings, 1985.

Kirkpatrick, Jeane. "Dictatorships and Double Standards." *Commentary* 68 (November 1979): 34–45.

Lal, Deepak, and Martin Wolf, eds. *Stagflation, Savings, and the State: Perspectives on the Global Trade.* Princeton, N.J.: Princeton University Press, 1988.

Maynes, Charles Williams, and Richard S. Williamson, eds. *U.S. Foreign Policy and the United Nations.* New York: Norton, 1996.

Milner, Helen V. *Resisting Protectionism: Global Industries and the Politics of International Economy.* New York: Oxford University Press, 1986.

Oye, Kenneth A., Robert J. Lieter, and Donald Rothchild. *Eagle Resurgent? The Reagan Era in American Foreign Policy.* Boston: Little, Brown, 1987.

Pearson, David F. *KAL 007: The Cover-Up.* New York: Summit, 1990.

Perry, Charles M., and Robert L. Pfaltzgraff, Jr., eds. *Selling the Rope to Hang Capitalism? The Debate on West-East Trade and Technology Transfer.* Washington, D.C.: Pergamon-Brassey's, 1987.

Phillips, Kevin. *The Politics of Rich and Poor: Wealth and the American Electorate in the Reagan Aftermath.* New York: Random House, 1990.

Report of the President's Special Review Board [Tower Commission Report]. Washington, D.C.: GPO, February 26,1987.

Rosenfeld, Stephen S. "The Guns of July [Reagan Doctrine]. *Foreign Affairs* 64 (Spring 1986): 698–714.

Rotberg, Robert I., and Thomas G. Weiss. *From Massacres to Genocide: The Media, Public Policy, and Humanitarian Crises.* Washington, D.C.: Brookings Institution, 1996.

Appendix

Secretaries of State, 1781–2001

[Biographic information through 1977 is from U.S. Bureau of Public Affairs, Office of Public Communication. The Secretaries of State; Portraits and Biographical Sketches. Department of State Publication 8921. Department and Foreign Service Series 162. Washington: Government Printing Office, 1978. The data after 1977 has been provided by the compiler and editors.]

Robert R. Livingston (1781–1783) born in New York City, November 27, 1746; graduated from King's College (now Columbia) in 1765; married Mary Stevens in 1770; admitted to the bar the same year; member of the New York Provincial Convention 1775; delegate to the Continental Congress 1775–1776, 1779–1780, 1784–1785; served on several congressional committees including the committee to draft the Declaration of Independence; delegate to the New York State constitutional convention, 1777, and with Gouverneur Morris and John Jay drafted that state's constitution; helped secure New York's ratification of the Constitution in 1788; served as head of the Department of Foreign Affairs, the forerunner of the Department of State, 1781–1783; administered the presidential oath of office to George Washington in 1789; in 1801 became U.S. Minister to France; while there, helped effect the 1803 Louisiana Purchase; member of the New York Canal Commission in 1811; patron and partner of Robert Fulton; died at his estate in Clermont, New York, February 26, 1813.

John Jay (1784–1790) born in New York City, December 12, 1745; graduated from King's College in 1764; admitted to the bar in 1768 and practiced law; married Sarah Van Brugh Livingston in 1774; member of the Continental Congress 1774–1779; as a member of the New York Provincial Congress in 1776–1777, aided in obtaining approval of the Declaration of Independence and in drafting the state constitution; Chief Justice of New York State 1777–1778; President of the Continental Congress 1778–1779; Minister to Spain 1779–1782; one of the Commissioners named in 1781 to negotiate peace with Great Britain, signed the treaties of 1782 and 1783; took office as Secretary for Foreign Affairs under the Continental Congress December 21, 1784, served until the establishment of government under the Constitution, and continued unofficially to superintend the Department until Jefferson took office as Secretary of State on March 22, 1790; during his tenure of office, treaties of commerce with Prussia and Morocco and a consular convention with France were negotiated; Chief Justice of the United States 1789–1795; Minister to Great Britain 1794–1795, negotiated and signed Jay's Treaty; Governor of New York 1795–1801; retired to his farm at Bedford, near New York City, where he died May 17, 1829.

Thomas Jefferson (1790–1793) born at "Shadwell," Goochland (now Albemarle) County, Virginia, April 13, 1743; graduated from the College of William and Mary in 1762; admitted to the bar and commenced practice in 1767; held various local public offices; member of the Virginia House of Burgesses 1769–1775; married Martha (Wayles) Skelton in 1772; member of the Continental Congress 1775–1776; prepared the first draft of the Declaration of Independence and signed the final Declaration; member of the Virginia House of Delegates 1776–1779; Governor of Virginia 1779–1781; again a member of the Continental Congress 1783–1784; one of three Ministers named in 1784 to negotiate treaties with European nations and the Barbary States; Minister to France 1785–1789; commissioned Secretary of State in President Washington's Cabinet September 26, 1789, entered upon his duties March 22, 1790, and served until December 31, 1793; as Secretary of State, successfully administered a policy of neutrality in the war between Great Britain and France; Vice President of the United States 1797–1801; President of the United States 1801–1809; retired to "Monticello," his estate in Virginia; engaged in literary, architectural, scientific, and agricultural pursuits; participated in the founding and served as rector of the University of Virginia; died at "Monticello," Albemarle County, Virginia, July 4, 1826.

Edmund Randolph (1794–1795) born at "Tazewell Hall," near Williamsburg, Virginia, August 10, 1753; attended the College of William and Mary; admitted to the bar and practiced in Williamsburg; appointed aide-de-camp to General Washington in 1775; member of the Virginia constitutional convention and Mayor of Williamsburg in 1776; married Elizabeth Nicholas the same year; Attorney General of Virginia 1776–1786; member of the Continental Congress 1779–1782; Governor of Virginia 1786–1788; delegate to the Annapolis Convention of 1786 and to the federal constitutional convention of 1787, member of the Virginia convention of 1788 that ratified the Constitution; member of the State House of Delegates 1788–1789; Attorney General in President Washington's Cabinet 1789–1794; commissioned Secretary of State January 2, 1794, entered upon his duties the same day, and served until August 20, 1795; as Secretary of State, directed the negotiation of the treaty of 1795 with Spain; moved to Richmond and resumed the practice of law; senior counsel for Aaron Burr in the treason trial of 1807; died in Clarke County, Virginia, September 12, 1813.

Timothy Pickering (1795–1800) born in Salem, Massachusetts, July 17, 1745; graduated from Harvard College in 1763; admitted to the bar in 1768 and commenced practice in Salem; held various local public offices; entered the Revolutionary Army as a colonel in 1775; elected to the State Legislature in 1776; married Rebecca White the same year; appointed Adjutant General and elected by the Continental Congress as a member of the Board of War in 1777; Quartermaster General of the Army 1780–1785; entered mercantile business in Philadelphia in 1785; organized Luzerne County, Pennsylvania, and represented it in the convention of 1787 that ratified the federal Constitution and in the state constitutional convention of 1789–1790; Postmaster General 1791–1795; Secretary of War in President Washington's Cabinet in 1795; Secretary of State ad interim August 20–December 9, 1795; commissioned Secretary of State December 10, 1795, entered upon his duties the same day, and served until May 12, 1800, when he was dismissed from office; as Secretary of State, opposed the French in the "XYZ Affair" of 1797–1798 and entered into preparations for war; became

Chief Justice of the Massachusetts Court of Common Pleas in 1802; Senator from Massachusetts 1803–1811; member of the State Executive Council 1812–1813; Representative from Massachusetts 1813–1817; died in Salem, January 29, 1829.

John Marshall (1800–1801) born near Germantown, in what became Fauquier County, Virginia, September 24, 1755; privately educated; officer in the Revolution; studied law at the College of William and Mary, admitted to the bar in 1780 and began practice; member of the Virginia Assembly 1782–1791 and 1795–1797; member of the state Executive Council 1782–1784; married Mary Willis Ambler in 1783; member of the Virginia convention of 1788 that ratified the federal Constitution; one of the "XYZ" commissioners of 1797–1798 to adjust differences with France; Representative from Virginia 1799–1800; commissioned Secretary of State in President Adams' Cabinet May 13, 1800, entered upon his duties June 6, 1800, and served until February 4, 1801; as Secretary of State, directed the negotiation of the reconciliation convention of 1800 with France; commissioned Chief Justice of the United States January 31, 1801, and took office February 4, 1801; continued as Secretary of State ad interim February 4–March 4, 1801; member of the Virginia constitutional convention of 1829; author of a five-volume biography of George Washington; during thirty-four years as Chief Justice of the United States, established the authority and prestige of the Supreme Court; died in Philadelphia, Pennsylvania, July 6, 1835.

James Madison (1801–1809) born at Port Conway, Virginia, March 16, 1751; graduated from the College of New Jersey in 1771; studied law and was admitted to the bar; elected to the Virginia constitutional convention and member of the state Assembly in 1776; member of the state Executive Council 1778–1779; member of the Continental Congress 1780–1783 and 1786–1788; Virginia House of Delegates 1784–1786; delegate to the Annapolis convention of 1786 and to the federal convention of 1787, where he played a major part in the framing of the Constitution; cooperated with Hamilton and Jay on a series of essays later published as *The Federalist*; member of the Virginia convention of 1788 that ratified the Constitution; Representative from Virginia 1789–1797; married Dolly (Payne) Todd in 1794; again a member of the House of Delegates in 1799; served as presidential elector in 1800; commissioned Secretary of State in President Jefferson's Cabinet March 5, 1801, entered upon his duties May 2, 1801, and served until March 3, 1809; during his tenure of office France offered and the United States accepted the Louisiana Purchase; President of the United States 1809–1817; retired to "Montpellier" (now "Montpelier"), his estate in Virginia; became rector of the University of Virginia in 1826; member of the Virginia constitutional convention of 1829; died at "Montpellier," Orange County, Virginia, June 28, 1836.

Robert Smith (1809–1811) born in Lancaster, Pennsylvania, November 3, 1757; moved with his parents to Baltimore, Maryland, at an early age; graduated from the College of New Jersey in 1781; served briefly as a private in the Continental Army; studied law, admitted to the bar in Baltimore, and soon had a large admiralty practice; one of the presidential electors of Maryland in 1789; married Margaret Smith in 1790; member of the Maryland Senate 1793–1795, and of the House of Delegates 1796–1800; sat in the Baltimore city council 1798–1801; served as Secretary of the Navy in President Jefferson's Cabinet 1801–1809; nominated, confirmed, and commissioned Attorney General in 1805, but did not serve; commissioned Secretary of State in President Madison's Cabinet March 6, 1809, entered upon his duties the same day, and served until April 1, 1811; as Secretary of State, negotiated the Smith Erskine Agreement of 1809, rejection of which by the British Government marked a turning point in the relations between the two countries, returned to Baltimore, where he filled offices in various private organizations; died in Baltimore, Maryland, November 26, 1842.

James Monroe (1811–1817) born in Westmoreland County, Virginia, April 28, 1758; attended the College of William and Mary 1774–1776; officer in the Continental Army; studied law under Jefferson 1780–1783; member of the Virginia Assembly in 1782 and 1786; member of the Continental Congress 1783–1786; attended the Annapolis convention of 1786; married Eliza Kortright the same year; admitted to the bar and practiced in Fredericksburg; member of the state convention of 1788 that ratified the federal Constitution; Senator from Virginia 1790–1794; Minister to France 1794–1796; Governor of Virginia 1799–1802; again Minister to France in 1803; served as Minister to Great Britain 1803–1807; headed a diplomatic mission to Spain 1804–1805; again elected to the Virginia Assembly in 1810; again Governor of Virginia in 1811; commissioned Secretary of State in President Madison's Cabinet April 2, 1811, entered upon his duties April 6, 1811, and served until September 30, 1814; both Secretary of War and Secretary of State ad interim October 1, 1814–February 28, 1815; again commissioned Secretary of State February 28, 1815, entered upon his duties the same day, and served until March 3, 1817; during his tenure of office the War of 1812 was fought and the Treaty of Ghent, which restored peace, was negotiated; President of the United States 1817–1825; retired to his farm in Virginia; presiding officer of the Virginia constitutional convention of 1829; died in New York City, July 4, 1831.

John Quincy Adams (1817–1825) born in Braintree (now Quincy), Massachusetts, July 11, 1767; studied in France and the Netherlands; served briefly as private secretary to the American Minister in Russia in 1781; secretary to his father during the peace negotiations with Great Britain 1782–1783; graduated from Harvard University in 1787; admitted to the bar in 1790 and practiced in Boston; served as Minister Resident to the Netherlands 1794–1797; married Louisa Catherine Johnson in 1797; Minister to Prussia 1797–1801; elected to the Massachusetts Senate in 1802; Senator from Massachusetts 1803–1808; professor of rhetoric and oratory at Harvard 1806–1809; Minister to Russia 1809–1814; head of the commission that negotiated the Treaty of Ghent with Great Britain in 1814; Minister to Great Britain 1815–1817; commissioned Secretary of State in President Monroe's Cabinet March 5, 1817, entered upon his duties September 22, 1817, and served until March 3, 1825; as Secretary of State, negotiated the treaty of 1819 with Spain for the cession of the Floridas and collaborated with the President in the formulation of the Monroe Doctrine; President of the United States 1825–1829; Representative from Massachusetts 1831–1848; author of many writings and speeches and a notable diary covering half a century; died in Washington, D. C., February 23, 1848.

Henry Clay (1825–1829) born in Hanover County, Virginia, April 12, 1777; attended public school; studied law in Richmond, Virginia; admitted to the bar and commenced practice in Lexington, Kentucky, in 1797; married Lucretia Hart in 1799; served in the state House of Representatives 1803–1806; Senator from Kentucky 1806–1807; served again in the state House of Representatives 1807–1809; again Senator from Kentucky 1810–1811; Representative from Kentucky and Speaker of the House 1811–1814; one of the Commissioners who negotiated the Treaty of Ghent with Great Britain in 1814; again Representative from Kentucky 1815–1821 and 1823–1825, and Speaker of the House 1815–1820 and 1823–1825; unsuccessful candidate for the presidency in 1824; commissioned Secretary of State in President John Quincy Adams' Cabinet March 7, 1825, entered upon his duties the same day, and served until March 3, 1829; as Secretary of State, negotiated a number of commercial treaties and sought unsuccessfully to have the United States participate in the Inter-American Congress at Panama in 1826; again Senator from Kentucky 1831–1842; Whig candidate for the Presidency in 1832 and in 1844; in retirement 1845–1848; again Senator from Kentucky 1849–1852; died in Washington, D.C., June 29, 1852.

Martin Van Buren (1829–1831) born at Kinderhook, near Albany, New York, December 5, 1782; attended local schools; admitted to the bar and commenced practice in Kinderhook in 1803; married Hannah Hoes in 1807; moved to Hudson, New York, where he was surrogate 1808–1813; served in the state Senate 1812–1820; chosen regent of the University of New York in 1815; state Attorney General 1816–1819, residing in Albany; delegate to the state constitutional convention of 1821; Senator from New York 1821–1828; Governor of New York in 1829; commissioned Secretary of State in President Jackson's Cabinet March 6, 1829, entered upon his duties March 28, 1829, and served until May 23, 1831; as Secretary of State, settled a long-standing dispute with Great Britain over West Indian trade and obtained important treaties with Turkey and France; served as Minister to Great Britain 1831–1832 on a recess appointment that failed confirmation by the Senate; Vice-President of the United States 1833–1837; President of the United States 1837–1841; unsuccessful candidate for the presidency on the Democratic ticket in 1840 and on the Free-soil ticket in 1848; retired to "Lindenwald," his country home at Kinderhook, New York, where he died July 24, 1862.

Edward Livingston (1831–1833) born at "Clermont", Columbia County, New York, May 28, 1764; graduated from the College of New Jersey in 1781; admitted to the bar in 1785 and practiced in New York City; married Mary McEvers in 1788 (she died 1801); Representative from New York 1795–1801; United States Attorney for the District of New York and Mayor of New York City 1801–1803; moved to New Orleans in 1804 and practiced law; married Louise Moreau de Lassey (née D'Avezac) in 1805; aide to General Jackson at the Battle of New Orleans; elected to the Louisiana House of Representatives in 1820; prepared a penal code for the state which, though not adopted, brought him fame; engaged in a protracted controversy with the federal government over title to land known as Batture Sainte Marie, which was finally decided in his favor; Representative from Louisiana 1823–1829; Senator from Louisiana 1829–1831; commissioned Secretary of State in President Jackson's Cabinet May 24, 1831, entered upon his duties the same day, and served until May 29, 1833; as Secretary of State, drafted the celebrated Nullification Proclamation of 1832; Minister to France

1833–1835; died at "Montgomery Place," Dutchess County, New York, May 23, 1836.

Louis McLane (1833–1834) born in Smyrna, Delaware, May 28, 1786; midshipman in the Navy 1798–1801; attended Newark Academy (now the University of Delaware); admitted to the bar in 1807 and commenced practice in Smyrna; married Catherine Mary Milligan in 1812; served in the War of 1812; Representative from Delaware 1817–1827; Senator from Delaware 1827–1829; Minister to Great Britain 1829–1831; Secretary of the Treasury in President Jackson's Cabinet 1831–1833; commissioned Secretary of State May 29, 1833, entered upon his duties the same day, and served until June 30, 1834; as Secretary of State, reorganized the Department, introducing systematic procedure into its operations; became president of the Morris Canal and Banking Company in New York City; moved to Baltimore, Maryland, where he was president of the Baltimore and Ohio Railroad Company 1837–1847; while holding the last-mentioned position, again Minister to Great Britain 1845–1846; delegate to the Maryland constitutional convention of 1850; died in Baltimore, October 7, 1857.

John Forsyth (1834–1841) born in Fredericksburg, Virginia, October 22, 1780; moved to Augusta, Georgia, with his parents; graduated from the College of New Jersey in 1799; admitted to the bar in 1802 and commenced practice in Augusta; married Clara Meigs in 1801 or 1802; became Attorney General of Georgia in 1808; Representative from Georgia 1813–1818; Senator from Georgia 1818–1819; Minister to Spain 1819–1823; again Representative from Georgia 1823–1827; Governor of Georgia 1827–1829; again Senator from Georgia 1829–1834; delegate to the anti-tariff convention at Milledgeville, Georgia, in 1832; earned the reputation of being one of the most powerful debaters of his time; commissioned Secretary of State in President Jackson's Cabinet June 27, 1834, entered upon his duties July 1, 1834, continued in office under President Van Buren, and served until March 3, 1841; as Secretary of State, brought to a successful conclusion a serious controversy with France regarding payment under the claims convention of 1831; died in Washington, D.C., October 21, 1841.

Daniel Webster (1841–1843, 1850–1852) born in Salisbury, New Hampshire, January 18, 1782; graduated from Dartmouth College in 1801; taught school; admitted to the bar in 1805 and commenced practice in Boscawen, New Hampshire; moved to Portsmouth, New Hampshire, in 1807; married Grace Fletcher in 1808 (she died 1828); Representative from New Hampshire 1813–1817; moved to Boston in 1816 and soon became known as one of the foremost lawyers and orators of his time; presidential elector in 1820; delegate to the Massachusetts constitutional convention of 1820–1821; member of the state House of Representatives in 1822; Representative from Massachusetts 1823–1827; Senator from Massachusetts 1827–1841; married Caroline Le Roy in 1829; nominated by the state legislature for the presidency in 1836; commissioned Secretary of State in President Harrison's Cabinet March 5, 1841, entered upon his duties March 6, 1841, continued in office under President Tyler, and served until May 8, 1843; as Secretary of State, negotiated the famous Webster-Ashburton Treaty of 1842 with Great Britain; again Senator from Massachusetts 1845–1850; commissioned Secretary of State in President Fillmore's Cabinet July 22, 1850, entered upon his duties July 23, 1850, and served until his death in Marshfield, Massachusetts, October 24, 1852.

Abel Parker Upshur (1843–1844) born at "Vaucluse," Northampton County, Virginia, June 17, 1791; attended the College of New Jersey and Yale College; admitted to the bar in 1810 and practiced in Richmond; member of the Virginia House of Delegates 1812–1813 and 1825–1827; married Elizabeth Dennis, who died; married Elizabeth A. B. Upshur in 1826; judge of the General Court of Virginia 1826–1829; delegate to the state constitutional convention of 1829; judge of the reorganized General Court 1830–1841; Secretary of the Navy in President Tyler's Cabinet 1841–1843; served as Secretary of State ad interim June 24–July 23, 1843; commissioned Secretary of State July 24, 1843, entered upon his duties the same day, and served until his death; as Secretary of State, reopened negotiations for the annexation of Texas; killed by the explosion of a gun aboard the U. S. warship Princeton on the Potomac River about fifteen miles below Washington, D.C., February 28, 1844.

John Caldwell Calhoun (1844–1845) was born at "the Long Canes settlement," in what became Abbeville County, South Carolina, March 18, 1782; graduated from Yale College in 1804 and from Litchfield Law School in 1806; admitted to the bar in 1807 and commenced practice in Abbeville, South Carolina; married Floride Bonneau Colhoun in 1811; gave up the practice of law and established himself as a planter; member of the state House of Representatives 1808–1809; Representative from South Carolina 1811–1817; Secretary of War in President Monroe's Cabinet 1817–1825; Vice President of the United States 1825–1832, resigned as Vice President; Senator from South Carolina 1832–1843; commissioned Secretary of State in President Tyler's Cabinet March 6, 1844, entered upon his duties April 1, 1844, and served until March 10, 1845; as Secretary of State, signed an abortive treaty for the annexation of Texas and aided in accomplishing annexation by joint resolution of Congress; delegate of South Carolina to, and presiding officer of, a railroad-and-waterway convention held in Memphis, Tennessee, in 1845; again Senator from South Carolina 1845–1850; author of voluminous writings and speeches; died in Washington, D.C., March 31, 1850.

James Buchanan (1845–1849) born at Cove Gap, near Mercersburg, Pennsylvania, April 23, 1791; graduated from Dickinson College in 1809; admitted to the bar in 1812 and practiced in Lancaster, Pennsylvania; served in the defense of Baltimore in the War of 1812; member of the Pennsylvania House of Representatives 1814–1816; Representative from Pennsylvania 1821–1831; Minister to Russia 1832–1833; Senator from Pennsylvania 1834–1845; commissioned Secretary of State in President Polk's Cabinet March 6, 1845, entered upon his duties March 10, 1845, and served until March 7, 1849; as Secretary of State, negotiated and signed the Oregon Treaty of 1846 with Great Britain, directed the negotiation of the Treaty of Guadalupe Hidalgo of 1848 with Mexico, and sought unsuccessfully to purchase Cuba from Spain; unsuccessful candidate for the Democratic presidential nomination in 1852; served as Minister to Great Britain 1853–1856; one of three United States Ministers who drew up the "Ostend Manifesto" of 1854; President of the United States 1857–1861; retired to "Wheatland," his country estate near Lancaster; never married; died at "Wheatland" June 1, 1868.

John Middleton Clayton (1849–1850) born at Dagsboro, Sussex County, Delaware, July 24, 1796; graduated from Yale College In 1815; attended Litchfield Law School; admitted to the bar in 1819, commenced practice in Dover, Delaware, and won a reputation unrivaled in the state; married Sarah Ann Fisher in 1822; member of the state House of Representatives 1824–1826; Secretary of State of Delaware 1826–1828; Senator from Delaware 1829–1836; delegate to the state constitutional convention of 1831; Chief Justice of Delaware 1837–1839; engaged in scientific farming near New Castle, Delaware, and gained a wide reputation as an agriculturist; again Senator from Delaware 1845–1849; commissioned Secretary of State in President Taylor's Cabinet March 7, 1849, entered upon his duties March 8, 1849, and served until July 22, 1850; as Secretary of State, negotiated and signed the Clayton-Bulwer Treaty of 1850 with Great Britain; resumed his agricultural pursuits; again Senator from Delaware 1853–1856; died in Dover, November 9, 1856.

Edward Everett (1852–1853) born in Dorchester, Massachusetts, April 11, 1794; graduated from Harvard University in 1811; pursued theological studies and received his M.A. in 1814; became pastor of the Brattle Street Unitarian Church, Boston, in 1814; studied and traveled in Europe 1815–1819, receiving his Ph.D. degree at Göttingen in 1817; occupied the chair of Greek literature at Harvard 1819–1825; edited the North American Review 1820–1824; married Charlotte Gray Brooks in 1822; Representative from Massachusetts 1825–1835; Governor of Massachusetts 1836–1839; Minister to Great Britain 1841–1845; president of Harvard 1846–1849; commissioned Secretary of State in President Fillmore's Cabinet November 6, 1852, entered upon his duties the same day, and served until March 3, 1853; as Secretary of State, declined a proposal of France and Great Britain that the United States enter into a convention with them guaranteeing to Spain the possession of Cuba; Senator from Massachusetts 1853–1854; became known as one of the greatest orators of his day; unsuccessful candidate for the Vice-Presidency on the Constitutional Union ticket in 1860; presidential elector in 1864; died in Boston, January 15, 1865.

William Learned Marcy (1853–1857) born in Sturbridge (now Southbridge), Massachusetts, December 12, 1786; graduated from Brown University in 1808; admitted to the bar in 1811 and commenced practice in Troy, New York; married Dolly Newell in 1812 (she died 1821); served in the War of 1812; recorder of Troy 1816–1818 and 1821–1823; became adjutant General of New York in 1821; state Comptroller 1823–1829; married Cornelia Knower about 1825; Associate Justice of the state Supreme Court 1829–1831; Senator from New York 1831–1833; Governor of New York 1833–1838; member of the Mexican Claims Commission 1840–1842; Secretary of War in President Polk's Cabinet 1845–1849; resumed the practice of law; commissioned Secretary of State in President Pierce's Cabinet March 7, 1853, entered upon his duties March 8, 1853, and served until March 6, 1857; as Secretary of State, negotiated or directed the negotiation of numerous treaties, among them the Gadsden Treaty of 1853 with Mexico and the reciprocity treaty of 1854 with Great Britain, and settled various delicate problems of international relations, among them the Koszta case with Austria, the Black Warrior case with Spain, and the Patrice Dillon case with France; died at Ballston Spa, New York, July 4, 1857.

Lewis Cass (1857–1860) born in Exeter, New Hampshire, October 9, 1782; attended Exeter Academy; went to the Northwest Territory in 1799; admitted to the bar in 1802 and practiced in Zanesville, Ohio; married Elizabeth Spencer in 1806; elected to the Ohio House of Representatives the same year; United States Marshal for the District of Ohio 1807–1812; served with distinction in the War of 1812, attaining the rank of brigadier general; Governor of Michigan Territory 1813–1831; Secretary of War in President Jackson's Cabinet 1831–1836; served as Minister to France 1836–1842; unsuccessful candidate for Democratic presidential nomination in 1844 and again in 1852; Senator from Michigan 1845–1848; Democratic candidate for the Presidency in 1848; again Senator from Michigan 1849–1857; commissioned Secretary of State in President Buchanan's Cabinet March 6, 1857; entered upon his duties the same day, and served until December 14, 1860; as Secretary of State, obtained British acceptance of the American construction of the Clayton-Bulwer Treaty and abandonment by Great Britain of its claim to a right to visit and search American vessels; returned to his home in Detroit, Michigan, and engaged in literary pursuits; died in Detroit, June 17, 1866.

Jeremiah Sullivan Black (1860–1861) born near Stony Creek, Somerset County, Pennsylvania, January 10, 1810; attended public schools; admitted to the bar in 1830 and began the practice of law; appointed Deputy Attorney General of Somerset County in 1831; married Mary Forward in 1836; served as President Judge of the Court of Common Pleas for the sixteenth judicial district 1842–1851; elected to the state Supreme Court in 1851 and reelected in 1854, by lot serving the first three years as Chief Justice; served as Attorney General in President Buchanan's Cabinet 1857–1860; commissioned Secretary of State December 17, 1860, entered upon his duties the same day, and served until March 5, 1861; as Secretary of State, instructed the principal United States representatives in Europe to use their best efforts to prevent recognition of the Confederate States; appointed United States Supreme Court reporter in 1861 and prepared Blacks Reports, in two volumes; moved to York, Pennsylvania, and resumed the practice of law; engaged in controversial writing, member of the Pennsylvania constitutional convention of 1872–1873; counsel for William Belknap in his impeachment trial in 1876 and for Samuel J. Tilden before the Electoral Commission in 1877; died in York, August 19, 1883.

William Henry Seward (1861–1869) born at Florida, Orange County, New York, May 16, 1801; graduated from Union College in 1820; admitted to the bar in 1822 and commenced practice in Auburn, New York, in 1823; married Frances Miller in 1824; member of the State Senate 1830–1834; Governor of New York 1838–1842; resumed the practice of law; Senator from New York 1849–1861; unsuccessful candidate for the Republican presidential nomination in 1860; commissioned Secretary of State in President Lincoln's Cabinet March 5, 1861, entered upon his duties March 6, 1861, continued in office under President Johnson, and served until March 4, 1869; as Secretary of State, handled with skill the delicate relations of the United States with foreign nations during the Civil War, and in 1867 negotiated and signed the treaty with Russia for the cession of Alaska to the United States; made a trip around the world 1870–1871 and was everywhere accorded an enthusiastic reception; retired to his home in Auburn in 1871, where he died October 10, 1872.

Elihu Benjamin Washburne (1869) born in Livermore, Maine, September 23, 1816; attended the common schools; held an editorial position on the *Augusta Kennebec Journal*; attended Harvard Law School in 1839 and was admitted to the Massachusetts bar in 1840; moved to Galena, Illinois, later the same year and commenced the practice of law; delegate to the Whig National Conventions at Baltimore in 1844 and 1852; married Adéle Gratiot in 1845; Representative from Illinois 1853–1869; commissioned Secretary of State in President Grant's Cabinet March 5, 1869, entered upon his duties the same day, and served until March 16, 1869, a period of only twelve days; served as Minister to France 1869–1877 and was the only official representative of a foreign government to remain in Paris during the siege of 1870–1871 and the days of the Commune; on his return to the United States, settled in Chicago, Illinois, and engaged in historical and literary pursuits; unsuccessful candidate for the Republican presidential nomination in 1880; president of the Chicago Historical Society 1884–1887; died in Chicago October 22, 1887.

Hamilton Fish (1869–1877) born in New York City, August 3, 1808; graduated from Columbia College in 1827; admitted to the bar in 1830 and practiced in New York City; married Julia Kean in 1836; Representative from New York 1843–1845; Lieutenant Governor of New York in 1848 and Governor 1849–1850; Senator from New York 1851–1857; president general of the Society of the Cincinnati 1854–1893; during the Civil War, on a Board of Commissioners of the federal government for the relief and exchange of prisoners; president of the New York Historical Society 1867–1869; commissioned Secretary of State in President Grant's Cabinet March 11, 1869, entered upon his duties March 17, 1869, and served until March 12, 1877; as Secretary of State, was one of the Commissioners of the United States who negotiated the Treaty of Washington of 1871 with Great Britain for the settlement of differences between the two countries, directed negotiations that resulted in the settlement of American claims against Spain, and signed the reciprocity treaty of 1875 with Hawaii; retired from public life; died at "Glen Clyffe," his estate near Garrison, New York, September 7, 1893.

William Maxwell Evarts (1877–1881) born in Boston, Massachusetts, February 6, 1818; graduated from Yale College in 1837; attended Harvard Law School 1838–1839; admitted to the bar in 1841 and practiced in New York City; married Helen Minerva Wardner in 1843; Assistant United States Attorney for the Southern District of New York 1849–1853; chairman of the New York delegation to the Republican National Convention at Chicago in 1860; member of a government mission to Great Britain 1863–1864; delegate to the New York State constitutional convention of 1867–1868; chief counsel for President Johnson in the impeachment trial of 1868; Attorney General in President Johnson's Cabinet 1868–1869; one of counsel for the United States before the tribunal of arbitration at Geneva 1871–1872; chief counsel for the Republican Party before the Electoral Commission in 1877; commissioned Secretary of State in President Hayes' Cabinet March 12, 1877, entered upon his duties the same day, and served until March 7, 1881; as Secretary of State, defined American policy with regard to an isthmian canal, took a strong stand toward Mexico in defense of American lives and property, and directed the negotiation of treaties with China relating to commerce and immigration; delegate to the International Monetary Conference at Paris in 1881; Senator from New York 1885–1891; died in New York City, February 28, 1901.

James Gillespie Blaine (1881, 1889–1892) born in West Brownsville, Pennsylvania, January 31, 1830; graduated from Washington College in 1847; taught school in Kentucky; married Harriet Stanwood in 1850; taught school and studied law in Philadelphia 1852–1854; moved in 1854 to Maine, where he purchased an interest in the *Augusta Kennebec Journal* and served on the editorial staff of the *Portland Advertiser*; one of the founders of the Republican Party; member of the Maine House of Representatives 1859–1862 and Speaker of the House 1861–1862; served as chairman of the Republican State Committee 1859–1881; Representative from Maine 1863–1876 and Speaker of the House 1869–1875; Senator from Maine 1876–1881; unsuccessful candidate for the Republican presidential nomination of 1876 and again in 1880; commissioned Secretary of State in President Garfield's Cabinet March 5, 1881, entered upon his duties March 7, 1881, continued in office under President Arthur, and served until December 19, 1881; Republican candidate for the Presidency in 1884; commissioned Secretary of State in President Harrison's Cabinet March 5, 1889, entered upon his duties March 7, 1889, and served until June 4, 1892; as Secretary of State, convened and presided over the First Pan American Conference in 1889; died in Washington, D.C., January 27, 1893.

Frederick Theodore Frelinghuysen (1881–1885) born in Millstone, New Jersey, August 4, 1817; graduated from Rutgers College in 1836; admitted to the bar in 1839 and practiced in Newark, New Jersey; married Matilde E. Griswold in 1842; city attorney of Newark in 1849 and a member of the city council in 1850; trustee of Rutgers College 1851–1885; representative of New Jersey at the peace congress held in Washington, D.C., early in 1861; Attorney General of New Jersey 1861–1866; Senator from New Jersey 1866–1869 and 1871–1877; member of the Electoral Commission of 1877 to decide the contested presidential election of 1876; resumed the practice of law; commissioned Secretary of State in President Arthur's Cabinet December 12, 1881, entered upon his duties December 19, 1881, and served until March 6, 1885; as Secretary of State, fostered commercial relations with Latin America, sent delegates to the Berlin Conference of 1884–1885 on the Congo, and opened treaty relations with Korea; died in Newark, May 20, 1885.

Thomas Francis Bayard (1885–1889) born in Wilmington, Delaware, October 29, 1828; attended private schools and an academy at Flushing, New York; studied law, was admitted to the bar in 1851, and commenced practice in Wilmington; United States District Attorney for Delaware 1853–1854; moved to Philadelphia, Pennsylvania, and practiced law there, returning to Wilmington in 1858; married Louise Lee in 1856 (she died 1886); Senator from Delaware 1869–1885; member of the Electoral Commission of 1877 to decide the contested presidential election of 1876; unsuccessful candidate for the Democratic presidential nomination in 1876, in 1880, and again in 1884; commissioned Secretary of State in President Cleveland's Cabinet March 6, 1885, entered upon his duties March 7, 1885, and served until March 6, 1889; as Secretary of State, paved the way for settlement of the Samoan question with Great Britain and Germany, arranged a solution regarding fisheries that allayed difficulties with Canada, and upheld the special interest of the United States in the Hawaiian Islands; resumed the practice of law in

Wilmington; married Mary W. Clymer in 1889; served as Ambassador to Great Britain 1893–1897; died in Dedham, Massachusetts, September 28, 1898.

John Watson Foster (1892–1893) born in Pike County, Indiana, March 2, 1836; graduated from Indiana University in 1855 (A.M. 1858); attended Harvard Law School; admitted to the bar in 1857 and commenced practice in Evansville, Indiana; married Mary Parke McFerson in 1859; served in the Union Army, attaining the rank of brevet brigadier general; edited the Evansville Daily Journal 1865–1869 and postmaster of Evansville 1869–1873; chairman of the Republican State Committee in 1872; Minister to Mexico 1873–1880 and Minister to Russia 1880–1881; established an international law practice in Washington, D.C.; Minister to Spain 1883–1885; special plenipotentiary to negotiate reciprocity agreements 1890–1891; agent of the United States in the Fur-seal Arbitration 1892–1893; commissioned Secretary of State in President Harrison's Cabinet June 29, 1892, entered upon his duties the same day, and served until February 23, 1893; as Secretary of State signed the abortive treaty of 1893 for the annexation of Hawaii; Commissioner for China in the negotiation of the treaty of peace of 1895 with Japan; Ambassador on special mission to Great Britain and Russia in 1897; agent of the United States before the Alaska Boundary Tribunal in 1903; represented China at the Second Hague Conference in 1907; author of numerous published writings; died in Washington, November 15, 1917.

Walter Quintin Gresham (1893–1895) born near Lanesville, Harrison County, Indiana, March 17, 1832; attended Indiana University; admitted to the bar in 1854 and practiced in Corydon, Indiana; married Matilda McGrain in 1858; elected to the state Legislature in 1860; served in the Union Army, attaining the rank of brevet major general of volunteers; opened a law office in New Albany, Indiana, in 1865; financial agent of Indiana in New York City 1867–1869; delegate to the Republican National Convention at Chicago in 1868; United States Judge for the District of Indiana 1869–1883; Postmaster General in President Arthur's Cabinet 1883–1884 and Secretary of the Treasury briefly in 1884; United States Circuit Judge for the Seventh Judicial District 1884–1893; unsuccessful candidate for the Republican presidential nomination in 1888; went over to the Democratic Party in 1892; commissioned Secretary of State in President Cleveland's Cabinet March 6, 1893, entered upon his duties March 7, 1893, and served until his death; as Secretary of State, advised against resubmission to the Senate of the annexation treaty of 1893 with Hawaii, and brought about the settlement of a dispute between Great Britain and Nicaragua; died in Washington, D.C., May 28, 1895.

Richard Olney (1895–1897) born in Oxford, Massachusetts, September 15, 1835; graduated from Brown University in 1856 (A.M.) and from Harvard Law School in 1858; admitted to the bar in 1859 and commenced practice in Boston, Massachusetts; married Agnes Park Thomas in 1861; member of the Massachusetts House of Representatives in 1874; Attorney General in President Cleveland's Cabinet 1893–1895; commissioned Secretary of State June 8, 1895, entered upon his duties June 10, 1895, and served until March 5, 1897; as Secretary of State, induced the British Government to submit to arbitration its dispute with Venezuela over the boundary between Venezuela and British Guiana, and insisted on the protection of American lives and property and on reparation for injuries in the disorders then prevailing in Cuba, China, and Turkey; resumed the practice of law; regent of the Smithsonian Institution 1900–1908; American member of the Permanent International Commission under the Bryan-Jusserand Treaty of 1914 with France 1915–1917; died in Boston, April 8, 1917.

John Sherman (1897–1898) born in Lancaster, Ohio, May 10, 1823; attended a local academy; admitted to the bar in 1844 and practiced in Mansfield, Ohio; married Margaret Sarah Cecilia Stewart in 1848; delegate to the Whig National Conventions of 1848 and 1852; moved to Cleveland, Ohio, in 1853; chairman of the first Republican convention in Ohio in 1855 and participated in the organization of the national Republican Party; Representative from Ohio 1855–1861; Senator from Ohio 1861–1877; Secretary of the Treasury in President Hayes' Cabinet 1877–1881; again Senator from Ohio 1881–1897; authority on matters of federal finance; unsuccessful candidate for the Republican presidential nomination in 1880, in 1884, and again in 1888; commissioned Secretary of State in President McKinley's Cabinet March 5, 1897, entered upon his duties March 6, 1897, and served until April 27, 1898; as Secretary of State, supported the American interpretation of most-favored-nation treatment in matters relating to international trade; retired from public life; died in Washington, D.C., October 22, 1900.

William Rufus Day (1898) born in Ravenna, Ohio, April 17, 1849; graduated from the University of Michigan in 1870; admitted to the bar in 1872 and commenced practice in Canton, Ohio; married Mary Elizabeth Schaefer in 1875; Judge of the Court of Common Pleas 1886–1890; appointed United States Judge for the Northern District of Ohio in 1889, but because of ill health resigned before taking office; served as Assistant Secretary of State 1897–1898; commissioned Secretary of State in President McKinley's Cabinet April 26, 1898, entered upon his duties April 28, 1898, and served until September 16, 1898; as Secretary of State, secured the neutrality of the nations of western Europe in the Spanish-American War and signed the protocol of 1898 for the cessation of hostilities; chairman of the United States Commission that negotiated and signed the treaty of peace of 1898 with Spain; Judge of the United States Court of Appeals for the Sixth Circuit 1899–1903; Associate Justice of the United States Supreme Court 1903–1922; Umpire in the Mixed Claims Commission, United States and Germany, 1922–1923; died at his summer home at Mackinac Island, Michigan, July 9, 1923.

John Hay (1898–1905) born in Salem, Indiana, October 8, 1838; graduated from Brown University in 1858; admitted to the Illinois bar in 1861; private secretary to President Lincoln 1861–1865; Secretary of Legation at Paris 1865–1867, Chargé d'Affaires ad interim at Vienna 1867–1868, and Secretary of Legation at Madrid 1869–1870; journalist with the New York Tribune 1870–1875; engaged successfully in the writing of verse and fiction; married Clara Louise Stone in 1874; Assistant Secretary of State 1879–1881; made frequent trips to Europe 1881–1896; co-author with John G. Nicolay of *Abraham Lincoln: A History* (10 volumes, 1890); Ambassador to Great Britain 1897–1898; commissioned Secretary of State in President McKinley's Cabinet September 20, 1898, entered upon his duties September 30, 1898, continued in office under President Roosevelt, and served until his death; as Secretary of State, supported the "open door" policy in China, prevented the dissolution of the Chinese Empire in 1900, obtained settlement of the Alaska-Canada boundary controversy, acquired a clear title to Tutuila, and secured by treaty the right for the United States to construct and defend the Panama Canal; died at his summer home at Newbury, New Hampshire, July 1, 1905.

Elihu Root (1905–1909) born in Clinton, New York, February 15, 1845; graduated from Hamilton College in 1864 and from New York University Law School in 1867; admitted to the bar in 1867 and practiced in New York City; married Clara Frances Wales in 1878; United States Attorney for the Southern District of New York 1883–1885; delegate to the state constitutional convention of 1894; Secretary of War in the Cabinets of Presidents McKinley and Roosevelt 1899–1904; member of the Alaskan Boundary Tribunal in 1903; commissioned Secretary of State in President Roosevelt's Cabinet July 7, 1905, entered upon his duties July 19, 1905, and served until January 27, 1909; as Secretary of State, created the American-Canadian International Joint Commission and negotiated arbitration treaties with twenty-four nations; Senator from New York 1909–1915; was counsel for the United States in the North Atlantic Coast Fisheries Arbitration in 1910; became a member of the Permanent Court of Arbitration the same year; president of the Carnegie Endowment for International Peace 1910–1925; president of the New York State constitutional convention of 1915; chief of a special mission to Russia in 1917; member of the committee of jurists which planned the Permanent Court of International Justice in 1920; delegate to the Washington Conference on Limitation of Armament 1921–1922; died in New York City, February 7,1937.

Robert Bacon (1909) born in Jamaica Plain, Massachusetts, July 5, 1860; graduated from Harvard University in 1880; after a trip around the world, commenced a business career with Lee, Higginson and Company of Boston in 1881; married Martha Waldron Cowdin in 1883; member of the firm of E. Rollins Morse and Brother of Boston 1883–1894; member of the New York firm of J. P. Morgan and Company 1894–1903; Assistant Secretary of State 1905–1909 and Acting Secretary while Elihu Root was in South America in 1906; commissioned Secretary of State in President Roosevelt's Cabinet January 27, 1909, entered upon his duties the same day, and served until March 5, 1909; as Secretary of State, obtained the advice and consent of the Senate to the canal treaties of 1909 with Colombia and Panama; Ambassador to France 1909–1912; became a Fellow of Harvard in 1912; made a journey to South America at the request of the Carnegie Endowment for International Peace in 1913; went to France in August 1914 and helped with the work of the "American Ambulance"; commissioned a major and detailed to General Pershing's staff in 1917; promoted to lieutenant colonel in 1918 and served as Chief of the American Military Mission at British General Headquarters; died in New York City, May 29, 1919.

Philander Chase Knox (1909–1913) born in Brownsville, Pennsylvania, May 6, 1853; graduated from Mount Union College in 1872; admitted to the bar in 1875 and practiced in Pittsburgh, Pennsylvania; Assistant United States Attorney for the Western District of Pennsylvania 1876–1877; married Lillie Smith in 1880; president of the Pennsylvania Bar Association in 1897; as counsel for the Carnegie Steel Company, took a prominent part in organizing the United States Steel Corporation in 1901; Attorney General in the Cabinets of Presidents McKinley and Roosevelt 1901–1904; Senator from Pennsylvania 1904–1909; unsuccessful candidate for the Republican presidential nomination in 1908; commissioned

Secretary of State in President Taft's Cabinet March 5, 1909, entered upon his duties March 6, 1909, and served until March 5, 1913; as Secretary of State, reorganized the Department on a divisional basis, extended the merit system to the Diplomatic Service up to the grade of chief of mission, pursued a policy of encouraging and protecting American investments abroad, and accomplished the settlement of the Bering Sea controversy and the North Atlantic fisheries controversy; resumed the practice of law in Pittsburgh; again Senator from Pennsylvania 1917–1921; died in Washington, D.C., October 12, 1921.

William Jennings Bryan (1913–1915) born in Salem, Illinois, March 19, 1860; graduated from Ilinois College in 1881 (A.M. 1884) and from Union College of Law in 1883; admitted to the bar in 1883 and practiced in Jacksonville, Illinois; married Mary Elizabeth Baird in 1884; moved to Lincoln, Nebraska, in 1887 and continued the practice of law; delegate to the Democratic state convention in 1888; Representative from Nebraska 1891–1895; edited the *Omaha World-Herald* 1894–1896; delegate to the Democratic national conventions in 1896, 1904, 1912, 1920, and 1924; Democratic candidate for the Presidency in 1896, in 1900, and again in 1908; raised a regiment of volunteer infantry in 1898 and was commissioned colonel; founded a weekly newspaper, *The Commoner*, in 1901; toured the world 1905–1906; engaged in editorial writing and delivering Chautauqua lectures; commissioned Secretary of State in President Wilson's Cabinet March 5, 1913, entered upon his duties the same day, and served until June 9, 1915; as Secretary of State, negotiated treaties "for the advancement of peace" with thirty nations; resumed his writing and lecturing; established his home in Miami, Florida, in 1921; opposed Clarence Darrow as counsel in the Scopes trial at Dayton, Tennessee, in 1925; died in Dayton, July 26, 1925.

Robert Lansing (1915–1920) born in Watertown, New York, October 17, 1864; graduated from Amherst College in 1886; admitted to the bar in 1889 and practiced in Watertown; married Eleanor Foster in 1890; associate counsel for the United States in the Bering Sea Arbitration 1892–1893; counsel for the Mexican and Chinese Legations in Washington 1894–1895 and 1900–1901; counsel for the United States before the Bering Sea Claims Commission 1896–1897, before the Alaskan Boundary Tribunal in 1903, in the North Atlantic Coast Fisheries Arbitration 1908–1910, and in the American and British Claims Arbitration in 1912; agent of the United States in the last-mentioned arbitration 1913–1914; instrumental in founding the American Society of International Law in 1906 and in establishing the American Journal of International Law in 1907; Counselor of the Department of State 1914–1915; Secretary of State ad interim June 9–23, 1915; commissioned Secretary of State in President Wilson's Cabinet June 23, 1915, entered upon his duties June 24, 1915, and served until February 13, 1920; as Secretary of State, protested against British blockade and contraband practices, and signed the treaty of 1916 for the purchase of the Danish West Indies and the Lansing-Ishii Agreement of 1917 with Japan; practiced international law in Washington, D.C.; died in Washington, D.C. October 30, 1928.

Bainbridge Colby (1920–1921) was born in St. Louis, Missouri, December 22, 1869; graduated from Williams College in 1890 and from New York Law School in 1892; admitted to the bar and practiced in New York City; married Nathalie Sedgwick in 1895 (divorced 1929); member of the state Assembly 1901–1902;

assisted in founding the Progressive Party and was a delegate to its conventions in 1912 and 1916; counsel for a joint committee of the New York Legislature in an investigation of the public-utility commissions and public-service corporations in 1916; special assistant to the United States Attorney General in antitrust proceedings in 1917; member of the American Mission to the Inter-Allied Conference at Paris the same year; member of the United States Shipping Board 1917–1919 and a trustee and vice president of the Emergency Fleet Corporation in 1918; commissioned Secretary of State in President Wilson's Cabinet March 22, 1920, entered upon his duties March 23, 1920, and served until March 4, 1921; as Secretary of State, forcefully enunciated American policy toward Soviet Russia and toward the mandates over former German colonies; practiced law in partnership with Woodrow Wilson in New York City 1921–1923; continued the practice of law; married Anne (von Ahlstrand) Ely in 1929; died in Bemus Point, New York, April 11, 1950.

Charles Evans Hughes (1921–1925) born in Glens Falls, New York, April 11, 1862; graduated from Brown University in 1881 (A.M. 1884) and from Columbia Law School in 1884; admitted to the bar in 1884 and practiced in New York City; married Antoinette Carter in 1888; professor of law at Cornell University 1891–1893; counsel for committees of the New York Legislature 1905–1906; special assistant to the United States Attorney General in the coal investigation in 1906; Governor of New York 1907–1910; Associate Justice of the United States Supreme Court 1910–1916; Republican candidate for the presidency in 1916; commissioned Secretary of State in President Harding's Cabinet March 4, 1921, entered upon his duties March 5, 1921, continued in office under President Coolidge, and served until March 4, 1925; as Secretary of State, presided over the Washington Conference on Limitation of Armament 1921–1922; member of the Permanent Court of Arbitration 1926–1930; chairman of the United States delegation to the Sixth Pan American Conference in 1928 and delegate to the Pan American Conference on Arbitration and Conciliation 1928–1929; judge of the Permanent Court of International Justice 1928–1930; Chief Justice of the United States Supreme Court 1930–1941; died in Osterville, Massachusetts, August 27, 1948.

Frank Billings Kellogg (1925–1929) born in Potsdam, New York, December 22, 1856; moved to Minnesota with his parents 1865; attended public schools; admitted to the bar in 1877 and commenced practice in Rochester, Minnesota; City Attorney of Rochester 1878–1881 and Olmstead County attorney 1882–1887; married Clara Margaret Cook in 1886; moved to St. Paul, Minnesota, in 1887 and continued the practice of law; government delegate to the Universal Congress of Lawyers and Jurists at St. Louis, Missouri, in 1904; member of the Republican National Committee 1904–1912 and a delegate to the Republican National Convention in 1904, 1908, and 1912; special counsel for the government to prosecute antitrust suits; president of the American Bar Association 1912–1913; Senator from Minnesota 1917–1923; delegate to the Fifth Pan American Conference in 1923; served as Ambassador to Great Britain 1923–1925; commissioned Secretary of State in President Coolidge's Cabinet February 16, 1925, entered upon his duties March 5, 1925, and served until March 28, 1929; as Secretary of State, was coauthor of the Kellogg-Briand Peace Pact of 1928; awarded the Nobel Peace Prize in 1929; resumed the practice of law in St. Paul; judge of the

Permanent Court of International Justice 1930–1935; died in St. Paul, December 21, 1937.

Henry Lewis Stimson (1929–1933) born in New York City, September 21, 1867; graduated from Yale University in 1888; attended Harvard University (A.M. 1889) and Harvard Law School 1889–1890; admitted to the bar in 1891 and practiced in New York City; married Mabel Wellington White in 1893; United States Attorney for the Southern District of New York 1906–1909; Secretary of War in President Taft's Cabinet 1911–1913; delegate at large to the New York State constitutional convention of 1915; served in the United States Army in France 1917–1918, attaining the rank of colonel; practiced law in New York City; special representative of the President to Nicaragua in 1927; Governor General of the Philippine Islands 1927–1929; commissioned Secretary of State in President Hoover's Cabinet March 5, 1929, entered upon his duties March 28, 1929, and served until March 4, 1933; as Secretary of State, was chairman of the American delegation to the London Naval Conference in 1930, and formulated the "Stimson Doctrine" with regard to Japanese activities in China; resumed the practice of law in New York City; Secretary of War in the Cabinets of Presidents Roosevelt and Truman 1940–1945; retired from public life; died at "Highhold," his estate in West Hills, Huntington Township, Long Island, October 20, 1950.

Cordell Hull (1933–1944) born in Overton (now Pickett) County, Tennessee, October 2, 1871; attended National Normal University, Lebanon, Ohio, 1889–1890; delegate to the Tennessee Democratic convention in 1890; graduated from Cumberland University Law School in 1891; admitted to the bar the same year and practiced in Celina, Tennessee; member of the state House of Representatives 1893–1897; served in Cuba as captain, Fourth Regiment, Tennessee Volunteer Infantry, in 1898; resumed the practice of law; judge of the Fifth Judicial Circuit of Tennessee 1903–1907; Representative from Tennessee 1907–1921 and 1923–1931; married Rose Frances (Witz) Whitney in 1917; chairman of the Democratic National Committee 1921–1924; Senator from Tennessee 1931–1933; commissioned Secretary of State in President Roosevelt's Cabinet March 4, 1933, entered upon his duties the same day, and served until November 30, 1944; as Secretary of State, sponsored a reciprocal trade program, was chairman of American delegations to numerous international conferences, and was United States delegate to the Moscow Conference in 1943; appointed a delegate to the United Nations Conference at San Francisco in 1945; awarded the Nobel Peace Prize the same year; retired from public life; died at the Naval Hospital, Bethesda, Maryland, July 23, 1955.

Edward Reilly Stettinius Jr., (1944–1945) born in Chicago, Illinois, October 22, 1900; attended the University of Virginia 1919–1924; married Virginia Gordon Wallace in 1926; associated with General Motors Corporation 1926–1934, becoming a vice president in 1931; associated with United States Steel Corporation 1934–1940, becoming chairman of the board of directors in 1938; chairman of the War Resources Board in 1939; member of the advisory committee to the Council of National Defense in 1940; chairman of the Priorities Board and director of the Priorities Division of the Office of Production Management in 1941; Lend-Lease Administrator, special assistant to the President, and a member of the Canadian-American Joint Defense Production Committee 1941–1943; member of the Board of Economic Warfare 1942–1943; Under Secretary of State 1943–1944; commissioned Secretary of State in President Roosevelt's Cabinet November 30, 1944, entered upon his duties December 1, 1944, continued in office under President Truman, and served until June 27, 1945; as Secretary of State, accompanied President Roosevelt to the Yalta Conference in 1945, and was chairman of the United States delegation to the United Nations Conference at San Francisco the same year; was United States representative to the United Nations 1945–1946; rector of the University of Virginia 1946–1949; died in Greenwich, Connecticut, October 31, 1949.

James Francis Byrnes (1945–1947) was born in Charleston, South Carolina, May 2, 1879; attended public schools; official court reporter 1900–1908; admitted to the bar in 1903 and practiced in Aiken, South Carolina; editor of the *Aiken Journal and Review* 1903–1907; married Maude Perkins Busch in 1906; solicitor for the Second Circuit of the State 1908–1910; Representative from South Carolina 1911–1925; delegate to all the Democratic national conventions from 1920 to 1940; practiced law in Spartanburg, South Carolina, 1925–1931; Senator from South Carolina 1931–1941; Associate Justice of the United States Supreme Court 1941–1942; director of the Office of Economic Stabilization 1942–1943; director of the Office of War Mobilization and Reconversion 1943–1945; accompanied President Roosevelt to the Yalta Conference in 1945; commissioned Secretary of State in President Truman's Cabinet July 2, 1945, entered upon his duties July 3, 1945, and served until January 21, 1947; as Secretary of State, accompanied President Truman to the Potsdam Conference in 1945, was United States member of the Council of Foreign Ministers at London in 1945 and at Paris and at New York City in 1946, and represented the United States at the Paris Peace Conference in 1946; practiced law in Washington, D.C., 1947–1950; Governor of South Carolina 1951–1955; died in Columbia, South Carolina, April 9, 1972.

George Catlett Marshall (1947–1949) born in Uniontown, Pennsylvania, December 31, 1880; graduated from Virginia Military Institute in 1901; married Elizabeth Carter Coles in 1902 (she died 1927); served in the United States Army 1901–1945, attaining the rank of general of the Army; saw overseas service in World War 1; married Katherine Boyce (Tupper) Brown in 1930; Chief of Staff of the Army 1939–1945; participated in the various World War II conferences of President Roosevelt with Prime Minister Churchill and with Marshal Stalin and Generalissimo Chiang Kai-shek; accompanied President Truman to the Potsdam Conference in 1945; special representative of the President to China with the rank of Ambassador 1945–1947; commissioned Secretary of State in President Truman's Cabinet January 8, 1947, entered upon his duties January 21, 1947, and served until January 20, 1949; as Secretary of State, was United States member of the Council of Foreign Ministers at Moscow and at London in 1947, and put forward the "Marshall Plan" for European economic recovery the same year; president of the American National Red Cross 1949–1950; Secretary of Defense 1950–1951; retired from public life; died in Washington, D.C., October 16, 1959.

Dean Gooderham Acheson (1949–1953) born in Middletown, Connecticut, April 11, 1893; graduated from Yale University in 1915 and from Harvard Law School in 1918; married Alice Stanley in 1917; an ensign in the United States Navy 1918–1919; served as private secretary to Louis D. Brandeis, Associate Justice of the

United States Supreme Court, 1919–1921; admitted to the bar and practiced in Washington, D.C., 1921–1933 and 1934–1941; Under Secretary of the Treasury in 1933; Assistant Secretary of State 1941–1945 and Under Secretary of State 1945–1947; resumed the practice of law; appointed by the President a member of the Commission on Organization of the Executive Branch of the Government in 1947; chairman of the American section of the Permanent Joint Defense Board 1947–1948; commissioned Secretary of State in President Truman's Cabinet January 19, 1949, entered upon his duties January 21, 1949, and served until January 20, 1953; as Secretary of State, was the United States member of the Council of Foreign Ministers at Paris in 1949, participated in the negotiation and signing of the North Atlantic Treaty of 1949, and served as chairman of the third session of the North Atlantic Council at Washington in 1950; resumed the practice of law; died in Sandy Spring, Maryland, October 12, 1971.

John Foster Dulles (1953–1959) born in Washington, D.C., February 25, 1888; graduated from Princeton University in 1908; attended the Sorbonne 1908–1909 and George Washington University Law School 1910–1911; practiced law in New York City 1911–1917; married Janet Pomeroy Avery in 1912; served in the United States Army 1917–1918, attaining the rank of major; resumed the practice of law; adviser to President Wilson at the Paris Peace Conference and a member of the Reparations Commission and Supreme Economic Council in 1919; delegate to the Berlin Debt Conferences in 1933, to the United Nations Conference at San Francisco in 1945, and to the United Nations General Assembly in 1946, 1947, 1948, and 1950; interim Senator from New York in 1949; consultant to the Secretary of State in 1950; special representative of the President, with the rank of Ambassador, to negotiate the Japanese peace treaty 1950–1951; commissioned Secretary of State in President Eisenhower's Cabinet January 21, 1953, entered upon his duties the same day, and served until April 22, 1959; during his six-year tenure he made some 60 foreign trips and journeyed a total of almost half a million miles; instrumental in expanding the free world alliance system; died in Washington, D. C., May 24, 1959.

Christian Archibald Herter (1959–1961) born in Paris, France, March 28, 1895; graduated from Harvard in 1915; attaché to U.S. Embassy in Berlin 1916–1917 and for two months in charge of U.S. legation in Brussels; married Mary Caroline Pratt in 1917; served in the Department of State from 1917–1919; secretary, U.S. Commission to Negotiate Peace, Paris 1918–1919; personal assistant to Secretary of Commerce Herbert Hoover 1919–1924; executive secretary of the European Relief Council 1920–1921; newspaper editor and associate editor 1924–1936; lecturer, Harvard University 1929–1930; served in the Massachusetts House of Representatives 1931–1943 and as Speaker of that body 1939–1943; Representative to the U.S. Congress 1943–1953 and head of a House select committee that helped pave the way for the Marshall Plan; Governor of Massachusetts from 1953 to 1957; served as Under Secretary of State 1957–1959 and commissioned Secretary of State in President Eisenhower's Cabinet on April 21, 1959, entered upon his duties April 22, 1959, and served until January 20, 1961; served as a trade negotiator in the administrations of John F. Kennedy and Lyndon B. Johnson; died in Washington, D.C., December 30, 1966.

Dean David Rusk (1961–1969) born in Cherokee County, Georgia, February 9, 1909; graduated from Davidson College in 1931; as a Rhodes Scholar studied at St. John's College, Oxford University 1931–1934; from 1934 to 1940 on the faculty of Mills College, Oakland, California and appointed Dean of Faculty in 1938; married Virginia Foisie in 1937; attained the rank of colonel during World War II and served as the deputy chief of staff for the China-Burma-India theater; assistant chief of the Department of State's Division of International Security Affairs in 1946; special assistant to the Secretary of War 1946; from 1947 to 1949 served in the Department of State as director of the Office of Special Political Affairs, which later became the Office of United Nations Affairs; in 1949 appointed Deputy Under Secretary of State; in 1950 appointed Assistant Secretary of State for Far Eastern Affairs; president of the Rockefeller Foundation 1952–1961; commissioned Secretary of State in President Kennedy's Cabinet on January 21, 1961, entered upon his duties the same day, continued in office under President Johnson, and served until January 20, 1969; helped deal with such problems as the Cuban Missile Crisis, the 1967 Arab-Israeli war, the Dominican Republic intervention, the "Pueblo" incident, the closure of the border between East and West Berlin, and especially the Vietnam war; became professor of international law at the University of Georgia in 1969.

William Pierce Rogers (1969–1973) born in Norfolk, New York, on June 23, 1913; graduated from Colgate University in 1934 and earned a law degree from Cornell University in 1937; married Adele Langston in 1936; Assistant District Attorney of New York County 1938–1942 and 1946–1947; served in U.S. Navy 1942–1946; counsel and chief counsel to the U.S. Senate Special Committee to Investigate the National Defense Program 1947–1948; chief counsel to the Senate Investigations Subcommittee of the Executive Expenditures Committee 1948–1950; practiced law 1950–1953; Deputy Attorney General 1953–1957; Attorney General 1957–1961; served as member of the U.S. delegation to the U.N. 20th General Assembly in 1965; member of the President's National Commission on Law Enforcement and Administration of Justice 1965–1967; U.S. representative to the United Nations in 1967; commissioned Secretary of State in President Nixon's Cabinet on January 21, 1969, entered upon duties January 22, 1969, and served until September 3, 1973; promoted a cease-fire in the Middle East in 1970 which lasted until the 1973 war; dealt with problems of security and cooperation in Europe; signed the Vietnam peace agreement; returned to the practice of law; received the Presidential Medal of Freedom October 15, 1973.

Henry Alfred Kissinger (1973–1977) born in Fürth, Germany, on May 27, 1923; emigrated to the United States in 1938; served in the U.S. Army in World War II; married Anne Fleischer in 1949—divorced in 1964; married Nancy Maginnes in 1974; earned his B.A. in 1950, M.A. in 1952, and Ph.D. in 1954 at Harvard University and was a member of the faculty from 1954 to 1971; consultant on foreign policy in the Kennedy and Johnson administrations; adviser to Governor Nelson Rockefeller of New York; named Assistant for National Security Affairs by President Nixon in 1968; in this position his many activities included participation in the 1972 presidential visit to the People's Republic of China and in the negotiations leading to the Vietnam peace agreement; commissioned Secretary of State in President Nixon's Cabinet on September 21, 1973, entered upon duties on September 22, 1973, continued in office under President Ford, and served until

January 20, 1977; among other accomplishments as Secretary of State, was instrumental in the signing of cease-fire agreements by Israel with Egypt and Syria in 1973; promoted policy of détente with Soviet Union, which included the signing of trade and arms agreements; dealt with problems of energy and economic cooperation; awarded Nobel Peace Prize in 1973.

Cyrus Roberts Vance (1977–1980) born in Clarkburg, West Virginia, on March 27, 1917; graduated from Yale University in 1939 and Yale University Law School in 1942; served in the U.S. Navy during World War II; married Grace Sloane in 1947; practiced law in New York City, 1947–1960 and 1967–1977; consulting counsel for the Senate Special Committee on Space and Astronautics in 1958; General Counsel for the Department of Defense 1961–1962; Secretary of the Army 1962–1964 and Deputy Secretary of Defense 1964–1967; President's special representative investigating the Detroit civil disturbances in 1967; served as special representative of the President in the Cyprus crisis in 1967; in 1968 was special representative of the President in Korea; negotiator at the Paris Peace Conference on Vietnam 1968–1969; commissioned Secretary of State in President Carter's Cabinet on January 23, 1977, entered upon his duties the same day, and served until April 1980. Vance's acheivements included negotiating a second strategic arms limitation treaty (SALT II) which the Soviet Union and promoting human rights whenever possible. He resigned in April 1980 because he disagreed with President Carter's policies on Afghanistan and Iran.

Edmund Sixtus Muskie (1980–1981) was born in Rumford, Maine, March 28, 1914; graduated from Bates College 1936 and from Cornell Law School 1939; admitted to Massachusetts Bar 1939, Maine Bar 1940, and United States District Court 1941; practiced law in Waterville, Maine 1940, 1945–1955; served in the United States Navy 1942–1945; member Maine House of Representatives 1947–1951, and Democratic floor leader of that body 1949–1951; married Jane Frances Gray in 1948; Governor of Maine 1955–1959; Senator from Maine 1959–1980; Democratic candidate for the vice-presidency in 1968; chairman of Senate Budget Committee 1974–1980; commissioned Secretary of State in President Carter's Cabinet in 1980, and served until January 20, 1981; as Secretary of State his negotiations secured the release of American hostages held by Iran until January 1981.

Alexander Meiggs Haig, Jr. (1981–1982) born in Philadelphia, Pennsylvania, December 2, 1924; graduated from the United States Military Academy 1947, the Naval War College 1960, and Georgetown University 1961; joined the United States Army in 1947, rising to the rank of General in 1973; married Patricia Antoinette Fox in 1950; deputy special assistant to the Secretary and Deputy Secretary of Defense 1964–1965; battalion and brigade commander in the Republic of Vietnam 1966–1967; Regimental Commander and Deputy Commandant of the United States Military Academy 1967–1969; Senior Military Advisor to the Assistant to the President for National Security Affairs 1970–1973; Vice-Chief of Staff, United States Army 1973; special emissary to Vietnam 1973; retired from United States Army 1973; Assistant to the President and White House Chief of Staff under Presidents Nixon and Ford 1973–1974; recalled to active duty in the United States Army 1974; appointed Commander-in-Chief, United States European Command 1974–1979; Supreme Allied

Commander Europe, NATO 1979; President and Chief Operating Officer, United Technologies Corporation 1980–1981; commissioned Secretary of State in President Reagan's Cabinet in January 1981, and served until June 1982. Haig's eighteen months in office accomplished little because of disputes with the "California friends" of President Reagan, who opposed the existing policy of détente with the Soviet Union.

George Pratt Shultz, (1982–1989) born in New York City, December 13, 1920; graduated from Princeton University in 1942 and from the Massachusetts Institute of Technology in 1949; served in the United States Marine Corps 1942–1945, attaining the rank of major, saw overseas service in the Pacific in World War II; married Helena Maria O'Brien 1946; faculty, Massachusetts Institute of Technology 1948–1957; Senate staff economist, President's Council of Economic Advisors 1955–1956 (on leave from MIT); professor of industrial relations 1957–1962, then dean 1962–1969, Graduate School of Business, University of Chicago; Secretary of Labor 1969–1970; director, Office of Management and Budget 1970–1972; Secretary of the Treasury 1972–1974; professor of management and public policy, Graduate School of Business, Stanford University 1974; executive vice-president 1974–1975, then president 1975–1979, Bechtel Corporation; vice-chairman, The Bechtel Group 1980–1982; commissioned Secretary of State in President Reagan's Cabinet in July 1982; served until January 24, 1989. Shultz loyally followed President Reagan's shift from seeing the Soviet Union as an "evil empire" to negotiating with Gorbachev. In accord with this change, Shultz participated in efforts to "roll back" communist gains in the Third World and led an anti-terrorist campaign, but after 1985 he achieved the 1987 agreement with Premier Gorbachev to eliminate all intermediate range missile (INF) in Europe.

James Addison Baker III (1989–1992) born in Houston, Texas on April 28, 1930; graduated from Princeton University, 1952; Lieutenant in U.S. Marine Corps; J.D., University of Texas School of Law at Austin, 1957; married Susan Garrett, August 6, 1973; national chairman, President Ford Committee, 1976; Andrews & Kurth 1957–1975; Under Secretary of Commerce, 1975; campaign chairman, presidential campaign for Vice President George Bush, August 1988–November 1989; Secretary of the Treasury, 1985–1988; Chief of Staff, 1981–1985; member of the National Security Council, 1981–1988; nominated Secretary of State, on November 9, 1988, confirmed by the Senate; sworn in January 27, 1989, and served until August 13,1992; chairman of the presidential campaign for President George Bush; as the first post–Cold War secretary, Baker's notable achievements were assisting the reunification of Germany, establishing the UN coalition against Iraq in 1990, enabling Arabs and Israeli's to negotiate in October 1991, and negotiating two strategic arms reduction treaties (START I and START II) with the Soviet Union and Russia.

Lawrence S. Eagleburger (1992–1993) born in Milwaukee, Wisconsin, August 1, 1930; married to Marlene Ann Heineman; B.S., University of Wisconsin, political science, 1952; M.S., University of Wisconsin, 1957; U.S. Army, 1952–1954; American Embassy, Tegucigalpa, Honduras, 1957–1959; political analyst, Department of State, Bureau of Intelligence and Research, 1959–1961; Language Training, Washington, DC, 1961–1962; Economic Section, American Embassy,

Belgrade, Yugoslavia, 1962–1965; special assistant to Dean Acheson and acting director of the Secretariat staff, 1965–1966; member, National Security Council staff, 1966–1967; Special Assistant to Under Secretary of State Nicholas Katzenback, 1967–1968; Executive Assistant to National Security Adviser Henry A. Kissinger, 1968–1969; political adviser and Chief, Political Section, U.S. NATO delegation, Brussels, Belgium, 1969–1971; Deputy Assistant, Secretary of Defense, 1971–1973; Acting Assistant Secretary of Defense for International Security Affairs; Executive Assistant to the Secretary of State, 1973–1975; Deputy Under Secretary for Management, 1975–1977; Ambassador to Yugoslavia, 1977–81; Assistant Secretary of State for European Affairs, 1981–1982; Under Secretary of State for Political Affairs, 1982–84; awards: Distinguished Civilian Service Medal; Department of Defense, 1973; Carr Distinguished Honor Award; Deputy Secretary of State, nominated on March 3, 1989; confirmed by the Senate on March 17, 1989; sworn in on March 20, 1989; Acting Secretary of State August 13, 1992– January 20, 1993. During six months as acting secretary, Eagleburger's main duty was to support President Bush's decision to intervene in Somalia.

Warren M. Christopher (1993–1997) born in Scranton, North Dakota on October 27, 1925; B.A. (*magna cum laude*), University of Southern California, 1945; LL.B., Stanford University (Order of the Coif), 1949; service in U.S. Naval Reserve, 1943–1946; married to the former Marie J. Wyllis; resident of California; law clerk, U.S. Supreme Court, for Justice William O. Douglas, 1949–1950; practiced law at O'Melveney & Myers, Los Angeles, California, 1950–1967; Deputy Attorney General, U.S. Department of Justice, 1967–1969; practiced law again at O'Melveney & Myers, 1969–1976; Deputy Secretary of State, U.S. Department of State, 1977–1981; chairman, O'Melveney & Myers, 1981–1993; nominated Secretary of State January 20, 1993 by President Clinton, served until January 22, 1997; as secretary, Christopher principally dealt with problems inherited from the Bush administration regarding Somalia, Haiti, and Bosnia; also negotiated the expansion of NATO to include Eastern European nations and opened U.S. diplomatic relations with Vietnam.

Madeleine Korbel Albright (1997–2001) born in Prague, Czechoslovakia, May 15, 1937; became Secretary of State on January 23, 1997; first female Secretary of State and highest ranking woman in the U.S. government; B.A., Wellesley with honors in Political Science; Masters and Doctorate from the Department of Public Law and Government, Columbia University; research professor of international affairs and director of Women in Foreign Service Program, Georgetown University School of Foreign Service; United States permanent representative to the United Nations (presenting her credentials at the UN on February 6, 1993); president, Center for National Policy; awarded fellowship, Woodrow Wilson International Center for scholars at the Smithsonian Institute, 1981–1982; senior fellow, Soviet and eastern European affairs at the Center for Strategic and International Studies; staff member on the National Security Council and White House staff member, 1978–82; senior fellow, Soviet and eastern European affairs at the Center for Strategic and International Studies; staff member on the National Security Council and White House staff member, 1978–1981; chief legislative assistant for Senator Edmund S. Muskie, 1976–1978; Albright's important efforts were hard-line policies that helped Serbs overthrow Slobodan Milosevic in October 2000 and negotiations to improve trade relations with China that were often tenuous due to China's human rights violations; she and President Clinton were less successful in resolving disputes and violence between Israelis and Palestinians following the signing of the Oslo Accords in 1993.

Index

A

Aahdi Muslims, 884
Aalawite Muslims, 972
Abaca, Sani, 1316
Abaellino (ship), 87
ABC-1 war plans, 548, 551, 567–568
A.B.C. mediation, 351–353
Abd al-Rahman Siwar al-Dahab, 1040
Abd el-Kader, 115, 153
Abdallah, Georges Ibrahim, 1098
Abdel Gamal Nasser. *See* Nasser, Gamal Abdel
Abdel Halim Kaddam, 1010
Abdul Aziz, sultan of Morocco, 225, 335
Abdul Gutíerrez, Jaime, 879–880, 887
Abdul Hamid II, sultan of Turkey, 225, 227, 333
Abdullah Emir, king of Transjordan, 618, 659
Abdullah II, king of Jordan, 1327
   Arab-Israeli mediation, 1334, 1335
Abdullah Tariki, 714
Abe, Shintaro, 1023, 1067
Abel, Rudolf, 726–727
Aberdeen, Lord, 116, 136, 139–140, 145–146, 149–150
Abhay, Kou, 712–713
Abiola, Mashood, 1316–1317
Abkhazia, Georgia Republic conflict, 1236, 1249–1250
abolitionists
   African colonization, opposition to, 152
   Texas recognition and, 125
abortion, U.S. opposition to funding of, 1013
Aboukir Bay, battle of (1798–1799), 45
Abraham, Herard, 1190, 1204
Abrams, Creighton, 780, 781, 790, 799, 810
Abrams, Elliott, 1108, 1141
Abrams v. U.S., 402
Abrego, Juan Garcia, 1273
absolute monarchy, 86–87, 95–96, 101, 115
   Jefferson opposition, 21
Abu Abbas, 1054, 1055, 1063
Abu Dhabi, oil embargo by, 826
Abu Musa, 1101
Abu Nidal, 945, 1060, 1101
Abubakr, Abdul Salam, 1316–1317, 1332
Acadia, Canada, 2
Accessory Transit Company (ACT), 163, 176–178, 182
Aceh, Sumatra, 1363

Acheson, Dean, 619, 626, 627
   Asian relations, 643–646
   Cuban missile crisis, 731
   pro-communist accusations, 638, 646, 647
   as secretary of state, 638–663, **659**
   Vietnam War, 764, **768**
Achille Lauro hijacking, 1053–1055, 1063
acid-rain, 1070–1071, 1150, 1186
Ackerman, Thomas J., 984
Acre, siege of (1799), 44
Act to Abolish the Slave Trade in the District of Columbia of 1850, 162
Adalia, Italian concessions, 380
Adamec, Ladislav, 1164, 1168
Adams, Charles Francis, 195, 197, 200–201, 219
Adams, Francis, 479
Adams, Gerry, 1255, 1260, 1313, 1319
Adams, J. M. G., 982
Adams, John, *39*
   American Revolution peace negotiation, 12, 14, 16, 89, 110, 117, 132
   Barbary powers and, 21–22
   as colonial moderate, 1
   day of prayer proclamation, 42
   Declaration of Independence and, 8–9, *9*
   diplomacy by, 14–15, 22
   French Convention of 1800, 52
   Haitian revolution and, 47–48
   Marshall as secretary of state, 50
   as minister to Great Britain, 21–23
   navy buildup request, 39, 42
   presidency, 39–44
   presidential election of 1796, 39
   presidential second-term defeat, 51
   son John Quincy, 17, 89
   undeclared war with France and, 39–43, 45–50
   as vice president, 26, 30
   W, X, Y, Z affair and, 41–42
Adams, John Quincy, 89–110, *99*
   British relations, softening of, 102
   British trade policy, 97–98, 100, 105, 109, 115
   on Chinese "tribute trade," 130–131
   diplomatic background of, 89
   Indian removal policies and, 109–110, 114
   Latin American independence and, 90–92, 103–104, 106
   as minister to Great Britain, 21–23, 89

B

ethnocentric Western views of, 130–131, 139, 180, 188

Ever Victorious Army, 198

extraterritoriality provision, 156

Formosa and, 180

French concessions in, 280–281, 285–286

French Indochina and, 237

German concessions in, 271, 274, 280, 389–390

gunboat diplomacy and, 179, 228

Hundred Days of Reform, 280, 284

India border war, 730

internal reform movement, 259

international loan consortium (1920), 429

Japanese 21 demands (1915), 359, 363–364, 365

Japanese concessions, 281, 298, 389–390, 396, 429, 442, 478

Japanese invasion of (1928), 463–464

Japanese invasion of (1931), 475–476, 488

Japanese invasion of (1932), 478–480

Japanese invasion of (1937), 513, 521

Japanese trade agreement (1871), 218

Japanese war (1894–1895), 257, 259

Korea, independence from, 223

Korea, withdrawal from, 240

Kuomintang (KMT), 347, 352, 458–459, 464, 464–467

Manchurian conflict, Mukden incident, 475–478, 485–486, 637, 643–644

Manchurian interests, 470–471, 475–476

Mao Tse-tung and communism. *See* Mao Tse-tung; People's Republic of China

May Fourth Movement (1919), 417

missionaries in, 63, 184, 191, 197, 294, 295, 296

Morgan railroad corporation sale, 323–324

most-favored-nation status, 136, 184–185

Nanking antiforeign riots, 458

nationalism, 320–321, 324–325, 342, 456. *See also* Chiang-Kai shek; Kuomintang (National People's Party)

Nine-Power Treaty (1922), 441–442

open-door policy, 134, 136, 139, 184–185, 274, 286, 364

open-door reaffirmation, 291–292, 294, 298, 311, 317, 441–442

opium trade and, 128–129, 131

Paris Peace Conference, 415–416

railroads, 266, 271, 280, 323–324, 336

Reorganization Loan (1913), 347

Revolution of 1911, 259, 342

Russia concession in, 280–281, 291

Russian treaties, 183, 266

Shanghai, internationalization of, 165

silver monetary standard, 498

Soviet repudiation of treaties (1924), 450–451, 457

steamship great circle route proposal, 168

Sung Chiao-Jen assassination, 347

Taiping Rebellion, 170, 181, 184, 191

Terranova incident, 97

Treaty of Tientsin (1858), 184–185, 188

tributary trade, 130–131

U.N. membership, end of, 643

U.S. business consortiums (1909), 336–337

U.S. claims convention signed, 186

U.S. commercial commission, 279

U.S. consul, first, 23

U.S. disavowal of opium trade, 128

U.S. extraterritorial rights ended, 578

U.S. goods, boycott of, 320–321, 324–325

U.S. immigration restriction, 231–232, 321

U.S. loan to (1938), 526

U.S. loan consortiums, 342, 346–347, 398

U.S. most-favored-nation status (1979), 874

U.S. resident commissioner, 132

U.S. trade treaties, 139, 184–185, 187–188

U.S. trade ventures, 19–20, 27

U.S. treaties revision (1927), 457

U.S. treaty with (1880), 231–232, 235

U.S. white paper, loss of China (1949), 641

warlordism begins (1916), 381

Western interests, increase in, 265–266

Western mercenaries, assistance of, 198

World War I, 355–356, 394–395

World War II, 551, 568–570, 575, 578, 580–581, 585–586, 591, 595–596, 609, 611

Yüan Shi-K'ai regime, 342, 347–348, 351–352, 359, 381, 395, 459

See also Formosa; Hong Kong

China Eastern Railway, 266

China Mail Steamship Company, 210

Chincha Islands, 202

Chinese Communist Party (CCP), 458–459, 466

Chinese Eastern Railway, 404, 451, 470, 501

Chinese immigration

exclusion advocates, 237

exclusion of, 244–245, 321

restrictions on, 231–232, 237

separate schools issue, 327–328

Chinese Trade Treaty (1980), 874

Ch'ing dynasty, 198, 259, 280, 301, 321, 325, 342, 381

Chiquita Brands International, 1329

Chirac, Jacques, Bosnia-Serbia war and, 1265–1266, **1328**

Chivez Mena, Fidel, 1152

Chivington, J. M., 204

Chivington massacre (1864), 204

chloroflurocarbons (CFCs)

ban on, 1151, 1177, 1225

ozone layer destruction, 1126

Choate, Joseph, 302, 312, 317, 330

Choi Zemin, 910

Chosen, Korea renamed by Japan, 337

Choshu daimyo, 200–201, 203, 210, 212

Chou En-lai, 673, 678–679, 693, 705

Kissinger meetings, 802, **803**, 806

Nixon visit, 808

on U.S.-People's Republic goodwill, 800–801

Chrétien, Jean, 1298

Chrétien, Jean-Loup, 946

Christ, Hans, 919

Christian Democratic Party (Chile), 796–797

Christian Democratic Party (El Salvador), 937–938, 1003, 1013, 1039, 1127, 1152

Christian Democratic Party (Italy), 973

Christian Democratic Party (West Germany), 615, 639, 951, 965, 1095

France (*Continued*)
    U.S. abrogation of treaties, 44
    U.S. alliance with (1778), 10–12, 16, 19, 31, 36
    U.S. Civil War and, 198–201
    U.S. credit extended to, 358
    U.S. debt repayment to, 28, 31
    U.S. deteriorating relations with, 36–39
    U.S. diplomatic overtures, 8
    U.S. independence recognition, 10
    U.S. normalized relations, 52–53
    U.S. quasi war with, 38–39, 50–53
    U.S. relations rupture, 121–123
    U.S. retaliatory duties, 95
    U.S. trade reciprocity and, 98
    Vietnam conflict, 671–672, 675–676
    Vietnam, control of, 237, 611, 617, 640
    W, X, Y, Z affair, 41–42, *43*
    West German relations (1980s), 1125
    West Indies trade restrictions, 21
    World War I, 354–356, 370, 377, 379, 389, 393–394, 399, 401,
        409, 411, 414, 415
    World War I debt to U.S., 483
    World War I reparations from Germany, 444–445, 452
    World War II, 524, 535–541, 568, 571, 589–593, 614
    Yugoslavian friendship agreement, 461
Francis, David R., 391, 394
Francis Ferdinand, archduke of Austria, assassination of, 352,
    353
Francis Joseph I, emperor of Austria-Hungary, 155, 333, 384
Franck, James O., 606
Franco-American Consular Convention of February 23, 1853,
    177–178
Franco-American Treaty of Alliance (1778), 10–12, 16, 19, 21,
    29, 48, 50
    abrogation of, 52–53
    de facto nullification, 38
    French reaffirmation of, 36
    Jay's Treaty and, 36, 38
    Monroe continuation diplomacy t, 37–38
    neutrality arguments in face of, 31–32
Franco-American undeclared war (1797–1800), 38–49
    Convention of 1800, 50–53
    peace delegation, 50
    three peace conditions, 48
Franco, Francisco, **529**
    Allies verbal appeal for coup of, 617, 652
    death of, 845
    Nazi-Fascist ideology, 509
    Spanish Civil War (1936), 506–508, 521, 528
    U.S. recognition of regime, 529–530
Franco-Prussian War (1870), 193, 214, 216, 222
Franco-Russian Alliance (1894), 255
François, Michael, 1254
François, Michel, 1359
Franham, Roger L., 358
Frank, Anne, 1042
Frank, Richard B., 602
Frankfurt National Assembly (1848), 155–156
Franklin (proposed state), 25

Franklin (ship), 49
Franklin, Benjamin, 6, 8–10, 14–17, 169
    Barbary powers and, 21–22
    as colonial moderate, 1
    as minister to France, 10, *16*, 21
Franklin D. Roosevelt (aircraft carrier), 626
Franklin, Noble, 601
Franks, Lonni Douglas, 809
Franz Joseph, emperor of Austria, 186
Fraser, Malcolm, 965
Frazier, Linda, 1008
Frederick William, king of Prussia, 156
Frederick William II, king of Prussia, 29
Free Democratic Party (Germany), 951, 965, 1071, 1095, 1188,
    1216
"free ships equal free goods," 39, 51, 62
free silver coinage, 254
Free Soil Party, 150, 156–157, 166, 174
free speech
    versus scandalous statements (1798), 45
    in wartime (1918), 401–402
free trade
    British adoption of, 149, 190
    Iran-former Soviet republics, 1213
    Latin American countries, 1198
    North American Free Trade Agreement (NAFTA), 1243–1244
    U.S. and Canada agreement, 1111–1112, 1142
    U.S. and Chile, 1367
    U.S. and Hawaii, 221
    U.S. and Jordan, 1367
    U.S. and Singapore, 1367
    U.S. and South Korea, 1222
    and World Trade Organization (WTO), 1288–1289
Free Trade Agreement (1987), 1111–1112, 1142
Freed, Donald, 655
Freedom Foundation, 716
Freedom of Information Act, 623
Freedom Party (Austria), 1341, 1354
freedom of the seas, 9
Freeh, Louis, 1288
Freeman, Orville, 750
Frei Montalvo, Eduardo, 796, 1245
Frelinghuysen, Frederick
    release of Blaine's War of the Pacific diplomatic
        correspondence, 234–235
    as secretary of state, 233–245
Frémont, John C., 179
French Assembly, 27
French Committee of National Liberation, 589, 591–592
French Community, 702, 712
French Convention of Peace, Commerce, and Navigation (1800),
    50–53
French Direct Action Group, 1049
French and Indian War, 2
French Indochina. *See* Indochina
French National Committee, 541
French Petroleum Company, 677
French Revolution, 21, 26–30, 86–87
French revolutionary wars. *See* Napoleonic wars

World War I reparations, 435, 443–444, 452–453, 468–469, 473, 474, 481–482, 498–499

World War II, 535–536, 539, 541, 544–546, 549–550, 553–554, 558–559, 567, 578, 581, 585, 588–593, 602–604

World War II negotiations and, 600, 602, 607–608

World War II post-war status, 615

World War II reparations, 600, 607

See also Prussia

Gerö, Ernö, 688–689

Gerolt, Baron, 156

Geronimo, 217, *217*

Gerry, Elbridge, *40*
French negotiations and, 40–42, *43*, 45–47
as vice president, 78

Gettysburg, battle of (1863), 200–201, 213

Ghana
independent state (1957), 692
Nkrumah overthrown, 752

Ghandi, Indira, 751

Gharekhan, Chinmoy, 934

Ghent, Treaty of (1815), 81, 83–85, 89, 92–93, 110, 160, 168

Ghmielewski, Waldemar, 1023

Ghorbanifar, Adnan M., 1099, 1102

Ghotbzadeh, Sadegh, 885

Gia Long, emperor of Annam, 197

Giap, Vo Nguyen, 671, 766–767, 809–810, 938

Gibraltar, 11, 16, 86
IRA attack, 1126

Gibson, Hugh, 358, 460

Giddi Pass, 844, 879, 940

Giddings, Joshua R., 131–132

Gierek, Edward, 798, 895–897, 918

Gila River, 154, 171

Gilbert, Prentiss, 477

Gilmer, Thomas, 138

Gingrich, Newt, 1256, 1271–1272

Ginzberg, Aleksandr, 1095

Giraud, Henri Honoré, 578, 580, 589, 591

Girodondin Party (France), 33

Giroldi Vega, Moisés, 1167

Gitlow, Benjamin, 420

Givin, William, 208

Gizenga, Antonio, 720

Gizikis, Phaidon, 828

Gjallico pyramid scheme, 1295

Gladstone, William, 199, 213

glasnost (Soviet societial openness), 1038, 1201

Glaspie, April, 1180–1181

Glass, Charles, 1095

Glass, Henry, 280

Glass-Steagall Act of 1933, 488

Glenn, John H., Jr., 727

Global Protection Against Limited Strikes (GPALS), 1176, 1203, 1217–1218

Glorious Revolution of 1688–1689 (G.B.), 1–2

Glynn, James, 157

Glynn, Martin H., 380–381

Godoy, Manuel de, 37, 57

Godwin, Doris Kearns, 764

Goebbels, Joseph, 622

Goering, Hermann, 622

Golan Heights
annexation to Israel, 930, 940
Arab-Israeli violence, 760, 793, 825, 832
peace mediation, 832, 1246, 1340, 1341

Golcher, Rinaldo, 1010

gold
in Alaskan Klondike, 266
Black Hills (Dakota) discovery, 224
California discovery of, 159–160
in Venezuela, 258

Gold, Harry, 647, 655

Gold Reserve Act of 1934, 494

gold reserves, Panic of 1893 and, 254, 255

gold standard
British abandonment (1931), 476
election of 1896 issue, 266
U.S. abandonment (1933), 487, 494
U.S. dollar to gold exchange suspension (1971), 804

Golder, Frank A., 202

Goldman, Allan, 819

Goldman, Emma, 422

Goldstein, Baruch, 1249

Goldwater, Barry, 720, 868, **868**
on mining Nicaraguan harbors, 999
presidential election of 1964 defeat, 742, **743**

Goliad, battle of (1836), 123–124

Golkar Party (Indonesia), 1335

Gold Coast Colony, becomes Ghana (1957), 692

Gomes, Francisco Costa, 834

Gómez, Eden Pastora, 969, 1007–1008, 1076–1077

Gómez, José, 390

Gómez, José Miguel, 327

Gómez, Max, 1085

Gómez, Maximo, 259

Gomułka, Władysław, 687, 690–691, 692, 798, 895

Gonçalves, Colores Vasco, 834

Goncharov, Sergei N., 646

Gondra Convention, 446

Gonzáles, Elian, 1339, 1350

Gonzáles, Juan Miguel, 1339

Gonzales Macci, Luis Angel, 1331

González, Carlos, 824

Goodman, Alan, 818

Goodman, Robert O., Jr., 990, **991**

Goranies, 1326

Gorbachev, Mikhail S.
Afghanistan troop withdrawal, 1081, 1128–1129, 1135–1136
on Arab-Israeli conflict, 1101
British visit by, 1029
Bush (G. H. W.), Malta meeting, 1165, **1165**
central government restructuring plan, 1190–1191, 1197, 1207
coup attempt (1991), 1201–1202
on East German reforms, 1161–1162
East German relations, 1101–1102
on ethnic nationalism, 1157
as executive president (1990), 1171
glasnost (Soviet societial openness), 1038, 1201

Chinese treaties revision, 456, 457

Colombo Plan for economic aid, 653

commercial treaty barriers, 27

Confederate recognition issue, 198–199, 206

Confederate warship construction by, 195, 197, 200–201, 206, 213, 218

Creole case and, 131

Crimean War, 172–174, 176, 178

Declaration of London (1908), 334, 354, 357

Declaration of Paris and, 178–179

Dutch war, 13

Egypt, occupation of, 235, 239, 283, 443

Egyptian alliance (1936), 507

Egyptian independence and, 442–443

Erskine Agreement (1809), 67–68

in European Common Market, 765, 807

Falkland Islands claim by, 117–119, 127–128, 632

Falkland Islands War (1982), 938–939

first minister to United States, 29

Franco-American Treaty of Alliance of 1778 and, 10

free-trade policies, 149, 190

French alliance, 317, 319

French cessions to, 2, 8

French trade treaty, 190

French Treaty of Amiens, 54

French wars, 1–2, 8, 11, 30, 38, 45–46, 55–57. *See also* Napoleonic wars

Gallipoli campaign against Turkey, 362

German entente with, 239

German relations (1930s), 261–262, 512–513

Great Depression economy, 476

Great Lakes demilitarization agreement, 89

Hong Kong, control of, 134, 165, 441, 533, 611, 1019

India under control of, 185

India independence initiatives, 502

international conference on Africa, 239

Ireland, partition of (1922), 443

Irish-British War (1919), 423, 443

Irish independence struggle and, 206, 215, 356, 379, 382

Irish Republican Army (IRA), terrorist attacks. *See* Irish Republican Army (IRA)

Japanese alliance, 259, 303–304, 533

Japanese trade and, 182–183, 203, 206

Jay as special envoy to, 34

Jay's Treaty provisions, 35

Joint High Commission (1871), 216, 218

Latin American influence of, 235

League of Armed Neutrality ended by, 53

Liberia, recognition of, 152

Libyan embassy, seizure of, 1001

Loyalist evacuation from New York, 17

Mediterranean Sea agreements, 242

mercantilism, 1–2, 86, 98

Mexican dictatorship and, 349–350

Mexican intervention and, 190–191, 195

Middle East oil interests, 432

minister to U.S., first, 29

Napoléon paper blockade of, 62

naval defense act, 247

navy. *See* Royal Navy (G.B.)

New Zealand as dominion, 292

North American Indian policies, 18–20, 29, 33, 35, 64

northeast boundary arbitration, 109–110, 116–117

northeast boundary settlement, 132–133

Northwest posts, 38

nuclear arms control, 771–772, 1086

nuclear test ban treaties, 736

nuclear weapons development, 661, 693, 1086

oil price cuts (1984), 1022

Opium War, 128, 129, 131, 133

Oregon boundary issue, 142–150, 219–220

Palestine issue, 396, 531, 531–532, 630–631

Panama Congress observer, 108

peace terms with France, Spain, and United States (1783), 17–18

Peel government, 144

People's Republic of China, recognition of, 809

Persian/Iranian oil holdings, 432, 449, 658

Pinkney recall from, 70

Polish uprising and (1863) and, 200, 202

privateering, 32

protective tariff laws (1932), 480

in Quadruple Alliance, 87

reactionary European alliances, rejection of, 96–98

restrictive naval controls, 12

Russian treaty on northwest Pacific coast boundary, 104

Samoa crisis and, 247–248

Samoa partition and, 293–294

Saudi Arabia, aircraft/arms sales to, 1052, 1133–1134

sealing controversy, 241, 242, 247

Siam independence and, 264

slave trade suppression measures, 63, 98–99, 103, 136, 141, 183–184, 186, 254

slavery issues, 92, 118, 131, 136, 138–141, 198–199

South Africa and, 263–264, 292

Soviet-Anglo break, 453

Soviet pipeline issue, 950, 955

Soviet recognition by, 453, 469

Soviet relations (1930s–1940s), 502, 574, 609, 644–645

Soviet relations (1980s), 1100

Spanish claim to Cuba and, 167

Spanish war potential, 28

Spanish wars, 2, 11, 16, 38, 58

stock exchange, deregulation of, 1090

Sudan as protectorate, 685

Suez Canal, control of, 223, 235, 239, 245

Suez crisis, 689–690, 693–694

Syrian break, 1090

terrorist (Muslims) incidents, 1001, 1090

Texas policies, 132, 137–140, 143

Tibet as protectorate, 317, 352

Trafalgar naval victory, 60

transatlantic cable, 207

transatlantic sailings, monthly, 90

transatlantic steamships, 141–142

in Triple Entente, 330

U.S. Anglophobia, 245, *245*

U.S. Anglo-Saxon unity policy, 260–261

H

Hyde de Neuville, Baron Guillaume-Jean, 97–98
Hyde, Henry, 979
hydrogen bomb (H-bomb), development of, 647, 663, 671, 761
Hypsilanti, Alexander, 96

I

I. Chang, 183
Ibn Saud, king of Saudi Arabia, 487–488
Ibrahim, Izzat, 1179
Iceland
    NATO defense facilities at, 658
    Reagan-Gorbachev meeting, 1059, 1086–1088, **1087**
    whaling violation, prohibition of, 1091
    World War II, 554, 557, 558
Ichiang Island, 679
Ickes, Harold, 622
Idris I, king of Libya, 784
Ii Naosuke, 190
Il, Kim Jong, 1253, 1310, 1319, 1350, 1366, 1369
Ileto, Rafael, 1093
Iliescu, Ion, 1168, 1175, 1364
Illinois
    American capture of, 11
    Black Hawk War (1832), 114
Illinois (steamer), 392
Imanyara, Gitobu, 1194
Imbros, 447
Imhausen-Chemical, Libyan plant, 1146
immigration
    of Americans to Texas, 105
    Chinese to United States, 211
    foreign labor encouragement (1864), 203
immigration regulation
    Chinese restriction/exclusion, 231–232, 235, 237, 244, 321, 451
    Chinese restriction/exclusion abrogated, 587–588
    communist-related restrictions, 422, 424, 435–436, 445–446, 651
    deportation of dangerous aliens, 44
    emergency quota act (1921), 436–437, 445
    Gentleman's Agreement with Japan, 329
    Immigration Bill of 1924, 450
    Japanese, 258, 450
    Japanese to Hawaii, 270
    McCarren-Walter Immigration and Nationality Act (1952), 662
    naturalization residency requirement, 36, 43–44
    quota limits (1965), 749
impeachment
    Clinton, 1308, 1320, 1327
    Nixon, 834
Imperial Chinese Railroad bonds, 963
Imperial Conference of Japan, 558–559, 564
imperialism
    anti-imperialists, 284
    British, 260–261
    European, *240*
    Italian, 264

social Darwinism and, 261
    United States, 254, 260
impressment, 46, 57, 61–65, 67, 71, *71*, 76–77, 92
Independence (aircraft carrier), 1276
Independent Motherland Party (Turkey), 985
India
    Bhopal carbon monoxide leak, 1027, 1091–1092
    British control of, 185
    Clinton visit, 1345
    Dalai Lama exile in, 705
    disqualification for office (1975), 842
    independence of (1947), 629
    independence initiatives, 502
    Kashmir dispute with Pakistan, 934, 1098, 1333, 1345
    Nixon visit, 783
    nuclear testing moratorium, 1317
    nuclear weapons development, 832, 1315
    opium trade, 128
    Pakistan nonaggression pact plan, 934
    Pakistan war (1971), 806, 807
    Pakistani airline downed by, 1335
    People's Republic of China border war, 730
    Soviet friendship treaty (1971), 803
    U.S. agricultural aid treaty, 750, 755–756
    U.S. economic assistance halted, 848
    U.S. economic sanctions (1998), 1315, 1317
    U.S. Four Point agreement (1952), 660–661
    U.S. uranium fuel to, 892
    U.S. wheat contribution mission, 755–756
    U.S. wheat sale to, 919
Indian Ocean, 120
    U.S. military defenses, 884, 893
Indian Removal Act of 1830, 114
Indian Springs, Treaty of (1826), 109, 114
Indiana
    action against Indians, 72–73
    Indian-settler lands boundary treaty, 36
Indians, American. *See* Native Americans
Indochina
    Dutch nationals expulsion (1957), 696–697
    French holdings in, 197, 201, 237, 264, 611
    in French Union, 617, 624
    Great Britain in, 168, 240
    Japanese occupation, 554, 563, 564, 610
    map (1896), *264*
    U.S.-France mutual defense agreement (1950), 654
    World War II, 554, 563, 564
    See also southeast Asia; *individual countries*
Indochinese Communist Party, 610
Indonesia
    Aceh independence rally, 1363
    East Timor independence conflict, 1335
    food and fuel aid to, 1312
    human rights violations, 1256
    independence of (1949), 645
    Islamic airline hijacking attempt, 912
    map of, 1312
    Suharto regime, 1312, 1314–1315
    West Irian secession conflict, 1363

Izetbegović, Alija, 1214, 1221, 1240, 1252, 1270, 1274, 1284–1285
Izurieta, Ricardo, 1365

J

Jackson, Andrew, 82, *91, 111*
   attack on Spanish Florida by, 90–91, 93–94
   Battle of New Orleans, 84–85, *85*
   British West Indian trade policy, 115
   Indian removal policy, 114
   nullification and, 120
   presidency of, 113–125, 127
   presidential election of 1828, 109, 110
   presidential election of 1832, 119
   reelection of, 119
   Senate censure of, 94
   tariffs and, 110, 119–120
   Texas policy and, 124–125, 132
Jackson, Francis James, 68, 70
Jackson, Henry, 836, 847
Jackson, Jesse, **991**
   Cuba relations and, 1011
Jackson, Michigan, 174
Jackson, Robert, 622
Jackson State College massacre, 791
Jacobins (France), 30, 33–34
Jacobsen, David P., 1051, 1092, 1360
Jagan, Cheddi B., 919
Jagow, Gottlieb von, 365, 366, 371–373
Jalapa, battle of (1847), 152
Jamaica, 11, 85
   U.S. cancellation of debt, 1201
James I, king of England, 2
James II, king of England, 2
James Monroe (ship), 90
Jameson, J. Franklin, 407
Jameson, Leander, 264
Jamestown (ship), 203
Jamestown, Va., 2
Janata Party (India), 1337
Jane's Defense Weekly, 1019
Japan
   anti-Western program, 203
   antiforeign, antishogun groups, assassinations by, 190, 193
   auto production. *See* automobiles
   British alliance, 259, 303–304, 533
   Chinese concessions, 281, 298, 389–390, 396, 429, 442, 478
   Chinese invasion (1928), 463–464
   Chinese invasion (1931), 475–476, 488
   Chinese invasion (1937), 513, 521
   Chinese trade treaty with, 218
   Chinese war (1894–1895), 257, 259
   closure of, 166
   diplomatic status of, 220, 228–229, 257–258
   economy stimulation package (1987), 1104
   Formosa occupied by, 209–210
   Germany anti-Comintern pact (1936), 510
   gunboat diplomacy, 201, 203, 206–207, 228

Hamaguchi assassination, 474
Hara, commoner as premier, 407
Hawaii-American annexation treaty, 270
Hawaii immigration restriction, 270, 272
Hirohito as emperor, 456, 481, 615
Hoover-Stimson non-recognition doctrine, 478
Hua Guofeng visit to People's Republic of China (1980), 891
Indochina occupation, 554, 563, 564, 610
internal struggle, 190, 193, 201, 203
Inukai assassination, 481
Korea, withdrawal from, 240
Korean interests, 323, 324, 334, 337
Korean trade interest (1983), 970
Korean treaty with, 223, 235
Lagoda incident (1849), 157, 166–167
Lansing-Ishii agreement (1917), 396, 429, 444
Manchuria conflict, Mukden incident, 475–476, 486–487
Manchurian interests, 323, 334, 337, 475–476, 478–480, 501, 513
Meiji Restoration of 1868, 173, 210, 212, 407
Monroe Doctrine extended to, 342
naval expansion (1921), 439, 499–500
naval parity demand (1935), 504
naval reduction, (1930), 472–473
nuclear accident (1999), 1336
"open door" policy, 182–183
Paris Peace Conference, 415–416
People's Republic of China, loan to (1984), 998
People's Republic of China, trade agreement (1978), 858
Perry trade overture to, 166–170, *169*, 172–173, *172*
Postal Convention of 1873, 220, 228–229
Root-Takahira Agreement (1908), 322, 334, 336
Russo-Japanese treaty (1905), 322–323, 324
Russo-Japanese war, 311, 316–317, 319–320
Ryukyu Islands control, 220
Shanghai attack (1932), 478
Shimonoseki incident, 201, 203, 207, 236–236
Shōwa era, 456
Sino-Japanese Treaty (1922), 442
Soviet border incidents, 522
Soviet Union, Toshiba sales banned, 1103
space exploration plans, 1042
Suzuki as prime minister, 892
Taft-Katsura Agreement, 322
Taisho period, 407, 456
terrorist incidents in, 1045
terrorist subway attack (1995), 1260
trade surplus reduction, five-year plan (1988), 1130
Treaty of Kanagawa, 172–173
21 demands on China (1915), 359, 363–364, 365
U.S. arbitration agreement (1908), 332
U.S. as commercial relations mentor, 185
U.S. commercial treaties, 172–173, 182–183, 185, 207, 228–229, 257–258, 338, 450, 533, 539
U.S. cultural/trade mission by, 190
U.S. extradition treaty, 240–241
U.S. goods, opening Japanese market to (1980s), 961, 1005, 1030–1031, 1040, 1100
U.S.-Japan automobile venture. *See* automobiles

M

Marcos, Ferdinand E. (*Continued*)
  Aquino (Corazon) elected president, 1068–1069
  Aquino (Corazon) overthrow attempt, 1079, 1093
  exile of, 1068, 1097
  fraudulent election (1984), 1005
  fraudulent election (1986), 1066
  plan for election of 1986, 1060
Marcović, Ante, 1170
Marcovich, Herbert, 763
Marcula (ship), 732
Marcy-Elgin Treaty (1854), 173–174
  U.S. termination of, 206
Marcy, William Learned, 164
  book of consular instructions, 176
  as secretary of state, 168–183
Marengo, battle of, 50
Maria de Gloria, queen of Portugal, 120
Mariana Islands, 626, 1091
Marina (steamer), 386
Marine Corps
  formation of, 44
  Mexico City capture, 153
  Samoan crisis and, *246*
  Tripolitan war success, *59*, 60
Maritime Canal Company of Nicaragua, 230, 289
maritime law, 9
Maritime Provinces (Canada), 22
Marjane, Kamel, 1369
Markarios, Archbishop, 714
Marković, Ante, 1208
Marković, Rade, 1366
Marques, Felipe Gonzáles, 954
Marquessas Island, 135
Marroquin, José Manuel, 310
Mars, U.S. landing on, 849
Marshall, George C.
  China diplomacy, 613, 618, 623, 625
  Marshall Plan (1947), 627–628, 631, 633
  resignation as secretary of state, 638
  as secretary of state, 625–638, **625**
  World War II, 527, 563, 570, 576, 579, 582, 602–603, 607
Marshall, Humphrey, 170
Marshall Islands, 1009, 1091
  U.N. membership, 1203
Marshall, John, *40*
  Burr treason trial and, 63
  French negotiations and, 40–43, *43*, 46
  as secretary of state, 50–52
Marshall, Thomas R., 382, 418, 521, 527
Marshall Islands, 626, 663, 897
  U.S. nuclear testing agreement, 953
Marshall Plan (1947), 627–628, 631, 633, 634, 648, 652, 660
Marti, José, 259
Martin, John Barlow, 747
Martin, Joseph A., 657
Martin, Lynn, 975
Martínez, Gustavo Alvarez, 998
Martinique, 11, 304, 543
Marx, Karl, 200, 413

Marxism
  compared to communism, 631–632
  and Russian communism, 397
Marxist Popular Front for the Liberation of Angola, 842
Mary II, queen of England, 2
Masaryk, Jan, **632**
Masaryk, Thomás, 408
Mashuda (ship), 86
Maskhadov, Aslan, 1284, 1292, 1337
Mason, James M., 196
Mason, John Y., 174–175
Mason, Richard B., 151
Masri, Zafir al-, 1069
Massachusetts
  American Revolution, 1
  colonial-British conflict, 4
  constitutional ratification and, 25
  Shays's Rebellion, 24
  trade discrimination against British, 22
  War of 1812 opposition, 77, 83–84
  Webster-Ashburton Treaty settlement, 132–133
Massachusetts Historical Society, 131
Massoud, Ahmed Shah, 1216, 1287
Mataafa, Chief (Samoan), 246, 248, 289
Matamoros, Mexico, 147, 149
Matek, Sirik, 789, 820
Mateos, Adolfo López, 704
Matsu (battleship), 441
Matsu Island, 678–679, 701–702, 1366
Matsudaira, Tsuneo, 477
Matsuoka, Tosuke, 551
Matta, Manuel A., 251
Matthews, George, 74
Mau-Mau uprising, 663
Maumee River, 18, 30, 33, 35
Maung, Maung, 1140
Maung, Saw, 1139–1140
Mauritania, independence of, 702, 712
Mauritius, 893
Maury, M. F., 168
Maverick missiles, 1113
Max, prince of Baden, 408, 409
Maxim Gorky (cruise ship), 1165
Maximilian, emperor of Mexico, 196, 208
May, Alan Nunn, 616
May First Movement (Philippines), 1093
May Fourth Movement (China), 417
Mayaguez, 841
Mayan Indians
  CIA connections with, 1260–1261, 1294
  as Guatamalan guerrillas, 1261
Mayo, Henry T., 350–351
Mayorski, Boris, 1328
Maza, Manuel Vincente de, 118
Mazowiecki, Tadeusz, 1160, 1189
Mazzini, Giuseppe, 155
M'Bow, Amadou-Mahtar, 1030
M'Bow, General, 990
Mead, Walter R., 1285

of Red Sea by Islamic Jihad, 1013
by U.S. of Nicaraguan harbors, 999–1001
by U.S. in Vietnam War, 757–758, 810, 811
of waterways Iran, 1109
Minuteman I, 1009
Minutemen silos, 935, 969
Miquelon Island, 2, 568
Miramon, Miguel, 186, 190
Miranda, Jorge Alberto, 1125
missile defense systems
antiballistic-missile defense (ABM), 756, 778–779, 786
Ballistic Missile Defense Organization (BMDO), 1239, 1255, 1287, 1331
Brilliant Pebbles missile defense system, 1176, 1203, 1217–1218
Global Protection Against Limited Strikes (GPALS), 1176, 1203, 1217–1218
National Missile Defense System (NMDS), 1331, 1350, 1369
Single Integrated Operations Policy (SIOP), 943, 1217–1218
strategic defense initiative (SDI), 966–967, **966**, 1009
Theater High Altitude Area Defense (THAAD), 1239, 1287, 1303, 1331, 1336
missiles
air-to-air missiles, 1017
antisatellite missiles, 1051
cruise missiles, 866, 877
deployment plans to NATO countries (1979), 877–878, 891
intercontinental ballistic (ICBM) missiles, 684–685, 694, 720, 778–779
intermediate-range ballistic missiles (IRBM), 684–685, 705, 967–968, 976, 978
long-range ground launched cruise missile, 1015
Maverick missiles, 1113
medium-range Pershing II missiles, 877, 908
Migetman missiles, 994
Minutemen silos, 935, 969
multiple independent reentry vehicles (MIRV), 786, 875
MX missiles, 874, 895, 922, 934–935, 959, 967–969, 972
NATO conference on (1957), 697
NATO dual-track policy, 908, 911, 962
Patriot-Roland missiles, 987
Pershing II missiles, 908
polaris missiles, 712, 720
precision guided reentry vehicle, 895
reduction of. *See* nuclear arms control
Scowcroft Commission (1983), 968–969
short-range nuclear missiles (SNF), 1155
Silkworm anti-ship missiles, 1103, 1113
single-warhead missile, 1065
Skybolt missile program, 733–734
submarine launching, 712, 720, 895
surface-to-air missiles (SAMs), 793
Tomahawk cruise missiles, 986
TOW anti-tank missiles, 1033
missing-in-action (MIA). *See* prisoners-of-war (POWs)/missing-in-action (MIA)
missionaries
in China, 63, 184, 191, 197, 294, 295, 296
El Salvador murder of (1980), 899, 906, 985, 1007
in Hawaii, 128

in Korea, 207
Liberia murder of (1992), 1224
in Persia, 235
Turkish plunder of property, 262
Mississippi
Indian removal, 109
opposition to Tariff of 1828, 111
Mississippi River
American Revolution negotiation terms, 11
Battle of New Orleans and, 85
British territory east of, 2
Indian removal west of, 114
navigation rights, 11, 20–21, 23, 25–26, 28, 37
northwest border, 56
as United States western boundary, 18
Mississippi River valley, 11, 24
Mississippi territory
organization of, 42
West Florida incorporation into, 75
See also Mississippi
Missouri, statehood as slave state, 95
Missouri (battleship), 610, **610**, 626
Missouri Compromise (1820), 95, 173
Missouri River, Lewis and Clark expedition, 57
Mitchell, George J., 1281, 1312–1313, 1319, 1348
Mitchell, William, 435, 437
Mitchell's Map of 1755, 117
Mitchell's Map of 1782, 110, 117, 132–133
Mitla Pass, 844, 879, 940
Mitsubishi Corporation
Chrysler Auto Corporation joint venture, 1053–1054
FSX fighter construction, 1111, 1148
Mitterand, François, 915, 948
on Atlantic Alliance, 961–962
reelection of (1988), 1129
Rwanda conflict and, 1183
Miyazawa, Kiichi, 1119, 1210
Mladenov, Petar, 1168
Mladić, Ratko, 1232–1233, 1248, 1256, 1260, 1266, 1284, 1302
M-19 movement, 910, 1057, 1129
Moawad, Rene, 1163
Mobile Act (1804), 58
Mobile Oil Company, 677, 1104
Mobutu, Joseph, 714, 750, 853–854
Model Treaty ("Plan of 1776"), 12, 20, 22
main points, 9
Modrow, Hans, 1164
on German unification, 1167
Modža, Milan, 522
Moffat, Jay Pierrepont, 516
Moffit, Ronnie Karpen, 881, 1174
Mohamed, Ahmed Yousef, 1280
Mohamed, Ali, 1358
Mohammed VI, sultan of Turkey, 408, 431, 447
Mohave Desert, 108
Moi, Daniel Arap, 1194
Mojaddidi, Sibghatullah, 1151
Moldavia, in Commonwealth of Independent States (CIS), 1208
Moley, Raymond, 489

Muslims (*Continued*)
  ethnic cleansing in Bosnia-Serbia war, 1215, 1218, 1220, 1232, 1266, 1271
  Kosovo slaughter (1912), 343
  Lebanon, 700–701
  Moroccan independence, 686
Mussolini, Benito
  Corfu invasion, 448
  Ethiopian invasion, 265, 503–505
  execution of, 603
  Fascist Republic of Italy, 582
  Four-Power Pact (1933), 489
  Hitler relationship, 499
  North Africa concessions, 500
  Rome protocol (1930), 472
  Roosevelt communication, 523, 530
mutual assured destruction (MAD), 756, 779, 812, 894
Mutual and Balanced Force Reduction (MBFR), 947
Mutual Legal Assistance Treaty (1991), 1197
Mutual Security Agency, 660
Mutual Security Treaty (1951), U.S.-Japan, 660, 708, 786, 1265
Muzorewa, Abel T., 877, 886
MX missiles, 874, 895, 922, 934–935, 959, 968–969, 972, 1140
Myanmar, Union of, formerly Burma, 1156
myths
  American idealism in China, 129
  Anglo-American 1823 agreement, 102
  Hartford Convention secession recommendation, 84

N

Naccache, Anis, 1070
Nagakubo, Aikichi, 671
Nagasaki, Japan, 157
  atomic bomb, 609
  as open port, 183
Nagorno-Karabakh region, Azerbaijan, reunification protests, 1125, 1133, 1213–1214
Naguib Bey, Mohammed, 662
Nagy, Ferenc, 640
Nagy, Imre, 689
Najera, Castillo, 562
Najibullah, Mohammad, 1075, 1136, 1148, 1210, 1216, 1287
Nakasone, Yasuhiro, **1031**
  American goods, opening Japanese market to (1980s), 961, 1005, 1030–1031, 1040
  "Buy American" speech, 1040
  China, development loan offer to, 998
  coalition cabinet of, 988–989
  elected to second term, 1023
  elected to third term, 1079
  end of term, 1115
  Korea, visit to, 970
  U.S. pressure for Japanese defense spending (1980s), 961, 994
Namibia
  Angola-based guerrilla bases, 989
  independence of (1988), 1144–1145

independence plans, 921, 1012
  map of (1981), 913
  Nujoma as first president, 1171
  South Africa border issue, 863–864, 893, 935
  U.N. supervised elections, 1164
  U.S. diplomats, murder of, 1000–1001
  Zimbabwe formula and statehood, 912–914
Namphy, Henri, 1066, 1118, 1139, 1190
Naniwa (ship), 270
Nanking, Treaty of (1842), 134, 136, 139, 165
Nano, Fatos, 1301
Nansen, Fridtjof, 416, 438
napalm firebombing, Vietnam War, 748
Napier, Lord, 181, 183
Naples, Kingdom of, liberal uprising (1821), 95–96
Napoléon I, emperor of France, 44, 49–51, 58, 62, 118
  abdications by, 81, 86
  Bayonne Decree (1808), 66
  Berlin Decree (1806), 62, 65, 69, 71–73
  confiscation of U.S. ships, 69
  Continental System, 62–63, 72, 74, 114
  control, 49–51, 54–56, 58–59
  deception of Madison by, 74–75
  decline of, 77–78
  Elba exile, 81
  Louisiana Territory sale, 55–56
  Milan Decree (1807), 62, 65, 69–73
  100 days return, 85–86
  peak of European power (1807–1812), 64
  Rambouillet Decree (1810), 69
  St. Helena exile, 86
  territories in Americas and, 54–55, 59, 85
  Trianon Decree (1810), 69–70
  victory over Austria, 68
  Waterloo defeat of, 86
  See also Napoleonic wars
Napoléon III, emperor of France, 153–154, 159, 164, 174, 186, 207
  British free-trade treaty and, 190
  Franco-Prussian War and, 216
  French colonialism in southeast Asia and, 197
  Italian unification and, 193
  Mexican empire establishment by, 195–196, 200, 202, 205
  Mexican withdrawal by, 206, *206*
  Polish uprising (1863) and, 200
  U.S. Civil War mediation offer, 199–200
Napoleonic wars, 30–31, 38, 44–45, 50, 54, 58–59
  Britain and, 78, 81–82, 85–86
  British blockade, 61–62
  British neutral trade curbs, 63
  British Trafalgar victory, 60
  Danish prize courts and, 114
  first Treaty of Paris, 81–82
  international alliances against Napoléon, 78–79, 86
  Rambouillet Decree (1810), 69
  return from Elba for 100 days, 85
  Russian campaign, 77
  Treaties of Tilsit, 64
  Treaty of Schonbrunn, 68

Nesselrode, Count, 103, 119
Nestlé, infant formula issue, 916
Netanyahu, Benjamin
    Arab-Israeli mediation, 1283, 1291, 1322, 1324
    election as prime minister, 1283
    Israel claim to Jerusalem plan, 1283, 1286, 1293–1294
    new West Bank housing units by, 1304, 1304–1305, 1336
    reelection bid, loss of, 1324, 1332
    on West Bank settlements, 1283
Netherlands
    Algiers, attack of, 88
    American independence recognition, 14
    American Revolution aid, 12–13, 15, 28
    British conflict, 11, 13
    French war with, 30
    Indonesia independence conflict, 645, 696–697, 728
    IRA attack, 1126
    Japanese trade and, 182–183, 203
    League of Armed Neutrality, 12
    Nazi invasion of, 539
    U.S. airline treaty (1992), 1221
    U.S. missile deployment, 1057
Neto, Agestino, 850, 913–914
Neuces River, 145, 147–148
Neuilly, Treaty of (1919), 423
Neumann, Klaus, 1326
Neurath, Konstantin von, 484, 499
neutrality
    American assertion of principles of, 187
    American delegation to Britain on, 62
    American legislation (1794), 34
    British-American treaty (1806), 63
    in British Falklands seizure, 127
    British maritime violations, 32, 34–35, 46, 61
    British recruitment violations, 176, 178
    "broken voyage" concept, 56–57, 62
    of Canadian border, 204
    Crimean War and, 173, 176, 178
    Cuban rebellion (1895) and, 260
    Danish-Prussian war and, 157–158
    Declaration of Paris (1856) and, 178–179
    Embargo of 1807 and, 41, 65–66
    Essex decision, 59, 61–62
    European League of Armed Neutrality, 12–13
    Franco-American Alliance and, 31
    French violation announcement, 38–40
    German Samoan aggression and, 244
    Greek independence war and, 96
    Hamilton and Madison writings on, 32
    Jay's Treaty and, 35, 38
    in Latin American anti-Spanish rebellions, 87, 89–92
    law revision, 126
    League of Armed Neutrality, 51
    London Declaration (1908), 334, 354
    Macon's Bill No. 2, 32
    Model Treaty, 9
    Napoleonic wars, 61, 65, 69, 72–73
    Panama Congress attendance and, 105, 107
    "police-type" peacetime navy resolution and, 102

Seward note on Trent affair and, 196–197
    trade with Spanish colonies, 41
    War of 1859 in northern Italy, 187
    wartime confiscation of goods prohibition, 22
    Washington's proclamation, 31, 34
    World War I, 353, 354, 370
    World War II, 502–505, 511–512, 522, 532, 536, 537
Neutrality Act of 1817, 89
Neutrality Act of 1818, 91–92, 173
Neutrality Act of 1838, 126
Neutrality Act of 1935, 502–503
Neutrality Act of 1936, 504–505
Neutrality Act of 1937, 512, 522, 537
Neutrality Act of 1939, 537
neutron bomb
    Carter cancellation of project, 859
    French development, 893
    Reagan production of, 918–919
Nevada (battleship), 564
Nevado del Ruiz volcano, 1057
Neves, Tancredo de Almeida, 1033
New Brunswick, Canada, 110
    Webster-Ashburton Treaty settlement, 133
New Democracy (Greece), 1043
New England
    Canadian boundary commission, 18
    disregard of 1813 embargo, 80–81
    protests against Embargo of 1807, 65–66
    textile manufacture, 110
    War of 1812 opposition, 76–78, 80–81, 83–84
    See also specific states
New Granada, 94
    antimonarchist agreement, 154
    See also Colombia; Ecuador; Venezuela
New Granada, Treaty of (1846), 151
New Hampshire
    British boundary dispute, 110, 117
    constitutional ratification and, 25
    trade discrimination against British, 22
    War of 1812 dissent, 83
New Jersey
    American Revolution and, 9, 12
    War of 1812 opposition, 76
New Jewel Movement (Grenada), 966, 982–983, 1028
New Korea Democratic Party, 1036
new look policy, Eisenhower, 669–670, 677, 678, 695, 710, 718
New Masses, 654
New Mexico
    Apache war in, 217
    popular sovereignty and, 162
    U.S. occupation of, 150
    U.S. purchase offer, 143
New National Party (Grenada), 1028
New Orleans, battle of (1815), 84–85, 85, 116
New Orleans (ship), 162
New Orleans, La., 2, 21, 23, 26, 37, 62, 116
    ceded to United States, 58
    Mafia murders, 249–250
    protest against Spanish execution of Crittenden, 163

Nuber, Franz von, 376
Nuccio, Richard, 1294
nuclear arms control
    Anti-Ballistic Missile Treaty (ABM) (1972), 812
    atomic energy control plan (1945), 611–612
    Baruch Plan, 619, 621, 624–625
    disarmament/test ban conferences, 703, 711, 728
    Gorbachev era, 1029, 1040, 1048, 1087–1088, 1093–1094,
        1099–1100, 1101, 1119–1121, 1175–1176, 1201
    Great Britain, 771–772, 1086
    inspection system proposal, 669, 728
    intermediate nuclear forces (INF), 986, 1099–1100, 1101
    for intermediate-range missiles, 967–968
    Johnson-Khrushchev era weapons cuts, 740
    Latin America, 757
    Middle East as nuclear-free zone, 1198–1199
    Nuclear Non-Proliferation Treaty (1969), 771–772, 786–787
    Nunn-Lugar program, 1207
    Poseidon submarine dismantling, 1044
    SALT I (1972), 785–786, 812, 852, 858
    SALT II, 812, 833, 836, 874–875, 899
    strategic arms reduction talks (START), 942, 947, 988
    Strategic Arms Reduction Treaty (START I), 1201
    Strategic Arms Reduction Treaty (START II), 1228, 1274, 1346
    test bans, 728, 736, 833
    theater nuclear forces (TNF), 897–898
    U.S.-Soviet collapse of negotiations (1984), 986, 993
    U.S.-Soviet violations allegations (1984), 993–994
    Vladivostok formula (1974), 835–836, 853
    walk-in-the-woods agreement, 961, 1028
    See also specific countries; specific treaties
nuclear attack
    antinuclear war groups, 911, 920, 924, 939–940, 943, 946, 953
    deterrence approach, 1306
    multilateral nuclear striking force, 735
    mutual assured destruction (MAD) as deterrent, 756, 779
    "no first use" declaration, 940
    nuclear winter from, 984, 1037
    Ogarkov self-defense theory, 1127
    Pentagon crisis relocation plan, 1037
    physicians group against, 910–911, 1062
    strategic defense initiative (SDI), 966–967, **966**, 1009
    survivalist extremist view, 938
    U.S. protracted nuclear conflict plan, 943–944
    U.S.-Soviet Union Hot Line, 735, 761, 805, 1011
    See also missile defense systems
nuclear development and testing
    dangers of, 728
    France, 893, 1268
    Great Britain, 661, 693
    India, 832, 1315
    Iraq, 1187
    Israel, 1085–1086
    Kennedy expansion, 720, 727–728, 733–734
    Marshall Islands-U.S. agreement, 953
    Nixon expansion goals, 778–779
    Pakistan, 957–958, 1156, 1242, 1253, 1261, 1315
    People's Republic of China, 761, 944, 1239–1240, 1241
    Soviet Union, 614, 642, 647, 668, 694, 756

    test ban treaties, 728, 736
    test detection system, 700
    test measurement systems, 1139
    U.S., 605–607, 620, **621**, 663, 671, 687, 727–728, 1094, 1236
    U.S.-Soviet joint tests, 1117, 1139
    See also Atomic bomb; Hydrogen bomb (H-bomb); Missiles
Nuclear Non-Proliferation Treaty (1969), 771–772, 786–787,
    1245, 1253
    permanent status of (1995), 1263
nuclear reactors
    first reactor (1942), 576
    Hanford reactor, closing of, 1093
    North Korea construction, 1272, 1302
    on-site inspection of, 1036, 1063
nuclear winter, 984
Nueces River, 104
Nujoma, Sam, 914, 1171
nullification controversy of 1832, 111, 116, 118–120, 192
Nunn Amendment, 1009–1010, 1116
Nunn, Sam, 1009, 1115–1116, 1130, 1138, 1186, 1192, 1207,
    1237
Nuremberg Laws, 526
Nuremberg War Crimes tribunal, 622–623
Nyasaland
    dissolution of, 739
    See also Malawi
Nye, Gerald P., 495, 502–503, 521–522, 537
Nye, Gideon, Jr., 180
Nyerere, Jules, 738
Nyers, Rezso, 1158, 1162

O

Oakley, Robert, 1227, 1233, 1240
Obando y Bravo, Miguel, 1119
Obasanjo, Olusegun, 1332–1333, 1352
Obeid, Abdul Karim, 1159
Oberdorfer, Louis, 1053
Obregón, Alvaro, 353, 358, 374–375, 448
O'Brien v. Webb, 446
Obuchi, Keizo, 1317, 1346
Ocalan, Abdullah, 1328–1329, 1342
Ocana, Gilberto Ocana, 1076
Ochab, Edward, 691
Ochirbat, Gambojavyn, 1179
Ochoa, Jorge Luis, 1274
Ochoa Vasques, Jorge Thuis, 1106
Ochoa Vasquez, Fabio, 1190
O'Connor, Charles, 220
October Manifesto, 324
Octobrists, 391
O'Daniel, John, 680
Odeh, Muhammad Saddiq, 1318
Odell, Harry L., 792
Oder-Neisse River, 797
Odinga, Oginga, 1194
Odría, Manuel, 636
OFF TACKLE, 641

Pfeiffer, Jack B., 721
Phalangist Christians
  Gemayel assassination, 950–951
  Israeli military support by, 944–945
  Muslim conflict in Lebanon, 839, 850, 852, 858–859, 950–951, 975, 995, 1043, 1079
  Palestinian refugees massacre by, 951–952, 963
Phat, Lan Van, 743
Phelps, William W., 247
Philadelphia, Pa.
  banquet for Marshall, 43
  Constitutional Convention, 24–25
  First Continental Congress, 5
Philadelphia (frigate), 57–58
Philadelphia (ship), 289
Philippine Communist Party (PKP), 620
Philippines
  annexation issue, 284–288, 290–291
  Aquino (Benigo) assassination, 976, 979, 1005, 1022–1023
  Aquino (Corazon) presidency. *See* Aquino, Corazon C.
  cessation to U.S., 283
  guerrilla forces (1990s), 1174–1175
  guerrilla war (1901), 300, 305
  independence of (1934), 494
  independence of (1946), 620–621
  independence in future decree (1916), 381–382
  independence movement, 272, 278–279
  independent republic declared (1898), 283
  Marcos as president, 904, 916
  Philippine Government Act (Organic Act), 305
  Spanish-American war (1898), 274, 278–284
  Spanish execution of nationalist leader, 267, 272
  U.S. aid refusal (1986), 1084
  U.S. airforce base, 565–566, 971, 1141, 1210, 1225
  U.S. mutual assistance pact (1950), 650
  U.S. mutual defense treaty (1951), 659
  U.S. naval base, 441
  U.S. use of military bases, 868, 971
  World War II, 554–555, 563–564, 565–566, 594–595, 599
Phillips, Isaac, 46
Phillips, Rufus, 737
Phillips, William, 538
Phnom Penh, Cambodia, 789, 791, 840, 868, 1205
Phoenix operations, 772
Phouma, Souvanna, 713, 718–719, 729
Pickering, Thomas, 971, 987, 1010, 1011
Pickering, Timothy, 36–37, 42–43, 46–47, 49–50
Pico, Andres, 151
Piedmont
  Austrian invasion of, 186–187, 193
  Declaration of Paris and, 178–179
Pierce, Franklin, 165
  presidency of, 166–179, 181
  presidential election of 1852, 166
Pierce, John, 61
Pierce, Samuel, 1077
Pietruszka, Adam, 1023
Pilar, Marcelo de, 267
Pilliod, Charles J., Jr., 1082

Piłsudski, Józef, 528
Pinckney, Charles Cotesworth, 38, 40
  French negotiations and, 40–42, 43, 45–46
  as minister to Spain, 54, 58–59
  presidential loss (1804), 58
  presidential loss (1808), 66
Pinckney, Thomas, 29, 37, 39
Pinckney's Treaty (1795), 37, 42, 54
Pineau, Christian, 686
ping-pong team (U.S.), invitation to China, 800–801
Pinilla, Rojas, 694
Pinkney, William, 62–63, 68–70
Pinkowski, Jósef, 906
Pinochet, Augusto
  CIA aid to, 881
  human rights violations, 1034, 1079, 1195, 1331
  indictment for murder, 1349, 1365
  junta by, 1319
  ouster of, 1141
  return to Chile (2000), 1343
  state of siege declared by, 1024–1025
pinyin, Chinese translations, 870–871
Pioneer space program, 699
Piotrowski, Grzegarz, 1023
piracy
  Barbary piracy, 21, 24, 34, 37, 53, 63
  slave trade declared as, 95, 98, 103
  by terrorists. *See* hijacking
Pitt, William, 27, 61
Pittman, Key, 498, 502–503, 532
Pittman-Bloom resolution of 1940, 543
Pitts, Earl Edward, 1275
Pius VII, Pope, 49
Pius XII, Pope, 538, 684
"Plan of 1776" (Model Treaty), 9, 12, 20, 22
Plan of Ayola, 359
Platt, Orville H., 299–300
Platt Amendment, 299–300, 304, 354, 497
Plattsburg, N.Y., 81
Plavsić, Biljana, 1289, 1302, 1306
Plaza Accord (1985), 1051–1052, 1065
Pleiku, South Vietnam, 744, 838, 840
Pleven, René, 654
Pleven Plan, 654
Phnom Penh, 789
Pochot, Philippe, 1070
Podesta, John, **1361**
Podgorny, Nikolay, 799
pogroms, Russia, 309
Poher, Alain, 782
Pohill, Robert, 1154
Pohl, Hugo von, 360
Poincaré, Raymond, 444, 452
Poindexter, John M., **1061**
  Iran-Contra affair, 1092, 1096–1097, 1102, 1116, 1172–1173, 1203
  as national security adviser, 1061
Poinsett, Joel, 102, 104–105, 110, 113, 115–116
Point Four Program, 638, 648

Proctor, Redfield, 275
Progressive (Bull Moose) Party, 344, 383, 426, 453, 636
Progressive Conservative Party (Canada), 885, 1016
Progressive People's Party (Germany), 395
Progressive Socialist Party (Lebanon), 852
Prohibition Party, 224, 231, 246, 252
Project Argus, 852
Project Democracy, 925, 945–946, 960–961, 1033
Project Elephant Herd, 1015
Project Enhance, 817
Project Independence, 828
Project Restore Hope, **1231**
Project Rhyolite, 852
Project 20, 030 Pyramid, 852
Prometheus (steamship), 163
Promo de Rivera, Miguel, 476–478
Promontory, Utah, 213
Prophet (Indian leader), 72–73
protective tariff, 109–110
    Fordney-McCumber Tariff (1922), 443
    of German Empire, 229
    of Great Britain, 480
    McKinley (1890), 248–249
    Morrill Tariff (1861), 193
    Payne-Aldrich Tariff (1909), 336
    Protective Tariff of 1816, 88
    Reciprocal Trade Agreements Act of 1934, 497–498
    in Republican platform, 180, 192–193, 215, 231, 246, 252, 266
    Smoot-Hawley Tariff (1931), 474, 490, 498
    specialty steel issue (1980s), 973, 992
    Tariff of 1883 and, 236
    for U.S. manufacturing, 215
    and U.S. trade imbalance (1980s), 915
    War of 1812 and, 88
Protestants, Northern Ireland conflict, 774
protests and demonstrations, anti-Asian immigrants, 231, *231*, 235, 244–245
protests and demonstrations (U.S.)
    antinuclear demonstrations and groups, 911, 920, 924, 946
    colonial grievances, 4
    Democratic Convention 1968, 773
    Embargo of 1807, 65–66
    Great Peace March (1986), 1091
    Jackson State College massacre, 791
    Kent State University massacre, 791
    Panic of 1837 and, 125
    poor people's campaign, 771
    Vietnam antiwar movement, 77, 745–746, 749, 763, 773, **790**, 791, 801
    War of 1812, 77
    World Trade Organization (WTO) meeting, 1339
Provisional Army, 45, 50
Provisional Revolutionary Government (PRG) (Vietnam), 816, 821
Proxmire, William, 823, 1068
Prussia
    Adams (John Quincy) as minister to, 48, 89
    commercial treaty, 20, 22
    Danish war, 156–158

French war, 29–30, 193, 214, 216, 222
German unification and, 156
in Holy Alliance, 87
League of Armed Neutrality, 12, 51
Napoléon, alliance against, 78–82, 86
Napoleonic victory over, 64
Polish uprising and, 200
in Quadruple Alliance, 87
in Quintuple Alliance, 87, 95–96
Seven Weeks' War with Austria, 207
See also Germany
Pruyn, Robert H., 201, 203, 207
"Psychological Operations in Guerrilla Warfare," 1021–1022
P'u-i, Henry, 480
Public Against Violence (Czechoslovakia), 1177
Pucnik, Joze, 1173
Puebla, battle of (1847), 152
Pueblo (spy ship), 766
Puerto Rico
    cessation to U.S., 282, 284
    import duties, 302
    independence movement, 652
    non-citizenship status, 302
    Spanish retention of, 99, 106
    as territory (1900), 294–295
Pueyrredon, Juan Martín, 90
Pugo, Boris, 1202
P'ui, emperor of China, 342
Pulitzer, Joseph, 263, 271
Punjab, India-Pakistan conflict, 1098
Put-in-Bay, 79
Putiatin, Count, 183–184
Putin, Vladimir
    Afghanistan border issue, 1355
    appointed acting president, 1340
    Chechnya conflict, 1337, 1340, 1343, 1345, 1350
    Clinton visit, 1349, **1349**
    election as president, 1345
    nuclear arms control, 1346
Putnam, William, 244
Pyatakov, Yuri, 512

Q

Qatar, 851
Qian Qichen, 1188, 1243, 1300
Qin Yong, 1316
Quadritite Agreement (1972), 798, 804, 812–813
Quadruple Alliance, 87, 120
Quang, Thich Tri, 752–753
Quang Tri, South Vietnam, 838
Quarantine Speech (1937), 514–515, 518
Quartering Act of 1765 (G.B.), 4
quasi war with France. *See* Franco-American undeclared war
Quat, Phan Huy, 747
Quavam, Ahmad, 617
Quayle, Danforth, as vice president, 1142, **1176**, **1193**, 1220
Quebec, Canada, colonial siege of, 6–7

Hungary invasion (1919), 420
Jewish persecution, 306
Little Entente, 436, 461
most-favored-nation status, 1104, 1125–1126
Nixon visit, 783–784
Second Balkan War (1913), 348
Soviet control, 623–624, 626
Soviet interests, 569, 614
Soviet military assistance treaty (1948), 633
Soviet withdrawal, 701
Transylvania and, 844
Treaty of Berlin and, 227
Treaty of Bucharest (1918), 401
World War I, 401, 407, 430
World War II, 546, 589
Romanies, 1326
Rome, Italian annexation of, 193, 216, 235
Rome, Treaty of (1957), 1061
Romero, Carlos Huberto, 879
Romero, Oscar Arnulfo, assassination of, 887, 1010, 1028, 1117, 1230
Rommel, Erwin, 549, 581
Rong Sam Len Island, 841
Ronning, Chester, 753
Roosevelt Corollary, 318–319, 468
Roosevelt, Eleanor, 637
Roosevelt, Franklin Delano
    arms embargo (1935), 502–506, 512, 514, 543
    Atlantic Charter (1941), 555–557
    Big Three Conference (1943), 586
    Cairo Conference (1943), 585–586, 587
    Casablanca Conference (1943), 579–580
    China relations, 526, 551, 569–570, 575, 578, 580–581, 585–586, 587–588, 591, 595–596
    Cuba policy, 489–491, 493–494, 497
    on currency stabilization, 488–489
    Czech crisis intervention, 522–523
    de Gaulle recognition by, 591–592
    death of, 603
    defense buildup, 522, 524–525, 530, 540, 543
    Fireside Chats, 547–548
    "Germany First" strategy, 542, 546, 548, 551
    Great Depression measures, 488–489, 494
    Greer incident, 557–558
    Hitler communications, 522–523, 530–531, 535
    Import-Export Bank, 494
    on isolationism, 540–541
    Japan, pre-war actions, 533, 539, 543, 550, 551–552, 554–555, 557–559, 562–564, 566
    Japanese-American relocation, 570–571
    Japanese declaration of war by, 566
    on Jewish massacre by Nazis, 525–526, 538, 589
    Latin American policy, 510–511
    lend-lease program, 548, 548–549, 554, 560, 576
    military draft, 545, 556–557
    moral embargoes, 503, 506, 507, 511, 538
    Mussolini communication, 523, 530
    national emergency declared (1941), 552–553
    presidency of (first term) of, 482–509, **483**

presidency of (second term), 509–546
presidency of (third term), 546–596
presidency of (fourth term), 596–603
presidential election of 1932, 482
presidential election of 1936, 509
presidential election of 1940, 546
presidential election of 1944, 596
Quarantine Speech (1937), 514–515, 518
Quebec Conferences (1943, 1944), 582, 593–594
Rainbow War Plans (1939), 531, 542
Soviet recognition by, 492
Soviet relations, 553–554, 560, 574, 576, 581, 583–587, 592–594, 602
on Spanish Civil War, 511, 529
Trident Conference (1943), 582
Washington (Arcadia) Conference (1942), 567–568
World War II, **556**, **583**, **587**
Yalta Conference (1945), 594, 599–601, **600**
Roosevelt, Kermit, 668
Roosevelt, Theodore
    Bull Moose Republican, 344, 383
    foreign affairs, approach to, 252, 263, 306, 317
    on 14 Points, 408
    on League of Nations, 388, 408, 409
    Nobel Peace Prize, 323
    Panama Canal, 303, 304, 310–311, 314–316
    Panama independence revolution, **314**
    Philippines war and, 273, 281, 305
    presidency of, 301–333
    president after McKinley assassination, 301
    presidential election of 1904, 318
    and presidential election of 1912, 344
    Rough Riders, 281
    Russo-Japanese peace conference, 322–323
    as secretary of navy, 273
Root, Elihu
    as delegate to Russia, 393–394
    naval reduction conference, 439
    resignation as secretary of state, 335
    as secretary of state, 320–335
    as secretary of war, 299, 300, 307–308, 312
    State Department document-location system by, 324
    State Department geographic divison, 332
Root-Bryce Treaty (1908), 332
Root-Cortés Treaty (1909), 334–335, 350
Root-Takahira Agreement (1908), 322, 334, 336, 364
Rosario, Strait of, 219
Rose, Michael, 1247
Rose, Sir John, 213–214, 216, 218
Rosen, Roman R., 322
Rosenberg, Ethel, 647, 655–656
Rosenberg, Julius, 647, 655–656, 1266
Rosenberg, Tina, 1318
Rosenthal, Elizabeth, 1316
Ross, Dennis, 1286, 1291
Ross, Robert, 82
Rost, Pierre A., 195
Rostow, Eugene, 755–756, 915, 960
Rostow, Walter W., 725–726, 736–737, **765**, 769

Savannah (ship), 94

Savimbi, Jonas, 913, 930, 1002, 1046–1047, 1068, 1083, 1117, 1145, 1223, 1234, 1295

Sawyer, Amos, 1278

Saxitonit, biological weapon, 787

Sayaf, Abdul Rasul, 1151

Sayre, Francis B., 497, 500

Scale, Patrick, 1074

Scammon, Richard M., 992

Schacht, Hjalmar, 498–499, 505

Schatz, Jesse G., 1039

Scheer, Robert, 922, 938

Scheidemann, Philipp, 395, 409

Schenck v. U.S., 401

Schiff, Jacob, 306, 309

Schleicher, Kurt von, 485

Schlesinger, James, 826, 829, 894, 968, 1105

Schleswig-Holstein, 157–158

Schley, Winfield S., 251, 279, 281

Schlieffen Plan, 355

Schmidt, Alfred, 1138

Schmidt, Helmut
on arms reduction, 908, 927
Brezhnev meetings, 893, 927
East German president meeting with, 929
end of chancellorship, 951
on NATO missile deployment, 877–878, 891–892
North-South conference, 923–924
reelection as chancellor, 897

Schmitz, Eugene, 329

Schneider, Commander, 372–373

Schneider, Rene, 797

Schofield, James M., 205

Schomburgk, Robert, 258

Schomburgk Line, 258, 261, 263

Schonbrunn, Treaty of (1809), 68

School of the Americas (Panama), 1018

Schröder, Gerhard, 1319–1320
Berlin as headquarters, 1335
Clinton visit, 1349
social entitlements issue, 1325

Schuman, Robert, 662

Schuman Plan (1952), 662

Schurman, Jacob G., 290–291

Schuschnigg, Kurt, 518

Schussel, Wolfgang, 1341

Schwarzenberg, Prince Felix, 155

Schwarzkopf, H. Norman
Mossadegh overthrown, 668
Persian Gulf War, 1180, 1194–1195

Schweiger, Walter, 363

Sciaroni, Bretton, 1317

Sclopis, Frederic, 219

Scobee, Francis R., 1065

Scoon, Paul, 982

Scotland, Pan-Am explosion over (1988), 1133, 1145, 1318, 1362

Scott, Charles S., 247

Scott, Winfield, 126, 128
Mexican War, 151–152, *152*, 153

as Whig presidential candidate, 166

Scowcroft, Brent, 967, 968, 1098–1099, **1193**
as national security adviser, 1152, **1176**, **1187**
People's Republic visit, 1157, 1166–1167

Scowcroft Commission (1983), 968–969

Scruggs, William, 258–259, 261

SCUD missiles, 1193

Sea Gull (ship), 162

Sea Isle City (tanker), 1113

Sea Shephard Conservation Society, 1091

Sea Stallion helicopters, 1107

Seabed Arms Control Treaty (1971), 799

sealing controversy
arbitration ruling against United States, 254
British-U.S. conflict, 241, 242, 245, 247
British-U.S. modus vivendi, 250
pelagic sealing prohibition, 339–340

SEALS, U.S. Navy, 1113

Sears, Isaac, 1, 4

Seattle Post-Intelligencer, 421

Seattle Star, 421

secession, 193–194
New England War of 1812 dissenting radicals and, 83
See also Confederate States of America

Second Bank of the United States, 88, 93

Second Continental Congress. *See* Continental Congress

Second International, 413

Secord, Richard V., Iran-Contra affair, 1092, 1116

Secret Committee. *See* Committee of Secret Commerce

Sécurité Intelligence Nationale (SIN), 1066

Sécurité Intelligence Nationale (SIN) (Haiti), 1066, 1204

Sedan, battle of (1870), 216

Sedition Act of 1798, 44–47

Sedition Act of 1918, 401

seismic method, nuclear test measurement, 1139

Seko, Mobutu Sese, 1288, 1297, 1327, 1369

Selassie, Haile, 831

Selective Service Act of 1917, 393

Selective Service and Training Act of 1940, 545, 556–557, 822–823

Selfridge, Thomas, 223

Semenov, Eugene (alias Kohn), 406

semiconductor chips, U.S.-Japan dispute, 1081, 1100

Seminole Indians, 88

Seminole War (1835–1843), 114

Semyonov, Vladimir, 947

Sen, Hun, 1122, 1135, 1157–1158, 1317–1318

Senate
Adams (John Quincy) opponents in, 107
Anglo-American slave trade suppression convention and, 103
Colombian-U.S. Panama Canal rights treaty rejection, 212
Jackson censure by, 94
Johnson (Andrew) impeachment trial, 211
Oregon 49th parallel compromise and, 149
organization of, 26
Texas annexation treaty rejection by, 139
Wilmot Proviso rejection, 150

Senate Foreign Relations Committee, 107, 210, 212–213
Sumner and, 217

Snow, Edgar, 753
Snow, Peter W., 128
"Snow Mountains" (Sangre do Cristos), 104
Snowe, Olympia, 975
Sobell, Morton, 655
Socarras, Prio, 661
social Darwinism, 261
Social Democrat Party (Germany), 395, 411–412, 615, 639, 951, 965, 1071, 1171, 1183
Social Democratic Party (Japan), 627
Social Democratic Party (Nicaragua), 1102
Social Democratic Party (Serbia), 1285, 1359
Social Revolutionists (Russia), 418, 427
socialism, rise of. *See* Bolsheviks; communism; communism in U.S.; Union of Soviet Socialist Republics (USSR)
Socialist Party (Bulgaria), 1177
Socialist Party (France), 506
Socialist Party (Italy), 973
Socialist Party (Japan), 1159
Socialist Party (Russia), 391
Socialist Party (U.S.), 392, 401, 420
Socialist Unity Party (East Germany), 616, 1162, 1166
Socialist Workers Party (Spain), 954
Socialized People's Self-Defense Forces (PSDF), 788
Sofaer, Abraham, 1115
Sokolovsky, Vasily D., 633
Sol, Armando Calderon, 1248
Sol Meza, Ricardo, 919, 1065
Solana, Javier, 1330
Solidarity
    beginning of, 897
    coalition with communists, 1160
    evolution of movement, 1160
    Polish trade union ban (1982), 953
    Reverend Popieluszko assassination, 1023
    See also Wałesa, Lech
Solomon, Gerald, 1067
Solomon Islands, World War II, 576, 594
Solorzano, Carlos, 454, 459
Solovyev, Yury F., 1153
Solzhenitsyn, Aleksandr, 831
Somalia
    civil war (1990s), 1191–1192, 1215
    Cuba relations, 856, 1191
    Ethiopia war, 855, 858, 947
    Hassan as president (2000), 1352
    map of (1991), 1191
    Mogadishu hostage crisis, 856
    Soviet break, 856
    U.N. forces/Pakistani peacekeepers, attack on, 1234–1235
    U.N. National Council plan, 1230–1231
    U.N. peacekeepers in, 1226
    UNOSOM II troops in, 1233, 1234–1235
    U.S. Blackhawk helicopters, attack on, 1240
    U.S. humanitarian mission, 1226–1227
    U.S. military aid to, 947, 1191, 1228–1229
    U.S. Quick Reaction Force, 1234–1235, **1235**, 1240
Somalia Democratic Salvation Front, 1191–1192
Somalia National Movement, 1191

Somaliland
    French territory, 702
    World War II, 549
Somoza, Anastasio, 865–866, 875–876, 1036, 1127, 1134
Son, Hoang Bich, 1067
Son Tay POW camp, 797
Sonnefeldt, Helmut, 784
Sonnino, Sidney, 365
Sonora, Mexico, 183, 188
Sons of Liberty, 1, 4
Soong, James, 1344
Sorenson, Theodore, 733, 1149
Soros, George, 1302
Soros Foundation, 1302
Sotels, Leopoldo Calvo, 907
Soulé, Pierre, 170, 174–176
"Sound Dues" (Denmark), 181–182
Souphanouvong, 729
South (U.S.)
    disputed 1876 electoral vote compromise and, 225–226
    expansionist Cuban annexation plan, 161, 163
    nullification doctrine, 118
    Reconstruction era, 204
    slavery issue and, 162, 186
    See also Civil War, U.S.; Confederate States of America; *specific states*
South Africa
    Angolan invasions by, 893, 920, 989, 1117–1118
    anti-apartheid groups. *See* African National Congress (ANC); Mandela, Nelson
    black African discrimination. *See* apartheid
    Boer War (1899), 292
    Canadian economic sanctions, 1046
    Clinton visit to, 1312
    constitutional reforms (1991), 1200
    democratic constitution (1996), 1280
    emergency decrees (1985), 1048
    interim nonracial government (1992), 1222
    Kruger Telegram, 263–264
    Mandela as president. *See* Mandela, Nelson
    media restrictions by, 1057
    mixed-blood citizens, limited rights for, 984, 1016
    Mozambique peace pact, 997
    Namibia border issue, 863–864, 893
    Namibian independence, 1144–1145
    Reagan on "reformist" government of, 1049
    U.N. membership (1994), 1250–1251
    U.S. economic sanctions, 1050, 1085
    U.S. economic sanctions lifted (1990s), 1200, 1244
    U.S. export restrictions eased, 935
    Verwoerd assassination, 753
South African Communist Party, 1169
South America. *See* Latin America
South Asian Association for Regional Cooperation, 1062
South Carolina
    disputed electoral votes (1876), 224
    Fort Sumter fall and, 194
    nullification, 120
    opposition to Tariff of 1828, 111, 120

"Star Spangled Banner, The" (national anthem), 82
Star Wars. *See* Strategic Defense Initiative (SDI)
Stark (guided missile frigate), 1103, 1107, 1153
Stark, Harold, 542, 546, 555, 558
Starodubtsev, Vasily, 1202
Starr, Kenneth, 1308, 1320
Starr, Richard, 947
State Department
　Acheson appointed secretary, 638, 638–663
　Adams (John Quincy) appointed secretary, 89
　Albright appointed secretary, 1291
　Bacon appointed secretary, 335
　Baker appointed secretary, 1152
　Baker resignation, 1220
　Bayard appointed secretary, 239
　Blaine appointed secretary, 232
　Blaine reappointed secretary, 247–251
　Blaine resignation, 252
　Bryan appointed secretary, 345
　Bryan resignation, 345, 365–366
　Buchanan appointed secretary, 142
　Byrnes appointed secretary, 605
　Calhoun appointed secretary, 138
　Cass appointed secretary, 180
　Central American canal rights and, 223
　Christopher appointed secretary, 1229
　Clay appointed secretary, 104
　Clayton appointed secretary, 157
　Colby appointed secretary, 425–426
　communist-infiltration accusations, 635, 638, 647, 650, 654–655
　consolidation of department, 324
　creation as first executive department, 27
　Day appointed secretary, 277
　Day resignation, 283
　Defense Department cooperation, 905–906
　diplomatic service formal organization, 176
　document-location system, 324
　Dulles appointed secretary, 664
　Dulles death, 705
　Eagleburger as acting secretary, 1220
　Evarts appointed secretary, 226
　Everett appointed secretary, 167
　Fish named as Washburne replacement, 213
　foreign loan control to, 439
　Foreign Service Department established, 451
　Forsyth appointed secretary, 120–121
　Frelinghuysen appointed secretary, 234
　geographic divisions of, 332
　Gresham appointed secretary, 253
　Haig appointed secretary, 903
　Haig resignation, 946–947
　Hay appointed secretary, 283
　Herter appointed secretary, 705
　Hughes appointed secretary, 435
　Hughes resignation, 453
　Hull appointed secretary, 487
　Hull resignation, 597
　Jefferson as first secretary, 26, 27–33

Jefferson resignation, 33
Kellogg appointed secretary, 453
Kissinger appointed secretary, 824
Knox appointed secretary, 335
Lansing appointed secretary, 366
Lansing resignation, 425
Livingston named as Van Buren replacement, 116
Loyalty Security Board (LSB), 654
McLane appointed secretary, 120
Madison appointed secretary, 52
Marcy appointed secretary, 168
Marshall (George) appointed secretary, 625
Marshall (George) resignation, 638
Marshall (John) appointed secretary, 50
Monroe named as Smith (Robert) replacement, 71
Muskie appointed secretary, 889
Olney appointed secretary, 260–267, 269
Pickering named as Randolph replacement, 36–37
policy-planning staff established, 627
Powell appointed secretary, 1370
Randolph appointed secretary, 33
Randolph resignation, 36–37
Rogers appointed secretary, 777
Rogers resignation, 824
Root appointed secretary, 320
Root resignation, 335
Rusk appointed secretary, 719
Seward appointed secretary, 193
Sherman appointed secretary, 269
Sherman resignation, 269, 277
Shultz appointed secretary, 946
slavery defense by, 136
Smith appointed secretary, 67
Standing Liaison Committee, 521
Stettinius appointed secretary, 597
Stimson appointed secretary, 467
transatlantic cable use, 207
Upshur appointed secretary, 135
U.S. embassies, safety plan for, 1052
Van Buren appointed secretary, 112
Vance appointed secretary, 851
Vance resignation, 889
Washburne appointed secretary, 212–213
Watson appointed secretary, 252
Webster appointed secretary, 130
Webster reappointed secretary, 162
state sovereignty
　Articles of the Confederation and, 13, 20
　Calhoun defense of, 111
　commercial regulation and, 22
　Embargo Act annulment and, 67
　fears of congressional commercial treaty powers and, 20
　Hartford Convention and, 84
　Indian removal policies and, 108–109, 114
　militia-raising powers and, 29
　secession and, 193
　Supreme Court rulings against, 32
　wartime military defense and, 84
　See also state's rights

Christian-Muslim conflict, 1166
Egypt border tension (1995), 1265
Egypt relations (1980s), 998
food relief, abuse of program, 1184
food relief, international, 1196
government overthrown (1985), 1040
independence of (1956), 685, 712
Libya relations (1980s), 997–998, 1040, 1166
as terrorist nation (1993), 1237, 1265
terrorists incidents in. *See* Israeli terrorist; Muslim terrorists;
    Palestinian terrorist
U.S. economic sanctions (1996), 1280
U.S. monitoring of Libya from, 976
Sudanese People's Liberation Army, 1166, 1184
Suez Canal
    British control of, 223, 235, 239, 242
    convention signing (1888), 245–246
    mining of Red Sea, 1013
    official opening, 214
    reopens (1975), 841
    territorial zones, 830
Suez Canal Company, 223
Suez Canal User's Association (SCUA), 689–690
Suez crisis, 688–690, 692
Suffolk (cruiser), 427
Sugar Act of 1764 (G.B.), 3
sugar imports, 221
Suh, Lee Bum, 980
Suharto, Mohamed, 1312, 1314–1315
Sukarno, Achmed, 645, 696–697, 728
Sukarnoputri, Megawati, 1337
Sulawesi (Celebes), 696
Sullivan Code (South Africa), 1104
Sullivan, James M., 356
Sullivan, Leon, 1104
Sullivan, Peter J., 212
Sullivan, William H., 870
Sullivans (destroyer), 1357
Sultan, Khalid bin, 1194–1195
Summer Language Institute, 910
Summers, Anthony, 775
Summers, Lawrence H., 1355
Summit of the Americas (1998), 1313
Summit Aviation, 1015
Sumner, Charles, 169, 208, 213–214, 216–218, 219
Sumulong, Lorenzo, 715
Sun Wen, 395
Sun Yat-Sen, 342, 347, 348, 352, 417, 466
Sung Chiao-Jen, assassination of, 347, 348
Sung, Kim Il, 642, 649, 652, 709, 876, 1242, 1244, 1253
Sunni Muslims, 972, 995
    Lebanon factionalism, 1041
    Taliban, 1320
    terrorism by, 1053
Sununu, **1193**
Super Etendard fighter planes, 1006
Superior (ship), 117
supersonic transport plane (SST), 800
Supreme Court, U.S., *Amistad* ruling, 130

Supreme War Council, 567
Supreme Worshipful Association of the Sons of the People. *See*
    Katipunan
surface-to-air missiles (SAMs), 793
Suriname, new constitition of (1987), 1118
Susan Loud (ship), 162
Suslov, Mikhail, 689
Sussex (steamer), 379, 381, 383
Sutherland, Richard K., 565
Sutherland, Thomas M., 1031, 1205
Sutterlee, F. W., 297
Suzuki, Zenko, 892
    U.S. pressure for Japanese military spending, 917, 937
Swank, Emory C., 823
Swanson, Claude, 942
Sweden
    League of Armed Neutrality, 51
    Napoleonic war, 78
Swift, John T., 231
Swiss Air hijacking (1970), 794
Sykes–Picot Agreement (1916), 379–380, 396, 531
Sylvester II, Pope, 858
Symington, Stuart, 695
Syndicate of Petroleum Workers, 519
Syria
    Arab-Israeli conflict *See* Arab-Israeli mediation; Arab-Israeli
        warfare and violence; Arab terrorism; Israeli terrorism
    Assad leadership. *See* Assad, Hafiz al-
    communist takeover crisis (1957), 694–695
    Golan Heights annexation to Israel, 930, 940
    Great Britain break with, 1090
    independence of (1945), 614
    Israel border dispute, 685, 755
    Jordan, attack of (1970), 795
    Jordan dispute (1980), 900
    Lebanon friendship treaty (1991), 1198
    Lebanon peace talks (1984), 996–997
    Lebanon peacekeeping by, 850, 1079
    Palestine Liberation Organization (PLO) expulsion, 972
    Palestine Liberation Organization (PLO) in, 961
    Soviet relations (1970s), 794–795
    spheres of influence (1916), 379
    U.S. pilot released (1984), 990
Szilard, Leo, 537
Szulc, Tad, 799, 832
Szuros, Mátyás, 1162

T

Ta-Kiang (merchant steamer), 203
Tachen Island, 679, 701
Tack, Juan Antonio, 830
Tacoma, 445
Tacubaya, Armistice of (1847), 152
Tadić, Dušan, 1297
Tadjikistan, in Soviet Union, 444
Taepo Dong-1 missile, 1318
Taft, George, 909

Tracy, Benjamin, 250, 251
Tracy, Edward A., 1205
trade. *See* commercial treaties; embargoes; free trade; interstate commerce; *specific tariffs and treaties*; tariffs
Trade Act of 1823, 98–99, 115
trade deficit (U.S.). *See* debt, national
Trade Expansion Act of 1962, 729–730
Trade Reform Bill of 1974, 836
Trading with the Enemy Act (1917), 396
Trafalgar, battle of (1805), 60
Trajkovski, Boris, 1365
Trans-Siberian Railway, 403–404, 426, 428
Trans-World Airways (TWA)
  explosion/planted bomb (1986), 1072
  hijacking (1970), 794
  hijacking (1985), 1044–1045, 1105
transatlantic cable, 207–208
transatlantic crossings
  regularly scheduled New York-Liverpool, 90
  steam-powered ship, 94, 141–142
Transcaucasia
  in USSR, 444
  World War I, 401
transcontinental railroad, 166
  completion of first (1869), 213
transcontinental telegraph, 195
Transcontinental Treaty of 1819, 94
Transits and Conventions, Treaty of (1859), 189
Transjordan, 618
transportation
  clipper ship transcontinental crossing, 90
  railroads, transcontinental, 166, 213
  steamship service, 141–142, 163
Transvaal, 264
Transylvania, 420, 430, 626, 844
Travis, William B., 123
Treasury Department, Hamilton as first secretary, 26, 27
treaties
  congressional powers and, 25
  Indian tribal lands and, 242
  invalidity of infringing state laws, 32
  negotiation model (1776), 9
  U.S. Constitution and, 178
  See also commercial treaties; *specific treaties by key word*
Treaty on Conventional Forces in Europe (1990), 1186
Treholt, Arne, 994
Trent affair (1861), 196–197
Trenton (ship), 247
Trenton, battle of (1776), 9
Trescot, William H., 231, 233
  War of the Pacific mediation, 234–235
trial by jury, 3
Trianon Decree (1810), 69–70
Trianon, Treaty of (1920), 430
tribute trade, Chinese, 130–131
Trident Conference (1943), 580, 582
Trident submarines, 895
Trieste, border dispute, 625, 670
Trimble, David, 1313, 1319

Tripartite Pact of 1940, 546–547, 553
Triple Alliance (1882), 235, 242
Triple Alliance (1902), 305
Triple Alliance (1907), 330
Triple Entente (1907), 330
Tripoli
  Barbary piracy, 21, 24, 37, 236
  capture of *Philadelphia*, 57–58
  commercial treaty, 40–41
  Dema capture and peace, 59–60, *59*
  indemnification from, 87
  Italian colony conflict, 305
  U.S. embassy attack (1979), 882
  U.S. naval action against, 53–54
Tripp, Bartlett, 293
Tripp, Linda, 1308, 1320
Trist, Nicholas P., 152–154
Trochu, Louis, 216
Troppau Protocol (1821), 96, 98
Trotsky, Leon
  defeat of White Russians, 444
  post-Revolution flight, 507
  Sisson Documents, 406–407
  See also Bolsheviks
Troup, George Michael, 108
Trudeau, Pierre, 874, 885, 939, 1016
Trujillo, César Gaviria, 1190
Trujillo, Rafael, 723, 746
Truk Island, 897
Truman, Harry S.
  assassination attempt, 652
  atomic bombing of Japan, 605–609
  atomic energy policy, 611–612, 614, 621
  China policy, 612–613
  containment policy, 669
  defense program investigation, 549
  European recovery assistance, 621, 626–631, 634–635, 638, 648, 660
  Korean War, 648–649, 652–658
  MacArthur dismissal, 656–657
  military draft, 658
  NATO war plans (Korea), 653–654
  on Palestine issue, 630–631
  Point Four program, 638
  Potsdam Conference (1945), 605–608
  presidency of, 603–663, **603**
  presidential election of 1948, 636
  pro-communist accusations, 646, 647
  Soviet relations, 604
  Truman Doctrine (1947), 626
  Vietnam policy, 611
  Wallace conflict, 622
  West German policy, 634–635
  World War II negotiation, 605–608, **606**
Trumbull, John, 6, *10*, *19*
Trumbull, Jonathan, 67
Truong Mountains, 837
trusts, 221
Truxtun, Thomas, 49

TRW Defense and Space Systems Group, 851–852
Tsantes, George, 985
Tseng Kuo-fan, 198
Tshombe, Moise, 711, 713, 720, 724–726, 733, 741
Tsingtao-Tsinan Railway, 271, 442
Tsushima Straits, battle of, 320
TTAPS report, 984
Tudeh Communist Party (Iran), 668
Tudjman, Franjo, 1169, 1173, 1183, 1200, 1221, 1232, 1258, 1267, 1270, 1274, 1342, **1342**
   corruption of, 1353
Tudjman, Stjepan, 1353
Tudor, Corneliu Vadim, 1364
Tuileries Palace (Paris), 29, 50
Tukhachevsky, M. N., 512
Tunis, Tunisia
   Barbary piracy, 21, 24, 37, 63
   commercial treaty with, 41
   French protectorate over, 232
   independence movement, 662
   Italian concessions, 500
   Palestine Liberation Organization (PLO) headquarters bombing, 1053
   Palestine Liberation Organization (PLO) in, 949, 972
   U.S. naval action, 60
   World War II, 581
Tupac Amaru Revolutionary Movement. *See* Shining Path
Tupper, Charles, 244, 245
Turabi, Hassal al-, 1237
Turco, Richard P., 984
Turgot, marquis de, 174–175
Turkey
   Armenian attacks on, 948, 975
   Armenians, massacre of, 258, 262, 266, 362, 458
   armistice of 1918, 408
   Atatürk leadership. *See* Atatürk, Kemal
   in CENTO, 705, 707
   Ciller, first woman president, 1236
   Colby railway concession, 341, 446
   Cyprus, Turkish Republic of, 985
   Cyprus independence and, 714
   First Balkan War (1912), 333, 343
   Gallipoli campaign against, 362, 374
   Greco-Crete conflict (1896), 266, 270
   Greco-Cyprus conflict (1964), 739
   Greco-Cyprus conflict (1974), 833–835
   Greco-Turkish war (1920), 431, 447
   Kurdish conflicts, 1118, 1204, 1328–1329
   Kurdish safe zone, 1196, 1201, 1219, 1248, 1282
   Menderes ousted, 710
   missionaries, attack on, 262
   Muslim fundamentalism, rejection of (1997), 1293
   nationalism, 431, 447
   NATO membership (1951), 660
   nuclear-free zone opposition, 1125
   opium trade, 128
   republic declared (1923), 448–449
   republican goverment overthrown (1982), 954–955
   as secular state, 448–449, 1293

   Serb attack of, 343
   Soviet interests, 621–622
   Sykes–Picot Agreement, 379–380
   terrorist incidents, 1083
   Treaty of Lausanne (1923), 447, 456–457
   Treaty of Sévres (1920), 431, 447
   Triolitan War with Italy, 340
   Truman Doctrine (1947), 626
   U.S. arms embargo, 834–835, 843, 865
   U.S. economic assistance (1980), 887–888
   U.S. economic assistance halted (1974), 834–835
   U.S. indemnity claim, 299
   U.S. military installation in, 705, 733, 835, 843, 887–888, 1201
   U.S. treaty of amity (1923), 447–448
   U.S. treaty of amity (1923) rejected, 456–457
   World War I, 362, 374
   Young Turk revolution, 333
Turkish Cypriot Republic, 985
Turkish Empire. *See* Ottoman Empire
Turkish National Union, 710
Turkmenistan
   in Commonwealth of Independent States (CIS), 1208
   natural gas pipeline, 1308
Turmenistan, in USSR, 445
Turner, David, 140
Turner, George, 312
Turner, Jesse, 1205
Turner, John N., 1016
Turner Joy (destroyer), 741
Turpie resolution, 277
Turpitz, Admiral von, 362
Tuscany, 54
Tutsi tribe, Hutu war with, 1183, 1250, 1262, 1287–1288, 1313–1314, 1334
Tutu, Desmond, 1049
Tutuila, 293
Tuyll, Baron, 100
TV MARTI, 1172
Twelfth Amendment, 52
Twenty-fifth Amendment, 825, 834
Twenty-second Amendment, 655
Twitchell, Karl S., 488
2 + 4 plan, 1181–1182
   German reunification, 1169–1170, 1174
Two Sicilies, Kingdom of the, 12, 118
Tydings, Millard, 653
Tydings Committee (1950), 650
Tydings-McDuffie Act of 1934, 494
Tyler, John
   expansionism and, 135, 140–141
   presidency of, 130–141
   protective tariff and, 132
   Texas annexation and, 132, 137
   as vice president, 129
Tyrrell, William, 350
Tzeki, battle of (1862), 198
Tz'u-hsi, empress dowager of China, 198, 280, 284, 295, 296–298, 301

U

Uganda
  Amin, military coup by, 799
  Amin overthrow, 854
  Entebbe hostage crisis, 849
  human rights violations, 854
Ugandan National Liberation Front, 854
Ugarte, Augusto Pinohet, 824
Ugaz, José, 1361
Ukraine
  anti-Bolshevik actions, 411, 414
  in Commonwealth of Independent States (CIS), 1208
  nuclear weapons, disposal of, 1241–1242, 1248, 1257
  Russia friendship treaty (1997), 1298
  Soviet interests, 444, 600
  U.S. economic aid to, 1248, 1257
  World War I, 401
  World War II, 528, 589
Ulam, Adam, 685–686, 697
Ulster Unionists (Northern Ireland), 1348, 1364
Ultranationalist Socialist People's Party (Serbia), 1366
U.N. Conference on Population, 1013
U.N. Convention on the Prevention and Punishment of the
    Crime of Genocide, 1068
U.N. Truce Supervisory Organization (UNTSO), 879
Underwood, Oscar, 438
Underwood-Simmons Tariff (1913), 349, 443
unemployment, Panic of 1837 and, 125
Ungo, Guillermo Manuel, 905, 1022, 1117
Unidad Popular (Chile), 796
Union Carbide, Bhopal, India carbon monoxide leak, 1027,
    1091–1092
Union of Democratic Forces (Bulgaria), 1168, 1177, 1205
Union Labor Party, 246
Union Pacific Railway, 213
Union Rights Party, 166
Union of Russian Workers, 422
Union of Soviet Socialist Republics (USSR)
  establishment of (1922), 444
  See also Soviet Union
Union for the Total Independence of Angola, 846
United Arab Emirates, oil price increase (1976), 851
United Arab Republic (UAR), 692, 698, 700
United Democratic Force (Bulgaria), 1296
United Fruit Company, 673–674
United Labor Party, 246
United Left (Peru), 1043
United National Front for an Independent, Neutral, Peaceful and
    Cooperative Cambodia Party, 1234
United Nationalist Democratic Organization (UNIDO), 1060
United Nations (U.N.)
  Angola as member, 850
  Atomic Energy Commission, 612, 615, 621, 624
  budget crisis of (1987), 1117, 1145
  charter ratified (1945), 605
  Chinese Nationalists and, 646
  disarmament commission (1952), 661
  divisions of, 605

East German membership, 816
first session (1946), 615
on Franco Fascist regime, 652
on Grenada War (1983), 983
International Court of Justice, 605, 637
Iran hostage crisis (1980), 885–886, 888
Israel condemned by (1980s), 846, 896, 941, 1184
on Israel withdrawal from Lebanon, 1016
Khrushchev's tirade (1960), 714–715
on Korean independence, 630
Korean partition, 642
on Korean War aims, 652
Mideast peace negotiations, 798, 800
Millennium Summit, 1354
Monetary and Financial Conference (Bretton Woods)(1946),
    592
Namibia peace plan (1978), 863–864
on Palestine partition, 630–631, 634
Palestinian Liberation Organization (PLO) as member, 848
People's Republic arms embargo, 658
People's Republic as member, 805–806
Relief and Rehabilitation Administration (UNRRA), 585
Six-Day War, 761, 764
on South Africa forces in Angola, 1117–1118
Soviet boycott of, 646
on Soviet invasion of Afghanistan, 884, 972
Spanish membership (1950), 652
Suez crisis, 690
Universal Declaration of Human Rights (1948), 637
U.S. dues owed to (1980s), 1117, 1139, 1145–1146
U.S. dues owed to (1990s), 1338
U.S. Pacific Islands Trust Territories, dissolution of, 1191
Vietnam denied membership, 850
Vietnam membership, 855
War Crimes Commission (UNWCC), 622
on West Bank policy of Israel, 896
West German membership, 816
World War II, 567
Zionism condemned, 845, 1208
United Nations Disarmament Conference (1984),
    1001–1002
United Nations Educational, Scientific, and Cultural
    Organization (UNESCO)
  British withdrawal from, 1030, 1061
  fund cuts (1981), 921
  Third World censorship issue, 921, 957, 983
  U.S. withdrawal from, 990, 1029–1030
United Nations Fund for Population Assistance, anti-abortion
    protests of funding, 1052–1053
United Nations Good Office Committee, 645
United Nations Observer Group, 1171
United Nations Security Council
  AIDS issue, 1370
  Albania peacekeeping, 1295–1296
  Israel, condemnation of, 1293–1294
  Persian Gulf War, 180, 1181, 1187–1188
  Sarajevo airport protection, 1218
  structure of, 605
  world security, increasing role in, 1211

W